WILDER TIMES

Wilder Times

THE LIFE OF BILLY WILDER

Kevin Lally

HENRY HOLT AND COMPANY
NEW YORK

Henry Holt and Company, Inc.
Publishers since 1866
115 West 18th Street
New York, New York 10011

Henry Holt® is a registered
trademark of Henry Holt and Company, Inc.

Library of Congress Cataloging-in-Publication Data
Lally, Kevin
Wilder times: the life of Billy Wilder / Kevin Lally.—1st ed.
p.   cm.
Filmography
Includes bibliographical references and index.
1. Wilder, Billy, 1906– . 2. Motion picture producers and
directors—United States—Biography. I. Title.
PN1998.3.W56L36 1996   95-33668
791.43'0233'092—dc20   CIP
[B]

ISBN 0-8050-3119-7

Henry Holt books are available for special promotions and
premiums. For details contact: Director, Special Markets.

First edition—1996

Designed by Kate Nichols

Frontispiece: Wilder tangos with Jack Lemmon's Daphne
during production of *Some Like It Hot* (PHOTOFEST)

Printed in the United States of America
All first editions are printed on acid-free paper.∞

1 3 5 7 9 10 8 6 4 2

FOR MY MOTHER AND FATHER,

HELEN AND WILLIAM LALLY

CONTENTS

PROLOGUE: *A WILDER OUTLOOK xi*

1. *A BOY NAMED BILLIE 1*

2. *THE VIENNA BEAT 8*

3. *BERLIN STORIES 14*

4. *DREAMS AND NIGHTMARES 36*

5. *ESCAPE TO PARIS 53*

6. *HOLLYWOOD HUSTLE 61*

7. *TEAMWORK 71*

8. *GARBO LAUGHS 81*

9. *THE DIRECTING ITCH 98*

10. *LOVE, WAR AND MURDER 118*

11. *LOST AND REDEEMED 142*

12. *FOREIGN AFFAIRS 163*

13. *PARTNERS AT SUNSET 186*

Contents

14. DIRECT FROM BROADWAY 216

15. FINDING A DIAMOND 247

16. HOTTER THAN EVER 277

17. AGAINST THE WALL 308

18. FROM IRMA TO INFAMY 327

19. WILDER BUT MELLOWER 356

20. PARTING SHOTS 390

21. A FINAL CLOSEUP 411

ACKNOWLEDGMENTS 425

FILMOGRAPHY 429

SOURCE NOTES 438

BIBLIOGRAPHY 463

INDEX 471

PROLOGUE

A Wilder Outlook

I T'S ONE OF THE MOST JARRING, HAUNTING, YET EERILY COM-
ical images in the history of movies: William Holden as the corpse of
screenwriter-turned-gigolo Joe Gillis, floating face-down in a Beverly Hills
swimming pool, fully clothed and arms akimbo. While newsmen swarm to
get a better look, the camera studies him from below the water's surface, a
humiliating expression of shock frozen on Holden's matinee-idol mug. "I
always wanted a swimming pool," says Joe, the hard-bitten narrator of Billy
Wilder's 1950 classic *Sunset Boulevard,* as he begins recounting the bizarre
events that led to his sordid death.

Joe Gillis is *not* the young Billy Wilder in Hollywood, though they
share a number of things in common: unemployment, creditors at their
heels, a shabby one-room apartment, a background in journalism, amateur-
gigolo duties, a cocky attitude and a quick facility with story ideas. But, no
matter how desperate, Joe's predicament was never comparable to that of
his creator, a Jewish exile from Nazi Germany who arrived in the movie
capital with only the flimsiest grasp of the English language. Neither was
Joe's talent: Chances are the hack writer of a tired baseball drama called
Bases Loaded wouldn't have amounted to much, even if he'd never had that
doomed encounter with a demented, former silent-screen goddess named
Norma Desmond.

The young Billy Wilder amounted to plenty, and fast. Within five years of his arrival in Los Angeles, he and partner Charles Brackett were the hottest screenwriting team in town, fashioning sleek, sophisticated comedies for Claudette Colbert and coaxing Garbo to laugh in the immortal *Ninotchka*. In 1942, Wilder seized control of his words by becoming one of Hollywood's first writer-director hyphenates; three years later, he won his first two Oscars, for writing and directing *The Lost Weekend*. By 1950, the year of *Sunset Boulevard*'s release, he could easily risk "biting the hand that fed him" (in Louis B. Mayer's words) by creating a Hollywood-insider's Gothic-horror story—and make wry melodrama out of his own early career anxieties.

Billy Wilder has been getting a lot of attention in the past few years—a Presidential tribute here, a lifetime achievement award there, not to mention a much publicized Andrew Lloyd Webber musical version of *Sunset Boulevard*. Some of that attention is simply by virtue of this eighty-nine-year-old writer-director's longevity—when you're one of the last survivors of Hollywood's fabled Golden Era, you're bound to get a certain volume of press. Dutiful reporters single out the Wilder classics—*Some Like It Hot, Double Indemnity, Sunset Boulevard, The Apartment, The Lost Weekend, Witness for the Prosecution*—and praise his nimble wit and his masterly story-telling skills, with maybe a passing mention of his astringent outlook on life. What they invariably fail to point out is the extent of his influence. Without Billy Wilder around to apply the lessons of his two great idols, Ernst Lubitsch and Erich von Stroheim, to the 1940s, '50s and '60s, the commercial Hollywood movie may never have matured so quickly.

In film after film, Billy Wilder tested the boundaries of what mainstream American moviegoers would accept. Before *Double Indemnity*, who would have dared construct a studio feature around a pair of lusty, homicidal lovers? Would anyone else have envisioned *The Lost Weekend*, a relentless novel tracing the downward spiral of a self-destructive alcoholic writer, as a viable movie prospect? Who else would have had the cheek to make *A Foreign Affair*, a romantic farce set in postwar Berlin, with a corrupt American army captain as its ostensible hero? What other émigré to Hollywood would be secure enough to uncover, in *Sunset Boulevard*, the dark, psychotic side of the movie industry's ego-gratification machine? These are the major beachheads from just the first of Wilder's four decades as a Hollywood writer-director.

By the late 1950s, Billy Wilder was generally considered the most successful filmmaker in town, with a string of box-office hits including *Stalag 17*, *Sabrina*, *The Seven Year Itch*, *Witness for the Prosecution* and the classic farce *Some Like It Hot*. In the spring of 1961, he became the second person in history to collect three Academy Awards in one night, for his comedy-drama about the underbelly of corporate America, *The Apartment*. Two years later, he risked building a comedy around a guilt-free French prostitute and had the biggest smash of his career with *Irma la Douce*.

No one shakes up Hollywood or becomes this wildly successful without paying a price. As Wilder's career approached its zenith, there were plenty of people eager to see it plummet. The Viennese native had a brittle sense of humor and a healthy ego, and often spoke his mind about the vanities of actors, the follies of studio executives and the faux pas of lesser filmmakers. Those who could stand the blast of his withering criticisms (or had the brains and talent never to be their target) loved being around this funny, erudite raconteur/imp; those who were less secure in his presence couldn't wait to see him fail.

Wilder was not just an artist, but a showman, and that too left him wide open to attack. "For me, the aim of a film is entertainment, to make it as amusing or thrilling as possible, and never pretentious," he once said. "I have always had more fear of pretentiousness than of failure." But Wilder also contends, "When people walk out of a theater, they should leave with something more than just having seen a two-hour-long film."

However strong his commercial consciousness, Wilder sometimes gave an audience more than they bargained for: disreputable and unsympathetic lead characters, startling gallows humor, a blistering view of the human condition. But because these elements appeared within the confines of a Hollywood studio film, often with an antihero learning a devastating moral lesson, Wilder's artistic integrity was questioned by some members of the critical community. Did Wilder lack the guts to see his pessimistic scenarios through to the bitter end? Was he cynically exploiting cynicism? Or was he sincerely trying to break new ground, and doing the job too well? "Every picture I make involves people making moral choices," he argues. "How can I show that without showing the seamy side of the world?"

While some faulted Wilder for not having the courage of his convictions, others just saw the seaminess and were deeply offended. "Bad taste" was a label that followed Wilder through much of his career, and the attacks really gained momentum as the culture approached the sea change of the midsixties. Wilder had a role in that change: Films like *Some Like It Hot*, *The Apartment* and *Irma la Douce* brought a mischievous new attitude to once taboo subjects like adultery, prostitution, office hanky-panky and even sexual identity. All three were hits; Wilder was exactly in sync with a mass audience tempted by the expanding sexual frontier.

Then came the Great Comeuppance, as Wilder found himself ahead of the curve by just a few years. *Kiss Me, Stupid*, a relentlessly bawdy modern-day variation on Restoration comedy, dared to suggest that a little adultery could be good for a marriage, and was met with the wrath of the Catholic church and critics anxious to solidify their family-newspaper credentials. Not just a box-office failure, but an *ignominious* box-office failure, *Kiss Me, Stupid* proved a devastating blow to Wilder's career. Ironically, in a very short time, this still vital filmmaker would be unfairly looked upon as "out of touch" with the very times he had influenced.

Having thrived under a studio system where, in theory, there was no such thing as a personal filmmaker, Billy Wilder put his personal touch on every movie he directed. Unlike the great majority of his American contemporaries, he is the co-author of all his films, first with Charles Brackett, then with a series of collaborators in the fifties, and finally with his long-running partner in comedy, I. A. L. Diamond. Elements of Wilder's life course throughout his motion-picture work: his Viennese heritage and memories of long-ago waltzes; his first professional experience as an aggressive young reporter; the curious lessons in male-female exploitation he learned as a gigolo/dancer in Berlin; the clash between the culture and elegance of Europe and the acquisitive energy of his adoptive homeland. So many of his characters are on the make, barely scraping by or struggling to hold their footing on the corporate ladder, that the impact of his often lean early years in Vienna, Berlin, Paris and Hollywood can't be minimized. And because so many Wilder scenarios involve elaborate masquerades and deceptions, it's impossible not to see these devices as a reflection of Wilder's own effort to make himself over as the ultimate American go-getter.

The so-called cynical side of Wilder's films is personal, too. Wilder can regale a room for hours with amusing stories, but he seldom talks about the central tragedy of his life: the loss of his mother and grandmother at Auschwitz. The Holocaust is never explicitly addressed in his films, and only hinted at in his satirical portrayals of the German mind-set. But Billy Wilder's firsthand knowledge of the misdeeds human beings are capable of has profoundly influenced the relationships he portrays in his films: Someone is always acting from a base motive, while someone else is being exploited.

What some regard as cynicism, others might call sensitivity. Wilder's close friend and frequent leading man, Jack Lemmon, says, "Billy is called an acid tongue because he is so sensitive to human behavior and so perceptive that he notices things that other people just don't notice. And he is able to point them out with a personal barb."

Wilder's wicked wit and hard-boiled characters do tend to obscure his softer side—but it's there, and it's genuine. His love of old pop and jazz standards suffuses his movies—the song "Isn't It Romantic?" turns up any number of times, though sometimes in a deliberately dark context. And, for an old cynic, Wilder has contributed some indelibly romantic movie moments: Audrey Hepburn running after Gary Cooper's departing train at the end of *Love in the Afternoon;* Melvyn Douglas in *Ninotchka* purring to Greta Garbo, "It's midnight—one half of Paris is making love to the other half"; Shirley MacLaine in *The Apartment,* racing across the Upper West Side of Manhattan after she realizes Jack Lemmon loves her.

Romantic/cynic. Entertainer/social critic. As Viennese as a Strauss waltz. As American as a home run. Billy Wilder is not only one of the most influential filmmakers in Hollywood history, but one of its most fascinating paradoxes.

A Boy Named Billie

E VEN AS HE APPROACHES THE AGE OF NINETY, BILLY WIL-
der has trouble sitting still. Wherever he is, he's already preparing to
be somewhere else—a gallery showing, dinner at Spago, another grudging
interview about *Sunset Boulevard,* another black-tie ceremony in his honor.
His restlessness, no doubt, stems from a bright and brittle mind and a long-
standing place in the most rarefied circles of the Hollywood social scene.
But it's more deeply engrained than that, too—traceable to a childhood
spent on the move, in a Europe on the verge of seismic change.

Billy Wilder was born as Samuel Wilder on June 22, 1906, in the town
of Sucha, in the province of Galicia, an area of Poland that was then part of
the Austro-Hungarian Empire. His father, Max, had married Eugenia
Baldinger in 1903; for Max, the union was a step up the social ladder, as he
was a lowly headwaiter in Kracòw while Eugenia's mother owned the Hotel
Zent'al in Nowy Targ, the last stop on the way up the Tatra mountain range
to the health spa of Zakopane. In 1905, the Wilders had their first child,
Wilhelm, whom his mother nicknamed Willie. When Samuel came along,
she immediately took to calling him Billie, in fond memory of the Buffalo
Bill Wild West show she had seen as a teenager during a long stay in New
York with her uncle, a Madison Avenue jeweler.

Following his marriage, Max Wilder went into the business of managing a chain of small cafés at various railway stations along the route from

Vienna to Lemberg. The family was constantly in motion, spending a few days at one café stop, then proceeding to the next. Once he accumulated some money, Max invested in a four-story hotel and restaurant in Kraców at the foot of the Wawel Castle, near Jagiellonian University, Poland's oldest educational institution, where Copernicus studied and the first globe to depict the American continent was created. Perhaps under Eugenia's influence, Max gave his new venture an English name: Hotel City. The hotel had a grand outdoor terrace, where guests would sit during the summer drinking coffee, eating Bundt cake and listening to a small orchestra play court-style concert music. Best of all, from little Billie's point of view, the place had a billiard room. "I grew up standing on chairs and playing billiards against the grown-ups," Wilder recalls. "There was always some sucker who did not know how to play billiards, whom I got to take for a few *krönen*. And sometimes, I even stole some of the tips left over for the waiters."

Hanging around the billiard room and the card tables, young Billie received an early education in games of chance and the vicissitudes of gambling. As for more cultural matters, Wilder notes, "My father had nothing to do with literature or music—he did not play an instrument, he did not read novels. But he did read newspapers—he was aware as to what was happening. The same thing with my mother. I did have an aunt who had a little library, who would talk to me about the German writers, who made me familiar with Zola, Dumas, made me read Thomas Mann. I also had an uncle, an army engineer in the First World War, who was an opera lover." That uncle, David Baldinger, also encouraged Billie to read up on the Greek classics and on Zionism, and urged him to stay away from *Der Ring des Nibelungen*. But as Wilder sums up, "That's about all the connection my family had with the seven arts."

By 1910, the family was doing well enough to own a home in Vienna in the upscale First District, next door to a historic fifteenth-century restaurant and a dazzling nineteenth-century Greek Orthodox church. The Wilders divided their time between their Vienna residence and their Kraców establishment, until a memorable day in 1914 when Max Wilder, in striped trousers and a cutaway, mounted the Hotel City bandstand and halted the orchestra to make a dire announcement. "Ladies and gentlemen, there will be no more music today," he informed the guests. "Our Archduke Ferdinand has been murdered in Sarajevo."

With one bullet, a great era was effectively ended. The Habsburg dynasty had ruled the land for more than 600 years, with the venerable Emperor Franz Josef presiding since 1848. As a child, Billie Wilder experienced a culture characterized by grace, refinement, harmony, aestheticism and a love of beautiful music—most particularly, the waltzes of Johann Strauss and his even more celebrated son. Austria-Hungary in those days was still the stuff of fairy tales—a grand, baroque never-never-land seemingly immune from the sweaty fever of the Industrial Revolution and the angry ethnic forces clashing outside its borders. The political assassination in what is now Bosnia punctured that insular existence. The Wilder family joined the frantic exodus from Kraców to Vienna, traveling in a horse-drawn carriage because the trains were completely full. Soon, Galicia was invaded by the Russians, and Wilder's birthplace of Sucha became an especially chaotic battleground, with the Russian and the Austrian forces constantly wresting control of the hapless hamlet from each other.

In 1916, Franz Josef died, and Wilder remembers watching the grand funeral cortege with his father, from the second floor of the Café Edison on Vienna's Ringstrasse. Military leaders and diplomats from all Austria-Hungary's allies were there, dressed in black uniforms and riding black horses. Max Wilder pointed to the coffin of Franz Josef, declaring, "There is the last of your old emperor." Then he called Billie's attention to a little boy riding behind on a white horse: "And there is your future emperor." Of course, that was not to be; the war was tearing apart the great Austro-Hungarian empire, drastically altering the map of Europe. Decades later, after the *Second* World War, Wilder, now a hugely successful director at Paramount Pictures, would be called on to give a personal studio tour to a visitor from his native Austria. His guest was a frail, prematurely aged-looking man in a wrinkled suit: Otto von Habsburg, the very same boy he had seen parading behind his fabled grandfather's coffin in Vienna. Instead of ruling half of Europe, he was in exile in America, making a humble career as a college lecturer on international relations.

Like everyone in Vienna during the war, the Wilders faced hardship and deprivation they had never known before. The British blockade of

Germany and Austria created shortages of food and fuel. Recalls Wilder, "I and my late brother, who was two years older, we would stand in line for fourteen, sixteen hours, and each of us would get three potatoes. . . . But we as children had an easier time than the grown-ups, because we were flexible: You'd go out to the country and grab a couple of eggs, and things like that. You went into the swapping business—I'll give you my watch for a half a ham, or whatever." Young Billie also earned money as a street cleaner, while his mother served in the Red Cross and his father performed guard duty for the army reserve.

When the war ended in November 1918, things only got worse. Angry mobs raided shops, toppled imperial statues, attacked and killed soldiers. Wilder remembers how the soldiers, and especially the officers, scampered into civilian clothes so as not to be held responsible for all the ongoing suffering. As the empire was divided up, Austria became increasingly vulnerable. Food was still woefully scarce, and nearly half the country's population was fighting for scraps in the overburdened, ailing city of Vienna.

"Then one day," says Wilder, "the spell was broken—the Americans came with the trucks with the flags. That was all started and organized by Herbert Hoover, later on our president, who was the head of the American Relief Committee. And suddenly there was white flour, there were eggs. It got us gradually out of the years of hunger."

The war, however, had taken a huge economic toll on the Wilder family. The Hotel City became a liability, and Max Wilder spent the rest of his days jumping from one quixotic business venture to another. "My father was a dreamer and an adventurer who sought something his whole life long without knowing exactly what it was," Wilder declares. "He dreamed about becoming rich and changing his fortunes by leaps and bounds." One day, Max announced to the family at lunch that he had entered a new business, importing Swiss clockwork. Two rooms in the house were converted into the office of the mysterious firm Frankel, Pytlak and Wilder. On another occasion, he sold the hotel in Kraców and bought a trout hatchery, even though he knew nothing about trout. The business failed, and ultimately the family was forced to move from its handsome home in the First District to a small residence on Billrothstrasse in the far less fashionable Nineteenth District.

One day, Billie found rather startling evidence of his father's fecklessness: an invitation to a party taking place at a boarding school attended by his son—a son the family didn't know existed. Billie instinctively took the card out of the morning mail and hid it away until his father came home. Max persuaded Billie to keep the news a secret. In return, Max usually turned a blind eye to his son's scams and scrapes.

On one such occasion, Billie broke a store window while playing "football" with a rock. After promising the shopkeeper he'd pay for the window, the boy went home and told his parents he needed extra money for a typing and stenography course he wanted to take at school. Billie's ruse caught up with him one Sunday when his father had to send an urgent letter and decided to test his son's newly acquired secretarial skills. Trapped, the boy pretended to take dictation, then clattered nonsense on his father's typewriter. But when Max saw the pathetic results, he didn't say a word. It was as if he already knew the lessons were a fraud and his son was whiling away the hours on the Prater football field, just as Billie knew about the many times his papa went to the racetrack instead of the office.

From the first time he stole the waiters' tips at the Hotel City, young Billie Wilder had a keen sense of just how much larceny he could get away with. He remembers pouring out his father's good wine just to get the deposit back on the bottle, and conspiring with a friend to steal some valuable stamps from an old, half-blind stamp dealer. "But he was not as old and not half as blind as we had believed, and he caught us," Wilder recalls. Luckily for the young thieves, they managed to flee before the man could report them to the police.

Billie looked for extra cash wherever he could find it. A prostitute who lived around the corner from the house on Fleischmarkt would give him two *kreuzer* to take care of her ill-tempered dachshund whenever she found a client, he remembers. It was easy enough money—until she was arrested in a police raid and the boy was left holding the dog.

Billie's money-raising schemes were motivated in large part by a new love: the movies. Until the family was forced to give up their home in the First District, a movie theater was just a few paces away, on the corner of Fleischmarkt and Rotenturmstrasse. And just as those American CARE packages helped fill Billie's stomach, the Hollywood movies now entering Austria fed his fantasies. His mother had thrilled to Buffalo Bill's Wild West show as a teenager; now, Billie immersed himself in the lore of the American West, and the adventures of screen heroes like Tom Mix, William S. Hart and Hoot Gibson. He roared at the comic mischief of Chaplin and Keaton, and idolized the dashing Douglas Fairbanks. "I remember hearing that during the inflation, he offered to buy Austria! He made a firm price of ten million dollars for the whole country—lock, stock and waltzes. We were by now a little country, but still . . . I liked this. Another millionaire would buy a French château, a Greek island. Not Fairbanks. He wanted a whole country. That is what I call class. He was my kind of a hero."

Like many teenagers, Billie had his first sexual misadventure at the movies. He was smitten with a girl named Greta whom he saw every day while playing tennis in the park. Billie turned for advice to his friend Egon, the one everyone looked up to because he had had the clap at age eleven. (It was later revealed to be the measles.) Egon gave him step-by-step instruction in seducing a girl: Invite her to the movies, buy her a piece of chocolate cake, take her hand in the darkened theater, then make your move. Easy as cake! For a while, the plan seemed to be working. Greta accepted his invitation (Wilder believes the main feature was Asta Nielsen in *Storms of Passion)*, and the cake, and Billie's hand. Then Billie let his hand wander, closer and closer to Greta's panties. Suddenly, the girl let out a piercing scream, and the lights went up. The usher found Billie, red faced, with a sickly smile of embarrassment, his hand frozen between Greta's locked knees.

Sex also got Billie in big trouble at school—or was it the first flowering of his passion for art? The boy was caught with a copy of an Egon Schiele nude. Unable or unwilling to see the finer points of one of Austria's great artists, Wilder's teachers deemed the sketch pornography. And so Billie was transferred to the Realgymnasium Juranek on Buchfeldgasse in the Eighth District, a school for "problem" students that specialized in science. Unfortunately for Billie, math and science were his weak subjects; otherwise, he was a fast reader who excelled in literature, history and languages.

The small, three-story school was situated on a narrow street, directly opposite the Hotel Stadion, an establishment that most often rented its rooms by the hour. Wilder says it took him three years to figure out exactly what went on inside the Stadion; after that, you couldn't keep him away from the classroom window. Billie could now identify all the hotel's working girls, and could easily tell which clients were married by the nervous way their eyes darted back and forth before entering the building.

Wilder remembers one particularly gorgeous redhead who fueled his classroom daydreams. Week upon week, he would fantasize about Red Fritzi, as he nicknamed her. Finally, upon reaching a certain maturity, he turned his dream into reality. He walked up to Fritzi, negotiated a price, and rented them a room in the Stadion under the pseudonyms Herr and Frau Finsterbusch (the name of his French teacher).

Behind Wilder's colorful boyhood exploits, there's a largely unspoken dark side—the inescapable consciousness of being part of Austria's Jewish minority. "There are many aspects to Austria," Wilder reflects. "It's a small country—seven-and-a-half million, of which two-and-a-half million are in Vienna; it's like a baby with an enormous head. . . . But I think that in the provinces, Nazism is strong, has been stronger than the German Nazism. Let us not forget that Mr. Hitler was Austrian. As they say now, the Austrians are absolute magicians—they have now convinced the world that Beethoven was an Austrian and Hitler was a German. I always get into terrible fights with the newspapermen there, because I remember my days in school. I remember the attitudes. The most famous Austrians, whether it be Schnitzler or Mahler or Schoenberg, they were Jewish. The source of anti-Semitism, the bloodline, is the lack of education. It is impossible to eradicate, it was impossible to do it two thousand or four thousand years ago. They were always on the march."

The Vienna Beat

WHEN A JEWISH MOTHER HAS TWO SONS, SAYS BILLY WILder, chances are while the boys are still in their strollers you'll hear "Hey, I would like you to meet my son the lawyer—and this is my son the doctor."

Wilder is explaining how, after graduation from the Realgymnasium Juranek, he found himself studying law at the University of Vienna. His mother had already been forced to abandon her dream of Willie's pursuing a career in medicine; he was in New York, getting his start as a manufacturer of women's purses. So, to make Eugenia happy, Billie plunged into the world of torts and statutes. It bored him to tears.

After three months, the eighteen-year-old Wilder dropped out of college. Today, the only regret the director has about that decision is the response it triggered in his 1970s biographer, Maurice Zolotow. For Zolotow, Wilder's departure from the university was a tantalizing mystery; surely, there had to be a *reason* for this abrupt change in the course of the young Viennese's life. Zolotow thought he found it in Ilse, a pretty, lively young clerk in a record store on the Ringstrasse. Billie came in regularly to listen to the new jazz imports from America and found a kindred spirit in the fashionable, fun-loving shop girl. They went out to dance halls together, and Billie got to show off his newly acquired skill at the tango and the fox-trot. They took long walks, spent hours over coffee. According to Zolotow, Ilse was the first great love of Wilder's life.

Then, said Zolotow, some friends spotted Ilse on the Kärntnerstrasse after midnight, heavily made up and soliciting customers. They told Billie and brought him out to Ilse's corner to see for himself. The student angrily confronted his girlfriend, and then turned away from her in shame. Soon after, Zolotow claimed, Wilder quit the university.

For Zolotow, the alleged Ilse incident was the central moment in Wilder's life, the Rosebud that climaxed the late author's 1977 biography. This youthful trauma, he said, explained Wilder's cynical view of life and his problematic attitudes toward women. It also accounted for all the prostitutes and shady ladies in the Wilder canon: Shirley MacLaine in *Irma la Douce*, Kim Novak in *Kiss Me, Stupid*, Barbara Stanwyck in *Double Indemnity*, Marlene Dietrich in *A Foreign Affair*, Jan Sterling in *Ace in the Hole*, Judi West in *The Fortune Cookie* and, most significantly, Geneviève Page as a spy named Ilse in *The Private Life of Sherlock Holmes*. One could just as easily argue, however, that there are at least as many wonderfully appealing and sympathetic women in Wilder's films, and many more *male* scoundrels than female. But why not let Wilder speak for himself?

"[Zolotow] came up with the most grammar-school version of a Freudian explanation," the director fumes. "In my youth, so he says, I fell in love with a girl and then found out she was a prostitute—therefore, I hate women."

Speaking frankly, Wilder asserts, "I knew the girl to be a hooker. She was very pretty, and I paid her. There were hookers in my life, but I was never in love with a hooker."

According to Wilder, the tedium of law was the sole reason he left school and decided to attempt a career as a newspaper reporter. Even his family wasn't terribly upset. The economy was in a shambles, and any extra income Billie could bring in would be welcome.

Why a reporter? "I don't know," Wilder shrugs. "I was pretty good at writing little stories and doing the school paper. I just had a hunch that it was an interesting life, not doing every day the same thing. I just knew that I would come in contact with different people, different cases—a burglary, a murder, a message from the Vatican to the archbishop in Vienna, I did all kinds of things. It was very interesting."

Wilder's breakthrough into the world of journalism sounds like something out of a sex farce, as his stories of his youth often do. After making endless rounds of Vienna's editing rooms, the young man went seeking a job at *Die Stunde*, a midday paper located at Canisiusgasse 9, not far from his parents' home on Billrothstrasse. Wilder arrived in the afternoon, and found the offices deserted except for some cleaning women. "Where is everyone?" the puzzled applicant inquired. "Try the first floor," replied one of the charwomen, grinning. Wilder went upstairs, and saw nothing but empty offices, their doors wide open. Then he heard a noise coming from inside a closed office. He knocked. No reply, just the same noise, "like someone who had asthma." He knocked again, then gingerly opened the door. A plump, short man with a pointy gray beard was sprawled on a sofa with a woman. The man jumped up, pulling on his pants. The woman pushed her dress back down over her knees, grabbed a steno pad and rushed into an adjoining room.

"What do you want?" the startled Casanova grumbled. Wilder stood his ground and answered, "I'm looking for work." Anxious to smooth over an embarrassing situation, the bearded man told the youngster a job was available. Wilder remembers his cocky reply: "Like they say, the right place at the right time."

The would-be lover was the fifty-year-old Hans Liebstockl, one of Vienna's leading theater critics. Liebstockl, who also wrote for the daily *Wiener Tagblatt*, was a major force at *Die Stunde*; that same year, he was named editor-in-chief of *Die Bühne*, the new theater weekly begun by *Die Stunde*'s colorful Hungarian publisher, Imre Bekessy. Despite their awkward first meeting, Liebstockl liked his new protégé, and praised his innate talent for turning a clever phrase. Wilder remembers one in particular that tickled his mentor—when a plump local Vienna celebrity died, Billie offered this parting salute in the obituary: "May he become as light as the earth."

A few notches above a yellow tabloid, *Die Stunde* nonetheless contributed its fair share of gossip and sensation to Viennese life. Reporting was expected to be punchy and terse, and a high premium was placed on snagging celebrity interviews. At first, Wilder wasn't allowed to do any writing—he simply made the rounds and telephoned in the facts. Most of his time was divided between covering sports and local crime—he and his counterparts from the rival papers would sit in a café near the police precinct, playing cards, chess or billiards; when a red light came on, that meant a story was breaking and it was time to get to work. For Wilder, the worst part of the job was visiting the family of, say, a murder suspect, making a show of consoling them but all the while scheming to get his hands on an exclusive photo of their errant child.

Another of Billie's regular beats was the Viennese Catholic archdiocese, where he got to know Cardinal Pacelli, later to be known as Pope Pius XII. Wilder also indulged his passion for sports by conducting in-depth interviews with football and tennis stars, and he was always on the alert for visits by celebrated Americans. One of his interviews was with the famed Hungarian playwright Ferenc Molnár; some thirty-five years later, a Molnár one-act farce would become the basis for Wilder's Cold War Berlin romp, *One, Two, Three.*

Wilder's late friend Walter Reisch (with whom he collaborated on the screenplay for *Ninotchka)* said the young journalist "developed a fantastic knack for getting interviews. For instance, the richest man in the world was Sir Basil Zaharoff—he sold arms to governments, to the fascists. Nobody ever saw this man. Billy found out he was going to make a two-hour stopover on the train in Vienna. He walked right onto his train and got the interview. That man was stupefied by such chutzpah."

Wilder's talent for tracking down celebrities was put to its greatest test in December 1925, when the editors of *Die Stunde* decided to run a special holiday section on the rise of Italian fascism. The nineteen-year-old was sent out to ask some of Vienna's most influential figures their opinions on the subject. And so, in one day, Wilder spoke to composer Richard Strauss, psychiatrist Alfred Adler, playwright Arthur Schnitzler and—briefly, very briefly—Sigmund Freud. In Wilder's recollection, Strauss praised the leadership qualities of Mussolini while Adler took the opportunity to psychoanalyze the Italian dictator. Schnitzler, meanwhile, predicted that fascism would never last. As for Freud, Wilder remembers going to the family apartment on Berggasse and presenting his card to the maid. "She let me wait in the salon, the living room—in Austria or Mittel Europa then, they had the apartment and the office together. Herr Professor was at lunch and she took the card inside to him." Through a crack in the door, the reporter could see the consulting room and the famous couch, which was much smaller than he had imagined. "Then the door opened and there he stood with the card in his hand. He said, 'You're a reporter with *Die Stunde*?' And I said, 'Yes, sir! Yes, Herr Professor!' And he pointed to the door leading out of the apartment and said, 'There's the door!' I took a deep bow and I thanked him very much for his kindness and I left!" Today, Wilder considers it something of an honor to have been ejected by Freud.

Because *Die Stunde* was a midday paper, the young reporter did most of his sleeping in the afternoon. He'd generally perform his legwork in the evening hours, arrive at the office well after midnight, and work on his copy till nine or ten in the morning. His hours made it difficult to carry on much of a romantic life, especially since he was now living in a small furnished room and subject to the prying eyes of his landlady. As it was forbidden to bring a girl home to his room, Wilder told Maurice Zolotow he often made love while standing in doorways, an uncomfortable compromise he claimed may have been the root cause of the severe back problems he developed later in his life.

In May 1926, Wilder sought out an interview that changed his life forever. Paul Whiteman, the American conductor popularly known as the King of Jazz, was staying at the posh Hotel Bristol in Vienna, taking a break from his European concert tour. "Whiteman gave four concerts," Wilder recalls, "in London, Paris, Berlin and Amsterdam. The first part was the big, standard hits; the second half was Gershwin's *Rhapsody in Blue*. He was in Vienna, and I interviewed him with my lousy English." To mollify his musically ignorant editor, Wilder came up with the angle of bringing Whiteman some recent songs by Viennese composers and getting the great bandleader's opinion of them. Among them was "Madonna, Du Bist Schöner als der Sonnenschein" ("Madonna, You Are Lovelier than the Sunlight"), which Whiteman liked so much he added it as an instrumental to his repertoire. It later emerged as the American standard "When Day Is Done."

Whiteman was disarmed by the eager young Viennese and his fondness for American jazz. Wilder, for his part, was thrilled to meet the King, who traveled with a black butler whose only job seemed to be winding up the conductor's portable gramophone. The reporter became Whiteman's personal tour guide to Vienna. At one point, Wilder recalls, "I said, 'Gee, I wish I could go to the concert in Berlin, but there's no way anybody would pay my ticket there.' In those days, you see, I did my reportage on foot or by streetcar—nobody had an automobile, only the publisher. But Whiteman liked me, and I went to Berlin on his invitation. I never went back to Vienna."

Wilder's expenses were paid by a man named Wrede, the organizer of the Whiteman tour and who also headed the music house Bloch & Erben, which published the song "Madonna." The reporter told *Die Stunde* he was taking a few vacation days and would return with an article on Whiteman's Berlin concert. But, in the back of his mind, he knew that wasn't going to happen. After all, he says, "Berlin was the dream of every journalist."

Berlin Stories

BERLIN IN 1926 WAS A HEADY PLACE FOR A VIENNESE JUST shy of his twentieth birthday. Determined to shake off the gloom of the war and its harsh aftermath, the city had become the new artistic mecca of Europe. Experimental theater was booming, cabarets served up wildly uninhibited entertainment, painters like George Grosz, Otto Dix and Max Beckmann were combining startling technique with wicked social criticism. The film industry, led by the extraordinary UFA studio, was making international waves with its revolutionary work, audaciously stylized masterpieces like F. W. Murnau's *The Last Laugh*, G. W. Pabst's *The Joyless Street*, and Fritz Lang's *Metropolis* and *Dr. Mabuse, the Gambler*. Berlin was also celebrated for its outlandish, eccentric street life. On Berlin's main shopping avenue, the Kurfürstendamm, one could watch a constant parade of libidinous creatures of all persuasions: men done up in high drag, women in men's suits, leather aficionados, hookers and hustlers of every age and variety. Mixed among them were homeless beggars, teenage waifs, amputees still wearing their medals from the war—reminders of the poverty, desperation and anger churning beneath the city's hedonistic surface.

Wilder didn't have to walk in on any lovemaking sessions to obtain employment in Berlin—he came with a letter of introduction from Dr. Krienes, the Vienna correspondent of the Scherl publishing house. He got a reporting job with the *Nachtausgabe*, found a furnished room on Pariser

Strasse and fell in love with a dancer in the Revue Girls named Olive Victoria. Wilder claims the affair cost him his job: After staying up all night with Olive, he was found asleep in a telephone box in the editing room and promptly fired. The reporter immortalized the romance in a poem, written in the form of a letter to Olive, which appeared in the July 1927 issue of *Revue of the Month* under the title "The Fifth from the Right." The paean was illustrated with a photo spread of the Revue Girls, an arrow pointing to Olive, for those who couldn't count.

Having lost his post at the *Nachtausgabe*, Wilder became a freelance writer for such newspapers as the *Berliner Zeitung am Mittag* (or *B.Z.*), *Tempo* and *Borsen Courier*, and the chic monthly magazine *Querschnitt*. His knowledge of American music was a valuable asset, since Berlin was at least as jazz-crazy as he was, and he found he could easily sell pieces on the hot musicians of the day like Gene Austin, Whispering Jack Smith and, of course, Paul Whiteman. And when Hollywood stars came to town, Wilder was there, aggressively pursuing a story. He interviewed the suave actor Adolphe Menjou, and wrote a slyly perceptive piece about Jackie Coogan, the child star who had charmed a worldwide audience in Charlie Chaplin's 1921 classic, *The Kid*. Wilder noted how Coogan's parents hovered over their prize child and, suspecting the worst, brazenly inquired about their plans for the boy's money. The Coogans declared the interview over, and Wilder wrote a story correctly implying that the boy's fortune was not in the best of hands.

As a reporter, Wilder had no compunction about asking the kind of nervy questions that made good copy. When he met with Cornelius Vanderbilt Jr. at the Hotel Adlon, the first thing he wanted to know was how much money the millionaire was carrying. As Wilder expected, the man didn't have a cent on him, since "anyone by the name of Vanderbilt has no need to carry any money." Vanderbilt and the young reporter then went for a walk and stopped for lunch. The millionaire ate three *buletten* and drank four beers—and Wilder paid.

Wilder always had his antennae out for an unusual story. One night, he attended the opening of a new play about Rasputin, and managed to sit behind Prince Youssopoff, the leader of his assassins. Wilder asked his opinion of the play. "Rubbish," the prince replied, adding that the author missed the real tragedy of the event. "And what is the real tragedy?" Wilder inquired. "We killed the wrong man," declared Youssopoff. "We should have killed Lenin. And Trotsky, too, while we were at it."

One of Wilder's story ideas backfired badly. The *B.Z.* agreed to a series on professional gamblers in Monte Carlo and their surefire systems for "breaking the bank." But on his first day on the Riviera, before he had written a single word, the young reporter managed to gamble away all his advance money. Wilder had to telegraph his mother for money for the trip home.

Dogged as he was, the reporter was nearly always short of money, and ever on the lookout for supplemental sources of income. (Wilder wryly comments that the best way to look good while starving is to wear a tight shirt collar: "You can scarcely breathe, but your cheeks become rosy and you look as if you're well nourished.") In October 1926, Wilder discovered a comparatively lucrative sideline, which he turned into the most talked-about piece he ever wrote as a journalist.

"It was going badly for me," his account begins. "I had literally not one *groschen* more. I stood on the Potsdamer Platz, without a coat, my knees shaking from cold and hunger. And it was raining, such a rain. . . . Then I heard behind me, 'Hello, Billie!' I will never forget this 'Hello, Billie!' for the rest of my life."

The greeting came from an old Vienna acquaintance named Robert, a Frenchman who had a dance act (Robert and Yvette) at the Hotel Eden. Seeing his friend's sad state, Robert suggested he think about becoming one of the Eden's gigolos, a dancer for hire. And so, out of a desire to both fill his stomach and seize upon a good story, Wilder entered the posh but grueling, singularly strange world of the *eintanzer*, or professional society dancer. The hours were 4:30 to 7 P.M. and 9:30 P.M. to 3 A.M.; salary was 5 marks a day, or 150 marks a month, plus tips.

Published in four installments in the *B.Z.* in January 1927, "Waiter, Bring Me a Dancer—The Life of a Gigolo" is comic, evocative and beautifully written:

In the hall. Completely filled. Cigarette fumes. Perfume and hair-oil. Powdered women from twenty to fifty. Bald heads. Mothers with underdeveloped daughters. Young men with loud cravats and bright spats. Hordes of families. Above, the jazz band lays into their instruments and jerks with the rhythm they make. . . .

Table 46: An old lady in a bottle-green dress, with long neck and egg-yellow hair; a little one with a pug nose. I stand before them, a second ass of the Buridian, beads of perspiration on my forehead, colors all playing about, helpless and shaking. Then I stiffly move my upper torso forward, against the one with the pug nose, purse my lips and say very softly: "May I ask the lady?" She grins at me and considers. I must look very stupid in this comical position, deep red head bent over to her. The little one raises herself, lays her round arm on my shoulder. We dance. . . .

I dance the entire five-hour tea with table 46. She in the bottle-green dress has asked about my name. Now she will come more often. "Dear God, no!" I think to myself. Around seven o'clock, I sit like a boxer after a k.o. on my stool in the corner. My God, I have to do this two times every day to get paid. For 150 marks . . .

I honestly earn my bread. Honestly and with difficulty. I dance painstakingly, but desireless, joyless, without thoughts, without opinion, without heart, without brain. Only animated by one desire, one thought: I want a couple of checkered slippers, a wide chair, and in them I want to sleep for all eternity. Amen.

The word "gigolo" conjures up another image than the one Wilder portrays in his exposé—the suave, smooth-talking opportunist who trades sex for money, then disappears from the picture. In Wilder's account, it's the Eden gigolos who are exploited and demeaned; Wilder keeps emphasizing the hard work, drudgery and awkward playacting of their odd profession. "It is no easy bread," Wilder writes. "Nothing that sentimental, tender natures could eat. Those who can bear it, can live off it. I have not starved." When gigolos turn up in Wilder's Hollywood films—William Holden in *Sunset Boulevard* and Charles Boyer in *Hold Back the Dawn* being the most prominent—their self-loathing is palpable; there's nothing blithe or casual about them.

Wilder's article contains only one episode with the promise of sex. A beautiful, dark-haired woman asks her dance partner to accompany her home at 3 A.M., even though they've barely spoken to each other. The cab drops them off at her home on the Kantstrasse. She turns to Wilder and asks, "Do you know who Kant was, anyway?" Oh, I see, Wilder thinks to himself. She still wants me to prove whether I really am so stupid. I will not spoil it for her. "Who Kant was? A Swiss national hero!" he responds.

Wilder writes: "She moves her mouth a little, lifts her hand and strokes my cheek, like a poor, wayward child. Then she wants to give me money. Thanks. Not now. She looks at me with surprise, then closes the door from inside. I pull my collar high and walk slowly through the rain toward home."

At least Wilder didn't starve during his two-month engagement at the Eden: Dancers were expected to dine there "like a guest." The young writer also managed to create a sideline within his sideline: A girlfriend named Margerie had recently returned from New York and taught him the hot new dance the Charleston. Mornings, she and Wilder would make house calls, carrying a portable gramophone; he would teach the wives the Charleston, and she would teach their husbands.

Wilder also used his gigolo gig to refine another talent. There were more agile dancers, better-looking dancers, Wilder admits, "but I had the best dialogue." "You come here every Tuesday, Thursday and Saturday," Wilder would tell his partner. "How do you know that?" she'd gasp. "Because it is so boring Mondays, Wednesdays and Fridays." Good practice for the romantic banter of *Ninotchka*, *Arise My Love*, *Sabrina*, *Love in the Afternoon* and countless other Wilder scripts—where sometimes the smooth talk is actually sincere.

"Because of some impudence," Wilder says in the memoir, he was fired from the Eden on December 15. It was the poet Klabund, listening to Wilder's gigolo stories at the Romanisches Café, a popular artists' and writers' hangout on the Kurfürstendamm, who encouraged the reporter to turn them into a newspaper series. For a brief while, his account was the talk of the town.

Despite the notoriety, Wilder still couldn't secure enough freelance assignments to make ends meet. He remembers how he would order breakfast at the Romanisches Café without having a cent in his pocket, in the hope that a friend would show up and he could borrow the money before the bill came due at the noon lunch hour. Wilder likens the tension to the showdown in his friend and fellow director Fred Zinnemann's western classic, *High Noon.*

Berlin café society consisted of all kinds of creative people: artists, actors, singers, dancers, poets, novelists, playwrights, journalists and film-makers. Mingling with movie people, Wilder learned of an alternative way to earn some money—as a *"neger"* (or "nigger"), the rude German word for ghostwriter. And so, Billy Wilder entered the film world, through a discreet side door.

Wilder explains the setup: "A ghostwriter is somebody who's very popular, who's working on three scripts at the same time. Ghostwriters would do considerable work without getting any credit. There's a joke I heard the other day: A writer is stuck with a script, and suddenly a genie appears. He says: 'I've been watching you, is there anything I can do?' He goes away, and comes back with a complete screenplay. The writer says, 'That's great,' and he's nominated for an award. The second time, the writer can't lick a story, and it's due the following Monday. The genie appears again, and comes back with a complete screenplay. The third time, the genie says, 'You know, I've done a lot of work for you.' The writer says, 'Well, you can have anything you want, I'm so goddamn grateful.' And the genie says, 'Could I have co-writer credit?' And the writer says, 'Well, fuck you!' That's the story of the ghostwriter. A good ghostwriter has talent and ideas, but equally important is to keep your mouth shut. . . .

"They took enormous advantage. In those days, they would get fifty thousand marks for a screenplay, and I would get two hundred fifty marks a week. But if I ever opened my mouth, I wouldn't have a job."

Wilder estimates he worked on some forty or fifty silent films in Berlin, all without a credit. (The quantity is deceptive, since the scripts never numbered more than thirty pages apiece.) Many were for Curt Braun, whom Wilder calls "a walking script factory." Braun took credit for hundreds of screenplays and kept a whole stable of writers toiling in secret for him. Despite Braun's exploitation, Wilder says his first film boss had an instinctive feel for what the public wanted and he learned a lot from him. Wilder also did considerable ghostwriting for Franz Schulz, who became best known in Berlin for the 1930 Erich Pommer hit, *Die Drei von der Tankstelle (Three from the Filling Station).* Unlike in the Hollywood system, writers generally worked at home, and Wilder remembers reporting mornings at nine to Schulz's residence on Jenaer Strasse near Bayrischen Platz. Sometimes, Schulz would go out at lunchtime and leave his young ghostwriter to continue the work, his stomach growling from hunger. Wilder says Schulz was so cheap that a big fight erupted between them over a liverwurst sandwich Wilder made for himself in Schulz's absence. Schulz deemed it "a breach of confidence," never admitting the possibility he wasn't paying his ghostwriter enough to afford his own lunch.

The memory sticks in Wilder's craw; he still enjoys telling tales of Schulz's stinginess: "When he came to America, he called himself Francis Spencer, so he wouldn't have to change the initials on his shirts." Wilder got some measure of satisfaction when he arrived for work one morning and Schulz greeted him with a pair of black eyes. " 'What happened?' I asked. He said he was having an affair with Mrs. Erich Maria Remarque, and Erich beat him up." (Wilder also brings up this story to set the record straight, since Maurice Zolotow cited rumors that *Wilder* had an affair with Mrs. Remarque. "I never saw her in my life!" he laments.)

By forgoing meals, Wilder somehow scraped enough money together to buy a used car, a khaki-colored Chrysler two-seater with a rumble seat and a wooden steering wheel. Half the time, however, he couldn't afford fuel, and the sporty vehicle would remain parked on the Kurfürstendamm for days.

Among the film-industry people Wilder befriended at the time was Joe Pasternak, the Hungarian later to be known as the producer of such Hollywood films as *Destry Rides Again, Anchors Aweigh, The Great Caruso, Love Me or Leave Me* and the Deanna Durbin musicals. Pasternak managed the Berlin branch of Universal Pictures along with Paul Kohner, who would later become one of Hollywood's leading agents, with a client list including Billy Wilder. Pasternak arranged for Wilder to serve as a tour guide for Allan Dwan, the pioneering Hollywood filmmaker who directed Wilder's hero Douglas Fairbanks in *Robin Hood*. Dwan had just married a Ziegfeld showgirl and was spending his honeymoon touring Germany. Wilder met with Dwan at the Hotel Adlon, and jumped at his offer of 100 marks per week. The only trouble was, all Wilder knew of Germany was Berlin. The money was too good to pass up, though, so the novice guide bought a Baedeker and furiously studied it at night.

The first stop was Dresden, and Wilder dutifully walked the Dwans through the Staatsgalerie and pointed out the museum's great holdings. Dwan cut the lecture short—he wanted to get back to the hotel and its bar. It was Prohibition time in America and, apparently, Dwan's main reason for coming to Europe was the opportunity to indulge his love of the double martini without looking over his shoulder. Dwan's wife tried to keep up with her fast-drinking husband; Wilder says he stuck to lemonade. The amateur guide's job was made all that easier; wherever they went, it was "fifteen minutes of museum, fifteen minutes of classical architecture, and four hours of martinis."

Easy money, until they got to Heidelberg. By this time, Wilder was faking his way through his lectures, zanily embellishing on his vague muddle of facts and figures. While touring an old castle, however, the trio crossed paths with a group of English tourists and their guide, and Wilder's ruse was instantly exposed. Dwan fired Wilder on the spot, adding, "Never trust a son of a bitch who doesn't drink!"

Later that year, 1927, Wilder secured a job as night editor for the *Börsen Courier* on Spittelmarkt, but this too was not fated to last. The young writer couldn't resist adding a sardonic line or two to the dull press accounts that landed on his desk. But one of his little jokes had some unexpected fallout. A man was given a disproportionately harsh sentence for stealing some empty egg crates around the time of Succoth, the Jewish Festival of Tabernacles; Wilder commented that perhaps the poor fellow only wanted to build his own tabernacle. Angry letters came in from Jewish readers, and Wilder was ultimately let go by his Jewish editor-in-chief, Emil Faktor. Wilder speculates that it wasn't so much his joke that caused offense, but the reference he made to a Jewish holy day in the headline; in these difficult times, assimilated Jews believed it was unwise to call too much attention to their religious rituals.

Wilder took his firing in stride, but 1927 brought a much more devastating blow. Max and Eugenia were preparing to join their son Willie in New York, and Max came to Berlin to say good-bye. During his stay, he was suddenly stricken with severe stomach pains; Max died of an abdominal rupture in the ambulance on the way to the hospital, in the arms of his younger son. Somehow, Billie found the money to give his father a decent burial, in the Jewish cemetery in Berlin's Schönhauser Allee.

Billie was now living in a small, third-floor room in the home of the York-Schulz family at Victoria Luiseplatz 11, today a drab-looking, gray cement apartment house. The tree-lined plaza is fairly inviting, but its central fountain is marred by graffiti, and there's even graffiti next to the plaque commemorating Wilder's early days there. (A plaque above Wilder's also identifies No. 11 as the home of composer Ferruccio Busoni.) As in Vienna, his domestic situation was bourgeois enough to make it difficult for a young, single man to carry on an active romantic life, but Wilder managed to keep a steady succession of girlfriends—including the daughter of Berlin's police chief.

The house at Victoria Luiseplatz is the source of two of Wilder's favorite anecdotes about his Berlin days. The writer's room was next to a bathroom with a faulty toilet, and he could hear the sound of the water running all night long. "Since I was young and romantic," he says, "I'd imagine it was a beautiful waterfall—just to get my mind off the monotony of it." Many years later, Wilder and his wife vacationed in Europe with Samuel and Frances Goldwyn and stayed at the Hotel Kaiserhof, a luxury hotel in Badgastein, next to a stunning waterfall. Lying in bed at night and listening to the sound of the water, the fantasies of Wilder's youth turned on him. "There I am in that resort," he winces, "and all I can think of is that goddamned toilet!"

In a much repeated story, Wilder credits his living situation at Victoria Luiseplatz with his first big movie sale. Next to his room lived the daughter of the housekeeper—the name was either Inge or Lulu. Her lover, Heinz, was the owner of a thriving lesbian bar, the Silhouette. One night, the young lodger was again being kept awake—not by the toilet, but by the sounds of lovemaking from the next room. Suddenly, a strange thump erupted, and the passionate noises stopped and turned into frantic whispers. Wilder heard the door to the room next door open, then through his own door a man entered, holding his pants and shoes in his hands. Outside the adjoining room, Wilder heard a knocking and the words, "It's me, Heinz!" Inge or Lulu let her boyfriend in, and he began screaming, "Where is he? I'll kill him!" while the stranger stood quaking in his underwear in Wilder's room. The two men quietly introduced themselves, and Wilder discovered he had no less a personage than Herr Galitzenstein, the head of Maxim Films, standing there, his very life in the ghostwriter's hands.

After lending Galitzenstein a shoehorn, Wilder grabbed one of the film scripts he had been trying unsuccessfully to peddle all over Berlin and handed it to the producer. "Bring it to my office tomorrow," Galitzenstein suggested. "Tomorrow you'll forget you ever met me," Wilder replied. "You must read it now!" When the producer said he didn't have his glasses, Wilder offered to read it out loud. Thus cornered, Galitzenstein agreed to buy the script sight unseen, gave Wilder 500 marks, and snuck out of the building, leaving behind his new acquisition. As the story goes, Wilder encountered Inge (or Lulu) the next day and told her: "Thank you for sending me Galitzenstein. But he is a small-time producer. Next time, please—Erich Pommer!"

The Galitzenstein incident may not have led anywhere, but Wilder's persistence and social networking were beginning to bring results. The author of "Waiter, Bring Me a Dancer" was an established presence at popular artists' gathering places like the Café Kranzler and especially the Romanisches Café, where it was hard to miss him banging out articles on his portable typewriter. In Berlin's lively coffeehouse circles, Wilder mingled comfortably with the likes of Thomas Mann, Bertolt Brecht, Mies van der Rohe, George Grosz and Fritz Lang. He became friendly with a rising cabaret performer and film actress named Marlene Dietrich. At the Kranzler, he was a frequent breakfast companion to Carl Mayer, the great German screenwriter of *The Cabinet of Dr. Caligari*, *The Last Laugh* and *Sunrise*.

The creative energy concentrated in Berlin was electric, and fraught with promise. Wilder learned that anything was possible when he gave some advice to his friend Erich Maria Remarque, then the editor of *Die Dame*, the most influential women's-fashion magazine in Germany. Remarque announced he was leaving his high-paying post to write a realistic novel about the ordeal of German soldiers during World War I. "Who cares about the war!" Wilder insisted, adding that Remarque would be crazy to give up his cushy job for such a dubious undertaking. The novel was *All Quiet on the Western Front*, a modern classic that also became the Academy Award–winning Best Picture of 1930. "I almost stopped it single-handedly," Wilder says, sheepishly.

Wilder's own breakthrough as a credited screenwriter finally happened in 1929, just as the silent-film era was about to come to a sudden halt. Having forgiven Wilder for the Allan Dwan fiasco, Joe Pasternak and Paul Kohner of Universal thought of the feisty writer when their American boss, Carl Laemmle, assigned them the task of setting up a directing vehicle in Germany for his nephew Ernst. The movie would feature Eddie Polo, a faded American action-serial star who had been working in Germany since 1926. Kohner and Pasternak each took credit for the idea of hiring Wilder—Kohner because he liked the young man's personality, Pasternak because Wilder supposedly owed him a thousand marks from a poker game.

One of Wilder's few solo writing credits, *Der Teufelsreporter* (loosely translated as *The Daredevil Reporter)* is a giddily enjoyable, completely inconsequential B movie. The film virtually begs not to be taken seriously, centering as it does on the kidnapping of thirteen American heiresses traveling through Germany. Eddie Polo plays a character named Eddie Polo, a reporter from the *Rapid Journal* who doubles as a fearless action hero; at one point, he calls in his report to the paper while firing a gun at the villains. The second half is virtually one continuous chase, and Wilder even makes sure the virginal heroines are stripped to their underwear before they are rescued. Today, apart from its Wilder connection, the picture is most notable for its location filming on the streets of Berlin and for the presence of the distinguished actor Robert Garrison, veteran of films for Pabst and Dreyer, as the main villain.

The same year as this trifle, Wilder became involved with one of the true landmarks of German cinema. It sprang from a conversation at the Romanisches Café, which Wilder recounted in a February 1930 article in the leftist newspaper *Montag Morgen:*

> "This thing has got to be made!"
> A small man springs up from a sitting position and bangs on the marble tabletop. The lemonade glasses shake. Moritz Seeler.
> We are five.
> A Herr Eugen Schüfftan, inventor of some world-famous film effects . . . looks at him with his mouth half-open: "Without money?"

"Without money!"

The third one, Robert Siodmak from Dresden (at first newspapers, then theater, then film distribution), finds it difficult not to laugh out loud: "Without a studio?"

"Without a studio!"

"So, completely off the cuff?" The question comes from Edgar Ulmer, twenty-four years old, emigrated for a half-year from Hollywood, where he was a designer for Murnau's *Sunrise*.

"Completely off the cuff!"

The fifth one is me, Billie Wilder: "Then we are set on this?"

"Yes, agreed. Off the cuff. Without a studio. Without money."

So began the Film Studio. At a coffeehouse table. In June, 1929.

The first named of the group, Moritz Seeler, was a diminutive thirty-five-year-old who, in 1921, founded the Junge Bühne (Young Stage), an avant-garde playhouse offering provocative works like Bertolt Brecht's *Baal* and Arnolt Bronnen's *Patricide*. Major stars, playwrights, directors and designers got their start at Seeler's little theater and moved on. Now, after years of struggle, Seeler was eager to establish himself as a film impresario.

Completely lacking in moviemaking experience, Seeler recruited one of the café regulars, Robert Siodmak, the twenty-eight-year-old son of a Galician furrier and banker, born while his parents were visiting Memphis, Tennessee, on a business trip. After an unsuccessful attempt to found a magazine in Germany, Siodmak became a stage actor and then secured work as a translator of silent-movie intertitles and as an editor and assistant director hired by his uncle, Heinrich Nebenzahl, producer of the hit Harry Piel action-detective films. To earn extra cash, he also returned to the publishing world—in the lowly position of advertising salesman for the illustrated magazine *Neue Revue*.

The two other brainstormers Wilder refers to were cameraman Eugen Schüfftan, the thirty-six-year-old creator of the patented Schüfftan process, a cinematographic breakthrough that used mirrors to blend live actors with elaborate miniatures in such films as Fritz Lang's *Metropolis*; and assistant director Edgar G. Ulmer, who, in addition to his duties as production-design assistant on the classic *Sunrise*, had been stage designer for the great theatrical director Max Reinhardt for six years and had worked on some low-budget westerns for Universal.

Despite the cries of "Without money!," a bare minimum of cash had to be rounded up for the Romanisches gang's film project. The financing came from any number of sources, depending on whose memory you trust. Siodmak asked for a loan of 5,000 marks (then roughly $1,400) from his uncle Heinrich, whose Harry Piel movies cost 200,000 marks apiece. Both Wilder and Siodmak (in his biography) say Nebenzahl came through with the full amount, but, according to Siodmak's younger brother Curt, the uncle "gave Robert 50 marks and told him to go ahead—that was the full amount of his financial contribution." A much bigger share of the movie's 9,000-mark budget, says Curt Siodmak, came from his own recent wind-fall—a 12,000-mark sale of a novel to the Scherl publishing house's illus-trated newspaper *Die Woche*. Then there is the recollection of Edgar G. Ulmer, who said *he* financed the bulk of the project with money he brought over from America. Despite all these possible benefactors, the team was somehow still short of cash. Wilder spoke in his 1930 *Montag Morgen* piece of finding a backer on the Friedrichstrasse: "We bluffed him with numbers. He believed 3 percent in our abilities, and 97 percent in the chance to have control over an improbably inexpensive film. We drew up ridiculously low calculations. Told him of waltzes and an army regiment that we had to have. . . ."

What is not in dispute is that the idea for the film originated with the younger Siodmak, who was not only a journalist and fiction writer but an engineer with the German railway. "I was trying to find a story that could be made into a film Robert could direct—his most ardent wish," says Si-odmak in his forthcoming autobiography. "A writer can get a break by writing a successful story or a book. But how does a director get his chance? He first needs a 'vehicle,' a story, which I hoped to supply for Robert, since he was brother, father figure and family to me."

Because the aspiring filmmakers had no money to pay professional actors, Curt Siodmak devised a story about ordinary, working-class Ber-liners on a Sunday outing, to be made with amateur performers on the streets of the city. The ninety-three-year-old writer, who lives today with his wife, Henrietta, on a ranch in northern California, is eager to set the record straight about his contribution to this historic film, which came to be known as *Menschen am Sonntag* (*People on Sunday*). No fewer than six future filmmakers of significance were connected with the project, and the story of its creation reflects the clash of healthy egos. The greatest rivalry, however, was between the Siodmak brothers. Robert told biographer Hans C. Blumenberg that his brother's idea "was never written up"; Curt says he wrote a fifty-page treatment. Once the film was completed, Curt notes, "Robert reluctantly put my name on the credits, but in such small lettering that it seems to underline Billy Wilder's name: 'After an idea by Curt Siodmak.' For Robert, one Siodmak's prominence in the film business, his, was quite sufficient. He never lost that obsession of sibling rivalry to the end of his life."

Robert Siodmak also slighted Wilder in the Blumenberg book; even though Wilder gets screenplay credit, Robert claimed he contributed only one gag to the film. But all other accounts contradict Siodmak's harsh assessment, indicating Wilder was very much part of the collaborative team. The sole screenplay credit, however, does seem a bit generous. In his 1930 *Montag Morgen* account, Wilder noted that the screenplay consisted of all of seven typewritten pages, but Curt Siodmak declares, "There was no screenplay. We devised scenes from day to day." Ulmer confirmed the same sentiment in a 1961 *Cahiers du Cinema* interview: "Billie Wilder did not write a true script. We would have one drink in the tavern and say, 'Next Sunday, we will do this and this.' We had a plot thread and defined characters. Our main weapon was that each person was responsible for his own part—even the assistant [Fred] Zinnemann could join in the conversation." One of the film's young "stars," Brigitte Borchert, remembers the same sort of freewheeling creative atmosphere: "Nothing written ever appeared. Often, we had to wait a long time in the morning in an outdoor restaurant between the railway station and the Wannsee swimming pool until the gentlemen of the shooting team worked out the day's scenes at the next table. They also debated during the many involuntary pauses that occurred because we could only shoot in sunlight. Even during the shooting, [Robert] Siodmak would shout instructions to us, things that had come to him in a flash."

The content, style and shooting method of *Menschen am Sonntag* perfectly meshed. The theme, "people on Sunday," was inspired largely by the fact that most of the cast and crew had regular jobs, and Sunday was generally the only day they could all assemble for the shoot. In response, the team developed the most basic of story lines: On a Saturday afternoon in Berlin, a wine merchant named Wolfgang makes a date for a Sunday excursion to the Nikolassee beach with a pretty young stranger, a film extra named Christl. The wine seller invites his best friend, Erwin, a taxi driver, and Erwin's wife, Annie, to join him. But come Sunday morning, lazy Annie refuses to get out of bed, and Erwin leaves a note for her to join them later. Christl, meanwhile, has invited along her pal Brigitte, a record-shop clerk. Christl becomes jealous when Wolfgang shifts his attention to Brigitte, but the two girls make up after their escorts ignore them to help two female strangers recover a lost paddle during a boating interlude. The quartet return to the city on a crowded bus, and Erwin discovers that his wife has slept the entire day. It's "a day like all the others," a title card notes, but "all the world lives for the return of Sunday."

After ten days of production, Wilder publicized the activities of the self-proclaimed Film Studio 1929 in an article in the newspaper *Tempo*.

We work at a fevered tempo. We have rented a rickety cart from a baker in Nikolassee and glide the equipment across the sand. Stand fourteen hours at the camera and tackle everything in an orderly manner. We ourselves watch the focus, kneeling the whole day in the sea, and if we are threatened by heatstroke, then we stick our heads in the water. I don't believe that the Chang or the Pamir expeditions had more willpower or suffered more privations. My God, such primitive means are placed at our disposal! While a few kilometers away, in Neue Babelsberg [site of the UFA studios], they are perhaps building the great sets for Nina Petrowna's* wonderful lies, we're here with a completely laughable sum of money to shoot a few truths that seem important to us.

Searching for a title, we vacillated for a long time between *Sommer 29* [*Summer 29*] and *Junge Leute wie alle* [*Young People Like Everyone*]. We finally decided on *So ist es und nicht anders* [*So It Is and Nothing Else*], because this title unequivocally said what we

---

* Wilder is referring to Erich Pommer's 1929 costume drama, *Die wundbare Luge der Nina Petrowna (The Wonderful Lies of Nina Petrowna).*

wanted: It is everything so completely different than what we have come to see in film; so uncomplicated, so little editing, so little drama and so little paper! . . . A totally simple story, quiet and full of the melodies that sound to us daily in all our ears. Without gags and without cleverly contrived situations. . . . We have proceeded on well-trampled highways toward a small and entirely unused, frighteningly lonely path: The sign says "Life."

Film Studio 1929 was a manifesto for a new kind of cinema, a rebellion against the melodramatic and comic conventions and fancy production values of UFA and the lesser German studios, even if the rebels were partly motivated by their inability to break into UFA's exclusive club. "It was a shallow time in German pictures," Wilder says. "The big companies that were making pictures, they were kind of lost in schmaltz."

People on Sunday did indeed contribute something different, although its innovations didn't come wholly out of the blue. The late film historian Siegfried Kracauer grouped it with a class of pictures called cross-section films, concerned with presenting a representative cross-section of German life. The first of these was *The Adventures of a Ten-Mark Note* (1926), produced by the great cinematographer Karl Freund and written by noted film theorist Béla Balázs. The film follows the titular bill as it changes hands, offering an excuse to observe settings as diverse as a factory, a pawnshop, a late-night café, a hospital and a ragpicker's makeshift home. Balázs also included a central love story to give the film some added structure.

The most celebrated of the cross-section films, however, was *Berlin, the Symphony of a Great City* (1927), an abstract portrait of daily life in Berlin, conceived by Carl Mayer and taken over by the experimental filmmaker Walter Ruttmann. Although completely lacking in narrative, the film was a great success with German audiences and remains a staple of college film classes.

The style of *People on Sunday* falls between these two antecedents, being neither fully abstract nor tied to a gimmick like a busy ten-mark note. Arguably, it takes the biggest risk, by introducing a quintet of appealing characters and then defying our expectation of building a traditional story around them. The film is also somewhat radical in its choice of ordinary working-class characters for whom high drama consists of deciding how to spend their Saturday night.

In his 1930 *Montag Morgen* account, Wilder chronicles the casting process: "At first, we thought about young actors. But the people had to be genuine. We searched. Seeler discovered in front of a Kurfürstendamm bar a chauffeur, taxi number 1A 10 088, Erwin Splettstösser. He was immediately cast. But Fraulein [Brigitte] Borchert thought that we meant something entirely different. We found her buying phonograph records. She was difficult to persuade; her family took us for white slavers. In spite of that, she came to the test shoot on Thielplatz. Also Christl Ehlers came—she had experience already, she had once been an extra at Dupont [a Berlin studio] and gave us her word of honor that she was on 'du' [familiar] terms with the cinematographer for [director] Lupu Pick. One [Wolfgang] von Waltershausen just fell into our arms—he was exactly what we needed." The five actors (the fifth being Annie Schreyer as the lazy wife) were paid ten marks a day.

Initially, direction of the film was headed by Rochus Gliese, the renowned stage and film designer whose credits included the classics *The Golem* and *Sunrise* (for which he was nominated for the very first Oscar for interior decoration). Seeler had long wanted Gliese to direct a film, and set up a meeting between the designer and Wilder. Gliese agreed to give the project a try, with Robert Siodmak as his assistant.

According to Brigitte Borchert, Gliese left after fourteen days of shooting because of "differences of opinion"—primarily with his imposed assistant and money conduit, Siodmak. As Siodmak exaggeratedly recalled the dispute, "Gliese shot so much film on the first day that I threw him out." Siodmak then promoted himself to director. As Wilder explains it, "Robert was the director for a very simple reason: When kids play football on a meadow, the one who owns the football is the captain—and he owned the camera."

The atmosphere didn't get any better. Robert Siodmak said something to offend Edgar Ulmer's American wife, and within days the Ulmers were on their way back to America. Then Moritz Seeler, fed up with the chaos, abandoned the company.

Schüfftan, meantime, brought in as his camera assistant a twenty-two-year-old former music and law student named Fred Zinnemann, whose only significant credit was an early Marlene Dietrich film, *I Kiss Your Hand, Madame*. In his autobiography, Zinnemann recalls Wilder as "a highly strung young man." Asked to elaborate on that statement, he replies, "It's very simple. Some people are high-strung and others are not. A racehorse is not the same as a plow horse. . . . During any filming, there's a certain amount of pressure, and everybody reacts [according] to their own character. His reactions were nervous. He was basically a nervous person. But there was nothing extraordinary, nothing clinical or pathological about it."

According to Zinnemann's memoir, Rochus Gliese and Edgar Ulmer weren't the only members of the team who experienced friction with Robert Siodmak. "We went to the location by bus and in the evening Billy and Siodmak took the exposed negative to the laboratory to be developed. One day they got into an argument and walked angrily off the bus, leaving the negative behind them—three days' work which was never seen again and had to be reshot."

In light of all the wrangling for credit, creatively and financially, on *People on Sunday*, it's refreshing to hear Zinnemann talk as humbly as he does about his role in this movie milestone. "As the assistant cameraman, your job is really mechanical. Your job consists of loading and unloading film, making sure that the film that has been exposed is properly labeled and sent to the lab, carrying the camera around, cleaning the equipment, cleaning the lenses, and taking the tripod to where the cameraman wants it. You wouldn't call it menial, but it's a very specific job of manual work. Creatively, I had nothing to do with it. And so I don't like to be presented as somebody who creatively had any kind of influence. I didn't." By the time *People on Sunday* premiered, Zinnemann was in Hollywood, working as an extra in *All Quiet on the Western Front*.

Zinnemann credits camera wizard Schüfftan, and perhaps Ulmer, as the only ones who really knew what they were doing. "All of us were pretty much amateurs," he says. But the results of this amateur undertaking were daring, refreshing. Using unknown and nonprofessional actors to play people very much like themselves brought a charming naturalism to this weekend amble. And, despite the disputed authorship, there's a rueful wit to the film that feels very much like the later Wilder.

In one vivid early sequence, Erwin the taxi driver waits impatiently for his wife to rouse herself from bed and get dressed for their Saturday night at the movies. But by the time she's ready, Erwin's buddy Wolfgang has arrived at the door, suggesting the two play cards. A fight erupts between husband and wife: He takes her prized photo of matinee idol Willy Fritsch from the wall and lathers it with shaving cream; she retaliates by attacking his Garbo picture with a curling iron. Wilder has always enjoyed putting mischievous topical movie references into his scripts; this was the first.

Later, the film has fun with the hoariest of movie clichés (even in 1929)—the camera that leaves two embracing lovers and pans toward the sky. As Wolfgang and Brigitte enjoy a secret rendezvous, the camera rises up to the trees, then (as if missing its target) descends back down to a pile of trash. At the end of the love scene, Brigitte removes a pine cone that has been poking her in the back. In 1929, Wilder described the filmmakers' attitude toward traditional movie notions of romance: "At the end of the film, we have a brief scene that perhaps says everything the clearest: After Saturday and after Sunday, entirely by chance our young ones stand in front of a suburban movie theater without seeing it. Behind a poster proclaims, 'Weekend Magic.' And that is the dissonance we want to show— between the weekend-film inside and the reality of the Sunday our five people have experienced."

People on Sunday is also fascinating for the candid portrait it presents of the Berlin middle class at work and play, before the conflicts of the coming decade would sour their idyll. One especially delightful sequence shows a cross-section of Berliners having their pictures taken at a photo booth; freeze-frames inserted into the film invariably catch the subjects with the most unbecoming expressions.

As both Wilder and Curt Siodmak note, *People on Sunday* anticipated the real-life, naturalistic approach of Italian neorealism by some fifteen years. Says Siodmak, "They did the same story in Italy, called *Domenica d'Agusto* [*Sunday in August*]. Sir Carol Reed in England made *Bank Holiday*. Different stories, but the nucleus was kids going out to the country and what happens when they come back. This is *Menschen am Sonntag*, and out of that came five people who made it internationally. If Hitler hadn't thrown us out, believe me, we would have created a German film industry that would have been competitive with Hollywood."

Schüfftan and Robert Siodmak completed editing the film on December 11, 1929. Now came the challenge of getting it shown. Wilder's 1930 account continues:

> We project it for the gentlemen of the great film companies. No one takes us seriously. The head of distribution swears that after thirty years' experience, he will resign his job if this film even receives a premiere somewhere—not to speak at all of a success. . . . A new backer appears. He will possibly finance a nighttime presentation. We show it to UFA. Brodnitz, the head of the theater division, gets to see it. And takes it. For the regular evening schedule at the U.T. Kurfürstendamm. We are flabbergasted.
>
> As we take a bow around 9 P.M., we don't know what is happening. Are we being taken seriously or laughed at? In any event, between 9 and 9:15, in the midst of so many heart palpitations, the idea for a new film appears.

Robert Siodmak remembered that "people applauded like crazy" at the end of the first performance. "The news of our success spread like wildfire. Within twenty minutes, a thousand people were lining up to see the film. . . . Seeler threatened to shoot me if I didn't come with him onto the stage. Finally I consented. As I made my way through the stage exit with difficulty after the last showing, hundreds of people shook my hand and congratulated me."

"For somebody who had never had his name on the screen, it was very exciting," Wilder says today. "The picture came at the right time."

Newspaper accounts of the period support Siodmak's description of the opening-night mania. "The public likes it," reported the *Lichtbild-Bühne*. "In the hugest crowds! A true storm of applause called the participants onto the stage." Critics were generally enchanted by the film's spare but artful approach to ordinary Berlin life. "We actually become touched," said another contemporary reviewer, "because we recognize ourselves and pity ourselves and rejoice in ourselves. The wonderful destiny of this Film Studio 1929, which we with our whole heart wish a long existence, lies in the splendid choice of the typical." *Der Abend* praised the filmmakers as "neutral but sensitive observers. Once, Paris was shown to us in an impressive, simple manner; now, we see Berlin without the shine of advertisements in lights and the crazy nightlife of the bars. The premiere audience was enthusiastic. Apparently, it was worth it to discover the everyday."

The influential critic Rudolf Arnheim had a decidedly more mixed reaction: "Photographically, the film contains a few wonderfully beautiful takes and ideas, but they are insignificant. A studio should be fresher, should attempt the most refined cinematographic art and be more daring in its choice of themes." Still, he added, "what this novice gets wrong is a thousand times more important than what is correctly made by a troop of dexterous film-industry manufacturers. We would sacrifice with an easy heart all the Hungarian rhapsodies of the Hugenberg privy councillors if every week we could see such an experimental film."

Siegfried Kracauer, in his definitive psychological history of the early German film, *From Caligari to Hitler*, was largely unimpressed. Even as he declared *People on Sunday* "one of the first films to draw attention to the plight of the 'little man' " he criticized it for its "noncommittal" political stance.

Still, there's no disputing that *People on Sunday* is a landmark, not only for its stylistic daring but for its astounding confluence of filmmaking talent. Robert Siodmak directed several more films in Germany until he fled in 1933, and went on to become one of the most notable of Hollywood's film noir directors, with such credits as *Phantom Lady*, *The Spiral Staircase*, *The Killers*, *The Dark Mirror* and *Criss Cross*. He returned to Germany in the mid-1950s and died in 1973. Siodmak's brother Curt also became a Hollywood director, but is best known as the screenwriter of such horror classics as *The Wolf Man*, *I Walked with a Zombie* and *The Beast with Five Fingers* and as the author of the novel *Donovan's Brain*. Edgar G. Ulmer found a cult reputation as an American B-movie auteur, most celebrated for *The Black Cat*, *Bluebeard* and the fatalistic low-budgeter *Detour*; he died in 1972. Eugen Schüfftan (1893–1977) immigrated to France in 1933, where he supervised the poetic lighting of Marcel Carné's classics *Bizarre Bizarre* and *Quai des Brumes;* he came to Hollywood in the forties and eventually won an Oscar in 1961 for photographing the Paul Newman pool-shark drama *The Hustler*.* Fred Zinnemann became a director of documentaries

* In the U.S., he was known as Eugene Shuftan.

and shorts before breaking into features in the 1940s; his long list of credits includes such renowned films as *High Noon*, *From Here to Eternity*, *The Nun's Story*, *The Sundowners*, *A Man for All Seasons* and *Julia*. A three-time Academy Award winner, he lives today in London.

Sadly, Moritz Seeler, the man who brought all this budding talent together, perished under the Nazis in 1942, at the age of forty-six.

FOUR

Dreams and Nightmares

LIKE MANY AN ACCLAIMED "ART FILM," *PEOPLE ON SUNDAY* did not enjoy a similar success outside Berlin and a few other big-city engagements. It was, after all, a radical departure from the glamorous escapism and melodramatic thrills that were the steady movie diet of an anxious German people. But even more crippling was its absence of sound: The makers of *People on Sunday* were lucky to secure *any* Berlin booking in February 1930, much less one on the fashionable Kurfürstendamm. The thunderous response to a singing Al Jolson in 1927's *The Jazz Singer* had rocked the film industry; virtually overnight, panicky American studios converted to primitive sound-recording processes. The first all-talking picture, *Lights of New York*, appeared in 1928, and by January of the following year the sensation had spread to German production, when the largely silent *I Kiss Your Hand, Madame* featured star Harry Liedtke miming to the hit title song. By November, the first all-talking German production, *I Have Loved You*, hit theaters, to be followed in December by UFA's first complete sound film, *Melody of the Heart*. In 1929, the German film industry produced 210 silent films and 14 sound or partial-sound films; by the next year, there were 111 sound films and 75 silent films, of which 15 were post-synchronized. The revolution had arrived.

With a certain wistfulness, Wilder notes, "We were just getting going when sound came in. In the silent era, there were some wonderful writers like Carl Mayer, like the ones in Russia, who were striving to dig a bit deeper. But then UFA started concentrating on films like *The Blue Angel*— that cost ten times as much as the little silent picture that we did. And so we had to go back to what the studios thought had a chance to make some profit. Our idea of doing pictures on a slightly higher level fell on its face."

Even though it was a remnant of a fading era, *People on Sunday* nonetheless brought immediate good fortune to its director. When the glowing reviews came out, Robert Siodmak recalled, "I locked myself in the toilet and cried with relief. The same afternoon, UFA called and engaged me." Siodmak was hired by writers' department head Robert Liebmann, a veteran screenwriter whose versatility extended from horror to adventure films, from sophisticated comedies to melodramas and operettas.

Wilder also got the attention of Liebmann, under quite different circumstances. Holding court at the Romanisches Café, Wilder was complaining in a loud voice about how the great Liebmann never gave a break to young talent. Then, a stranger came over and introduced himself as the very same Liebmann. Wilder remembers him saying, "Look, if you know so much, okay, we'll put you to work on a script."

Wilder was still ghostwriting, and prior to receiving his first onscreen UFA credit, he made an unsung contribution to his first sound film, UFA's *Ein Burschenlied aus Heidelberg (A Student Song from Heidelberg)*. A musical vehicle for matinee idol Willi Forst, this story of romance between an American coed and a German student was credited to Viennese playwright, novelist and composer Ernst Neubach.

Wilder's first official UFA credit was *Der Mann, der seinen Mörder sucht* (*The Man Who Looked for His Murderer*), a black comedy directed by Robert Siodmak and adapted by Wilder, Curt Siodmak and Ludwig Hirschfeld from a play by Ernst Neubach, with additional inspiration from a Jules Verne story. The Siodmak brothers had already caused a stir at the studio with a surrealistic twelve-minute short, *Der Kampf mit dem Drachen* (*The Battle with the Dragon*), about a poor lodger who is tormented by his gorgonlike landlady until he can't take it anymore and accidentally kills her; a jury of his peers, all oppressed lodgers, sets him free. Filmed in one day, this fantasy/satire outraged the UFA board but found a champion in studio head Erich Pommer.*

With *Der Mann*, Robert Siodmak continued in this experimental mode. An offbeat comedy, the film begins with its main protagonist, Hans Herfort (Heinz Rühmann), standing forlornly in front of a mirror with a gun pointed to his head. The sound of breaking glass distracts him from his suicide attempt; a burglar has broken into the apartment. When the intruder grabs his gun, Hans doesn't resist but declares he *wants* to be shot. As the burglar tries to take his leave, Hans offers him 10,000 marks—his life insurance premium—if the thug will kill him. Finally, they agree, and it's a most civilized transaction: Hans types up an agreement while the burglar dictates, and when Hans starts to play a lament on his piano, his hired killer insists on something more jaunty. By midnight, they decree, Hans will be dead.

That evening, however, everything changes. Treating himself to a final meal at a lively nightclub, Hans falls in love with the winsome Kitty (Lien Deyers) and decides life isn't so bad after all. Meanwhile, the burglar makes a series of hapless attempts to fulfill his contract: He plants a bomb in a package in Hans's topcoat, but an unfortunate thief steals the bundle; he wires Hans's living-room chair with an electric-shock device, but the contraption backfires on him. Thoroughly demoralized, the amateur hit man hands the assignment over to his syndicate. When Hans tracks him down and tries to cancel their deal, the would-be assassin is unable to tell him the identity of the new hired killer. But, as fate would have it, Hans has a nasty confrontation with the police and winds up in a jail cell with his new assassin—who, possessing only Hans's address, doesn't recognize his target.

The movie climaxes with a potentially lethal misunderstanding: When Hans sees Kitty with an older man, he gives up hope once again and spills the beans to his killer. But Kitty hasn't been cheating, she's been pleading with the insurance-company director to intercede on Hans's behalf. The confusion is cleared up just as the assassin is about to toss a bomb at Hans;

* Some Wilder filmographies say *Der Kampf mit der Drachen* was based on an uncredited idea by Wilder, but Curt Siodmak insists the film was inspired by a confrontation he had with a friend's landlady. More recent Wilder filmographies, including the one in an authorized German biography, do not list the film.

an explosion erupts, and the final image is of Hans and Kitty saying "I do" in a wedding ceremony in the wreckage of Hans's bombed-out apartment.

In an article he wrote at the time, Robert Siodmak hailed *Der Mann, der seinen Mörder sucht* as a new kind of German picture: a "grotesque film" conceived as a tribute to the "insane improbabilities" and heightened slapstick of great American silent comedians like Buster Keaton, Charles Chaplin and Harold Lloyd. Even though its morbid opening and overall premise may seem particularly Germanic, *Der Mann* is not so distant from the darker preoccupations and cavalier brutality often found in the work of the silent era's comic geniuses, especially Keaton. The film may begin in the depths of despair, but it quickly turns desperately "pro-life," and the frantic nature of Hans's quest to live is the engine that drives the comedy. It's the kind of predicament that will be refined to perfection nearly thirty years later in Wilder's most renowned comedy, *Some Like It Hot.*

Like *Der Teufelsreporter, Der Mann* features a high-speed chase through the streets of Berlin, this time in a careening ambulance. The movie is also highlighted by its striking, slightly off-kilter rooftop sets, its expressionistic use of shadows and its surprisingly adept sound mixing. Less serendipitous is its annoying reliance on goofy sound effects—heavy emphasis on timpani and toy whistles—to underline every sight gag. The music is credited to the otherwise brilliant Friedrich Holländer, already celebrated for writing Marlene Dietrich's "Falling in Love Again" and the rest of the *Blue Angel* score, who makes his acting debut as the chairman of an underworld song society, conducting with a revolver in his hand.

Berlin's film critics were delighted by the picture. Wilder's old haunt, *B.Z.*, called *Der Mann* "a well-crafted grotesque with extremely funny ideas. . . . Robert Siodmak has directed with such élan that laughter is always on his side." *Tempo* observed, "The camera gets a bit tipsy, it dances and jumps to Holländer's music," and praised the movie's "freshness, exuberance and superior wit." *8-Uhr-Abendblatt* declared it "a film of utmost cultivated black humor . . . with the most splendid ideas, with loving invention and execution of humorous terror."

The reviews, however, did not impress the public. Rühmann, who went on to become one of Germany's most popular film stars of the 1950s and '60s and who played a key role in Wim Wenders's *Faraway So Close* before his death in 1994, said about the experience: "We amused ourselves so much with our own gags that we often had to stop the takes for laughing. When the film got to the cinemas, nobody laughed anymore. This comedy à la *The Ladykillers* was too strange for the audience—we were thirty years too early."

Despite the film's box-office failure, Wilder found favor with UFA chieftain Pommer. "We worked at Pommer's villa outside Berlin," Curt Siodmak recalls. "He was very tough, but he protected us from the studio. He used to put out one mark in pennies, and whoever had a good idea would get one penny, three pennies, five pennies. And at the end of the evening, whoever had the most pennies won the day." Siodmak remembers the restless Wilder pacing back and forth in Pommer's office, catching the coins the producer threw his way. With his quick mind, Wilder was most often the winner of this odd creative contest.

"Pommer was not a man to have soft moments and make big friends," Wilder notes. "He was a very sober, very talented man—but there were no laughs there."

In 1931, Wilder began to make up for the countless screen credits denied him as a ghostwriter. In addition to *Der Mann, der seinen Mörder sucht*, he received onscreen credit for three films—*Ihre Hoheit befiehlt* (*Her Majesty Commands*), *Der falsche Ehemann* (*The Counterfeit Husband*) and *Emil und die Detektive* (*Emil and the Detectives*)—plus a story-idea acknowledgment for *Seitensprünge* (*Extramarital Escapade*).

Both *Ihre Hoheit befiehlt* and *Der falsche Ehemann* hinged on a device Wilder would return to many times in his film career: the masquerade. *Hoheit*, co-written with Paul Frank and UFA's formidable Robert Liebmann, is a typically light-headed German operetta set in an imaginary Bavarian principality drenched in nostalgic whimsy. Käthe von Nagy plays the mischievous Princess Marie-Christine who, bored with the palace routine, decides to mingle with the proletariat at a working-class ball. There, posing as a court manicurist named Mizzi, she meets and falls in love with the handsome Lieutenant von Conradi of the palace guard (Willy Fritsch), himself pretending to be a lowly delicatessen worker named Karl. The princess reveals her crush to the prime minister, who forbids any further contact with Karl and insists she go forward with an arranged marriage to the absentminded Prince von Leuchtenstein. Marie-Christine, meantime, recognizes Karl leading the guard outside the palace and continues to romance him as Mizzi, while impishly ordering his promotion to major. The new major, meanwhile, is recruited by the prime minister to seduce the princess away from Karl (his own alter ego!). Still pining for Mizzi, von Conradi suffers the indignity of another unearned promotion—to general. The picture ends with the hapless Prince von Leuchtenstein arriving embarrassingly late for a grand court ceremony, then refusing to dance with the princess. Marie-Christine instead waltzes with von Conradi, and hands him a dance card saying, "Mein Karl." To the amazement of the court, the princess and the general ride off together.

As fluffy as the film is, it somehow managed to seize the attention of Hollywood. Two years later, *Ihre Hoheit befiehlt* was remade as *Adorable*, a Fox vehicle for Janet Gaynor, featuring several of the same sight gags: the endless assembly line of palace chefs, all to prepare a simple soup; the use of comic dissolves as Karl's uniform acquires more and more medals and epaulets. It even uses the same composer, Werner Richard Heymann, though the lyrics in English must be heard to be believed: "You're so completely adorable / Is the way to your heart explorable? / Will this night be divine or deplorable?"

Wilder reteamed with Paul Frank on the screenplay for *Der falsche Ehemann*, in which identical-twin brothers with completely opposite personalities switch roles. Peter Hannemann is a dull Berlin manufacturer of the sleeping tonic Somnolin; his brother Paul (played by the same actor, Johannes Riemann) is the dynamic owner of a ski resort in the Swiss Alps. Peter's indifference to his wife, Ruth, prompts her to take off on a romantic escapade with the violin-playing gigolo Tartakoff; by coincidence, they wind up at Paul's resort. Paul, meantime, makes a surprise visit to Berlin, and persuades his brother to mind the resort while he whips Peter's business into shape: He changes the name of the tonic to Energin and launches a successful marketing campaign for this hot new elixir. At the resort, Peter falls for Ines, a wealthy guest's daughter who believes he is really Paul—an oddly clumsy and awkward Paul. Events come to a full boil when the real Paul returns, and all the principals get caught up in a mad chase through the corridors of the resort. The violinist is disposed of, a newly energized Peter reunites with his wife, and Paul proposes to Ines.

This lightweight comedy was well received by the German public, despite the bland performance of the underfed-looking Riemann in the lead roles. The pace is brisk and the gags are often amusing, particularly the satire of marketing scams as Somnolin becomes Energin. And, for the first time, you can sense Wilder mastering the mechanics of breakneck farce, a talent that would fully flower in movies like *Some Like It Hot* and *One, Two, Three*.

Seitensprünge further explored the subject of adultery—a matter that was no big deal to German audiences in 1931, but would land Wilder in the biggest mess of his career some thirty-three years later in America. Director Stefan Szekely's film is the simple story of a bourgeois couple, set in their ways, whose marriage is devastated by the aftermath of a night on the town. Uncle Emil, a high-living businessman visiting Berlin, takes Robert and Annemarie Burkhardt out to his favorite nightclub, the Andalusia, where he introduces his guests to the featured act, sultry tango dancers Carlo and Lupita. (As Robert watches the performance, Carlo becomes a big blur; Annemarie has the same focus problem with Lupita.) Carlo invites Annemarie to dance, while Lupita partners with Robert; the husband and wife are so besotted, they return the next day for private "dance lessons." Before you can say rumba, both Robert and Annemarie are recklessly taking off for romantic getaways with their new lovers. But soon, the bloom is off the rose the tango dancers clutch between their teeth: Robert has trouble keeping up with his fiery partner, and not only won't she light his cigar the way his wife does, she wants *him* to light her cigarette! Annemarie, in turn, sees Carlo's true colors when he starts expecting her to pick up the tab for dinner. In the end, the Burkhardts reconcile, the implication being that this extramarital escapade has done a world of good for their marriage. Wilder may not have written the actual screenplay—Ludwig Biro, B. E. Luthge and Karl Noti did—but the unsentimental attitude toward the institution of marriage is consistent with his later work, and the movie certainly makes apt use of his experience as a dancing gigolo.

Of all Wilder's German sound films, *Emil und die Detektive* is the most satisfying. It is also one of the few on which he received a solo writing credit, even though Wilder was working from a screenplay already turned in by the original book's author, Erich Kästner, and his collaborator Emeric Pressburger (who would later form a celebrated partnership with Michael Powell on such film classics as *The Red Shoes* and *Black Narcissus*). After Kästner's children's book became a huge popular success in 1928,

UFA bought the film rights and hired the author to work on the adaptation. According to Kästner, he and Pressburger crafted a good screenplay but delivered it too early. With time to kill, UFA executive Robert Liebmann handed the project to Wilder, who, in Kästner's words, "embellished the story and . . . vulgarized it." After much heated argument, the film's producer, Günther von Stapenhorst, director Gerhard Lamprecht and Liebmann promised that all three writers would be credited on the finished film—a promise that was not kept. Kästner never forgave Wilder, but Pressburger and Wilder remained good friends.

The film is generally faithful to Kästner's original story of a young boy named Emil from the small town of Neustadt who is robbed of 140 marks while traveling by train to see his grandmother in Berlin. In the big city, the innocent boy is befriended by a clever gang of street kids, who keep a constant eye on the thief and eventually expose his crime. When it's discovered that the crook is wanted for bank robbery, Emil is hailed as a hero.

Kästner's charge that Wilder "vulgarized" his charming story most likely stems from one outlandish touch. In the book, Emil simply falls asleep in the train compartment, and when he wakes up from a crazy dream his money—pinned inside his coat—is gone. Wilder instead has the stranger on the train (played with oily menace by Fritz Rasp of *Metropolis* fame) offer Emil a hallucinogenic bonbon, which the boy accidentally swallows. What follows is a drug-induced nightmare in the expressionistic UFA style: The stranger's evil eyes cast beams of light through the newspaper he's reading; the train compartment becomes very long and very high; an umbrella carries the boy up above the city toward an exploding clock tower. Emil's dream in the book was equally wild, but retained a childlike whimsy; the tainted candy gives the incident on the train a sinister edge beyond the realm of children's literature. (In another piece of business added by Wilder, the kids try to administer to the crook a dose of his own drug, to no avail.)

Even with Wilder's changes, the film is a vivid realization of the Kästner story, with an appealingly natural cast of young actors and a marvelous feel for the streets of Berlin as experienced by a boy seeing their wonders for the first time. Filming entirely on location, director Lamprecht captured a precious moment in time that's as lovely and fascinating as the footage in *People on Sunday*. The film was a huge critical and popular success and toured the American art-house circuit later that year. It was subsequently remade twice in English, in a British version and a 1964 Walt Disney production starring Walter Slezak.

BILLIE WILDER'S FINANCIAL STATUS WAS IMPROVING SIGNIFI-cantly. He moved to a new apartment in the tonily named Sachsisches Palais (Saxony Palace) on Sachsischen Strasse. Thanks to his friendship with the lyricist and screenwriter Max Kolpe (later Colpet), whose brother was a Bauhaus-schooled architect, he was able to furnish his apartment in the Bauhaus style with pieces by great names like Mies van der Rohe, Gropius and Breuer. Wilder even had enough spare cash to begin collecting works by some of the artists of Berlin's thriving gallery scene, the beginning of a passion that continues to this day.

Hans Feld, a colleague from Berlin's AAFA film studio, remembers the day Wilder bought a new car and couldn't resist gloating: "[Billie] sat nonchalantly on a corner of my desk and said, completely by-the-by, 'Imagine, I was traveling today along the Friedrichstrasse and saw (he named a successful screenwriter). And, you know, he was going on foot.' "*

Wilder would spend his summer weekends and holidays at either the posh Hiddensee island spa or the less fashionable Heringsdorf family spa. At Hiddensee, he would pass the time with the composer Franz Wachsmann (who changed his surname to Waxman after he arrived in Hollywood) and his married mistress. Whenever her husband came on the scene, says Wilder, she'd move into Wilder's room, and the conspiring writer would pretend he had been rooming with Wachsmann the whole time.

Wilder savored this life and, to keep gainfully employed, took Robert Liebmann's credo to his writers to heart: "Just don't be boring!" Even so, he tends to dismiss his German efforts. "Do I have to talk about them?" he groans. "They were all lousy." If pressed, the only one he'll single out for

---

* Feld also reveals that Wilder wrote for AAFA a film that does not appear in any of his official filmographies: *Aus dem Tagebuch einer schönen Frau (From the Diary of a Beautiful Woman)*, later released as *Das Abenteuer der Thea Roland (The Adventure of Thea Roland)*. It was the first film directed by Hermann Kosterlitz, who later went on to a successful career in America under the name Henry Koster, with such credits as *The Bishop's Wife, Harvey* and *The Robe*.

praise is *Emil und die Detektive:* "That was pretty good." Then again, Wilder is a tough critic of his own work, claiming he never watches even his most celebrated films and dismissing most of his later, less financially successful pictures. In his view, films generally don't stand the test of time very well. Back in 1979, he commented, "The other day, I saw Murnau's *The Last Laugh* again on television, script by the great Carl Mayer. . . . So naïve, the whole story, and so exaggerated! For that time, it may have been good, for that time it was a wonderful story, wonderfully designed by Murnau. Or *Potemkin.* Or a film like *M*—that was a terrific idea back then, daring and courageous, but today it would be made completely differently. . . . A great picture that was painted three hundred years ago is still a great picture today. But with film, it is an entirely different matter—very few retain their impact over the years. Nearly everything can be made better today, but no painter today can paint as well as Chardin painted his still lifes in the eighteenth century."

Of all the factors that date Wilder's German output, none is as detrimental as their songs. Just as audiences today find it hard to believe that the cloying musical numbers in Marx Brothers comedies were at one time a big selling point, so too it's sometimes difficult to get past the operetta conventions that were a staple of German film in the early 1930s. Remembers Wilder, "You had producers saying that you had to find a place for six or eight songs and then, in conversations with the composers and lyricists, you had to try to fine-tune what the character of those songs should be, whether they helped the story and how the connection with the theme of the story could be established. But you always had to make compromises. And often it was that the songs had not helped the plot, that they only interfered with the development of the story and unnecessarily held it up."

The most successful musical Wilder worked on in Berlin was a 1932 concoction called *Ein blonder Traum* (*A Blonde Dream*), a vehicle for three of the country's biggest stars—Willy Fritsch, Willi Forst and the multilingual, British-born Lilian Harvey. Fritsch and Forst play Berlin window cleaners, both named Willy, who become rivals for the attention of Jou-Jou (Harvey), a homeless former circus acrobat with dreams of stardom in Hollywood, fueled by a promise from an American producer named Merryman. The two Willys bring Jou-Jou to their home, a pair of abandoned railway cars filled with zany decorative touches. Wooing the girl, Willy I promises her a life of stability, Willy II a life of excitement. When Merryman comes to Berlin, Jou-Jou discovers that the man who offered her a movie contract was a fraud; she pleads her case with the real Merryman and is rudely turned away. But Willy II makes such an impassioned speech in her defense that Merryman offers *him* a contract, clearing the way for Jou-Jou and Willy I to settle down together.

Along with the chance to write for three popular stars, *Ein blonder Traum* gave Wilder the opportunity to learn from "the best popular German scriptwriter of the time"—his new collaborator, Walter Reisch. Oddly enough, it was Wilder who introduced Reisch to Erich Pommer—Reisch had managed to forge a successful career outside the powerful UFA. Calling Wilder "Pommer's favorite writer," Reisch recalled, "Billy was the life of the party. Pommer adored him, always had him around, always listened to him."

Within the limitations of the German musical genre, Wilder and Reisch came up with consistently clever business for *Ein blonder Traum*, such as the fight between the two Willys that opens the film—little physical insults that accelerate into an all-out brawl, a blatant homage to Laurel and Hardy, but deftly handled by the two stars. Also terrific is Willi Forst's speech to Merryman, an amusing précis of an actor's woes: ". . . then she plays a great farewell scene, believes the audience is having their hearts torn to pieces—and someone sneezes. Aaahchooo! And all the people laugh. Tell me, is that a life? Waking early when one really wants to sleep, eating zwieback with lemons when one has such an appetite for pig's knuckles with sauerkraut."

Best of all is the elaborate dream fantasy in which Jou-Jou imagines that a locomotive has attached itself to her railway-car home and is taking her through Europe, under the Atlantic Ocean, and across America to Hollywood. Director Paul Martin uses a patently fake miniature train: For the ocean sequence, he splits the screen horizontally between real waves and the toy train coursing along the sea bottom, amidst huge tropical fish. When the train gets to New York, it circles around a distorted skyline and the Statue of Liberty leans over and waves hello. Arriving in Hollywood, the two Willys are caked with dirt while Jou-Jou emerges in a spangly white dress revealing a bare midriff. But once she arrives at the studio, Jou-Jou's subconscious fears take over: As she performs for the Hollywood bigwigs, her slippers turn into huge clown shoes, and her singing voice runs the gamut from a high squeak to a froggy croak. The sequence clearly reflects Wilder's own hopes and fears in 1932.

"Back then," he notes, "there was hardly a screenwriter or director who did not say: 'I would really like to go to Hollywood!' Painters had always felt drawn to Paris or Rome, and for us it was the capital of films. . . . One always asked oneself, 'Am I good enough to write in Hollywood? Am I good enough to direct in Hollywood?' "

If *Ein blonder Traum* seems to arbitrarily choose a mate for Jou-Jou, it's the fault of Lilian Harvey and her powerful beau, UFA head Erich Pommer. The original ending had the two Willys going off together rather than split up their partnership over a woman; Harvey took that as an insult to her feminine allure, and Wilder and Reisch were sent back for a rewrite. Despite the compromise, the film is as preoccupied with male bonding as it is with male-female romance, a strand that also runs through such Wilder films as *Double Indemnity, Some Like It Hot* and *The Front Page.*

Its dated quality notwithstanding, *Ein blonder Traum* deserves to be seen today, not only for Wilder and Reisch's imaginative touches but for its showcasing of three charismatic performers. Harvey, especially, is a neglected talent—a handsome and highly capable singer, dancer and comedienne, fluent enough to play in French and English versions of the movie (which were filmed simultaneously with different costars).

That same year, Wilder earned a solo writing credit on another musical, *Es war einmal ein Walzer* (*Once There Was a Waltz*), with a score by the famed Viennese operetta composer Franz Lehàr. As *Ein blonder Traum* tries to make poverty as cheerful as possible with songs like "Somewhere in the World There's a Bit of Happiness" and "We Don't Pay Rent Anymore," *Walzer* also acknowledges the depressed times while maintaining a sunny attitude. The plot centers on the pending arranged marriage between banker's son Rudi Moebius and heiress Lucie Weidling, with each family secretly bankrupt and thinking the other is going to be its financial salvation. The bride- and groom-to-be are each in love with someone else, and flee to Berlin with their partners. At the close, the failed Moebius bank has been transformed into a café, employing all four principals. The title song expresses the movie's wistfully nostalgic theme: "Once there was a waltz, once there was a Vienna / They were such beautiful times, but now they are gone / Everything has an end, good luck often brings sorrow / So then return with a waltz to those beautiful times."

Wilder's next project, *Scampolo, ein Kind der Strasse* (*Scampolo, a Girl of the Street*), was his first collaboration with his friend Max Kolpe. Based on a play by the Italian Dario Niccodemi, it centers on a homeless Berlin girl who sleeps in telephone booths and does odd jobs for a local laundry. One day, she is sent to the nearby Pension Royal to settle an old bill and instead becomes smitten with the debtor: Maximilian, a financier who has fallen on hard times. Scampolo helps Maximilian keep one step ahead of his creditors by pawning a pair of cuff links and allowing herself to be courted by the pension's good-natured concierge, Gabriel. She also persuades Maximilian to open his own language school and promotes it into a success. Romance between the two seems to be blossoming, but then Maximilian explodes when Scampolo accepts a new dress and parasol from one of her customers, a wealthy banker. While returning the dress to the banker's office, the girl intercepts a hot stock tip and anonymously relays it to Maximilian. Maximilian strikes it rich and makes plans to relocate to London. The closing scene finds Scampolo running to deliver a package of laundry to Max before his plane takes off; she pours out her heart to him, and the two fly off together.

Scampolo is played by the petite twenty-two-year-old German film star Dolly Haas, who would later have a renowned New York stage career and would marry the Broadway caricaturist Al Hirschfeld. With her short hair and striped pullover, she looks a bit like Jean Seberg did in Godard's *Breathless*, and she has the same ebullient, gamine quality Audrey Hepburn displays for Wilder in *Sabrina* and *Love in the Afternoon*. In fact, Wilder might have been thinking of the ending of *Scampolo* when he staged the classic final clinch in *Love in the Afternoon;* both feature an innocent young woman running after a much older man and being carried off to a new life. (The two movies open nearly identically, too, with morning scenes of the city and sanitation trucks spraying water.)

Despite a rather dull performance by Karl Ludwig Diehl as Maximilian, *Scampolo* stands out as the first Wilder script to deal more seriously than comically with the complexities of longing between men and women. It's a crude blueprint for the later, more sophisticated romances, but fascinating in its combination of wish-fulfillment fantasy and the German reality of homelessness and financial ruin.

Wilder and Kolpe collaborated again on *Das Blaue vom Himmel* (*The Blue from the Sky*), a much lighter and slighter movie. At least the concept is somewhat original: an operetta set in the Berlin U-bahn (or subway) system. The movie's ingenue is Anni Muller, the pretty new cashier at the Wallenstein Platz stop, who proves such a distraction that she has all the commuters singing and dancing and jamming up the station. Before long, she's leading a marching band out of the subway and into the woods. A thunderstorm erupts, and Anni—obviously not the smartest of girls—takes shelter under a tree. There, she has a chance encounter with one of her customers, Hans, an aviator whose plane has just crash-landed. Anni and Hans fall for each other, but their conflicting work schedules keep them apart except for brief lovemaking sessions in the phone booth outside the U-bahn station. Anni is then pursued by Herr Piper, the owner of the Tabu cigarette factory; but instead of giving in to the millionaire, she persuades him to hire Hans as an advertising skywriter. The usual misunderstanding occurs when Hans sees Anni with Piper, but all ends well when he lands the skywriting job, writes, "I love you, Anni!" in the sky and takes off with his lover into the blue. An innocuous throwaway, *Das Blaue vom Himmel* is notable only for its look at the inner workings of the Berlin U-bahn system, and for its lesson in how to beat a fare by "borrowing" your fellow passenger's ticket.

Wilder's final German efforts appeared in 1933. He teamed once again with Max Kolpe on *Madame wünscht keine Kinder* (*Madame Wants No Children*), based on the novel by Clement Vautel and already filmed in 1926 by Alexander Korda with Marlene Dietrich in the lead role. The comedy centers on Madelaine, the inexhaustibly athletic wife of Felix Rainer, a pediatrician. Felix adores children and is eager to start building his own family; Madelaine, however, is a sports fanatic and hates the idea of children cramping her style. Right from the honeymoon—a trip to a tennis tournament in Cannes—everything in the couple's life is arranged around her obsession: The dining-room furniture is used for table tennis; the hoped-for children's room is devoted to gymnastics. Adding to Felix's irritation is the constant presence of Madelaine's tennis partner (and platonic friend), Adolf. In desperation, Felix turns to an old flame—arousing Madelaine's jealousy and a new allegiance to the cause of motherhood.

Perhaps Wilder, a sports nut himself and no great believer in big families, deep down admired Madelaine. Or perhaps with Madelaine he was trying to satirize the new German mania for physical perfection. More likely he saw *Madame wünscht keine Kinder* as a ready-made commercial vehicle, even if it didn't have Marlene Dietrich.

Wilder's last German script, co-written with his onetime ghostwriting boss Franz Schulz, is among his most interesting. *Was Frauen träumen* (*What Women Dream*) begins with a near wordless sequence as the elegantly dressed Rina Korff (Nora Gregor) walks along a fashionable shopping street, trailed by an expensive car. She stops at a jewelry store window and an orgasmic look comes over her face. In the store, she points to a glove and says it must belong to the woman who just went out the door. While the manager runs after the customer, she goes to work. Rina is a kleptomaniac.

But there's more to it than that. Every time Rina steals, a swank-looking gentleman named Levassor (Kurt Horwitz) is right behind her, ready to pay for the purloined merchandise. "The lady has an exciting way of choosing my gifts for her," he jokes. But Levassor has his own agenda: He wants Rina as his lover, and he wants to use her talent to pull off a major diamond heist.

Competing for Rina's soul is Walter (Gustav Fröhlich), a young amateur detective who believes in the essential goodness of this mysterious woman. But Levassor seems to have Rina under some kind of spell—will she be strong enough to break it?

Wilder and Schulz bring a refreshing aura of fun to this tale of pathology. Peter Lorre, in a distinct change from his child-killer role in Fritz Lang's *M*, turns up as a neighbor of Walter's, a zany cop who's always a step behind and forever getting trapped in his own handcuffs. Lorre and Gregor share an amusing scene as Rina shows off her special gifts—offering him a cigarette from his own stolen case, lighting it with his stolen lighter and handing over his borrowed gun.

Director Geza von Bolvary stages one especially stylish sequence depicting Rina's struggle: While she watches a nightclub performance, a woman with huge, expensive earrings sits in front of her. We see the chorus reflected in the jewelry, and closeups of Rina's face and clenched fists as she fights temptation. A few seconds later, and one earring is gone. Has she succumbed? No, she's playfully strung two earrings on her neighbor's left ear.

With its handsome production values and eccentric mix of light and dark plot elements, *Was Frauen träumen* caught Hollywood's attention; the following year, Universal Pictures produced a remake, *One Exciting Adventure*, starring Binnie Barnes.

OF ALL THE FILMS WILDER WROTE IN GERMANY, TWO HAVE particularly unpleasant associations: *Scampolo* and *Madame wünscht keine Kinder*. Both were directed by Hans Steinhoff, who went on to make one of the Nazi era's most vile propaganda films, *Hitlerjunge Quex*. Understandably, Wilder doesn't mince words when discussing him: "He was a shit, Steinhoff—a man without talent. He was a Nazi, a hundred-percenter. But there were many Nazis who had talent. I would never say that Leni Riefenstahl had no talent—her *Triumph of the Will* was an enormous undertaking. She had the most extras in the world, everything was at her disposal, and it was considered a great piece of propaganda. As for Steinhoff, he was an idiot—not because he was a Nazi, but he was also a very bad director."

Anti-Semitism was always a presence in Wilder's life, going back to his days in Vienna. But, especially within the cosmopolitan circles that encompassed the young writer, the brown-shirted National Socialists were considered at worst a minor annoyance, a laughably petty fringe group. The biggest talk they had ever created in movie circles stemmed from the time Joseph Goebbels's troops set white mice loose in the UFA Theatre on Nollendorfplatz during the 1931 German premiere of *All Quiet on the Western Front*, in protest against the film's pacifist message, and succeeded in getting the picture banned by the minister of the interior.

Through the end of 1932, Wilder notes, "nobody took Hitler very seriously. In 1932 there was an election, and the National Socialists, the Nazi party, lost about thirty-five seats [in the German Parliament, the Reichstag]. And we just thought: 'Well now, they've finally seen through that man, they've finally grasped the basic idea of Nazism.' But what happened then was one of the little caprices of mother history."

Wilder offers his own nutshell version of Adolf Hitler's rise: "The son of [President] Hindenburg was involved in some kind of monetary scandal, and in order to blow out that fire, Hindenburg demoted the liberal chancellor, General Schleicher, and appointed Mr. Hitler out of nowhere. Mr. von Hindenburg was slightly gaga at that time—he was promised the constitution would stay the way it was and you could vote for different parties. But to grab all the power, Mr. Hitler got hold of a young Dutchman who was slightly out of his mind, locked him up in the Reichstag and started the fire there. And Mr. Hitler said: 'You see what the Communists have done? There will be no other parties, only the National Socialist Party.' All of that came very suddenly—and very ruthlessly."

Wilder's response to the sea change in Germany was just as quick—and just as coolly pragmatic.

FIVE

Escape to Paris

O N JANUARY 30, 1933, THE DAY ADOLF HITLER WAS NAMED
chancellor of Germany, Billie Wilder was vacationing with his latest
girlfriend, Hella Hartwig, in a ski resort in Davos. An athletic girl with
short black hair, Hella was the daughter of the well-to-do owner of a
pharmaceutical firm in Frankfurt an der Oder. Hella rented two furnished
rooms from a middle-class family on the Kurfürstendamm and met Wilder
at a party. Hella liked fast cars and dancing, but she and Billie could also
have fun doing something as simple as playing dominoes with the regulars
at Walter Reisch's place. The trip to Davos was Wilder's first skiing excursion—and the beginning of a harsh new chapter in his life.

Billie and Hella were having lunch at a ski chalet when news of Hitler's
appointment came over the radio. Wilder declared the vacation over, but
he instinctively knew that more than a holiday had just come to an end.

The National Socialists basked in their newfound status, no longer
hesitant to assert their identities or their power. Wilder was startled one
day to see his garage attendant wearing a swastika armband. Even more
chilling was the Nazis' increasingly brutal "street theater." Wilder remembers sitting in a coffeehouse, commiserating with friends about the terrifying new climate. "We were saying: 'Where can we go? What can we do?'
And I saw eight or ten SS men in uniform beating an old Jew to death. I
made a move, and my friends held me back, saying: 'They'll kill you as

well—you can't help him.' That was when I knew how it was going to go, and *I* wasn't going to be there."

Wilder discussed the situation with Hella, and she agreed that the best course was to leave the country as soon as possible. He sold off most of his wonderful Bauhaus furnishings and got rid of his car, an American Cabriolet Graham-Paige. He moved out of the apartment on Sachsischen Strasse and lived out his last days in Berlin in a small single room at the Hotel Majestic on Brandenburgischen Strasse.

Wilder remembers one frightening morning around four when two plainclothes detectives entered his room. All he could think about was the anti-Hitler brochure he had been reading the night before in bed. Luckily, as he fell asleep, the tract had fallen in between the bed and the wall. In their cursory inspection, the police never saw it.

On the night of the Reichstag fire, Billie and Hella sat in the outdoor area of the Café Wien on the Kurfürstendamm, roughly where Hotel Kempinski stands today. It was an unseasonably warm evening, which only made their farewell to the city that much more bittersweet. The following night, the lovers boarded the train for Paris, just one step ahead of the authorities, according to Wilder.

The young writer never even considered returning to Austria. "A lot of my friends had a fear of going into a country where they didn't speak the language," he recalls, "so they went to Vienna or Prague, which was very shortsighted. Anybody who had listened to the speeches knew Hitler would want Austria and the Sudeten part of Czechoslovakia. I sensed that it was best to go as far as possible."

Wilder was indeed wise to leave so quickly. On April 1, Hitler promoted a boycott of Jewish-owned shops, stationing brownshirts outside their entrances to intimidate potential customers. By April 7, all Jews were dismissed from civil-service jobs. A few weeks later, the Law Against Overcrowding of German Schools severely cut back the number of Jews at higher institutions of learning. Despite these blatant manifestations of Hitler's hatred, many Jews in Germany continued to believe they could ride out the anti-Semitic storm.

The atmosphere at Wilder's old studio, UFA, was also changing—not surprisingly, since the majority of the company's stock was controlled by weapons manufacturer Alfried Krupp, one of the National Socialist Party's most ardent supporters. As Hitler consolidated his power, UFA newsreels became increasingly worshipful of the charismatic *Führer*, and feature filmmakers were warned not to deal in themes or subtext that implied even the faintest criticism of the new Nazi regime. By the time Wilder's final German film, *Was Frauen träumen*, premiered to coincide with Hitler's birthday on April 20, the names of Wilder and co-writer Franz Schulz were deleted from the programs and publicity materials.

Billie and Hella arrived at Paris's Gare St. Lazare, most likely on the morning of March 1. Wilder's entry was made easier by the fact that he was still an Austrian national, with an Austrian passport, which meant he was in no danger of being deported back to Germany. All he had brought was one suitcase, and a thousand American dollars tucked away in his hatband. Hella, meanwhile, had concealed a small sack filled with gold coins—which she neglected to tell Billie about until it was absolutely necessary.

Since neither had the proper visas, the pair had to keep a low profile. They wound up living in the Hotel Ansonia at 8 rue de Saigon, near the Arc de Triomphe—a haven for film-industry refugees from the Nazi juggernaut. Billie and Hella's neighbors included the actor Peter Lorre, plus several old friends and colleagues: Friedrich Holländer, the composer of *The Blue Angel*; Franz Wachsmann, the composer of *Scampolo*; and Wilder's frequent writing partner, Max Kolpe.

Only a handful of German film-industry exiles were able to secure positions approaching their status back home. After UFA chieftain Erich Pommer fled Germany, he landed a producing post at Fox's studios in France. Fritz Lang, meanwhile, was such a celebrated master of artistic spectacle that Joseph Goebbels invited him to take over UFA, despite the fact that Lang was half-Jewish; Lang, however, immediately boarded a train for Paris, and quickly found work directing Ferenc Molnár's *Liliom*, starring matinee idol Charles Boyer.

Most of the refugees, however, were forced to begin from scratch. All of Wilder's accomplishments of the last several years were effectively erased, and he was again foraging for ghostwriting jobs. The ex-Berliner was fluent in French, but he thought in German, which created double the work: writing scripts in his native language, then translating them into the parlance of his adopted home.

The atmosphere of longing and dread at the Hotel Ansonia was captured years later by Erich Maria Remarque in his novel *Arch of Triumph*, which became a 1948 Hollywood film starring Ingrid Bergman, Charles Boyer and Charles Laughton. Wilder had less reason to fear deportation than his neighbors, but the Ansonia—despite its colorful and gifted residents—was a dreary, depressing place to pass one's days after the heady café life of pre-Hitler Berlin. Wilder's fondest memory of the period is going to the Davis Cup tennis matches between France and England at the Roland Garros Stadium with the newly arrived Walter Reisch.

By chance, Wilder notched his first directing credit during his stay in Paris. He collaborated with two Ansonia neighbors, Max Kolpe and former Berlin newspaper editor and critic Hanns G. Lustig, on a screenplay about young car thieves, *Mauvaise Graine* (*Bad Seed*). Kolpe remembers how the film almost fell apart after the trio had worked three months on the screenplay. "Everything looked perfect. But there was a producer who wanted to cast his girlfriend in the main female role. [Billie] made a screen test and the result was catastrophic. The two other producers realized it, but the third one was the financial backer. He threatened to take back the money if the girl didn't play the role. But that didn't matter to [Billie]. We would rather pay back the money than be involved in such a transaction. Unfortunately, the producers accepted the arrangement. One seldom saw a sadder bunch, trotting along the banks of the Seine back to the hotel. . . .

"But three days later, there was a great surprise. We could shoot the film, we could pick and choose the person we wanted. The old backer had taken off, but the other two producers had managed to interest some others in the project. The main female role was played by the then almost unknown Danielle Darrieux."

Most of the money for the shoestring production came from Edouard Corniglion-Molinier, a World War I aviation hero who had been recruited by the writers' Hungarian partner, Alexander Esway. With no volunteers stepping forward, Esway and Wilder shared directing chores, filming either outdoors or inside a converted garage; even scenes taking place in a living room were shot in the garage. "We had to improvise," Wilder says. "We didn't have money enough for the hotels to stay overnight. It was tough."

The seventeen-year-old Darrieux had been making films since age fourteen, *Mauvaise Graine* was her eighth picture. Three years later, she would become an international star opposite Charles Boyer in *Mayerling*, following with such successes as *The Rage of Paris*, *La Ronde*, *Le Plaisir*, *Five Fingers* and *The Earrings of Madame De*. In *Mauvaise Graine*, she had the tasty role of Jeanette, a young seductress who distracts men while her fellow gang members steal their cars. The first time we see Jeanette at work, Wilder employs some visual shorthand reminiscent of one of his idols, Ernst Lubitsch: The girl sashays down the street, a car following close behind her. Then, for a few seconds, our view of her is obscured by a passing horse-drawn van. When we see her again, she's sitting next to the driver of the car. It's a witty means of showing that Jeanette is very good at working her wiles, without delving into clumsy or sordid details.

Wilder's unwavering desire for a car of his own is expressed in an opening title card that states: "One out of eight Parisians owns a car. Henri is one of the seven others." Henri (Pierre Mingand), unlike most Parisians, has known the pleasure of driving—but his wealthy father has taken away his car. Late for a date, the spoiled young man steals some wheels, but is caught by a gang of thieves and brought back to their garage headquarters. There, he is befriended by Jean la Cravate (Raymond Galle), who, as his nickname reveals, has a strange passion for filching neckties. Henri also gets cozy with Jean's sister Jeanette and, telling his father he has entered the auto business, joins the gang.

Without a budget for back projections or other studio trickery, Wilder and Esway nonetheless went ahead with a car chase—"live on the streets, at high speed," Wilder says. "It was very exhausting." This bare-bones action sequence occurs midway through the film, after the resentful leader of the gang tampers with the car Henri is to drive to Marseilles, and Jeanette at the last minute decides to accompany him. The lovers survive the inevitable crash and, after hitching a ride to Marseilles in a hay wagon, decide they've had enough of the criminal existence and plan a new life abroad. Henri returns to Paris to try to persuade Jean to join them, but he declines. Soon after, the picture takes a dark turn when Jean is killed in a police raid on the garage. In the finale, Henri gives Jeanette the tragic news about her brother, and the sad but resolute couple board a ship to America.

Perhaps to compensate for its budgetary limitations, the movie makes frequent use of relatively inexpensive optical effects like wipes, dissolves and superimpositions—the kind of flashy devices Wilder would seldom employ in his Hollywood career. *Mauvaise Graine* also gets an energy transfusion from its syncopated jazz score by Franz Wachsmann, whose next collaboration with Wilder would be the Oscar-winning score for *Sunset Boulevard* in 1950.

With no access to a soundstage, Wilder and Esway had made "out of necessity, a forerunner of Nouvelle Vague and cinema verité—long before Rossellini, Godard, Resnais and Truffaut," Wilder says with some degree of cocky pride. "It got very good reviews, and it was surprisingly lively."

Critic Andrew Sarris observes, *"Mauvaise Graine* fills a tantalizing gap in Billy Wilder's filmography. It is a small, slight, restless comedy-melodrama of disturbingly mixed moods, possibly a reflection of Wilder's own state of mind in the turbulent Europe of the 1930s. . . . There is also a great deal of Paris and the French countryside, all the way down to Marseilles, on view in the lyrical traversals of a camera in exile."

Wilder had joined the fraternity of film directors, but "I cannot say that it made me happy," he declares. The strain of making a crime picture with no studio resources and almost no money was too great. And, after all, the real pleasure came from the writing, not from coddling actors and rushing to meet a shooting schedule. But even if he became as proficient in French as he was in German, would he—as part of the lower creative tier of refugees from Hitler—ever be accepted enough by the French to fulfill the promise of his Berlin career? Like any other tidal wave of refugees, Wilder and his fellow ex-Berliners felt they were tolerated but never completely welcome. Like the protagonists of *Mauvaise Graine*, he, too, fantasized about sailing away to the promise of America.

"On the whole," Wilder claims, "the deals were made at the Café Fouquet on the Champs d'Elysées. That's where everybody met, where everybody promised, but nobody showed up later when it came time to pay. It was kind of a gypsy life for a picture-maker."

Wilder had little option but to keep writing, and one of his story ideas became his ticket to Hollywood. While at UFA, the young writer had become friendly with one of the studio's most valued directors, Joe May. Born Joseph Mandel in 1880, May led a charmed life. The son of a millionaire, he managed to squander nearly all of his late father's fortune on cars, women and Vienna nightlife, then came back from the brink of bankruptcy by investing in a successful new fertilizer. He married a beautiful actress named Mia and directed her in his first film, but his career was halted by the outbreak of World War I. According to Wilder, May secured an early release from the army by promoting to the Austrian ministry of war an outlandish plan to confound the Russian troops by projecting ethereal photographs of his wife in the sky. Wilder insists that the Austrian government actually gave May money for the scheme, with which he financed several comedies and launched his career at UFA. May went on to direct a popular series of lavish melodramas starring his wife, and made his biggest success with 1929's *Asphalt*, a gritty drama about the romance between a traffic cop and a prostitute. After a brief stay in Paris, May was offered a producing post at Columbia Pictures.

Wilder sent May an outline for a musical called *Pam-Pam*. Like *Mauvaise Graine*, it was the tale of a relative innocent caught up in a world of crime—in this case, a gang of counterfeiters holing up in a shuttered theater. The heroine is a young actress from Scarsdale, New York, who is looking for work. The counterfeiters pretend to be theatrical producers, and send the girl out to the bank to change some bogus hundred-dollar bills, telling her to keep twenty dollars per hundred for herself. Then, feeling guilty about the ruse, they decide to put on a show spotlighting the girl. Needless to say, her stage debut is a big success.

May liked this latest variation on the Wilder masquerade, and so did Columbia. In December 1933, the studio offered the refugee one-way transportation to Hollywood and a salary of $150 a week to write the *Pam-Pam* screenplay. Wilder leapt at the chance. "My dream all along was to get to Hollywood, which would have happened even without Hitler," he declares.

Wilder claims May sent him a telegram requesting that he bring with him from France some items that couldn't be obtained in America— namely, 120 bottles of Anjou wine, three bidets, two hair sieves "for spinach straining," and three dress-coat vests by Knize (an expensive European tailor). Wilder says he cabled him back that there was a fourteen-day wait for the vests and that the wine wouldn't last the journey. "As for the bidets, I recommend handstands in the shower." Wilder recycled the same joke decades later, at the expense of his wife, Audrey, when he was in Paris shooting *Love in the Afternoon*.

On January 22, 1934, Wilder said good-bye to Hella and boarded the

Aquitania for New York, with a mere eleven dollars in his pocket. During his voyage, he began his campaign to learn English by reading some American novels he had bought in Brentano's in Paris, works by Ernest Hemingway, Thomas Wolfe and Sinclair Lewis that he had already read in their German translations.

The ship arrived in New York harbor around eleven at night, several hours late due to a heavy snowstorm. He was met by his brother, Willie, whom he hadn't seen in twelve years, and Willie's wife. Billie's first glimpse of the city, its landmarks glittering at midnight and blanketed in snow, was a magical one.

Billie stayed at his brother's house in Baldwin, Long Island. He woke up next morning to a distinctively American sight. Looking out the window, he noticed a Cadillac stopping at the house next door—a boy got out of the car, threw a newspaper toward the porch, and ducked back into the car. The Cadillac then proceeded a few yards to the Wilders' house, the boy got out and delivered another paper. A newspaper boy in a Cadillac? Wilder thought. Is this America? Billie's sister-in-law later explained that the boy usually delivered the papers on a bike, but because of the snow, he had arranged for his father's chauffeur to help him make his daily rounds—and continue to earn his own money.

Two days later, Billie Wilder was on the Twentieth Century to Los Angeles, ready to embrace the West—but the West was still a forbidding place for its new breed of pioneers.

Hollywood Hustle

BILLY WILDER CAME TO CALIFORNIA AS ONE OF THE FIRST arrivals in a second wave of moviemaking emigrants from Europe. This group was encumbered by very different circumstances than the first wave of bold, successful talent of the 1920s like Ernst Lubitsch and F. W. Murnau, who had been recruited by studio heads eager to acquire some of their artistic cachet. The second band of émigrés, which later included Wilder's *Menschen am Sonntag* collaborators Robert and Curt Siodmak, generally had not yet established international reputations.* "We didn't come because we were invited like the first group," Wilder notes. "We came to save our lives."

No studio emissaries were there to greet Wilder's train when it pulled into downtown Los Angeles's Second Street station—only Joe May, his one link with this sun-drenched new world. Wilder boarded with May and his vivacious wife Mia in their Spanish-style house, complete with swimming pool, on Courtney Avenue in the Hollywood Hills district where stars like Charles Laughton also resided. He paid them $75 a week for his room and Mia's Old World cooking, reassuring Austrian dishes like *leberknodelsuppe*, or liver noodle soup.

---

* Two important exceptions were Fritz Lang, the director of *Metropolis* and *M*, who came over under personal contract to David O. Selznick, and G. W. Pabst (*The Threepenny Opera*), whose brief Hollywood career was an unmitigated failure.

That $75 was half of Wilder's weekly salary at Columbia Pictures, where he went to work on the American version of *Pam-Pam*. Columbia, located at 1438 Gower Street off Sunset Boulevard, was then the least prestigious and most parsimonious of the major studios, run with a stern eye toward the bottom line by the notoriously crass Harry Cohn. On his first day, Wilder was brought in to see Sam Briskin, Cohn's second-in-command, who somehow had gotten the impression that his new trial scribe was an American. He made no attempt to hide his impatience with the Austrian's halting attempt to speak English and sent him cowering back to the writers' quarters.

Columbia employed some of the brightest and most promising writing talent around, but its second-tier status required that many be hired on a project-by-project basis. The roll call included James M. Cain, who had just unveiled the steamy, controversial crime novella *The Postman Always Rings Twice*; the legendary wit Dorothy Parker; acclaimed playwright Sidney Kingsley; future studio bigwig Dore Schary; and such major screenwriting talents as Jo Swerling, Norman Krasna, Sidney Buchman and Frank Capra's writing mainstay, Robert Riskin.

Wilder says he did most of his work on *Pam-Pam* at home, with the help of an American translator fluent in German. A Viennese friend, Reginald LeBorg, who later directed such B films as *The Mummy's Ghost* and the *Joe Palooka* series, also helped the young writer with his English.

"Like a fool," Wilder says, "in my high school years I chose French as a foreign language and not English, because that was then *la langue diplomatique*, the diplomatic language."

Wilder says you learn a language the way you learn to swim—"by jumping into deep water." To further his mastery of English, he consciously shied away from the European refugee colony and tried to acquire new American friends, and spent as much time as he could listening to the radio, especially to sports results and soap operas like *Dear John* and *As the World Turns*.

Despite the Hollywood novice's best efforts, *Pam-Pam* was ultimately rejected by the studio. "It never got beyond a draft of a screenplay, with no final dialogue or anything like that," Wilder says. "It did not work anyway, even if it had been in perfect English. They liked the original story, but they did not like what I did with it. It's forgotten, I hope never to be brought out again and made into a picture, because it would be very naïve today."

Suddenly jobless, Wilder could no longer afford to live with the Mays and, to make matters worse, his six-month visitor's visa was about to expire. In order to obtain an immigration visa, Wilder had to leave the United States and apply for reentry. He crossed the border and rented a hotel room in Mexicali, the nearest city with a U.S. consulate. The unemployed writer joined the ranks of other European émigrés waiting for permission to enter the States; because each country was given a different quota, some of the people Wilder met had been waiting for years. Their desperation, and the squalid conditions they were forced to live in, would find their way into Wilder's screenplay for the 1941 release *Hold Back the Dawn*, in which a Hungarian gigolo in Mexican limbo obtains his visa by seducing and marrying a naïve American schoolteacher.

Wilder movingly described his own experience with the immigration office in Mexicali when he received the prestigious Irving R. Thalberg Award for lifetime achievement in production at the 1988 Academy Awards ceremony. "As they showed me into the office of the consul," he recalled, "I was drenched in sweat. It was not the heat. It was the panic, the fear. I knew that I needed a whole bunch of documents—affidavits, official proof of former residence, sworn testaments that I had never been a criminal or an anarchist. I had nothing—zilch! Just my passport and my birth certificate and some letters from a few American friends vouching that I was honest. It looked hopeless.

"The consul—he looked a little bit like Will Rogers—examined my meager documentation. 'Is that all you have?' he asked. And I said yes. I had to explain that I had to get out of Berlin on very short notice, like twenty minutes. A neighbor had tipped me off that two men in uniform had been looking for me. I had just enough time to throw a few things in a suitcase and get on the night train to Paris. The consul just stared at me and said, 'How do you expect me to . . . with just these papers?' And I told him, 'I tried to get them from Nazi Germany but they just would not respond. Of course, I could get them if I went back to Germany. Then they would naturally put me on the train and ship me off to Dachau.'

"He just kept staring at me and I was not sure whether I was getting through to him. . . . Finally he asked me, 'What do you do? I mean, professionally?' And I said, 'I write movies.' He said, 'Is that so?' He got up and started pacing, kind of behind me, but I felt he was measuring me. Then he came back to the desk, picked up my passport, opened it and took a rubber stamp and went [pounding], handed me back the passport and said, 'Write some good ones.' That was fifty-four years ago. I've tried ever since. I certainly did not want to disappoint that dear man in Mexicali."

That night, Wilder said he regretted that he didn't remember the name of the man whose act of benevolence helped make possible his career in American film. Later, he was told the consul in Mexicali had been on vacation at the time; the early booster of Billy Wilder's movie hopes appeared to be a vice-consul named Meyers.

Safely back in Los Angeles, Wilder still needed a place to live. He found it in an ornate, castlelike hotel on Sunset Boulevard near Laurel Canyon, Hollywood's fabled Chateau Marmont, then a mere five years old. Ann Little, the Chateau's manager, told Wilder that, for less than half of what he had been paying the Mays, he could rent their "loveliest small suite"—actually a cramped, poorly lit room containing a Murphy bed. Wilder moved in, and for a time shared these spare accommodations with another refugee, Peter Lorre. Wilder has often said that he and Lorre were so poor their entire day's nourishment frequently consisted of a shared can of tomato soup. "His real name was Löwenstein, Hungarian descent," Wilder remembers. "He was a very nice, funny guy—an intelligent man. . . . We were friends—later on a little bit less, when I found out he was a dope addict."

In Little's recollection, "We didn't see much of Mr. Wilder for the longest time. He stayed in his room and worked till all hours of the night. I can't remember a time when I didn't see a light coming from beneath his door as I would make my evening rounds. That young man was much too hard on himself."

But a former desk clerk, in addition to recalling Wilder's determination to hone his English by reading and listening to the radio, saw another side of the young writer. "What I remember most about him was that he had a very busy social life. I doubt if he dated the same girl twice. He was quite the ladies' man."

By this time, Joe May had brought his services over to Fox, and landed Wilder a writing assignment on the film he was directing there for transplanted producer Erich Pommer: *Music in the Air*, a Jerome Kern/Oscar Hammerstein II operetta starring silent-film star Gloria Swanson. Still billed as "Billie Wilder," the young hopeful shared his first American screenwriting credit with Howard I. Young on this musical trifle, set in a fanciful Bavaria light-years removed from the troubled nation Wilder had left behind. The impossibly bucolic village of Ebensdorf is home to elderly concertmaster Dr. Lessing, his pretty daughter Sieglinde, and her wide-eyed boyfriend Karl, the town schoolteacher and Lessing's lyricist. Having written what he believes is a potential hit song, Lessing journeys to Munich, accompanied by Sieglinde and Karl, to look up his old school chum Weber, now a leading music publisher and agent. In Weber's office are Frieda (Swanson), a vain, temperamental operetta diva, and her lyricist lover Bruno. Frieda and Bruno have a major row, and Frieda goes after the naïve Karl to make her paramour jealous, while Bruno seduces Sieglinde and arranges for her to star in his new operetta, despite her total lack of stage experience. Frieda tries to persuade Karl to escape to Venice with her, but the shy teacher runs back to his little village. Sieglinde, meantime, proves ill prepared for Munich stardom, and Frieda returns in glory as her last-minute replacement. Both sets of lovers are reunited in the end, while Lessing celebrates the debut of his catchy ditty as part of Bruno's operetta.

Music in the Air is slight, painless, and even sometimes amusing, thanks largely to the vivacious playing of Swanson, who proves herself a perfectly adept sound-era comedienne with a decent light-operetta singing voice. Her scenes bickering with her lover and flirting with Karl are the movie's high points, but have little to do with Wilder, who was still struggling with a new language and most likely contributed mainly ideas for gags and bits of Bavarian color. Unintentional hilarity is provided by the near handsome Douglass Montgomery, fresh from George Cukor's film of *Little Women*, who spends most of the movie in knee-length pants and delivers Karl's lines with goofy inflections reminiscent of Martin Short's Ed Grimley character.

Despite its sporadic moments of fun, *Music in the Air* was neither Swanson's big comeback nor Wilder's big break. Work opportunities became more scarce. Wilder's old friend from Berlin, Joe Pasternak, was now a hotshot at Universal Pictures, but he was unable to get Wilder a job there; Pasternak speculated that it was because studio head Carl Laemmle was an unusually short man and didn't want anyone even as tall as the average-sized Wilder working there. In 1935, Wilder had but one screen credit, *Lottery Lover*, on which he received $200 a week for five weeks' work. Co-written with Wilder's old ghostwriting boss Franz Schulz, the Fox production is a forgettable tale of romantic mishaps, directed by another former Berliner, William Thiele. Lew Ayres plays a sailor aboard the training ship U.S.S. *Alaska*, docked in France, who is the lucky winner when the crew pools their money and selects one of their ranks to wine and dine a comely Parisian dancer. But the reluctant Ayres faces competition from a Russian prince and the dancer's old flame, an American captain. Meanwhile, a chorus girl from Canada is recruited to woo away the prince; in the course of her duties, she discovers she's really in love with Ayres. It's all as tired and formulaic as it sounds; the only recognizable Wilder touch is the repeat of a visual gag from the French *Mauvaise Graine*, as a passing truck obscures the details of an open-air seduction. The basic idea of *Lottery Lover* would be recycled years later, with greater box-office success, for the 1959 Tony Curtis–Janet Leigh military comedy *The Perfect Furlough*, directed by Blake Edwards.

With *Lottery Lover*, Wilder said farewell to the name Billie, having been informed by his new American friends that his mother's pet name for him had a peculiarly feminine ring. From now on, it would be "Billy." Whatever the name, he still couldn't find work.

Things became so bad for Wilder that he reverted to his old ghostwriting mode, working with director Raoul Walsh on *Under Pressure*, a macho story of "sandhogs" building a tunnel between Manhattan and Brooklyn, who in their spare time get roaring drunk and fight over the same woman. Victor McLaglen and Edmund Lowe starred. The unsung writer calls the result "idiotic" and is perfectly content with his lack of credit.

By design, Wilder had maintained a distance from the German émigré colony in Hollywood, which tended to gravitate to the Santa Monica home of Salka Viertel, an outgoing screenwriter and former actress—she can be seen opposite her close friend Greta Garbo in the German-language version of *Anna Christie*—and wife of the director Berthold Viertel. Most of the guests who gathered at the Viertel *kaffeeklatsches*—artists like Thomas Mann, Bertolt Brecht, Bruno Frank and Ludwig Marcuse—already had established significant reputations in Germany, and most dreamed of going back after the fall of Hitler. As for Wilder, "I was here because I wanted to stay here. I had landed in my dream city."

But now, out of inactivity and loneliness, Wilder began to attend the fashionable Viertel gatherings and ingratiate himself with their social circle. Among the familiar faces was Erich Pommer (now ensconced at RKO and living in Beverly Hills), who bet the starving young writer $75 at a poolside party that he wouldn't jump into the water fully clothed. Wilder, of course, took the dare, making sure to first demonstrate his dancing prowess on the diving board. Wilder insists it was just a simple wager, not a demeaning act of charity, but $75 could buy an awful lot of tomato soup.

Wilder's romantic life also took an auspicious turn in 1935, when he agreed to a blind dinner date set up by the American wife of a screenwriting friend, Jacques Théry. His partner for the evening was Judith Iribe, a tall, beautiful, sophisticated brunette from a prominent California family—in fact, her uncle was the state's lieutenant governor. Judith's father, George Coppicus, headed the Columbia Artists agency, representing world-renowned musicians like Arturo Toscanini. Her mother, Maybelle, had years ago divorced Coppicus and married Paul Iribe, a Basque caricaturist and designer who had worked as the art director for Cecil B. De Mille until he was fired in 1927 over creative differences during the filming of *The King of Kings*. Paul and Maybelle then went to France, where he opened a shop selling his custom-designed jewelry and furnishings. The marriage hit the rocks in 1933, when Maybelle learned of Paul's year-long affair with Coco Chanel, and Maybelle returned with her children to America.

Having spent her teen years abroad, Judith was fluent in French and impressed Wilder with her culture, her style, her wit and her strong opinions. And, like her stepfather, she too was a talented artist. Wilder was smitten.

Around this time, the Hollywood hopeful also found a valuable, if short-lived, writing collaborator. At the Viertels, he met and befriended Oliver H. P. Garrett, a writer of action films who came from a well-to-do New England family. Together, they worked on two screenplays, a spy adventure called *Gibraltar* and a musical love story entitled *Encore*. Garrett, who traveled in swank circles, pitched the stories to the principals of Pioneer Films, a new production company devoted exclusively to Technicolor movies: the millionaires John Hay Whitney and Cornelius Vanderbilt Whitney, and Merian C. Cooper, the adventuresome producer/director (with Ernest B. Schoedsack) of *King Kong*. Wilder and Garrett signed a long-term contract with Pioneer, and suddenly the young Austrian was $5,000 richer.

Wilder used his windfall to finance a return trip to Europe. He had an awkward, uneventful reunion with his ex-lover Hella in Paris, then went on to Vienna to visit his family. His mother had married a businessman named Siedlisker, and neither felt threatened enough by the rantings of Hitler to consider leaving their comfortably settled existence. It was the last time Wilder was ever to see his mother.

Wilder returned to Los Angeles on December 23, 1935, and was hit with an unexpected surprise: There was no room for him at the Chateau Marmont. "I forgot to notify Miss Little," Wilder recalls. "The hotel was absolutely booked up. I had my belongings there in the cellar or wherever it was. I found out that there was a ladies' toilet giving onto the lobby, with a swinging door—not even a lock. There was a little anteroom with a couch, and then there were six toilets. So I said, 'I'll stay here until . . . when are you going to have room?' And she said, 'After the twenty-sixth or twenty-seventh.' So I stayed in the ladies' room, which got very embarrassing. People would come in, look, and say: 'There's a man asleep there.' It's the only time I had a bedroom with six toilets."

Early in 1936, Pioneer Films released its second Technicolor production, *The Dancing Pirate*, to savage reviews and miserable business. Cowed by their humiliating failure, the Whitneys had second thoughts about their new filmmaking venture, and within weeks Pioneer folded.

Once again, Wilder was out of a job, but he continued to write on spec. He paired up with the Broadway playwright Hy Kraft on a comedy called *Champagne Waltz*, familiar territory for Wilder as it involved an American jazz musician in Vienna whose hot band becomes fierce competition to the waltz palace next door. Paramount-allied independent producer Lester Cowan bought the screenplay, giving Wilder and Kraft a $2,000 advance on $10,000. Cowan subsequently abandoned the project, but made it up to Wilder by securing him a $250-a-week position as a contract writer at Paramount. There, Wilder set to work adapting *Champagne Waltz* for one of the era's rising stars, Fred MacMurray. As often happened at the studio, the script was ultimately taken from Wilder and the final version, released in 1937, credited to Don Hartman and Frank Butler. Wilder soon found himself back on the musical beat, developing with his friend Jacques Théry *Rhythm on the River*, a Bing Crosby vehicle with a theme echoing the Austrian's own creative frustrations: Crosby and Mary Martin play ghost-writers who, unbeknownst to each other, collaborate on all the hit songs credited to a famous but artistically barren composer (Basil Rathbone). Once again, the script was taken away from Wilder, and final screenplay credit for this 1940 release went to Dwight Taylor.

Wilder's initial assignments at Paramount may have been unrewarding, but the work was steady, and today he looks back on his tenure there with fond regret for what has been lost. "It was not quite as difficult as it is now. At Paramount, where I spent eighteen years, they had 104 writers under contract. It was on the fourth floor, the writers' annex-annex. Every Thursday, I was to deliver eleven pages written on yellow paper. Everybody was working—not all the scripts were made, naturally—but they made like fifty pictures a year. Now you make a picture with a studio, and even if it's a very inexpensive picture, namely $30 million, they're looking over your shoulder, they're kibitzing, they're afraid, they make you feel that if this picture's not a hit, the studio must be sold, and the policemen will be fired and the secretaries will starve to death. They don't leave you alone. Back then, we decided this is the kind of picture we want to make and those are the actors we'd like to have, and then you went off and started writing the screenplay. The first thing [the executives] saw were the rushes, still not comprehending fully what those little holes on the side of the celluloid were for.

"Still, they sometimes had a desire to put their foot down, to show who is running this goddamn studio. They would come with suggestions for titles. They would run the rushes, as I witnessed one time: The guy who was running MGM, we came for dinner, and they were running the rushes in the living room. And there was the head of the studio and his wife and there were three kids picking their noses, twelve, fourteen, fifteen years old, saying, 'Oh, that's a lousy leading man.' You are exposed to those things. But, in any case, there was not all of this tension. I think that if *Jurassic Park* had turned out a failure, the whole of the United States would be shaking—

it would be a catastrophe of the first order. And now, we can see that we're doing very well, because the picture's going to make one billion dollars all around the world."

It would be some time before Wilder would be privy to the domestic enclaves of studio executives, but a meeting in the summer of 1936 would start him on the path to unimagined success. It was July 17, to be exact, when Paramount writers' department chief Manny Wolf called Wilder into his office to discuss a very tantalizing proposition. Ernst Lubitsch, one of the studio's most celebrated directors and a personal idol of Wilder's, was planning to make a new version of the Alfred Savoir stage farce *Bluebeard's Eighth Wife*, which had been filmed once before with Gloria Swanson in 1923. Wilder knew the play, and Wolf knew Wilder had some cosmopolitan wit to contribute to the project. But even more auspicious was Wolf's plan to team Wilder with one of the studio's veteran writers, a nattily attired, urbane fellow named Charles Brackett. No one, with the possible exception of Manny Wolf, could have predicted that Charles Brackett and Billy Wilder would become the most successful screenwriting duo of the 1940s.

SEVEN

Teamwork

CHARLES BRACKETT AND BILLY WILDER HAD VIRTUALLY nothing in common apart from a shared fondness for cribbage and the intricacies of the English language. Brackett, fourteen years Wilder's senior, came from old money. The son of a New York state senator, he was a graduate of Williams College and Harvard Law School. While Wilder's political leanings were toward Roosevelt New Deal liberalism, Brackett was a longtime conservative Republican. Where Wilder was brash, restless and eager to socialize, Brackett was courtly and reserved. Wilder hated closed doors, Brackett felt uneasy with them open. Wilder paced while he brainstormed, Brackett sat utterly still.

Unlike Wilder, Brackett came to Hollywood with established literary credentials. During his last year at Harvard Law School, he had had a three-part serial published in the *Saturday Evening Post*. He continued to write fiction while a member of his father's Saratoga Springs law firm. Then, in 1926, *New Yorker* editor Harold Ross hired him as drama critic, and his theater reviews over the next three years earned high praise. Soon after leaving *The New Yorker* to work on his third novel, Brackett was summoned to Hollywood by RKO to write dialogue for the burgeoning sound film industry. The initial experience of dealing with the whims of studio bureaucrats soured him on the movie business, and he returned east. But, a few years later, Brackett was back, with a staff writing job at Paramount, where he worked on such instantly forgettable projects as *College Scandal*, *Enter Madame* and *Rose of the Rancho*. Up until the summer of 1936, his most distinguished screen credit was *Piccadilly Jim*, an adaptation of a P. G. Wodehouse story starring Robert Montgomery.

Despite the differences in their backgrounds and personalities, Wilder and Brackett immediately hit it off. Of course, any potential conflict was secondary to their desire to please their director, Ernst Lubitsch. Identical in age to Brackett, Lubitsch had come to America in 1922, after a string of successful historical German silents had established him as one of Europe's most acclaimed directors. In Hollywood, he was celebrated for bringing an unprecedented subtlety and sophisticated wit to the portrayal of sexual relations, a tastefully suggestive quality that came to be known as the "Lubitsch touch."

For Wilder, collaborating with Lubitsch was like taking classes with a master craftsman. (Today, the student keeps a sign hanging in his office, designed by Saul Steinberg, with large-script letters reading, "How would Lubitsch do it?") Lubitsch always had an uncredited role in shaping the screenplays of his films, and *Bluebeard's Eighth Wife* was certainly no exception. As Wilder and Brackett would quickly discover, he could be extremely demanding. "Does it ring the bell? Is this the best we can do?" Lubitsch would constantly implore. In one scene, the Claudette Colbert character escapes Gary Cooper by diving into the Mediterranean. Lubitsch wanted one perfect word Colbert could shout before making her dive, a surefire laugh-getter. The trio couldn't come up with one. Over and over, the director would pantomime Colbert's dive, then gaze over at his writers, hoping inspiration would strike them. They moved on, but days later Lubitsch kept coming back to that elusive word. They never found it.

Wilder rang a bell with Lubitsch at their very first script session when he suggested the ultimate "meet cute" scene for Colbert and Cooper. The young writer proposed that the two protagonists meet in the men's clothing section of a department store: "The boy is trying to buy pajamas, but he sleeps only in the tops. He is thrifty so he insists on buying only the tops. The clerk says he must buy the pants too. It looks like a catastrophe. Then the girl comes into the shop and buys the pants because she sleeps only in the pants." Lubitsch and Brackett were duly impressed: It was not only a clever opener, but a crafty means of planting erotic images of the two leads in the audience's collective mind without violating the Production Code. Months later, Wilder admitted that he himself was a tops-only sleeper, and had been waiting for just such a chance to use this idea.

Wilder found a kindred comic spirit in Lubitsch as well as a mentor. The younger man recalls one particular Lubitsch gag early in the film, as Gary Cooper stops in front of a haberdashery in Nice. A placard in the window reads, "English spoken. Si parla Italiano. Man spricht Deutsch." And finally: "American understood." "That is one of the tiny, wonderful Lubitsch touches," Wilder beams. "I still remember Lubitsch inserting 'American understood' with his pen in our script." It's also exactly the kind of verbal jest that would turn up in many subsequent Wilder films, and in his oft quoted private and public conversations.

Wilder would also take inspiration from the sly manner in which Lubitsch circumvented the Production Code censors. "Lubitsch totally ignored whether the censorship was strict or lax. I don't remember ever having seen a nude scene in a Lubitsch picture, nor a scene where people are rolling in the hay. Now you go see a picture, and already under the titles there is coital action—under the titles! My wife would say: I think that is his left knee. I'd say: No, that's the right breast. But he never got himself in that position. His mind did not work in that direction. He would tell you enough to titillate you—he would tell the audience there was sex last night by only photographing the way the couple attacked breakfast, the way they looked at each other, the way they broke a croissant. . . . Lubitsch let you know what happened, and it could not be censored—you could not put your finger on it."

Above all, Wilder learned from Lubitsch to respect the intelligence of the moviegoer. "Unlike those [directors] who say two plus two equals four," Wilder notes, "Lubitsch says two plus two—that's it. The public has to add it up for themselves."

Brackett, meantime, provided a stable foundation for Wilder's fecund talent. With his East Coast literary background, he helped the young Austrian isolate the very best of his torrent of comic ideas and guide him past the pitfalls of a language he was still in the process of mastering. "[Brackett] spoke excellent English," Wilder enthuses. "He was a very classy guy, a couple of pegs above the ordinary Hollywood writer. He was very patient with me, but he also insisted on my English becoming less ridiculous than it was then. I went to a good school—it lifted my street English a few pegs.

"What was good about our collaboration was: Two collaborators who think exactly alike is a waste of time. Dialogue or whatever comes from: 'Not quite, but you are close to it. Let's find something that we both like. This is a little bit too cheap, this is too easy. This character is not developed. I am a Roosevelt man and you are a Republican.' Unless there are sparks that fly, it is totally unnecessary to have a collaborator." In time, those "sparks" would ignite shouting matches, even the occasional thrown object. To outside observers, however, the two men's individual personalities coalesced so well on paper they were often jokingly referred to as "Brackettandwilder."

Bluebeard's Eighth Wife commenced production on the Paramount lot on October 11, 1937, more than a year after Wilder and Brackett's first meeting, and finished shooting in January at a total cost of $1.3 million. Most critics regard it as lesser Lubitsch, and indeed there is a sense of sweaty desperation surrounding its manic battle of the sexes. Gary Cooper plays Michael Brandon, a wealthy American womanizer vacationing on the Riviera. When he and Colbert's Nicole de Loiselle meet at the pajama counter, Michael vows to make the comely French girl his wife. She resists, until her father (Edward Everett Horton) convinces her that marrying Michael is the only way the family can get out of its current financial doldrums. On the wedding night, Nicole is horrified to discover that Michael has already been married seven times; this arrogant American has a habit of collecting wives and offering one-million-franc divorce settlements once he grows tired of them, which never takes very long. Dubbing Michael "Bluebeard," Nicole refuses to consummate the marriage, and eagerly awaits her divorce papers. With *The Taming of the Shrew* at his side, Michael tries to conquer his bride, but gives up after six months and grants the divorce. By that time, however, Nicole realizes she's fallen in love with Michael and, divorce papers in hand, tries to win him back. She tracks Michael down to a sanatorium outside Paris and, all else failing, buys the place with her divorce settlement and orders her ex-husband put in a straitjacket until he admits he wants her, too.

Colbert and Cooper both give vivacious performances, Lubitsch's direction and the Paramount production design are typically stylish, and the Brackett-Wilder screenplay is bright and energetic. Where *Bluebeard's Eighth Wife* falters is in its awkwardly fabricated situation. The conflict comes not out of character but out of the deterministic demands of the farcical reverses. The Cooper and Colbert characters are almost never in sync, and the continual denial of romance gives the film an overall feeling of brittleness; surely, few other comedies of the thirties resolved their central relationship with a touch of bondage and discipline!

Wilder's private romantic life at this time was somewhat more placid than that of the bickering lovers in *Bluebeard*. On December 22, 1936, he married Judith Iribe, and they moved into a suite at the Marmont. Then, for a time, they lived in Judith's mother's house on De Longpre Avenue in West Hollywood. Subsequently, they found an apartment on South Camden Drive in Beverly Hills. With their mutual sense of style and appreciation of fine art, Judith and Billy seemed to be an ideal couple. But in the coming years, Billy's success and heightened social standing would have an unexpected effect on his brilliant, headstrong wife.

Wilder's other marriage—to Charles Brackett—continued to thrive; in fact, their second project together proved to be one of the brightest comedies of the 1930s. Based on a story idea by Edwin Justus Mayer and Franz Schulz, *Midnight* was also the first American Wilder script to utilize his trademark device of the masquerade. Claudette Colbert was once again the heroine, and this time her character, American chorus girl Eve Peabody, is in far worse financial straits than her Nicole in *Bluebeard's Eighth Wife*. As the film opens, Eve arrives at Paris's Gare de l'Est on a rainy night, dressed in a spectacular gold-lamé gown. "Can I get your luggage?" a porter asks. "I wish you would," Eve laughs. "Where is it?" he wonders. "Municipal pawnshop, Monte Carlo," says the glamorous high roller as she runs off into the downpour. A sympathetic taxi driver named Tibor Czerny (Don Ameche) helps Eve make the rounds of the city's nightclubs in search of a singing gig, to no avail. When Tibor starts to take a bit too much interest in her welfare, Eve flees, and inadvertently crashes an exclusive society recital and winds up posing as the "Baroness Czerny." There, she catches the eye of socialite Georges Flamarion (John Barrymore), who books a suite for her at the plush Ritz Hotel. The arrangement is not what it initially seems: Georges has noted that playboy Jacques Picot (Francis Lederer), the lover of his wife, Helen (Mary Astor), has taken an avid interest in Eve, and he plans to recruit the comely interloper to break up Helen's affair by inviting Eve to a weekend party at his country estate. Georges's seething wife suspects Eve is an impostor, and is about to expose her when Tibor, who has been desperately searching for Eve, enters the party as her husband, "Baron Czerny." Eve is attracted to Tibor but can't picture a future with a humble cabdriver; Tibor, meanwhile, is ready to try anything to win Eve away from Jacques and his snobbish circle. The Flamarion estate has become a madcap battleground.

Intricately structured and brimming with wit, *Midnight* is the first great Wilder-Brackett screenplay. Just as Wilder piqued interest with the pajamas in *Bluebeard's Eighth Wife*, there's something immediately arresting about a woman in a slinky, glittery gown who has but a *centime* to her name. On the surface a merry, sophisticated lark, the film gathers substance from its echoes of Wilder's own odyssey, setting out for Hollywood with—he says—eleven dollars in his pocket and trying to break into the heady, exclusive club of filmmakers. Wilder knows something of the high-wire act an Eve Peabody performs to survive, and it shows in the writing.

The title *Midnight*, of course, is derived from *Cinderella*—at one point, Eve even declares, "Every Cinderella has her midnight"—and, for the first half at least, Eve's adventure does have the unreality of a fairy tale. Barrymore, in his last great screen performance, is her impish fairy godfather, magically installing her in that lavish Ritz suite and granting her an expensive new wardrobe and her own chauffeur. Fortunately for Eve, the shoe fits—she has the charm and flair to wow Georges's society cronies and to send his wife into a green-eyed frenzy.

The arrival of Tibor, who saves Eve from a "midnight" humiliation, brings the fairy tale back down to earth and turns it into a brilliant comedy of manners. That night, Eve rejects Tibor's marriage proposal, and their morning-after breakfast confrontation is a classic of farcical double-crossing. Trying to hasten Eve's departure, Tibor fabricates a story about their child "Francie" contracting measles back in Budapest. (There's a hilarious closeup of a phony telegram with a crude drawing of a speckle-faced little girl and the message "Pleez cum home—Francie.") Eve, in turn, conspires with Georges in staging a fake phone call from Hungary; in an early example of the acid Wilder wit, Georges—from a phone in another room—tells Eve it wasn't measles after all: "It's just a plain case of alcohol poisoning. The baby must have had one highball too many. She was out all night. We picked her up in the gutter." In retaliation, Tibor marches up-stairs, dons his cabbie's garb, and prepares to reveal all to the breakfast circle. But Eve heads him off by telling her new friends that Tibor is subject to a strain of madness in the Czerny family. (As an engagement present, Eve recalls, his grandfather gave them "one roller skate, covered in Thousand Island dressing.") So, no matter how hard Tibor tries to expose the masquerade, Eve's society pals simply brush it off and continue with their breakfast until Tibor loses his temper and gets conked on the head with a saucepan.

After this comic highpoint, the rest of *Midnight* is a bit of a letdown. Eve comes to her senses and is ready to settle down with Tibor, but the cabbie is too angry to forgive her. The pair enter a bogus divorce proceeding in order to free Eve to marry Jacques. But Eve's heartfelt plea about the mental cruelty of her "husband" touches Tibor, and he finds an ingenious way to bind them together forever in their phony marriage. The ending is protracted, but wraps up all the story's loose ends with satisfying efficiency.

With *Midnight*, Wilder and Brackett blossomed as a writing team, but not everyone was quick to recognize their achievement. Producer Arthur Hornblow Jr., in a move common at Paramount and other studios, gave the script to staff writer Ken Englund for a polish. Dissatisfied with the result, Hornblow handed it back to Wilder and Brackett for a rewrite. The pair simply retyped the original script, with a few small adjustments, and submitted it to Hornblow. This time, he was thoroughly pleased. The essential point of the process was to massage Hornblow's ego.

Hornblow's was not the only ego Wilder and Brackett would have to confront on *Midnight*. For Wilder especially, dealing with director Mitchell Leisen was a daily trial. Best known at the time for directing *Death Takes a Holiday* and Preston Sturges's script of *Easy Living*, Leisen was a former set designer whose keen eye for production detail was a welcome asset at a studio famed for the creamily opulent look of its films.* Thanks to Colbert's box-office appeal, *Midnight* was given a generous budget of $1 mil-

---

* Leisen replaced Paul Iribe, Judith Wilder's late stepfather, when he was fired as designer of Cecil B. De Mille's *The King of Kings*.

lion, money well spent on lavish sets like the Flamarion estate. Photographed by one of Hollywood's masters, Charles Lang, *Midnight* has a sparkly elegance that fully complements its contemporary fairy-tale feeling.

Leisen knew how to give *Midnight* chic style, but Wilder had no confidence in the flamboyant, bisexual director's sense of story. He always felt that Leisen was more interested in costumes than dialogue, that he preferred to sit with the dress cutters than to consult with his writers.

Shortly before his death in 1972, Leisen defended himself to biographer David Chierichetti. "Billy Wilder was a middle European fresh from the old country, and most of my fights were with him. Having done eight years of psychoanalysis, I knew that a character had to follow a certain emotional pattern. I'd say, 'Billy, you have this guy doing something that is completely inconsistent. You suddenly introduce a completely different emotional setup for this character, and it can't be. It has to follow a definite emotional pattern.' Well, Billy couldn't figure this one out, but Brackett could. Brackett was sort of a leveling influence. He would referee my quarrels with Billy." Leisen also recalled that "Billy would scream if you changed one line of his dialogue."

Writer Maurice Zolotow got an earful when he sought Wilder's response to Leisen's claims. "He didn't know shit about construction," Wilder fumed. "And he didn't care. All he did was he fucked up the script, and our scripts were damn near perfection, let me tell you. Leisen was too goddamn fey. I don't knock fairies. Let him be a fairy. Leisen's problem was that he was a stupid fairy. He didn't have the brains to see that if Charlie and me, if we put in a line, we had a goddamn reason for putting in that line and not a different line, and you just don't go and cut a line or a piece of action to please some actress, at least without putting another line or action in its place." Wilder also contended that "Charlie hated him as much as I did. . . . It was Arthur Hornblow who refereed our fights."

Wilder's comments were embarrassingly politically incorrect, even when he first uttered them in the midseventies. One can't excuse his characterization of Leisen, but such taunts were common among heterosexual men of his generation. And it probably wasn't so much Leisen's personal demeanor that annoyed him, but what it represented in the one-sided power play between writer and director. How could he deal with a man so absorbed in the design elements of the movie? How could he take seriously anything he had to say about the script? This was no Lubitsch, no veteran master of the perfectly chiseled comic gem. This was Leisen, a clubfooted dandy who, in the non-writer-friendly hierarchy of the studio system, had absolute authority to tell Wilder and Brackett to go to hell.

In fact, Leisen's direction serves *Midnight* beautifully—one can't imagine a more handsome, polished, well-paced and sophisticated handling of Wilder and Brackett's material. But Wilder insists, *"Midnight* is perfect only because I fought [Leisen] every step of the way."

One enthusiastic fan of the *Midnight* script was John Barrymore, who by this point in his alcohol-fogged career was generally disinterested in the quality of his movie projects. Initially, the onetime matinee idol received only his "sides," the portions of the script requiring his participation. But he was so delighted by what he read, he sent his actress wife, Elaine Barrie, to Wilder and Brackett's office to pick up the entire screenplay.

Barrie was given a small role in the film, as a hat shop owner, primarily to keep her husband in line. Despite his dependence on cue cards, Barrymore came through with a wonderfully playful performance; nevertheless, he still found occasion to misbehave. One day, he was discovered relieving himself in the women's bathroom. "This is for ladies," the outraged visitor scolded him. Barrymore turned around and replied, "So is this." With Barrymore acting like Barrymore, Claudette Colbert insisting as usual on being photographed on her left side only, and Mary Astor straining to hide the fact of her pregnancy, Mitchell Leisen had his hands full without the tirades of Billy Wilder.

After the urbane humor of *Midnight* and *Bluebeard's Eighth Wife*, Wilder and Brackett were inexplicably assigned something at the opposite end of the sophistication spectrum: *What a Life*, the first of the series of teen comedies featuring Paramount's answer to Andy Hardy, Henry Aldrich. Adapted from the hit Broadway play by Clifford Goldsmith, which then became a very popular radio series, *What a Life* is an oddly mournful comedy about a slow-witted, socially impaired New Jersey high schooler, played here by Jackie Cooper. The routine plot finds Henry being harassed by campus bully George Bigelow (James Corner) and being pursued by the plain Barbara Pearson (Betty Field). Henry's ardor increases when Barbara is given a makeover by the principal's sexy secretary, but by that time

Barbara has accepted George's invitation to the big spring dance. When George makes improper advances, Barbara says she'll go to the dance with Henry after all, but now Henry's mother says he can't go unless he does well on an upcoming history exam. Henry gets caught cheating on the test, loses Barbara and, what's more, is accused of stealing instruments from the school music room. Fortunately, the boy has a champion in the open-minded young assistant principal, who believes Henry's classroom doodles reveal artistic talent. All ends happily the night of the dance, as Henry exposes the thief, wins back Barbara and appears to be bound for art school.

Sluggishly directed by Jay Theodore Reed, *What a Life* is an anomaly in the Brackett-and-Wilder canon. The subject matter—suburban teens, and not very bright teens at that—is utterly alien to the worldly writing pair. The film's only tenuous connection to Wilder's later, skeptical output is that, up until its cheerful conclusion, it offers an unusually glum view of American high school life. Henry, however, provides few opportunities for Wilder and Brackett to exercise their wit, since he's a whiny, subpar student who, befuddled by *Hamlet,* complains to his teacher, "Some people can make sense out of anything if it isn't interesting."

Proving there's no accounting for an era's taste, Henry Aldrich would go on to appear in ten more feature films, from 1941 through 1944, with Jimmy Lydon taking over for Cooper by the third outing, *Henry Aldrich for President.*

In no time at all, Wilder and Brackett were back in their element, as Ernst Lubitsch beckoned with a new project he was preparing at MGM. Moving from the banal to the sublime, the screenwriters abandoned the world of New Jersey high school underachievers for the magic of Paris and the mystique of a beautiful Russian named Ninotchka.

Garbo Laughs

ERNST LUBITSCH HAD BEEN WANTING TO MAKE A MOVIE with Greta Garbo for years, as Garbo's close friend Mercedes d'Acosta confirms in her autobiography when she describes the first meeting between the director and the charismatic star in 1932. Lubitsch embraced Garbo and told her, in his thick German accent, "Greta, vy don't you tell those idiots in your studio to let us do a picture together? *Gott*, how I vould love to direct a picture with you!" Garbo's weary reply: "You tell them, Ernst. I'm far too tired to talk to studio executives."

The union finally happened in 1939, on a project that had already passed through several hands before it found its way to Lubitsch. *Ninotchka* originated from a three-sentence story idea scribbled in a notebook by the Hungarian writer Melchior Lengyel: "Russian girl saturated with Bolshevik ideals goes to fearful, capitalistic, monopolistic Paris. She meets romance and has an uproarious good time. Capitalism not so bad after all." Gottfried Reinhardt, son of the legendary Austrian theater director Max Reinhardt and then assistant to director Sidney Franklin, brought Lengyel's story to MGM. Lengyel worked for a time on the screenplay, mainly contributing the supporting characters of the three Russian commissars whose inefficiency prompts the heroine's trip to Paris. Feeling Lengyel had arrived at a dead end, Reinhardt brought in two new writers to toil on separate drafts: Jacques Deval, author of the play *Tovarich*, a comedy about

Russian exiles in Paris that had been made into a 1937 Claudette Colbert film; and S. N. Behrman, screenwriter of the Garbo films *Anna Karenina* and *Queen Christina*. Behrman, in particular, made several significant contributions to the story: key sequences at the Eiffel Tower and in the male lead's apartment, and the restaurant scene in which Ninotchka finally learns to loosen up. George Cukor was scheduled to direct the film, but David O. Selznick's massive Civil War epic beckoned and he was soon gone with the wind.

Garbo, who was attached to the film pending approval of the script, also had unofficial approval of the movie's director. With Cukor's defection, she named two replacement choices: Lubitsch and Edmund Goulding. Even though Goulding had directed Garbo memorably in *Grand Hotel* in 1932, the studio opted for Lubitsch. Unsatisfied with Behrman's work, Lubitsch brought in Walter Reisch, Billy Wilder's friend and former Berlin mentor and collaborator. Behrman had Ninotchka in Paris to make a deal concerning a Siberian nickel mine; Reisch turned it into a matter of czarist jewelry. Behrman and Reinhardt thought the jewelry subplot was hackneyed; Lubitsch argued back that jewelry was more photogenic than nickel mines. Tempers swelled, and in short order, both Reinhardt and Behrman were off the project.

With those personnel conflicts settled, Lubitsch arranged to borrow from Paramount his *Bluebeard's Eighth Wife* team, Wilder and Brackett. Working very closely, as he always did, with his writers, Lubitsch honed *Ninotchka* into one of the era's wittiest and worldliest comic-romantic screenplays.

The pairing of Garbo and Lubitsch was still not a *fait accompli*. The Swedish recluse had serious doubts about her drunk scene in the film—she wasn't certain she could do it or whether it was the right image for her; what's more, she didn't like the idea of playing drunk in front of other actors. Garbo came to the studio for a discussion with Lubitsch, but refused to leave her car. So Lubitsch climbed inside the vehicle and, after two hours of easing her fears, Garbo agreed to give *Ninotchka* a try. Production began on May 31, 1939.

Lubitsch later called Garbo "probably the most inhibited person I ever worked with. When you finally break through the inhibitions and she really feels a scene, she is wonderful. But if you don't succeed in making her feel it, she can't do it cold-bloodedly on technique."

Lubitsch held off shooting Garbo's drunk scene till near the end of production, promising to make whatever accommodations the star needed to feel comfortable but insisting the sequence was essential to the film. With the utmost patience and tact, he guided her through the scene, building up her confidence and gradually getting her to relax. As much as he could, he isolated Garbo and costar Melvyn Douglas, shooting the extras separately and intercutting them into the action. In the end, Lubitsch felt it was worth all the trouble. "She played it beautifully," he declared. "So real. Not the routine of an actor who uses the customary tools. That's why it's so charming."

Because Garbo was so self-conscious, the set of *Ninotchka* was extremely restricted: No visitors were allowed, and even the presence of "nonessential" personnel like screenwriters was frowned upon. Nonetheless, both Wilder and Brackett would sneak onto the set to watch the legend at work. Whenever the crew surmised that Garbo was sensing either man's presence, a prop or a piece of scenery was quietly placed in front of his prying eyes.

AS THE OPENING TITLES CHARMINGLY ADMIT, *NINOTCHKA* "takes place in Paris in those wonderful days when a siren was a brunette and not an alarm . . . and if a Frenchman turned out the light it was not on account of an air raid!" The film begins as three comical emissaries from the Russian Board of Trade—Kopalski, Buljanoff and Iranoff—debate whether to check into the luxurious Hotel Clarence or the dreary Hotel Terminus that Moscow has assigned them. Convincing themselves that Lenin would approve (and bewitched by visions of French chambermaids), they opt for the former. The three delegates are in Paris to sell the court jewels of the exiled Grand Duchess Swana (Ina Claire), who promptly receives word of the mission from Count Rakonin, a fellow exile who works as a waiter at the Clarence. Swana's lover, Leon (Melvyn Douglas), confronts the Russian visitors, challenges their ownership of the jewels, and insinuates that a French court would likely side with the glamorous grand duchess. Leon introduces the troika to wine, women and decadent Western pleasures, and is just about ready to finalize a 50-50 settlement for his client when word arrives that a new envoy is en route to Paris to oversee negotiations. That envoy, of course, is Nina Ivanovna Yakushova, the beautiful but unbending bureaucrat who will come to be known more affectionately as Ninotchka.

Ninotchka and Leon have a chance meeting on a traffic island outside the hotel and, his curiosity much aroused, he becomes her guide to the marvels of the City of Light. As rigid as the Russian seems, she nonetheless agrees to accompany Leon to his apartment. ("You might be an interesting subject of study," she coolly informs him.) They kiss, and Ninotchka finds the experience "restful," requesting an encore. A phone call from Ninotchka's comrades not only interrupts their lovemaking, but reveals their identities to each other. Leon must work extra hard to regain Ninotchka's trust, but he and Paris ultimately transform the dogmatic Russian envoy into a woman giddy with love.

Ninotchka's passionate interlude is cut short when the jealous grand duchess gets hold of the jewels and blackmails the envoy into ending the affair and taking the first plane back to Russia. The heartbroken Ninotchka immerses herself in her work, and tries unsuccessfully to refuse an order to go to Constantinople to investigate the drunken antics of her former colleagues. There, she discovers that Kopalski, Buljanoff and Iranoff have opened a Russian restaurant together, and Leon is behind it all. Unable to get a visa for Russia, he's brought Ninotchka to him, and now he's threatening to turn every Russian commissar into a restaurateur unless she agrees to stay. "Well," Ninotchka shrugs, "if it's a choice between my personal interest and the good of my country, how can I waver? No one shall say Ninotchka was a bad Russian."

NINOTCHKA WAS THE HAPPIEST WORKING EXPERIENCE OF Wilder's pre-directing career; once again, he was collaborating with his idol, Ernst Lubitsch, on a project tailored to a star he first paid homage to in 1929's *Menschen am Sonntag*. In interviews, Wilder relishes pointing out the Lubitsch touches in *Ninotchka*, particularly the visual device of a rather absurdly elongated Parisian woman's hat that signals a decisive change in the heroine's outlook. When Ninotchka first sees the hat in a shop window, just after her arrival in Paris, she grumbles, "How can such a civilization survive which permits their women to put things like that on their heads? It won't be long now, comrades." After she falls in love, Lubitsch's camera finds the Russian envoy locking her bedroom door and sheepishly pulling the same hat out of the bottom drawer of her bureau. No words needed to be spoken.

Ninotchka also never underestimates the intelligence of the audience by assuming an unfamiliarity with the political forces and socioeconomic doctrines at work in the world of the late 1930s. It ridicules the oppressiveness and deprivation of Stalinist Russia at a time when it was still fashionable to show enthusiastic support for the Soviet experiment, but it has ample regard for its heroine's strength and dignity as a representative of an alien dogma. Wilder, Brackett and Reisch's screenplay also sees things from the other side, coming down hard on the social injustice and greed of the czarists and tweaking capitalism for its shallow value system. The film dives into a political morass and manages to offend only those most deserving of being offended. Wilder's clear-eyed vision of the world and its follies was surely a large contributing factor to *Ninotchka*'s smooth negotiation of such treacherous thematic waters.

In *Ninotchka*, character is a function of politics, but with such wit that the players are seldom less than full-blooded human beings. The exception, perhaps, is Ninotchka before her romantic flowering. "The last mass trials were a great success. There are going to be fewer but better Russians," she announces to her comrades in one of the more cold-blooded gag lines in the Wilder-Brackett canon. Fortunately, most of the laughs at the expense of Ninotchka's dogmatism are of a more gently satirical variety. Failing to comprehend why a railroad porter should want to carry her bags, she lectures him, "That's no business. That's social injustice." "That depends on the tip," is his hilariously down-to-earth reply. In Ninotchka's view, the spectacular lights of Paris are a waste of electricity, and when Leon insists he can't help flirting, she puts him in his place with a two-word directive: "Suppress it!"

Still, Ninotchka is seen as something of a superwoman (she mounts the Eiffel Tower's 1,083 steps by foot before Leon arrives by elevator) and her cause is a just one. In their climactic confrontation, Ninotchka tells the grand duchess that the Russian people paid for her jewels with their blood and their lives—a point the writers leave rightfully unchallenged. In terms of the filmmakers' sympathies, there's simply no contest between the strikingly handsome, robust, idealistic Ninotchka and the vain, spoiled, superficial (and considerably older-looking) Swana.

Wilder, Brackett and Reisch try their best to achieve a balance, through the occasional jab at capitalism ("They accumulate millions by taking loss after loss," a skeptical Buljanoff surmises during business negotiations) and a warm appreciation of Ninotchka's comradely instincts and the Russian culture. (Gourmand that he is, the Russia Wilder loves is the Russia of borscht, beef stroganoff, blinis and sour cream.) Still, *Ninotchka* is decidedly pro-West, with "West" defined in terms of romance, style and freedom to speak your mind. When Ninotchka returns to Russia, the film shows her dutifully marching in a parade dominated by portraits of Stalin, sharing a drab apartment with two women (and a stone-faced neighbor who periodically passes through to use the washroom) and having a reunion "feast" with her former Parisian comrades—each one brings an egg so they can share an omelette. Fair or not, the visual contrast between shabby Russia and swank Paris proved irresistible to the filmmakers.

Wilder's own political leanings were to the left. Besides being very much a Roosevelt Democrat, he supported the Loyalists in Spain and counted a number of Communists among his friends, not an exceptional occurrence in 1930s Hollywood. As a Russophile, he regretted some of the jokes in *Ninotchka*. As a satirist, he couldn't help himself. "I've always wanted to see Odessa," he told *Life* magazine's Lincoln Barnett in 1944, "and now I'm afraid we never will." Chimed in Brackett, "I can last a long time without seeing Odessa."

Of course, if *Ninotchka* were only about politics, it wouldn't have made a *kopeck*. The attraction of the film is summed up in its tag line, the notion that got the project started in the first place: "Garbo Laughs!" (a follow-up of sorts to *Anna Christie*'s declaration in 1930, "Garbo Talks!"). Wilder, Brackett and Reisch artfully deliver on the promise of S. N. Behrman's idea for the restaurant scene, in which Leon unsuccessfully tries to make Ninotchka laugh by telling her a series of bad jokes, then hits a gusher of suppressed laughter when he accidentally falls backward in his chair. From this point on, Garbo is radiant, displaying an elatedness that is altogether refreshing, coming as it does from the screen's reigning tragedienne. It's a natural, joyful Garbo the public hadn't seen before—a mood that affected her offscreen life, too. "Never since I had known her had I seen her in such good spirits," wrote Mercedes d'Acosta. "She used to come for me as usual after shooting, and we walked in the hills. At least I walked, but she more often ran and danced. She laughed constantly. . . . It was fascinating to see how by playing a gay role rather than a sad one her personality changed."

If the romance of *Ninotchka* has a shortcoming, it's in the casting of Melvyn Douglas as Leon. Douglas is perfectly adept at delivering the screenplay's plentiful seductive patter, but he lacks a certain sex appeal (which would have been amply supplied by Lubitsch's preferred choice for the role, Cary Grant). As played by Douglas, there's something a little too slimy about Leon's elaborate come-ons; a woman less sheltered than Ninotchka might never have given him a second look. But Leon does get to utter one of the most shamelessly romantic speeches Wilder and Brackett would ever write, the one that begins, "Ninotchka, it's midnight—one half of Paris is making love to the other half," and ends with "Surely you feel some slight symptom of the divine passion . . . a burning of the lips that isn't thirst but something a thousand times more tantalizing, more exalting, than thirst?" "You are very talkative" is Ninotchka's accurate reply.

Like many of Wilder's later protagonists, Leon is a roué, a gigolo, a scoundrel. But unlike those antiheroes, he falls immediately, deeply and sincerely in love; once he's smitten, Leon no longer cares what happens to the grand duchess and her coveted jewels. *Ninotchka* would be one of the rare Wilder scripts in which the romantic pursuer lays all his cards on the table, with no disguises or hidden agendas.

As the opening titles hint, the romantic Parisian milieu of *Ninotchka* was fast becoming a thing of the past. It's still a shock, in this elegant romantic comedy, to see Germans giving the Hitler salute as Kopalski, Buljanoff and Iranoff search for their presumably male superior at the train station. In the end, the Russians must make their new home in Turkey, not in a France engaged in war. Ninotchka, at the height of her joy, expresses best the elegiac mood of the film and its makers: "The revolution is on the march. . . . Bombs will fall, civilization will crumble. But not yet, please. Wait. What's the hurry? Give us our moment. Let's be happy."

Behind the scenes, Ernst Lubitsch and Billy Wilder were becoming intimately involved with the effects of the European revolution. Around the time of *Ninotchka*'s opening, Lubitsch and agent Paul Kohner formed the European Film Fund, uniting Hollywood's émigré community in a sponsorship program for impoverished new film-industry refugees. Members like Wilder, Walter Reisch, William Dieterle, Salka Viertel, Gottfried Reinhardt and Conrad Veidt contributed time and money to the fund, but the real powerhouse behind the project was Kohner, who used all his agent's pull to secure short-term, minimum-salary contracts for the new arrivals, many of them renowned writers back home, at studios like MGM, Warner Bros., Columbia and Universal. Seeing their desperation made Wilder doubly thankful he had fled Europe as early as he did.

NINOTCHKA PREMIERED ON OCTOBER 6, ONE MONTH AFTER France and Britain declared war on Germany. The reviews were uniformly ecstatic. Frank S. Nugent in *The New York Times* called *Ninotchka* "one of the sprightliest comedies of the year," adding "nothing quite so astonishing has come to the [Radio City] Music Hall since the Rockefellers landed on Fiftieth Street." He praised "the superb rightness of Garbo's playing" and said her deadpan comic approach had "the assurance of a Buster Keaton." Howard Barnes of the *Herald Tribune* noted "an added verve and color to [Garbo's] personality . . . which makes her even more magically lovely than in the past."

The film was a modest box-office success, earning $2.2 million worldwide on a $1.3 million investment. Half of that money came from foreign tallies, a major accomplishment when taking into account that the film's political satire got it banned in such countries as Italy, Bulgaria, Estonia and, for a short time, France.

In the 1939 Oscar race, *Ninotchka* was overshadowed by the monumental *Gone with the Wind*, as were all the other candidates in that remarkable film year: *Wuthering Heights, Mr. Smith Goes to Washington, Stagecoach, The Wizard of Oz* and *Goodbye, Mr. Chips* among them. The film was in the running for Best Picture, Garbo was up for Best Actress (losing to Vivien Leigh), and Brackett and Wilder earned their first Oscar nominations, along with Reisch, for Best Screenplay (losing again to the powerful *Wind*).

Lubitsch, in spite of a stylish comeback, was not nominated for Best Director.

Years after Garbo's retirement from the screen in 1941, Wilder was driving his car when he spotted the enigmatic star jogging along Rodeo Drive. "I stopped and said, 'Miss Garbo? This is Billy Wilder. How would you like to come over to my house? It's around the corner on Beverly Drive.' She looked all sweaty and she said, 'That would be won-der-ful.' So we went to my place. My [second] wife was upstairs, and I went up and said, 'Audrey, we have a guest downstairs. She would like to have a drink.' She said, 'Who?' And I said, 'Greta Garbo.' And she said, 'Oh, go fuck yourself.' I said, 'No, I swear.' Garbo sat down and we talked. She had three martinis of pretty good size. She was pretty strong." Wilder eventually worked up the courage to ask the question on everyone's mind: "Are you or aren't you going to make another picture?" The fabled beauty responded, "I will make a picture, but only if I can play a clown." "Why would you want to play a clown?" Wilder wondered. "Because I don't want to show my face," the age-conscious star insisted. "I would have a mask. . . ." "You mean, not even at the end?—" But before Wilder could get the words out, Garbo shook her head no. "So," she continued, "you have a story with a clown?" "Not at the moment," was Wilder's disheartened reply.

SHORTLY BEFORE *NINOTCHKA* WENT INTO PRODUCTION, Judith Wilder informed her husband that she was pregnant. The Wilders had moved out of their apartment on Camden Drive and into a rented Tudor house on Chevy Chase in Beverly Hills. Now, it was time to buy a house, a secluded countrylike place in the aptly named Hidden Valley, off Coldwater Canyon. Judith, an avid gardener and horseback rider, loved the tranquility and natural splendor of their new home. But Billy began to feel the move was a mistake—in Hidden Valley, he was too distant and isolated from the Hollywood social circle he relished. It was a long drive to the studio, and just as long a drive to the chic industry parties where Billy was now a welcome guest.

For Judith, that was all just fine. She had grown bored with Hollywood society, with all the industry talk, with fashion and decor and gourmet meals. She'd rather spend a quiet time savoring her new Eden, and when she socialized, it was usually for some political purpose. Stunned by the events happening in Europe, she believed in activism, not the frivolous fantasy world that Billy and his Hollywood cronies were in the business of creating.

Judith gave birth to twins, named Vincent and Victoria, on December 21, 1939. Tragically, Vincent died in infancy. Judith and Billy doted on their surviving girl, but the new responsibilities they shared did little to make their marriage stronger.

AFTER THE HEADY THRILL OF WORKING WITH LUBITSCH ON one of his most celebrated pictures, Wilder and Brackett returned to Paramount, again in the service of producer Arthur Hornblow Jr. and director Mitchell Leisen. They set to work on an original screenplay called *La Polonaise*, a drama that directly reflected Wilder's anguish over the fate of his mother and other family members back in Europe. The story revolved around an American athlete who journeys to Warsaw to find his grandmother and becomes caught up in the war when she refuses to leave with him; the title was taken from the fact that a Warsaw radio station continued to play Chopin's "Polonaise" as the Germans invaded the city. Maria Ouspenskaya was set to play the grandmother, but the production was forced to wait until male lead William Holden fulfilled a commitment at Columbia Pictures.

With *La Polonaise* postponed, the team of Wilder, Brackett, Leisen and Hornblow accelerated plans to make another wartime-themed tale, *Arise, My Love*. This new project would retain Wilder and Brackett's trademark romantic sophistication, but mingled with unaccustomed gravity and political urgency.

Arise, My Love (the title is taken from the Song of Solomon) began as an original screenplay by John S. Toldy and Benjamin Glazer, chronicling the snag-filled romance between an American fighter pilot, recently freed from a Spanish prison, and a provincial French girl. Fed up with the chaos in Europe, the American, after much coaxing, persuades the girl to flee with him to the States. The script ends with the pilot declaring to his love, "They can never touch us now"—just seconds before their United States–bound ship is attacked.

Paramount sent the script back for a radical overhaul by two writing teams: Toldy and Glazer, and, working completely separately, Wilder's old friend Jacques Théry and his partner, a fan magazine writer named Katharine Hartley (Ketti) Frings. In both versions, the French girl was changed to a feisty American reporter assigned to Europe, most probably inspired by Ernest Hemingway's third wife, Time-Life correspondent Martha Gellhorn. The new Toldy-Glazer draft concentrated on the pilot's escape from the Spanish prison, with the reporter pretending to be his wife. The Théry-Frings treatment focused on the couple's post-Spain romance and their thwarted attempts to get married and flee Europe.

Now it was Wilder and Brackett's turn. Expanding on the notion of the reporter masquerading as imprisoned pilot Tom Martin's spouse, Paramount's crack writing team—in their first daring fusion of light and darkness—transformed a grim firing-squad scene into an occasion for droll comedy.

Indeed, the opening scenes of *Arise, My Love* are unsettlingly schizoid. The film begins on an overhead shot of a prisoner being led to his execution in a sun-baked courtyard; the camera slowly closes in on a tiny, barred, ground-floor window. Inside, Tom Martin (Ray Milland) is playing cards with a fidgety priest; the prisoner takes time out from his cocky banter only to listen to the sound of the guards ordering their men to fire. The guns explode, and the shadow of Tom's dead comrade darkens the ground outside the window. The priest tries to persuade the pilot to repent for shooting down twelve enemy planes in the Spanish Civil War, but Tom's only regret is that he wasted his life "in some palooka preliminaries in Spain just before Hitler and Chamberlain warm up for the main event." Suddenly comes the extraordinary news that Tom has been granted a pardon by the highest military authorities, who have been persuaded by the desperate entreaties of his wife. What's even more extraordinary, as Tom confides to the priest, is that he isn't married.

Waiting in the prison governor's office is Augusta "Gusto" Nash (Claudette Colbert, in a situation not unlike her charade as the Baroness Czerny in *Midnight*). "Oh, Tom, it's you! It's your funny old face!" she swoons, embracing a puzzled Tom, who responds with a mischievously extended kiss. Once alone together, Gusto explains that she's a reporter for the Associated News, syndicated to 400 American newspapers. By posing as

Tom's wife, she figures she can land a great human-interest story; saving him from certain death seems to be merely an incidental side benefit.

Gusto succeeds in springing Tom, but the authorities soon catch on to her deception, and the pair is forced to make a breathless escape in a stolen plane, low on gas and with enemy aircraft on their tail. Tom still finds time to brush up on his seduction skills. "If it's going to be our last hour, why not spend it like sensible people?" he argues. Gusto warns that the last time a man got fresh with her, she bit his nose. A few close calls later, Gusto and Tom land safely in Bayonne—she with a first-class scoop, he with a bandage above his nostrils.

As this synopsis reveals, *Arise, My Love* offers a curious mix of comic banter and high-stakes drama—the same formula as escapist adventures ranging from *Gunga Din* to *Raiders of the Lost Ark*, except here the threat is all too real and contemporary. The script's wavering moods would have been a challenge for any director; Mitchell Leisen's difficulty in creating a consistent tone only added to Wilder's catalogue of complaints against him.

Following its exciting opening escape, *Arise, My Love* takes on a cozier rhythm of romantic wariness and seduction. Arriving in Paris, Gusto is ordered to do a fifty-thousand-word profile of Tom, which leads to a double-entendre-filled encounter in his hotel room as she gets the place ready for photographers while he thinks she's come to make up. "What's the best setup? . . . What about that chair?" Gusto wonders, as Tom glances over at the more conventional bed in the next room. "You'll love it when you see it in the Sunday supplement," the reporter enthuses, leading Tom to ponder what's happened to America since he left.

The photo session over, Gusto remains all business, but Tom complains that it's eight o'clock and Paris is waiting. Recalling Melvyn Douglas's vision of the city at midnight in *Ninotchka*, he proclaims, "On the Champs Elysées the lights are bursting into bloom; in the great restaurants wines are growing cold. Orchestras are limbering up their fingers and women all set for their rendezvous stand putting perfume behind their ears." The pilot persuades Gusto to continue her interview at Maxim's ("red plush and gilt and women's shoulders, the slow waltz, the fireworks of crêpes suzettes") while he waits for a fictitious Romanian dinner date. By night's end, Gusto is smitten, but she insists on returning to her typewriter, claiming love always hits her too hard and she musn't let it get in the way of her career.

As Gusto wrestles with her erotic urges, her editor arrives with big news: thanks to her recent headline-grabbing adventure, she's been named the syndicate's Berlin correspondent. Gusto boards a train for Berlin the next day, and is surprised and flattered when Tom shows up on the same train. But it's not love he's after (or so he says); the pilot is bound for Warsaw, where he plans to join the Polish Air Force. Before they go on to their individual destinies, Tom impulsively pulls the emergency brake, enabling the couple to enjoy a three-day idyll in the French countryside. Filmed on a lush forest set, their getaway is a peaceful, sensuous fantasy; ironically, they're among the few people in Europe who haven't heard that Hitler has invaded Poland.

Despite the lure of the European crisis, Gusto and Tom resolve to return to America and settle down as a conventional bourgeois couple. But, just like in the previous scripts, their ship is sunk. Tom joins a makeshift air squad searching for the enemy sub, and when Gusto sees the excitement in his eyes, she pretends to be bitten by the reporting bug and calls in a scoop to her office in Paris. The pair go their separate ways, to be reunited months later during the fall of Paris. His arm permanently injured in Norway, Tom tells Gusto he's returning to the States to become an air force flight instructor; she announces she's joining him, and will use her talent and experience to rouse the American public to join the fight for freedom.

Wilder and Brackett make three direct but entirely divergent references to the title over the course of the film. "Arise, my love, and carry me away," is Tom's private prayer when he needs his plane to lift him away from danger. Later, Gusto purrs, "Arise, my love," while coaxing Tom to take her to the safety of America. But most significantly, in the closing moments, she chants, "Arise, my love," as a challenge to her readers and the American movie audience. "Arise, my love," says Wilder, with his partner Brackett, to the country he now calls home.

Prior to 1940, few Hollywood features acknowledged the ugly turmoil that was erupting in Europe. A handful had used the Spanish Civil War as a dramatic backdrop, such as *Last Train from Madrid* in 1937 and *Blockade* in 1938. The potential Nazi threat was sensationalized in 1939's *Confessions of a Nazi Spy*, and that year also brought the film of Robert E. Sherwood's Pulitzer Prize–winning play *Idiot's Delight*, about the denizens of a hotel near the Italian border. But *Arise, My Love* was among the first Hollywood efforts, along with Alfred Hitchcock's *Foreign Correspondent* and Charles Chaplin's *The Great Dictator* (all released in 1940), to explicitly call for American intervention against the fearsome rise of Nazism and fascism. With the blessing of Hornblow and the Paramount hierarchy, Wilder was able to play a part in alerting the country to the evil juggernaut rolling across Europe and threatening the lives of his own family in Vienna. The whole filmmaking team strove to make *Arise, My Love* as timely as possible; the picture began shooting on June 24 and was in theaters by mid-October, and Colbert's closing speech was filmed last to reflect the day's headlines. (In fact, the ending was reshot to make her words "a little more political and less personal," in response to audience reactions at sneak-preview screenings.)

Paramount's position on *Arise, My Love* was never unqualifiedly coura-geous; even something as innocuous as Tom dubbing a rat in his Spanish prison cell with the nickname Adolf didn't make the final cut. And, ever alert to the bottom line of international grossing potential, the studio took extra precautions to shield its investment against foreign protests. As Para-mount executive Luigi Luraschi noted in a letter to Production Code chief Joseph Breen, "I advised you we were shooting extensive protection takes on all of the political aspects so that, if necessary, we could release the picture in any territory we wanted, eliminating all political cracks. . . . The Foreign Department has now decided to make full use of these protec-tion takes for the release of the picture in all Latin American territories." The revised *Arise, My Love* was ultimately approved in all Latin American republics except Brazil, which ordered additional cuts Paramount deemed "very unreasonable." In a spring 1941 missive to Breen, Luraschi described Brazil's reaction as "a positive indication of the pro-Axis tendencies of that government," and noted that this information was being forwarded to the State Department.

Politics wasn't the only censorable content in *Arise, My Love*; so was the healthy sex drive of Tom and his air force cronies. The Breen Office nixed lines like Tom's last request for "a couple of blonds à la mode, served with soft music from the next cell," and voiced objections to the double entendres of the first hotel-room scene between Tom and Gusto. Fair enough. But a letter from Breen to Motion Picture Producers and Distributors of America head Will Hays reveals just how hysterical and perverse the guardians of the nation's movie morality could sometimes be. "There is a scene in this picture," Breen huffed,

> which, in our judgment, is a new low in purported screen entertainment. It is a scene, set down in a private bathroom, in which three men participate in a conversation. Shock No. 1 comes at the opening of the scene, when it appears that one of the men *is seated on a toilet* [emphasis in original]. Later on, of course, we discover that he has really been sitting on a washstand bowl. Shock No. 2 is suggested by several scenes of Ray Milland in the bathtub *shaving himself.* The camera angles on these several scenes are pitched in such a way as to come as near as possible to the exposure of Mr. Milland's sex organs. . . . This whole sequence and, more especially, the scenes of Milland in the bathtub, constitute in our judgment the most shocking exhibition of consummate bad taste which we have ever seen on the motion picture screen.

However far director Leisen went in his appreciation of the youthful Ray Milland's physique, it seems more than a bit odd today that the sight of a toilet and a man in a bathtub could put Joe Breen in such a state of apoplexy. Perhaps Breen's rage was triggered by a small joke of Leisen's. As the director recalled, "If I was afraid something in a scene might not pass, I'd insert another line in the same scene that was absolutely outrageous. . . . In *Arise, My Love*, when Ray is taking a bath, I had one of his buddies look into the bathtub and say, 'I didn't know you were Jewish.' Of course, they made me cut it out, but they never noticed the line I was trying to keep in." With a few alterations, the bathtub scene did indeed survive, along with this forceful exchange:

> TOM'S BUDDY: You heard what Hitler said on the radio, didn't ya? "I have but three desires in my heart—peace, peace and peace!"

TOM: And next day he took Czechoslovakia. Tomorrow it will be Poland, Hungary, Romania. We'll get another crack at those big boys. War is coming, and I can smell it!

Despite the gravity of its backdrop, *Arise, My Love* was often a giddy production. Leisen insisted on using real alcohol in the scene where Tom and Gusto get drunk on champagne and crème de menthe (Brackett's awful notion of a sophisticated new drink), with the expected messy results. The two stars got along beautifully, though Milland began the film believing Colbert hated him after the terrible experience of their first picture together, *The Gilded Lily.** Colbert, as always, insisted on having only the left side of her face photographed—which put cinematographer Charles Lang in a quandary, since Milland favored his left side, too.

As Milland recalled, "Brackett and Wilder didn't hang around. . . . When we ran into an impasse and couldn't shoot a scene, we called them up and they came down to the set. Then they went back to their office where they could fix it, no matter what the problem was. Billy was wild and flamboyant, while Charlie was the quiet one. He had a calming influence on Billy. They were inseparable."

Arise, My Love proved a successful gamble for Paramount, but was not without its detractors. *The New York Times*'s lordly film critic, Bosley Crowther, branded it "a synthetic picture which attempts to give consequence to a pleasant April-in-Paris romance by involving it in the realities of war— but a war which is patently conceived by someone who has been reading headlines in California."

Wilder himself remembers, "We got many letters. What made it kind of a ticklish situation—I don't know how many letters came to the studio saying, 'How dare you!'—was that the war was not on yet. That was before Pearl Harbor. Oh sure, there were here and there graffiti and a stink bomb thrown. But it was a good picture. If it was not, Paramount would have taken back all the copies so as not to offend the German-American audience."

---

* In fact, Colbert had requested Milland after the studio's first choice, Joel McCrea, proved unavailable.

LESS THAN THREE WEEKS AFTER *ARISE, MY LOVE* BEGAN shooting, Paramount announced it had canceled *La Polonaise*, betraying a certain residual fear of films dealing too closely with the war in Europe. Wilder and Brackett's next film for Leisen and Hornblow would deal much more obliquely with the European tragedy, but would also have more personal resonances for Wilder than any project he had worked on to date. And, perhaps because it was so personal, it would be the film that would propel Wilder toward a nearly impossible goal for Paramount staff writers—the chance to direct his own material.

The Directing Itch

HOLD BACK THE DAWN WAS THE FIRST WILDER SCRIPT TO feature what would become a staple of his movie output: the antihero. In Georges Iscovescu, Wilder shows what happens when a dashing playboy is shut away from the pleasures of high society and confronted with the cold realities of a world at war. Georges, played by Charles Boyer, is a smooth Romanian ballroom dancer and gigolo who left Europe for the promise of a secure new life in the United States. But, like many of his compatriots, he didn't reckon on the American quota system, which allows only a prescribed number of refugees per country. Stuck in a squalid Mexican border hotel, Georges awaits an immigration visa, a process that could take as long as eight years. There, he meets his lusty former dancing partner Anita (Paulette Goddard), who suggests a way out of his trap: Why not, as she did, gain entry to the United States by seducing and marrying an American (and then file for divorce)? Georges goes for the plan, and eventually finds the perfect patsy: Emmy Brown (Olivia de Havilland), a bookish spinster schoolteacher from Azusa who is in Mexico on a Fourth of July field trip with her class of bratty young boys. When a comical collision forces Emmy to put her station-wagon school bus in a garage for repairs, Georges shrewdly hides an essential part so that she has no choice but to stay in Mexico overnight. That's all the time the professional gigolo needs to work his sleazy magic on the vulnerable teacher. By morning, the pair are married, and now Georges simply has to wait four weeks to obtain the proper entry papers from Washington.

Emmy goes back to her job in the States, but returns unexpectedly a few days later with the news that she's been given a week off for a honeymoon. To Georges's chagrin, her visit coincides with that of a dogged immigration officer, Hammock (Walter Abel). Georges flees town with Emmy on the pretext of a romantic honeymoon journey, which accidentally takes them to a small village celebration in honor of the patron saint of brides and bridegrooms. The atmosphere is enchanting, and Georges finds himself genuinely falling for his sweet, guileless new bride.

Georges's change of heart is bad news for bad girl Anita, who has already gotten them bookings as dance partners in America. She vindictively exposes Georges's real motives to Emmy, who, despite this devastating news, nobly defends her husband before a skeptical Hammock. Returning home to Azusa, the mortified Emmy crashes her car and is critically injured. On hearing the news, Georges crosses the border illegally and races to be by her side. Emmy recovers, and Georges's dramatic demonstration of his love clears the way toward a new start in America.

Hold Back the Dawn began life as a screenplay proposal by Ketti Frings entitled *Memo to a Movie Producer*, loosely based on her own marriage to German refugee Kurt Frings, a former European lightweight boxing champion. Though married to an American, Kurt Frings was not permitted to enter the United States, because he had falsified a date on a visa application. "I work in Hollywood, but I live and love in Tijuana," is how his wife began her original thirty-three page treatment, written in the form of a letter to a film producer. In it, Ketti Frings related the real-life stories of her immigrant neighbors in Tijuana, all possessed of what she called a "beautiful hunger," the hunger for freedom. Among them were the boxer Jack Doyle and his actress wife, Movita; the Polish-Jewish composer Gabriel Robles; a talented Czech art director named Emil Mannhof, and the brothers of Warners' successful film director, Hungarian Michael Curtiz. Frings envisioned her film as "the *Grand Hotel* of the border, *Grand Hotel* and *The Last Mile* all mixed together."

Paramount bought the rights to Frings's story, which she expanded to one hundred pages and subsequently adapted into her first novel, entitled *Hold Back the Dawn*. In Frings's version, her two lead characters, Jennifer

True and Eric Osler, are very much in love; the only thing that keeps them apart is her fan-magazine-writing career in Hollywood. Wilder and Brackett created a much more interesting, darker conflict—one that would understandably prompt Kurt Frings to threaten to sue Arthur Hornblow and Paramount Pictures for defamation of character.

Wilder and Brackett's radical new take on the Kurt Frings character may have been influenced by an ominous letter from the Treasury Department's Bureau of Narcotics to Kenneth Clark of the Motion Picture Producers and Distributors, which branded Frings as "a notorious international character," without bothering to offer any specifics. Frings's situation had been deemed important enough to be taken up by the House and the Senate, who passed a bill permitting the immigrant's entry, which was then vetoed by President Franklin Roosevelt. The nephew of a Catholic cardinal who had publicly denounced Hitler, Frings may have been considered too potentially controversial a figure in these strange days of interventionist/isolationist squabbles. In any event, Paramount paid attention when the Bureau of Narcotics warned that their Frings project "may do more harm than good"; two months later, Wilder and Brackett turned in a script with an amoral gigolo, not a romantic hero, at its center.

The Paramount duo's handiwork still retains a number of Ketti Frings's ideas, such as the community of immigrants eager to prove their devotion to America. (Two Frings characters, a pregnant wife and an old woman determined to die in the United States, are combined into one, a pregnant woman who schemes to have her baby just across the border.) Brackett and Wilder also borrowed Frings's device of a car wreck, which spurs the hero to risk arrest to be with his injured lover. Most interestingly, the film retains the "memo to a movie producer" notion, opening with the Boyer character crashing the real Paramount lot and telling his story to a filmmaker named Saxon (played by Leisen, who takes a break from directing the real Veronica Lake in a scene from his previous film, *I Wanted Wings*.)

Wilder was able to bring firsthand knowledge to the story's portrait of an unnamed Mexican border town suffused with heat, grime and desperate characters. But, no matter how much Georges complains about the flies and the baking sun, the Mexican plaza depicted in the film appears relatively clean, benign and downright attractive. The Mexican ambassador, it seems, had gotten an advance peek at the script and filed a complaint with the State Department about the image of Mexico *Hold Back the Dawn* was going to convey. Paramount, Leisen and Hornblow readily complied with the government's request not to put Mexico in too unflattering a light, thus diluting some of the dramatic urgency of Georges's need to escape to America.

Through Georges, Wilder also tapped into his memories of working as a dancer-for-hire in Berlin. (Before Production Code vetting, Georges declared, "My papers give my occupation as a dancer—but I did very little dancing"; in the film, he says, "My papers give my occupation as a dancer—which is correct in a general way.") Wilder's portrait of the typical European gigolo is merciless. In one sense, Georges is a descendant of the many smooth sexual adventurers and scoundrels in the films of Ernst Lubitsch. But the Romanian émigré must face a reality—exodus, homelessness and poverty—that Lubitsch's stylish scamps never had to cope with. Essentially a selfish, swellheaded bastard, Georges deals with tough times by becoming a calculating predator. His exploitation of the unworldly Emmy is crueler than even Lubitsch's most mischievous games. Shamelessly, he tells Emmy she resembles a woman who broke his heart, who compelled him to flee halfway across the world. When Emmy wakes up in the lobby of the hotel, where she and her class are spending the night, Georges is there in the opposite chair, gazing moonfully at her. He declares his love ("It's not this kiss I want, it's all your kisses") and instructs her to look at her finger, onto which he has slipped a wedding ring borrowed from Anita. ("No, the left one," he corrects her, in a comic touch that wickedly underscores Emmy's haplessness.) Telling her she needn't worry, the ring is just an impulsive fantasy, he walks out the door, confident she'll come running after him. She does, gushing, "Other people are lonesome, too— so lonesome they almost give up waiting." In voiceover, Georges sums up his victory: "I'd thrown some crumbs of romance before a hungry heart. The trap was set. She never had a chance."

If Boyer felt altogether comfortable playing such a cad, one aspect of Wilder and Brackett's script was judged beneath his dignity. Early in the film, Boyer was to point his walking stick at a cockroach crawling down his hotel-room wall. "Where are you going?" he was to demand. "You're not a citizen, are you? Where's *your* quota number?" The day the scene was shot,

Wilder spotted Boyer while eating lunch at the studio canteen and inquired how the production was going. The star revealed that, at his request, the cockroach bit had been cut. "A normal human being doesn't talk to an insect," he complained. Wilder was furious, but Boyer's sensibilities were given first priority by Leisen and the studio, even though the cockroach encounter could have played a crucial early role in humanizing Georges for the audience. But Wilder got his revenge, as only a writer could. The last third of the screenplay was yet to be completed, and so Wilder and Brackett conspired that if Boyer wouldn't speak to a cockroach, he wouldn't speak at all. As the story progressed, de Havilland's Emmy would become more and more loquacious, with Boyer's Georges sitting silently by, listening to her earnest soliloquies.* Her role thus bolstered, de Havilland went on to win her first Oscar nomination for Best Actress.

Hold Back the Dawn sets a pattern for many Wilder films to follow, with its pragmatic, largely unsympathetic central figure who comes to acknowledge his moral disintegration on the road to either redemption or death. At the same time, the movie contains passages that are far more blatantly sentimental than anything in Wilder's later directing canon, including romances like *Sabrina* and *Love in the Afternoon*. Georges's neighbors at the Hotel Esperanza are especially innocuous, a collection of humble "salt of the earth" types, broadly defined as characters and united by their gushing enthusiasm for American democracy. There's the bearded history professor and his demure daughter; the tubercular composer and his sweet-tempered, pregnant wife; the impatient French barber who discovers he is a direct descendant of Lafayette (and therefore an honorary citizen of the United States)—all thinly designed as comic and heart-tugging counterpoints to the main story. Wilder and Brackett's writing would never be quite this wholesome again, and Leisen's earnest handling of these scenes was surely one of the factors that turned Wilder so fervently against him.

The film's portrait of Emmy is much more persuasively heartfelt. De Havilland, always the beacon of purity in films like *Gone with the Wind* and *The Adventures of Robin Hood*, was again typecast, but her Emmy undergoes

---

* One year later, in *The Major and the Minor*, Wilder couldn't resist tweaking Boyer once again. "Look, Mommy," says a little girl, reading the cover of a fan magazine, " 'Why I Hate Women,' by Charles Boyer."

a subtle transformation from sheltered spinster to a woman of backbone, mature self-knowledge and blooming sex appeal. As easily trapped as she is by Georges's slick routine, it also takes courage to lower her emotional defenses and take a risk on committing to a relative stranger. Emmy's vibrant, unconditional devotion unnerves Georges, plunges past his shell of corruption. In one telling moment, Emmy tells Georges how proud she is of her new Romanian surname: "This is America—for the Rockefellers and the Joneses, for the McGonagles and the Frankfurters, for the Jeffersons and the Slovinskis. . . . It's like a lake, clear and fresh, and it will never get stagnant while new streams are flowing in." Georges argues back, "You people are building pretty high dams to stop those streams." "Just to keep out the scum, Georges," replies Emmy, unknowingly cutting right through to Georges's feelings of self-disgust.

From that moment on, Georges begins to become an honorable man. He desperately looks for ways not to consummate his marriage, feigning back trouble after he and Emmy prepare a makeshift wedding bed in her school bus. He returns to the border town with a new agenda, resolved not to hurt Emmy and perhaps even ready to turn their paper marriage into something genuine. Georges's respect for his new wife is sealed when, crushed by the news of his deceit, she nonetheless refuses to expose him. This would not be the last time a Wilder protagonist was saved from the brink by a morally superior woman.

It would also not be the last time an actor would thank Wilder and Brackett for a crucial role in their career. Without the efforts of the writing team, de Havilland, then under contract to Warner Bros., never would have been cast. According to de Havilland, she had just had her appendix removed and was recuperating at the home of her friends, the actress Geraldine Fitzgerald and her husband, Edward Lindsay-Hogg. Brackett invited the Lindsay-Hoggs to a Sunday lunch and, when told they were tending to de Havilland, insisted they bring her along, despite her continuing discomfort. "I've been trying to find her for days," Brackett told Fitzgerald. Over lunch, Brackett gave de Havilland a rough draft of the script, instructing her to tell no one else but him if she wanted the part. When she said yes, Brackett and the Paramount front office were primed to pull a fast one on Jack Warner. Knowing Warner wanted Fred MacMurray for a film, Paramount's executives coolly listened to a roster of names offered in exchange, then pretended to halfheartedly accept de Havilland, knowing all along she was Brackett's first choice for Emmy. "[Jack] was sure he'd gotten the better of the deal," de Havilland recalls.

De Havilland's Oscar nomination was one of six awarded to *Hold Back the Dawn*, including nods in the categories of Best Picture and Best Screenplay (Wilder and Brackett's second nomination).

DESPITE THE ACCOLADES FOR *HOLD BACK THE DAWN*, WILDER was unhappy with the film and determined to gain more control over his work. "I was a pest then," Wilder recalls. "I would go on the set and see how a director screwed up a scene, did not even know what the scene was about. I did not become a director because I loved being with actors and polishing scenes and giving them ideas—no, I would have been a very happy writer. But the directors—some of them were very good, but some others just missed the point. Somebody asked me once, 'Is it important for a director to know how to write?' I said, 'No, but it helps if he knows how to read.' "

It wouldn't be easy making the transition to directing. Among Paramount's cadre of writers, only Preston Sturges had taken the leap successfully, with his 1940 hit *The Great McGinty*. The studio frowned on Wilder's incursions onto the set; once filming began, he and Brackett were supposed to be confined to their office, generating their next script.

Then came an unexpected opportunity to learn from a master. Samuel Goldwyn, who had built the independent studio bearing his name into one of the most successful creative forces in Hollywood, was not getting value for money from his top star, Gary Cooper. Goldwyn had signed Cooper a few years earlier to a nonexclusive contract, but the actor kept having his hits at other studios. So Goldwyn lit on the idea of borrowing Paramount's hottest writing team to work their magic on Cooper, and contacted William Dozier, head of the studio's story department. Dozier saw Goldwyn's request as a great opportunity to snag Cooper for Paramount's upcoming prestige production of Ernest Hemingway's *For Whom the Bell Tolls*. Goldwyn agreed to the trade, as long as Paramount threw in some cash and a one-picture loan of Bob Hope. "Gives you an idea of the value of people," Wilder notes sardonically. " 'I'll give you Bob Hope, plus the writing team—whatever their name is—and you give us Gary Cooper, and you've got a deal!' "

Wilder unearthed a story idea from his Paris days entitled *From A to Z*, polished it with a Paramount junior writer named Thomas Monroe, and sent it to the mogul. Goldwyn called the next day, saying his wife, Frances, had read the story and liked it. Wilder, acting as his own agent, asked for $10,000 for the rights. Goldwyn balked, then agreed to pay $7,500 right away, and the remaining $2,500 when the project was made.

Wilder agreed to work for Goldwyn on one condition: that he be allowed on the set throughout the filming, to observe firsthand the working methods of director Howard Hawks. Skilled at both fast-paced comedies and rugged action films, Hawks by this time had a string of impressive hits behind him, including *Scarface, Twentieth Century, Bringing Up Baby, Only Angels Have Wings*, and *His Girl Friday*. He had just finished shooting *Sergeant York*, which would win Gary Cooper an Oscar.

Recalls Wilder, "After the script for *Ball of Fire* was finished, I took kind of a leave of absence for two months and stayed behind, somewhere up the ladder, watching how Hawks went about it, how he connected scenes (he was a very fine technician, you know), how he made every scene have three acts. The thing I learned from Hawks is: Make it simple. I learned that crazy, absurd, unheard-of camera setups are not going to make a director. It's going to remind the audience that there was a big crew that was tilting the camera. There's a whole group of directors that photographs a living room through the fire in the fireplace. And I've always said: Whose point of view is that? Maybe Santa Claus, I don't know."

A playful takeoff on *Snow White and the Seven Dwarfs* (its characters even move like the Disney septet as they take their jaunty morning constitutional through Central Park), *Ball of Fire* concerns an eccentric group of academics who've been stuck in a Manhattan town house for nine years writing a definitive new encyclopedia. (Their late benefactor, the inventor of the toaster, commissioned the project when he discovered that the *Encyclopaedia Britannica* devoted thirty pages to Thomas Edison and none to him.) The leader of their circle, Bertram Potts (Cooper), comes to the realization that their sheltered lifestyle has made his entry on slang hopelessly out of date, and decides to conduct some field research. His travels take him to a jazz club headlining Gene Krupa's orchestra and a brassy singer/stripteaser named Sugarpuss O'Shea (Barbara Stanwyck). Bertram leaves his card with the singer, and that same night she turns up on the professors' doorstep as a research volunteer; what she doesn't tell Bertram and his colleagues is that she's hiding out from an aggressive district attorney who wants her to be a witness against her gangster boyfriend, Joe Lilac (Dana Andrews).

The saucy Sugarpuss provides a welcome disruption to the professors' staid routine—especially when she starts a conga line—and Bertram himself is besotted after one electric kiss. Inexperienced in love, he proposes to the singer. Sugarpuss is encouraged to play along by Joe, who's just proposed to her himself, knowing a wife can't be forced to testify against her husband. Posing as Sugarpuss's father over the phone, Joe asks that the nuptials be held in New Jersey, where he and his thugs are hiding out; hopefully, the police will never suspect that the blushing fiancée in the strange wedding party crossing the George Washington Bridge is the notorious Sugarpuss O'Shea. His cargo delivered, Joe brutally lowers the boom on Bertram, who returns to his Manhattan enclave in shame. But Sugarpuss, deeply moved by Bertram's wholehearted devotion, refuses to marry Joe, leading to a showdown at the professors' mansion in which brains prove mightier than brawn.

Working in an altogether different, lighter key, Wilder and Brackett fashioned a mirror image of the situation in *Hold Back the Dawn*, with the sex roles reversed. This time, it's the man who is innocent, naïve, unworldly—Cooper in his Mr. Deeds mode, but with a head full of arcane knowledge. Here, it's the woman who has the sexually adventurous past, who cynically exploits a trusting victim to obtain a temporary safe harbor. And once again, the power of flowering, genuine love inspires the predator to see into his/her soul and rediscover his/her humanity.

Ball of Fire's unexpectedly poignant side is a tribute to the empathetic power of Barbara Stanwyck, who not only makes Sugarpuss a memorably sassy and vibrant New York character but also reveals her tender side, without jarring inconsistencies. Cooper's Bertram is more of a caricature— his pixilated closeup when he discovers he's in love is priceless—but the actor also makes a satisfying transition to deeper emotions after Bertram is so thoroughly humiliated. Much of the pleasure of *Ball of Fire* comes from the matchup of two superb comedians who also happen to be exceptionally good actors.

A frothy change from Wilder and Brackett's two previous films, *Ball of Fire* was an ideal opportunity for the writing partners to indulge their mutual love of wordplay. For Wilder especially, it brought back memories of his first years in the United States as a self-consciously foreign screenwriter struggling to master the American vernacular. The movie offers a bountiful smorgasbord of 1940s slang, which the writers researched by hanging out at soda fountains, dance halls, baseball grandstands and the Hollywood Park racetrack. At one high school soda fountain, the team reportedly paid $8.30 for seventy sodas, while picking up such expressions as "a slight case of Andy Hardy" (for "getting sentimental") and "sucker for succotash" (someone who likes old jokes). The movie includes such arcane argot as "oolie droolie," "plenty gestanko" and "clip the mooch," and at one point Cooper's character draws an absurd diagram illustrating the many offshoots of "corn" and "hick." Wilder and Brackett also saddled Cooper with their humorous version of the kind of excessively ostentatious academic language an unworldly scholar like Bertram might utter. Cooper complained that it was "gibberish that doesn't make any sense," warning, "I can't memorize it if it doesn't mean anything." He stormed into Goldwyn's office demanding a story conference, and was overheard to say, "Two-dollar words, okay, but not *ten*-dollar words!"

Wilder and Brackett's language games turned out to have plenty of box-office appeal, landing *Ball of Fire* among the top twenty grossers for 1942, the year of its national release. The critics were also charmed, with *The New York Times*'s Bosley Crowther calling it "a wholly ingratiating lark" and noting that the film "had the customers jumping with enjoyment at the [Radio City] Music Hall. In the Oscar race, Stanwyck was nominated as Best Actress, and Wilder earned a second 1941 nomination in the original story category (shared with Thomas Monroe).

The film a success, Wilder phoned Goldwyn about the remaining $2,500 which was still due him. The producer said he remembered nothing about an additional $2,500, asking if Wilder had anything in writing. Wilder slammed down the phone in anger. Ten minutes later, Goldwyn called back to say his wife had no recollection of the $2,500 either. Furious, Wilder told Goldwyn to go to hell, and if they ever met again, to just pretend they didn't know each other. Another ten minutes, another call from Goldwyn: "Look, Billy, I don't want people going around Hollywood saying I'm not honest. Come on over, right now, and pick up the . . . fifteen hundred dollars."

However tightfisted, Goldwyn was eager to use Wilder's services again—but only as a screenwriter. The producer called in Wilder one day and asked him if he had any ideas for a big-scale production. The writer suggested a movie about Nijinsky. Goldwyn had no idea who that was, so Wilder told him the story of the great Russian dancer and his stormy relationship with his lover, the impresario Diaghilev. Goldwyn was nonplussed when he realized Wilder was proposing a film about two homosexuals, but Wilder pressed on, recounting how Nijinsky was placed in an insane asylum, under the delusion he was a horse. The producer thought Wilder himself was insane, but the cocky writer left the meeting insisting the movie would have a happy ending: Nijinsky would win the Kentucky Derby.

Despite his doubts about Goldwyn's intellect, Wilder and the producer became friendlier as the years went by—they socialized often, and even vacationed together with their wives. But they would never again work together, with the exception of one weekend when Wilder and Brackett did an uncredited emergency polish on Goldwyn's 1947 fantasy hit, *The Bishop's Wife*. The producer offered the team $25,000 for their trouble, but when it came time to settle up, Wilder and Brackett decided that since most of the fee would be eaten up in taxes, they would tell Goldwyn they had done the work as a matter of courtesy—no money need change hands. Goldwyn's reply: "That's funny. I've come to the same conclusion."

Around the time of *Ball of Fire*, another famed producer took advantage of Wilder and his creative bounty. Sam Spiegel, who would later produce such classics as *The African Queen, On the Waterfront, The Bridge on the River Kwai* and *Lawrence of Arabia*, had known Wilder when he worked as a publicist for Universal in Berlin. Having acquired a dismal track record as a producer in France and England, he was now ensconced in a small office at the Goldwyn studio and desperate to make his mark in Hollywood. When he spied Wilder on the Goldwyn lot, he saw his chance. Spiegel had a good relationship with William Goetz, the acting studio head at 20th Century–Fox, if only he had a story idea he could offer him. . . . Wilder, feeling sorry for Spiegel, remembered the last, unproduced screenplay he had written for Erich Pommer at UFA, in collaboration with Walter Reisch. It was an episodic piece about a tailcoat and what happens as it is transferred from owner to owner. Spiegel got the script out of Germany, and sold the idea to Fox. The result, with no onscreen credit given to Wilder and Reisch, was *Tales of Manhattan*, a charming film boasting a sensational lineup of stars: Charles Boyer, Rita Hayworth, Henry Fonda, Ginger Rogers, Charles Laughton, Edward G. Robinson, Paul Robeson and Ethel Waters.

Wilder refused payment for his old handiwork, but Spiegel wouldn't hear of it. Finally, Wilder mentioned some designer chairs he had spotted in a Beverly Hills shop window. Spiegel said it was a deal, and he also offered to buy Reisch a new phonograph with speakers set in the wall. Reisch, who was building a house in Bel Air, had the holes drilled for his deluxe new sound system. By the time of the charity premiere of *Tales of Manhattan*, neither the phonograph nor the chairs had arrived. The writers boycotted the screening, sending Spiegel an acerbic telegram in which they described sitting in Wilder's chairs listening to Reisch's record player; the only trouble was the draft coming through the walls. Eventually, the writers' gifts arrived—along with the bills.

At least one producer was as good as his word: Wilder cites Paramount veteran Arthur Hornblow Jr. as a major supporter in his quest to become a director. He also gives thanks to a fellow writer who helped clear the way. "I was the number-two writer who became a director. The number-one writer, timewise, was Preston Sturges, a very fine writer.* He succeeded, and so they decided to give me a chance. But in those days, you know, we made fifty pictures [at one studio]. The pictures that I made in the beginning, they were never over a million dollars. The most expensive picture I made was something like two and a half million, for let us say a big picture like *Sunset Boulevard*. Two and a half million was already enormous then, because, I have to remind you, the entire production including the release and the advertising of *Gone with the Wind* was five million dollars. Now they would spend five million dollars on advertising a big picture just in America."

---

* Wilder's statement is true for Paramount, but over at Warner Bros. Sturges was preceded by John Huston and his landmark 1941 directorial debut, *The Maltese Falcon*.

Letting Wilder direct was a relatively low risk for Paramount. "Their idea was: 'We'll give Wilder a picture, let him choose the subject, and it will not be expensive, under a million. Very probably he will fall on his face and then come back like a good boy and go up to the fourth floor where he is writing with Brackett.' But I knew not to do something artsy-smartsy, like most writers do, with crazy setups that don't fit. I chose a very marketable product, *The Major and the Minor*."

The idea was brought to Wilder's attention by Joe Sistrom, a young Paramount executive who enjoyed playing bridge with the studio's star writer. It came from a 1921 *Saturday Evening Post* story by Fannie Kilbourne called "Sunny Goes Home" (adapted two years later by Edward Childs Carpenter as the Broadway play *Connie Goes Home)*, about the comical train ride of a nineteen-year-old actress who looks twelve. Wilder and Brackett turned the heroine into a slightly older woman named Susan Applegate from Stevenson, Iowa, struggling to make ends meet in New York City. After one year and twenty-five different jobs, Susan is not in the mood for a customer's amorous advances when she turns up for an appointment as his professional scalp masseuse. Admitting failure, she decides to pack her things and head straight back to Stevenson and the arms of Will Duffy, the "plain, honest, slow-witted lug" who runs the feed-and-grain store there.

All through her desperate days in New York, Susan has held on to an envelope containing $27.50, her train fare back to Iowa. But when she arrives at Grand Central, she finds the fare has risen five dollars. Rather than begging or waiting to save up the difference, Susan takes her cue from a little girl paying half fare: She heads for the ladies' room and emerges dressed as a rather dicey facsimile of a twelve-year-old girl, complete with pigtails, bonnet and a balloon. With the help of a shifty stranger posing as her father, Susan secures a ticket, but it's a rocky ride from New York to Stevenson.

Many at the studio were dubious about the premise, especially after the filmmakers took the calculated gamble of casting thirty-year-old Ginger Rogers in the role of Susan. In truth, getting Rogers was a real coup for a first-time director, since she was a major box-office star from her magical partnership with Fred Astaire and she had just won the Oscar for her dramatic work in *Kitty Foyle,* Hornblow and Brackett corralled Rogers during a lunch break on the set of *Roxie Hart*, and she liked their description of the plot—it reminded her of ruses she used to pull as a fourteen-year-old performer traveling cross-country by train with her mother. Rogers's positive response was a particular relief to Brackett, since she had recently turned down the lead in *Ball of Fire*, claiming she only wanted to play "ladies." (Hearing that, Sam Goldwyn screamed at her agent, Leland Hayward, "You tell Ginger Rogers ladies stink up the place.")

Wilder was also being represented these days by Hayward, whose client list included luminaries like Greta Garbo and Ernest Hemingway. Even so, Rogers insisted on a meeting with Wilder before accepting him as director, and she was duly charmed by his "wonderful sense of the ridiculous." Wilder then secured Rogers's costar, Ray Milland, by following his car from the Paramount gate after work one day and inquiring at a traffic light whether he'd be interested in appearing in his maiden directing effort. Milland, having enjoyed his role in *Arise, My Love*, was game.

Rogers had already played a young girl in flashback scenes in *Kitty Foyle*, but could she really pass as a twelve-year-old? No, not by a long shot. But that's part of the joke of *The Major and the Minor*, as it would be in later Wilder comedies utilizing improbable disguises like *Some Like It Hot* and *Irma la Douce*. Scrutinized by two very suspicious train conductors, Susan claims to be of big-boned Swedish stock, from a family with a history of gland trouble. ("My brother Olaf's six foot two, and he's only in the second grade.") Caught smoking on the platform, Susan flees the conductors and takes refuge in what she thinks is an empty compartment. There, she encounters courtly Army Major Philip Kirby (Milland), whose bad eye not only keeps him from seeing through Susan's disguise, but is also keeping him out of active duty and consigned to a tutoring post at the Wallace Military Institute in High Creek, Indiana. "Uncle" Philip insists the frightened girl spend the night in his lower bunk, a good deed that is punished the next morning when the major's huffy fiancée Pamela (Rita Johnson)—who is also the daughter of his superior officer—meets the train and sees a strange woman in his compartment. Philip insists that "Sue-Sue," as Susan calls her alter ego, accompany him to the institute so that he can clear up the misunderstanding. And so the masquerade continues, with Susan fending off the advances of randy young military cadets and teaming up with Pamela's feisty, bookish younger sister Lucy (Diana Lynn) to foil Pamela, who's been secretly pulling strings to keep Philip at home and out of the war.

Despite Wilder's intentions, *The Major and the Minor* is hardly a safe commercial bet. Predating Vladimir Nabokov's sensational *Lolita* by thirteen years, it flirts with the taboo theme of pedophilia, but in such an ingeniously tasteful way that no one in 1942 voiced the faintest objection. It's obvious that Susan Applegate is no child; it's clear that Major Kirby is a good, kind and honorable man. And yet, beginning the instant they meet, there's a sexual subtext in the bond between doting Uncle Philip and baby-talking Sue-Sue. Because we (and anyone else who isn't myopic or obtuse) are privy to the information that Susan is a mature woman, her night in the major's compartment is fraught with the possibility of grown-up passion erupting; the fact that she's dressed as a little girl just makes the situation all the more naughty.

Throughout the ensuing masquerade, Major Kirby is always the perfect gentleman, the ideal father figure. But something else is going on beneath his controlled façade, and this is where Wilder is at his most subtly subversive. Midway through the film, the major calls Sue-Sue into his office to caution her about the effect she's having on his cadets—they're like moths attracted to a lightbulb, he explains. Before long, he's gushing about her eyes, her "good straight legs," that "little red head" of hers. Gazing at her with just his bum eye, he can envision her as a grown woman, and she's a knockout. Philip's sudden bumbling nervousness reveals that he's having thoughts that are utterly off-limits.

"I was just talking about it with a friend," Wilder confirms, from a distance of fifty-two years. "I said, 'You know, the basic theme of that silly story that comes from the *Saturday Evening Post*, it is exactly *Lolita*!' Not knowing what it is, we did have scenes where the guy says, 'Oh my God, look at that girl, how bright she is, how nice she looks, what a good figure she has—what a shame, how wonderful it would be if she were fifteen or twenty years older.' Mr. Nabokov never saw the picture, so this is just kind of a coincidence, but it amuses me."

Susan's real identity is revealed to the jealous Pamela at a school dance where, in a typically topical and hilarious Wilder touch, the girls bused in from Miss Shackleford's School all sport Veronica Lake peekaboo hairdos (as does the spinsterish Miss Shackleford). As luck would have it, the visiting father of one of the cadets is the same scalp-massage client (Robert Benchley) who propelled Susan's flight from New York. Scratching his head in puzzlement, he makes the connection and confides in Pamela, who arranges Sue-Sue's discreet, unceremonious departure from the institute before she has a chance to explain things to Philip. But, as far as Pamela is concerned, the damage is already done: Impersonating Philip's fiancée on the phone, Susan has succeeded in getting Philip an assignment overseas and, in effect, ruining his marriage plans.

The finale brings yet one more impersonation, as Susan, home in Stevenson, pines for her lost love, then is startled to receive a phone call from him saying he's in town and eager to see Sue-Sue before he catches a train for the West Coast. Susan sends her mother (played by Rogers's real-life mother, Lela) to the attic, and dons her apron and glasses for Philip's visit. During a tender conversation, Susan learns from Philip that Pamela has dumped him for a cadet's rich banker father. The closing moments find Susan, in her comeliest grown-up dress, standing conspicuously on the train-station platform, a suitcase at her feet. She catches Philip's attention and kisses him, and his delighted "Sue-Sue!" hints that he's wanted that precocious little girl from the first moment his bum eye saw her.

The Major and the Minor is an extremely confidently directed first film, but Wilder wasn't so confident at the beginning. On the Sunday before shooting commenced, the novice director visited Ernst Lubitsch and confessed that he was so nervous about his first day that he was running a fever and afflicted with diarrhea. Lubitsch assured him, "I've directed fifty pictures, and I'm still crapping in my pants on the first day." To further cheer up his former writer, Lubitsch arranged for an envoy of Hollywood's German directors—himself, William Wyler, William Dieterle, E. A. Dupont and Henry Koster, along with Preston Sturges and Michael Curtiz—to visit the set as production opened in early March 1942. Nothing was accomplished that day, but Wilder knew he was in good company.

One of the director's most essential assets on this first film was his editor, Doane Harrison, who had worked on the Leisen films and whose career went all the way back to the Hal Roach comedies of the silent era. Working closely with Harrison, Wilder learned how to preplan each shot as part of a total editing scheme.

"I've learned how to shoot elegantly, so that the seams don't show,"

Wilder declares. "And I always shoot very fast—I'll shoot in one day instead of two, with the understanding that, should I, after seeing it in the rushes, think that I require more shooting, I'm going back and doing it. But I don't do it to be covered,* *a priori.* No, I just shoot the way I think it's going to look. And when I'm finished with a picture, there's very little celluloid left on the cutting-room floor. I'm using everything. Other people cover themselves: First comes the long shot of everyone sitting around the table, then there comes a medium shot, then over this shoulder, over that shoulder, then a closeup of the same thing, and the actors have to repeat the same words for all those angles, thirty times. No, I just . . . more or less, I overlap one or two speeches, but I know the way it's going to go and I hope that it's going to work."

In an unusual creative partnership, Harrison was a constant presence on Wilder's sets until his death in 1968, always nearby to consult on what shots were needed to complete the day's shoot. Beginning with *Sunset Boulevard* in 1950, his title became "editorial supervisor" or "editorial adviser." From *The Seven Year Itch* in 1955 until *The Fortune Cookie* in 1966, he was Wilder's associate producer. "Doane Harrison was one of the great influences of my life," Wilder says wistfully. "I went to the Doane Harrison College, and I miss him very much."

THOUGH MUCH LIGHTER IN TONE THAN HIS TWO PREVIOUS films written for Paramount, *The Major and the Minor* still makes an effort to reflect the increasing gravity of the world situation. The film is pointedly set seven months before the attack on Pearl Harbor, and the calculating Pamela earns extra hisses for selfishly striving to keep her fiancé safely at home. "Philip is an impetuous soul who insists that war is impending and he must be in it. Such nonsense!" she writes to an influential friend in Washington. The comedy also takes on a poignant undertone with our knowledge that the institute's callow cadets are bound to fulfill their destinies less than a year after their lusty interlude with Sue-Sue, and with the fact that Philip himself is on his way to active duty as the film ends. Susan has made that choice possible for Philip, and, unlike Pamela, she's willing

---

* Film term for having all the footage and angles required to create a coherent sequence.

to sacrifice her own happiness to the greater good of the nation, settling for a quickie Las Vegas wedding before her man ships overseas. Still, one has to wonder what wartime fate is in store for Philip and all the students and personnel of Wallace Military Institute if a thirty-year-old Ginger Rogers can fool them so completely into believing she's a preadolescent girl.

"My God, those were the great naïve days," Wilder says of the movie's improbable masquerade. "Now you couldn't do it anymore!" In 1942, the critics and the public happily suspended their disbelief, creating a major hit for the first-time director. In *The New York Times*, Bosley Crowther called *The Major and the Minor* "a very cunning film," hailing "a script which effervesces with neat situations and bright lines" and singling out Rogers's portrayal as "one of the best characterizations of her career." The *New York Post*'s Archer Winsten complained, "The trouble with *The Major and the Minor* is that too many people in the audience laugh too much and too loud. You miss lines which, if they are as amusing as the ones that are heard, ought not to be missed." He also noted, "When faced with such a high level of achievement in a single film, you naturally look for the director. This brings us to the maiden effort of Billy Wilder, who, like Preston Sturges, has made the jump from the successful writing of screen stories to the even more successful directing of them. He has what it takes, and it is something that causes anticipation for his future efforts." *Variety* chimed in along the same lines, stating that "Wilder shows a keen knowledge of comedy and dramatic values that rate him other important assignments."

Rogers also received some of the best reviews of her career in a nondancing role. (Actually, her brightest moment in the movie comes when Sue-Sue seduces a cadet away from his switchboard duties with a disarming tap-dancing routine; "I can dance," she nonchalantly declares.) In the mid-1970s, Rogers complained to Maurice Zolotow that Wilder never publicly gave her credit for helping to launch his directing career, and that he seemed to go out of his way to avoid her at social occasions. A few years later, Rogers was at Wilder's side at the Film Society of Lincoln Center's tribute to the director. "This one film we made together meant a great deal to me, and I suspect to Billy, too," she told the audience. "Any actress knows that nothing is more challenging and difficult than making comedy look effortless. But when you have as skilled a director as Billy and a script as sparkling as the one he wrote with Charles Brackett, your work is made so much easier." Rogers went on to recall that whenever Wilder was pleased with a take, he'd invariably shout, "Champagne for everyone!" She praised her director for bringing "European sophistication and all-American wit and energy" to the Hollywood film world, but, perhaps still conscious of past slights (real or imagined), she added, "I like to think that I was able to give something back in return with the part I played in the Americanization of Billy Wilder."

Indeed, the disproportionate status of Ginger Rogers and Billy Wilder in 1942 may be seen in their salaries: She received a handsome $175,000, while his directing fee was a mere $9,800. (Wilder and Brackett also split a $50,000 script fee.) And Paramount was still hedging its bets just months before production: A preliminary budget dated December 20, 1941, listed Rogers and Milland as stars, Arthur Hornblow as producer, and "director unknown."

The Major and the Minor, incidentally, produced one of the most celebrated one-liners in movies, as Robert Benchley suggests to an unreceptive Ginger Rogers, "Why don't you get out of those wet clothes and into a dry martini?" "That was purely Benchley," says Wilder. "He said it one day to another character around the Algonquin Table, in real life."*

Brackett, of course, was also a member of the fabled Algonquin circle of wits, and Wilder remembers how his crony Benchley used to arrive at the studio each day carrying a huge bag filled with a potpourri of the latest books, which he devoured whenever he was not needed on the set.

With *The Major and the Minor*, Billy Wilder had achieved a rare professional breakthrough, a decisive blow for the brotherhood of Hollywood screenwriters. But his personal life in 1942 was far from triumphant. War was raging in Europe, and Wilder feared the worst for his mother and the rest of the family he left behind. Meantime, his new American family was falling apart. The Wilders had moved out of Hidden Valley and were now situated more in the center of things, in a big, handsome house on fashionable Beverly Drive in Beverly Hills. Judith and Billy grew increasingly

---

* Authorship of the gag remains in question. Maurice Zolotow says Brackett overheard the comic actor Charles Butterworth try out the line at a party. But Butterworth can be heard uttering the exact same phrase in Mae West's 1937 comedy *Every Day's a Holiday*, whose script is credited to West. Thus, Mae West may actually be responsible for another of the most quoted come-on lines besides her "Come up and see me sometime."

distant. She painted and attended meetings and, in a throwback to her old style, opened a clothing boutique on Rodeo Drive. Billy, now a successful writer-director, immersed himself further in his career and the industry's heady social scene. Naturally, that scene included many beautiful women—actresses, non-actresses and would-be actresses. In time, Wilder wouldn't even make a secret of his extramarital flings, openly accepting calls from various women in the midst of his script sessions with Brackett. Wilder was now a bona fide movie director, and barely a married man.

TEN

Love, War and Murder

With *The Major and the Minor*, Wilder had fash-ioned a lighthearted crowd-pleaser that still found a graceful way to acknowledge the grave challenges facing America and the world in the early fall of 1942. In a characteristic change of pace, Wilder's second film as a director (with Brackett now taking over as producer) dealt directly with the war, though in a manner that distinguished it from the many more conventional war movies on studio rosters in 1943. Containing minimal scenes of action, *Five Graves to Cairo* is a character-driven drama of the North African conflict, in the same spirit as that year's more celebrated Oscar winner, *Casablanca*. Wilder himself is quick to credit *Casablanca* as the superior film, but *Five Graves* still rates as one of the more intelligent and restrained efforts of the Hollywood World War II propaganda machine.

Five Graves is a radically altered remake of *Hotel Imperial*, a World War I espionage stage play by Hungarian émigré Lajos Biro, screenwriter of *The Last Command, The Private Life of Henry VIII, The Scarlet Pimpernel* and several comedies for Ernst Lubitsch. Biro's drama had been filmed twice before, in a 1927 German silent version directed by Erich Pommer and starring Pola Negri, and a 1939 Hollywood version directed by Robert Florey *(Murders in the Rue Morgue)* and featuring Isa Miranda and Ray Milland. The property had a strong personal resonance for Wilder, since it not only dealt with a hotel atmosphere like the one in which he was raised, but took place in the very region where he was born, Galicia. It was Biro who suggested that his play could be updated to the current crisis in North Africa, and so Wilder and Brackett began crafting a melodrama in which the mastermind of Germany's Africa campaign, Field Marshal Erwin Rommel, would be a major character.

The shooting script was completed on December 17, 1942, just six months after the British defeat at Tobruk, the event that gives rise to the movie's eerie and tragic opening. A tank rolls haphazardly across the Libyan desert, with a dead soldier slumped over its exit hatch. Inside, other soldiers sit or hang motionless, in a grotesque tableau shrouded by exhaust fumes. But one soldier lurches forward and awakens: Corporal J. J. Bramble (Franchot Tone). Climbing over his dead comrades to get some air, he is pitched out of the moving ghost tank, and left to crawl through the desert toward shelter. He finds it at the ravaged Empress of Britain Hotel in the outpost of Sidi Halfaya, abandoned by all of its staff except for the nervous Egyptian proprietor Farid (Akim Tamiroff) and his French chambermaid Mouche (Anne Baxter). The sunstroke-afflicted Bramble's arrival is swiftly followed by that of German Army Lieutenant Schwegler (Peter Van Eyck), the advance man for the fearsome Rommel (Erich von Stroheim). Bramble quickly dons the clothes of the hotel's clubfooted waiter, Paul Davos, who was killed in the previous night's air raid. Schwegler takes a special interest in the waiter, and soon enough Bramble learns why: Davos was a spy for the Germans. Bramble vows to take advantage of his proximity to Rommel and kill him, but his plan is foiled by Mouche, who wants to plead with Rommel for the release of her soldier brother from a German prison. The next morning, a group of captured British officers arrives at the hotel, and Bramble is given instructions to continue his masquerade and try to unearth some of Rommel's military secrets. As Davos, Bramble is to be escorted to Cairo, but first he must discern the exact locations of Rommel's "five graves"—the supply depots hidden in the desert that are crucial to the success of the field marshal's campaign. As Bramble eventually learns, the secret, keyed to Rommel's map of Egypt, is deceptively simple, but before he can leave in safety, Schwegler discovers the body of the real Davos, who had been buried in the basement rubble. Bramble kills Schwegler, and Mouche—who had been given false promises of help by the lusty German lieutenant—takes the blame until Bramble is out of the Germans' grasp.

The film ends with Bramble returning victorious to Sidi Halfaya and paying a sad homage to Mouche, who has been beaten to death by Rommel's men.

Once again, masquerade plays a central role in a Wilder film, but in a much more solemn context than in *Midnight*, *The Major and the Minor* or even the opening scenes of *Arise, My Love*. Here, the comic possibilities of assumed identity are replaced by the thrill quotient of espionage, as an English officer assumes the role of a dead waiter who in reality was a spy for the Germans.

Corporal Bramble may maintain the most intricate tangle of deceit in *Five Graves to Cairo*, but he's not alone. The gutless Farid shifts his allegiances according to who is in power, exchanging a Union Jack for a swastika just as the proprietor in the original play switched a portrait of Emperor Franz Josef for one of Czar Nicholas. Cowering before the Germans, he even apologizes for being Egyptian, blaming that unfortunate fact on his parents. Mouche gives Bramble the impression that she, too, is an amoral opportunist who will offer herself to whoever holds the power; only later does he learn that her motives are pure, driven by the desire to save her imprisoned brother. Schwegler pretends to be concerned for Mouche and her brother, but the official telegrams he shows her from Berlin are just a fraud designed to get her into his bed. Even the fictionalized Rommel is a practiced deceiver, having posed as an archaeologist to plant his valuable stashes of fuel and ammunition.

Like *Arise, My Love* and *The Major and the Minor*, *Five Graves to Cairo* makes a sincere argument for self-sacrifice in the face of a dire world crisis. With the character of Mouche, Wilder takes that argument to an even higher level. Through much of the film, the French chambermaid is nakedly hostile to the English officer—she blames the British for abandoning her brothers (one died, one was captured) at the battle of Dunkirk, and constantly has to be persuaded not to expose Bramble's charade to the German occupiers. Ultimately, in the movie's most eloquent, mature and plainspoken passage, Bramble tells Mouche, "In Tobruk, I saw them in the hundreds. In Sebastopol, they were ten deep. In Athens, they're dying of starvation, four hundred a day. For what, Mouche? So that somebody like you can hold a tin cup to a victorious lieutenant, begging for a pfennig's worth of pity? It's not just one brother that matters, it's a million brothers.

It's not just one prison gate that might sneak open for you, it's all the gates that must go." Before this speech, Mouche was prepared to suffer any degradation for the sake of her brother; now, she not only sacrifices all hope for her kin, but bravely puts her own life at risk to save Bramble's mission. The film's soberly pragmatic viewpoint is especially striking in light of its director's own personal anguish over what had become of the family he left behind in Europe while he was building a reputation in Hollywood.

Wilder also refused to let personal emotion distort his portrayal of the German enemy. *Five Graves to Cairo* is notable for its unsensationalized, nonstereotypical view of Rommel and his cohorts. Although he first appears barking rigid instructions to Farid and Mouche, handsome Peter Van Eyck as Schwegler makes a legitimate romantic rival to Bramble for Mouche's attentions. He seems like such a gentleman at times that Wilder and Brackett almost fool you into believing there's a Nazi who can empathize with the concern of a young Frenchwoman for her captured brother.

As for Rommel, the film treats him with deference, respecting him as a brilliant tactician and mighty opponent. Much of this has to do with the casting of von Stroheim (fresh from the Broadway production of *Arsenic and Old Lace*), who didn't much resemble the real Rommel but brought powerful iconic associations to the part, for both the audience and Wilder. Von Stroheim was one of the great figures of the Hollywood silent era, a visionary directing genius whose disregard for the economic realities of the business brought his career crashing to a halt. In 1943, many in the audience would still remember him as "The Man You Love to Hate," the villainous Hun of World War I melodramas, and as the star and director of such silent-film triumphs as *Foolish Wives* and *Blind Husbands*. Von Stroheim's waterloo was *Greed*, a masterly film version of Frank Norris's classic naturalistic novel *McTeague*, which clocked in at 8 hours and was chopped down to 2 hours and 20 minutes by enraged MGM executives. His directing career ended in humiliation, with abrupt firings from his last two films, *Queen Kelly* (1928) and *Walking Down Broadway* (1932).

"I was always a great fan of Stroheim," Wilder enthuses. "Through a friend of mine who worked for Universal in America but was in Berlin at the time, I got an autographed photograph, which I still have."

Wilder remembers the day von Stroheim arrived on the set of *Five Graves.* "I was shooting exteriors with the tanks in the desert near Yuma. I came back to my office and they said, 'Mr. Stroheim has arrived—he's upstairs in the wardrobe department.' So I just rushed upstairs, clicked my heels, introduced myself, and there's that joke—which is true—where I said, 'This is a very big moment in my life, the idea that I, the autograph hunter, that I should now be directing the great Stroheim.' And he just didn't say anything. Then I said, 'Your problem, I guess, was that you were ten years ahead of your time.' And he looked at me and he said, 'Twenty.' "

Some of that hero worship creeps into Wilder's filming of von Stroheim: He gives him a grand star introduction, viewing him from above as Bramble and Schwegler watch Rommel from a nearby stairway. As he paces back and forth issuing a communiqué to Hitler, the back of his thick bald neck fills the screen. Wilder doesn't show his face until he finishes the memo and reveals that he is indeed the mighty Rommel (and the formidable von Stroheim). "You know, he was not an actor—he was just a personality," Wilder opines. "Standing with his stiff fat neck in the foreground, he could express more than almost any actor with his face."

The later arrival of captured British officers recalls the mood surrounding von Stroheim's performance in Jean Renoir's *La Grande Illusion* some six years earlier, as a German commander presiding over French prisoners during World War I.[*] One of the high points of *Five Graves* is Rommel's luncheon for the officers, in which the German field commander takes delight in conducting a game of Twenty Questions regarding his military strategy. Rommel reveals to the enemy the existence of his stores of fuel and ammunition; their whereabouts, alas, is Question 21 (but only by Rommel's unfair count). The good-humored, civilized nature of the session is a sign of Wilder's maturity and restraint; with every reason to despise the Nazis, he could still portray their human side. Wilder takes pains to note that he was a Nazi-hater, not a German-hater, and that he wanted to make

---

[*] The connection to *Grand Illusion*'s vision of wartime professional courtesy is probably no accident: In an early fifties poll of filmmakers and critics conducted by the Festival Mondial du Film et Beaux Arts de Belgique, Wilder named the Renoir classic as his sixth favorite film of all times.

a film which acknowledged that the German officers in Africa still behaved as officers.

Of course, as a former silent-movie heavy, von Stroheim did not over-look the pomposity, arrogance and ill temper inherent in the movie's por-trait of Rommel. The field marshal had already suffered a decisive defeat at El Alamein before the film went into production, so there was a certain built-in satisfaction for the American World War II audience in watching him swagger and boast. Still, von Stroheim's portrayal of Rommel was chilling enough to provoke this paean from *New York Times* critic Bosley Crowther, in an otherwise disgruntled evaluation of the film: "It's a good thing the German armies and Field Marshal Rommel in particular had been chased all the way out of Africa before *Five Graves to Cairo* opened at the Paramount yesterday, else the performance by Erich von Stroheim of the much touted field marshal in it might have been just a bit too aggressive for the comfort of most of us. As a matter of fact, it is still on the terrifying side. For Mr. von Stroheim has all other movie Huns backed completely off the screen. Just as he was in the last war, he is still the toughest German of them all."

Wilder recalls, "There was something very odd and yet noble and dignified about him. He wasn't a 'von' or anything like that, he had a very heavy accent from the rougher suburbs of Vienna, but it didn't matter—he had style." The director gave his esteemed star a wide berth when it came to details and ideas for his character—after all, it was this same painstaking concern for infinitesimal details that had led to his downfall at MGM. It was von Stroheim who suggested that his watchface be covered in lattice-work, since this was how World War I officers protected the glass from shell splinters. In makeup, he asked that the upper part of his forehead be made whiter, to highlight the effect of Rommel's always being out in the sun with his cap on. He also insisted on wearing real German field glasses and a real Leica camera—loaded with film—around his neck. "Why the film?" Wilder asked. "An audience always senses whether a prop is genuine or false," von Stroheim contended. The star even got Paramount to grant him the right to supervise all uniforms he was to wear during the produc-tion, provided they didn't conflict with the studio's own research into au-thenticity.

Wilder ran into a Stroheim-sized problem when it came time to shoot the opening scene of the ghostly tank roaming the desert. The director had found a large, virgin sand dune in Yuma, Arizona, which would convincingly represent the vast Libyan desert. But when the crew arrived at four A.M. for the start of shooting, they found tire marks all over their beautiful sand; they hadn't realized that an army training camp was located nearby. With no time to lose, Wilder sent crew members to Yuma to buy as many brooms as they could find. And so, a detail of about a hundred sweepers, including Wilder, his crew, actors and citizens of Yuma, set to work brushing the desert clean of all telltale marks.

Five Graves to Cairo was Wilder's first collaboration with cinematographer John F. Seitz, who made his reputation shooting the silent films of Rudolph Valentino and would go on to photograph three of the director's most celebrated films, *Double Indemnity, The Lost Weekend* and *Sunset Boulevard*. Wilder praises Seitz's willingness to experiment and fail; in preparation for the Yuma shoot, he photographed the desert at night just to see how far he could push his camera. The footage came out nearly black. Seitz's painstaking efforts, however, earned him an Oscar nomination, and the movie also received nominations for interior decoration and Doane Harrison's editing.

Along with von Stroheim's imposing Rommel, *Five Graves* features a sturdy if uncharismatic performance by Franchot Tone, intelligent work by the young Anne Baxter, and the broad buffoonery of Akim Tamiroff as the fidgety Farid. The movie is also notable for the appearance of Fortunio Bonanova (the singing teacher from *Citizen Kane)* as an opera-loving Italian general who is treated just slightly more sympathetically by Wilder and Brackett than he is by the haughty Germans in the film. (General Sebastiano is assigned the room next to the bathroom whose plumbing *doesn't* work.) The writers have fun with the barely suppressed hostility between the Germans and their Italian allies: Rommel constantly puts down the ineffectual Italian general, while Sebastiano laments, "Can a nation that belches understand a nation that sings?"

The satirical sideshow offered by Tamiroff and Bonanova wasn't to the liking of Bosley Crowther, who felt such comic elements were out of place in a film about a timely and somber situation. "*Five Graves to Cairo* is probably the most conglomerate war film to date. It has a little something for everyone, provided you don't give a darn," he huffed. This would be the first, but far from the last, time a charge of tastelessness would be hurled at a Billy Wilder film.

Paramount's only objection to the picture was its title. An in-house contest came up with the following alternatives: *North Africa*, *Appointment in Africa*, *Hellfire Pass*, *Tunisia*, *Afrika Korps*, *Africa Aflame*, *Desert Fury*, *Beyond the Line of Duty* and *One Came Back*. Paramount executive Sam Frey suggested shortening the title to *Five to Cairo*, removing the troublesome word "Graves." For Wilder and Brackett, the most egregious suggestion was *Rommel's Last Stand*. "We would have nothing to do with any picture so baptized," the writers warned in a studio memorandum. Wilder and Brackett held firm, and the studio's $880,000 investment went out with its intriguing original title.

In 1959, Charles Brackett would voice his own retrospective objection to the film after viewing it on television, labeling it "a top-notch melodrama on which hangs a dreadful smell of propaganda." In a 1976 interview, Wilder weighed in with his own evaluation: "Nobody said it was *The Battleship Potemkin* or *Intolerance*, but I thought it was a good, entertaining hunk of celluloid. It worked."

WILDER'S NEXT FILM, HOWEVER, WOULD CATAPULT HIM TO A new level of respect from his Hollywood peers. It would also be the first public sign of discord in the seemingly ideal working relationship he had with Charles Brackett.

Double Indemnity first made the Hollywood rounds shortly after James M. Cain wrote it as a serialized novella for *Liberty* magazine in 1935. Cain had made a spectacular and controversial debut the year before with *The Postman Always Rings Twice*, a story of passion and murder centered on an itinerant worker and a roadside café owner's unhappy wife. Cain's agent, James Geller, sent to the major studios mimeographed copies of his client's follow-up yarn, about an insurance salesman caught up in a beautiful customer's scheme to profit from her husband's murder. Within days, MGM, Warner Bros., Paramount, 20th Century–Fox and Columbia were all competing for the property, which Geller had priced at what he now believed was a low $25,000. But suddenly, thanks to the Production Code, all bids were withdrawn. In a letter to Louis B. Mayer, Joe Breen of the Hays

Office warned, "The general low tone and sordid flavor of this story makes it, in our judgment, thoroughly unacceptable for screen presentation before mixed audiences in the theater." He added, "I am sure you will agree that it is most important . . . to avoid what the Code calls 'the hardening of audiences,' especially those who are young and impressionable, to the thought and fact of crime." Carbon copies of the letter were also sent to Jack L. Warner, David O. Selznick and Paramount's John Hammell. Over at Fox, the screenwriter Nunnally Johnson devised a radically altered outline of the Cain story that was deemed acceptable by the Hays Office, but nothing came of it. For the foreseeable future, any film version of *Double Indemnity* was out of the question.

Eight years later, *Double Indemnity* was scheduled to come out for the first time in book form, as part of the Cain collection entitled *Three of a Kind*. Cain's new agent, H. N. Swanson, resubmitted the story to the big studios, and this time it found a champion in Joe Sistrom, the same eagle-eyed Paramount executive who unearthed "Sunny Goes Home" and helped spur the creation of *The Major and the Minor*. Sistrom urged Wilder to read the novella, and Paramount's hot new director was hooked.*

Brackett, however, was not at all convinced. "Too grisly" was his verdict, and he went off to produce something a bit more elegantly chilling, the haunted-house tale *The Uninvited*. At this point, there was still no guarantee the Hays Office wouldn't find *Double Indemnity* as objectionable as they did in 1935. The novella was resubmitted and Breen's response to Paramount's Luigi Luraschi was virtually identical to the one he wrote to Mayer; apparently, the Hays Office not only didn't believe in changing with the times, it didn't even make the effort to use new words. Cain later saw the "new" Hays Office missive and called it "perhaps as stupid a document as I have ever read—for it made not the slightest effort to ascertain whether the picture could be filmed with the changes commonly made in a novel when it is prepared for the screen. But Wilder, [Paramount executive

---

* Cain told a different, more populist version of the story: "One day Billy Wilder couldn't find his secretary. The relief girl said, 'Well, Mr. Wilder, I think she's still in the ladies' room reading that story.' Wilder said, 'What story?' About this time she came out with *Double Indemnity* pressed to her bosom—she'd just finished it and had this ga-ga look on her face—and Wilder snatched the book from her and took it home and read it. The next day I had an offer $15,000."

William] Dozier and Sistrom are not easily frightened men, and they decided to make a try at it. Price, however, became an important factor—the
studio holding quite naturally that with so much uncertainty as to its Hays
approval, it could not afford to get very deeply involved for the material."

Ultimately, the Hays Office proved surprisingly receptive once Paramount submitted a partial screenplay; Breen approved *Double Indemnity* on
the whole, with a few caveats about the film's portrayal of the disposition of
the victim's body, a proposed gas-chamber execution scene, and the skimp-
iness of the towel the female lead wears in her first scene. Until his death,
Cain would always speak bitterly about the Hays Office and its edicts, and
about the $10,000 he believed they owed him from the original asking price
of *Double Indemnity*. "It is not only the principle of the thing with me but
the money," he fumed.

Wilder says he wanted Cain to collaborate with him on the screenplay,
but the novelist was unavailable; Cain claimed he was never asked. Sistrom,
a voracious reader, suggested another writer of hard-boiled fiction—Raymond Chandler. Born in Chicago, Chandler spent most of his youth in
England and settled in California while in his early twenties. Fired from his
job in the oil business during the Depression, he began writing fiction, and
published his first novel in 1939: *The Big Sleep*, featuring the world-weary
private eye Philip Marlowe. By 1942, two of his subsequent novels were
loosely adapted into films: *Farewell My Lovely* emerged as *The Falcon Takes
Over*, and *The High Window* became the B movie *Time to Kill*. In 1943,
Chandler was still known chiefly to readers of popular crime fiction and a
small but growing segment of the literary cognoscenti; the erudite Wilder
had never heard of him. But when he read *The Big Sleep* and some Chandler
stories from the pulp magazine *Black Mask*, he was impressed by his lively
descriptive style. (Wilder relished details like the old man who had hair
growing out of his ears "long enough to catch a moth," and another whose
thinning hair was "like wild flowers fighting for life on a bare rock.") Such
descriptions, Wilder was well aware, could not be photographed, but
Chandler had other useful qualities. He knew how to write marvelously
pungent dialogue and, because he had grown up in England, his ear (like
Wilder's) was sharply attuned to the nuances of American slang.

It also helped that Chandler specialized in stories set in Los Angeles, a
perfect qualification for the gritty L.A. milieu of *Double Indemnity*. Review-

ers often linked Chandler with two other contemporary writers of note in the crime genre: Cain and Dashiell Hammett. Chandler had a degree of respect for the latter, but Cain he couldn't abide. In a letter to his publisher, Chandler said of Cain: "He is every kind of writer I detest, a faux naif, a Proust in overalls, a dirty little boy with a piece of chalk and a board fence and nobody looking. Such people are the offal of literature, not because they write about dirty things, but because they do it in a dirty way."

Chandler readily set aside his feelings about the Cain oeuvre when Paramount approached him to help adapt *Double Indemnity* to the screen. He saw working for Hollywood as a golden opportunity, but had no idea how golden. Not realizing he was going to be collaborating with Wilder, he demanded a flat fee of $1,000 and said he'd need at least a week to write the screenplay. Wilder and Sistrom looked at each other in amazement.

Wilder describes his disappointment on his first meeting with Chandler: "I was very startled. I had imagined, after reading *The Big Sleep*, a kind of Philip Marlowe. I envisioned a former private detective who had worked his own experiences into literature, like Dashiell Hammett. Now before me stood an awkward, pale-skinned elderly man, who created a somewhat eccentric impression. He wore a frayed, checkered tweed jacket with leather patches on the elbows, and gray, worn-out flannel trousers. He had a sickly complexion, like everyone who buries himself in drink."

Chandler was also a complete novice when it came to screenwriting. After their first meeting, Wilder told him to take the novel home and, using *Hold Back the Dawn* as a model of screenwriting style, begin work on the adaptation. The following Monday, an overeager Chandler came in with some eighty pages of a nearly complete script, while Wilder had worked on three pages of the opening scene. The Chandler script, in Wilder's view, was filled with useless camera instructions. "He had that idiotic idea that if you know about 'fade in' and 'dissolve' and 'closeup,' and 'the camera moves into the keyhole' and so on, that you have mastered the art of writing pictures. He had no idea how these things were done." Wilder tossed the manuscript aside and informed Chandler they'd be working together, slowly and meticulously.

Taking pity on the naïve author, Joe Sistrom arranged for H. N. Swanson, Cain's agent, to represent him on his Paramount deal. Chandler would be earning not $1,000, but $750—per week, for a minimum of thirteen weeks.

The money was more than Chandler had ever dreamed of making, but he never got used to the notion of working nine-to-five in a studio office building, or of writing with a collaborator—especially one of Wilder's colorful temperament. With Paramount as his longtime second home, the writer-director had acquired a number of idiosyncratic work habits he wasn't about to alter. He seldom sat still, but would pace back and forth like a restless animal, brandishing a malacca cane, which sometimes swung uncomfortably close to Chandler's head. He wore his hat indoors, which Chandler regarded as the height of rudeness. Even more uncivil was his habit of retreating to the bathroom more often than a normal bladder required—Wilder traditionally went there to have a smoke or stimulate his thinking process, but more and more it was to retreat from his fussy collaborator.

"He did not like me very much," Wilder admits. "He was in Alcoholics Anonymous, and I think he had a tough time with me—I drove him back into drinking. Also he didn't like it because I was a bachelor then [actually, Wilder was still married at the time] and I had all the pretty girls at Paramount and he had nothing.* So he complained that I wasn't serious about the script—I was very serious about the script! But I did not dedicate my entire life to writing scripts—I also had a private life. In one interview he says that everything he knows about picture-making he learned from me, and in another he says that I was Prussian, that I was commandeering him around."

Age was also a contributing factor to the tense atmosphere: Wilder was thirty-seven and playing mentor to his fifty-five-year-old colleague. And while Chandler struggled with his alcoholism, sneaking drinks from a pint bottle in his briefcase, Wilder could drink at lunch and in late afternoon and easily retain his creative focus.

For his part, Wilder couldn't decide which he hated more: Chandler's sour disposition, or the foul odor emanating from his pipe, which hung in the air like a poison-gas cloud because Chandler liked the windows closed.

---

* Chandler was married to a woman twenty years his senior whom he no longer slept with.

One day, about three weeks into their collaboration, Wilder yelled, "Ray, would you raise the window, just this once?" A few days later, Chandler did not show up for work; instead, he sent a memorandum, scribbled on yellow manuscript paper, to Joe Sistrom. "It was a letter of complaint against me," Wilder says. "He couldn't work with me anymore because I was rude. I was drinking, I was fucking, I was on the phone with four broads. With one I was on the phone—he clocked me—for twelve and a half minutes. I had asked him to pull down the venetian blinds—the sun was beating into the office—without saying, 'Please.' " Chandler's missive included an ultimatum cataloguing all the forms of behavior Wilder had to renounce before they could continue working together, including the waving of his cane under Chandler's nose. "Magnanimously, he did not request that I remove my hat in my office," Wilder muses. For the sake of the film, Wilder apologized and the collaboration continued, though not without occasional aftershocks.

Later, in a letter to his publisher Hamish Hamilton, Chandler said working with Wilder "was an agonizing experience and has probably shortened my life, but I learned from it as much about screenwriting as I am capable of learning, which is not much." Chandler went on to describe the frustration of working in an arena where "too many people have too much to say about a writer's work. It ceases to be his own. And after a while he ceases to care about it."

"Chandler had no idea about the structure of a picture," Wilder contends, "nor the structure of a novel—it always ends somewhere with millions of questions, it is not tidy. But the descriptions, the dialogue, are absolutely first-rate."

Despite Chandler's limitations as a film scenarist, the screenplay of *Double Indemnity* is much more efficiently structured for dramatic effect than the novella. Cain himself admitted that "my story was done very slapdash and very quick—I had to have money. I had made a lot of money, but I had to pay it all out to liquidate something I had hanging over my head. I was flat broke. To make money quick I thought, well, you can do a serial for *Liberty*, and the idea for this thing popped into my head."

Though some observers surmise that *Double Indemnity* is based on the headline-making Ruth Snyder–Judd Gray murder case of the 1920s, Cain said it was inspired by an anecdote told him by journalist Arthur Krock about a veteran newspaper proofreader assigned to spot suggestive typo-graphical errors who, one night, couldn't resist letting a lewd headline go to print. Cain hit on the notion of an ace insurance salesman who, having noted all the possible ways someone could cheat his company, similarly decides to tempt fate when he meets a sultry L.A. woman with plans to murder her spouse and collect on his accident insurance. Insurance man Walter Neff (Huff in the book) strangles H. S. Dietrichson (Nirdlinger in Cain's original) while Dietrichson's wife, Phyllis, drives him to the railroad station to catch a train for his college reunion. Walter then poses as the victim and jumps off the train's observation car at a prearranged location where he and Phyllis deposit her husband's body, making it look as if he suffered a fatal fall.

Up to this point, the film is fairly faithful to the source material, but the novella then gets caught up in some very murky plot convolutions that Wilder and Chandler were wise to abandon. Soon after the murder, Phyllis takes up with Nino Zachetti, the lover of her teenage stepdaughter, Lola. Walter, who has grown fond of Lola and lost whatever trust he had in Phyllis, resolves to kill his co-conspirator and sets up a rendezvous in Grif-fith Park. But Phyllis shoots Walter first, and Lola and Nino, who were also in the park, are charged with attempted murder—*and* become prime sus-pects in the prior killing. Feeling sorry for the innocent Lola, Walter con-fesses to the insurance-company claims investigator, Keyes. Then, Walter learns from Keyes that Phyllis is a mass murderer, a former nurse responsi-ble for the deaths of Lola's mother and of several infants left in her care. Nino is the son of the doctor who was blamed for Phyllis's crimes, and he fell in love with Lola while investigating her mother. Rather than deal with the publicity from a murder trial, Keyes arranges passage on a steamer for Walter and Phyllis before revealing their guilt to the police and clearing Nino and Lola. Reunited for the last time, Walter and Phyllis make a suicide pact and prepare to leap into the ocean.

The film's narrative thread is much clearer. Gone are Phyllis's history as a lethal nurse and all the overcrowded intrigue in Griffith Park. With satisfying symmetry, Walter and Phyllis have their fateful rendezvous in the same living room where they first met. Walter plans to shoot Phyllis and frame Nino, but Phyllis shoots first, from a distance. Unable to fire a second shot, she tells Walter it's because, for the first time, she loves someone. Walter's icy response is to fire into her at point-blank range. As in the book, Walter confesses to Keyes, but it's now the highly poignant finale of the story.

Cain heaped praise on the changes Wilder and Chandler made to his story. "I had to see *Double Indemnity* probably half a dozen times in various connections, and I was never bored. I must say Billy Wilder did a terrific job. It's the only picture I ever saw made from my books that had things in it I wish I had thought of. Wilder's ending was much better than my ending, and his device for letting the guy tell the story by taking out the office dictating machine—I would have done it if I had thought of it."

One thing Wilder did hope to keep was Cain's staccato, seemingly naturalistic dialogue. Chandler, however, insisted the words had to be re-written. Wilder decided to bring in a third party—Cain himself—for a story conference. As Cain remembered it, "To try and prove his point [Wilder] got three contract people up, and they ran through these scenes with my dialogue. But to Wilder's astonishment, he found out it *wouldn't* play. Chandler said, 'I tried to tell him, Jim,' with that easy familiarity they have out in Hollywood; even first meeting me he called me by my first name. 'Jim, that dialogue of yours is to the *eye*.' I said I knew my book is to the eye, although I *could* write to the ear. Chandler said, 'I tried to explain it to Billy.' "

No doubt much of the brash, punchy effectiveness of the dialogue and narration in the film is owed to Chandler's skill, but Wilder cautions, "I'm a very good dialogue writer, if I say so myself. I adopted the Chandler technique, and quite a few Chandlerian lines for which he gets credit, they came from me, a Mittel European. That does not mean that he was not enormously helpful—he was as helpful as he was grouchy, which was all the time." As an example of his imitation Chandler, Wilder cites this exchange between Walter and Phyllis: "What's your name?" "Phyllis—you like it?" "Well, let me drive it around the block a couple of times."

The collaboration produced some of the most memorable banter in any Wilder film, as in the highly charged scene where Walter acts on the erotic signals Phyllis seems to be sending him minutes after they've first met.

Phyllis: "There's a speed limit in this state, Mr. Neff—forty-five miles an hour."

Walter: "How fast was I going, Officer?"

"I'd say around ninety."

"Suppose you get down off your motorcycle and give me a ticket."

"Suppose I let you off with a warning this time."

"Suppose it doesn't take."

"Suppose I have to whack you over the knuckles."

"Suppose I bust out crying and put my head on your shoulder."

"Suppose you try putting it on my husband's shoulder."

"That tears it."

Grabbing his hat, Walter sets an appointment with Phyllis's husband for the following evening and asks if Phyllis will be there, too: "Same chair, same perfume, same anklet?"

"I wonder if I know what you mean," Phyllis responds.

"I wonder if you wonder," smirks Walter.

In an extremely rare and gracious gesture by the studio, Raymond Chandler remained under contract during the filming of *Double Indemnity*, and not one word of the script was permitted to be changed without his approval. Despite the nine-to-five routine, Chandler began to feel very much at home at Paramount; at lunch, he would sit at the writers' table, where "I heard some of the best wit I've heard in my life." But as he became more social, his drinking increased. By the time *Double Indemnity* was released, he was again feeling bitter about Hollywood. He published an angry piece in the November 1945 *Atlantic Monthly* entitled "Writers in Hollywood," in which he complained that the screenwriter has "the status of an assistant picture-maker, superficially deferred to (if he is in the room), essentially ignored, and even in his most brilliant achievements carefully pushed out of the way of any possible accolade which might otherwise fall to the star, the producer, the director." Among Chandler's catalogue of complaints was that he was never invited to the studio preview of *Double Indemnity*. "Of course he was invited," Wilder rebuts. "He couldn't come because he was lying drunk under a table at Lucey's," referring to a then popular Hollywood restaurant.

Since by late 1945 he was working once again with Wilder, Charles Brackett felt compelled to respond in print to Chandler's bilious article, claiming Chandler's books were not good enough, nor his films bad enough, to justify his accusations. In a 1953 interview, Chandler, his Hollywood career behind him, had cooled enough on the subject to name his favorite of the films with which he had been associated: "Without question, *Double Indemnity*, which I wrote for an odd little director with a touch of genius, Billy Wilder."

WILDER AND CHANDLER'S DECISION TO HAVE THE PROTAGO-nists of *Double Indemnity* mortally wound each other was one of the key factors in their script obtaining Hays Office approval, since the Production Code still demanded that criminals pay onscreen for their transgressions. Even so, this was groundbreaking territory for Hollywood—a seminal film noir in which the two "romantic" leads conspire to murder. One clear indication of *Double Indemnity*'s daring was the trouble Wilder had in casting those two roles. Among the actors Wilder says turned down the part of Walter Neff were Alan Ladd, James Cagney, Spencer Tracy, Gregory Peck and Fredric March. The director also recalls pursuing George Raft; since Raft didn't read scripts, Wilder had to tell him the story. As he described the planning of the murder, Raft stopped him and queried, "When do we get to the lapel part?" "What lapel?" a confounded Wilder asked. "You know," said Raft, "the part where he turns over his lapel and flashes his police badge." "There is no lapel," Wilder insisted, and the conversation ended there. (With equal discernment, Raft had also turned down the part of Sam Spade in John Huston's *The Maltese Falcon* just a few years earlier, much to that movie classic's benefit.)

Ultimately, Wilder wanted a sympathetic actor to play Walter, someone with a decent, average-Joe image that would accentuate the salesman's descent into immorality. And so he turned to Fred MacMurray, a Paramount contract player (and sometime saxophonist) who had starred as the go-getting bandleader in Wilder's script of *Champagne Waltz* and carved a moderately successful career as an unthreatening romantic-comic lead. MacMurray, too, had serious qualms about playing a killer, and doubts about his qualifications for the role. "I had to talk Fred MacMurray into it," recalls Wilder. "It took me days! He said, 'My God, this requires acting!' I said, 'Yeah, it does require acting, I know what you mean. But you have the kind of personality where you just have to behave. You don't have to act, just behave.'"

According to Maurice Zolotow, MacMurray was in the middle of contract-renewal negotiations with Paramount and agreed to take this unseemly role as a form of leverage against the studio, thinking they'd never really let him do it. Instead, says Zolotow, Paramount decided to "punish" MacMurray by agreeing to this potentially career-damaging assignment. The irony, of course, is that *Double Indemnity* would be by far his best-remembered and most fulfilling work in motion pictures.

Wilder's first choice for Phyllis was Barbara Stanwyck, and she, too, required a measure of prodding. According to Stanwyck, "I said, 'I love the script and I love you, but I am a little afraid after all these years of playing heroines to go into an out-and-out killer.' And Mr. Wilder—and rightly so—looked at me and he said, 'Well, are you a mouse or an actress?' And I said, 'Well, I *hope* I'm an actress.' He said, 'Then do the part.' And I did and I'm very grateful to him."

Wilder speaks glowingly of his *Double Indemnity* femme fatale: "She was a terrific performer with great discipline. She knew her lines, she never muffed, she knew everybody else's lines! She read the script once and she had it. It was very easy to work with her. She knew what I wanted and she gave it to me in spades."

Wilder decked Stanwyck out in a long blonde wig, "to complement her anklet . . . to make her look as sleazy as possible." The wig isn't terribly convincing, but it does give a severity to the hardened Phyllis, even if Paramount production head Buddy De Sylva was overheard to say, "We hired Barbara Stanwyck, and here we get George Washington."

Edward G. Robinson was also hesitant to sign up for *Double Indemnity*, but for a different reason than MacMurray's and Stanwyck's. The role of the brilliant insurance investigator Keyes was significantly beefed up from the novel, but it was still the third lead, a momentous step downward for an actor who had been a motion picture star since *Little Caesar* in 1930. Still, Robinson admitted to himself that "at my age, it was time to begin thinking of character roles, to slide into middle and old age with the same grace as that marvelous actor Lewis Stone." It also helped, as Robinson freely confessed, that instead of a decrease in pay, he would be receiving slightly more money than usual. Indeed, for forty-eight days of work, Robinson would receive the same amount, $100,000, as Stanwyck would for sixty days. (MacMurray's salary was virtually the same, $101,666 for sixty-one days.)

Wilder's salary, too, was escalating, though not to the heights of his stars'. His directing fee rose from $16,500 for *Five Graves to Cairo* to $26,000 for *Double Indemnity*, while his writing fee jumped from $31,500 to nearly $44,000.

The film began production on September 27, 1943, with John Seitz again overseeing the camerawork. Here, for the first time, Wilder as director was able to tap into his Berlin roots, giving the film a look subtly reminiscent of German expressionism, with dramatic deployment of light and shadow. As moody and heightened as the lighting scheme was, Wilder sought a degree of realism for the settings, filming exteriors in real Los Angeles locations and, in his words, "dirtying up" the sets. "I wanted to get away from what we described in those days as the white-satin decor associated with MGM's chief set designer, Cedric Gibbons," Wilder remembers. "Once the set was ready for shooting . . . I would go around and overturn a few ashtrays in order to give the house in which Phyllis lived an appropriately grubby look, because she was not much of a housekeeper. I worked with the cameraman to get dust into the air to give the house a sort of musty look. We blew aluminum particles into the air, and when they floated down into a shaft of light it looked just like dust."

Even more than the visual scheme, it's Fred MacMurray's voiceover account that gives *Double Indemnity* a rueful, fatalistic air—Cain was right to single out Walter's Dictaphone confession as a powerful narrative device. However insecure MacMurray may have been about his talent, his haunted, self-deprecating, haplessly tough interpretation of Walter—both on- and offscreen—anchors and defines *Double Indemnity*. Chandler and Wilder's prose is as heightened as the shadowy look of the film, but Mac-Murray makes us believe in Walter as an L.A. archetype—the middle-class huckster/bachelor whose slick, cocky outward show wards off the pain of introspection. But Walter is more self-aware than he appears; his recording to Keyes brims with disgust over his erotic weakness and amoral recklessness.

According to 1940s movie conventions, the way Phyllis's ankle bracelet cuts into her leg would be enough to explain why Walter succumbs to temptation. The lust factor in *Double Indemnity* is indeed considerable, but there's more to Walter's psyche than facile film noir motivations. Phyllis is just the catalyst for feelings that have been churning inside Walter for years; it's clear from the smooth, cool, almost languid way he peddles insurance that he's lost whatever satisfaction he may have once had in his work. Phyllis's murder plan is titillating not just because it's uttered by a seductive woman, but because the suggestion itself is dangerously thrilling. It's a way to bring some excitement, something *real*, back into Walter's life. This restlessness, this anxiousness to escape a workaday rut—a character trait shared by the movie's peripatetic director—would color the actions of many other Wilder antiheroes in years to come.

Wilder has called *Double Indemnity* a love story, but he's not talking about the relationship between Walter and Phyllis—rather, it's the bond between Walter and his mentor. Keyes sees great potential in the sharp salesman, so much so that he tries to sell Walter on the idea of becoming his chief investigative assistant (at a cut in pay, but Keyes insists the intellectual rewards are so much greater). Keyes's proposal, however, comes at the exact same time that Phyllis informs Walter by phone that her husband has decided to take that fateful train trip. Even without the distraction of a murder pact, Walter could never have become another Keyes—a man soured on women after investigating his fiancée's disreputable past. When Keyes finally bears witness to Walter's foul deeds, he's like a disappointed father—or even a disappointed lover. Wilder pointedly establishes a ritual between the two men whereby Walter always has a match ready to light Keyes's cigar. As Walter lies bleeding just outside the office, he tells his colleague, "Know why you couldn't figure this one? . . . Because the guy you were looking for was too close—right across the desk from you." "Closer than that, Walter," is Keyes's heartfelt reply. "I love you, too," Walter responds. He tries to ignite a last cigarette, and Keyes strikes the match.

This encounter was so powerful and apt—"you couldn't have a more meaningful scene between two men," Wilder says—that the director felt obligated to end the picture there, cutting an elaborate gas-chamber sequence that cost the studio a reported $150,000 to film. He had included all the clinical details of such an execution—the pellet dropping into a bucket of acid and releasing the deadly gas; the doctor standing outside the glass, listening to a stethoscope attached by a long tube to the prisoner's heart.

Keyes, too, is outside the chamber, and at the end of the scene he pulls out a cigar, fumbles for matches, and the horror of Walter's death registers on his face.

"I was very proud of the scene," Wilder attests, "but nothing can make you prouder than conciseness." He now realized that the gas-chamber sequence, filmed prior to those intimate moments with MacMurray and Robinson, was anticlimactic, superfluous. With the new ending, Wilder would also sidestep the Hays Office's single biggest objection to the picture, since they regarded the execution scene as "unduly gruesome" and predicted that it would never be approved by local and regional censor boards. Keyes's call for an ambulance and the police, despite the ambiguous outcome, would suffice.

Wilder also circumvented the censors by filming the murder in an oblique manner: Phyllis pulls the car into a dark side street and, at a signal of three honks of the horn, Walter rises from his hiding place in the back and strangles her husband. Wilder keeps the camera trained on Phyllis's face; a slight jerk of her head and a satisfied smile indicate the deed has been done.

The murder sequence also includes what Wilder claims is the first use of one of the movies' most familiar suspense devices—one he discovered by pure accident. The director had just finished shooting the scene of the lovers returning to their car after disposing of the corpse of Phyllis's husband, and was about to leave for a lunchtime appointment. "I went to get my car from the garage at Paramount," he recalls, "and it wouldn't start. I ran back into the studio, shouting, 'Hold the setup!' " Wilder reshot the scene and added agonizing tension by having the car's engine fail several times as Phyllis turns the ignition key. As Alfred Hitchcock would also discover in films like *Psycho*, such moments create a strange complicity in the audience, as they find themselves empathizing with the wrongdoers and hoping they'll get away with murder.

DOUBLE INDEMNITY HAD ITS FIRST PUBLIC PREVIEW IN APRIL 1944 at the Fox Theatre in the Westwood section of Los Angeles. The audience, many of them film-industry people, was riveted. As the crowd filed out, Wilder spotted James Cain standing alone in a corner of the lobby; Cain embraced the director and effusively praised the film. Also caught up in the enthusiasm was Paramount Pictures, which promoted the film with the bizarre tag line *"Double Indemnity*—The Two Most Important Words in the Motion Picture Industry Since *Broken Blossoms,"* evoking the memory of a 1919 D. W. Griffith silent classic that couldn't be more unlike their steamy new melodrama. Alfred Hitchcock responded to Paramount's claim with a good-natured telegram to the director: "Since *Double Indemnity*, the two most important words are Billy Wilder."

When the film opened in early September, the reviews were largely positive, though the content of the story made some critics uncomfortable. In a mixed notice in *The New York Times*, Bosley Crowther called the picture "steadily diverting, despite its monotonous pace and length." He complained that the two lead characters "lack the attractiveness to render their fate of emotional consequence," but he also felt the movie possessed "a realism reminiscent of the bite of past French films."

The *New York Herald Tribune*'s Howard Barnes was much more enthusiastic, calling *Double Indemnity* "one of the most vital and arresting films of the year," and praising Wilder's "magnificent direction and a whale of a script." The trade paper *Variety*, meanwhile, said the film "sets a new standard for screen treatment in its category."

Despite (or perhaps because of) its groundbreaking reputation, *Double Indemnity* was not a big box-office hit. Nonetheless, it scored seven Oscar nominations—including Best Picture, Best Director, Best Actress and Best Screenplay—in the following year's Oscar race, a surprisingly strong showing for a film about two killers. The Oscar derby gave Wilder a chance to play one of his frequent industry pranks in response to David O. Selznick's pompous trade ad for *his* big Oscar contender, *Since You Went Away*, in which he ran gushing quotes from "distinguished" members of society and politics. Wilder took out an ad saying:

**THIS IS WHAT
A DISTINGUISHED RESTAURATEUR THINKS**

Dear Mr. Billy Wilder:
I certainly do appreciate the opportunity you gave me to see your picture *Double Indemnity*. It held my attention. It held my wife's

attention. It held my sister-in-law's attention. It certainly was a good picture, one of the best pictures we have seen in several days.

Sincerely,

George Oblath

OBLATH'S:

The Best Food for Less Money and Utmost Effort for Service

(Oblath's, it should be explained, was the rather humble luncheonette across the street from the Paramount Studios.)

Selznick was not amused, but he did send Wilder a letter suggesting that the director invite Selznick's eighty-year-old aunt in East St. Louis to a screening. Since she had never been to a movie, she could truthfully say that *Double Indemnity* was the best movie she had ever seen.

Wilder's biggest competition on Oscar night was not from Selznick but from his own studio. Paramount had a huge hit in *Going My Way*, director Leo McCarey's sentimental tale of a parish priest played by Bing Crosby. This was the movie Paramount was encouraging its employees to vote for, since it was still going strong in theaters and *Double Indemnity* had long ago closed. Adding insult to injury, *Going My Way* costar Barry Fitzgerald had earned nominations in both the Best Actor and Best Supporting Actor categories, effectively stealing a possible nomination from either Edward G. Robinson or Fred MacMurray.

Come Oscar night, Wilder sat quietly as *Going My Way* took the Oscars for Best Screenplay and Best Director. When the night's big award was announced, and McCarey rose to collect his trophy as producer of the year's Best Picture, Wilder couldn't resist sticking his foot just slightly into the aisle. "Mr. McCarey . . . stumbled perceptibly," he gleefully recalls.

WHILE BILLY WILDER WAS ACCEPTING PLAUDITS FOR *DOUBLE Indemnity*, another Wilder was surfacing in a more obscure corner of the movie industry. Billy's brother, Willie, had relocated from suburban Long Island and was now making a modest attempt to follow the path of his celebrated younger sibling. Modest may be too kind a word. At first calling himself William Wilder, then W. Lee Wilder to avoid confusion of their names, Willie produced one of the earliest films by director Anthony Mann, later to win renown for his intelligent series of westerns starring James Stewart and epics like *El Cid* and *The Fall of the Roman Empire*. W. Lee persuaded his brother's Rommel, Erich von Stroheim, to star in the title role of *The Great Flamarion*, a low-budget melodrama about a sharpshooter who performs a vaudeville act with a married couple. A la *Double Indemnity*, the film begins with a dying von Stroheim relating how he was seduced by the wife into staging a fatal onstage "accident" involving her husband—and then was betrayed by the vixen. Competent but unexciting, the movie is mainly of interest today for the performances of von Stroheim and Dan Duryea as the ill-fated husband.

In the 1950s, W. Lee would produce *and* direct several more bargain-basement items: *Phantom from Space*, about an invisible alien in Los Angeles; *The Snow Creature*, in which a Himalayan yeti wrangles with U.S. Customs officials; and *Bluebeard's Ten Honeymoons*, a British production starring George Sanders as the lethal lover. Billy Wilder has seldom mentioned his brother or his obscure movie career, apart from calling him "a dull son of a bitch" at a 1976 American Film Institute seminar.

Lost and Redeemed

I T WAS THE TITLE THAT FIRST PIQUED WILDER'S ATTEN-
tion: *The Lost Weekend.* Traveling by train from Los Angeles to New
York, the director spotted Charles Jackson's novel at a railway kiosk during
a Chicago stopover and bought a copy to pass the time. By the time he
arrived in New York, his mind was made up. Wilder called Brackett in Los
Angeles and asked whether he was ready to work with him again. Finding
his former partner in a receptive mood, he told him to pick up the Jackson
book and read it. He then called Buddy De Sylva, and urged Paramount to
inquire about the film rights.

What attracted Wilder to *The Lost Weekend*, the searing account of five
days in the life of a failed New York writer battling alcoholism? The director's initial answer is tinged with his fabled cynicism. "To begin with, not
only did I know it was going to make a good picture, I also knew that the
guy who was going to play Don Birnam—Ray Milland, the drunk—was
going to get the Academy Award. Because for the people who are watching
pictures, if you are a cripple, if you stammer, if you are a hunchback, if you
are an alcoholic, they think that this is acting. You cannot win an Academy
Award when you play Cary Grant parts. Nothing is astonishing there,
coming in and saying 'Tennis, anyone?' " Wilder's words may be flip, but
that doesn't mean they're not true: Witness the recent Oscar victories for

Daniel Day-Lewis as the paralyzed writer in *My Left Foot* and Dustin Hoffman as the autistic savant in *Rain Man*.

But Wilder also sensed that *The Lost Weekend* could be a landmark film "if I could go a little bit deeper, and for the *first time* in pictures show an alcoholic who's not a comedian, who doesn't fall down and do stupid things, if I could draw the audience's attention to the fact that this guy's sick and he has to have it or he's going to die in the gutter. (Like we say in the picture, 'One drink is too many and a thousand are not enough'). And at the end of the picture, I didn't have him cured or anything like that. He just says, 'I'm *trying* not to drink.' And [his girlfriend] says, 'Yeah, you're trying not to drink, like I'm trying not to love you.' The last thing he does is throw his cigarette into a glass of scotch and soda—but it's left questionable, will she succeed and get him off that stuff forever? One drink that he refuses is not going to do it.

"I talked to alcoholics, I went to AA, I talked to doctors, and it was pretty accurate. This was the first time you didn't have the drunk [stumbling] upstairs at four in the morning, and the wife says, 'My God, you have a brain operation today,' and he says, 'I completely forgot,' and he puts on his hat and walks out of the apartment backward. There's nothing funny about a drunk."

Some people at Paramount saw nothing funny about backing a property like *The Lost Weekend*, even if the novel was a 1944 best-seller. Among the strongest naysayers was Y. Frank Freeman, head of West Coast production, a conservative former theater owner who was out of town when De Sylva bought the book for his star writer-director. ("Y. Frank Freeman," Wilder muses, "a question nobody can answer.") On his return, Freeman demanded to know why the studio was getting involved with such a dreary, sordid, uncommercial piece of material. Wilder seized the moment and, in a grim executive conference, accentuated the love-story aspect of *The Lost Weekend*. He came up with a "meet cute" to rival the pajama scene in *Bluebeard's Eighth Wife*, as Birnam exits the opera early to fetch a bottle in his topcoat pocket and is given the leopard-skin coat of the woman he is destined to fall in love with. Well aware of Hollywood realities, Wilder also emphasized the "happy" ending, which today he insists is no conclusive ending at all. Ultimately, the director won over the one executive he needed most—Barney Balaban, Paramount's top man.

But other battles still had to be waged. The Hays Office notified the studio it would never approve a film about a drunken weekend without drastic revisions. Paramount assured the Production Code monitors it would come up with an ending in line with their standards and, in an unusually bold move, commenced production on October 23, 1944, before sending the Hays Office a single page of the script. That same day, the studio submitted a partial screenplay, citing "certain technical difficulties" related to the production. Strangely enough, Joe Breen's main objection to the first section of *The Lost Weekend* he received was not to its depiction of alcoholic binging but to the character of Gloria, a "hostess" at Don's favorite bar who has designs on the fancy-talking writer. "The characterization of Gloria as a prostitute is definitely unacceptable," Breen complained. "Perhaps defining her as a buyer who entertains out-of-town visitors would solve this problem."

Paramount also had to contend with the fears of another influential group: the liquor industry. Three weeks after production began, Freeman received a letter from Stanley Barr, executive vice-president of Allied Liquor Industries, Inc., a national public-relations firm, voicing his "very serious concern" about the film's possible adverse effect on his clients. "There is an almost certain probability that the film version will be distortedly used against our industry and those engaged in it," Barr predicted, warning that "professional prohibitionists will not have the slightest hesitancy in pointing to the leading character in *The Lost Weekend* as typical of anyone who sips a mild and occasional cocktail or the working man who has a glass of beer with friends at his neighborhood tavern." To bolster his argument, Barr cited impossibly rosy liquor-industry statistics that, out of an estimated 40 million consumers, "less than one percent are reported to overindulge." He concluded with the hope that "perhaps you are already planning to use a forceful and plainly stated preamble . . . which will eliminate all our fears."

In a *New York World-Telegram* interview, Brackett tried to deflect some of the liquor industry's potential objections: "I guess the distillers are watching nervously to see what we are doing with the picture. They won't find it an argument for prohibition because we're not dealing with the average drinker at all. . . . We are making the movies' first attempt to understand a drunkard, a chronic alcoholic, and interpret what goes on in his mind. This has been done with an opium smoker, so why not with a drinker?"

Wilder graciously denies that his tumultuous experience working with the closet-alcoholic Raymond Chandler had any influence on the writing of *The Lost Weekend*, but for Brackett the project had deep and painful personal resonances. For years now, Brackett had been coping with his wife Elizabeth's severe alcohol dependency; she had been hospitalized several times and almost never appeared in public. One of Brackett's daughters was also an alcoholic, and would later be killed after tumbling down a flight of stairs while drunk. Brackett also had ample experience helping literary cronies like Dashiell Hammett, Scott Fitzgerald and Dorothy Parker through drunken episodes. "How many of us have found ourselves separated from a friend by his excessive alcoholism?" Brackett told the *New York Sun* while expressing a compassionate desire to re-create the "strange and sometimes beautiful things" that occur inside an alcoholic's head.

Much of Charles Jackson's copious detailing of his hero's inner turmoil, however, had to be sacrificed in adapting *The Lost Weekend* to film. Wilder and Brackett removed any mention of one particularly crucial incident in the novel: the young Don Birnam's banishment from his college fraternity over a passionate letter he wrote to an idolized upperclassman. Was it a case of innocent hero worship, part of Don's lifelong effort to come to terms with his father's desertion? Or was it something deeper, more explicitly sexual? Though Jackson remains ambiguous about the matter, Don's sexual uncertainty arises several times in the novel and is as key to his character's alcoholism as his creative paralysis.

Asked about the omission, Wilder argues, "Look, I had enough problems already making an alcoholic a sympathetic character. If on top of that, he also was a homosexual. . . . One problem's enough. Now we've got everything, right?" Wilder and Brackett did allow one hint of the book's gay subtext to sneak through, retaining the character of the fey Bellevue male nurse Bim, played with insinuating effectiveness in the film by Frank Faylen.

While written in the third person, Jackson's novel has a virtuosic stream-of-consciousness quality as it approximates Birnam's paranoid rants, delusions of literary grandeur, bouts of sudden depression, and feverish dreams and hallucinations. Brackett and Wilder wisely avoided attempting a cinematic equivalent of Jackson's brilliant prose digressions, but they clearly knew a strong visual image when they saw one. No doubt one of the great attractions the book held for Wilder was the opportunity it offered to create several powerful set pieces: Birnam's desperate, futile Yom Kippur journey up Third Avenue to find an open pawn shop that will take his typewriter;* the fall down a flight of stairs that leads to a terrifying night in the alcoholic ward of Bellevue Hospital; Don's bloodcurdling hallucination of a bat swooping down on a mouse that peeps through a crack in his bedroom wall. Even the forceful opening image—a secret bottle hanging by a string outside Don's apartment window—is taken from the book, although, significantly, that image appears in the novel's more pessimistic final pages.

Wilder's first choice for the demanding role of Don Birnam was José Ferrer, whom he had just seen as Iago opposite Paul Robeson in a Broadway production of *Othello*. But this was one instance where he couldn't convince the studio: Buddy De Sylva said audiences would reject the lead character if he wasn't a handsome matinee-idol type. Wilder conceded the point.

At De Sylva's suggestion, the part was offered to the costar of the first film Wilder directed, Ray Milland. De Sylva sent the book to the actor with a note saying, "Read it. Study it. You're going to play it." After an hour's reading, Milland recalled, "The book began to repel me. . . . Its subject was one I knew very little about. Alcoholism. I could not abide being in the company of people who were drunk; they made me tense and very nervous."

After a few days, Milland discussed the Jackson novel with his wife, Mal, admitting that it was "beautifully written but depressing and unrelieved." Most troubling of all, however, was that "it's going to call for some pretty serious acting and I don't know whether I'm equipped to do it." Milland credited his wife with urging him to accept the challenge.

---

* This plot point recalled Wilder's early days in Berlin, when he would leave his portable typewriter as collateral with a man named Nietz to whom he owed a large sum of money; in time, the young writer actually preferred storing the machine with Nietz to lugging it around with him.

Before shooting began, Milland went on a diet of dry toast, coffee, grapefruit juice and boiled eggs, to give himself the appropriately haggard look of a man who habitually forgets to eat. Insecure about his ability to play a convincing drunk scene, he experimented by drinking too much bourbon and reading portions of the script to his visiting in-laws; the evening ended with him hugging a toilet bowl and being put to bed.

Upon his arrival in New York, Milland obtained permission to spend the night anonymously in the psychiatric ward at Bellevue Hospital to prepare for one of the movie's most harrowing sequences. The actor recalled that of the fifteen men in the ward that night, the majority, for some odd reason, were from the advertising profession. Around midnight, a new inmate was brought in, kicking and screaming, and setting off the other patients. "From across the room a long undulating howl started, the sound that coyotes make at night in the high deserts of Arizona," Milland remembered. The actor decided he had had enough, and quietly managed to slip out the front entrance—only to be picked up by a policeman and promptly returned to Bellevue.

Cast opposite Milland was Jane Wyman, in her first major film role after supporting parts in films like *My Favorite Spy* and *Princess O'Rourke.* "We wanted to get away from the suffering type," Brackett stated. "We wanted a girl with a gift for life. We needed some gusto in the picture." What Brackett didn't mention at the time was that the role had already been turned down by both Katharine Hepburn and Jean Arthur.

Wilder cast a mischievous-looking brunette chorus girl named Doris Dowling as the hot-blooded Gloria. Doris's sister Constance had come to Hollywood first, landing roles opposite Danny Kaye in *Up in Arms* and Nelson Eddy in *Knickerbocker Holiday.* Doris followed, and secured a contract with Selznick International Pictures but no feature assignments; *The Lost Weekend* marked her movie debut, and the beginning of a romance with its director. Wilder let Dowling know she had the part in characteristically acerbic fashion. As Dowling told the *New York Sun,* "It hadn't occurred to me there was a part for me in that picture. But one day we were lunching at Lucey's. Mr. Jackson said it was too bad I wasn't a more common type so I could play Gloria. And Billy never even looked up. He just said, 'She is.' That's all. Just 'She is.' I almost went crazy with excitement."

PRODUCTION OF *THE LOST WEEKEND* INCLUDED CONSIDER-able location shooting in New York. Even though the Paramount lot contained artful New York streetfronts, Wilder believed that "in our own minds, these sets were movie props and they created a mental hazard. We felt that we had to have the actual locale stretched out before us. We wanted the real Empire State Building hovering over the backgrounds. We wanted the sound of the trains of the old Third Avenue elevated rumbling over our heads. We couldn't get these things on the Paramount back lot. Nor could we duplicate Milland's nightmarish trek through the milling crowds anywhere else but on the spot."

Wilder used a shot of the actual apartment building where Charles Jackson lived with his brother, and filmed Don Birnam's flight from Belle-vue in front of the real hospital, while duplicating its alcoholic ward in detail on a Hollywood soundstage. He shot one day at P.J. Clarke's, the landmark Fifty-fifth Street tavern where Jackson liked to drink, before deciding the el noises would interfere with the filming; he then built a replica at Paramount so exacting that Robert Benchley would come in every day at five and ask for a shot of bourbon. Howard Da Silva, cast as the bartender, would invariably oblige.

The movie's location tour de force was Don Birnam's calvarylike journey up Third Avenue. Wilder filmed Milland during regular business hours from cameras hidden inside large packing crates, slow-moving delivery trucks and empty storefront windows. An unshaven, sickly looking Milland would wait inside a cab until an "all clear" signal was given by an assistant director, and another small portion of his typewriter pilgrimage would commence; sometimes Milland himself would tap on the packing crate to let the suffering cameraman inside know it was time to start shooting. Most passersby didn't recognize the anguished fellow trudging up the avenue, with a few exceptions. In the middle of one take, a young woman rushed up to the star and asked for his autograph. Milland tried to convince the girl he wasn't an actor, but she wasn't buying. Wilder says she wouldn't go away until he himself intervened and promised her Milland's autograph.

Milland, in his memoirs, recalled filming another shot in which Birnam leans exhausted against an antique shop window. Looking up, the actor spotted two women, a friend of his wife and another acquaintance, eyeing him, then scurrying away in embarrassment. A few nights later, Milland received an anxious call from his wife, Mal, reporting sympathetic calls from friends and the appearance of newspaper gossip-column items claiming that the actor was on a drunken binge in New York. After Milland explained Wilder's hidden-camera setup, his wife urged him to do some damage control. "Within thirty seconds," Milland said, "I had the unit publicity man on the blower, and ten minutes after that, I was talking to the head of Paramount publicity in Hollywood. Talking, hell! I was roaring."

EVEN THOUGH *THE LOST WEEKEND* ABANDONS THE PSYCHO-logical complexity of Jackson's novel to become the story of a man with the world's worst case of writer's block, visually it is one of Wilder's most adventurous films. The decision to film in New York gives a documentarylike authenticity to Don Birnam's struggle, while John Seitz's camerawork reveals more German expressionist influence than any film in Wilder's canon—an appropriate stylistic choice given the hero's mood swings and hallucinatory travails. (The shot in which Don's mind transforms the entire drinking cast of *La Traviata* into swaying overcoats containing his whiskey bottle could have come straight from a 1920s German film.)

Indeed, *The Lost Weekend* is one instance in which Wilder shows real glee in discussing his visual scheme. He's proud of the movie's narrative shorthand: the bottle hanging outside the window, which instantly tells you of Birnam's desperation; the moist rings left on the bar by the writer's whiskey glasses, an efficient way to show the passage of time and the speed of Birnam's descent. Wilder justly points out one of the movie's most effective and haunting shots: After Birnam frantically tears through his apartment in search of a hidden stash, he sinks into a chair and looks up at the ceiling. There, he sees the looming, magnified silhouette of a bottle, sitting in the chandelier.

For the startling scene in which Birnam develops *delirium tremens*, Wilder and Brackett found themselves employing a bona fide bat wrangler. "The bat-and-mouse sequence was wonderfully put together by the backroom boys at the studio," Wilder recalled. "We may have old-fashioned directors, money-mad financiers and stupid front offices, but we have a tremendous back lot. All those guys, the technicians, the prop men, the special-effects men, these are the strength of Hollywood."

THE LOST WEEKEND FINISHED SHOOTING AT THE END OF December 1944, and was given its first public showing at a sneak preview in Santa Barbara. Wilder knew he had created a challenging picture, but nothing could have prepared him for the reaction that night. "The people laughed from the beginning," Wilder recalls. "They laughed when Birnam's brother found the bottle outside the window, they laughed when he emptied the whiskey into the sink." Customers walked out in droves, and by the end the crowd of one thousand was down to a tenth that size. Preview cards were handed out, and the verdicts ranged from "disgusting" to "boring." Wilder claims that one patron left the theater proclaiming, "I've sworn off. Never again." "You'll never drink again?" he was asked. "No, I'll never see another picture again."

Wilder remembers Paramount executive Henry Ginsberg comforting him: "We make good ones. We make bad ones. Don't worry about it." But Wilder couldn't stop worrying; *The Lost Weekend* looked like the first big setback of his brief directing career.

Composer Miklos Rozsa thought the temporary music score was the chief culprit. "The opening shots of the New York skyline had some jazzy xylophonic Gershwinesque music (in the Hollywood musical vernacular, New York means Gershwin)," he remembered. Rozsa felt the choice was "disastrously inappropriate," and he got Wilder and Brackett's okay to write a score utilizing the eerie electronic sounds of a theremin.

In the wake of the Santa Barbara disaster, Paramount's top brass talked of cutting their losses and putting the $1.3 million movie on the shelf. That option was made even more tempting by a secret $5 million offer from the liquor industry to buy up the negative via a dummy corporation claiming to acquire foreign distribution rights to the film. "If they would have given *me* the $5 million, *I* would have burned the negative," Wilder jokes today.

FACED WITH SUCH TERRIBLE OMENS, WILDER WAS IN AN EX-tremely receptive mood when he was asked by Elmer Davis, head of the

Office of War Information, to join the army's Psychological Warfare Division in Germany. Back in November 1944, the Allied Expeditionary Forces' Supreme Headquarters had issued a decree halting all film and theater activities in occupied areas of the Third Reich. On May 12, 1945, a few days after Germany's surrender, the decree was lifted, as long as no former Nazis were permitted to work in the German movie business or on German stages. The army needed someone to oversee this "de-Nazification" program, and when Davis read a lengthy *Life* magazine profile of Wilder and Brackett detailing Wilder's German film background, he found his man.

Wilder reported to an office in the Fisk Building in New York City, a huge room containing hundreds of desks, not unlike the vast office he would depict years later in *The Apartment*. At one of those desks, a dyspeptic-looking bureaucrat skimmed through the new recruit's papers. He seemed annoyed that Wilder had been given the rank and income of a colonel, even though he had never served in the army before. He honed in on the new colonel's $6,500 annual salary and demanded to know what Wilder had been earning in civilian life. Wilder replied, "Twenty-five hundred dollars," but before he could finish, the official banged on his desk and started screaming about corruption and government waste, vowing that someone would be held accountable. Wilder waited for the tirade to end, then calmly told his interviewer that his civilian salary had been $2,500 a *week*. The red-faced bureaucrat said nothing, but simply stamped Wilder's papers and handed them back to him.

Wilder was briefed on his new duties and left for Europe in a Dornier seaplane on May 9, the day after VE Day. The plane landed in Limerick, Ireland; from there, Wilder was put on a bus to another airport and then flew to London. "Everything was terribly clandestine," he recalls.

In London, the director got his first, shocking glimpse of the damage caused by the air war over that ailing city. Then it was on to Paris, and a brief reunion with his old flame, Hella. He stayed at Hotel d'Astorg on rue d'Astorg, opposite the United Artists building. Wilder remembers how a French chef there transformed the American soldiers' K rations—"a kind of dog food"—into the most delectable cuisine.

While in Paris, the director met a colonel named Voss who had been up for Wilder's job, even though he didn't speak a word of German. Voss told Wilder he suspected he was a candidate solely on the basis of his being born in Hollywood. Outside of serving as a chauffeur for a member of the Warner family, he had never had any connection to the film industry. The army seemed to need Wilder even more than it was letting on.

Wilder and his colleagues' ultimate destination was Bad Homburg, where they set up headquarters in a former school for railroad engineers. There, they attempted to screen out any actors, directors, producers or writers who had been eager participants in the entertainment side of the Nazi propaganda effort. Wilder was perfect for the job, since he had kept abreast of the bleak changes in his once beloved German film industry and could easily identify people like the actor Werner Krauss, who specialized in grotesque Jewish stereotypes in such films as *Jud Suss.*

Wilder was also one of the few army personnel there who could speak German. One day, he was handed an application from Oberammergau, filled out in German, asking permission to stage the Passion play. With a little digging, he discovered that the troupe consisted exclusively of former Nazis, and that their Jesus, Anton Lang, had been an elite member of the SS. Wilder's answer: They could perform the Passion play, but only on condition that they use real nails.

The new colonel spent most of his time confined to the office, but one day his superior officer, Brigadier General Robert A. McClure, sent him and three soldiers out on a special mission—to bring back a carload of liquor for the unit. And so, Wilder and his companions raided restaurant wine cellars and requisitioned their contents, traveling as far as Salzburg, Austria. Even though the war was over, the quartet still rode in fear of the Nazi resistance fighters Goebbels had bragged of. Their anxiety seemed justified when, journeying through Austria, they heard gunshots and Wilder ordered his buddies to get out of the jeep and lie on their stomachs. When they got to Salzburg, Wilder discovered to his embarrassment that the "shots" had come from champagne bottles exploding in the heat.

For most of the summer, the Americans had not been allowed to enter Berlin, which was largely under control of the victorious Soviet army. Wilder remembers flying over the bombed-out city with a cameraman: "It looked like the end of the world. . . . The summer of 'forty-five was very, very hot—it was the hottest summer in Berlin that anyone could remember. Thousands of corpses must have lain under the wreckage, the stink in the heat was intolerable. In the *Landwehrkanal* [militia canal] swam the dead; in the *Schrebergarten* [vegetable gardens] lay putrefying corpses."

Finally permitted to enter the city, Wilder and a young driver went searching in the Soviet sector for the Jewish cemetery in the Schönhauser Allee where Wilder's father was buried. The cemetery was a complete shambles, filled with shell craters, charred trees, tank tracks, tall grass and crumbling headstones. As Wilder and his driver entered the cemetery, two men came toward them: a rabbi and a haunted-looking grave digger who reminded Wilder of the actor Conrad Veidt. When Wilder told them he was looking for the grave of his father, the rabbi said it wouldn't be easy to find, as the cemetery had been the scene of a tank battle. The rabbi then told of living four desperate years in the underground. When the Russians came, he and his wife joyfully ran to meet them. But their liberators turned out to be Mongolians, who proceeded to rape and kill the rabbi's wife. Wilder looked over at his driver, an eighteen-year-old redheaded Irish boy from Louisiana. Even though the boy didn't understand a word of the conversation, tears were streaming down his face. Wilder never found his father's grave.

While in Germany, Wilder received confirmation of his worst fears: His mother, Eugenia, his stepfather and his grandmother had all perished in Auschwitz. He had last seen them ten years ago, when it still seemed possible that the Jews in Vienna could be sheltered from the lunacy over-taking Germany. So much had changed: Billy Wilder had not merely es-caped to America but conquered it, while the blood relatives he left behind had suffered terribly and disappeared without a trace.

Wilder reflects on the singular horror of the Holocaust: "There are anti-Semites all around the world, some of them in very high positions. But no country made it legal, and even obligatory, to kill the Jews. I mean, if you kill a Jew in Alabama, the populace is outraged: 'Where was the law?' 'What happened?' It's a whole different story. . . . I know the decent ones [in Germany], I know the indecent ones, I know the ones who stood out-raged, but within themselves there was a little jubilation: one Jew less. But then, I don't think the world behaved very well after it became public knowledge that they had concentration camps. I think it could have done more. I could have maybe saved my mother—but I didn't dare because then there would have been one more."

A key part of Wilder's mission in Germany was to impress upon the population the barbaric nature of the Nazi regime they had obeyed. The most dramatic way to do that was through film—the shocking footage the Allies had shot of the liberation of the concentration camps, with their skeletal survivors and piles of corpses. Wilder remembers one especially terrible image from the liberation of Bergen-Belsen: "There was an entire field, a whole landscape of corpses. And next to one of the corpses sat a dying man. He is the only one still moving in this totality of death and he glances apathetically into the camera. Then he turns, tries to stand up, and falls over . . . dead. Hundreds of bodies, and the look of this dying man. Shattering!"

A documentary filmmaker named Hanus Borger, a lieutenant in the Psychological Warfare Division who had immigrated to America in 1938, was handed the task of combining the Allied footage with the Nazis' own captured film of prisoners digging their own graves. In August 1945, he turned in an 86-minute rough edit to the Office of War Information's London branch. Deciding Borger's version was too long to be of practical use, the OWI gave the film to Wilder, with instructions to pare it down to less than 30 minutes.

Over scenes of the rallies and the camps, the living and the dead, a narrator read the somber words of Professor Oskar Seidlin: "They had to die because of the willingness of the German people to follow criminals and madmen—without resistance. . . . At the Party rally at Nuremberg, I shouted, 'Heil!' And then one day when the Gestapo fetched my neighbor, I looked the other way: 'This is not my business.' Do you remember? 1933 . . . 1936 . . . 1939. I was there. What have I done to prevent it?"

The film was titled *Todesmuhlen (Death Mills)*, and Wilder determined to show it to as many Germans as possible. One of his OWI colleagues argued that German audiences would be so caught up in denial, they'd convince themselves the footage was Hollywood/Jewish trickery. And so Wilder put *Death Mills* to a Hollywood-style test: a preview screening.

"The preview occurred in the autumn of 1945 in Würzburg," recalls the director. "First we showed an old film, a harmless operetta with Lilian Harvey. Afterward, we asked the audience to remain seated and watch the following film. We told them there were preview cards and pencils outside with which they could write their opinion of the picture they were about to see. . . . There were 500 people in the audience; at the end, only about 75. Not one card was filled out, but every pencil was stolen."

Wilder devised a draconian solution to the walk-out problem, which his superiors permitted him to try out in Frankfurt. During the occupation, German citizens could not buy bread or meat without special food cards; for a brief period, they could not get these cards validated without first having sat through a screening of *Death Mills*.

In January 1946, *Death Mills* played for one week in all cinemas in Bavaria. A Foreign Office report described the general reaction as "hushed, with many sighs, tears and turnings away. The audience left quietly at the end, and very few who attended appeared to doubt the veracity of what was shown." At one showing, the report noted, an American agent in plain clothes tested the crowd by shouting that the film was nothing but propaganda, and was immediately threatened by his fellow audience members.

In spite of these positive signs, Wilder remained skeptical. Throughout his travels in Germany, he said with pointed irony, "I never met a single Nazi. Everyone was a victim, everyone had been a resistance fighter."

But in one darkly amusing incident, the returning émigré witnessed the kind of blind obedience to authority that had helped create the Nazi terror. Wilder and some fellow army personnel were speeding along the Kurfür-stendamm when they nearly ran into a pedestrian, who shouted "Asshole!" in German after their Jeep screeched to a halt. Wilder got out and told the angry stranger that he shouldn't assume that someone in an American uniform didn't understand words like that—and that the man would *never* speak that way to a Nazi. Wilder told the fellow to stay put while he reported the incident to the military police. He and his buddies then drove off, thinking nothing more of the encounter. A few hours later, they passed the same intersection, and the man was still standing there, forlornly wait-ing for the authorities.

Wilder experienced his own intimidation when it came time to meet his Soviet counterparts in the eastern sector of Berlin. An American lieu-tenant translated as the director was introduced to two Russian colonels, one of whom had a goatee like Trotsky and crossed eyes like the silent comic Ben Turpin. When told Wilder was a Hollywood filmmaker, the cockeyed Russian suddenly turned and left the room. As Wilder sat there in silence, paranoia set in: What if the Russian colonel checked his file and saw that he had written *Ninotchka*, with its wicked barbs at Mother Russia? After about ten minutes, the colonel reentered the room, with a big smile on his face. His sidled up to his colleague, pointed at Wilder, and said: "*Mrs. Miniver!*" The pair hurried over to Wilder, shook his hand, hugged him and kissed him on the cheek, shouting: "Mr. Wyler, we have seen all of your films! Especially *Mrs. Miniver*! Your films are wonderful!" Of course, the Russians had him confused with his contemporary William Wyler, the director of not only *Mrs. Miniver* but *Wuthering Heights, Dodsworth, Jezebel, The Little Foxes* and, soon, the Oscar-winning *The Best Years of Our Lives.* Wilder simply nodded and accepted the unearned praise, never more grateful for the confusion that often arises between the two directors. (As Wilder once joked, "Monet, Manet—who cares?")

Wilder had the Russians' beloved movie on his mind when he wrote a lengthy report on August 16 entitled "Propaganda Through Entertainment," which was sent to Davidson Taylor, head of the Film, Theater and Music Control Section, and to Colonel William S. Paley, deputy chief of the Information Control Division (and in civilian life, the president of CBS). *Miniver*, Wilder said, was a perfect example of the kind of hybrid of entertainment and propaganda that was needed to reeducate the German population most effectively. Newsreels and documentaries were of value, to be sure, but it wasn't until Wyler's film and its heart-tugging tale of a family coping with the air war over London that America truly appreciated what was at stake in Europe. The film "did a job no documentary, no fifty newsreels could have done," Wilder stressed in his report.

The same lessons applied in Germany. Wilder advised that attendance was good for newsreels and documentary fare, but wondered, "Will the Germans come in week after week to play the guilty pupil?" Already, he noticed German audiences dozing through newsreels, only to awaken for Rita Hayworth in *Cover Girl*. "*Cover Girl* is a fine film," Wilder noted in the report. "It has a love story, it has music and it is in Technicolor. However, it does not particularly help us in our program of reeducating the German people. Now *if* there was an entertainment film with Rita Hayworth, Ingrid Bergman or Gary Cooper, in Technicolor if you wish, and with a love story—only with a very special love story, cleverly devised to help us sell a few ideological items—such a film would provide us with a superior piece of propaganda: They would stand in long lines to buy and once they bought it, it would stick. Unfortunately, no such film exists yet. It must be made. I want to make it."

With that, Wilder proposed an idea for a simple love story between an American GI and a German girl. He then described an encounter he had with one of the women clearing away the rubble on the Kurfürstendamm. "I am so glad you Americans have finally come," she told him, "because now you will help us repair the gas." When Wilder remarked that, yes, it would surely be nice to get a warm meal again, the woman shook her head. "It is not to cook," she corrected him. "We will turn it on, but we won't light it. Don't you see? It is just to breathe it in, deep." "Why do you say that?" "Because we Germans have nothing to live for anymore." Wilder couldn't help picturing the drama of this woman in his head, but in his version the woman would turn on her reactivated stove—and light a fire under her meager allotment of a few potatoes, having found "something new to live for." The message of the film would be, in General Eisenhower's words, "that we are not here to degrade the German people but to make it impossible to wage war . . . give them a little hope to redeem themselves in the eyes of the world."

As for the GI, Wilder declared, "I shall not make him a flag-waving hero or a theorizing apostle of democracy. As a matter of fact, in the beginning of the picture I want him not to be too sure of what the hell this war was all about. I want to touch on fraternization, on homesickness, on the black market. Furthermore, (although it is a 'love story'), boy does *not* get girl. He goes back home with his division while the girl he leaves behind 'sees the light.' There shall be no pompous messages."

With palpable eagerness, Wilder reported: "I have spent two weeks in Berlin. . . . I found the town mad, depraved, starving, fascinating as background for a movie. My notebooks are filled with hot research stuff. I have photographed every corner I need for atmosphere. I have talked to General Gavin, the commanding general of the 82nd Airborne Division, now the main occupying U.S. troops in Berlin; he assured me of every cooperation. I have lived with some of his GIs and put down their lingo. I have talked to Russian WACs and British MPs. I have fraternized with Germans—from bombed-out university professors to three-cigarette chippies at the Femina [Bar]. I have almost sold my wristwatch at the black market under the Reichstag. I have secured the copyrights to the famous song 'Berlin kommt wieder' ['Berlin Will Come Back Again']. I think I am quite ready now to sit down with my collaborator and start writing the script."

The majority of Wilder's communiqué reads like the transcript of a Paramount pitch meeting. The Austrian-American colonel had done his duty; now it was time to get back to the business of making movies—while channeling the profound experience of the past few months into his art. He speculated that some 85 percent of his proposed $1.5 million film project could be shot on Hollywood soundstages, with perhaps three weeks of exterior shooting in Berlin using a skeleton crew of eight. He also stressed that his services were no longer needed in Berlin: "In my opinion, no production of German pictures is possible in the near future. It will take some time to vet prospective producers, to assemble stars, writers, directors and crews. As for the equipment, most of it has been stolen or destroyed. . . . As we are not here to produce films ourselves, but only to *control* the ones the Germans will be producing, I am suggesting in my report that we shall find a man who will be sitting in Berlin, together with the British and Russians, and whose job it will be to read all proposed scripts, to check on policy and to watch out that no fascist thought or Nazi propaganda gets on their celluloid. I don't think that the Division will need me for this kind of passive job. . . . I frankly feel that my further stay in Bad Homburg would be stealing money from the Government."

Wilder calculated that, if he were immediately given a green light on his proposed "propaganda-entertainment" film, he could have the completed product ready by the beginning of 1946. Paley and Taylor approved the idea, but once Wilder returned to the States, other priorities took hold. By January, he was caught up in a new Paramount movie and hoping to get to the Berlin project by the end of 1946; meanwhile, he wanted some policy guidelines from the State Department. By this time, the government was beginning to lose its enthusiasm for Wilder's propaganda-entertainment concept: A memo from Eric T. Clarke, the new chief of the Film, Theater and Music Control Section, stated, "With a $1.5 million budget, Wilder's chief market must be for U.S. people at home. But would his picture, showing that there is hope for Germany, help convince them that Congress should continue to support the occupation? If not, where is its importance to ICD [Information Control Division]? Wilder's thought of making his picture in Hollywood is questionable. He is already too far away from his subject. The ideas he set down last August, the scenes he saw, do not seem so typical today and must seem less so tomorrow. The German scene is changing; our attitudes change, too.

"Of course," Clarke added, in a mercenary frame of mind, "if Wilder proposed to have the picture made in Germany with the acculated [*sic*] Marks, that would be something else again."

The final offshoot of Wilder's Berlin adventure wouldn't be ready until 1948—and it was nothing like the government-sanctioned propaganda his army superiors originally envisioned.

While in Berlin, Wilder began getting startling reports from the Paramount brass that his nightmare concoction, *The Lost Weekend*, was finding new champions in its current round of screenings. The director was anxious to join the salvage operation. There was only one hitch: To get out of the army and out of Germany, Wilder needed the signature of his immediate superior, Bill Paley. Unfortunately, says Wilder, Paley had lost some $2,000 to him in gin-rummy games at headquarters in Bad Homburg, and didn't want Wilder to leave until he had recouped his money. So, systematically, Wilder began to lose—"and with an opponent like Paley, it wasn't easy," he says. Once the debt was pared down to $700, Paley signed the necessary papers and Wilder was on his way back to Hollywood.

IMMEDIATELY ON HIS RETURN, WILDER GRANTED AN INTERVIEW to the *New York Times* in which he described the Allies' plan to oversee the reconstruction of the German film industry. (Putting the great UFA back together would be tricky, he noted, since the soundstages were in the American sector and the power plant was on Russian turf.) Bearing surprisingly little malice, he emphasized that "the Germans are thirsting for information about America and the rest of the outside world."

Urged by a Paramount publicist to trumpet *The Lost Weekend*, Wilder was his usual irreverent self. "If *To Have and Have Not* established Lauren Bacall as The Look, then *The Lost Weekend* certainly should bring Mr. Milland renown as The Kidney," he quipped.

Turning more serious, the director noted, "Charlie and I think we have made an interesting and good film, but probably could have done even better if we didn't have to do so much winking at the audience over the shoulders of the Hays Office."

That fall, *The Lost Weekend* also had to contend with the even more stringent demands of local censor boards, particularly in the pro-temperance state of Ohio. The Ohio board asked for the elimination of Bellevue orderly Bim's line about the Prohibition era, "Prohibition—that is what started most of these guys off," along with another reference to "narrow-minded, small-town teetotalers." In an interoffice memo, Paramount executive Russell Holman expressed outrage at the request, declaring that Bim's speech "simply states a fact: Alcoholic wards were much more crowded in Prohibition days. . . . If a character in a book or a motion picture cannot state an opinion, there would be no more books or motion pictures. If a censor, who possibly has a contrary opinion, can eliminate [such a line], the whole institution of a free press and freedom of speech is in danger." Holman vowed to fight the cuts "very vigorously," noting that the film had been "extremely well-received at all previews. Of hundreds of cards, not one made complaints along the lines of Ohio." Ultimately, however, Paramount lost the battle with the Ohio bluenoses.

Curiously, Paramount was also warned that in Britain the picture would require "drastic modification" before a censors' certificate could be issued. The eventual solution was a subtitle for the British release—*The Lost Weekend: Diary of a Dipsomaniac*—and special trailers alerting delicate Britons to the film's unsavory content:

Ladies and gentlemen . . .

As this is a most unusual subject for screen presentation, we have been requested to warn you of the grim and realistic sequences contained in this unique diary carrying such a powerful moral.

Eyeing a publicity boon in the British Board of Censors' queasy reaction to the film, and still wary of its stateside prospects, Paramount took the unusual move of premiering *The Lost Weekend* in London on October 5. The critical response was sensational. "London is on a praise binge for *The*

Lost Weekend," said the *Hollywood Reporter.* "Even with the paper shortage, it's gotten more comment than any picture since *Gone with the Wind."*

Back in the States, the heat was off on one crucial front. The Joint Committee of the Allied Liquor Industries resolved that the best way to deal with the imminent release of *The Lost Weekend* was to keep a low profile, expressing no public opposition to the film and issuing no public statements unless they were specifically requested. Later, according to Wilder, the distributors of the better brands would praise the film because its hero "drank only the cheapest stuff he could buy."

The Lost Weekend opened in New York on November 16, to the best notices yet of Wilder's career. Bosley Crowther called it "a shatteringly realistic and morbidly fascinating film . . . a *chef d'oeuvre* of motion picture art," with the sole caveat that the reasons behind Birnam's addiction are not sufficiently explained. Howard Barnes in the *New York Herald Tribune* proclaimed *The Lost Weekend* "a milestone in moviemaking . . . every inch a cinematic masterpiece." *Cue* deemed it "a deeply stirring and memorable picture," in the same league as films like *The Informer, The Grapes of Wrath* and *The Ox-Bow Incident* (and, it should be noted, less durable fare like *Wilson*).

James Agee, one of the era's toughest, most astute film critics, wrote a *Nation* review mingling praise with serious qualifications. Calling the movie "unusually hard, tense, cruel, intelligent, and straightforward," Agee yet found nothing that was "new, sharply individual, or strongly creative." Agee questioned whether Wilder or Milland really knew much about the kind of well-bred, failed artist they were portraying, and he criticized the movie's lack of depth while acknowledging that even the novel didn't have a clear handle on Birnam's psychology. For the exacting Agee, the film just didn't possess the visual and aural virtuosity to truly capture the varying moods and sensations of a desperate alcoholic. His mixed but respectful review, however, ends on a mischievously comic note: "I understand that liquor interesh: innerish: intereshtsh are rather worried about thish film. Thash tough."

Wilder and Brackett's most upbeat critic was none other than Charles Jackson, who gushed, "I had absolutely nothing to do with the filming of my book, so I can say this frankly: It's my fourth favorite motion picture of all time. The first three are *The Informer, All Quiet on the Western Front* and

The Gold Rush." Echoing James M. Cain on *Double Indemnity,* Jackson added, "They thought of things I wish I'd thought of first—they were that good."

Much to everyone's surprise, *The Lost Weekend* was a box-office hit, ultimately bringing in $4.3 million in domestic rentals to the studio— placing it among the top sixty films of the 1940s. The movie became easily recognizable fodder for the nation's comics and columnists, despite Wilder's contention that "there's nothing funny about a drunk." *Life* magazine claimed that "Let's lose a weekend" had become a new catchphrase for going out for a drink. Ray Milland complained that he couldn't order a cocktail in a restaurant without hearing wisecracks from the waiters and reported being passed in his car by a group of sailors and their girlfriends who leaned out their window yelling, "Still on that bender?"

The jokes continued at the following March's Oscar ceremony, where *The Lost Weekend* was up for seven awards, including Best Picture, Best Actor and Best Director. "It's Four Roses against Old Granddad," Bob Hope said of the contest between Milland and Bing Crosby in *The Bells of St. Mary's,* the heavily nominated sequel to 1944's big winner, *Going My Way. The Lost Weekend* had already swept the New York Film Critics' awards for picture, actor and director, and was a strong Oscar favorite. Even the liquor industry, putting the best face on the situation, joined in the Oscar campaign: A House of Seagrams ad stated, with ironic fervor, "Paramount has succeeded in burning into the hearts and minds of all who see this vivid screen story our own long-held and oft-published belief that . . . *some men should not drink!,* which might well have been the name of this great picture instead of *The Lost Weekend."*

This time around, Wilder triumphed over Leo McCarey and his lovable clergymen. *The Lost Weekend* took the awards for screenplay, director (presented by William Wyler), actor and Best Picture. Composer Miklos Rozsa, with three nominations in the same category, won for his score for Alfred Hitchcock's *Spellbound,* though Rozsa later said he preferred his work on the Wilder film. Wilder, Brackett and their victorious team celebrated at Romanoff's, and the next morning their colleagues at the studio paid them a special tribute by hanging dozens of bottles outside the windows of their Paramount office. For Wilder, it was a euphoric moment to rival any of Don Birnam's highest flights of fancy.

TWELVE

Foreign Affairs

T*HE LOST WEEKEND* WAS A LUCKY FILM FOR BILLY WIL-
der, beyond the Oscars and the enhanced respect of his peers. This,
after all, was the picture on which the thirty-eight-year-old director met
the love of his life, a strikingly beautiful twenty-two-year-old Paramount
contract player named Audrey Young.

Despite the fact that his lover Doris Dowling was working on the same
film, Wilder couldn't help noticing the slender brunette who reported for
two days' extra work on the scene in which Don Birnam gets thrown out of
Harry and Joe's Bar for stealing money from a woman's purse. The daughter of a used-car dealer and a Hollywood wardrobe supervisor, Audrey had
grown up in Los Angeles and gotten her first taste of show business when
her mother brought her along to the studio. As a youngster, she took tap,
singing and diction lessons, and made her professional debut as a chorus
girl in the touring company of *George White's Scandals.* She performed in
the chorus of various New York cabaret shows, then found herself back in
Hollywood as a Paramount extra and bit player. Audrey was given the full
studio makeover—she even agreed to have her nose altered to make her
profile more camera-friendly. She tried to hone her talents by studying
acting with the stage actress Josephine Hutchinson, but concluded that she
didn't really have what it takes to be a film star, or even a worthy supporting player. Her private singing lessons with the coach Glenn Raikes proved

much more encouraging. When she reported to the *Lost Weekend* set, most of her film work to date had consisted of walk-ons in musicals.

As Audrey entered the piano-bar set, Harry Barris, a friend of Wilder who was one of the Paul Whiteman Orchestra's original Rhythm Boys vocal group, was at the keyboard rehearsing the standard "You Were Mine," which he would perform in the film. The young extra leaned on the piano and listened; when she turned around, the director was standing behind her. After a brief, awkward exchange, Audrey, desperate for something to say, told the great Wilder that Barris's song always made her cry. Amused, the director said he had to go attend to something, but he'd be back in a moment to see if she was in tears yet. "Believe me," Audrey told Maurice Zolotow, "I can't act worth a damn. I just have no talent in that direction, but when Billy came back, there I was crying and I just couldn't stop."

That was enough for Billy to ask Audrey on their first date—a discreet date, since he was still married, and still very much involved with Doris Dowling. Audrey and Billy went out on several more dates, and one night he even escorted her home to her parents' house at the decidedly unfashionable intersection of La Brea Avenue and Washington Boulevard. "I'd worship the ground you walk on—if you lived in a better neighborhood," Billy quipped. "Just think of it as East Beverly Hills," Audrey shot back.

Audrey's role as the hat-check girl at Harry and Joe's Bar never made it to the final cut, though Wilder insists you can see her arm in a corner of the frame, as Ray Milland is handed his hat and shown the door. Audrey wound up getting a much more useful career boost from Abbott and Costello: She landed her first substantial part playing Marjorie Main's daughter in the comedy team's movie *The Wistful Widow of Wagon Gap*, and was hired as a singer in their stage show at New York's Roxy Theatre. That gig became the launching pad for a solo nightclub act. For the time being, she and Billy Wilder went their separate ways. Perhaps things had worked out for the best, she thought. After all, everyone *knew* Billy Wilder was destined to wed Doris Dowling once his bad marriage was ended.

Billy's long army stint in Europe proved the final catalyst for his wife, Judith. On September 26, 1945, shortly after his return to America, the Wilders announced their separation. One week later, just days before *The*

Lost Weekend's triumphant premiere in London, Judith sued her husband for divorce on the grounds of extreme cruelty. The marriage had been effectively over for some time now: While Judith painted and did ceramics and tended to their home on Beverly Drive, Billy went out to parties and bridge games, openly fielded phone calls in his Paramount office from various girlfriends, and began the affair with Dowling that was one of Hollywood's worst-kept secrets.

Though the fling continued for another two years, Wilder says he was never all that serious about the temperamental Dowling and certainly never considered marrying her. Apart from her appearances in the gossip columns, Dowling's only other claim to fame during this period was a sultry role in the Alan Ladd melodrama *The Blue Dahlia*, written by Wilder's former nemesis, Raymond Chandler. Doris's sister Constance was also turning up in the papers as the paramour of rising film and theater director Elia Kazan. No doubt it made irresistible copy: "Dowling Girls Snag Hollywood Honchos." Wilder's divorce was granted in 1947, but soon after he and Dowling broke up and his former *Lost Weekend* star was bound for Rome, where she costarred in the Italian neorealist classic *Bitter Rice*; she also appears in Orson Welles's *Othello*. Her last significant show-business credit was the 1964–65 TV fantasy sitcom, *My Living Doll*.

Judith stayed in the Beverly Drive house a short while, but soon announced her engagement to a writer and cabinetmaker named Badner. Wilder's ex-wife and daughter lived for a time in a brownstone in Brooklyn Heights, then returned to Los Angeles, settling in Laurel Canyon. Eventually, they moved upstate to Mill Valley, where Victoria attended San Francisco State College and majored in English and anthropology. Judith devoted most of her time to painting at their house on Stinson Beach and still resides in northern California. Victoria, known as Billi to her family and friends, married a San Francisco high school teacher named Fiorenzo Gordine, with whom she had a daughter named Julie. Victoria later divorced Fiorenzo and went on to marry Tony Settember, a former race-car driver. The couple—like Judith—live today in northern California.

Billy Wilder never talks about his first wife, his daughter or grandchild in interviews—just as his films tend to avoid traditional notions of family. On the rare occasions when children appear in Wilder movies—*The Seven Year Itch*, *One, Two, Three* and *The Fortune Cookie* being the most prominent examples—it's usually to illustrate the annoyances of a bourgeois domestic life. Real parental devotion only surfaces in his two Audrey Hepburn films, in the sheltering presence of screen fathers John Williams and Maurice Chevalier.

In Maurice Zolotow's account, Vicki Wilder recalled the many presents her father gave her—a Lionel electric-train set, a TV set, an MGA sports car, even a 2½-month trip to Europe. She remembered being taken to Broadway musicals and horse shows and posh restaurants and star-studded Hollywood parties. But she also admitted, "My daddy is a hard person to get to know. I worship him but I cannot seem to get close to him. He is kind and generous but he can't say 'I love you.' . . . He isn't a physically expressive man. I don't know why this is, but that doesn't mean he doesn't have deep feelings."

WITH *THE LOST WEEKEND*, WILDER HAD WON NEAR UNI-versal acclaim, claimed the Oscar, and even earned the top prize at the first postwar Cannes Film Festival. He and Brackett were kings of the Paramount creative hierarchy, earning between them $4,500 a week; Wilder jokingly said they were "the happiest couple in Hollywood," and the phrase became the headline of a lengthy *Life* magazine profile of the pair. Their studio quarters consisted of three rooms: a reception area for their secretary, Helen Hernandez, decorated with stills from their films; an office they dubbed "the game room," where they would go to relax and play cribbage; and the largest office, christened "the bedroom," where they brainstormed ideas and polished their scripts. The oak-paneled room was equipped with a fireplace, plush sofas and chairs, a large table, and a bust of Shakespeare. During the early stages of a project, very little actual writing was done; they'd toss ideas around while eating or lying down, constantly interrupted by visits from actors and fellow writers. Then, in the final phase of their work, the accumulated details of the script would be committed to paper, with Brackett writing it all out in longhand on yellow pads.

When *The Lost Weekend* wrapped at the end of 1944, Wilder and Brackett began considering a number of projects which never came to fruition: a Danny Kaye musical called *The Count of Luxembourg*; a Ferenc Molnár play named *Olympia*, intended as a comeback vehicle for Greta Garbo; and a film of Jules Verne's *Around the World in 80 Days*, which would surface a decade later as an Oscar-winning Mike Todd spectacular. Clearly, they were looking for something very different from the edgy, black-and-white nightmare odyssey of Don Birnam. They finally found it in a brightly colored piece of turn-of-the-century Austrian musical fluff called *The Emperor Waltz*.

The Emperor Waltz is a throwback to Wilder's earliest Hollywood screenwriting days, when he was pigeonholed into the Bavarian ghetto of innocuous Mittel European musicals like *Music in the Air* and *Champagne Waltz*. Wilder says he and Brackett created the film as a favor to Paramount, which was eager to have a new vehicle for one of its biggest contract stars, Bing Crosby. But, surely, there was also the appeal of tackling something in the spirit of Wilder's idol and mentor, Ernst Lubitsch, who was still active but battling serious heart problems. *The Emperor Waltz* was Wilder's first conscious attempt as a director to evoke the famed Lubitsch touch, with its romantic sophistication and sexual playfulness. Unfortunately, Lubitsch-style comedy and the laid-back, all-American folksiness of Bing Crosby were an ill-fitting combination.

Wilder filmed *The Emperor Waltz* at Paramount and at the Jasper National Park in the Canadian Rockies from June to September 1946 (though the picture wouldn't be released until 1948, in April in Great Britain and July in the United States). The movie is set some forty years in the past, right around the time of Wilder's birth, and thus can be seen as a mildly irreverent memoir of the collapsed empire of the director's childhood. An opening title crawl reveals just how seriously Wilder intends the reign of the Emperor Franz Josef to be taken: "On a December night, some forty-odd years ago, His Majesty Francis Joseph the First, Emperor of Austria, Apostolic King of Hungary, King of Bohemia, Dalmatia, Croatia, Slavonia, Galicia, and so forth and so forth, was giving a little clambake at his palace in Vienna." Already, Wilder is so eager to bring an American spin to the subject, he anglicizes Franz Josef's name and reduces a royal ball to a clambake.

Shot in rich Technicolor, the film immediately impresses with its handsome production value—Paramount spared no expense in rewarding its new Oscar victor, allotting him a reported $4 million. The opening scene is Wilder's biggest directorial setup to date—a lavish palace gala crashed by nervy American Virgil Smith (Crosby). Nearly two thirds of the story is told in flashback by a minor observer, the gossipy old Princess Bitotska (Lucile Watson), who recounts Virgil's first outrage against the empire some months ago. A salesman from Newark, New Jersey, Virgil has journeyed to Vienna to try to secure the Emperor's endorsement of an amazing new contraption, the phonograph machine. The task is far from easy: Jittery palace guards promptly eject the drummer, thinking the device is a bomb. During the melee, Virgil meets the Countess Johanna von Stolzenburg-Stolzenburg (Joan Fontaine) and her father, the Baron Holenia (Roland Culver), who have been summoned to the court to arrange the mating of their purebred black French poodle Scheherazade with the Emperor's aging dog. Scheherazade and Virgil's scrappy mutt Buttons get into a fight, and Virgil pursues the countess, demanding but not receiving an apology (although he does brazenly steal a kiss). To their dismay, the countess and the baron find that Scherherazade's encounter with Buttons has left her deeply terrified of other dogs. The palace vet, a Freud disciple named Dr. Semmelgries (Sig Ruman), says the only way to cure Scheherazade is by having her make up with Buttons. The two dogs not only make up but become downright intimate, as do Virgil and the countess—all it takes is a little Crosby crooning to make Johanna swoon.

Virgil finally receives his audience with the Emperor—this time for the purpose of asking permission to wed Johanna (though he does bring along the phonograph). The Emperor, convinced Johanna couldn't possibly be happy with a salesman from New Jersey, makes a proposition: He'll endorse the phonograph if Virgil promises to break things off with the countess. Virgil, convinced that the Emperor is right about the couple's future prospects, accepts the deal and pretends to Johanna that he was only interested in gaining access to Franz Josef all along.

Here, the film picks up where it began, with Virgil begging for a rapprochement with the countess, if only for the sake of his miserable dog, Buttons. Their reunion coincides with a big event in the lonely Emperor's life—the imminent arrival of Scheherazade's prized litter. But when the puppies arrive, they're anything but purebred—Buttons has spoiled the succession. Anxious to preserve his social position, the baron tells the Emperor the pups were born dead and orders the pathetic whelps drowned. But Virgil saves them in the nick of time and, in the midst of the ball, delivers them to a surprisingly doting Emperor. The American tells Johanna he's loved her all along and was wrong to doubt their future together, and the reunited lovers dance to "The Emperor Waltz."

Although a box-office hit in its time, today *The Emperor Waltz* is among the least celebrated films in the Wilder canon. Wilder has always dismissed the movie, saying of his "favor" to Paramount, "No good deed goes unpunished." He hated his first dealings with Technicolor, complaining, "Everything looked like it was in an ice-cream parlor. . . . Even the dialogue sounded wrong in color." Like the operettas of the director's Berlin days, the picture has dated in a way other Wilder films have not. Crosby's mercifully few songs are for die-hard fans only, and there's a quaintness to the musical interludes that's wholly appropriate to the turn-of-the-century setting but makes the movie something of a trial for contemporary viewers. Wilder does have fun, though, with the image of the Viennese as a music-obsessed people: Whenever Crosby starts to sing, there's usually a multitude of strangers joining in. At one point, a chauffeur, a chambermaid and a pudgy clerk stage an impromptu ballet in Virgil's hotel lobby, and all the townspeople seem to have instruments within easy reach. It's as if Wilder is giving a final, ambivalent kiss-off to his years of Bavarian fluff.

The movie's chief stumbling block is Crosby. He's perhaps too aptly cast as a gauche American—his cavalier, unflappable personal style fits this slick Yankee huckster, all right, but Crosby doesn't have the charm to make Virgil also work as a romantic lead. (With typical Wilder bluntness, Princess Bitotska complains that Virgil has "ears like a bat, and the rest of him like a plucked duck.") Early in the film, during their first fight, Virgil steps up to the countess and plants a fat kiss on her mouth, and there's a queasy impropriety to the moment a more appealing actor might have avoided. When Johanna falls for Virgil as he serenades her, we have to take it on faith that she sees something in this arrogant crooner that we don't. The sexual tension the movie hinges upon is all in the script, not in the playing. There's more real passion onscreen between Fontaine's poodle and Crosby's mutt.

Indeed, Wilder continually uses the dogs to blatantly mirror what's going on between his human characters: Virgil and Buttons are different kinds of American mutt, and Johanna and Scheherazade are both high-strung aristocrats brought down by love. For two weeks, the two couples rendezvous on an island near the palace, and it's implicit that both sets of lovers are involved in behavior the Hays Office would never approve of. This was Wilder's rather blunt variation on the Lubitsch touch, prompting at least one pundit of the day, *Cue*, to complain of "several inexcusably vulgar and belabored additions to the main thread of the story—among them, a leering, snickering canine romance."

The dogs come to represent more than a visual code for sex, however—they also symbolize the movie's preoccupation with class and privilege. Virgil and Buttons may be ugly, low-bred Americans, but they represent the future. As the Emperor himself tells the drummer, "Ultimately, the world will be yours." Comparing himself and his kind to snails, he notes, "They are majestic creatures, with small coronetted heads that peer very proudly from their tiny castles. They move with dignity. I imagine they have a great sense of their own importance. But you take them from their shells and they die."

If Wilder feels any nostalgia for the world of his dotty Franz Josef, he makes his position clear in the movie's very curious final reel. Only a mind as wicked as Wilder's could conceive of a comic climax built around the near drowning of newborn puppies, but there's an even darker subtext to the baron's deed. Wilder's ostensibly innocuous portrait of the Vienna of his youth, his first film after returning from Nazi-devastated Europe, is suddenly jarred by echoes of the recent past. "Orders have been given!" Dr. Semmelgries shouts as Virgil absconds with the innocent pups. "They're not pure enough for you, not quite your sort, freaks!" Virgil scolds the Emperor after careening past his kneeling subjects. Is such a reference to the Nazi Holocaust tasteless in this frivolous context, or is it a brazen subversion of Hollywood's sugar-coated fantasy image of Austria, the birthplace of Hitler? If anyone has the right to make that judgment call, it's Billy Wilder.

The Emperor Waltz is the first Wilder-directed film to touch on what would become a recurring personal theme: the clash between European sophistication and all-American directness. His allegiances would change from film to film, but in this instance Wilder exhibits real fondness for Virgil Smith and his blithe dismissal of matters of birthright and social station. As much as Wilder cherished Europe and its bracing culture, he felt more American than ever after seeing the aftereffects of a war triggered by notions of ethnic supremacy. In theory at least, everyone was welcome in America. As Wilder told *The New York Times* in 1988, "There is one great difference between America and all the other countries. If you want to become a French citizen, a Swiss citizen, they say: 'What do you mean? *We* were born here.' If you *don't* want to become an American citizen, they say, 'What's the matter? Aren't we good enough?' It's the basis of my love for America."

With *The Emperor Waltz*, Wilder happily wore the mantle of big-budget Hollywood director. His wish, for now, was Paramount's command. The Canadian location needed more trees? So be it! The lake required a small island for the rendezvous of the lovers and their dogs? No problem! At a cost of $90,000, crews constructed an island hideaway out of oil drums, dirt and rocks. Wilder denies, however, that he had any of the real-life scenery painted to order: "Painting trees red is an Antonioni trick," he said in a 1969 interview. "Like Hitchcock in *The Trouble with Harry*, it was a question of putting leaves on trees when they weren't already there. I don't much care for shooting in a naturalistic way outside. In the studios, the degree of control I have is greater, and I feel much freer."

One of the first people to see a rough cut of *The Emperor Waltz* was the man who inspired it, Ernst Lubitsch. The two filmmakers had grown so close that Wilder actually lived for a week in Lubitsch's big house in Bel Air, soon after his divorce from Judith. The arrangement didn't last, the younger director says, because both men had various girlfriends entering the house and Wilder felt they were starting to get in each other's way.

The master's reaction to *The Emperor Waltz* may be one reason Wilder speaks so ill of the film today. According to biographer Scott Eyman, Lubitsch had proposed to friends a variation on a comic notion he used in *Heaven Can Wait*, in which a couple got along so poorly they could only communicate through a go-between. Wouldn't it be funny, Lubitsch said, if the go-between were a dog? When the director saw all the canine-surrogate business in *The Emperor Waltz*, it seemed awfully reminiscent of his own concept. "The son of a bitch has taken my story!" Lubitsch angrily hissed to his friend Mary Loos.

Lubitsch's opinion notwithstanding, the reviews for *The Emperor Waltz* were generally kind. In *The New York Times*, Bosley Crowther, who had quibbled about *Five Graves to Cairo* and *Double Indemnity*, sounded like a studio publicist when he said, "*The Emperor Waltz* is a project that should turn the Blue Danube to twinkling gold." Acknowledging that the idea was a meager one, he felt Wilder and Brackett made up for it with casualness, charm and "a great deal of clever sight-humor." *Variety* predicted that "*The Emperor Waltz* should solve any ticket buyer's entertainment problem. That's the only problem it attempts to resolve, and the way it goes about it is strictly enjoyable." Even hard-to-please James Agee admitted, "At its best this semi-musical is amusing and well shaped, because Charles Brackett and Billy Wilder have learned a fair amount from the comedies of Ernst Lubitsch. In general it is reasonably good fun. At its worst it yaps and embraces every unguarded leg in sight."

On November 30, 1947, seven months before the U.S. premiere of *The Emperor Waltz*, Ernst Lubitsch died of a massive heart attack shortly after making love to an attractive blond. Charles Brackett delivered the eulogy, and Wilder was one of the pallbearers. After the burial at Forest Lawn Cemetery, Wilder and William Wyler walked down a hill to their cars. "No more Lubitsch," Wilder said, just to break the silence. "Worse than that," Wyler replied, "no more Lubitsch films."

WHILE *THE EMPEROR WALTZ* MADE OBLIQUE REFERENCE TO Wilder's experience of postwar Germany, his next project would engage the subject head-on. Wilder was still toying with his army-report idea of a romance between an American GI and a German girl when Brackett brought him a seventy-two-page screen story treatment called *Love in the Air* by Irwin Shaw (later, the celebrated author of *The Young Lions*) and his brother, David, which begins by proclaiming, "The Second World War was not only witness to the most enormous movement of material goods in the history of the world; it also saw the greatest mass movement of lust in recorded time." The Shaws' story concerned a young air force captain, engaged for five years to a girl in Iowa, who accompanies a young, pretty congresswoman on a world tour of army installations. As the legislator discovers, the captain has girls in every corner of the globe, from London to Moscow, Cairo to Sydney. Ultimately, the captain realizes that every one of his women pales next to his vibrant traveling companion, and he proposes marriage.

By the end of May 1947, Wilder, Brackett and a writer named Robert Harari had come up with their own forty-eight-page treatment, very loosely based on *Love in the Air* and incorporating Wilder's notion of the German/American romance to form a most provocative love triangle.* The congresswoman was no longer particularly young, pretty, or passionate about anything but serving the American people with absolute rectitude. As the Brackett/Wilder/Harari treatment described her, "Before Phoebe Frost went into politics, she had been a notary public—one of those who, prior to putting her seal on a document, had to see the signatory actually sign it, and inspect the signatory's birth certificate, and verify the seal of the notary certifying the birth certificate."

Meanwhile, the German girl of Wilder's original vision had become much more than a simple *fraulein*. Now, she was Erika von Schlütow, cabaret singer extraordinaire and former consort of the German high command. Cheekily, Wilder had Erika involved in a steamy affair with an American army captain, John Pringle, who has only the vaguest suspicions of his paramour's past affiliations. As luck would have it, Pringle gets stuck being an escort to Congresswoman Frost, who is in Berlin to investigate reports of fraternization between the occupying American Army and the women of Germany.

As the staunchly Republican Phoebe, Wilder cast Jean Arthur, the fresh-faced comedienne beloved for her work in film classics like *Mr. Smith Goes to Washington*, *Only Angels Have Wings* and *The More the Merrier*; having been embroiled in a dispute with Columbia Pictures boss Harry Cohn, Arthur would be making her first film in four years. Captain Pringle was to be played by John Lund, a gruff-voiced leading man whose only prior movie credits were *To Each His Own*, *The Perils of Pauline* and *Variety Girl*.

Only one woman could play the Erika of Wilder's dreams—his old Berlin friend, Marlene Dietrich. It would take some persuading. During the war, Dietrich had become an authentic American heroine, bravely and tirelessly entertaining the troops advancing through Europe. (When Wilder asked her if she'd ever slept with General Eisenhower, she replied, "How could I? He was never at the front.") The German-born actress was

---

* The final screenplay is credited to Wilder, Brackett and Richard Breen.

the first woman ever to be awarded the U.S. government's Medal of Freedom, the highest possible civilian honor. For someone who had campaigned so fiercely against Hitler, the idea of playing a Nazi was repellent. Initially, she turned down Wilder's offer but, as Dietrich says in her autobiography, "at that time, I didn't know that you can't refuse Billy Wilder." (Wilder denies one story that he used reverse psychology to win over Dietrich, by showing her a screen test of June Havoc in the role and asking her advice on Havoc's German accent.)

As Dietrich's daughter Maria Riva recalls it, "She hated the character, the whole idea, but trusted Wilder and needed the money. She left for Hollywood in '47, quite sure that once she had designed the clothes, sung the [Frederick] Hollander songs, and made sure that 'Billy won't insist that the woman was really a Nazi during the war,' *A Foreign Affair* would become a Dietrich film."

Wilder already had some startling aerial footage of the ruins of Berlin from his army tour in 1945. Now, he would have to obtain the permission of the War Department to do some background filming in the still devastated city. Wilder's contacts helped clear the way without close scrutiny of his new script. As Paramount's Luigi Luraschi wrote to studio colleague Russell Holman, "We know that the film people in Berlin are friendly [*sic*] disposed to us, and particularly to Billy because of past associations. We also know that Erich Pommer, who handles the production of German pictures by German civilians, is likewise disposed."

Wilder left on the S.S. *America* in late July 1947 and, after a brief stay at the George V Hotel in Paris, joined a small second-unit photography crew in Berlin. There, they shot back-projection footage for several key sequences: in Nollendorfplatz and Wittenbergplatz, for Captain Pringle's jaunty drive through the ruined city; outside the Tiergarten, as Yank soldiers fraternize with the *frauleins*; and past landmarks like the Reichstag, as Pringle's superior Colonel Plummer narrates a sardonic capsule history of the Third Reich. Two hundred extras were also employed for long shots of the black market near the Brandenburg Gate.

Studio work on *A Foreign Affair*, at one time known as *Operation Candybar*, commenced at Paramount on December 1. Arthur would be paid $185,000, with Dietrich getting $110,000 and Lund $25,000. (No longer overtaken in salary by his stars, Wilder received $116,000 for directing and

$89,000 for writing; Brackett's paycheck was $131,000). Dietrich didn't think much of her costars: According to her daughter, she called Lund "that piece of petrified wood," and branded Arthur "that ugly, ugly woman with that terrible American twang." (It didn't help that Arthur had her hair in a severe bun throughout the film.)

Arthur, a notoriously insecure performer, immediately felt threatened by the bond between her director and Dietrich. One night, Arthur rang Wilder's doorbell, accompanied by her husband, the producer Frank Ross. "What did you do with my closeup?" she screamed at her befuddled director. "What closeup?" Wilder asked. "The closeup where I look so beautiful," she moaned, going on to accuse Wilder of destroying it at Dietrich's behest. In fact, says Wilder, there was no such closeup.

Wilder recalls another difficult encounter with his star during the filming of a scene in which Phoebe gets drunk in the underground nightclub where Erika performs and winds up getting tossed in the air by some rowdy soldiers. The director recommended using a double, as he wanted Phoebe to be handled roughly and thrown up high. Arthur said she had never yet used a double, and insisted on doing the stunt herself. Wilder shot the scene, as boisterously as he had envisioned it. After the take, Arthur threw back her head and gave the director a piercing look. "What will you require next from me, Mr. Wilder?" she inquired loudly, to a round of sympathetic applause from the crew and extras.

A FOREIGN AFFAIR OPENS WITH A REAL SHOCK TO THE AUDI-ence's system—Wilder's footage of the incredible devastation to his fondly remembered Berlin, contrasted with the touristlike utterances of an American congressional delegation flying overhead. With down-home bluntness, a Texas congressman says the city looks "like pack rats been gnawing at a hunk of old moldy roquefort cheese." Congresswoman Frost, meanwhile, is sitting apart from her colleagues, scribbling in a notebook. Informed the plane is over Berlin, she announces, "One thing at a time" and, in a clever visualization of Wilder and Brackett's original "notary public" depiction of Phoebe, she proceeds with an elaborate ritual of folding her notebook, capping her pen, putting away her eyeglasses, locking her briefcase, closing her key holder, etc. It's like an anal-retentive precursor of Art Carney's

Honeymooners shtick, and it tells us everything we need to know about the character in mere seconds. When she finally does get a glimpse of the carnage below, her response is a laughably inadequate "Golly!"

The Americans in *A Foreign Affair* consistently respond to the tragedy of Berlin with disconcerting lapses of sensitivity. As Pringle drives through bombed-out areas of the city toward a romantic rendezvous with Erika, he whistles "Isn't It Romantic?" When Colonel Plummer (Millard Mitchell) conducts an official tour, he fires one glib wisecrack after another. ("That's the first time in history a man ever gave himself the hotfoot," he says about the Reichstag fire.)

Critics, then and now, were often outraged. James Agee thought much of the film was "in rotten taste," while contemporary critic Richard Corliss found Plummer's guided tour especially irksome, complaining, "The rise and fall of the Third Reich is capsulized into a monologue on Nazi architecture, with each building prompting a puerile gag."

One mustn't forget, however, that Wilder began as a reporter, and what seems callous or condescending in these American characters may be just a reflection of things he saw and heard during his tour of duty in postwar Germany. The debate among the politically diverse U.S. delegation before their plane lands in Berlin, for example, is as lively as anything one hears on today's Sunday-morning news forums. ("If you give a hungry man a loaf of bread," barks the pro-labor liberal, "that's democracy. If you leave the wrapper on, it's imperialism.")

What's surprising about *A Foreign Affair* is how evenhanded it is in portraying all three sides of its postwar-Berlin triangle. No one is particularly likable, yet—as Jean Renoir once said—everyone has his (or her) reasons. For someone whose family suffered so much at the hands of the Germans, Wilder is remarkably sympathetic to their plight, even to the point of acknowledging a certain undying verve. After the jolt of those aerial shots of Berlin, could even a 1948 audience remain unmoved by the subsequent scenes of eager, thronging black-market traders near the Brandenburg Gate, or the squalor of Erika's torn-up living quarters? Thoroughly demoralized, the former enemy population is easy prey for the libidinous American military presence. In a world of moral absolutes, Congresswoman Frost might be justified in tsk-tsking all she surveys: soldiers and *frauleins* cozying up by the dozens, baby carriages proudly sporting

American flags. But in a ghost of a city like postwar Berlin, the old rules of conduct simply don't apply. Even the sexist, gleefully exploitative American soldiers can be forgiven their peccadilloes; as Colonel Plummer argues, "You can't pin sergeant's stripes on an archangel."

A Foreign Affair is centrally about the indoctrination of Phoebe Frost—symbolizing a sheltered America—into this terrain of harsh postwar realities. The contrast between Phoebe and the worldly, bitter Erika is memorably expressed when the congresswoman, posing as a giggly *fraulein*, enters Erika's smoky star venue, the Club Lorelei, escorted by two girl-hungry soldiers she's encountered. With composer Frederick Hollander at the piano, Dietrich sings "Black Market," a brilliant Brechtian tune that combines the decadent defiance of pre-Hitler Berlin with the cold facts of the present crisis. The lyrics are both bleak and sultry:

> *I'm selling out, take all I've got—*
> *ambitions, convictions, the works.*
> *Why not?*
> *Enjoy these goods,*
> *for boy, these goods*
> *are hot!*

Exquisitely staged and lit, the Dietrich performance has a soul and authenticity that make Arthur's exaggerated harrumphing seem even more inappropriate and absurd. The two women will later become rivals over the unworthy Pringle; Wilder's genius stroke is his shaping of a comic romantic triangle into a metaphor for the confrontation between a paternalistic, innocent America and a war-ravaged, unsentimental Germany.

The plot mechanics are set in motion when Phoebe, having heard rumors that Erika is a former member of Hitler's inner circle and is now being shielded by an American officer, demands something be done during a briefing with Colonel Plummer. When Plummer insists that Erika's situation is a delicate security matter, Phoebe turns to Pringle—whose smooth talk at the Lorelei has led her to believe he's "the only soldier I can trust"—in her quest to get some answers. The congresswoman and the captain keep a stakeout outside Erika's building, and the two women meet face to face when Pringle accidentally signals to his German paramour by hitting the horn on his Jeep. Pringle manages to alert Erika to what's happening, and she wickedly taunts the prim legislator: "I see you do not believe in lipstick . . . and what a curious way to do your hair, or rather not to do it." At this moment, we note a different side of Phoebe, a surprisingly vulnerable side. Rather than express outrage, she succumbs to vanity. "I suppose I do look awful without makeup. We were only allowed sixty pounds of luggage, we had to eliminate unessentials."

Right then, Pringle calculates that Phoebe can be seduced away from her pious mission. "Who wants perfume?" he unctuously assures her. "Give me the fresh wet smell of Iowa corn right after it rains." Iowa, in fact, is a running joke throughout *A Foreign Affair*; for Wilder, it's the very kernel of American ingenuousness and bland, well-meaning, untested virtue. During their stakeout, Phoebe waxes nostalgic about pickled peaches and 4-H clubs while Pringle grimaces, then delivers one of Wilder's shockingly modern, black-comic gems: "We had the lowest juvenile delinquency rate in the country till two months ago. A little boy in Des Moines took a blowtorch to his grandmother. Fell clear down to sixteenth place—it was humiliating." Even Iowa, it seems, is not immune to the horrors of the post-war era.

One of *A Foreign Affair*'s best-written scenes comes just after Phoebe's initial encounter with Erika, when she determines to search for the army's files on the singer in the middle of the night. As Phoebe pores through the file drawer and Pringle awaits his imminent exposure, the captain launches a preemptive strike in his own defense: ". . . during the war [a soldier] couldn't go fast enough for you. Get on that beachhead, get through those tank traps, get across the Rhine. Step on it, step on it. Faster, a hundred miles an hour, twenty-four hours a day, through burning towns and down smashed autobahns. And then one day the war is over and you expect him to jam on those brakes and stop like *that*! Well, everybody can't stop like that. Sometimes you skid quite a piece, sometimes you go into a spin and smash into a wall or a tree and bash your fenders and scrape those fine, shiny ideals you brought from back home."

Pringle goes on to question whether straitlaced Phoebe is qualified to sit in judgment on men whose innocence has been vanquished by the chaos of war. She responds by confessing her own loss of innocence to a liberal Southern Democrat colleague who seduced her in an effort to swing her vote. Pringle sees his opening and closes in on Phoebe. She tries to filibuster him, reciting "Paul Revere's Ride" and blocking his way by opening one file drawer after another, but the captain traps her in a corner between two drawers and gives her a deep kiss. The congresswoman yields the floor.

Like Georges Iscovescu in *Hold Back the Dawn*, and, later, Linus Larrabee in *Sabrina* and Leonard Vole in *Witness for the Prosecution*, Pringle exploits the desires of an innocent woman to serve his own pragmatic ends. Bewitched by the captain and his declarations of love, Phoebe lets the von Schlütow investigation slide; she even goes to the black market and sells her typewriter for a spangly, ill-fitting black evening dress. ("It's like a circus tent in mourning for an elephant that died," she laments.)

To celebrate their last night together in Berlin, Phoebe prods the captain into taking her to the wicked Lorelei, where she proceeds to get very drunk while listening to a jealous Erika sing another cogent Hollander song, "Illusions." Pringle is called away to an urgent meeting with Colonel Plummer, but the congresswoman continues to party, leading the club's entire clientele in a rousing chorus of her campaign theme song, "Ioway (That's Where the Tall Corn Grows)." This magical night comes to an abrupt close when the Lorelei is raided and Phoebe, accompanied by Erika, is carted off to the police station. Erika uses her clout with the German authorities to protect Phoebe from a public scandal, but not without a price. She brings the American back to her apartment and, coyly whistling one of Phoebe's favorite tunes, "Shine On, Harvest Moon," reveals that they're both after the same man. "Four hours ago, you were in a position to have [Pringle] court-martialed and send me to a labor camp," Erika taunts Phoebe at the end of a fiery speech about surviving the war. "Not now. Not anymore. Now you're one of us." After a final confrontation with Pringle, Phoebe walks off into the ruins of Berlin. Like Erika, she is now stripped of illusions.

One of the ironies of Wilder and Brackett's screenplay is that, just as Pringle has been exploiting Phoebe's innocent love to save his ass, the army has been using Pringle. The captain's affair with Erika is no secret to military brass; on the contrary, they've been hoping his indiscretion will help flush out one Hans Otto Bergel, a Nazi bigwig who is her former lover. Consequently, Pringle is ordered to forget Phoebe and continue playing the sitting duck until their prey is captured. In a suspenseful closing scene in the Lorelei, Bergel is apprehended in the nick of time. Colonel Plummer explains the charade to Phoebe, who reunites with Pringle while Erika works her considerable charm on her starstruck military-police escorts.

A FOREIGN AFFAIR'S ONE INSURMOUNTABLE DEFECT IS ITS insistence that Pringle develops a real fondness for the spinsterish Phoebe. The captain and the congresswoman begin the film on such opposite ends of the propriety spectrum that their eventual romance is never convincing. It's certainly no fault of Arthur's—she adroitly softens Phoebe's edges and makes her more engaging and comically touching as the film proceeds, while remaining true to her essential dowdiness. No, it's more a case of Wilder painting himself into a narrative corner by making Pringle such a bluff tough guy. To go from Dietrich's iconic vampishness to Arthur's small-town guilelessness is like quitting hard drugs cold turkey, and Wilder never gives Lund the cathartic jolt to make such a radical withdrawal believable. Instead, Pringle's transition comes in subtle increments that don't quite add up. There's the captain's pleasantly startled look when Phoebe gives him an enthusiastic series of good-night kisses. Then, his unabashed admission to Erika that he and Phoebe like to hold hands and sing "Shine On, Harvest Moon." Then, the tender way he adjusts Phoebe's gaudy evening gown and creates a shawl from an armchair slipcover. None of these little niceties, however, is consistent with the randy pre-Phoebe Pringle, the one who takes the birthday cake the congresswoman brought him from an old flame in Iowa and cynically trades it on the black market for a mattress for his German mistress's hovel, the one who purrs to Erika, "Why don't I choke you a little, break you in two, build a fire under you, you blonde witch." It's just too far a stretch to have Pringle eagerly shack up with a temptress holding dubious wartime credentials *and* succumb to the corn-fed adoration of a Phoebe Frost. Even Wilder seems to realize his error when, in the movie's final moments, Pringle nervously backs away from Phoebe's advances—in exactly the way she retreated from him in the army file room.

Still, if *A Foreign Affair* falters, it's from honorably attempting too much—to create wicked caricatures *and* make them human and poignant. Erika, Pringle and Phoebe are all wonderfully rich archetypes, representing the survivors, the warriors and the observers of a great and tragic epoch. Wilder's genius is in making their three-way skirmish so funny and full of personal emotion.

FROM THE BEGINNING OF THE PROJECT, BRACKETT DISAPproved of his partner's unflattering portrait of the U.S. Army presence in Berlin. Wilder felt he was just scratching the surface and, to this day, he believes there's nothing particularly outlandish about his lusty *Foreign Affair*. "The affair with the German girl?" he responds. "They were not in bed. Of course, he did swap the cake that his fiancée in Iowa sent him through Jean Arthur, he swapped it for a mattress because he could be having Marlene but there was no bed to be had. But driving a mattress in his Jeep through the destroyed Berlin—there's nothing censorable in that. An American officer, a German girlfriend—corrupt—and a mattress. A man doesn't want to go sleepless in Seattle. We just got away with it. There were very few times where I had to cut something because I lost a battle. I was not laughing behind their back—'Ha, ha, ha, they don't know what I did.' No. I have my own censorship that tells me this is ugly, this is *schmutzig*, this is dirty, it's not worth it, it degrades the picture, it degrades the writer and director—don't do it."

Wilder is bemused about questions of good taste in his films—and just a little envious—in light of everything that has come since his heyday. "If you are wondering how I got away with [*A Foreign Affair*], how did the Italians get away with *Last Tango in Paris*? I was not even in the same neighborhood, not even on the same planet! You remember how Miss Pauline Kael—somebody quoted it again because he did not like me—said that when she saw *Sunset Boulevard*, it made her puke? I always wanted to ask her: How did you feel about that butter job in *Last Tango in Paris*? Mr.

Ber-to-lucci—I kind of admired his nerve, because I could not even tell that to the front office."*

Despite Wilder's assertions, *A Foreign Affair* did not have a smooth ride with the Production Code Administration. They objected to the portrayal of a U.S. congresswoman getting drunk in an underground nightclub, hanging from the ceiling and getting arrested. They protested the depiction of occupation personnel dealing on the black market. They scorned the "over-emphasis on illicit sex that seems to run through most of the script," demanding that "it will be clearly indicated that John brings the mattress to Erika's apartment for some other reason than making the bed more comfortable." They picked apart Hollander's "Black Market" lyrics, deleting phrases like "thousand little pleasures."

Wilder and Brackett agreed to eliminate a number of offending lines, such as "There's the kind of dish makes you wish you had two spoons," and a reference to Congress as "a bunch of boobs that flunked out of law school." But, as often happened, the filmmakers found that by conceding on minor details they could distract the censors from the larger fight. Even when viewed today, their Berlin farce is remarkably irreverent.

A FOREIGN AFFAIR DEBUTED AT NEW YORK'S PARAMOUNT Theatre on July 1, 1948, to mostly positive reviews. For once, Bosley Crowther got it absolutely right when he noted, "Under less clever presentation, this sort of traffic with big stuff in the current events department might be offensive to reason and taste. But as handled by the Messrs. Brackett and Wilder . . . it has wit, worldliness and charm." The *New York Post*'s Archer Winsten declared it "Hollywood's most thoroughly enjoyable picture of the year," while *The New Yorker* confessed, "Except for an occasional nagging thought that maybe Berlin isn't precisely the proper locale for a farce these days, I had a pretty good time."

But a number of critics fell into the Agee camp of offended sensibilities. The *Morning Telegraph*'s Leo Mishkin complained, "I just don't think the

---

* Kael's review of *Sunset Boulevard* is actually mostly positive—perhaps Wilder is reacting to her statement that "the whole enterprise exudes decadence like a stale, exotic perfume." The *Last Tango* reference harks back to Kael's highly publicized rave review.

notion of an Army captain playing around with a woman once connected with Hitler's entourage lends itself very well to farce." And *Cue*'s review oozed with vitriol, branding the picture "a gutter romance as messy as a bagful of soiled laundry" and its three central characters "thoroughly repulsive."

This sort of outrage went on for decades. In his 1975 book on screenwriters, *Talking Pictures,* Richard Corliss said, "This is the kind of film that can turn one away from a director's or writer's entire body of work. *A Foreign Affair* offers Wilder at his most vile." Corliss spends almost half his review complaining about Wilder's treatment of Jean Arthur, who he says is "photographed with all the gentleness of a mug shot." In his influential ranking of directors in *The American Cinema,* critic Andrew Sarris also singles out the way in which Wilder "thoughtlessly brutalizes" the veteran star.

Sarris and Corliss act as if Arthur had no say in the creation of Phoebe Frost when, from that fussy comic ritual she performs in the opening minutes, it's clear she and Wilder are on the same wavelength. True, Phoebe never gets to let her hair down—maybe Wilder thought that was too much a cliché—but she does become increasingly charming and vulnerable as the film proceeds. Some forty years after the fact, Wilder says, Jean Arthur called him from her home in Carmel after seeing *A Foreign Affair* on television. It was a wonderful film, she gushed—even her closeups were wonderful. Could he ever forgive her for her behavior? Wilder answered that there was nothing to forgive.

Whether Arthur could forgive Dietrich is another question, for in *A Foreign Affair* the German star gives one of the great iconic performances of her film career. At the age of forty-six, the 1930s femme fatale never looked better in her form-fitting spangled gowns, and her musical performances are among her most spirited and hypnotic. Whatever hesitation she had about playing a notorious Nazi, it doesn't show in the rich complexity, wit and larger-than-life allure she brings to the role of Erika; in fact, her nonjudgmental approach to the character probably added to the controversy surrounding Wilder's satire. Universally praised by the critics, Dietrich's performance landed her on the cover of *Life.*

Predictably, the U.S. military was not amused by Wilder's unabashed treatment of its activities overseas. Exhibition of the picture in postwar

Germany was banned by American occupation forces. Stuart Schulberg, who worked with Erich Pommer in evaluating films, said, "We could not excuse a director who played the ruins for laughs, cast Military Government officers as comics, and rang in the Nazis for an extra boff." He called Wilder "crude, superficial, and insensible to certain responsibilities which the world situation, like it or not, has thrust on 'America's Ambassador of Good Will'—the movies," adding, "Berlin's trials and tribulations are not the stuff of cheap comedy."

"I was in the army and I was in Berlin," Wilder argues, adding that had the military voiced any objections beforehand "I would have said: 'All right, this is fiction, but let me tell you things that I observed that are absent.' It is not just the American or the Russian occupiers that behave like this. Every occupying, victorious army rapes, plunders, steals—that is a rule that goes way back to the Persians."

A Foreign Affair finally opened in Germany in 1977, to enthusiastic critical and popular support. "They loved it," Wilder says. "It was not so much anti-German—it was anti-Nazi. The Dietrich character was much smarter than a Nazi-convinced female."

In the States, *A Foreign Affair* did only modest business, most likely because it was such a difficult film to pin down. No doubt many Americans were dubious about a romantic farce set in postwar Berlin, and others likely took the side of critics who were put off by Wilder's assault on American institutions. Nonetheless, the film was nominated for two Oscars, for its screenplay and for Charles B. Lang Jr.'s artful, atmospheric photography. (That same year, *The Emperor Waltz* was nominated for its costume design and musical score.) Dietrich, nominated but once for an Oscar, in 1931, was overlooked again.

IN THE MIDST OF FILMING *A FOREIGN AFFAIR*, WILDER began receiving late-night phone calls from a familiar voice. Audrey Young had gotten the break of her life, as a singer with the great Tommy Dorsey Orchestra. But the schedule of one-night stands was grueling, and the charm of hanging out with the boys quickly wore thin. Feeling lonely late one night after a gig in Pennsylvania, Audrey picked up the phone and dialed Billy's home number—collect. Billy welcomed the call, even though he had to be on the set early the next morning. Audrey phoned several more times—always collect—from various gloomy hotel rooms, and Billy was always glad to take the call, even if he was already fast asleep. He barely spoke of the film—he was more interested in Audrey's life on the road. To his amusement, Audrey had picked up the latest musicians' slang on her travels, phrases like "gone" and "real gone." "What does this mean? 'Gone'?" Billy would ask. Like a scene out of *Ball of Fire*.

Audrey returned to Los Angeles in February, just as *A Foreign Affair* was wrapping production, and she and Billy began dating again. In April, after completing post-production, Billy planned a vacation in Europe accompanied by his friend, the director Anatole Litvak. Audrey told him to have a wonderful time, but was miserable at the thought of Billy going away without her. But when he came back, in an uncharacteristically heartfelt moment, he told Audrey how much he had missed her. For the first time, Audrey believed they might actually have a future together.

THIRTEEN

Partners at Sunset

IF CHARLES BRACKETT HAD PREVAILED, *SUNSET BOULEVARD* might have been the laugh riot of 1950. Always eager to attract a mass audience, Wilder's partner envisioned their new project as a frothy comedy about the misadventures and ultimate triumph of a faded silent-movie queen seeking a comeback in modern-day Hollywood. Their first choice for the role was none other than Mae West, the salty sex farceur who had been one of Paramount's biggest box-office draws in the 1930s but had not made a picture since 1943.

True to form, Wilder wanted to do something with more edge, and his cause was furthered when West turned down the project, incensed by the idea of playing a woman past her prime. The director found a new ally in D. M. Marshman Jr., a *Life* magazine reporter and film critic who often sat in on Wilder's afternoon bridge games. Marshman had a suggestion: What if Brackett and Wilder's silent-movie goddess began an affair with a young man—say, a struggling screenwriter, perhaps from the Midwest? Now *there* was an idea with some cheek, some daring—on that basis, Marshman was invited to join the team.

Describing the genesis of the script, Brackett noted, "Wilder, Marshman and I were acutely conscious of the fact that we lived in a town which had been swept by a social change as profound as that brought about in the Old South by the Civil War. Overnight, the coming of sound brushed gods and goddesses into obscurity. We had an idea of a young man stumbling into a great house where one of these ex-goddesses survived. At first we saw her as a kind of horror woman . . . an embodiment of vanity and selfishness. But as we went along, our sympathies became deeply involved with the woman who had been given the brush by 30 million fans."

Even with Marshman's extra input, Wilder and Brackett had trouble determining where their dramatic setup would lead. Then, one day, while discussing Balzac's *Père Goriot*, Wilder had a sudden brainstorm: "Suppose the old dame shoots the boy?" Publicly, Brackett called this stroke of inspiration "a wonderful, splendid, beautiful thing." But in reality, *Sunset Boulevard* was slipping away from him. Like *A Foreign Affair* before it, it was becoming darker, and more identifiably a Wilder film. Joe Gillis, the writer who ruefully exploits the wealth, loneliness and delusion of former cinema legend Norma Desmond, was as close to a movie alter ego as Wilder would ever create, harking back not only to his early years of struggle in Hollywood but to his gigolo stint in Berlin. (Joe and Wilder also share a background in journalism.)

Asked about the resemblances, Wilder seems weary of the question. "I was never mistaken for an undertaker," he huffs, referring to the first meeting between Joe and Norma. "I was never taken in by a lady with gushing oil wells." Regaining his patience, he urges, "Look, any writer, even if he writes about characters that don't correspond with him but remind him of somebody he knew, draws—willingly or subconsciously— on things he has seen and lived through. Just because he was a writer. . . . I *was* a writer at the very beginning, I had leather patches on my elbows not because it was chic but because there were holes in them. I submitted God knows how many scripts and synopses and was turned down, sure. But it was not quite as difficult then as it is now." Wilder seems almost envious of his *Sunset Boulevard* hero; for all Joe Gillis's career frustration, at least he had the advantage of an ongoing studio system to go up against.

As Wilder more freely admits, Joe's romance with a smart, attractive Paramount story analyst named Betty Schaefer also had a real-life connection, reflecting the director's own deepening relationship with Audrey Young. Like Audrey, Betty was a child of Hollywood, the daughter of a studio wardrobe woman. (Unlike Audrey, Betty also had a father in the business, a studio electrician.) And both Audrey and her screen counterpart had taken acting, diction and dancing lessons, and even had nose jobs, in the vain hope of launching a movie career.

"Come clean, Betty," Joe insists. "At night you long for those lost closeups, those gala openings." "Not once," Betty urges. "What's wrong with being on the other side of the cameras? It's really more fun." Sweet, levelheaded Betty is the antidote to the ego-driven dementia of Norma Desmond and her world, and Wilder's personal tribute to the woman who was about to become the most important partner of his life.

Nancy Olson, the then twenty-year-old UCLA student and Paramount contract player who portrayed Betty, cautions against too literal a comparison between the two women. "Only part of Betty Schaefer's story is modeled on Audrey. Really, Audrey and I are completely different people. Billy just used the fact that she had grown up with parents and grandparents who were part of the movie industry, and I think that she had had her nose operated on or something. He used all those very human, specific details to help make the character fuller, but the person was different. I don't think that Audrey would have ever been so naïve. She would have caught on to what Joe Gillis was about long before this character did. She was much more sophisticated a person."

As Maurice Zolotow has suggested, the Joe/Norma relationship also surely mirrored some of what Wilder was feeling as he grew increasingly serious about a woman sixteen years his junior. While Joe's plight recalls the director's own days of hunger, Norma Desmond's passion taps into something more immediate: Wilder's growing love for Audrey, tempered by doubts about their age discrepancy and the bitter lessons of his first, failed marriage. However mad she may be, Norma's dependence on Joe, both as professional collaborator and rejuvenating lover, is heartbreakingly real. The poignant side of Norma Desmond might not have emerged without Wilder's own concurrent struggle with questions of love and commitment.

After Mae West rejected the film that Brackett and Wilder were keeping under wraps with the joke title *A Can of Beans*, Wilder made a pilgrimage to the legendary Pickfair estate to woo one of the silent era's most beloved and prosperous stars, Mary Pickford. Now, however, the story concept had evolved to the point where the Joe Gillis role was at least as important as Norma Desmond. Pickford and her actor husband, Buddy

Rogers, were intrigued by this Hollywood tale, but insisted that Norma must be the movie's centerpiece if it was to serve as Pickford's big comeback vehicle. Wilder saw signs of potential trouble in the veteran star's haughty attitude and still girlish manner, and gingerly backed away from the situation. "I suddenly stopped reading [the script] and just said, 'You know, Mary, you can play anything. You really can. You can act rings around any actress. But, Mary, I just realized this is not on your level. It's not up to your caliber.'" It was a snow job worthy of Joe Gillis.

Next, Wilder went to Pola Negri, the vivacious Polish star of such silent dramas as Ernst Lubitsch's *Madame Dubarry* and *Forbidden Paradise*, but the part came too uncomfortably close to the truth of her own forgotten glory—and besides, her accent was impenetrable.

It was fellow director George Cukor who came up with a name Wilder had somehow overlooked: Gloria Swanson. The former Mack Sennett comedienne and star of the silent classics *Male and Female* and *Sadie Thompson* had crossed paths with Wilder fifteen years earlier on his first Hollywood film, *Music in the Air*. Then, she was a movie goddess hoping for a comeback and he was a novice screenwriter, but unlike Norma Desmond and Joe Gillis, they had minimal contact. Now, Wilder was a celebrated filmmaker, and Swanson, a well-maintained fifty-two, was hostess of a local TV talk show in New York.

Wilder almost lost another Norma when Swanson was summoned to Paramount for a screen test. "I was revolted," the onetime silent diva told Maurice Zolotow. "Never made a test in my life." It was particularly galling that the request came from Paramount—"my old studio, you know, the one you might say I built," fumed Swanson. At the time, Brackett and Wilder had only a handful of pages to show the actress—in her various recollections, as few as three or as many as twenty-six—and the writers weren't even sure who would be killed at the end. Swanson said she recognized that Norma was a good part, but she was also "horrified" by the story's "anti-Hollywood" tone.

Again, Cukor came to the filmmakers' rescue. He reminded Swanson that Brackett and Wilder were the hottest creative team in Hollywood and insisted that Norma would be the greatest role of her career, adding, "If they ask you to do ten screen tests, do them, or I'll personally shoot you." Swanson relented, and the test went splendidly.

Brackett and Wilder now had their Norma but, on April 11, 1949, two weeks before shooting was to begin, they lost their Joe. The filmmakers had cast a magnetic young actor from the New York stage, Montgomery Clift, just before he shot to movie stardom in Howard Hawks's *Red River.* As production loomed closer, Clift got cold feet, claiming he was incapable of playing a man in a relationship with a woman twice his age. In truth, *Sunset Boulevard* may have been too uncomfortably close to reality, for Clift was involved in a romantic affair with aging torch singer Libby Holman, whose own turbulent life (including the accidental shooting death of her husband, an R.J. Reynolds tobacco heir) rivaled that of Norma Desmond.

Whatever the reason, Clift was gone, leaving the filmmakers in a desperate scramble to replace him. Wilder turned first to Fred MacMurray, whom he had so successfully cast against type in *Double Indemnity*, but MacMurray was squeamish about playing a kept man. Then, in a surprising move, the director offered the part to Gene Kelly—but MGM wouldn't hear of releasing its big musical star. Finally, Wilder honed in on Paramount contract player William Holden, whose early splash in 1939's *Golden Boy* was followed by ten years of forgettable and minor movie roles. Wilder had run into Holden occasionally on the studio lot, but knew little about the actor; after a few drinks together, he decided Holden had the depth and intelligence to be a persuasive Joe Gillis.

As Holden biographer Bob Thomas tells it, Holden read the uncompleted *Boulevard* script and told Wilder, "I like it. I'll do it. Let's go!" But Wilder recalls Holden being resistant to playing second fiddle to a has-been like Gloria Swanson; according to Zolotow, studio head Henry Ginsberg had to order the actor to play Gillis. Whatever initial resistance there was on either side, Wilder was pleased with the final outcome. "I liked his performance enormously," he smiles. "He looked like a writer, he wore the suits like it, he talked like it."

There was one hitch in the combination of William Holden and Gloria Swanson. Holden was just turning thirty-one, and Gillis was supposed to be a callow twenty-five. Swanson, meanwhile, looked years younger than fifty-two. The former silent star balked at the suggestion that she be made up to seem older; a woman like Norma Desmond would have maintained her looks, she argued. In deference to Swanson, Holden's hair and makeup were altered to make him appear younger.

Wilder cast his ingenue, Nancy Olson, on pure instinct. "He had seen my screen test at the studio," she recalls. "I don't know if he saw the little picture that I did. Paramount had loaned me to 20th Century–Fox for a picture called *Canadian Pacific* with Randolph Scott, who was older than my father—*much* older than my father. They cast me as an Indian half-breed, and I was a Scandinavian, blond, blue-eyed girl. It was during the summer, so it didn't interfere with school. So I went back to school, and then the studio told me that I was going to do this film with Bill Holden and Gloria Swanson—I didn't know who she was.

"Billy cast me without really talking to me, which seems, when I look back and think about it, rather strange. But he was looking for a particular quality. Also, I'd been having lunch a couple of times a week at the commissary, and he had lunch there every day. He was probably observing me carefully, and I was not even aware of it.

"By the way," Olson continues, "I don't think that my persona—i.e., the Betty Schaefer character—is typical of any of his films. That girl is not someone who truly interests him. . . . And yet, he was extremely precise in casting me in that role. I was to be an obvious juxtaposition to Gloria, to Norma Desmond—I was to be a *complete* contrast. That's what he wanted in my tone of voice, in the way I looked, in my manner, in the fact that I was a student at UCLA, which therefore gave me a credibility that I could be a writer. . . . It was all very apparent to him. He put me in the role, and I never had the feeling that he was dissatisfied."

The novice actress found the Wilder working atmosphere "extremely friendly, extremely professional, extremely down-to-business, but with a great spirit of fun and joy." Looking back, Olson laughs, "I was too stupid to realize how lucky I was. And certainly too inexperienced."

Another critical casting choice was Erich von Stroheim. Six years had elapsed since *Five Graves to Cairo,* and now Wilder felt comfortable enough with the onetime silent-film titan to ask him to take what some regarded as a cruelly demeaning role. Max von Mayerling is Norma Desmond's imperious butler and chauffeur; midway through the story, we discover he is also her ex-husband and former director. In the film's most audacious intermingling of art and real life, von Stroheim was once Swanson's director on *Queen Kelly,* a provocative 1928 silent feature financed by Swanson's then lover, Joseph Kennedy, who removed von Stroheim and temporarily abandoned the project with the advent of sound. When Norma Desmond unveils a giant movie screen in her living room, the film she chooses to demonstrate that "we didn't need dialogue, we had *faces*" is *Queen Kelly*.

Von Stroheim was not insulted by his assignment—he treated it with as much diligent seriousness as his own great silent-film roles. It was von Stroheim's idea that Max would be the author of the ever flowing fan letters that keep Norma's illusions of undying fame alive. But Wilder drew the line at von Stroheim's suggestion that Max be shown washing Norma's lingerie and caressing it in lascivious closeup—the sort of touch that outraged and titillated viewers of early von Stroheim classics like *Foolish Wives* and *Blind Husbands*. Von Stroheim was on less secure ground when it came to his driving scenes. "Erich didn't know how to drive, which humiliated him," Swanson recalled, "but he acted the scene, and the action of driving, so completely that he was exhausted after each take, even though the car was being towed by ropes the whole time." Despite the tow car's assistance, von Stroheim still managed to crash the vintage auto into the Paramount gate.

The von Stroheim/Swanson connections are not the only elements of real Hollywood lore in *Sunset Boulevard*. Wilder recruited yet another director, Cecil B. De Mille, for the scene in which Norma returns to the Paramount lot, thinking the studio wants to talk about her huge, inept screenplay of *Salome* when all they want to do is rent her vintage Isotta-Fraschini car with the leopard-skin upholstery. De Mille, a silent-era survivor who prospered by catering to the mass audience's taste for broad, lavish epics simultaneously condemning and showcasing sex and violence, is seen on the set of the Paramount film he was directing at the time, *Samson and Delilah*. When Norma descends on his soundstage, he's kind and solicitous—he has a history with her, just as he has with the real Gloria Swanson, whom he directed in *Male and Female* and *The Affairs of Anatol*. In a backhanded compliment, Wilder noted, "De Mille . . . was total perfection. He was disciplined and gave a subtler performance, I thought, than any of the actors in the films he directed ever gave." De Mille was paid $10,000 for one day's work. "Then we required one more closeup," Wilder recalls. "I asked him to come back and do it. He understood. It was the shot outside the stage where he says good-bye. He came back. For another $10,000."

Wilder had also hoped to get Hedy Lamarr, the costar of *Samson and*

Delilah, to appear as herself, being told by De Mille to surrender her chair to Norma. But Lamarr's asking price was $25,000; as Wilder remembers it, even the use of her name would have cost $10,000. And so, Norma winds up sitting in De Mille's chair, for that memorable shot where a boom mike ruffles the peacock feather in her hat and she angrily pushes it away.

Adding to the film's pungent atmosphere of moldering nostalgia, Wilder hired three former silent-film greats for the cameo roles of Norma's bridge partners, whom Joe rudely nicknames "the Waxworks": Anna Q. Nilsson, who starred in Raoul Walsh's first feature, *Regeneration*; H. B. Warner, who played Christ in De Mille's 1927 *The King of Kings* and was Swanson's leading man in *Zaza*; and the great silent clown Buster Keaton, still a few years away from his mid-fifties rediscovery. "Waxworks is right," Swanson recalled Keaton muttering, to peals of laughter from the bridge party.

For the climax, Wilder wanted to show Hollywood's two reigning gossip columnists, Hedda Hopper and Louella Parsons, fighting to use the phones in the Desmond mansion. Hopper quickly agreed, but Parsons, worried about being upstaged because her rival was a former actress, declined the offer.

At one point, the New Year's Eve party scene was slated to include Hollywood songwriters Jay Livingston and Ray Evans, singing a specially commissioned tune, "The Paramount-Don't-Want-Me Blues." (Sample lyric: "I got those David-Selznick-needs-me / And-though-Dore-Schary-heeds-me / It's-my-laundry-job-that-feeds-me blues.") Perhaps mercifully, Livingston and Evans didn't make the final cut.

All of these real reel-life elements give *Sunset Boulevard* an immediacy and authenticity like no "inside Hollywood" film before it. As Wilder matured as a director in the 1940s, his mise-en-scène became more and more documentarylike: the gloomy off-roads of L.A. in *Double Indemnity*; the desperate trek up Third Avenue in *The Lost Weekend*; the shocking ruins of Berlin in *A Foreign Affair*. Now, his documentarian impulse extended to his characters.

Swanson saw that vividly when she tried to calm De Mille's fears about his *Sunset Boulevard* acting assignment by telling him to just be himself. "I grasped with fearful apprehension, for the first time, that the same certainly applied to me to a great extent, that I would have to use all my past experience for props, and that this picture should be a very revealing one to make, something akin to analysis. Billy Wilder deliberately left us on our own, made us dig into ourselves, knowing full well that such a script, about Hollywood's excesses and neuroses, was bound to give the Hollywood people acting in it healthy doubts about the material or about themselves, depending on their individual security. The more you thought about the film, the more it seemed to be a modern extension of Pirandello, or some sort of living exercise in science fiction."

That same harsh reflection of reality even extended to Holden. How far, after all, was Joe Gillis from a studio contract player floundering in unrewarding film roles? When Holden told his director he was having trouble getting a handle on the character, Wilder replied, "That's easy. Do you know Bill Holden? . . . Then you know Joe Gillis."

The Paramount gate, the set of *Samson and Delilah*, the fabled Schwab's Pharmacy, the streets of L.A.—all these actual locations play key roles in Brackett and Wilder's Hollywood story. But one location stands apart from the movie's verisimilitude: Norma Desmond's big, decaying mansion, which stood not on Sunset but *Wilshire* Boulevard. Built for $250,000 in 1924 by William Jenkins, the Renaissance-style structure was bought by J. Paul Getty in the thirties and given to his second wife as part of their divorce settlement. The swimming pool was added for the film, on condition that the studio pave it over and restore the grounds after shooting was completed. But the former Mrs. Getty decided she liked the pool and accepted it as a gift from Paramount (with a few alterations); it later made another famous appearance in the 1955 James Dean movie, *Rebel Without a Cause*. In 1957, the mansion was torn down, to be replaced by the twenty-two-story Getty Oil Company office building.

The Desmond estate is larger than life, certainly larger than anything in Joe Gillis's mundane, bitter life of cramped garden apartments, studio rejections and close escapes from creditors. But, even more than the sultry, film noir L.A. of *Double Indemnity*, Norma's domain conjures up Wilder's Germanic film roots. Just as his compatriots Edgar G. Ulmer and Curt Siodmak enriched the American horror film, Wilder taps into the Gothic tradition to make of *Sunset Boulevard* an unsettling hybrid of modern Hollywood story and macabre fright yarn. After all, this is a movie that begins with a corpse floating face-down in a swimming pool, the camera looking up at his grotesque expression of shock. What's even more startling is that the victim is narrating the story of his own demise.

Images of *The Old Dark House, Frankenstein, Dracula* and countless haunted-house tales spring to mind as Joe Gillis turns into the long drive-way of the Desmond home, after eluding two repo-company goons in a high-speed chase. Joe assumes the place is abandoned, observing on the soundtrack, "A neglected house gets an unhappy look—this one had it in spades." But then, a woman's voice calls out, "You, there! Why are you so late?" Hidden behind the blinds of her second-story window, with only her sunglasses clearly in sight, she looks a bit like the gauze-wrapped Invisible Man. A bald man with a daunting German accent summons Joe to the front door—another horror staple, the eerily faithful manservant. "If you need any help with the coffin, call me," he mysteriously offers.

Before he can explain himself, Joe is beckoned up the massive marble staircase, past rutted columns and ornate candelabra. Norma Desmond stands in near darkness outside her bedroom door, her head wrapped in a spotted turban. She leads Joe into her riotously baroque chambers, past her swan-shaped bed, toward a roaring fireplace and the massage table where a small body lies beneath a shawl. A hairy arm swings down from the table; then, Norma uncovers the frozen face of her dead pet monkey, seen in freakish closeup. Joe has been mistaken for the man from the pet mortuary. With our knowledge of Joe's fate, the monkey's corpse, just a few feet from Norma's bed, is a chilling harbinger of things to come.

That night, other images of dread will appear: the living-room pipe organ that plays its own spooky tunes with the wind; the rats swarming at the bottom of Norma's empty swimming pool; the moonlit burial of the monkey, with Norma and Max in ghostly long shot. (A favorite Wilder anecdote has cinematographer John F. Seitz asking how to light the scene. "Oh, just your usual monkey funeral shot," the director offhandedly re-plied.)

"The atmosphere of the picture was a bit ghoulish," Swanson noted in her memoirs, but no one element is quite as otherworldly as her Norma. The character's alien quality is partly the result of her mastery of an art that has outlived its usefulness—the art of silent-film acting. Cloistered from the world of "talk, talk, talk," she can no longer separate her obsolete style of performance from her everyday style of living. When something angers or excites her, she takes on the mask of the silent diva, her eyes flaring, her fingers dancing. Unlike Wilder, who started in silent films, came to Hollywood speaking a foreign tongue and became one of its master wordsmiths, Norma refused to face the onslaught of sound. Instead, she retreated into her glorious past: The mansion is overrun with photos of Norma/Swanson in her prime and, for entertainment, she watches her old films, never tiring of the genius of their magnetic star.

Joe likens Norma to a sleepwalker, "still sleepwalking along the giddy heights of her lost career." Sustained by the fan letters Max secretly writes, she fancies herself still capable of playing the seductive Salome, as if time has stopped. Of course, for any great star, time *does* stop—the alchemy of celluloid passing through a projector at 24 frames per second produces immortality. It's even happening right now to Joe Gillis—we know he's dead, but there he is, reliving his odyssey so vividly that we forget the cold fact of his extinction. Onscreen, Norma possesses immortality, but, unable to cope with changing technology and the public's fleeting love, in her daily routine she's become one of the living dead.

When Norma discovers Joe is a writer, she lashes out at the enemy with a graphic harangue: "You've made a rope of words and strangled this business. But there's a microphone right there to catch the last gurgle, and Technicolor to photograph the red, swollen tongue!" Still, she's attracted to this young, handsome, insolent intruder, and demands he stay and read her mountainous *Salome* script. Joe thinks he's getting the better end of the deal: a place to stash his car and hide out from the loan company, plus more pocket money than he's had in months. But Norma already has her own predatory agenda: Joe wakes up the next morning in the room above her garage to find all his belongings have been moved in. (Norma's also paid the three months' back rent on his apartment.) Gradually, Joe becomes more entrapped. When the repo men find Joe's car and tow it away, Norma has the vintage Isotta-Fraschini restored to running order. On one of their outings with Max, Norma declares she's sick of Joe's bargain-basement wardrobe and takes him into town to buy an expensive new suit, a tux and a topcoat. (Joe's sense of degradation is heightened when an oily clerk suggests a more costly vicuña coat instead of camel hair: "After all, if the lady's paying . . ." In the next scene, Joe wears the vicuña.)

As if summoned by Norma, heavy rains leak through the ceiling of

Joe's garage apartment and force him to move into the mansion. Then, on New Year's Eve, Norma throws a fancy-dress party, complete with string orchestra, all for a single guest: Joe. The pair tango to "La Cumparsita," echoing Wilder's own days as an *eintanzer* attending to lonely older women. An hour later, Norma is drunk and Joe is feeling distinctly uneasy. Having heard enough of the faded star's extravagant plans for their future, Joe makes the mistake of insisting he has a life of his own, maybe even a girl he's crazy about. The argument escalates, and Norma staggers to her room. Joe grabs his coat and hitchhikes into town, in search of a real New Year's Eve party.

The blowout thrown by Joe's old buddy, assistant director Artie Green (Jack Webb), is a giddy contrast to the arid, oppressive realm of Norma Desmond. Joe, absurdly overdressed in his tux, enters a throng of raucous young people on the margins of the movie industry. There, he once again meets Betty Schaefer, the Paramount story analyst who rejected his tired baseball story, *Bases Loaded*, and helped accelerate the financial crisis that led him to Norma. But Betty's been looking over some of Joe's old scripts, and sees some potential in a story fragment about a struggling teacher. Clearly, Joe's been shut away with Norma too long—a little shop talk with Betty quickly sets off a sexual current, even if Betty *is* engaged to Artie. Joe's respite is short-lived, however, once he calls Max to have his belongings sent over to Artie's and learns that Norma has slit her wrists with his razor blade. Joe hurries back to the mansion to find Norma in bed sobbing, her bandaged wrists on prominent display. "I'll do it again! I'll do it again!" she cries in response to his attempts to calm her. Then, "Auld Lang Syne" comes on the radio. Joe approaches her bed and wishes her a tender Happy New Year. Norma's hands reach up and pull Joe down by the collar of his vicuña coat. They kiss. The emotional trap has been sealed.

In the next scene, the Joe Gillis we've known has already died. Wilder gives us our first "beefcake" shot of Holden, emerging from the now filled swimming pool, as Norma relaxes in the sun. It's clear the diva has gotten what she perhaps wanted all along: Joe has forfeited all traces of rebellion and become her bed partner. What motivates Joe? Fear? Pity? Greed? Surely not love—at best, what he feels is an awed respect for Norma's dynamism and former Hollywood majesty. In the fullest sense, Joe has become a kept man—a particularly sordid brand of antihero by 1950's repressed standards. Wilder was again testing the limits of Hollywood's Production Code, and this aspect of *Sunset Boulevard* evokes the ground-breaking silent work of one of its revered participants: Erich von Stroheim. Gigolos, opportunists and extramarital offenders were all an essential part of the risqué, cosmopolitan world of early Stroheim classics. Joe Gillis is a direct descendant of that tradition, but with a more tragic soul.

Interestingly, as Joe sacrifices his spirit, Norma regains some of her humanity. Invigorated by love, she begins to resemble a real woman—her histrionics have become noticeably subdued. Norma even exhibits a sense of humor—putting on a private show for Joe, she follows a rather embarrassing frolic as a Mack Sennett bathing beauty (another echo of Swanson's actual past) with a persuasive slapstick imitation of Charlie Chaplin.

Norma's brief interlude of relative normalcy ends the moment she comes to believe Cecil B. De Mille and Paramount Pictures want her back, and her descent into madness accelerates when she discovers Joe has been moonlighting on a script, "an untitled love story," with Betty. Her rabid possessiveness prompts Joe to shatter her illusions, leading to the movie's stark poolside killing. By film's end, Norma is completely insane, caught up in the delusion that the newsreel cameras waiting at the foot of her staircase are studio cameras photographing her first scene in *Salome*. "I'm ready for my closeup, Mr. De Mille," she announces, as Max directs her descent and her face melts into the lens like some supernatural vision from a Val Lewton horror movie.

"A dozen press agents working overtime can do terrible things to the human spirit," De Mille confides to an assistant after his awkward reunion with Norma earlier in the film. He remembers Norma as "a lovely little girl of seventeen with more courage and wit and heart than ever came together in one youngster." De Mille's observations are crucial to our understanding of the monster she has become. Thanks to Swanson's oversized performance, that monster is a unique hybrid: madwoman, dominatrix, succubus, age-obsessed ghoul and needy, overgrown child. Norma is also uniquely a creature of Hollywood, its ego gratification and its cruel fickleness.

Wilder recently observed that the tragedy of *Sunset Boulevard* is especially tied to the era in which it was made: "What made it work would not work in pictures today. . . . Back then, you could still dramatize, and have as a very valid background, the demise of silent pictures. In other words, this was when we had big stars like John Gilbert, who just disappeared with the advent of the talkies. And of course, Gloria Swanson was one of them. To dramatize that today, with some star who's simply out of the spotlight—it's not as good as having someone who was one of the biggest stars here, but suddenly there are no parts for her."

The movie is equally, of course, the tragedy of Joe Gillis, the failed screenwriter whose plans to return to his home state of Ohio are forever altered when he turns up that fateful driveway. The words could just as easily describe Wilder the new immigrant when Joe tells us how Betty Schaefer reminds him of his younger self: "She was so like all us writers when we first hit Hollywood, itching with ambition, panting to get your names up there. Screenplay by . . . Original story by . . . Audiences don't know somebody sits down and writes a picture—they think the actors make it up as they go along." In a typical Wilder moment of climactic nobility, Joe, consumed with shame, pretends Norma's money means more to him than Betty's love and sends her away crying, just before he packs his bags and leaves Norma. Unfortunately, as the gun-toting Norma hisses, "No one ever leaves a star."

DESPITE THE LAST-MINUTE CHAOS OF REPLACING MONTGOM-ery Clift, *Sunset Boulevard* "was one of those pictures that started falling into place," Wilder recalls. "After one weekend, we knew we had something."

"This was very risky storytelling," notes Olson, "risky in the sense that it was a little bizarre and it could have been farcical if it had not been played for ultimate reality. . . . But this had a kind of purity of intent, right from the beginning. Everybody just stuck to that, and it worked."

Wilder was particularly impressed by Swanson's artistry and gutsiness, and he showed his appreciation by having the entire cast and crew wear Chaplin-style derbies the day after she filmed her imitation of the Little Tramp. Later, during the shooting of her scene with the stuffed chimpanzee, Swanson pulled away the shawl covering the animal's face and was amused to find a derby perched on its head. On completing her final shot, Norma's indelible descent down the grand staircase, Swanson burst into tears. "I had a party planned for this last day," she recalled, "but then and there the cast and crew gave me one instead, right on the set. Everyone was in a great state of emotion."

Olson says that Swanson "was thrilled to be working with some of her old colleagues like De Mille and Keaton. As far as von Stroheim's presence on the set was concerned, it was interesting; he was so remote, so proper and polite. She was very correct with him, but also very easy. I found her easy with me, too. She had a lovely, graceful demeanor." Swanson was even thoughtful enough to remain in sight on the set as Olson filmed closeups of her character's devastating, climactic phone conversation with the jealous Norma. "She did it out of wanting everything to be right," Olson notes.

Behind the camera, Wilder's relationship with his writing partner wasn't nearly as cordial. Brackett was increasingly uncomfortable with the morbid, grotesque touches Wilder was adding to their latest creation. For Brackett, the most egregious was the brief montage Wilder had filmed showing Norma's radical preparations for her big-screen "return," complete with steam cabinets, electric treatments, rough massages and bizarre facial masks. Brackett felt the sequence was in poor taste and demanded it be cut. Wilder refused to budge.

The partners also bickered over a hole in their plotting. Recalls Wilder, "We had the ending of *Sunset Boulevard* blocked out, we knew this man who wanted a swimming pool, got a swimming pool, died in a swimming pool. We knew that she was going to shoot him. The script was not yet finalized; the last ten minutes—we had it but it needed work. [Brackett] was working on it and came to me and said he found the solution as to how this woman who is suicidal, and everybody is very careful about having no locks in the doors and no razors around, how she has a gun to shoot him. Brackett and Marshman came up with this very complex thing—that she got the gun from the old doorman at Paramount who recognized her. I said, 'Charles, this is too long, this is not gonna work.' And he said, 'Well, how are you gonna do it?!' I said, 'She says to him, "I got myself a gun," and she lifts the pillow and there's a gun there. How she got it, nobody knows. I don't give a shit. . . . I'm not going to go into side plots.' I said, 'Look, if it is a plot point and it gets too complicated, we can't use it. Let's just throw it away—she says, "I got myself a gun." ' " Once again, Wilder prevailed.

One section of *Sunset Boulevard* that Brackett objected to, however, never made it to the final release prints. The studio held a sneak preview of the film in January 1950 in Evanston, Illinois, and the audience reaction was a distressing surprise. As originally conceived, the film opened outside the receiving entrance of the Los Angeles County Morgue, as an ambulance pulls up and the body of Joe Gillis is deposited into a room with a dozen extras lying under white sheets. (Wilder filmed at the actual morgue, and remembers the workers there eating breakfast on the same slabs where the corpses rested.) An attendant writes out a name tag and places it on the new arrival's big toe. Slowly, the sheets covering the various corpses become transparent, and we can see William Holden and his dead neighbors: a young boy, a black man, an elderly fat man, etc. In voiceover, the corpses begin a conversation. The fat man says he was about to sign a lease on a retirement bungalow when he succumbed to a heart attack. The boy tells how he bet his friends he could stay underwater for more than two minutes—"and I did, too." The black man wants to know if Satchel Paige beat the White Sox. And then Joe Gillis starts narrating his strange Hollywood odyssey.

Just as in the disastrous first screening of *The Lost Weekend*, the audience took the wrong cue from the action onscreen. "At the moment they wheel [Holden] into the morgue and tie the name tag on his big toe, I heard laughter greater than I have ever heard in my life," Wilder remembers with sorrow. "The people roared with laughter. 'Aah' and 'hooo' and 'hah.' Today I know that, because nearly all humans are very ticklish on their big toe, they could not stop themselves from laughing."

Minutes into the film, the director skulked out of the auditorium and sat dejectedly on some steps leading to the rest rooms. Soon, a well-dressed woman passed by. Hoping for the best, Wilder asked what she thought of the picture so far. "I never saw such a pile of shit in all my life," was her blunt reply.

A second preview in Great Neck, New York, was equally bleak, prompting Wilder to scuttle his elaborate opening and begin the film with its celebrated voiceover by Holden as Joe's corpse floats in Norma's swimming pool. The startling shot of the openmouthed Holden hovering facedown in the water was filmed using what Wilder terms "an amazingly simple trick": A mirror was placed on the bottom of the pool, and a camera positioned above the water filmed his reflection.

Sunset Boulevard was previewed with its new opening in Poughkeepsie,

New York, and this time the audience got it. Then, in April 1950, it had its most important word-of-mouth screening, for an audience of Hollywood cognoscenti at a theater on the Paramount lot. "I've never seen so many prominent people at once in the projection room at Paramount as I saw [that night]," Wilder says. "Word was out that this was a stunner, you see. After the picture ended, there were violent reactions—from excitement to pure horror."

Gloria Swanson had a different memory of the evening: "These affairs are known for being morbidly restrained, devoid of the slightest overt reaction, but that night the whole audience stood up and cheered." Mary Pickford, she was told, was too overcome to stick around, but one fellow actress made her feelings very public: Barbara Stanwyck knelt down before Swanson and kissed the hem of her dress.

Louis B. Mayer wasn't nearly as taken with the film; in fact, he was outraged. The powerful head of MGM confronted Wilder outside the theater, shouting, "You bastard! You have disgraced the industry that made you and fed you. You should be tarred and feathered and run out of the country." (Wilder also remembers hearing something about horsewhipping.) The director's reply has variously been reported as "Fuck you" or the somewhat more creative "Go shit in your hat."

To this day, Wilder doesn't understand what made Mayer so upset. "It was not anti-Hollywood," he insists. "As a matter of fact, a cold fish like Mr. Cecil B. De Mille wants to withhold the truth from Swanson—he wants to protect her, he behaves very warmly toward her, very sympathetically. The writer, Holden, was writing schlock, and that girl who put him on the right track, she was right. I don't say anything derogatory about pictures. There's no filth, no dirt, no *National Enquirer* gossip—nothing. All the other Hollywood pictures, they're all about the casting couch. I've never seen one in my life. I don't do *that* kind of a picture. Look, the same thing happens in the aluminum business, it can happen in the families of dentists. . . ."

No matter Mayer's reaction, *Sunset Boulevard* became one of the year's most highly praised films. Thomas M. Pryor, in *The New York Times*, said, "*Sunset Boulevard* is that rare blend of pungent writing, expert acting, masterly direction and unobtrusively artistic photography which quickly casts a spell over an audience and holds it enthralled to a shattering climax." *Newsweek* saw fit to put the film and Gloria Swanson on its cover, six weeks prior to the movie's August opening. And James Agee called it "a very courageous picture" and "Hollywood craftsmanship at its smartest and at just about its best," while expressing reservations about its general audience appeal and about Wilder and Brackett's seeming inability to work from far inside themselves as artists. A strong minority opinion was filed by Philip Hamburger in *The New Yorker*, who deemed the film "a pretentious slice of Roquefort" and scorned the writers' "unhealthy contempt for aging stars."

Opening on August 10, 1950, *Sunset Boulevard* posted a nonholiday all-time house record of $166,000 at New York's Radio City Music Hall. Its seven-week total of $1,020,000 was the sixth-largest gross ever tallied at the landmark movie palace. But, to a degree, James Agee was right: Once out in Middle America, the film was at best a modest but unspectacular success.

Come Oscar time, *Sunset Boulevard* proved it had made a big impression in Hollywood with eleven nominations, including Best Picture, Best Director, Best Story and Screenplay, and nominations for all four of its principal players. Like Norma Desmond, Erich von Stroheim couldn't put his glorious past behind him; he threatened to sue Paramount for placing him in what he regarded as the demeaning supporting actor category.

Ironically, *Sunset Boulevard* found itself competing against another lavishly praised picture about an aging star—Joseph L. Mankiewicz's *All About Eve*. Each film took home a screenplay Oscar, but *Eve* grabbed the big trophies for Best Picture and Best Director while *Sunset Boulevard* had to console itself with Oscars for art direction and for Franz Waxman's evocative music score.

"Swanson didn't get it, Holden didn't get it, the director didn't get it," Wilder counts off, "but it is one of those pictures that gets better with time." Still mulling over the rivalry, he adds, "I think that people remember it better than *All About Eve*—a very good picture, and a very wonderful talent. It's a big shame that he kicked the bucket, Joe Mankiewicz. A very, very fine picture."

On Oscar night, much of the press attention focused on Gloria Swanson, who, along with the ferocious Bette Davis in *All About Eve*, lost to relative newcomer Judy Holliday in *Born Yesterday*. "It slowly dawned on me that [the press] were unconsciously asking for a larger-than-life scene or, better still, a mad scene," Swanson complained in her memoirs. "More accurately, they were trying to flush out Norma Desmond."

Although the role propelled her back into the public eye, Swanson lamented, "I had played the part too well. I may not have got an Academy Award for it, but I had somehow convinced the world once again of the corniest of clichés—that, on very rare artistic occasions, the actor actually becomes the part. Barrymore *is* Hamlet. Garbo *is* Camille. Swanson *is* Norma Desmond. Most of the scripts I was offered dealt with aging, eccentric actresses." Indeed, Swanson had only a handful of film roles after *Sunset Boulevard*, and her last appearances were in the 1973 TV movie *The Killer Bees* and as herself on a plummeting jet in *Airport 1975*. Her remarkably successful silent-film career notwithstanding, Gloria Swanson remains Norma Desmond in the minds of the great majority of moviegoers.

Unlike Swanson, Bill Holden's career skyrocketed after *Sunset Boulevard*. Nancy Olson tells the story of a young actor asking Holden for advice on becoming a star. "Well, you gotta have *it*," Holden is said to have answered. "What is *it*?" inquired the actor. "*It* is *Sunset Boulevard*," was Holden's terse reply.

Olson, who immediately costarred with Holden in three more pictures and would soon be married to composer Alan Jay Lerner, continues, "What happened was wonderful and fascinating. Bill emerged as a man of many colors. Now he was showing us that he could portray weakness and dishonesty, a little bit of depravity, sadness, lostness. Something happened to him after *Sunset Boulevard*—he became an honest-to-goodness, real star. And something more important happened to him. He caught the attention of Billy Wilder and became a true friend of Billy's."

As one friendship was forming, another was falling apart. For all their publicity as "the happiest couple in Hollywood," Charles Brackett and Billy Wilder had never had much in common, apart from their pride in their craft and their fondness for cribbage and word games. At the beginning, the elder Brackett had been something of a father figure, helping Wilder with his faulty English and protecting him from the Paramount bureaucracy. "Billy was a little in awe of Charles, and as far as I know, he's the only person Billy has ever been in awe of," says Barbara Diamond, the widow of Wilder's other longtime writing partner, I. A. L. Diamond.

"Charlie came from a certain kind of elaborate WASP background that Billy found a little intimidating."

The dynamic of the relationship changed considerably through the 1940s. Brackett bolted from one of Wilder's most celebrated projects, *Double Indemnity*. Wilder became an Oscar-winning director, and his return to Berlin to witness firsthand the brutal consequences of the war was a profoundly sobering experience. The human cruelty he observed gave rise to the dark sensibility of *A Foreign Affair* and *Sunset Boulevard*. Never a particularly patient man, Wilder was finding it harder than ever to deal with Brackett's squeamishness and trifling objections to his partner's increasingly skeptical outlook.

"Collaboration is like a box of matches," Wilder observes. "You take out a match and you strike it and you light your cigarette. But if you do that often enough, the surface on which you strike . . . it does not catch anymore—it is all used up. . . . It was a series of—never, never screaming fights, we still remained friends—but I thought I maybe needed another striking surface."

Maurice Zolotow says all the team's workaday intimates—their secretary, Helen Hernandez, Paramount executives William Dozier and Henry Ginsberg, production associate William Schorr—knew the breakup was coming, and that Wilder himself had broached the subject to Brackett years earlier. However, shortly before his death in 1969, in a bitter interview with writer-director Garson Kanin, Brackett insisted the announcement came as a complete shock. "I never knew what happened, never understood it, we were doing so well," Brackett lamented. "But we met one morning, as we always did, and Billy smiled that sweet smile of his at me and said, 'You know, Charlie, after this, I don't think we should work together anymore. I think it would be better for both of us if we just split up.' I could say nothing. It was shattering. And Billy—you know how he is, bright and volatile—got right into the business of the day, and we said no more about it. But it was such a blow, such an unexpected blow. I thought I'd never recover from it. And, in fact, I don't think I ever have."

Brackett insisted he and Wilder never had a serious quarrel, and said he would have gladly settled for just being his producer. "I loved working with him," he maintained. "It was so stimulating and pleasant. And such fun."

Wilder claims he wasn't alone in desiring the breakup; some Paramount executives, he says, thought the studio could get twice as many scripts by splitting up the team. But Brackett went on to sign a deal with 20th Century–Fox, where he produced *The King and I*, *Ten North Frederick* and *State Fair*, and co-wrote and produced *Niagara* and *Journey to the Center of the Earth*. In 1953, he, *A Foreign Affair* co-writer Richard Breen and *Ninotchka* co-writer Walter Reisch won the Oscar for their story and screenplay for *Titanic*. He also served in the prestigious post of president of the Academy of Motion Picture Arts and Sciences from 1949 to 1955.

After the split, Wilder and Brackett continued in public forums to demonstrate immense respect for each other. When Herbert G. Luft, a film editor, TV producer and survivor of the Dachau concentration camp, deemed Wilder's Hollywood output as "anti-American" in the fall 1952 *Quarterly of Film, Radio and Television*, it was Brackett who came to the defense of his former partner. Luft grumbled, "Like many Germans [*sic*], Wilder depicts only the weaknesses and the shortcomings of the American people, ridicules their habits, but never senses the strikingly salubrious strength of this vibrantly young republic." Brackett essentially told Luft to lighten up. "Predominant among Billy Wilder's qualities is humor—a fantastically American sense of humor," he countered. "It was the outstanding trait of the young man with whom I started to work some seventeen years ago. He was sassy and brash and often unwise, but he had a fine, salutary laugh. Also, he was in love with America as I have seen few people in love with it."

Brackett found himself in the unexpected position of championing the very films that had contributed to the breakup. Answering the charge that *Sunset Boulevard* "flays some of the finest creators of the silent screen," he said, "It merely records that time, which flays us all mercilessly, has not spared them." As for *A Foreign Affair*, he sounded downright enthusiastic about its portrait of American soldiers abroad: "There's larceny in their hearts, and fun in them and health in them. Does Mr. Luft want a glimpse of the truth about those young men? No. It evokes that horrid sound of laughter." Brackett never gave a more gracious performance in support of Billy Wilder.

In 1962, Wilder dramatically voiced his concern for his former partner when Brackett's Fox contract was abruptly canceled during a radical reorganization of the studio hierarchy. Wilder called a press conference at which he stated, "I cannot imagine any self-respecting artist, whether director, writer, actor, producer or musician, going to work for 20th Century–Fox under its present administration." In a wire to Fox president Darryl F. Zanuck, Wilder was even more blunt: "The sooner the bulldozers raze your studio, the better it will be for the industry," he jeered. Wilder's actions yielded some embarrassing publicity for Fox and were a boon to Brackett, who was paid for the remaining two years of his contract.

IRONICALLY, WILDER'S PROFESSIONAL MARRIAGE TO BRACKett headed toward the rocks just as he was considering making a commitment to Audrey Young. All through the early stages of preparing and shooting *Sunset Boulevard,* Audrey, in her words, "begged" a reluctant Billy to marry her. Midway through production, Billy told her he would give her his decision when the picture was finished—but, for now, she would have to be patient. No longer touring, Audrey visited the set every day—a welcome guest, since she and Billy were very much in love. One night, toward the end of filming, the couple went to a small dinner party at Romanoff's to celebrate the engagement of *Sunset* co-writer Marshman. Just before they entered the restaurant, Billy proposed.

The wedding was an extremely low-key, spontaneous affair. After *Sunset* wrapped, Billy and Audrey went on a road trip to Nevada with their friends the married designers Charles and Ray Eames, with a vague plan of getting married somewhere along the way. Billy stopped at a jewelry store in Encino and bought a plain gold band for less than twenty dollars. The party traveled all morning, and arrived in the small town of Linden, Nevada, at noon on June 30, 1949. "This looks like a good place for a marriage," Billy announced. They located a justice of the peace, and Ray Eames put together a bouquet from some backyard flowers. Audrey had brought a pretty dress, but Billy refused to let her change out of her blue jeans. "Either you get married like this, or you don't get married at all," he ordered her. Was this some kind of test? Audrey got married in her blue jeans. The wedding was reported the next day by columnist Louella Parsons, who called Audrey "one of the prettiest girls in town."

The couple went on to Lake Tahoe, and Audrey remembers them staying at an unfashionable old hotel, where they found an old pair of socks under the bed. Next morning, Billy and Charles Eames passed the time taking photos of Nevada landscapes until Audrey insisted Charles take some portrait shots of her and Billy. "I can't say that I really had a romantic time on my honeymoon, but it was beautiful, beautiful," Audrey recalled. "We remained there two days and then we drove home to Los Angeles." In retrospect, she concluded that Billy was self-conscious about getting married a second time and wanted to make as little fuss as possible out of the occasion. Despite its humble beginnings, the union of Billy Wilder and Audrey Young has been one of the longest-running marriages in Hollywood.

SINCE HIS ARRIVAL IN AMERICA, BILLY WILDER HAD ALWAYS worked with a writing partner, and he wasn't about to change. But after all those years of deferring to the elder Brackett, perhaps it was time to switch roles. The director found the first of a string of writing colleagues while listening to a play on his car radio. It was written by a thirty-three-year-old with no movie experience, Walter Brown Newman. Wilder called him in for a meeting. Newman was quiet but a good listener, which suited Wilder the raconteur just fine. He told Newman an idea he had for a movie about a Mafia boss with an embarrassing tendency to break out crying. The gangster seeks help from a psychiatrist and winds up spilling his most incriminating secrets. The punch line: Once the mobster is cured, he'll get rid of the shrink.

Newman laughed and agreed to develop the idea with his new mentor, but they couldn't make it work. So Wilder came up with another notion—an English nobleman who makes a fortune on the side as a television wrestler, the "Masked Marvel." Wilder thought it would make an ideal vehicle for Charles Laughton, and Newman recalled a meeting with the great, rotund actor during which Laughton literally fell out of his chair laughing. Unfortunately, the writing partners couldn't get the Masked Marvel concept to go anywhere. They agreed to go their separate ways, but not before Newman slipped in a story idea of his own: the tragedy of Floyd Collins.

In January 1925, Floyd Collins was exploring a cavern in Kentucky when he was trapped by falling rock. Still able to talk to the outside world, he was interviewed by a cub reporter from the *Louisville Courier-Journal;* his story became a national sensation, drawing thousands upon thousands of the curious to the cave-in site. As the media circus grew bigger, Floyd became weaker, and he died after eighteen days below ground.

After mulling it over for a week or two, Wilder contacted Newman and told him they'd be working together on a contemporary variation on the Collins incident. Joining in the sessions would be Lesser Samuels, a Paramount contract writer who was also a former newspaperman. Wilder himself would be tapping into all he'd learned about aggressive reporting as a journalist in Vienna and Berlin during the same period when the Collins story broke. The project, initially dubbed *The Human Interest Story,* came to be known as *Ace in the Hole.*

Instead of a cub reporter, the movie centers on Chuck Tatum (Kirk Douglas), a cocky newshound who has been canned from eleven big-city papers for reasons ranging from drunkenness to fooling around with an editor's wife. Tatum's convertible breaks down outside Albuquerque, New Mexico, which seems as good a place as any to try to get his career back on track. He offers his services to Mr. Boot (Porter Hall, the man on the train with Fred MacMurray in *Double Indemnity),* the milquetoast editor of the *Albuquerque Sun-Bulletin.* "I'm a two-hundred-and-fifty-dollar-a-week newspaperman," he announces. "I can be had for fifty." After getting the honest dirt on Tatum's past, Boot hires him for sixty.

Cut to Tatum's one-year anniversary at the *Sun-Bulletin,* a depressing milestone since he still hasn't found the big story that will propel him out of this arid burg. It's also the occasion for yet another colorful Wilder monologue, as the reporter bemoans the scarcity of chopped chicken livers, the New York Yankees, or even an eighty-first floor to jump from. To give Tatum a change of scenery, Boot sends him and young reporter Herbie Cook (Bob Arthur) out to cover an area rattlesnake hunt. What Tatum finds instead is a nest of human vipers.

On the road near the desert outpost of Escudero, Tatum and Herbie encounter Lorraine Minosa (Jan Sterling), a world-weary bleached blond who seems unusually nonchalant about the fact that her husband, Leo (Richard Benedict), has just been trapped in a mountain cave-in while looking for Indian pottery for his trading post. Smelling a story, Tatum is the first to enter the cavern and find Leo, who is stuck under a huge rock but remains in good spirits. Tatum takes Leo's picture and files a story high-lighting the fact that the mountain is an ancient Indian burial ground. "Ancient Curse Entombs Man" the next morning's headline blares, and soon tourists start flocking to the cave-in site. A construction engineer tells Tatum he can have Leo out in sixteen hours, but Tatum conspires with the corrupt local sheriff (Ray Teal) to prolong this golden opportunity by tak-ing the slower course of drilling through the top of the mountain. Tatum also promises the sheriff glowing coverage for his reelection campaign in exchange for sole access to Leo. That same morning, Lorraine prepares to leave her dead-end marriage while her husband can't chase after her, but Tatum convinces her she'd be a fool to abandon Escudero just as the place is getting hot.

Lorraine becomes an instant entrepreneur, charging admission to the burial site, selling souvenirs, and renting out space to a traveling carnival. The reporter has to literally wipe (or slap) the smile off her face to make her look the grieving wife. Tatum quits the *Sun-Bulletin* and sells his ser-vices to the New York paper that once fired him, but his big story doesn't have the ending he needs. Leo is dying, and the rescuers can't get to him in time. His ace in the hole's pathetic struggle haunts Tatum and, in an angry confrontation with Leo's unfeeling wife, the reporter is stabbed in the stomach with a pair of shears. Understandably distracted, Tatum neglects his news reports, and when Leo succumbs after six days of entombment, the human-interest story evaporates. Tatum offers up his confession to his New York paper, but no one will listen. He returns to the *Sun-Bulletin*, and peddles his services for nothing before collapsing to the floor, in a huge closeup.

WILDER, NEWMAN AND SAMUELS WORKED ON THE SCRIPT throughout the spring and early summer of 1950, with a production start date of July 10. An early draft shows Wilder still hanging on to the *Sunset Boulevard* idea of a talking corpse, in this case Tatum's being loaded onto a railway baggage car. "When you write the obit, lay it on the line!" his voice urges Boot and Herbie. "All you got on me! What I wanted and how bad I wanted it—put that in! What I did to get it—that goes in, too! Friendship—pity—conscience—don't let any of those things stop you! I never let them stop me!" Wilder also toyed with the idea of making Lorraine even greedier, having her beg Tatum not to reveal Leo's death so the carnival could run one more weekend. In one version, Lorraine is run over by a carnival truck; in the finished film, she simply walks away aimlessly amid the dust of the departing crowds.

Because Chuck Tatum dies in the end, the Production Code office was easy on the film, although it cautioned that the final scenes "would need a proper voice for morality." Their biggest concerns were with the mixture of "Indian medicine ceremonies with legitimate praying for the trapped man" and with the sheriff's pet baby rattler, since "many exhibitors have expressed their dislike for scenes showing snakes on the screen."

The $1.8 million picture was shot in forty-five days, many of them on location in Gallup, New Mexico. (The cave interiors were built on a soundstage.) Logistically, it was Wilder's most ambitious project yet, with some shots requiring 1,200 extras and 600 cars and trucks.

Kirk Douglas came to *Ace in the Hole* following his star breakthrough in *Champion*, bringing his usual high energy and intensity. "Working with Billy is *exciting*," he enthuses, "a kind of excitement I haven't found much with others—it's like working with a guy on a high wire. Holy Christ, it's dangerous, but somehow you feel you're not gonna fall. For example, he never had a full script—I never saw it. That was exciting: Gee, where's the other part of it? He knew and he eventually gave it to us, and you did it. And Billy has such a brilliant sense of humor—in all things, there was always that quick wit. I remember when I first approached the part, I said, 'Look, Billy, I think I'm being a little too tough with the character. I think maybe I ought to start out easy.' He said, 'Kirk, give it both knees. Both knees!' "

In one scene, Douglas gave it everything, to his costar's regret. The sequence called for Tatum to hand Lorraine her husband's anniversary gift, a cheap fur stole. Lorraine tosses it to the floor in disgust. Tatum picks it up and wraps it tightly around her neck. Douglas told Jan Sterling to let him know if he was choking her too much. They filmed the scene, and Douglas suddenly noticed that Sterling's face was blue. She fell to the ground and Douglas picked her up and slapped her face. "Why didn't you tell me I was squeezing too hard?" he cried. Sterling answered, "I couldn't. You were choking me."

Sterling brought just the right plain/pretty look and working-class attitude to the marriage-weary Lorraine. In return, Wilder gave her two of the movie's most memorable lines. "I've seen some hard-boiled eggs in my day," she tells Tatum, "but you—you're twenty minutes." And when Tatum orders her to go to Mass and make it look as if she's praying for her husband, Lorraine shoots back, "I don't go to church. Kneeling bags my nylons." Wilder credits the latter gem to his wife, Audrey.

Absent Charles Brackett's mellowing influence, *Ace in the Hole* became the most uncompromisingly bleak picture of Wilder's career since *Double Indemnity*, with two misanthropic leads whose relationship was even more deeply rooted in the desire for money than in the Cain story.

Wilder was so successful in portraying Tatum as a heel that many critics were unconvinced by the character's attack of conscience in the movie's final third. "Too cynical to believe even his own cynicism" was Andrew Sarris's verdict when he consigned Wilder to the "Less Than Meets the Eye" category in his 1963 ranking of American directors. (Sarris has since recanted, with sincere apologies.) But Wilder's antiheroes are never *just* heels; he understands their human frailty too well to deny them the potential for self-examination. No matter how repellent their behavior, Wilder usually provides a hard-knock backstory to show they haven't arrived at this moral quagmire all on their own—whether it's Georges in *Hold Back the Dawn*, Joe in *Sunset Boulevard*, or a Nazi adornment like Erika in *A Foreign Affair*.

Wilder even allows a tough cookie like Lorraine her excuses. Just out of the army, Leo found his wife working in a Baltimore saloon. "He told me he had a hundred sixty acres in New Mexico and a big business," she gripes. "Look at it! We sell eight hamburgers a week and a case of soda pop, and once in a while a Navajo rug." Every time she tries to break free from her stifling marriage, the love-struck dope tracks her down. Sure she's bad, but five years in Escudero can do terrible things to the human spirit.

The film is a little less explicit about Tatum's demons—one suspects they're a combination of restless ego and a weakness for alcohol, like Don Birnam's in *The Lost Weekend*. Tatum tries to start fresh in a humble setting, but New Mexico won't give him a break. Extending poor Leo's ordeal is a calculated risk for someone whose profession thrives on human tragedy. "Good news is no news," Tatum instructs rookie reporter Herbie.

However shady his past, Tatum has never before—we assume—been responsible for a man's death. As it becomes clear Leo's a goner, the reporter is constantly reminded of his sin by the pious atmosphere of the Minosa home, by the mirror image of Lorraine's venality, and most of all by the simple good-heartedness of Leo. When Leo is given his last rites, the camera closes in on the guilt-ridden Tatum, who is also dying. The change in Tatum is subtle, incremental—there's nothing superficial about Wilder's attitude, and it's certainly not a cop-out.

The primary villain in *Ace in the Hole* isn't Tatum or Lorraine, but the public's hunger for sensation, and the media's eagerness to feed it. It goes without saying that the theme Wilder explored in 1951 is timelier than ever in this era of tabloid-style stories like O. J. Simpson, the Menendez brothers, Tonya Harding and Lorena Bobbitt dominating the news media. The circus surrounding the Leo Minosa rescue effort is itself an essential character in *Ace in the Hole*, and its swelling size is one of the film's most artfully handled devices.

ACE IN THE HOLE OPENED AT NEW YORK'S GLOBE THEATRE on June 30, 1951, to largely negative notices. John McCarten in *The New Yorker* deemed it "a compound of unjelled satire, half-baked melodrama, and dialogue in which not even a dowsing rod could discover a vein of wit," and called Douglas "certainly the most preposterous version of a reporter *I've* ever seen." Bosley Crowther labeled it "one of the truly challenging pictures of this year," and praised "a spectacular job of visioning the monstrous vulgarity of mob behavior." But the *New York Times* critic took strong exception to the movie's distorted view of journalism: "the simple fact is that no reporter could get away with such a badly arrogant crime as the fellow engineers in this picture. The responsible elements wouldn't permit such a thing."

In a minority rave, *Saturday Review* hailed the film's integrity, linking it with *Greed*, *The Informer* and *The Treasure of the Sierra Madre*, "pictures that have come from Hollywood with an utter disregard for box-office values or potentialities." (Charles Brackett, in his 1952 treatise on Wilder, also found some literary antecedents for the film, stating that it was "in the vein of American self-criticism which has been a major current in our national literature since the days of *The Octopus* and *The Pit* and *The Jungle*.")

Saturday Review was certainly right about *Ace in the Hole*'s box-office value: It was the first indisputable flop of Wilder's career. Returns were so bad, Paramount took drastic action. Recalls Wilder, "Behind my back, because I was making a picture in Paris at the time, Mr. Freeman, head of the studio, changed the title from *Ace in the Hole* to *The Big Carnival*—like this is going to attract people. Without asking me! It was one of the reasons I left Paramount.

"It was a very good picture, with a strong, well-worked-out story," Wilder notes. "But people did not want to know, they don't want to be told that if there's an accident on the street and somebody's dying, before people go call for a doctor, they'll look at that tragedy with a curious morbidity. That's what I had there—the circus upstairs, the songs, people getting drunk and having fun. . . . I would say it was not an easily digestible subject—people were not running to the hors d'oeuvres to eat them, because they felt a little bit guilty.

"Having been at it for a long time," Wilder declares, "I don't delude myself. Usually when a picture doesn't work, you go around and you say: It was ahead of its time. The release was too close to Christmas. It was too close after Christmas, because people had spent their money on presents. It was a failure because there was so much sun and people wanted to go to the beach. And then it was a failure because it rained and nobody's on the streets. All kinds of excuses. The excuse in this picture must be that I chose a subject—the one split second when you decide what to do—and apparently it was the wrong picture for the time."

Kirk Douglas also reflects on the movie's failure. "I've often thought one reason why it wasn't a big smash here in the States was because, at that time, TV was not a very important factor—newspapers were important. And this, don't forget, depicted a ruthless newspaper man."

In a 1970s interview, screenwriter Walter Newman blamed the picture's timing. "It wasn't ahead of its time so much as it came out at a peculiar time. It came out in 1950 [*sic*], I believe, at the height of the McCarthy period and we had some very trenchant observations to make about certain aspects of hoopla involving most tragedies in our country, all countries, I suppose. We were shafted unmercifully by most of the newspapers—the heavies were newspaper men—and suddenly every newspaper man and every reviewer became a member of the State Department and said, 'How will this film look abroad?' "

Ace in the Hole looked quite good abroad, generating solid box office and high critical praise. London trade journal *Today's Cinema*, for instance, called it "American filmmaking at its most brilliant." Later that year, the film won the Golden Lion, the top prize at the Venice Film Festival.

"I ran into Billy many, many years later on the Goldwyn lot," Newman remembered. "I hadn't seen him for a while and he said, 'Boy, I really lost studio power on that one.' And then he said, 'Fuck 'em, it was the best thing I ever did.' " In his 1963 *Playboy* interview, Wilder called *Ace in the Hole* "the runt of my litter."

In spite of its domestic box-office failure, *Ace in the Hole* earned an Oscar nomination for its story and screenplay. Newman, who died in 1993, went on to write the screenplays for Otto Preminger's *The Man with the Golden Arm*, the hit comedy *Cat Ballou* and the Richard Gere drama *Bloodbrothers*, the latter two also gaining him Oscar nominations. Working with Wilder, he said, was "enchanting, illuminating, constantly exciting, filled with laughs, filled with good talk, constant surprises. . . . I think he's the very best of us in all departments." Newman never collaborated with the director again, but he always savored the memento Wilder gave him after their noble flop: the malacca cane Gloria Swanson twirled as Chaplin in *Sunset Boulevard*.

FOURTEEN

Direct from Broadway

BILLY AND AUDREY WERE LIVING BACK AT BILLY'S OLD address, 704 North Beverly Drive, now that Judith had moved east. The first years of marriage weren't easy for the former band singer, sixteen years her husband's junior and so new to his dazzling social circle. Their low-key hcneymoon had given her some inkling of what to expect: no sentimental gush and plenty of wisecracks. Legend has it that one morning she came in at breakfast and announced their first anniversary. "Please," Billy replied, "not while I'm eating."

Audrey's biggest rival for Billy's attention was the studio. A workaholic, he was apt to be up till all hours worrying over every detail of the next day's shooting. And, now that he had broken up with Charles Brackett, Billy had taken on the added burden of being his own producer. Audrey saw him through the disastrous first preview of *Sunset Boulevard* (and its eventual triumph), through the anxiety of finding a new collaborator, through the scathing reviews and dismal box-office returns for *Ace in the Hole*. Billy was not one to easily shake off problems and setbacks—the new bride would have to grit her teeth and learn to cope with his changing moods.

It was also clear to Audrey that she had married one of the smartest men in Hollywood. Billy could hold forth on a vast range of subjects—art, literature, politics, history, sports, movies, food, fashion, you name it. He could pinpoint the missing condiment in a gourmet meal, recommend a hot new gallery or advise on the best maker of Italian shoes. Audrey would have some catching up to do.

Billy's friends didn't make it easy. Having kept a scorecard of his various conquests over the past decade, they took bets on how long this folly of a marriage to a band singer would last. Marlene Dietrich was especially cruel. Though she and Billy had never been lovers, Dietrich took an instant dislike to the new Mrs. Wilder. Early on, at a dinner party, she made a big show of asking Audrey's astrological sign. Told it was Cancer, she announced, "Cancer and Gemini, they don't go well together." Gemini, of course, was Billy's sign. Despite the friction, Dietrich was a frequent houseguest at the Wilders' whenever she was in Los Angeles.

The competition from living legends like Dietrich must have fired up Audrey, because she learned quickly how to compete in this heady new climate. She began reading up on history and current events, so she and her erudite husband could have more to talk about at night than studio gossip. She studied French, boned up on modern art. And, mindful of her husband's gourmet appetites, she went to cooking school and became a master chef, adept at all kinds of international cuisines—powerful agent Irving "Swifty" Lazar, a close friends of the Wilders, called her "the best cook in Hollywood." Lazar said Audrey would make chicken paprika with fresh-ground paprika, and turn bland kasha dishes into something savory and exotic. "Out at their beach house, out at Trancas, she won't have a servant," Lazar recalled. "I've seen her serve drinks and prepare a meal of many courses for eight people—and all by herself." Much to Billy's delight, she could whip up a marvelous dinner for four or six on just a few hours' notice—and she truly seemed to enjoy it.

In time, the Wilders became known for throwing the best parties in Hollywood, soirees packed with famous faces and brimming over with laughs and spirited conversation. And, as a capper to each evening, a space in the room would clear and Audrey would entertain the crowd with a selection of American standards, in a clear, lilting voice. The parties were so celebrated that Truman Capote's unfinished novel about American high society, *Answered Prayers*, included a chapter called "And Audrey Wilder Sang."

The hardest thing for Audrey to accept was Billy's decision not to have another child. At forty-three, perhaps he felt he was too old to take on the responsibilities of fatherhood again, especially now at this major juncture in his movie career. Audrey acceded to Billy's wishes and, fortunately, became good friends with his daughter, Vicki, as she entered adolescence.

WITH THE FAILURE OF *ACE IN THE HOLE*, BILLY WILDER was anxious to recover his clout. Though his own philosophy was that you're as good as the best thing you've ever done, he knew that in Hollywood the prevailing wisdom was that you're only as good as your last picture.

At first, Wilder tried to get as far away as possible from the downbeat tone of *Ace in the Hole*. He rang up veteran comedy writer Norman Krasna, an old friend who had won an Oscar in 1944 for writing the Olivia de Havilland film *Princess O'Rourke*, which he also directed. Wilder had an idea for a comeback vehicle for Stan Laurel and Oliver Hardy, in which they would play movie extras during the early silent-comedy era. The picture would begin with a longshot of the big Hollywood sign in the Hills, with Laurel sleeping inside one "O" and Hardy in another. The two writers worked on the screenplay for a month before Krasna walked out. Wilder, it seems, was dominating their sessions and, what's worse, Krasna just couldn't take his good-natured but brutal insults. Krasna and Wilder remained friends—they even occasionally sought each other's help when stuck on a screenplay—but any long-term collaboration was out of the question.

Wilder then turned to another old friend and Hollywood veteran, Edwin Blum, who was also a frequent tennis and bridge partner. They worked for a time on the Laurel and Hardy movie, but the project fell apart when Oliver Hardy became ill.

What to do next? Back during the filming of *Ace in the Hole*, Wilder told the press he was developing a new Berlin comedy, with Marlene Dietrich as a one-legged prostitute. This idea too disappeared into vapor— perhaps Paramount objected to the notion of not getting all their money's worth out of Dietrich's gams.

Wilder now suggested something even more daring: a musical version of *Camille*, set in Harlem. Lena Horne would play a light-skinned prostitute who has an affair with a white navy lieutenant who doesn't know his real father is black. Paul Robeson and Tyrone Power had agreed to play father and son, and the score would be by the great Duke Ellington. Once again, Wilder would be pushing the studio envelope. Sadly, after several weeks, he and Blum abandoned the project.*

The desperate director finally hit upon the right property during a trip to New York. *Stalag 17*, written by Donald Bevan and Edmund Trzcinski and directed by José Ferrer, opened at the Forty-eighth Street Theatre on May 8, 1951, and was an immediate smash. Despite the fact that it was an all-male drama set in a German *stalag*, or prisoner-of-war camp, Wilder saw possibilities in the play and had Paramount buy the film rights for a low $50,000. A year before, he had told the *Los Angeles Times*, "I always make things very tough on myself by not going out and buying a successful stage play or novel, but starting instead from scratch." Finally, he was being easy on himself. Or so it seemed.

Stalag 17 would be the first of a successful run of stage adaptations for the director. Wilder has minimized the challenge of transferring a play to film, but in his case the work is always extensive. As a master of story construction, he can't resist tinkering with the original, often radically re-working the property, as he did with the James Cain novella of *Double Indemnity*. *Stalag 17* is no exception.

The play text describes the central protagonist, Sefton, as "a handsome but sullen young man dominated by an animosity toward the world in general and toward Price [a fellow prisoner] in particular. . . . His back-ground has been in the world of 'dog eat dog,' and survival has been his chief goal, 'back home' as it is now in the prison camp." The perfect Wilder antihero, but Wilder opted to make him even more disagreeable — so much so that co-author Trzcinski, who had a small role in the film, refused to speak to the director afterward.

In the play, Sefton's main breach of the barracks code of honor is trading with the German guards for food. In Wilder and Blum's concep-tion, Sefton is one smart American entrepreneur. He's got an entire conve-nience store tucked away in his foot locker, and his "business enterprises"

---

* Among other unrealized projects Wilder considered in the early fifties were an adapta-tion of Evelyn Waugh's black comedy *The Loved One* (later filmed in 1965); a story set in Palestine; and a Yul Brynner vehicle about a Soviet ballet dancer in Venice.

include a literal rat race on which the prisoners place bets, a homemade distillery, and charging a fee to view the Russian women's shower room through a telescope. Sefton is such an icy cool operator he sets down a wager on whether two fleeing prisoners will successfully escape. (They lose their lives, he wins a pile of cigarettes.) Sefton justifies his behavior by the fact that most of his possessions were stolen when he was first interned, but he's now made an entire career out of exploiting his neighbors' weaknesses and desperation.

In the play, Sefton is equally alienated but his political sympathies are clear: He enjoys reading the German death lists in the "Jerry" newspapers. But Wilder wouldn't allow *his* Sefton any jingoistic anti-Nazi speeches—that would defeat the whole purpose of the story. As an outsider and a seeming collaborator, Sefton is the first to be suspected when the German guards' knowledge of hiding places and escape plans makes it apparent that there's a spy in the barracks. Sefton's position worsens with the arrival of Lieutenant James Dunbar, who brags about how he secretly set fire to a German ammunition train after his capture. Recognizing Dunbar as a millionaire's son from his native Boston who tried to use his influence to dodge the draft, Sefton is openly hostile to the new prisoner. When the Nazis arrest Dunbar for sabotage, the barracks concludes that Sefton ratted on him and gives him a vicious beating after lights-out. Only two people in the room know Sefton is innocent—Sefton and the real spy.

For Wilder, the attraction of *Stalag 17* was in proving that someone as self-interested and antisocial and stubbornly iconoclastic—someone as suspect—as Sefton could still be worthy of an audience's respect. "He is the black marketeer in Stalag 17. He bet them cigarettes and whatever he could for self-aggrandizement, but then when the chips are down, you slowly change your opinion about him. You need that kind of twist. Suddenly you see that the guy they have beaten up because they think, as the audience does, that he is a shit . . . slowly, slowly he emerges as a superhero."

The timing of the film, in the midst of the McCarthy witch-hunts, was surely no coincidence. Wilder's politics had always leaned toward the liberal, and he was never one for dogmatic platitudes. "I was not a blind, idiotic patriot, you know. I came to America because I loved Roosevelt . . . but I was a critic of Roosevelt, too."

In the late 1940s, Wilder didn't hesitate to lend his support to the

Committee for the First Amendment, a group of prominent Hollywood figures including John Huston, William Wyler, Humphrey Bogart, Burt Lancaster, Gene Kelly and Judy Garland who issued a protest against the methods of the House Committee on Un-American Activities. A more dramatic moment came when Leo McCarey recommended that the Screen Directors Guild vote by a show of hands on whether Guild members should agree to take a loyalty oath in order to hang on to their jobs. As John Huston recalled the scene, "I looked on in amazement as everyone in the room except Billy Wilder and me raised their hands in an affirmative vote. Even Willie Wyler, who was sitting out of my sight, went along. Billy was sitting next to me, and he took his cue from my action. When the negative vote was called for, I raised my hand, and Billy hesitantly followed suit. I doubt if he knew why, but he could tell he was in deep trouble from the muted roar that followed. I am sure it was one of the bravest things that Billy, as a naturalized German [*sic*], had ever done. There were 150 to 200 directors at this meeting, and here Billy and I sat alone with our hands raised in protest against the loyalty oath."

Today, Wilder believes he was largely protected from any harassment from the government by being so closely linked with Charles Brackett, whose longtime conservative Republican credentials and standing in Hollywood were impeccable. It also helped that Wilder himself had done his service with the Army's de-Nazification program, even if the resulting *A Foreign Affair* was not the kind of American propaganda the Truman administration had been looking for.

As *A Foreign Affair* showed, Wilder was too inclined to see several sides of an issue to fall into line with something like the new anti-Communist mania. *Ace in the Hole* had already explored the psychology of mass hysteria, and now *Stalag 17* attacked the same rush to judge within the more confined setting of a POW camp.

INITIALLY, WILDER WENT ALONG WITH THE STUDIO'S NOTION to cast Charlton Heston in the lead. But the more Sefton evolved, the clearer it became that Heston's upstanding persona would not be suitable. The director next approached his *Ace in the Hole* star, Kirk Douglas. "I was young and stupid," says Douglas. "I saw the play, and there were things about it I didn't realize. How stupid I was not to take into account the ingredient of Billy Wilder."

William Holden was on his way to New York to do some publicity, and Wilder asked him to check out the play. On his return, Holden reported that he walked out after the first act—he thought the play was dull and Sefton was just a con man without real motivation. Wilder told him to wait and read his script, and emphasized how much he wanted him for Sefton. Aware that the production had originally sought Heston, Holden smirked, "Second choice again, huh?" "You didn't do so badly the last time, Bill," the director reminded him. Holden eventually accepted the assignment, and agreed to downplay his matinee-idol looks with an unflattering crew cut. He had only one request: Couldn't he have a line or two showing Sefton's contempt for the Germans? Wilder declined.

Wilder made a number of vital changes to the play in addition to Sefton's scams. The camp commandant, never seen in the show, was now a significant presence. The hollow chess pieces and the knotted-lamp-cord signal by which the spy and Nazi Corporal Shultz communicate were Wilder's invention. So was the use of smoking Ping-Pong balls to create a diversion during a crucial moment. The unveiling of the real spy is also much better handled—interrogated by Sefton, he says he was eating dinner when the attack on Pearl Harbor was announced, when it was lunchtime in America.

Although he added a number of camp exteriors and scenes in the commandant's office, Wilder did not "open up" the play per se. "Sometimes opening up a play can ruin it," Wilder says, citing *The Diary of Anne Frank* as a movie that suffered from the loss of the stage's feeling of intimacy. "So, too, in *Stalag 17* I wanted the audience to experience the confinement of the prisoners and therefore shot no scenes outside of the prison compound."

Stalag 17 began filming at Paramount on February 4, 1952, with the authentically muddy compound exteriors shot at the Snow Ranch in Calabasas, California. "This was one of the easiest films of my life," Wilder says. "No affectations, no elaborate setups, good black-and-white photography, shot quickly [in less than two months]. But you never felt it said: 'Great artist at work!' "

Great art it's not, largely because Wilder indulges in some broad comic relief that seems grimly out of place. From the original Broadway cast, Wilder hired actor Robert Strauss for the role of Animal, a slovenly, Betty Grable–obsessed GI who spends most of the movie stomping around in dirty long johns. Paired with Broadway recruit Harvey Lembeck as the stock New Yahk wise guy Harry Shapiro, Strauss mugs incessantly, in a performance that earned a supporting Oscar nomination but is painfully unfunny today. In the right context, with the right writing, Wilder's taste for broad comedy can be bracing (i.e., *Some Like It Hot*). Here, it's just an irritant.

Much more successful is Sig Ruman, the royal vet from *The Emperor Waltz* and the memorable Concentration Camp Erhardt in Ernst Lubitsch's controversial but brilliant Nazi-themed comedy, *To Be or Not to Be*. As Corporal Shultz, Ruman arrives at just the right combination of unctuous cheeriness and hidden menace; he's the perfect embodiment of the German who refuses to take personal blame for the Nazi terror, both a target of ridicule and a symbol of moral bankruptcy.

Just a few years after casting Erich von Stroheim and Cecil B. De Mille in *Sunset Boulevard*, Wilder again recruited a fellow director, Otto Preminger, for the role of Commandant Oberst von Scherbach. Born the same year as Wilder, Preminger grew up in Vienna in more rarefied social circles, as the son of the attorney general of the Austro-Hungarian Empire. He began his show-business career as an actor in several productions by theater director Max Reinhardt, and graduated to directing for the stage. Preminger directed his first film in Austria in 1931, immigrated to the United States and made an unauspicious American directing debut in 1936 with a film called *Under Your Spell*. He alternated between acting and directing until his 1944 breakthrough, the haunting mystery-romance *Laura*, and followed with a series of moody melodramas including *Fallen Angel*, *Whirlpool* and *Where the Sidewalk Ends*, plus the costume drama *Forever Amber* and the soapy romance *Daisy Kenyon*. Preminger was also closely linked to Ernst Lubitsch, having finished two films begun by the master: *A Royal Scandal* and (after Lubitsch's death) *That Lady in Ermine*.

Preminger was the very definition of the director-as-autocrat; he had a terrible reputation for constantly berating his actors and crew at the top of his voice. According to Hollywood legend, Preminger once attempted to put a nervous performer "at his ease" by leaning into his face and screaming, "Relax!!!" Tony Curtis claims Wilder told him that on Preminger's first day of shooting *Stalag 17*, Wilder jokingly tried out the same routine on the fidgety director.

"He always forgot his lines," Wilder himself recalls. "He was very strict when he was a director, but he himself. . . . He said, 'Forgive me, I'm a little rusty,' and in the evening he always sent you three pounds of caviar. Very generous. But the actors, the extras who played the soldiers, they had worked for him before and he treated them miserably. So, in back of the apologizing Preminger looking in this direction, are all these extras looking at me and doing this [Wilder raises his middle finger]: 'Give it to him!' "

What Wilder gave Preminger instead was an established screen persona that he was able to parlay into a sideline as his directing career evolved toward bigger-scale productions like *Carmen Jones, The Man with the Golden Arm, Porgy and Bess, Anatomy of a Murder, Exodus, Advise and Consent* and *The Cardinal*. Preminger, playing up his Hun-like image, became a fixture on TV talk shows and even made some young new fans as the villain Mr. Freeze in the *Batman* TV series.

In *Stalag 17*, Preminger's best moment is a sly visual gag worthy of Lubitsch. Pacing back and forth in his office in his stockinged feet while interrogating Lieutenant Dunbar, von Scherbach places a call to his superiors in Berlin to inform them of his catch. Before the call goes through, the commandant summons an officer to help put on his boots—all for the purpose of having Berlin hear the sound of his heels clicking together. At the end of the conversation, he has his boots removed once again.

Wilder would rather satirize his Germans than demonize them. Yes, they're fully capable of cold-blooded murder, as in the shooting of the two escaping prisoners in the film's first five minutes. But Wilder prefers to accentuate their human foibles, suggesting that an absurdly rigid, imperious and humorless mind-set is the chief reason that the Nazis lost the war.

The movie saves most of its contempt for Price (Peter Graves), the barracks security officer who is unmasked as a German-born informer. As a diversion while Sefton and Dunbar escape, Price is tied to some tin cups and thrown out into the dark of the compound, where he is shot to death. Despite Production Code threats that such an example of deliberate collective murder would never be approved, the scene remained intact.

To the end, Sefton acts out of self-interest—never a fan of Dunbar, he says he's helping him escape in order to collect a big reward from his rich family. Sefton's last words to his comrades as he descends into the escape tunnel are: "If I ever run into any of you bums on a street corner, just let's pretend we never met before." But Wilder undercuts the moment by having Sefton reemerge and give his barracks-mates a smile and a friendly salute. After everything Sefton's done and had done to him, the gesture is out of character. This is one of the few instances when the charge of being "too cynical to believe even his own cynicism" sticks; Wilder seems too willing here to stroke and comfort the mass audience, even if it is only for a matter of seconds.

The strategy worked, however. *Stalag 17*, which opened early in July 1953, was an instant hit, generating in excess of $10 million in its first year of release. In a rave, Bosley Crowther judged the picture "humorous, suspenseful, disturbing and rousing," and thoroughly enjoyed the comic antics of Strauss and Lembeck. *Life* deemed it "the finest comedy-drama out of Hollywood this year" and Holden's Sefton the year's most memorable movie character. The *New Yorker* critic, who hated the play, said the movie "doesn't do much to enhance my opinion of the thing," but liked Holden and admitted that Wilder "has seen to it that there are few lulls in the action."

Stalag 17 was passed over in the 1953 Oscar race for Best Picture, but Wilder earned his fourth Best Director nomination, losing to his old *People on Sunday* cohort Fred Zinnemann for *From Here to Eternity*. In the Best Actor race, Holden's hard-bitten performance won against impressive competition: *Eternity* stars Burt Lancaster and Montgomery Clift, plus Marlon Brando in *Julius Caesar* and Richard Burton in *The Robe*. "I really thought Burt would win," Holden told biographer Bob Thomas. "I honestly believed that Burt did the best acting of the year, and I told him so when I saw him one night at Chasen's. I felt adequate in *Stalag 17*, but I was never really simpatico with Sefton." Holden's feelings didn't stop him from enjoying a post-Oscar celebration at Romanoff's, where he kidded Wilder, "I knew it all the time." The next morning, Holden woke up in his favorite easy chair, still wearing his tuxedo, with the gold statuette in his lap.

With *Stalag 17*, Wilder had reasserted his power at Paramount, but the film would create irreparable damage between the director and his studio three years later. "I was making *Love in the Afternoon* in Paris," Wilder remembers, "and I got a letter from the head of distribution saying, 'We've got good news. The Germans are crazy about *Stalag 17*. They would like to release it, but we have to make one little change: The spy that is hiding among them is not a German—make him a Pole.' And I just said: 'Fuck you, gentlemen. Haven't you got any shame? You ask me, who lost his family in Auschwitz, to do a mistake like this? Unless somebody apologizes, forget about my contract. Good-bye, Paramount.' Nobody apologized, and I left Paramount. But it remained the way it was in the American picture."

Initially banned by the German Self-Censorship Board back in 1953, *Stalag 17* was finally given official approval for exhibition in Germany in 1960, but with an opening disclaimer stating that "the visitors to the film understand that this picture is not typical [of all German prison camps] but only one example." On its own, Paramount added the message, "This is another time and these events could not happen again." The release of *Stalag 17* generated considerable print in the German press debating that very question. Curiously, a ban on *Stalag 17* lasted even longer in Spain, until the end of 1964.

Though they had created a hit, Edwin Blum opted not to continue working with Wilder, considering himself "little more than his butler." Blum had made some vital suggestions, but *Stalag 17* was Wilder's show. Though the director kept Blum on as an adviser through the end of post-production, an unusual courtesy to a mere co-writer, Wilder was clearly the boss—and a deeply sarcastic one at that. It was time once again to change partners.

By contrast, making *Stalag 17* brought Wilder and William Holden even closer together. The summer after production wrapped, Holden visited Europe for the first time, accompanied by his actress wife, Ardis (known to the public as Brenda Marshall), and Billy and Audrey. Wilder made sure they stopped in Paris, Berlin and Vienna, and arranged a hectic itinerary of sightseeing and museum-going. After a particularly exhausting day of touring landmarks and climbing a mountain in Bad Ischl, Austria, Holden told Wilder he planned to sleep in the next day. But at six the next morning, Wilder was on the phone, insisting Holden report to the hotel lobby. "We made four important stops that day, and it was one of the most wonderful days of my life," Holden later said. The quartet finally ended up in one of Wilder's favorite relaxation spots, the Badgastein spa near Salzburg.

IN THE FALL OF 1952, A YOUNG, DELICATELY BEAUTIFUL BELgian-born actress named Audrey Hepburn was creating a stir of excitement inside the executive offices of Paramount Pictures. Paramount brass had just viewed some rough footage from William Wyler's new romantic comedy-drama *Roman Holiday*, and they sensed the arrival of an enchanting new star. Finding the right follow-up vehicle suddenly became a top priority. The search ended with *Sabrina Fair*, a new play by Samuel Taylor* destined for Broadway with Margaret Sullavan in the lead. Her biographer, Alexander Walker, says Hepburn found the play; Wilder insists *he* urged the studio to buy it. In any event, it was a rare instance of a stage play going into film production *before* its Broadway opening.

Then forty, Taylor had enjoyed a previous Broadway success in 1950 with *The Happy Time*, a comedy about an eccentric French-Canadian family. To the playwright's profound dismay, Wilder did not regard his new effort as anything close to a sacred text; in fact, he dismantled it like a piece of broken machinery. Taylor's comedy hadn't made it to Broadway yet, and already it was unrecognizable as a film. After a few weeks of queasy collaboration, Wilder's newest partner quit. Taylor recovered just fine, though: His later credits included the book for the Richard Rodgers musical *No Strings* and a co-writing credit on the Alfred Hitchcock classic *Vertigo*.

With half of a first draft in his possession, Wilder went looking for a new co-writer. He then remembered his buddy William Holden telling him how much he liked the script of the new film he was shooting over at MGM, *Executive Suite*. Its author was a thirty-two-year-old first-time screenwriter named Ernest Lehman.

A native of Manhattan, Lehman began as a fiction writer and attracted Hollywood's attention when his stinging novella about Broadway press agents, *Sweet Smell of Success*, debuted in *Cosmopolitan*. Paramount signed

* Previous biographies have confused the playwright with Sam Taylor, a 1920s screenwriter whose credit for a 1929 version of *The Taming of the Shrew* read: "By William Shakespeare. Additional dialogue by Sam Taylor."

Lehman to a one-year contract, and soon he was a fixture at the studio writers' lunch table, where Wilder and his colleagues had a long-standing tradition of playing the Word Game, a contest to fill a grid with words using only letters called out by the players.

"I was the new guy in town," Lehman recalls today from his inviting den in the heart of Bel Air. "I was the buttoned-down New Yorker, with my Brooks Brothers shirts and suits and lapel handkerchief. In those days if you'd never had a picture on the screen, you were hot—you hadn't done anything yet to destroy your reputation. I was a Manhattanite, graduate of City College, lived on the South Shore [of Long Island], a freelance writer, writing novelettes like *Sweet Smell of Success* and *The Comedian*. I kind of had a reputation—an ex–press agent, sort of a New York smart-ass—and I think that probably appealed to Billy."

Nothing came of Lehman's year at Paramount, and he wound up at MGM working on *Executive Suite* with producer John Houseman. Then, MGM optioned *Sweet Smell of Success*. Lehman remembers leaving his house for the studio one morning to start work on that film. "And before lunchtime came, Don Hartman, the head of Paramount, called Dore Schary, the head of MGM, and said Billy Wilder would like to know whether Ernie would be willing to come over and work on *Sabrina*—would you lend him to us? So Dore called me, and I agreed to go over and see Billy. I got in the car and drove from MGM to Paramount—and stayed there! When I came home that night, I was on a Paramount picture. A very unusual experience—to start at one studio in the morning, and end the day at another studio.

"I didn't get to watch them shoot *Executive Suite*," Lehman notes. "I was busy sitting in Billy's house on Beverly Drive, working from breakfast to midnight, until finally we had to start shooting the picture. And then it would be working at lunch and on the way home to dinner, and then from dinner to midnight, desperate because if we didn't come up with something, we wouldn't have anything to shoot the next day."

The writing of *Sabrina* fell behind schedule because Wilder as producer had nabbed three busy stars and was forced to begin filming by September 1953. The director had hoped to get Cary Grant to star opposite the twenty-four-year-old Hepburn, but the ageless leading man turned him down. Tony Curtis remembers Wilder telling him the dispute focused on a simple prop. "Billy said, 'In the film, you're going to play the older brother.' Cary said, 'That's okay.' And Billy said, 'At one point you're going to come in with an umbrella.' And Cary said, 'I don't think I want to carry an umbrella. I don't need that kind of a prop.' And Billy said, 'You must use it, because I wrote it.' And Cary said, 'Well, I won't do it with an umbrella.' And so he didn't. It was only because of ego."

Grant's surprising replacement for the role of high-powered New York businessman Linus Larrabee was Humphrey Bogart, in a decided change of pace from his usual tough-guy persona. With Bogart in place, Wilder recruited Bill Holden—just finishing up *Executive Suite*—for the lesser part of Linus's playboy brother, David. The casting was a lucky stroke, since both Holden and Hepburn would win Oscars the next spring (for *Stalag 17* and *Roman Holiday*, respectively), giving *Sabrina* the extra cachet of featuring three recent Academy Award winners.

Recalls Lehman, "Bill, at the end of his day's shooting of *Executive Suite*, used to come over and have a cocktail with us at Billy's house. Billy used to get furious, because Bill Holden would take me over to a corner and very quietly tell me what went on during the day's shooting on my picture. Finally, one day, Billy said, 'Tell me, Bill, are there any *jokes* in *Executive Suite?*' "

Lehman finds it hard to believe today, but he's certain he never read Taylor's play. "By the time I was on the movie, Billy didn't want to hear about it." Indeed, of all Wilder's theater adaptations, *Sabrina* is the most radically altered. In the play, Linus (portrayed in New York by Joseph Cotten) is a passive observer, always on the sidelines, who encourages the romance between Sabrina Fairchild, the family chauffeur's daughter, and his younger brother, David, as an amusing experiment. In the film, however, Linus takes an active, calculated role in sabotaging the affair, purely for business reasons invented by Wilder and Lehman. He woos Sabrina himself, in order to prevent her from breaking up a pending marriage of convenience between David and a sugar-cane heiress considered valuable to Larrabee Industries' future. Thus, Linus joins a long line of Wilder cads who profess love while hiding selfish ulterior motives.

The change is consistent with Wilder's philosophy of movie characterization. "Virtue is not photogenic," he insists. "A man leaving his apartment opens a drawer, takes out a handkerchief and puts it in his pocket. But if he opens the drawer and takes out a gun and puts in his pocket, you've got a scene. I love to have situations where people are entering rooms through windows, not through doors. It carries suspense, it carries some kind of excitement and also it is easier to act. You know, the most difficult line for an actor is to open the door and say: 'Tennis, anyone?' That's a deadly line. But to come to the door and say: 'I just got the call. This is the moment. Don't forget the submachine gun.' That's a situation. But 'Tennis, anyone?'—how can you, even if you're Cary Grant? 'Tennis anyone?' would only be a good line if somebody comes in in a wheelchair."

Like the play, *Sabrina* the film opens with fairy-tale-like narration: "Once upon a time, on the North Shore of Long Island, some thirty miles from New York, there lived a small girl on a large estate." The youthful Hepburn (much better cast than the play's aging Margaret Sullavan) sits in a tree, wistfully gazing at the Larrabees' posh gathering to celebrate the annual six-meter yacht race, an artificial-looking full moon over her shoulder. Slightly tomboyish, the chauffeur's daughter has long mooned over the handsome, carefree David Larrabee (William Holden, his hair dyed a comical-looking blond), who barely notices her as he accompanies his latest bubbleheaded conquest to a love match on the indoor tennis court. Sabrina's dreams are further discouraged by her father (John Williams), a conservative member of the servant class who scorns any effort to rise above one's station in life. In accordance with her father's plans, Sabrina is to leave the next morning for a two-year stint at the best cooking school in Paris. "I'm not telling you that you have to be a cook as [your mother] was, or that you have to marry a chauffeur like me," Fairchild admonishes her. "But you know how I feel about it. Your mother and I had a good life together—we were respected by everyone. That's as much as anyone can want in this world. Don't reach for the moon, child."

Rather than finish her packing, Sabrina writes a farewell note to her father, retreats to the mammoth Larrabee garage, shuts the door and turns on the ignition of the eight limos and roadsters parked there. By chance, Linus discovers the girl before carbon-monoxide poisoning can overtake her. Just as the older Larrabee brother saves her from suicide, in Paris Sabrina is revived by the platonic interest of an elderly baron who escorts her to the opera, museums and charity balls. Upon graduation, Sabrina can write to her father, "I have learned how to live, how to be in the world and of the world, and not just to stand aside and watch. And I will never, never again run away from life—or from love, either." Decked out in a chic suit and white cloche, Sabrina returns home, as promised, "the most sophisticated woman at the Glen Cove station."

By chance, Sabrina's great unrequited love, David, passes by the train station as she waits to be picked up by her father. The glib playboy offers her a ride, never recognizing the chauffeur's daughter but thoroughly entranced by this comely glamour girl. It's only when he pulls into his own driveway and the rest of the household help comes out to greet her that David realizes Sabrina's true identity. That night, at yet another of the Larrabees' lavish parties, David dumps his fiancée to dance with his alluring new catch, and he even arranges one of his notorious champagne rendezvous on the indoor tennis court. But first, David must deal with the wrath of his cranky, elitist father; in the heat of the argument, Linus urges his younger brother to sit down—right on the champagne glasses David has hidden in his back pants pocket. With a painful crunch, David is suddenly put out of commission, and Linus takes charge of the Sabrina problem. Meeting on the tennis court, Linus and Sabrina have an instantly palpable sexual tension—as Linus will explain several times, "It's all in the family."

With Linus Larrabee, Wilder returns to an archetype—the emotionally stunted American giant of industry—he first explored in Lubitsch's *Bluebeard's Eighth Wife*. Variations on this character would reappear in *Love in the Afternoon* and *Avanti!*, with lower-echelon types in *The Apartment* and *One, Two, Three* adhering to the same blindered corporate ethic. Interestingly, in light of Wilder's own background, *Sabrina, Love in the Afternoon* and *Avanti!* all explicitly set up a conflict between American hustle and expediency and European refinement and insouciance. With Sabrina, Linus intends to be all business, even if it means breaking the heart and spirit of a naïve, vulnerable young woman. The schism between them is first made evident when the subject of Paris arises during their first boat ride together:

SABRINA: Maybe you should go to Paris, Linus.
LINUS: Paris?
SABRINA: It helped me a lot. Have you ever been there?
LINUS: Oh yes, once. I was there for thirty-five minutes.
SABRINA: Thirty-five minutes!?

LINUS: Changing planes. I was on my way to Iraq for an oil deal.

SABRINA: Oh, but Paris isn't for changing planes—it's for changing your outlook, for throwing open the windows and letting in . . . letting in "La Vie en Rose."

LINUS: Paris is for lovers. Maybe that's why I stayed only thirty-five minutes.

It's hard now to picture Cary Grant in the role of Linus; with him, *Sabrina* would have been an entirely different picture—more conventionally romantic and far less complex. Linus might have been just as reserved and repressed, but Grant would have made him seem more a daffy eccentric along the lines of his *Bringing Up Baby* milquetoast than someone with Bogart's authentic pain. Arguably, Bogart's casting makes *Sabrina* less airy and comic than it ought to have been, but in other ways it renders the film richer.

"I kind of liked the idea of having Bogart," Wilder reflects today, "because it's against the grain. Nobody suspected that he was going to wind up with Audrey Hepburn. He makes a deal for his brother to marry the daughter of a rich, complex-owning family, but then he himself falls into a trap. It's not the common thing, that Bogart wins against the more attractive Holden—except maybe for one reason, that he got the bigger salary. That's why he got the girl."*

Thanks to Bogart's innate soulfulness, Linus's charade never seems as fully hard-hearted as Joe Gillis's with Norma Desmond or John Pringle's with Phoebe Frost. For all his boardroom bravado, Linus cuts a rather pathetic figure in the romance department. Though he's about to make a killing with a revolutionary new plastic, the elder Larrabee son is completely out of touch with current fashion: Preparing for that first date with Sabrina, he even contemplates wearing his old Yale sweater and beanie. He does, however, cart along an antiquated gramophone, which bleats the old novelty song, "Yes, We Have No Bananas"—not exactly the ideal accompaniment for a romantic boat ride, though Sabrina finds it charming. When the girl tries out a more appropriate tune, Linus asks her to stop the music—the song brings back painful memories he doesn't care to discuss.

* Bogart received $300,000, compared to Holden's $125,000.

Suddenly, the sequence turns into a strange, enigmatic (and possibly fraudulent) confessional that seems specially designed for the melancholy Bogart mystique. "No man walks alone from choice," Linus laments, claiming that he once stood on his office's window ledge for three hours, contemplating suicide over yet another lost love. No further details are ever offered.

Lehman remembers agonizing over the pivotal scene in the movie when Linus admits his chicanery to Sabrina late at night in his office. "That scene had to be shot after Bill Holden left the picture, because he had to fly off to an aircraft carrier in the Pacific to make *The Bridges of Toko-Ri*. We showed Bill Holden getting punched in the jaw and flying down the board of directors' table, and saying to Bogart: 'Then you *are* in love with her, here's your hat, here's your cane, there's a tugboat waiting, get moving.' We had to do that before we had conceived what happened between [Sabrina and Linus] in the office the night before. That was desperation time, it really was."

Not only did the scene have to cover a huge amount of emotional territory—Sabrina discovering two boat tickets for Europe and professing her love, Linus confessing his deceit, Sabrina running off—but Wilder and Lehman fought over the director's insistence that his two leads should sleep together in Linus's office apartment. "I absolutely wouldn't let Billy do it," Lehman declares. After all, *Sabrina* was a modern-day fairy tale, and people don't copulate in fairy tales. "He was furious. He said, 'You're a middle-class Jewish prude.' I said, 'You just can't do it—I'll never forgive you.' And I stubbornly prevailed."

For Lehman, the collaboration was fraught with personality conflicts. One of Wilder's biggest sore spots was his new partner's aversion to exotic cuisine. "There I am in the house every day, turning down the food, driving Billy crazy," Lehman sighs. "Headcheese! What is headcheese? Calves' brains! Tripe! The inner lining of a cow's stomach?!

"We went cross-country by train because Doane Harrison wouldn't fly. . . . We had three days to work on the train, to catch up. We were on the way to the Long Island estate of [Paramount president] Barney Balaban to shoot on location, and Irving Lazar—Swifty—presented Billy with this pound of the best beluga caviar. And the first thing we do is go into the dining room to start eating the caviar. I said, 'Not me.' 'What do you mean, not you?' 'I don't eat caviar.' 'You don't eat caviar?!' And as the result of my not eating caviar, we spent three days on that train going cross-country, staring at each other or out the window—not one word was mentioned about the picture."

Just before their arrival in New York, Wilder told Lehman to pack away some towels from their New York Central Railroad compartment. "All our grips were taken up to Billy's suite, and the porters were standing around waiting for their tips. I opened up my bag and said, 'Billy, what do you want me to do with these towels you had me steal from the New York Central?' What a thing to say! He was stunned.

"I was passive-aggressive," Lehman admits, "covertly getting back at him for all the things he would overtly say to me, like, 'You're a Yankee fan? Typical underdog rooting for the overdog!'"

Lehman still cringes at the memory of his partner's comments after Wilder went, against the writer's wishes, to a sneak preview of *Executive Suite*. Lehman was so nervous about the reaction to his first screen credit that he arranged to leave town for Palm Springs early the following morning. But before he could get away, the phone rang. It was Wilder. "He said, 'Ernie, I saw your picture last night. You were a noble salmon swimming upstream against the tide of a dreary subject.' That whole weekend in Palm Springs, I kept writing letters to Billy Wilder—how could he do a thing like that to me? I never sent the letter. The film made all the ten-best lists, as did *Sabrina*. But I felt kind of crushed. You notice how I remember the words? Because everything Billy says is such an aphorism. He doesn't speak normal language—he doesn't have to think of it either, it comes just like that."

Midway through the shoot, Lehman had what he terms "a mini–nervous breakdown" from the long hours and the pressure of trying to churn out sparkling pages of script just hours before they were scheduled to be filmed. "I started crying," he recalls, "and Billy came over and put his arm around me and said, 'Nobody's ever worked harder than you. I want you to call a cab, go home, and just go to bed.' The doctor came to my house and gave me an injection, put me to sleep for thirteen hours. Billy must have told some lies to the studio, and they shut down for a day. I was told not to work, but Billy sneaked over to the house. Suddenly my wife says, 'The doctor's here!' Billy snuggled into the den and closed the door. And the doctor looked me over and said, 'You're okay.' And as he walked out the door, he said, 'You can tell Mr. Wilder to come out now.' He must have seen his car."

The pressure was getting to Wilder, too, in the form of severe back trouble. "I used to go with Billy to his doctor, and I'd hear him screaming with pain inside," says Lehman, adding with a guilty grin, "and I'd be standing out in the corridor, trying to suppress gleeful laughter."

The insane workload continued to the very end. As Lehman describes it, "There came that night when, at four in the morning, after we had paced up and down the streets of Beverly Hills trying to come up with a solution to the next day's scene, we just couldn't find it. We woke up the assistant director and told him to cancel the calls and make other cast calls instead and shoot closeups and retakes and things like that to cover up what we couldn't do. Overscheduled, we were finally ordered by the studio that on that Saturday the picture would end shooting, no matter what. This was it. What hadn't been written was the scene where Fairchild is driving Sabrina to the *Liberté*. It's a two-shot, all in one take. And we had to write it during the lunch hour. We were in Billy's office and suddenly I started hearing loud noises outside, out in the big courtyard at Paramount. I looked down and there were people playing touch football. So I threw up the window and I leaned out and shouted, 'Shut up down there, you god-damned idiots, we're working!' And it turned out to be Martin and Lewis. I closed the window and they didn't stop. Billy said, 'Come on, Ernie, we have to do this scene!' And I said, 'I can't work with this noise.' So I called the studio police. I said, 'You've got to go and stop them. We're writing a scene and we have to finish it.' 'Martin and Lewis? We can't tell *them* to stop playing football.' And I called D. A. Duran, who was like second in command at Paramount, and he said, 'Martin and Lewis? We can't tell them to stop playing football.' Meanwhile, Billy's going crazy with this nutty writer of his. Finally, I called the head of the writers' department, John Mock. He said, 'Tell you what, you two come here and use my office.' That's what we did. We wrote the scene and Billy started shooting it right before dinnertime. John Williams kept blowing his lines. There was nothing to cut to, so each time you had to start all over again. Billy shot about seventy-two takes, and at 9:30 that night, finally, he got one take which went perfectly from beginning to end. We looked up at the heavens and shouted 'Fuck you' and it was over."

Along with a grueling schedule, Wilder had to deal with the grumblings of one very unhappy star: Humphrey Bogart. Bogie knew he was second choice for the role of Linus, which he had accepted at the urging of his and Wilder's mutual friend, Swifty Lazar. He was ill at ease wearing Larrabee's striped trousers and derby and carrying around an umbrella—it was quite an odd stretch after all those years of trench coats and guns. Worst of all, he felt alienated from the cozy camaraderie that had developed among Wilder, his good friend Holden and the disarming Hepburn. "He was totally excluded," says Ernest Lehman. "We all used to go into Bill Holden's dressing room at the end of the day's shooting and drink and enjoy ourselves, and Bogie would be off in his dressing room with his dresser. Also, he felt Billy had promised to take care of him, and now Billy was in love with those closeups of Audrey Hepburn, as who wouldn't be. I think Bogie came off very well, was treated very well, but apparently he was an irritable sort of guy with a lot of people, not just Billy." The movie tough guy was especially cranky late in the afternoon; Bogie's personal assistant, Verita Petersen, always knew to have a scotch and soda ready for him as he entered his dressing room at 5:30.

Bogart discovered that the best way to annoy Wilder was to make fun of his Viennese accent, responding to his directions with a hearty "*Jawohl!*" and clicking his heels. (He later told a *Time* magazine reporter, "Wilder is the kind of Prussian German with a riding crop. He's the type of director I don't like to work with.") One time, he asked Wilder if he had any children. When the director answered that he had a teenage daughter, Bogie pointed to a section of the script and sneered, "Did she write this?"

Wilder told journalist Ezra Goodman he was never intimidated by Bogart's barbs. "I learned from the master, Erich von Stroheim, and this was just child's play. I'm in the major leagues. Bogart was a bore. You have to be much wittier to be that mean." Wilder, for his part, got back at Bogart by helping fuel the rumor that, contrary to what his star had been told, the film would end with Holden winning the love of Hepburn. Since he and Lehman were writing as they filmed, Wilder was able to string Bogart along to the end of production.

Bogie even picked on Hepburn, yelling at her to stay home nights and learn her lines when she flubbed a scene. (Wilder claims that the actress actually conspired with him to hold up completion of the day's work whenever he was running short of screenplay pages.) As for Holden, Bogart taunted him with nicknames like "Lover Boy" and "Smiling Jim," accused him of mugging and questioned his talent.

Lehman, too, felt the wrath of Bogart. The writer came down from his office to the soundstage with some pages he had just rewritten, but neglected to make enough copies to go around. Without thinking, he handed the new pages to Wilder and Holden, but none to Bogart. Furious at the accidental slight, Bogie screamed, "Get this City College writer out of here and back to Monogram where he belongs!" "I had to walk away, his rage was so violent," wonders Lehman. "Talk about frothing at the mouth!" Then Wilder intervened. "There will be no further shooting on this picture until Mr. Bogart apologizes to Mr. Lehman," he formally announced in front of 150 witnesses. Finally, Bogart walked over to the embarrassed young writer and invited him to share a drink in his dressing room.

Frankly terrified of Bogart, Hepburn found all the support she needed from Wilder and Holden. Wilder remembers, "I saw the test that Wyler made with her for *Roman Holiday*, and I was in love with her, I just absolutely was crazy about her. And I told her one day when we were shooting: 'You know, Audrey, when we got you, I didn't know you very well, but you came on the set and everybody, whether it was a grip, an electrician, an extra, the camera crew, the actors, certainly myself, we all fell in love with you. And (as I said at Lincoln Center)* my problem was a tremendous one, because I was not only in love with you but I speak in my sleep. But fortunately, fortunately, my wife's first name is Audrey as well. So I got away with it.' "

At the time, Wilder told the press, "After so many drive-in waitresses in movies—it has been a real drought—here is class, somebody who went to school, can spell and possibly play the piano. The other class girl is Katharine Hepburn. There is nobody else." With more than a little sexist 1950s irreverence, Wilder also observed, "Titism has taken over the country. This girl single-handed may make bozooms a thing of the past."

Holden was even more smitten with his costar. Ernest Lehman remembers accidentally walking in on the two in one of their trailers and how abruptly they drew apart. Their mutual attraction was obvious to the crew,

---

* At the 1991 Film Society of Lincoln Center tribute to Hepburn.

but they struggled to keep their affair a secret—after all, Holden was married with two young children, and Hepburn was America's demure new princess. Still, it wasn't an uncommon sight to see Hepburn riding the green bicycle Wilder had given her, on her way to a private rendezvous with her costar. Holden and Hepburn continued to see each other after *Sabrina* wrapped; Holden even brought her home to dinner with his wife, Ardis. Holden's marriage had been in serious trouble for years, but as he and Hepburn pondered their future together, the actor revealed that he had had a vasectomy shortly after his second son was born. Audrey passionately wanted children and determined to end the affair.

SABRINA DEBUTED ON SEPTEMBER 25, 1954, THE SAME DAY AS Hepburn's wedding to actor Mel Ferrer. The notices were enthusiastic and the lines were long. Bosley Crowther pronounced it "the most delightful comedy-romance in years," swearing he hadn't enjoyed a romance so much since *It Happened One Night* twenty years before. *Variety* called it "a socko romantic comedy" and also thought that Bogart was "socko" and Hepburn would "have audiences rooting for her all the way." *Time* opined that *Sabrina* was "never less than glittering entertainment," but cautioned, "somehow a certain measure of lead has found its way into the formula." Curiously, the *Time* critic felt that Bogart had all the best scenes, while praising Hepburn with faint damns: "Hepburn's appeal . . . is largely to the imagination; the less acting she does the more people can imagine her doing, and wisely she does very little in *Sabrina*. That little she does skillfully."

Most critics, however, were thoroughly charmed by Hepburn, and she earned an Oscar nomination, losing to Grace Kelly in *The Country Girl*. Though the picture wasn't nominated, Wilder was in the Best Director competition yet again (he lost to Elia Kazan for *On the Waterfront)* and he shared a screenplay nomination with Lehman and Taylor. The film was also nominated in the cinematography, art direction and costume categories, winning the latter prize for Edith Head—even though several of Hepburn's most striking dresses in the film were designed at the actress's request by the great French couturier Hubert de Givenchy, who became an essential contributor to the Hepburn "look."

Wilder remained close to both Hepburn and Holden, and he even made up with Bogart a few years later. Wilder visited Bogie as he lay dying of cancer, and he was impressed by the actor's bravery. "He bore his agony silently and with great dignity," Wilder says.

Though they never worked together again, Wilder also maintained his friendship with Ernest Lehman—in fact, Lehman's next assignment, adapting the musical *The King and I* to the screen, came about after Wilder recommended him to his former partner, *King and I* producer Charles Brackett. From there, Lehman went on to a remarkably successful movie career, writing such celebrated films as *Somebody Up There Likes Me*, *North by Northwest*, *West Side Story*, *The Sound of Music* and *Family Plot*, and adapting and producing *Who's Afraid of Virginia Woolf?* and *Hello, Dolly!*.

"Billy and I meet at least annually when the Laurel [screenwriting] Awards committee gets together to decide who might be this year's winner," says Lehman. "He's always very friendly and gentle and kind. . . . In fact, when I was a first-time producer doing *Who's Afraid of Virginia Woolf?*, he very kindly offered to have lunch with Mike Nichols, who didn't know the front end of a camera from the back end, the wunderkind of Broadway. He gave him all the hints he could about being a first-time director. He was very generous and helpful."

As someone who worked long, long days with Wilder, Lehman can speak authoritatively on the filmmaker's reputation as a cynic. "I would call him more of a realist than a cynic, and at times not a realist but a romanticist. Certainly in *Sabrina*. Even the so-called cynical big-businessman. Isn't that interesting? [Linus] talks about putting shoes on children's feet and sending them to school and factories going up. The so-called greedy capitalist expresses his ambitions in very romanticized terms. Billy a cynic? No, I never think of him as a cynic. I think of him as a man who sees life as it really is and expresses what he sees in rather acerbic terms which make him sound cynical. He doesn't sound like Bill Clinton on a political campaign."

WILDER REMAINED ON THE BROADWAY BEAT WITH HIS NEXT project, which came together thanks to the aggressive Swifty Lazar. The superagent was at a party when he overheard MGM executive Kenneth MacKenna discussing the studio's imminent movie deal for the sexy stage hit *The Seven Year Itch*. MacKenna couldn't get over it: The play's relatively unknown author, George Axelrod, wanted the great Billy Wilder to direct the film! Swifty got to work in a hurry. Wilder liked the idea of making this comedy about a marriage-weary New York book editor and his tempting new upstairs neighbor, so Lazar brokered a deal for the director. Swifty told Axelrod of Wilder's enthusiasm, and landed the playwright as a client, too. Then came word that Marilyn Monroe's agent, producer Charles Feldman, desired the property for America's new sex goddess. Wilder and Lazar wanted Monroe, but she had an exclusive contract with 20th Century–Fox. Lazar arranged for Fox to pay $500,000 for the movie rights (twice what Wilder had just shelled out) and, for the first time in fourteen years, Wilder went to work for a studio other than Paramount.

Axelrod's admiration for Wilder was tempered somewhat when his director and writing partner suggested they use the play script as a doorstop. Axelrod fared better than Samuel Taylor, however: Much of the original structure of the play remains, along with a fair amount of its dialogue. The biggest and most critical difference was one that neither Wilder nor Axelrod wanted, and one that neither could prevent.

The term "seven year itch," which soon entered the American vernacular, refers to the sexual restlessness supposedly felt by men after seven years of married routine. Its victim here is one Richard Sherman (Tom Ewell), a glum, ordinary-looking editor who specializes in transforming respectable texts into lurid come-ons for the twenty-five-cent paperback market. (In the film, *Little Women* becomes *Secrets of a Girls' Dormitory;* in the play, *The Scarlet Letter* is about to be redubbed *Adultress.*) As the film opens, Richard sends his wife and obnoxious young son off to a resort in Maine while he stays behind in the sweltering New York summer heat. Richard's plans to work quietly and temperately at home are disrupted by the arrival of the new upstairs tenant (Monroe), a voluptuous aspiring actress with a sweet disposition and a low-wattage brain. After the Girl—she's never named—knocks a tomato plant off her balcony and almost brains Richard, the editor invites her down for a drink and begins fantasizing about the possibilities. Will Richard scratch his itch? In the play, he does; in the film, he never finds relief.

The stumbling block, as usual, was the Production Code. As a November 1953 memo from Code Administration director Geoffrey Shurlock

Three-year-old Billie Wilder (center) with his parents, Eugenia and Max, and brother Willie, 1909. (BILLY WILDER)

The young reporter and budding screenwriter in Berlin, 1929. (BILLY WILDER)

A scene from *Menschen am Sonntag (People on Sunday)*, the groundbreaking 1930 German film written by Wilder and directed by Robert Siodmak.
(STIFTUNG DEUTSCHE KINEMATHEK)

Regie: Gerhard Lamprecht · Buch: Billy Wilder

Emil und die Detektive

EIN FILM NACH EINEM ROMAN VON

ERICH KÄSTNER

Emil and the Detectives, which Wilder adapted from the classic children's novel by Erich Kästner, was a popular and critical success in Germany.
(STIFTUNG DEUTSCHE KINEMATHEK)

Facing page, bottom: Fred MacMurray goes to the gas chamber as Edward G. Robinson looks on in the deleted final scene from *Double Indemnity*.
(MUSEUM OF MODERN ART)

The 35-year-old Wilder makes his directing debut with the Ginger Rogers comedy, *The Major and the Minor.* (MUSEUM OF MODERN ART FILM STILLS ARCHIVE)

Right: Wilder casts a wary eye at Raymond Chandler during the making of *Double Indemnity*. (UCLA RAYMOND CHANDLER COLLECTION)

Wilder with his first wife, Judith, and daughter Victoria in the mid-1940s. (BILLY WILDER)

Oscar winner Ray Milland, with Wilder's paramour Doris Dowling, in a scene from *The Lost Weekend*. (PHOTOFEST)

Bette Davis presents the Oscar for Best Screenplay to Wilder and Charles Brackett for *The Lost Weekend*. Wilder also won his first Best Director Oscar, and the film was named Best Picture. (ACADEMY OF MOTION PICTURE ARTS AND SCIENCES)

Wilder returned to Berlin twice after the war, first as a colonel with the U.S. Army's Psychological Warfare Division, then as a civilian filmmaker preparing a satire on U.S.–German relations. (MUSEUM OF MODERN ART)

Preparing *A Foreign Affair*: Jean Arthur, Wilder, Brackett, John Lund, dialogue director Ronnie Lubin, and Marlene Dietrich.
(MUSEUM OF MODERN ART)

Gloria Swanson returns to Paramount as silent-screen legend Norma Desmond in Wilder's 1950 classic, *Sunset Boulevard*.
(MUSEUM OF MODERN ART)

Kirk Douglas plays doomed reporter Chuck Tatum in "the runt of Wilder's litter," *Ace in the Hole*. (FILM FORUM)

Wilder enjoys a dance with the young Audrey Hepburn during the filming of *Sabrina*. (CULVER PICTURES)

The making of a pop icon: Wilder supervises the celebrated subway vent scene during a nighttime filming session for *The Seven Year Itch* with Marilyn Monroe on New York's Lexington Avenue. (CULVER PICTURES)

Maurice Chevalier visits Wilder and Jimmy Stewart during production of *The Spirit of St. Louis*. (MUSEUM OF MODERN ART)

Audrey Wilder prepares to film a cameo appearance opposite Gary Cooper in *Love in the Afternoon*. (MUSEUM OF MODERN ART)

Cooper, Wilder, and Audrey Hepburn take a break while filming
Love in the Afternoon. (MUSEUM OF MODERN ART)

Charles Laughton, Marlene Dietrich, Tyrone Power, and Wilder form a
close circle during the making of Agatha Christie's *Witness for the Prosecution*.
(MUSEUM OF MODERN ART)

Cozying up to Marilyn Monroe—a good day on *Some Like It Hot*. (PHOTOFEST)

Best Director presenter Gina Lollobrigida and Best Picture presenter Audrey Hepburn flank Wilder and I.A.L. Diamond after *The Apartment*'s big Oscar victory. Wilder became the second person in history to win three Academy Awards in one night. (ACADEMY OF MOTION PICTURE ARTS AND SCIENCES)

Wilder (left) with star Horst Buchholz and crew during production of the Cold War farce, *One, Two, Three,* in Berlin. (STIFTUNG DEUTSCHE KINEMATHEK)

Billy and Audrey, flush with success in the early '60s. (PHOTOFEST)

Wilder rehearses Lou Jacobi (left),
Jack Lemmon, and Shirley MacLaine
in a scene from *Irma La Douce*,
his biggest box-office hit.
(MUSEUM OF MODERN ART)

Wilder gives waitressing lessons
to Kim Novak during production on
the notorious *Kiss Me, Stupid*.
(MUSEUM OF MODERN ART)

Wilder directs Robert
Stephens, Colin Blakely, and
Genevieve Page in his
ambitious box-office failure,
*The Private Life of
Sherlock Holmes*.
(MUSEUM OF MODERN ART)

Wilder with two of his best
friends and favorite stars,
Walter Matthau and Jack
Lemmon.

Fred MacMurray, Matthau, Lemmon, Hepburn, and Tony Curtis celebrate the life and work of Billy Wilder at the American Film Institute's Life Achievement Award ceremony in 1986. (PHOTOFEST)

Billy and Audrey, amidst the Wilder art collection at their apartment on Wilshire Blvd. (JIM MCHUGH)

declared, the play was "flatly in violation of the Code clause which states that adultery must never be the subject of comedy or laughter." Within a year, Wilder and Axelrod had a script that basically passed Code muster: The Girl sleeps in Richard's bed, but only because his apartment is air-conditioned; Richard spends the night on the living-room sofa.

Wilder had hoped to add a Lubitsch-like touch to indicate that the pair had indeed slept together. "I could have done it very easily," he states. "I went to [Fox chairman Darryl] Zanuck and Feldman and I said, 'Look, unless they do it, we have no picture. . . . I would just like to have one tiny little scene where the maid of the Tom Ewell apartment is making the bed and finds a hairpin. . . . That's all I want, nothing more.' The whole aspect of the picture would have changed." Wilder lost the battle, and today regrets having made the movie under "straitjacketed" conditions.

But even if the director had gotten his way, *The Seven Year Itch* would likely remain a minor Wilder picture. The titillating qualities that made the comedy a long-running stage success in the 1950s no longer apply, and what's left is a rather undynamic, claustrophobic case study of an agitated milquetoast.

True to form, Wilder, working with Axelrod, improves on the original with some amusing gag lines: Richard plays some Rachmaninoff for the Girl and she identifies it as classical music "because it doesn't have a vocal." She describes getting her toe stuck in her bathtub faucet, and how embarrassed she was in front of the plumber because she didn't have any polish on her toe nails. And a health-food restaurant scene provides an excuse for the hilariously hangdog character actress Doro Merande to champion the cause of nudism.

The film retains the fantasy elements of the play, giving Wilder the opportunity to break free of the boundaries of Richard's apartment and to explore the full screen in his first CinemaScope picture (his second in color). Wilder can't resist parodying his friend Fred Zinnemann's celebrated seaside love scene in *From Here to Eternity*, with Richard stumbling into the ocean as the sequence ends. Wilder's postmodern sense of mischief also finds expression as Richard and the Girl go out to see *The Creature from the Black Lagoon* and, in a weirdly Pirandellian moment, Richard tells a visitor, "Maybe it's Marilyn Monroe!" after he lets it slip that there's a blond in the kitchen.

Wilder's casual reference to Monroe's celebrity shows what an icon of sex she had already become. *The Seven Year Itch* makes a significant contribution to that iconography, and she in turn carries the film to a higher plane. Monroe's delivery has seldom been better, and she was never more vibrant, alive and sexy. Her breathy recital of the Girl's TV commercial for Dazzledent toothpaste ("I had onions for lunch. I had garlic dressing at dinner. But he'll never know, because I stay kissing sweet—the Dazzledent way.") is an essential Monroe moment, and even people who've never seen the film know the classic image of the sex goddess standing over a subway grate, her ecru pleated dress hoisted by a blast of air. In the original play, Monroe's character was smarter—she even had a passing acquaintance with Sartre—but here she's adorably daffy, a woman who keeps her underwear in the icebox on hot summer days. It's a comic gem of a performance, even if it probably added to Monroe's struggle to be accepted by the public for her brains as well as her beauty.

Behind the scenes, a crisis was erupting in Monroe's life, spurred by the filming of the celebrated scene with the subway grate. Production began on September 13, 1954, with a brief schedule of location filming in New York, designed to maximize publicity for the movie. The first setup was simple: Marilyn calling out to Ewell from an upper-floor window at 164 East Sixty-first Street. The second, filmed from one to four on the morning of September 15, was a more elaborate affair. A mob of photographers and close to two thousand bystanders swarmed round the Trans-Lux Theatre on Lexington Avenue and Fifty-second Street to catch a glimpse of the blonde goddess as a giant electric fan swooped up her dress to reveal her gorgeous legs and tight white panties. Production assistants told the crowd that as long as they stayed behind the barricades, photographs of Monroe's unveiling were definitely permitted. The result was the kind of worldwide publicity a studio dreams about. This brilliant media event was the brainstorm of Monroe's friend Sam Shaw, the production's official still photographer, who had always envisioned Marilyn and her raised skirt as the main image for the movie's ad campaign. Indeed, the early-morning shoot was arranged largely for publicity purposes; the bulk of the scene was reshot later inside Fox's Hollywood studio, where crowd noise wouldn't drown out the dialogue. In the finished film, Monroe's dress rises just above her knees; the mob on Lexington Avenue and readers of the next day's papers got to see a lot more of their favorite sex symbol.

Unfortunately for Monroe, one of the bystanders that morning was her husband, Joe DiMaggio. Powerful columnist Walter Winchell had phoned the baseball great in Beverly Hills the day before and advised him of the circus that was about to take place. DiMaggio immediately booked a flight to New York, but thought better of attending the shoot and decided to wait for his wife at the bar of the St. Regis Hotel. But Winchell tracked down DiMaggio and, seeing a juicy story in the making, cajoled him into a visit to the Lexington Avenue location. As DiMaggio watched his wife's skirt go flying up over and over to the loud cheers of the crowd, he became enraged; Wilder said his face had "the look of death." Later that morning, after the shoot, Monroe and DiMaggio had a terrific fight. The star's hairdresser, Gladys Whitten, remembered seeing bruises on Monroe's shoulders. Two weeks later, Monroe filed for divorce.

The events of September 15 had an adverse effect on the film, too. Standing under the wind machine all night had given Monroe a chill. Costar Ewell recalled, "She was shaking like hell that night." The star caught a severe cold that, combined with her depression over the collapse of her marriage, caused her to call in sick for four days that September. The movie wound up going thirteen days over its original thirty-five-day schedule.

Wilder had had his problems with actors before, but never with one so insecure, erratic and unpredictable. Sometimes Monroe would deliver her lines perfectly on the first or second take; at others, she would continually stumble over the same few words. To Wilder's annoyance, her longtime drama coach, Natasha Lytess, was always off camera giving her hand signals. And, to Wilder's total amazement, one day his star reported to the set several hours late, claiming she couldn't find the studio—a studio that had been her daily workplace for the past several years.

Nonetheless, says Wilder, "it was worth going through hell. It was worth making eighty or ninety takes of the same thing, because when you did it and it was right, it was the best it could be." For Wilder, part of what made it all worthwhile was Monroe's "flesh impact," a palpable quality that makes it seem as if you could reach out to the screen and touch her. Yes, she brought a lot of emotional baggage to the set and she was hardly ever on time, but as Wilder once said, "I have an Aunt Ida in Vienna who is always on time, but I wouldn't put her in a movie."

One person who never had a bad word to say about Monroe was her costar, Tom Ewell (or Tommy Ewell, as he's billed onscreen). The Kentucky-born actor, then best known in films for his role in George Cukor's 1949 *Adam's Rib*, had originated the role of Richard Sherman on Broadway (opposite the relatively little known Vanessa Brown) and played it for some 730 performances. In his view—at least the view he gave to the press—Monroe was a total professional, possessed of intelligence, sensitivity and "an eagerness to find out what our director wanted."

Unbeknownst to Ewell, one thing the director wanted was another actor in the part of Richard Sherman. Recalls Wilder, "I tested a young actor in New York and I liked him very much. He was kind of a revelation—I never saw a leading man like this before. But they wouldn't go for that—I was not making the picture all by myself." The actor's name was Walter Matthau.

Matthau confirms the story. "Yeah, I did a screen test. I think it was with Gena Rowlands. And after I did it, [Billy] said, 'What did you think?' And I said, 'Well, I felt rushed.' He said, 'No, that's not rushed—that's pace. When you see the rushes tomorrow, you'll see.' I saw it the next day, and I said, 'Yeah, you're right. Good pace.' He said, 'Well, you've got the part, 83–10.' Then Tom Ewell got the part. Three years later, I saw him someplace and I said, 'What happened to the 83–10?' He said, 'Didn't you ever bet on an odds-on favorite and lose?' "

Wilder hastens to note that Ewell "is a very good actor," and indeed he gives a highly proficient comic performance that launched a durable career in movies (most memorably opposite another 50s blonde bombshell, Jayne Mansfield, in *The Girl Can't Help It*) and TV (*The Tom Ewell Show* and *Baretta*, among them). But he's perhaps too aptly cast as a plain-looking drudge; he lacks the quirky charisma that Matthau would have brought to the Monroe matchup.

Cast as Ewell's good-natured wife was Evelyn Keyes, the ex-wife of Wilder's close friend John Huston, a pert actress best known for her roles as Scarlett O'Hara's younger sister in *Gone with the Wind* and opposite Larry Parks in *The Jolson Story*. No doubt Keyes's casting made for some interesting conversations at the Wilder home, since the actress had had a brief romance with the director back in the 1940s, according to writer Peter Viertel. Also on hand in the newly created role of a nosy superintendant was *Stalag 17* Oscar nominee Robert Strauss, hammy as ever. And character actor Oscar Homolka turns up as one of Richard's writers, a cocky German psychiatrist who complains that he's running fifteen minutes early because a patient jumped out the window in the middle of a session—another Wilder gag at the expense of Sigmund Freud.

When *The Seven Year Itch* wrapped production on November 4, producer Feldman organized a huge party in Monroe's honor at Romanoff's, in part to try to persuade the star not to leave him for new agents at MCA. The remarkable guest list included Clark Gable, Humphrey Bogart, Gary Cooper, Claudette Colbert, Darryl F. Zanuck, Jack Warner, Sam Goldwyn and, of course, Wilder and Axelrod.

The movie premiered on June 1, 1955 (Monroe's birthday), at New York's Loews State, where a four-story cutout of Marilyn in her high-flying skirt drew crowds and stopped traffic. A few weeks after the opening, 20th Century–Fox quietly removed a couple of moments of racy footage in order to receive a "B" rating ("morally objectionable in part for all") from the Catholic Legion of Decency. One cut came in the fantasy sequence in which Richard imagines the Girl with her toe stuck in the bathtub faucet; no longer would the plumber drop his wrench and grope around in the soapy water to retrieve it. Also deleted was a line from the subway-grate scene, when Monroe says she feels sorry for "you men in your hot pants." One shot was added to the film, weakening the running joke about an award-winning photograph Monroe's character posed for on the beach. In the original version, the audience is led to presume Monroe is nude; now, the audience sees the photo in question, with the sexpot sprawled out in a modest 1950s bathing suit.

Like most reviewers of the day, Bosley Crowther singled out the spectacle of Monroe in her revealing Travilla costumes as the main reason audiences would want to flock to the film. Crowther felt Monroe's presence overwhelmed the play's dominant interest in Ewell's sexual torment, but then admitted "there is a certain emptiness and eventual tedium to the anxieties of Mr. Ewell." In a mostly negative appraisal, *Time* complained about the laundering of the play, but hailed Monroe's comic style as "reminiscent of a baby-talk Judy Holliday." *Variety* also noted the compromising of the play, but dubbed the comedy "a funny picture and a money picture." The industry bible's prediction came true: *The Seven Year Itch* was Wilder's second most successful film of the 1950s, with some $6 million in rentals to the studio (or roughly $12 million in box office).

Right after *The Seven Year Itch*, George Axelrod set to work on another Monroe vehicle, which marked a dramatic breakthrough for the sex star: *Bus Stop*, the film adaptation of William Inge's play about a naïve cowboy and a saloon singer. Axelrod also wrote the screenplays for the acclaimed 1960s hits *Breakfast at Tiffany's* and *The Manchurian Candidate*, and he wrote and directed the darkly comic 1966 cult film *Lord Love a Duck*. In a recent interview, Axelrod declared, "Billy is, was, a wonderful teacher. I learned about art, food, everything. I didn't learn about writing so much. I learned about real life. Culture." What he did learn about writing included two cardinal rules: "Thou Shalt Not Bore," and "Anything is Permitted." "Billy gave me the courage to do some of the nutty stuff we did in *The Manchurian Candidate*," Axelrod insists. The two remain close friends to this day, and even collaborated briefly on an unrealized screenplay idea in the early 1990s.

As for Marilyn, she was positively gushy when it came to Wilder. "He's a wonderful director," she declared. "I want him to direct me again, but he's doing the story of Charles Lindbergh next, and he won't let me play Lindbergh." It would be four years before Monroe and Wilder worked together again, on a shoot that would make *The Seven Year Itch* seem like pure heaven.

FIFTEEN

Finding a Diamond

WITH THREE HIT PICTURES IN A ROW, WILDER WAS ONCE again among the most bankable filmmakers in Hollywood, at the top of the list of candidates for hot movie properties. Instead of originating bold new projects like *Sunset Boulevard* and *Ace in the Hole*, he was increasingly allowing himself to be part of a package assembled by aggressive agents and producers—especially now that his relationship with Paramount Pictures was reaching its end. The strategy paid off handsomely with *The Seven Year Itch*, resulting in the most popular film of the director's career to date. But it was also his least personal, too. George Axelrod's play may have piqued a certain mischievous interest in the effect of a Marilyn Monroe on a married man, but it had only the most superficial connection with Wilder's deeper concerns as a writer: the masks people adopt to survive, the psychological journey of a flawed protagonist. The compromises with the censor only made the distance between the director and the material that much greater.

Wilder's next picture again found him playing the role of filmmaker-for-hire. Of all the titles in his canon, it is the least recognizable as a Billy Wilder film—in truth, it's largely indistinguishable from a long line of handsomely mounted, respectful, somewhat stodgy movie biographies. Its name is *The Spirit of St. Louis*.

This ambitious account of the first solo airplane flight across the Atlantic by American folk hero Charles Lindbergh on May 20–21, 1927, chiefly owes its existence to an old friend of Wilder's, Leland Hayward. The former agent to the stars had sold his business to the Music Corporation of America in the mid-1940s and become equally successful as a Broadway producer, with such hits as *A Bell for Adano, State of the Union, South Pacific* and *Mister Roberts* to his credit. When Lindbergh's chronicle of his landmark flight was published in 1953 and became an immediate best-seller, Hayward snapped up the movie rights for $1 million. A history buff, Wilder was receptive when Hayward asked him to direct his forthcoming production, despite the notoriety of Lindbergh's friendly official visits to Nazi Germany in the late 1930s.

From their first meeting with the "Lone Eagle," the producer and director realized they were dealing with a most unconventional hero. Lindbergh was staying in Pasadena, some thirty miles away, and agreed to come to Wilder's house for Sunday dinner. Hayward's wife suggested picking up the aviator at his hotel, but Hayward said there was no need, assuming Lindbergh had a car and chauffeur at his disposal. Just after four, the famous guest arrived, dressed in a gray suit and high-top shoes, and apologized for being three minutes late—he had underestimated the length of the walk from the bus stop, itself nearly a mile. "You took the bus?" Wilder asked. Yes, the pilot explained, when he was in a strange city he liked to travel by public bus; that way, he could watch and listen to ordinary people unobserved. To maintain his anonymity, Lindbergh had not allowed himself to be photographed for some twenty years; in fact, his contract with Warner Bros. stipulated that he would not be party to press interviews or photo sessions.

Once they secured their subject's cooperation, Wilder and Hayward consulted on the phone with Lindbergh at least once a week. But the filmmakers found they could go only so far in their portrayal of the secretive hero. "I was interested [in doing the film] because he seemed like a wonderful character," says Wilder, "which did not turn out to be, because I was not allowed to deviate even one inch from the book. I could not delve into his private life, I could not touch the kidnapping of his baby or his visits in Germany. I talked to him about it, but we didn't touch on it. So it turned out to be a one-dimensional character. There are some very good things [in the film], but it leaves you unfulfilled.

"He was a very silent man," Wilder continues. "When we talked about the script, he gave his opinions in a very short yes or no, or I don't think so. It was not my happiest experience, where I could let my imagination grow, because there was always that iron curtain there."

At one point, Wilder and Lindbergh took a commercial plane from New York to Washington so that they could study the pilot's original single-engine craft, the *Spirit of St. Louis*, which was on display at the Smithsonian Institution. When the plane ran into rough weather, Wilder leaned over to his companion and joked, "Wouldn't it be embarrassing if we crashed and the headlines said, 'Lone Eagle and Jewish Friend in Plane Crash'?" Lindbergh smiled, acknowledging the director's sly reference to his German excursions. Giving Lindy the benefit of the doubt, Wilder says he always suspected the aviator might have been acting as a spy for U.S. Army Intelligence during his controversial trips abroad.

The star of *The Spirit of St. Louis* was another old friend of Hayward's: Jimmy Stewart. The actor and the producer first met in 1935 as copilots in a cross-country airplane race; at one point in their bachelor days, they even shared a house together. Stewart, an accomplished pilot and a war hero, wanted the role of Lindbergh badly, but the forty-seven-year-old star knew that Hayward considered him too old to play the then twenty-five-year-old aviator. The filmmakers' first choice for the role was John Kerr from the Broadway success *Tea and Sympathy*, but the young actor turned them down, objecting to Lindbergh's right-wing politics. Then, Stewart's cause was boosted when his eighty-four-year-old father, having remarried, came to Hollywood on his honeymoon. The Haywards, the Stewarts and the newlyweds celebrated together at a local restaurant, and before long the elder Stewart was lecturing the producer on why his son was the perfect actor to play Lindbergh—age be damned. "After my dad's outburst, Hayward took to asking me to lunch with Billy Wilder," Stewart recalled. "I could hardly eat. They watched everything I did and every forkful I lifted. They were studying me, thinking about my age." Finally, Hayward relented and, in a desperate effort to look younger, Stewart shed five pounds from his lanky frame and dyed his hair and eyebrows reddish blond. Adding to Stewart's insecurity, Wilder continually teased the actor that the only reason he got the role was because he had a pilot's license.

Initially, Wilder worked on the screenplay with another old friend,

Charles Lederer, the screenwriter of the 1931 *Front Page* and its remake, *His Girl Friday*, as well as *Kiss of Death* and *The Thing*. But relations between the two veterans quickly grew strained, and soon Wilder was searching for yet another partner. By chance, he read a rave *Los Angeles Times* review of a TV drama written by a former stage actor named Wendell Mayes. Working on gut instinct, Wilder told Hayward to recruit the unknown writer, at a salary of $1,000 a week. The thirty-five-year-old Missouri native leapt at the offer, and Wilder liked his genial enthusiasm. In fact, Mayes was such an easygoing type he later graduated, on Wilder's recommendation, to a successful three-film relationship with Otto Preminger, as the screenwriter of *Anatomy of a Murder*, *Advise and Consent* and *In Harm's Way*.

After months of preparation, with $2 million already spent (most of it on replicas of Lindbergh's plane), Wilder and Mayes still had only forty pages of script. Understandably nervous, Jack Warner insisted on seeing their handiwork. Wilder refused—he never showed an unfinished script to anyone, not even Jack Warner. But he was willing to compromise—he would come up to Warner's office and give a verbal account of the work-in-progress. The mogul was greeted not only by Wilder, but by Mayes and Hayward. Mayes narrated the story and read the dialogue, Hayward improvised a musical score, and Wilder simulated the sound effects—the revving of the engine, the whirring of the propeller, the wind whooshing past the plane. The zany performance wiped away Warner's bad mood, and he left his filmmakers in peace.

Wilder and Mayes faced the tough challenge of giving visual interest and variety to Lindbergh's 33½-hour solo flight from New York to Paris, which takes up the entire second half of the film. Their solution was a continual series of flashbacks, beginning the night before takeoff, as the young pilot struggles unsuccessfully to get some sleep in a Long Island hotel room. We see Lindbergh as an airmail pilot parachuting out of his plane in a snowstorm, then honing his ideas for a craft that will successfully take him across the Atlantic, pitching his scheme to some St. Louis bankers, and overseeing the building of the streamlined plane at the low-key, hands-on Ryan Aircraft Factory in San Diego. Once the *Spirit of St. Louis* is in the air, we get more biographical vignettes: Lindbergh's purchase of his first plane, his barnstorming days in the Midwest, etc. The flashbacks are generally lively and flavorful, but fail to overcome an inherent problem: The movie is still basically the chronicle of one man stuck in a cockpit for a day and a half, and we already know how his daring adventure ends.

That said, the most effective moments in *The Spirit of St. Louis* are those that dramatize the perils of Lindbergh's journey. The takeoff from mud-soaked Roosevelt Field is masterfully filmed, as the plane labors to become airborne, passing the safety marker and snagging electrical wires along the way. Wilder also generates high suspense when the pilot succumbs to sleep over the Atlantic and the *Spirit of St. Louis* circles in a downward spiral, closer and closer to the ocean waves; the crosscutting between Stewart's face and the wayward plane is worthy of Hitchcock. Over the course of the film, Lindbergh copes with fog, ice, a broken compass, engine trouble—all made more palpable by Stewart's deeply committed performance and a special-effects team that earned the film its only Oscar nomination.

Through much of the flight, Stewart performs in silence, accompanied by an interior monologue on the soundtrack. But, desperate to get his leading man talking, Wilder turned to a variation on the discarded cockroach scene in *Hold Back the Dawn:* Up till Newfoundland, Lindbergh holds court with a stowaway fly. Unlike Charles Boyer, Stewart didn't object to talking to an insect, although he later told a reporter, "My first instinct on seeing a fly in a plane would be to hit it or kill it. They're the ugliest things in the world."

Wilder also considered adding an element of sex to the film, after hearing a rumor that the reason Lindbergh didn't sleep before his journey was because a reporter had arranged for a willing waitress to visit the virginal pilot in his room. Whatever thought Wilder had of introducing the mystery girl, no one on the production dared ask Lindbergh for his approval. The only female presence in the final film is the Lindbergh groupie who lends the pilot her compact mirror, an encounter loosely based on fact.

UNUSUAL FOR WILDER, THE PRODUCTION FILMED ITS FINAL scenes first—the arrival of an exhausted Lindbergh at Paris's Le Bourget Airdrome, which was reconstructed at Guyancourt, outside Paris. In a letter to Warner Bros. on September 9, 1955, Hayward described the elaborate shoot as "a real hysterical night, with the five thousand French extras and the enormous, enormous crew. We took a chance on the weather and it looked like we'd blown a fortune. It started to rain early and I want to tell you, you could have bought the picture for a quarter when it started to rain with this airport covered with these goddamned French extras. But luckily it stopped and we got some terrific shots." Hayward further reported that "after they ran across the fields about ten times, screaming and yelling, the five thousand began to get dissipated a little bit. Toward four or five in the morning, quite a few had been nipping at the bottle." Hayward hastened to add that, with Charles Eames acting as a montage adviser, Wilder was preparing his shots "with complete exactness."

During a break in the grueling night shoot, a short, elegant man walked up to Wilder and asked, "Why are you doing this? This is a job for the second-unit director." It was Alexandre Trauner, the Viennese-born art director, famed for his work on such classic French films as *Quai des brumes* and *Children of Paradise* (the latter an especially remarkable achievement, since he was a Jew in occupied Paris). Within months, Trauner would be re-creating the interior of Paris's Ritz Hotel for Wilder's *Love in the Afternoon*, the first of many splendid collaborative efforts.

One thing Wilder and Hayward hadn't planned on during their stay in Paris was trouble from Jimmy Stewart, but the actor was tired and irritable, having just come off a grueling shoot on Alfred Hitchcock's *The Man Who Knew Too Much*. The filmmakers wanted Stewart around so they could photograph him in the *Spirit* replica, actually flying over Paris and other locations like Cherbourg, Le Havre and Ireland. The actor insisted the shots could be captured just as well or better in a studio, with back projections. As Hayward reported to Warner Bros., "His big point was that this is the most important picture in his whole life and it's essential to him to look as physically well as possible. He left the day after the Hitchcock picture and says he needs two or three weeks of absolute rest. I pointed out that the beds at the Ritz [in Paris] are very comfortable. He said he couldn't rest here, he hated Paris, the food made him sick, his wife had the trots. . . ."

After several days of arguments, Stewart got up in the middle of a dinner with Hayward, went straight to the airport and flew to New York.

Once there, he went directly to bed, complaining of exhaustion. Hayward and Wilder subsequently got him on the phone and asked him if he wanted out of the picture. Stewart said no, doing the Lindbergh story was a life-time ambition, and he would soon see them back in New York. Wilder and Hayward never got their shots of the star in the air over Europe.

"I've known Stewart longer than anyone," Hayward wondered, "and I've never seen him behave in the irrational, ridiculous, kind of crazy fashion he did in Paris." But all Stewart wanted, at age forty-seven playing twenty-five, was to make sure he was still ready for his closeup.

The French police were yet another problem. Hayward noted that, while shooting *Around the World in 80 Days* in Paris, the flamboyant producer Mike Todd had had all the parked cars in the Place Vendôme illegally towed, angering the city's law-enforcement officials. In the shadow of that incident, all eyes were on the *Spirit of St. Louis* replica flying over Paris. Hayward was warned that the plane had been spotted traveling below the prescribed altitude of 900 feet; if it happened again, the plane would be confiscated by the French government.

By September 25, the movie was already well over budget. Hayward wrote to Jack Warner, "There is no escaping the fact that this is probably the most difficult picture that anyone has tried to make—logistically, technically, and every other way it is a bitch." But the producer assured the studio boss, "Billy is as competent and thorough and conscientious a man as I have met in the business."

Wilder's crew covered some 25,000 miles tracing Lindbergh's journey, capturing CinemaScope footage of New England, Nova Scotia, New-foundland, Greenland, Ireland and France. "The technical problems were enormous," Wilder said in the mid-1960s. "We had to cover such a vast area . . . and we had to keep trying to keep in touch with Paul Mantz, who flew the plane, and you'd have to ground it to discuss the technical facts, and the weather didn't match. I've never done an outdoor picture before or since—I'm not an outdoor man."

Wilder may not consider himself much of an outdoorsman, but that didn't stop him from accepting a bet with Stewart that turned him into an amateur daredevil. After the director jokingly complained about having to hire a double to do a Lindbergh wing-walking stunt, claiming anyone could perform such a simple feat, Stewart dared Wilder to make good on his boast. And so Wilder strapped himself to the struts of a vintage World War I monoplane, and stood on its wings for a ten-minute ride at 800 feet.

The Spirit of St. Louis cost $6 million, an enormous sum for its day. Thanks to the extensive aerial location photography, Wilder had more than ten times the footage he needed, an editing dilemma he had never faced before. The final film clocked in at two hours and fifteen minutes, and would have run longer had Wilder and Hayward not decided to cut a dream sequence in which Lindbergh lands in Paris and no one is there to greet him, and a subplot in which the pilot's barnstorming pal, Bud Gurney, has a flying accident. But, after viewing the completed film in Jack Warner's private screening room, everyone connected with *The Spirit of St. Louis* sensed that no amount of trimming would save the picture. Something fundamental was missing.

With so much money at stake, the Warner Bros. publicity department worked overtime to create public awareness of their big Lindbergh movie. In a convenient piece of timing, Stewart—who began the film as a colonel in the Air Force reserve—was nominated to the rank of brigadier general. Hayward, Wilder and Jack Warner used all their clout to make the Los Angeles premiere of the movie at the Egyptian Theatre one of the grandest in Hollywood history. Among the 1,500 guests on April 11, 1957, were many of the day's top movie names, including Clark Gable, Gary Cooper, Burt Lancaster, Natalie Wood, Charlton Heston, Kim Novak, Jayne Mansfield and Jane Russell. The event was broadcast on nearly all the radio and TV networks, with special features on such popular shows of the day as *Lux Video Theatre, House Party, Truth or Consequences* and *Today*. The *Hollywood Reporter* billed it as "the biggest TV-radio audience in Hollywood premiere history."

The hoopla was partly an attempt to overcome the tepid audience response to *The Spirit of St. Louis*'s American debut at Radio City Music Hall in New York, which had kicked off with a gala charity premiere on February 21. The early reviews acknowledged the painstaking, often gripping re-creation of the flight across the Atlantic, but invariably found fault with the movie's portrayal of the Lone Eagle. "We see very little of his basic nature, his home life or what makes him tick," Bosley Crowther complained. *New Yorker* critic John McCarten said that while the book revealed Lindbergh to be "a fairly subtle character," in the film he "hasn't much more depth than one of those beamish young men you encounter on Air Force recruiting posters." And Hollis Alpert in *Saturday Review* singled out one of the picture's more curious elements: the emphasis on a St. Christopher medal a friend hides in the pilot's lunch bag. "Lindbergh flew to Paris, so the movie implies, and found God," Alpert scoffed. True enough. Unlike in *Ace in the Hole*, where Wilder used religious imagery with subtle effectiveness, the miraculous medal is the kind of clunkily "up-lifting," old-style-Hollywood device Wilder managed to avoid through most of his career.

Warner Bros. mustered enough critics' quotes to make *The Spirit of St. Louis* look like an event *(Redbook* deemed it "one of the best films ever made") and sent Stewart on a hectic cross-country promotional tour via the private plane of the president of United Airlines. But the public wasn't interested—perhaps it was a combination of Lindbergh's faded celebrity and a certain jadedness about what he accomplished, or maybe it was just the film. *The Spirit of St. Louis* took in only $2.6 million in box office, not even half of its production cost. Jack Warner would call it "the most disastrous failure we ever had."

BEFORE *THE SPIRIT OF ST. LOUIS* TOOK ITS NOSEDIVE, WILder went back to work at Columbia Pictures, the studio that first welcomed him as a fresh-off-the-boat immigrant. It was still being ruled by the same gauche tyrant, the dreaded Harry Cohn. Jerry Wald, a producer at Columbia, invited Wilder to come work on the movie version of the Rodgers and Hart Broadway musical *Pal Joey*, based on John O'Hara's stories of a shady nightclub impresario. Wilder moved into a three-room suite at the Gower Street studio, and began formulating ideas along the lines of the original's younger man/older woman relationship. Naturally, *Sunset Boulevard* came to mind, and with it the notion of casting Mae West as the woman; for her young lover, he pictured the most talked-about actor in Hollywood, Marlon Brando. Wilder proposed his concept to Cohn over a long lunch in the studio commissary. Cohn hated it. Who wanted to see an over-the-hill cartoon like Mae West in *Pal Joey*? The leading lady had to be sexy, voluptuous, *young*—someone like Rita Hayworth. A little more than a week after he had settled in at Columbia, Wilder received word via Jerry Wald that things weren't going to work out with Harry Cohn. Wilder also got a bill for the lunch.

If Columbia wouldn't have him, there were plenty of places in town that would. In fact, Wilder had a commitment waiting on the back burner. Around the time his relationship with Paramount was beginning to crumble, he had joined his friends John Huston and William Wyler in a bold and risky move, signing a contract with Allied Artists, the independent company formerly known as Monogram Pictures. Throughout the 1930s and '40s, Monogram had been one of Hollywood's leading producers of B pictures, the low-budget bottom halves of theater double bills. In 1946, as the market for B pictures began to decline, Monogram launched Allied Artists, a subsidiary devoted to higher-grade offerings. But, compared to the big-studio releases, Allied Artists' output was painfully humble—films with semi-name actors, produced on an average budget of $200,000, and never based on the kind of literary or stage property the public might recognize.

By 1954, the Monogram name was dead, and the revamped Allied Artists was determined to play with the big boys. The company's evolution came largely through the efforts of three brothers, Harold, Marvin and Walter Mirisch, all with backgrounds in theater exhibition. Youngest brother Walter was the first to arrive at Monogram; hired in 1945 as assistant to company president Steve Broidy, he created the successful series of *Bomba, the Jungle Boy* pictures and was named executive producer in 1951, at the age of twenty-nine. Harold, the oldest of the trio, had been head of Warner Bros.'s Wisconsin theaters and chief film buyer for the RKO circuit before joining Monogram in 1948 as vice-president of distribution. Marvin was the last to come aboard, in 1952 as assistant secretary; before that, he had been branch manager for Grand National Pictures and cofounder (with his eldest brother, Irving) of Theatres Candy Company, one of the nation's largest theater concession operations.

Putting all his sales experience to good use, Harold managed to sign individual deals with three of the country's top motion-picture directors, mainly by promising them hefty profit shares and generous stock options in the company. First out of the gate was William Wyler, with the 1956 Oscar-nominated Quaker drama *Friendly Persuasion*. Meanwhile, John Huston planned to make Rudyard Kipling's *The Man Who Would Be King* with Clark Gable and Humphrey Bogart, but was forced to cancel the project when Bogart became too ill to work.*

Wilder's Allied Artists picture was drawn from his memories of a 1931 German movie based on Claude Anet's novel *Ariane* (already filmed once before in 1926). It starred Elisabeth Bergner as an innocent young cello player in czarist Russia who is in love with an older Frenchman; what Wilder remembered most vividly was the closing scene, an emotional farewell between the two lovers at a railway station.

Preliminary work on *Love in the Afternoon*, as the new *Ariane* came to be known, began in 1955, while Wilder was in the midst of preparing *The Spirit of St. Louis*. Once again, he was testing out a new writing partner—a conservatively dressed, bespectacled gentleman with the curious name of I. A. L. Diamond. As self-effacing and taciturn as Wilder was brash and extroverted, surely this Diamond would be lucky to get through one film with the imposing Austrian.

Itek Dommnici, as he was first known, was born on June 27, 1920, in Ungheni, Romania (now Moldavia). At the age of nine, he and his family settled in the Crown Heights section of Brooklyn. His father, who arrived several years earlier, changed the family name to the more American-sounding Diamond, while a teacher who didn't like the sound of "Itek" took to calling the young boy "Isidore." An exceptionally bright child, he not only acclimated to his new life in New York, but won a scholarship in a metropolitan-area mathematics competition. Diamond went on to Columbia University, where he edited the *Spectator* and wrote skits for the university variety show. Right out of college, he ventured to Hollywood, where he cranked out screenplays for an array of forgettable films, including *Two Guys from Milwaukee*, *Two Guys from Texas* and *The Girl from Jones Beach*. Until he partnered with Billy Wilder, his most notable credit was as one of the writers of the 1952 Howard Hawks comedy, *Monkey Business*.

The story behind Diamond's eye-catching initials varies. Sometimes Diamond claimed that they meant nothing at all; at others, he suggested they stood for Interscholastic Algebra League, in tribute to his early academic triumph. Jack Lemmon believes the initials were born during

---

* The film was finally realized in 1975, with Sean Connery and Michael Caine.

Diamond's newspaper days. "The editor said, 'I. Diamond is o byline, and Isidore is too long—add something to it.' So he put down I. A. L. Diamond and the editor said, 'Fine. What the hell is the A. L.?' And Diamond answered, 'Abraham Lincoln—who knows?'" Whatever their origin, the initials made a good conversation piece; years later, during the rise of Black Muslim militancy, Wilder joked that Diamond ought to consider changing his name to I. A. L. X.

Diamond was a junior writer at Paramount in the 1940s when he first met Billy Wilder, according to his elegant widow, Barbara, who lives today in an unpretentious house on a quiet street in Beverly Hills. The partnership began to take shape, she says, when agent Swifty Lazar engineered a meeting between the two men in Wilder's office. Wilder enjoyed the humor columns Diamond had been writing for the Writers Guild newsletter, but he really became convinced about the younger man's talent after watching two skits he wrote for the annual Writers Guild awards dinner in 1955. One was a parody of the "Fugue for Tinhorns" from *Guys and Dolls*, with three agents hawking their writer clients. The clincher was a sketch in which two writers—one seated at his typewriter, one pacing furiously—agonize over just the right adverb for the stage directions accompanying a line of dialogue. "Quizzically?" one writer offers, to no reply. "Truculently?" The search continues. "With mixed emotions." "With great surmise!" And finally, "How about quizzically?" This was a man after Wilder's own language-loving heart.

"Billy was sitting with Ernie Lehman at that dinner," recalls Barbara Diamond, "and he kept asking Ernie who had written various things—Iz had done an enormous amount of the show. Afterward, Ernie came up to Iz and said, 'Are you going to start working with Billy or something?' I think it was already in the works."

Unlike some of Wilder's prior collaborators, Diamond wasn't intimidated by the caustic, celebrated director. "My husband had enormous pride but no ego," his widow reflects. "Without saying anything against George or Ernie or any of the others . . . Billy is like a force of nature, he's a centrifugal force. When he walks into a room, he becomes the center of the room—it's the source of his power as a director, as a matter of fact. And this is very, very difficult for many people to handle. Iz had absolute confidence in his own ability, in his own skills, in his art, whatever you want to call it. He was not in the least bothered by this facet of Billy, so it was possible for him to work with him. And once that was accepted, Billy didn't treat him the way he treated some of his other collaborators.

"Their relationship was purely business. Billy used to make everybody else play tennis with him. Iz just went in and said, 'I don't play tennis or do any of that stuff.' "

Initially, the two worked apart. Wilder told Diamond his plans for *Love in the Afternoon* and, while work continued on *The Spirit of St. Louis*, Diamond began composing an outline, with the setting of *Ariane* changed to modern-day Paris.

As *LOVE IN THE AFTERNOON* TOOK SHAPE, WILDER ENVI-sioned Cary Grant for the role of the older lover. But once again the cautious matinee idol demurred. "Maybe he thought I was a Nazi," Wilder ponders—jokingly, since Grant was a personal friend. "I never made a picture with him, and I really liked him enormously. I liked what he did, which seems to be so easy—it's a very difficult thing to be a leading man in a comedy. The part that he was absolutely ideal for was in *Ninotchka*—it's very sad that we did not see Garbo with the best of the light comedians. It was just not to be. And I can't have him back now."

With Grant out of the picture, Wilder contemplated casting Yul Brynner, who was filming his signature role in Charles Brackett's movie version of the musical *The King and I*. Now the character would be an exotic international playboy, along the lines of the world-famous Aly Khan. Wilder sent Diamond out to interview Jack Warner's daughter, Doris Vidor, a leading Beverly Hills socialite who frequently played hostess to Khan. Vidor began describing Khan's charm, his knowledge of fashion and horses, then suddenly stopped midsentence. "To tell you the truth," she sighed, "Aly Khan is a fucking bore."

At last, Wilder determined to model the character after Howard Hughes, making him a wealthy industrialist with an eye for the ladies. The part was similar to the sexually capricious millionaire at the center of Wilder's first film for Ernst Lubitsch, *Bluebeard's Eighth Wife*. And so, nearly two decades later, the director cast the same actor, Gary Cooper. For the role of Ariane, his first and only choice was Audrey Hepburn.

Even though most of the story takes place indoors, Wilder opted to film it entirely in Paris, at the Studios de Boulogne. "We could have made this picture just as well in Hollywood," he admitted at the time. "But why not be in Paris? Besides, it's a picture about life here, and I think that living here in Paris all this time is good for the picture."

Hepburn came in almost directly from filming *Funny Face* opposite Fred Astaire. Once again, she was playing the love interest of a much older man, but unlike her tense experience with Humphrey Bogart in *Sabrina*, working with Coop was a joy. Any initial trepidation she felt about the screen legend was erased when Wilder scheduled a dance scene early in the shoot. Cooper was such a poor dancer that Wilder called him "Hopalong Nijinksy," putting Hepburn immediately at ease.

On her arrival in Paris, Hepburn also received encouragement from Maurice Chevalier, whose role as her father was his first American film assignment in twenty years. A telegram from Chevalier read: "How proud I would be, and full of love I would be, if I really had a daughter like you." However gracious, the veteran French musical star was not particularly well liked by the French crew, who couldn't forget his eagerness to continue entertaining during the wartime occupation.

A surprise addition to the cast—prominently featured in one scene but allowed not one word of dialogue—was Billy's wife, Audrey. "We needed a handsome, statuesque brunette, very elegant, who is at the opera with Gary Cooper," Wilder notes. "And she did it for me. She never worked in another picture of mine—except for her arm in *The Lost Weekend*."

Wilder has happy memories of the *Love in the Afternoon* shoot, with the possible exception of a picnic-in-the-grass sequence on an island on the Chevreuse River. First, fog delayed the action, then mosquitoes invaded the location. Take after take was ruined by the noise of overhead planes bound for Orly Airport. "I never knew a seducer's work could be so hard," Cooper deadpanned. More serious were the angry protests that erupted in Paris over the Russian invasion of Hungary in the fall of 1956, which climaxed with the firebombing of the Soviet embassy. A member of the film crew was injured in the melee and died later in a Paris hospital.

WILDER AND DIAMOND'S *LOVE IN THE AFTERNOON* SCRIPT retains the experienced-older-man/virginal-young-woman dynamic of the original novel (and Ariane's cello playing), but adds much that is new. A major new character is Ariane's father, Claude Chavasse (Chevalier), a Parisian private investigator specializing in gathering evidence of marital infidelities for suspicious spouses. A big portion of Chavasse's caseload is taken up with one Frank Flannagan (Cooper), an American millionaire with a string of female conquests all over the globe. The detective has gathered photographic evidence of Flannagan's latest dalliance for a grieving husband (John McGiver), who vows to shoot the aging playboy dead during the coming night's rendezvous at the Ritz Hotel. (Chavasse's reaction is to demand immediate payment of his fee.) Ariane overhears their conversation and, unable to convince the French police there's anything extraordinary about an irate husband stalking his wife's lover, rushes to the hotel to save the handsome philanderer she's admired in her father's photos. The young virgin takes the place of the cheating wife, falls under Flannagan's spell and becomes his four o'clock "appointment," pretending to be a woman of equally deep sexual experience and never revealing her name.

All too soon, Frank leaves Paris, and a year passes before the lovers see each other again, meeting by chance at the Paris Opera House. At first, Flannagan doesn't even recognize the "thin girl," but their four o'clock rendezvous resume. Ariane finds the best way to keep Frank interested is by inventing a list of exotic former lovers (basically culled from her father's files); the ploy sends the hypocritically jealous Frank into a drunken tailspin. Sweating out his hangover in a Turkish bath, he encounters the husband who tried to kill him, who recommends the services of Chavasse. The detective puts the pieces together and glumly reveals to Flannagan the identity of his mystery lover. For her own good, Frank breaks it off with Ariane and buys a train ticket for the Riviera. In the memorable closing scene, Ariane runs after Frank's train, her tears betraying her real emotions as she insists she'll get along just fine. Frank lifts the girl onto the train, leaving behind Chavasse, whose final narration (at least in American prints) reveals that the couple got married in Cannes.

Love in the Afternoon is Wilder's most conscious attempt to create a film in the spirit of Ernst Lubitsch, from its Continental setting to its mischievously adult treatment of sex to its casting of Cooper and especially Chevalier, a star of several 1930s Lubitsch musicals. Perhaps the most Lubitsch-like touch is the band of gypsy musicians Flannagan hires to accompany his seductions, even when the occasion is al fresco. When the band begins playing "Fascination" ("that piece of Viennese schmaltz"), you know Frank is almost ready to consummate. When they file out of the hotel room, it's fifties shorthand that something naughty is about to happen behind closed doors. Ernest Lehman may have kept Audrey Hepburn innocent in *Sabrina*, but now there was no denying that America's favorite gamine was a woman with grown-up desires.

As in *Sabrina*, Wilder pairs a sheltered Hepburn with an aging American businessman, with one huge difference: Bogart's Linus Larrabee is all work and no play, while Frank Flannagan is all play and very little work. But they're still both essentially uncultured Yanks who become more decent and compassionate men through the love of a European-bred woman. For all his professed fondness for his adopted country, Wilder could still be sharply critical of America's deficiencies of soul in the postwar materialistic age. "They're very odd people," Ariane says of Flannagan and his ilk. "When they're young, they have their teeth straightened, their tonsils taken out, and gallons of vitamins pumped into them. Something happens to their insides. They become immunized, mechanized, air-conditioned and hydromatic. I'm not even sure whether he has a heart." "What is he—a creature from outer space?" asks Ariane's goofy would-be boyfriend. "No," she announces, "he's an American."

Like Linus, Frank uses Ariane—but at least he's honest about his cavalier treatment of the women in his life. It's Ariane, thinking he can only be attracted to a woman of the world, who carries on the deception—and then discovers what a powerful tool she has to get under the millionaire's skin. But Ariane's motives are so pure, her masquerade has no dire consequences. When Frank discovers who his lover really is, he briefly tries to obscure his feelings and carry on with his empty playboy life. But his heart won't let him play the game—it's been won over by this strange, thin girl.

Powered by its emotional finale and the endearing charm of Audrey Hepburn, *Love in the Afternoon* is arguably the most romantic film of Wilder's career. But how much more romantic it could have been had Wilder persuaded Cary Grant to take the role of Frank Flannagan. Cooper certainly had a lot of the qualities the part required: sophistication, comic flair, a certain offstage notoriety as a lady-killer. Wilder remembers what an immaculate dresser Cooper was and how beautifully he moved, qualities he attributes to Dorothy di Frasso, the European countess who befriended the actor in his early western days and gave him a sense of style. Of all the actors he worked with, Wilder says, only Marilyn Monroe had as magical a relationship with the camera. "When you watched me shooting a scene with Gary Cooper, it didn't look like anything. But when you saw it on screen in the rushes, there was an added something going on—some kind of love affair between the performer and the celluloid."

And yet . . . Cooper was fifty-five when he made *Love in the Afternoon*, only three years older than the seemingly ageless Grant, but his gaunt, lined features made him look like a man in his sixties. Wilder contends that Cooper was more like Flannagan in real life than the upright western hero the public loved in *High Noon*, but the movie's visual scheme reveals a director well aware of his male lead's ebbing sex appeal, since Cooper is often photographed in shadow or through gauze. Hepburn may have thought her costar's looks were "astounding," but there's still a startling age difference between the two—especially today, when older leading men with much younger female love interests are less accepted as a matter of course. Even at the time, several critics felt Cooper was too old to be playing a womanizer. *Saturday Review*'s Hollis Alpert, after conceding that "no heart is too old or withered for romance," couldn't help dwelling on the practicalities of the relationship between Ariane and Frank. "With more than a thirty-year age differential, what about children, what about the future . . . ?" he wondered. The reviewer for *Cue* complained that Wilder "has miscast long, lanky, lethargic, leathery, and (let's be frank about it) no-longer-youthful Gary Cooper as a gay young dog. . . ."

Cue was none too kind to the film in general, branding it "a rather long and slow business" and a "two-hour juvenile-seduction joke." But *Cue* was in the minority. Bosley Crowther began his review with a declaration that might have made even Wilder blush: "The pedestal on which the reputation of Ernst Lubitsch has been sitting all these years will have to be relocated slightly to make room for another one. On this one we'll set Billy Wilder." *The New Yorker* raved, "Everyone involved in the enterprise seems truly to have entered into its antic mood—a mood set with brilliance and gaiety by Billy Wilder . . . and I. A. L. Diamond."

Despite the Lubitsch-like subtlety of Wilder's approach, *Love in the Afternoon* met some friction en route to the nation's theaters. The Catholic Legion of Decency gave the film a "B" rating, grumbling that it "tends to ridicule the virtue of purity by reason of undue emphasis on illicit love." According to *Variety*, Wilder had shot an alternate ending in which the two leads go their separate ways, but the Production Code Office insisted that they get together and that it be made clear they were off to the altar. (European release prints didn't bother with the disclaimer.) Industry censors also objected to a suggestive reference to Pepsi-Cola's ad slogan "Pepsi-Cola Hits the Spot" (Flannagan is a Pepsi executive, among other interests), but the line remains in the finished film.

Wilder also had to contend with some in-house meddling by Allied Artists chief Steve Broidy. "What are we going to do about the title?" Broidy demanded. "What kind of a title is *Love in the Afternoon*?" Dumbfounded, Wilder replied, "So we have a common denominator, tell me the best title you've ever heard." After a moment, Broidy suggested *Wichita*—the name of a low-budget Allied Artists western that was doing good business. "If *Wichita*'s a good title," Wilder answered back, "then you have a lot of good titles—*Seattle*, *Kansas City* . . ." Finally, Wilder walked out of the executive's office, threatening to take his title and never come back. After an hour or two, Broidy tracked down the director and sheepishly asked, "Can't you take a joke?"

Despite the rave reviews, *Love in the Afternoon* did only modest box-office business—delivering a severe blow to Allied Artists' venture into higher-profile pictures. With limited capital at its disposal, the company had sold off foreign distribution rights to finance both the $3 million *Friendly Persuasion* and the $2.1 million Wilder film. Unfortunately for AA, neither Gary Cooper vehicle was the sort of domestic smash hit that would propel the company into the big time.

Harold Mirisch acted fast. Within a month of *Love in the Afternoon*'s August 1957 opening, he finalized a twelve-picture deal with Arthur Krim, the president of United Artists, and announced the formation of the Mirisch Company, a new production company based at UA headquarters at the Samuel Goldwyn Studios in Hollywood. Founded in 1919 by Mary

Pickford, Douglas Fairbanks, Charles Chaplin and D. W. Griffith, United Artists had been in bad straits itself until just a few years earlier, when Krim and his partner, Robert Benjamin, turned the company around with an aggressive program of financing and distributing pictures and sharing profits with outside producers. Because it was not a studio per se, and thus charged no studio overhead costs and allowed greater creative freedom, UA became an attractive home base for some of Hollywood's brightest producers and directors. Within a year of their taking over the company, Krim and Benjamin had UA in profit, and they were soon releasing some of the decade's most distinctive films, pictures like *The African Queen, High Noon, Marty* and *Sweet Smell of Success.*

The Mirisches and UA were an especially good fit. Just as UA gave unusual latitude to the producers whose films it distributed, the Mirisch Company wanted to, in its own words, "enable the filmmaker to do the thing he most wants to do—concentrate completely on the films, on what appears on the screen, and let a small, effective organization handle all the other complex matters that are part of making a movie, ranging from negotiating contracts and financing, to persuading actors to work under the Mirisch banner, to arranging pre-production logistics and, perhaps most important, taking the completed film and supervising its merchandising on a coordinated, worldwide basis." The first filmmaker to sign with the Mirisch Company was Billy Wilder.

Coincidentally, Wilder was already preparing a picture for United Artists, independent of the Mirisches. Veteran B-movie producer Edward Small had acquired film rights for a hefty $430,000 to *Witness for the Prosecution*, mystery queen Agatha Christie's long-running stage adaptation of her short story, and brought it to UA. Rejected by director Joshua Logan, hot off *Picnic* and *Bus Stop*, the project came to Wilder through two longtime friends. Small's producing partner was Arthur Hornblow Jr., the man who gave Wilder his first directing break at Paramount. What's more, Marlene Dietrich, who was campaigning hard for the central role of the enigmatic Romaine Vole, wanted Wilder to be her director.

Wilder told Hornblow, "If we had to invent someone to be the ideal woman for Romaine, we would have to invent Dietrich," but Small wasn't convinced. Small, who planned to follow *Witness* with a production of *Solomon and Sheba*, wanted an actress he could cast in both films, and was talking with both Ava Gardner and Rita Hayworth. Hornblow informed Small, "Billy would go for Ava in the part, perhaps with Jack Lemmon, but doesn't think Hayworth could play it all [a reference to the disguise trickery in the film], and I agree."

First choice for the male lead was William Holden, who was not available. Then Hornblow and Wilder offered the part to Tyrone Power, who expressed reservations about taking on a character he was sure would be overshadowed by the two other leads in the film. "Nevertheless," Hornblow wrote to Small, "he said the promise of the show was so exciting that, with a strong setup, he was sure that he would find himself in a very good enterprise." Complicating the Power situation was the fact that he was a year late in delivering two pictures from his own production company to Harry Cohn's Columbia Pictures, and had already been granted postponements to perform in two plays.

With Power a question mark, inquiries went out to Richard Burton, Jack Lemmon, Glenn Ford, Gene Kelly (who was eager to establish his dramatic credentials) and the then unknown Roger Moore. Wilder suggested Kirk Douglas, partly because he had liked his work in *Ace in the Hole* and partly because he had introduced Douglas to Dietrich and watched a brief romance kindle between them. None of these casting choices materialized. Finally, producer Small offered Power $300,000 per film to star in both *Witness* and *Solomon and Sheba*. By January 1957, Power and Dietrich were set, along with a third star: Charles Laughton.*

The filmmakers had at first considered hiring Francis L. Sullivan, who had originated the role on stage, for the part of defense attorney Sir Wilfrid Robarts. But Wilder decided the film required an actor of a stature equal to Power and Dietrich's. Into the bargain, he also secured the services of Laughton's droll wife, Elsa Lanchester, for the newly created role of Sir Wilfrid's overly attentive nurse, Miss Plimsoll.

Working from a preliminary screenplay adaptation by Larry Marcus, Wilder teamed with a new partner, Harry Kurnitz, a longtime screenwriter whose credits included *Shadow of the Thin Man, See Here, Private Hargrove, One Touch of Venus, The Inspector General, The Man Between* and *Land of the*

---

* Power's salary far exceeded that of his costars. Dietrich earned $100,000 and Laughton $75,000, while Wilder's directing fee was $100,000.

Pharaohs. The forty-eight-year-old Kurnitz was also an author of detective novels under the pen name Marco Page, and thus a logical sounding board for ideas on how to improve on Agatha Christie. Kurnitz was erudite, sophisticated, a great talker—but nowhere near the kind of workaholic Wilder was. Seven years later, Kurnitz wrote a profile of Wilder for *Holiday* magazine which described the sensation of "being cooped up with Billy in a small room for some twenty stimulating weeks":

> though I kept no day-to-day record, interested persons who open 20th Century–Fox's *Book of Martyrs* more or less at random are likely to come on text or pictures conveying the nature of my experience. . . .
>
> Billy's associates sometimes have a hunted look, shuffle nervously, and have been known to break into tears if a door slams anywhere in the same building. He has a fierce, monomaniacal devotion to whatever project is in the typewriter or before the cameras; he is a fiend for work and to some people's dismay he works nearly all the time. In fact, having concluded an arduous project of his own, Billy's idea of a restful vacation is to join some colleagues (or even casual acquaintances) who are having script trouble and work for nothing on *their* story for a few weeks. Nor does the fact that he is not being paid make him easier to please. If anything, Billy the Philanthropist is even more demanding than Billy the Pro. "Let's face it," one of the recipients of his literary generosity once commented ruefully, "Billy Wilder at work is actually two people—Mr. Hyde and Mr. Hyde."

Kurnitz may have felt besieged by Wilder, but the director adored his three stars. Marlene, of course, was an old and dear comrade. Wilder insists there was never anything romantic between them, but "something much deeper"—a wonderful friendship. And, contrary to her cool public image, "she was a great cook—actually, she was a German *hausfrau.* She loved to wipe your floor, to scramble your eggs, God knows what. But she was nothing like the unreachable vamps of the time—not that mysterious quality that Garbo had. But she was a very, very big star and she made an enormous impact."

You can always get a choice quote from Wilder about Marlene Dietrich. He told German director Helmut Dietl, "She was Mother Teresa, only with better legs," adding, "she was beautiful, inside and outside, particularly in uniform. As we hit Berlin in the summer of 1945, we were both in American uniform. Naturally, hers was from Chanel."

The admiration was mutual. Late in her life, Dietrich called Wilder "the cleverest man I have ever met," and in her autobiography she had this summation of his craft: "Billy Wilder was a master builder who knew his toolbox and used it in the best way possible to set up the framework on which he hung the garlands of his wit and wisdom."

Wilder got a kick out of throwing dinner parties and encouraging Dietrich to shock his guests with stories of her many affairs back in Berlin, with both men and women. Dietrich's daughter, Maria Riva, says of the Wilders, "They were good friends, listened to her endless yearnings, kept her secrets, could be trusted." But as Riva continues her account, Dietrich's jealousy of Wilder's young wife is palpable. "All they do, those two, is sit in front of the television set!" Riva remembers her mother complaining. "Billy even eats in front of it. They both sit there like Mister and Missus Glutz from the Bronx, little mennubles—eating their frozen dinners! Unbelievable! That's what happens to brilliant men when they marry low-class women! Sad!"

Dietrich could also be a harsh critic of Wilder at work. In a long, detailed letter to her daughter, she dissected the many things she thought were wrong about Wilder's handling of the courtroom scenes in *Witness*. The Old Bailey set looked too new, the extras included "no middle-class English faces . . . no characters who go to murder trials but nice California good-looking ladies." She lamented that Tyrone Power's immaculate wardrobe and appearance were completely wrong for the unemployed defendant he was playing. "I am photographed harshly so that nothing reminds anyone of my usual beauty," she argued with her usual modesty, "and there sits a Hollywood LEADING MAN so out of character and his beautifully manicured hands with ring and cuff links and watch lie on the edge of the prisoner's box."

Laughton, too, was a target of her simmering discontent. "By now Laughton is codirecting me with Billy. He is a sly fox and Billy who is 'in love' with him does not notice what he is doing. Through his advice I was made to yell in the first courtroom scene which I think disastrous as I have no place to go."

At fifty-five, Dietrich was concerned not only with the nuances of her performance but with preserving the glamorous mystique she would keep up into her early seventies. "She was a great lighting technician, she learned that from Sternberg," Wilder notes. "For me it's a bit odd when an actress tells me, 'I don't think the key light is in the proper position.' Nobody knows about key lights!" Wilder's reaction was: "Be my guest! You light it, but you explain it to the gaffer, the head electrician. Don't make an enemy out of me!"

In *Witness*, despite her complaints about harsh lighting, Dietrich still seems remarkably young, thanks in large part to her secret helpers—flesh-colored tabs that were glued to her skin and pulled back tight to accentuate those famous cheekbones. One crucial sequence, however, required the star to look completely unappealing. (Readers who aren't in on the mystery should skip ahead.) Christie's tricky plot had Christine (as Romaine was now called) donning the guise of a dark-haired, slovenly Cockney woman. The big question wasn't whether Dietrich could hide her looks—makeup people can do wonders—but whether the German-born actress could pull off a convincing Cockney accent. Prior to filming, both Laughton and Noël Coward became her personal dialect coaches, with Coward reporting in his diary, "It is not easy to teach Cockney to a German glamour-puss who can't pronounce her Rs but she did astonishingly well." Indeed, many who see the finished film remain unconvinced that the dark mystery lady *is* Dietrich or that it's her real voice, although attentive listeners can still detect those telltale Rs.

Dietrich's observation that Wilder was "in love" with Laughton was not far from the truth. The director was a longtime fan of the rotund star of *The Private Life of Henry VIII*, *Mutiny on the Bounty*, *The Hunchback of Notre Dame* and other screen classics, but he'd never encountered a performer this bountifully gifted.

Wilder calls Laughton the best actor he's ever worked with, and backs up that bold statement with some fondly remembered examples. One time, the director was filming jurors' reaction shots, and Laughton volunteered to read all the script's speaking parts. "You don't want to do this, Charles," Wilder said. "It's donkey work, the script girl can do it." But Laughton insisted, and offered amazingly accurate cameos of his fellow actors. "I wish I'd had it in the picture," Wilder enthuses.

The director also recalls Laughton's meticulous preparation for his climactic courtroom monologue. The duo began rehearsing at six in the evening, each time making minor adjustments. "At nine o'clock we were at version number twenty-one," Wilder recalls. "Nine o'clock! And he got better and better and better. 'Now let's remember all of that, now do what you did before.' And next morning he said, 'I have it!' Version twenty-two. And that's the one we shot."

Wilder once noted that "you can tell how good an actor is by looking at his script. If he's no good, it will be neat as a pin. Charles's was filthy, it looked like a herring had been wrapped in it. He had obviously digested it and regurgitated it—whole!"

Along with digesting scripts, Laughton was getting fatter on Dietrich's home cooking. A tongue-in-cheek Dietrich appreciation Laughton wrote for the *Los Angeles Herald & Express* mostly concentrated on the elaborate lunches she whipped up for her colleagues, from Hungarian goulash to Wiener schnitzel to beef stroganoff. Whatever complaints she may have had about Laughton's "codirecting" efforts and Power's vanity, Dietrich still had enormous affection for her costars.

Wilder and Hornblow's regard for Tyrone Power was so high, they had made a special trip to Mexico City to the set of *The Sun Also Rises* in May 1957 to determine how soon their leading man would be available to work on their film. For Wilder, the handsome star of *Blood and Sand* and *The Razor's Edge* was another class act. "He was one of those rare occurrences in Hollywood," the director told Power biographer Hector Arce. "He was an absolutely total gentleman. The one thing I admired more about him than anything else was his manners.

"With very rare exceptions do I get close to actors," Wilder continued. "I try to keep it like a lawyer-client relationship. Ty became a close friend. The picture we did together was one of the few joys of my professional life."

Dietrich, as often happened with her costars, was also enamored of Power. To the actor's discomfort, she flirted with him constantly, and even bought him an expensive gold cigarette case. But, Wilder declared, "Everybody had a crush on Ty. Laughton had a crush on him. I did, too. As heterosexual as you might be, it was impossible to be totally impervious to that kind of charm."

FOR THE SECOND FILM IN A ROW, WILDER WORKED WITH ART director Alexandre Trauner. Having reproduced the Ritz on a Paris sound-stage, Trauner was now set the task of creating a persuasive facsimile of London's Central Criminal Court, commonly known as the Old Bailey, on Stage 4 of the Goldwyn Studios in Hollywood. The replica was built to scale, 43 feet by 56 feet, with a 27-foot-high ceiling, at a cost of $75,000. Though constructed of real Austrian oak, the set had movable panels and floor sections, thus allowing Wilder to shoot from any vantage point he desired. As impressive as his accomplishment was, Trauner humbly told observers, "The reality is better than the fake."

Wilder and Kurnitz, however, were determined to enhance Agatha Christie's handiwork. "Christie plotted like a god," Wilder observes, "but there were no human beings—they were cardboard. That's why we changed a lot of things in the picture. And she wrote me a letter and sent me a photograph saying it was the only good picture ever made of any of her material."

The screenplay retains the basic construct of the Christie whodunit. Unemployed war veteran and aspiring inventor Leonard Vole (Power) is about to be charged with the murder of Emily French (Norma Varden), an aging spinster he befriended, and seeks the counsel of Sir Wilfrid, a cele-brated London barrister. Leonard, who has inherited all of the victim's money, visited her the night of her death, but he says his wife, Christine, will attest that he was home at the time of the murder. Christine, however, appears decidedly less devoted to Leonard than her husband believes, and rather indifferent to backing up his alibi. In fact, when Christine finally takes the stand, she's an eager witness for the prosecution. Sir Wilfrid's case appears to be lost until a strange Cockney woman appears, eager to sell some love letters of Christine's that prove she's out to get her husband. The barrister exposes Christine's sham in court and clears Leonard of the crime. But there are more twists to come. (Again, skip ahead if you want to preserve the mystery.) Believing her word as his wife would never have saved her husband, Christine has engineered an elaborate masquerade, pretending not to love him and creating the Cockney woman and the letters. As it turns out, Leonard *is* guilty and Christine knows it; the supposedly agile Sir Wilfrid has been one step behind them all along. What Christine doesn't know is that Leonard has his own plans to run off with a younger woman. In the final moments, the spurned wife fatally stabs Leonard with a knife from the evidence table.

Wilder's biggest contribution to Christie's original was to transform Sir Wilfrid into a funny, endearing, flawed human being. The screenwriters had the portly lawyer returning from hospital as the film opens, with strict orders not to put any strain on his fragile heart. They also gave him a chatty, overbearing nurse, from whom Sir Wilfrid struggles to hide his continuing devotion to cigars and brandy, offering lots of opportunities for Laughton to spurt comic venom at his real-life wife. Sir Wilfrid intends to make good on his promise to stick to a diet of bland civil lawsuits, until he spies the cigars in Leonard's breast pocket and gets sucked into another high-profile murder case. Sir Wilfrid's heart condition adds both comedy and a certain undercurrent of suspense to the movie, though the barrister not only survives his humiliation but seems invigorated by the thought of defending cunning Christine at the movie's close.

Wilder and Kurnitz also added Sir Wilfrid's ploy of shining the light from his monocle into the faces of his interrogation subjects as a surefire means of detecting whether they're telling the truth. The monocle trick reveals nothing, however, except for the fact that Wilfrid is more a showman than an astute judge of character.

In the play, Leonard met and married Christine, an actress, while stationed in Hamburg after the war. Wilder expands that morsel of information into an entire flashback sequence which becomes a homage to both *The Blue Angel* and the director's own *A Foreign Affair*. Dietrich, at fifty-five still capable of vamping an audience of GIs, performs "I May Never Go Home Anymore," a reworking of "On the Reeperbahn Half Past Midnight," a old German tune written by one of her former Berlin acting cronies, Ralph Arthur Roberts. (Soon after, Dietrich recorded the song and put it in her nightclub act.)

Apart from this Hamburg interlude, *Witness for the Prosecution* may not seem like a particularly personal project for Wilder, but another of his can't-miss adaptations of a proven stage success. Part of the attraction, too, was the chance to work in a new genre. "I get bored being in the same rut," the director insists. "I admire Hitchcock, but I couldn't work like him, because he made the same picture every time. I told myself, 'Now, I'm going to make a picture that's better than Hitchcock,' and I did *Witness for the Prosecution*, let us say. Or, 'I can make a better picture than—I don't know—Capra.' I hop around like a chessman, always with different prospects. . . . I like to make different sorts of pictures. Spielberg does the same thing—either he does the dinosaurs or he does the Nazis. He will find out that that's the only way. It's very difficult to copy or to parody a picture of mine, because you never quite know what you're going to see."

Still, *Witness*'s connections to Wilder's previous work are strong. The mystery genre naturally lends itself to the director's preoccupation with disguise and deception—in fact, the audience's ultimate enjoyment of the film stems from a masquerade's success in fooling them, too. No one in the Christie tale is what they seem on the surface—not even the self-proclaimed legal dynamo, Sir Wilfrid.

In this instance, the masquerade involves hiding one's very essence. Leonard Vole is all charm and maligned innocence but, as his rodent surname hints, he's the biggest cad in the Wilder canon—and, considering the competition, that's saying a lot. Christine appears to be all ice and malice, but she's actually a fool for love, altogether willing to sacrifice her freedom for the husband who saved her from a harsh future in Germany. When everything falls apart, she's as much a woman scorned as Phyllis Dietrichson, Norma Desmond and Lorraine Minosa; like them, in one furious moment she takes her revenge on the man who's cast her aside.* But of all the heroines in Wilder melodrama, Christine is the most purely a victim.

When *Witness for the Prosecution* finished shooting in August 1957, the UA publicity wheels were already spinning. Studio publicists made a big deal of the fact that the final ten pages of the screenplay were being kept under wraps (even though the play had been seen worldwide) and alerted columnists that armed guards were being stationed on the set during filming of the finale. Secrecy pledges were enforced at early preview screenings, where the film met a sensational response. At a command performance in

---

* Wilder says he prefers a knife for screen killings. "I hate the noise of a gun," he insists. "I am such a delicate creature."

London, producer Hornblow even got the royal family to agree to sign a secrecy oath. Meanwhile, Wilder and Power took the picture to Germany, where they cabled back, "We killed them in Berlin. It's getting monotonous. Shall we take it to Moscow?"

Back in New York, the film had its first word-of-mouth screening in late November at the UA projection room, followed by a party at "21," for an exclusive guest list including Dietrich, Rex Harrison, Douglas Fairbanks Jr., Merle Oberon, Clifton Webb, Oscar Hammerstein II, Moss Hart, Joseph L. Mankiewicz, Truman Capote, Alan Jay Lerner, Irene Selznick, Kay Kendall, Sam Spiegel, George Axelrod, Leland Hayward, Arlene Francis and Bennett Cerf.

Witness opened in December with an exclusive run in Los Angeles to qualify for the Academy Awards, and in February in New York. The reviews were generally ecstatic and box office was brisk, ultimately bringing in close to $8 million. Bosley Crowther commented that "for a courtroom melodrama pegged to a single plot device . . . *Witness for the Prosecution* comes off extraordinarily well," singling out Wilder's direction and Laughton's performance for special praise. Both *Cue* and *Saturday Review* felt Wilder had improved on the play, while *Newsweek* called it a "masterful melodrama." *The New Yorker* said the picture "builds up quite a head of suspense," but good-naturedly complained that Laughton "goes about his forensic duties with all the groaning, moaning, snorting, sniffing, heaving and drooling that the script (and the director) will bear. . . . [Laughton] dominates the proceedings with the satisfaction of an old ham that has found the right platter."

In London, *Times* critic Dilys Powell was more appreciative of Laughton's talents. "Sidling and pouncing, wheedling or letting the great voice roar out, the artful master of the monologue employs every trick in his famous old box; fascinated, your eyes can't avert themselves from the huge wattled face, from the small, pale, well-shaped lips pouring out honey and comic vituperation."

Laughton's performance also caught the eye of the Oscar committee, securing him his third nomination for Best Actor. Elsa Lanchester was also in the running for supporting actress, and the movie earned nominations for Best Picture and Best Director (Wilder's sixth appearance in that category). As with *A Foreign Affair*, Dietrich deserved but failed to win a nomination; fully expecting Academy laurels, she had already arranged for the recorded introduction to her Las Vegas nightclub act to include a reference to her Oscar bid. That year, the big winner was David Lean's *The Bridge on the River Kwai* as the *Witness for the Prosecution* contingent went home empty-handed.

When *Witness* wrapped, Wilder, Power and Laughton didn't want the fun to end. They flew to Paris, rented a car and drove through Europe together, stopping at one of Wilder's favorite relaxation spots, the spa at Badgastein. From there it was on to Vienna and Berlin, with plenty of sightseeing, hiking and gourmet eating. "We laughed all the way," Wilder recalls. "It was the Three Stooges in Europe." One year later, while filming *Solomon and Sheba*, Tyrone Power suffered a severe heart attack and died at the age of forty-four.

Soon after his return from Europe, Wilder told the *New York Times* his plans to reunite with Laughton on the story of Colonel Alfred Redl, the Austrian head of the secret service who was convicted of selling military secrets to the Russians during World War I. The homely Redl's downfall was his powerful attraction to a young, handsome lieutenant, which compelled him into increasingly reckless behavior. Laughton, a repressed homosexual, became increasingly uncomfortable with the subject, finally telling Wilder he couldn't see himself playing the role under any circumstances. For Wilder, it would simply have been a fascinating tragedy of unrequited love. Nearly two decades later, the Redl story was filmed by the Hungarian director István Svabó, with Klaus Maria Brandauer in the title role.

Late in 1961, Wilder approached Laughton again, with an offer to play the role of the tavern proprietor Moustache in his forthcoming film of the hit stage musical *Irma la Douce*. But early the following year, when Laughton fell in his tub and broke his shoulder, doctors discovered he had cancer. All through his final year, the actor clung to the hope that he would remain strong enough to play the role. Wilder remembers Laughton telling him, "Don't listen to whatever they tell you, it's not true. I'll prove it—come and see me at my house." Says Wilder, "I went that lunchtime. He had had his male nurse dress him up, comb his hair, shave him, maybe even put a little makeup on him, and he was sitting in a chair by the swimming pool. He said, 'Now look at me. Do I look like someone that's going to die?' And he got himself out of the chair and he walked round the pool. He must have been in tremendous pain, but he just wanted to say to me, 'Wait.' This was one of the finest performances, I tell you. I was very touched." Laughton died on December 15, 1962, wearing a thick white moustache for the Billy Wilder film he would never make.

Wilder, of course, remained friends with Marlene Dietrich, but in her declining years it wasn't an easy relationship to maintain. In a 1988 television interview, he revealed how hard it now was to get close to the reclusive star: "When I'm in Paris, I always phone her. She disguises her voice, usually as a Czech cook or a French maid: 'I will geeve Miss Dietrich the mess-*sage*.'

" 'Come on, for Christ's sake, Marlene, we know it's you! . . . Marlene, I'll come up, I want to see you. I'll blindfold myself, how about that?'

" 'I'll call you Monday.' On Sunday she phones: 'Tomorrow is out—I have an eye appointment in Neuilly.'

" 'All right, I'll see you Tuesday.'

" 'Tuesday I thought you were leaving.'

" 'I can postpone my departure.'

" 'No, no, leave if you have to.' "

Despite these wary games, Dietrich, shortly before her death in 1992, told German journalist Hellmuth Karasek that of all the people she knew, the one she would most want to spend an evening with was Billy Wilder. "But not one evening—many evenings."

Hotter than Ever

WILDER'S TWO-PICTURE DEAL WITH THE MIRISCH COM-
pany was a generous one. He would be paid a director's fee of
$200,000 per picture, plus 17½ percent of the gross after the breakeven
point (determined as twice the movie's negative cost). Wilder's share would
rise to 20 percent when the film grossed $1 million beyond breakeven. In
addition, he was given final cut and virtual control over all the production
elements. "All the Mirisch Company asks me is the name of the picture, a
vague outline of the story and who's going to be in it," Wilder declared.
"The rest is up to me. You can't get any more freedom than that."

Wilder could also work with other production entities if he chose.
Around the time the Mirisch pact was announced, he was also in talks with
the UA-based Hecht-Hill-Lancaster outfit (producers of *Marty* and *Sweet
Smell of Success)* about two projects, the Colonel Redl film and a reunion
film with George Axelrod called *The Catbird Seat.* Neither materialized.

At Mirisch, Wilder began developing a new Audrey Hepburn vehicle
based on Louis Verneuil's stage farce *My Sister and I,* but the project lost its
momentum due to Hepburn's contractual commitments to Paramount.
Wilder's back-up idea sounded far less promising. It originated with Robert
Thoeren, an old Berlin friend turned Hollywood screenwriter who had
been urging the director to remake *Fanfaren der Liebe (Fanfares of Love),* an
obscure 1932 German musical comedy he had co-written. "We got a print

of the German original and ran it," Wilder told critic Stanley Kauffmann. "It was quite poor, a rather heavy-handed Bavarian *Charley's Aunt*, replete with dirndls and lederhosen. And yet there was that platinum nugget: two male musicians latching on to an all-girl band."

The nugget was buried amid a whole series of broad comic episodes in which the starving musicians do anything to get work—don blackface to enter an all-Negro ensemble, put on gypsy garb to blend with a band of gypsies, and so on. Wilder would begin the film from scratch, but first he needed the right collaborator.

WHEN *LOVE IN THE AFTERNOON* WRAPPED IN PARIS, I. A. L. Diamond returned to Hollywood to work on a Danny Kaye musical for MGM, *Merry Andrew*. "Fresh from the experience with Billy, he had his normal studio experience," states Barbara Diamond. "He wrote a picture in which an uptight, prissy schoolteacher finds a little lost dog in a field and immediately becomes transformed. But the producer decided the picture got off to too slow a start with somebody prissy, so he put a musical number up front and destroyed what plot there was. Billy called almost immediately after that and said, 'I've got an idea.' " From that moment on, in a partnership spanning some thirty years, Iz Diamond would have control over his material, because Billy Wilder was there to protect it.

Diamond liked Billy's idea of making something airy and all-American out of the heavily Germanic *Fanfares of Love*. But how to sustain the notion of two guys infiltrating an all-girl orchestra? Almost immediately, Wilder concluded it had to be "an absolute question of life and death." At first, the writing duo considered having the boys witness a murder in their bookie's office. Then, at the end of a brainstorming session, Diamond pointed out how the stage classic *Charley's Aunt* was always done as a period piece— "because when all the costumes look peculiar to us, a guy in drag looks no more peculiar than anybody else." The next morning, Wilder proclaimed that Joe, the movie's womanizing saxophonist, and Jerry, his easily manipulated, bass-fiddle-playing pal, would be witnesses to Chicago's infamous St. Valentine's Day Massacre of 1929.

"Suddenly, we were in business," Diamond recalled. "Because the period thing gave us all the other elements, you know, characters and backgrounds that we hadn't even thought of at that point. And I think that's what really made the picture, the bootleggers and the millionaires in Florida and all that." Diamond dubbed the project *Some Like It Hot*—little realizing that the title had already been used for a 1939 Bob Hope comedy for Paramount. But, since pre-1948 Paramount films were now owned by the Music Corporation of America, and MCA represented Billy Wilder, the proper clearances were easily obtained.

Wilder's first choice for the part of Jerry was Jack Lemmon, an Oscar winner for *Mister Roberts* but not a major box-office name. As Lemmon recalled at the 1986 American Film Institute Life Achievement Award tribute to Wilder, "I had my first real conversation with Billy Wilder in 1958. . . . I was in a little restaurant having dinner and Billy came over and reintroduced himself.* He said, 'Okay, we got this story here, we got two musicians and they witness the St. Valentine's Day Massacre. And they see the killers, but the killers see them. So they gotta disguise themselves in order to save their lives, which means you're gonna be in drag for 85 percent of the film. Do you wanna do it?' I said, 'I'll do it. I will *do* it! Under any circumstances.' Because it was Billy Wilder."

It wasn't quite that simple: Lemmon was under exclusive contract to Columbia Pictures and, besides, United Artists preferred a bigger name. The first star to come aboard was Tony Curtis, someone Wilder felt could play either of the lead roles. Then, UA suggested Frank Sinatra, and Wilder made a lunch date with the crooner. But Ol' Blue Eyes developed a sudden aversion to mascara and never showed up. For a while Mitzi Gaynor, coming off the success of *South Pacific*, was being considered for the female lead, but then the director received a friendly letter from Marilyn Monroe, saying she'd like to work with him again. Wilder and Diamond rushed Monroe a two-page outline of their new project, but not before beefing up the role of band singer Sugar Kowalczyk (aka Sugar Kane). Within weeks, Monroe signed on at a salary of $300,000 plus a hefty 10 percent of the gross profits.

With Monroe involved, Wilder was now free to pursue Lemmon. To obtain a temporary release from his contract with stingy Columbia boss

* The two had met briefly during *The Seven Year Itch*, and again when Lemmon was being considered for the Ty Power role in *Witness for the Prosecution*.

Harry Cohn, Lemmon agreed to do four more films for the studio at his old salary—he thinks he may still owe them one. For *Some Like It Hot*, Lemmon and Curtis each received $100,000.

Lemmon says many in the industry were calling the project "Wilder's folly." "Boy, we were really pushing an envelope—there wasn't anybody who didn't think Billy was crazy. The film was considered to be very expensive and the subject completely risky, putting your two leading men in drag for over 80 percent of the film and taking what was a five-minute burlesque sketch, in the opinion of most people, and trying to stretch it into a two-hour farce." David O. Selznick, after hearing Wilder describe the comedy's St. Valentine's Day Massacre setup, warned, "You can't make it work. Blood and jokes do not mix."

Lemmon's friends at the time feared his career would be ruined by people concluding he was gay or a closet transvestite, but the actor decided not to worry about audience perceptions. "The only way to play it was to let it all hang out and just go, trusting that Wilder would say 'Cut' if it got out of bounds."

Tony Curtis says he had no hesitation about getting into drag as Joe's alter ego Josephine, declaring, "It never dawned on me to think of it as anything but a unique and interesting part." Wilder, however, says that when the two actors were first fitted for their costumes and wigs, Lemmon eagerly showed off his new identity as Daphne, while Curtis had to be dragged out of the dressing room. "Mr. Curtis, he grew into it," recalls Wilder, "but you could see, going to the commissary, Lemmon came in like he was Mae West and Tony Curtis was slithering along the wall." Eventually, Curtis agreed to join Lemmon in an acid test of their feminine masquerade: They sauntered into the ladies' room of the studio dining hall. As Lemmon tells it, no one batted an eyebrow.

At one point, Wilder brought in a celebrated female impersonator he remembered from his younger days in Europe to tutor the two stars. Ironically, it was Lemmon who gave "Barbette" a hard time. The veteran drag performer showed her pupils how to walk like a woman by crossing one foot over the other, but Lemmon refused to follow instructions. "You didn't want them both doing the same shtick," Lemmon declares. "I was clumsy, I was an asshole, the shoes were killing me, my ankles were turning. But Tony could carry it off with a great aloofness; he just put his head up in the air and pouted his lips. His Josephine was fearless about it, but my Daphne was scared shitless." Indeed, Curtis has a fond regard for his *Some Like It Hot* alter ego: "I enjoyed seeing that kind of elegant, aloof, you-can't-fuck-me woman. I'm not a pushover."

Concluding that Curtis and Lemmon's masquerade would be less believable in color, Wilder hedged his bets by electing to shoot *Some Like It Hot* in black-and-white. Curtis also cites the massacre scene as a factor—he says Wilder told him, "If I do it in color, I'm going to have to use ketchup as the blood and people will know it's phony. But if I do it in black-and-white, it will enhance and maintain the tension." Monroe's contract with her regular studio, 20th Century–Fox, stipulated that all her films be shot in Technicolor, but after viewing gaudy color tests of her two costars, she agreed to deprive her fans of a flesh-and-fantasy-colored Marilyn.

Wilder had coped with Monroe's caprices on *The Seven Year Itch*, but nothing could have prepared him for the painfully neurotic creature he encountered a mere four years later. Monroe was perfect for the role of the emotionally bruised but ever hopeful lead singer of an all-girl jazz band in the year 1929. The star's husband, playwright Arthur Miller, thought a new Wilder comedy might be just the thing to cheer Monroe following her recent miscarriage. Whether *Some Like It Hot* had any therapeutic value for America's reigning sex symbol is an open question, but the experience was a thoroughly traumatic one for her director.

First there was the problem of Monroe's flagrantly excessive tardiness, which surfaced even before shooting began. A welcoming dinner party given in her honor by Harold Mirisch of the Mirisch production company was spoiled when she and Miller arrived at 11 P.M., after everyone had eaten. During early wardrobe and makeup tests, she showed up for a 1 P.M. call 2½ hours late, and finally emerged from her dressing room after six, with the crew already headed home.

Once production commenced, the pattern remained the same. Curtis and Lemmon would spend hours in makeup getting ready for a 9 A.M. call, then have to wait till noon or later for Monroe to show up. Once the star arrived, there was no guarantee she would be capable of delivering a performance. She'd stop cold in the middle of a take, obeying some inner voice only she could comprehend. Always hovering nearby was Monroe's acting coach, Paula Strasberg, wife of the method-acting teacher Lee Strasberg, whispering in her ear, "Relax." As Curtis remembers the scene, "You had to go through Paula for everything, so Marilyn could never fully connect with anybody she was acting with." And at the end of a take, Monroe's eyes would bypass her director and go directly to her guru, seeking her approval. On one such occasion, Wilder responded to the slight by standing up and inquiring in a loud voice, "How was that for you, Paula?" He may have put Marilyn's confidante in her place, but he didn't endear himself to the star. Later on in the filming, as Wilder approached Monroe with a suggestion, she growled, "Don't talk to me now. I'm thinking about how I'm going to play the scene!"

Co-author I. A. L. Diamond recalled the day Monroe emerged from makeup two hours late, carrying a copy of Thomas Paine's *The Rights of Man*, then proceeded to lock herself in her dressing room. After fifteen minutes, Wilder sent assistant director Hal Polaire to fetch her. He knocked on her door and called, "We're ready for you, Miss Monroe." In the spirit of Paine, the star shouted back, "Fuck you!"

At times, Monroe was in command of her craft and capable of making a real contribution to the creative team. After seeing the first day's rushes, in which Sugar was introduced amid her fellow band members, she told Wilder what her character needed was a memorable entrance. The next day, the writers came up with the movie's indelible first look at Sugar, as she sashays down the railway platform ("like Jell-O on springs," marvels Lemmon) and a burst of steam strikes her derriere.

Lemmon remembers a lengthy shot in which Sugar snuggles into Daphne's upper railway berth being done in one perfect take, and Wilder too recalls at least one lucky morning of filming with Monroe outside the handsome Victorian-style Coronado Hotel in San Diego (doubling for 1920s Miami): "We had a scene on the beach with Tony Curtis pretending to be a member of the Shell Oil family—one-and-a-half to two pages of dialogue in the open air. There was a naval station [nearby] and every ten minutes a jet flew over. I told myself it would take about four days—I tried to film between takeoffs. Second take, everything was there, every sentence of two pages—not a letter, not a comma left out. We finished in eighteen minutes, and I had planned on three days' shooting."

But more often than not, working with Marilyn went like this: "Once," says Wilder, "she had only one sentence, 'It's me, Sugar,' and we needed eighty-three takes. 'Sugar, it's me!' 'It's Sugar, me!' After the thirtieth take, I said, 'Look, Marilyn, we'll write it down—it's so easy.'

" 'I don't want to read it, it will throw my next line.'

"She then enters, looks around, opens a drawer, and says, 'Where's that bourbon?' We wrote the sentence in every drawer. Eighty-three takes! After the sixtieth take, I said, 'Marilyn, come on, relax. Don't worry.'

" 'Worry about what?' "

Wilder may not have realized how thoroughly dependent Monroe was at the time on liquor, sleeping pills and other painkillers. (After each scene, Monroe would call out for coffee and her secretary would bring her a thermos bottle which, according to Curtis, contained straight vermouth.) For the first time since *Sabrina*, Wilder's own working day took a personal toll. He himself began to turn to drink, and the tension of all those flubbed takes and wasted hours aggravated his back troubles. "I did not dare even to suggest recasting," Wilder says. "I lived with it, and I wanted to die with it." There was nothing Wilder could do but somehow finish the film. As he once observed, "We were in midflight, and there was a nut on the plane."

Tony Curtis also suffered from Monroe's hazy unprofessionalism. One of the movie's most memorable comic interludes has Curtis's character posing as an impotent millionaire so that Sugar will pour all her energy into seducing him. This hilariously erotic encounter required take after take after take, with Curtis getting wearier and wearier just as Monroe finally began to warm to her task. Ultimately, Wilder used the takes where Monroe shone and Curtis looked tired, since, the director was forced to admit, the audience's eyes always gravitated to Monroe. As demoralized by the shoot as Wilder, Curtis likened his love scenes with the sex goddess to "kissing Hitler."

Today, Curtis tries to put the best face on the situation. "It was a problem, but I never found it a problem. That was my day's work. I had to come in and lie under that girl and have champagne poured all over me," the actor jokes. "You can't tell in any of the scenes that there were any problems. I got along with everybody, including Marilyn. Only at the end was it impossible to deal with, because *she* was impossible to deal with.

"At the beginning, we had a lot of fun. Marilyn didn't socialize with us on the set. She would stay in her dressing room and only come out when she was ready to go to work. It wasn't like: Let's go to lunch or take a drive down Melrose, like Jack and I used to do. But we had our moments of joy and pleasure. I even took Marilyn into the ladies' room once."

Letting that mysterious revelation float in the air, Curtis continues, "But, you know, Marilyn, sweet Marilyn, she wasn't quite as funny as you imagine. It was hard for her at that point to laugh and be at ease. There was another tempo going on in that poor woman. And Billy did the best he could, all through it. He's a brilliant man, to put up with all that and not allow it to affect the making of the movie. We had a dinner party one night at my house, and Billy came up and his back was disconnected—terrible pains in the back. Everybody said, 'Well, maybe it's because of Marilyn.' We even called a doctor, 'cause he couldn't walk. And I'll never forget, the doctor was going to give him a shot in the back to relieve the pain, and he looked at the doctor and said, 'Do you have a license to practice?' "

"It was not intentional," Lemmon says of Monroe's erratic behavior. "Marilyn was totally screwed up and very unhappy. She had also had a miscarriage, and then had another one right after the film. But we didn't know that she was not feeling well—she didn't tell anybody."

To maintain his sanity, Lemmon says, "I made an adjustment where I said I'm not going to let this get to me." Whenever he had a scene with Monroe, he was determined to be ready on the first take and ready on the fiftieth—whatever it took. Lemmon says he and Curtis used to bet on how many takes Monroe would have to do before a shot was completed; Curtis, the more pessimistic of the two, usually won. "But it was easier for me," Lemmon insists, "because, in the second half of the film especially, Tony has the majority of the scenes with Marilyn, and I'm off with a rose in my mouth dancing with Joe E. Brown and having fun. I didn't have the problem of long scenes with her—I had very short scenes with her. Tony had the problem, and he did let it get to him, though I don't think it hurt his performance at all."

SOME LIKE IT HOT WOULD BE THE FIRST OF SEVEN COLLABO-
rations between Lemmon and Wilder, and while the star owes much of his subsequent good fortune to Wilder's casting savvy, *Some Like It Hot* in turn owes much of its success to Lemmon's comic inspiration.

Lemmon and Wilder's long-standing mutual admiration began soon after *Some Like It Hot* commenced filming. Wilder came to regard his new star as "the actor's actor, the divine clown," someone who found acting as natural as breathing. "Hell, the man can do anything," Wilder told *Coronet* magazine in a 1966 interview. "He'd never touched a bass fiddle before I tossed him one for *Some Like It Hot*. In fifteen minutes he looked as if he'd been playing it all his life."

Lemmon's gifts helped *Some Like It Hot* sail through some hazardous comedic waters. The actor saw Jerry as a guy who "never stopped to think once in his life," who reacts to situations rather than acting upon them. Not only is he the perfect dupe, but his innocence leads him to believe in his masquerade so thoroughly that he has to stop and remind himself, "I'm a boy, I'm a boy . . ." Ironically, it's the handsome Curtis who actually manages to pass for a reasonably attractive flapper-era female; Lemmon, by contrast, is one step removed from clown-face, or at least the exaggerated makeup of a silent-movie clown like Harry Langdon, making his character's sexual confusion that much more palatable to a 1959 audience.

The on-set chemistry between actor and director is best illustrated by a story Lemmon loves to tell about the filming of the classic morning-after scene following Jerry's night of tangoing in the arms of aged millionaire Osgood Fielding III (veteran comic Joe E. Brown). Just before the cameras rolled, Wilder handed his star a pair of maracas and told him to shake them vigorously after each line. Lemmon thought his director was crazy, but he cooperated. Only later did he realize what a practical piece of direction this was: When Jerry announces, "I'm engaged," the audience screams with laughter, and the business with the maracas helps fill the space between gag lines. The ploy works again when Joe asks, "Why would a guy want to marry a guy?" and Jerry responds, with a beatific smile, "Security." Wilder's genius is that the maracas not only solve a technical problem, but they also remind the audience of the earlier, equally hilarious scene in which Lemmon and Brown danced till dawn. And, however resistant Lemmon may have been to shaking those maracas, he does it with such joyous abandon it makes the sequence doubly memorable.

Lemmon cites the train sequence as another example of the craft of Billy Wilder. "In general, Billy would cover a scene in one setup—he'd move the people in the camera, and very often just eliminate cuts, so that the audience wouldn't even think about it, and just keep that camera wherever he felt the audience's eye should be at that moment. I believe that we go deep, deep into the film, all the way into the train sequence, before there's a single closeup of me on the screen. And then, when he does suddenly cut to a closeup, the audience doesn't know why but it knocks them on their ass—and that's me looking out of the upper berth as all the girls are walking back and forth in their little nighties. I've got my hands under my chin and my fingers drumming my cheeks and a grin from ear to ear, and I look like I've just been locked in a candy shop, all alone. And the audience goes bananas. Until then, he didn't use a closeup. As he once said to me, a closeup should really mean something—it's like a hit in the solar plexus."

IT WAS TONY CURTIS'S JOB TO TAKE ON THE REQUISITE ROLE of the Wilder scoundrel, though in a more comic mode than usual. He's Dean Martin to Lemmon's Jerry Lewis, Bud Abbott to Lemmon's Lou Costello—but with an extra fillip of sex appeal. Curtis says the combination clicked from the very first day.

"Lemmon and I looked at each other, and we both knew instinctively that we could help each other. And we did, we kind of supported each other through the whole film, emotionally, physically. When he stopped moving, I started moving. When he was talking, I stopped. When I started, he would stop. In some of the scenes, the way we play it, we're like two good musicians. Without even verbalizing it, we made it possible for Jack and I to kind of play melody and bass at the same time. And the nice thing about those two parts was that we could switch from melody to bass and bass to melody. We were constantly doing that. In that scene where he says to me, 'Why would you go on the yacht with that dirty old man?' and I say, 'I'm not going—you're going,' Jack became the straight man for a minute. Then when I come in the bedroom and he says, 'I'm engaged.' 'Who's the lucky girl?' 'I am.' All these scenes had counterbalances, and that's the exquisite writing of Billy Wilder and Izzy Diamond."

Even so, Curtis feels his function was largely to act as straight man to Lemmon and Monroe. "But doing that," he notes, "I had to bring to [the character] another level of consciousness, an inner drive. I never, never forgot the motivation, the motivating factor—that I had seen a murder and

I could be killed. And what I did was take that feeling and double it up onto Billy—I didn't want Billy to get mad at me! The Joe I play is right on target, doesn't fool around, isn't fucking around—he is just coming to grips with what the reality of the problem is. And that's the way I played it. I didn't stop for jokes, I didn't stop for anything, I just made sure that my tempo was maintained."

Curtis's Joe is a smooth talker with little moral conscience, especially in the way he bullies and exploits his good-natured partner. Jerry may be the first to get cozy with Sugar (in that hilariously intimate upper-berth scene), but it's Joe who gets under her skin, after listening to her sad tales of affairs with cheating saxophone players and her dreams of meeting and marrying a gentle, bespectacled Miami millionaire. Once in Miami, Joe purloins a navy-style blazer and yachting cap and dons a pair of glasses, to become the spitting image of Sugar's ideal millionaire. (Curtis came up with the idea of doing an exaggerated imitation of his idol, Cary Grant—"a huge, wonderful plus for the picture," says Wilder.*) Sugar falls instantly for Joe's bogus Shell Oil heir, and Joe strong-arms Jerry into spending a night ashore with the lecherous Osgood while he borrows the millionaire's yacht for a moonlight rendezvous with Sugar.

Through most of *Some Like It Hot*, Joe is little more than a selfish louse. His response to Sugar's private litany of sorrow is to hatch a scheme destined to hurt her once again. Sugar's strenuous effort to arouse the "shy" millionaire was the ultimate wish-fulfillment fantasy for the legions of drooling Monroe fans, but there's a cruel undercurrent to this farcical seduction scene. Perhaps Monroe had good reason to continually flub her lines, since once again she was being treated as a mere object of lust. Indeed, she later confided to her friend and publicist Rupert Allan that Sugar was just the sort of role she thought she had said good-bye to years before.

Even late in the film, Joe is disturbingly cavalier about his charade with the singer. "It's going to break Sugar's heart when she finds out I'm not a

---

* "It's not even Cary Grant," says Curtis, "it's a phony English accent—that's the way I look at it. That was the joke, and *still* is the joke, because there are many people today who don't know who Cary Grant is. When they see *Some Like It Hot*, they see a guy trying to masquerade as some kind of an Englishman." Wilder later screened the film for Grant, who, says Curtis in his best Grant imitation, reacted, "I don't talk like that!"

millionaire," he admits, adding, "That's life. You can't make an omelette without breaking an egg." Yet moments later, after Joe and Jerry spy the Chicago gangster Spats Colombo (George Raft) in the lobby of their hotel, Joe makes a parting gesture of pure generosity. He places a "ship-to-shore" call to Sugar's room to tell her he's going away, and sends over the diamond bracelet Osgood has given "Daphne." "We did the right thing," Joe insists to Jerry. "No tricks, no mirrors, nothing up my sleeve. It's on the level this time."

As with all Wilder antiheroes, Joe arrives at a decisive, humanizing moment of truth—in this instance, it's one of the most audacious screen moments the writer-director ever devised. In the midst of fleeing from Spats's gang, Joe hears Sugar's voice coming from the ballroom, singing a deeply felt rendition of "I'm Through with Love." Joe, in drag, steps up to the bandstand and, indifferent to the consequences, kisses Sugar full on the lips. Brushing away her tears, he tells her, in his real voice, "None of that, Sugar—no guy is worth it." Leave it to Wilder to stage Hollywood's first passionate "lesbian" kiss, but one that is fully justified by the character demands of his story. Though Curtis may have felt he was "kissing Hitler," his climactic encounter with Monroe is one of the tenderest, most emotionally satisfying gestures in any Wilder film.

Not satisfied with one *coup de cinema*, Wilder segues into another. In the even more celebrated final scene, Joe, Sugar, Jerry and Osgood flee Miami in a speedboat, destination unknown. Joe warns Sugar, "You don't want me. . . . I'm a liar and a phony. A *saxophone* player—one of those no-goodniks you've been running away from," but she refuses to be dissuaded. Jerry, still dressed as Daphne, has a bigger burden to unload. He tries to do it gently: "I'm not a natural blond. . . . I smoke. I smoke all the time. . . . I can never have children." Osgood remains unfazed. Giving up, Jerry removes his wig and nudges the millionaire. "I'm a man!" he confesses. "Well, nobody's perfect," Osgood replies blissfully, in the famed closing line, which Wilder always takes pains to attribute to Diamond. In a classic instance of writers not grasping the quality of their own work, Wilder and Diamond regarded those last words as a temporary gag, hoping to come up with something better on the set. Of course, they never did—or could.

The brilliance of *Some Like It Hot's* final moments doesn't reflect the chaos that was going on behind the scenes with its two writers. As Barbara

Diamond reveals, "Nothing was ever quite as frantic as *Some Like It Hot*. They started shooting before they finished the script many times, but they never started shooting on any other picture without a very clear notion of where they were going, scene by scene." On *Some Like It Hot*, however, "they hadn't the faintest idea how they were going to end it. Two days before they had to shoot the ending—because of Marilyn's problems they had to finish her up—they had to arbitrarily decide whether the boys were going to be in men's clothes or women's clothes in the final scene. It was written not quite the night before."

With an unmasking as its memorable punch line, *Some Like It Hot* is the quintessential example of that Wilder staple: the masquerade. Nearly everyone (with the possible exception of Osgood) is pretending to be something they're not. Joe and Jerry, obviously, are trying their hilarious best to pass as women, tottering on high heels, swiveling their hips and going out of their way to be genteel. Then there's Joe's second masquerade as Shell Oil Jr., juxtaposed against Sugar's pretense that her band, Sweet Sue and Her Society Syncopators, consists of wealthy Vassar and Bryn Mawr girls performing for a lark. Even the mobsters who descend on Miami in the third act would have you believe they're attending a convention of "Friends of Italian Opera."

The film itself is also something of a masque—a fond tribute, complete with familiar faces, to the Hollywood sound era's first decade. The opening chase between vintage police cars and a black hearse holding a cache of bootleg liquor might have been lifted intact from a 1932 Warner Brothers B movie, so accurately does Wilder capture the rough-hewn black-and-white look and frantic feel of the gangster genre's heyday. Along with George Raft as the dreaded Spats Colombo, you'll find the thirties' ultimate cop/priest, Pat O'Brien, as his nemesis, federal agent Mulligan. These two icons of law and disorder make an invaluable contribution to the movie's texture but, paradoxically, their presence serves as a constant reminder that you're watching a film that's well aware of its own screen lineage. "Where did you pick up that cheap trick?" Raft's Colombo barks at a young hood who keeps flipping a coin in the air. Of course, it's a Raft trademark, and, to add to the irony, the hood is played by Edward G. Robinson Jr. (who is in the film only because his father was supposed to be in it—in the mob-boss role brilliantly played by Nehemiah Persoff). Add

Joe E. Brown (himself a frequent drag performer in films) to the mix, plus Curtis's Grant impression, and *Some Like It Hot* becomes an unabashedly larger-than-life celebration of movie lore—set in 1929, the year of Wilder's own Berlin screenwriting debut.

But there's one unmistakable 1950s ingredient in *Some Like It Hot*, the source of much of the iconic power the movie still holds today: Monroe. As Wilder acknowledged in a recent TV interview, "No matter how much you suffered, when you saw the rushes—you cannot see it with the naked eye on the set—it was just like night and day. It looks like nothing, and then when it goes on the screen, it all comes out in neon lights. It's fantastic, how celluloid loved Monroe. Just incredible."

The character of Sugar is in many ways strikingly close to what we know of the private Marilyn—Wilder had to be conscious of the parallels. The desperation of Curtis's Joe and Lemmon's Jerry is not the only dark strand in this deceptively light screwball comedy; equally sobering is the melancholy, battered spirit of Monroe's Sugar. The band singer has been badly used by so many weaselly men, she's cloistered herself in an all-girl caravan and drowned her romantic yearnings in bourbon. Monroe's foggy delivery as she recounts Sugar's troubled past can't help evoking her own struggles with girlhood trauma, insecurity, drug dependency and suffocating celebrity. "I'm tired of getting the fuzzy end of the lollipop," she wearily declares.

In spite of his behind-the-camera hair-pulling, Wilder somehow managed to get a real performance out of his erratic star. She's gamely funny in the shipboard seduction scene, and poignant in her longing for a fantasy savior. Most memorable of all is her quivery, soulful rendition of "I'm Through with Love" on the nightclub stand, while a nearly transparent, glittery Orry-Kelly gown clings to her ample curves. The heartbreaking Sugar Kowalczyk is surely one of the key elements in the enduring Monroe persona.

TOWARD THE END OF FILMING, ARTHUR MILLER INFORMED THE director that his wife was pregnant, and requested she be let go at four-thirty each afternoon. Wilder's reply: "She never shows up until after twelve! Arthur, bring her to me at nine and you can have her back at eleven-thirty!'"

Some Like It Hot wrapped on November 6, 1958, several weeks late and $500,000 over budget. Its total cost had climbed to $2.8 million, a high figure for a comedy in 1958, and one due entirely to the vagaries of its troubled star. Wilder was so bitter over the experience that, when his wife, Audrey, hosted a lavish dinner party in celebration of the movie's completion, Mr. and Mrs. Arthur Miller were not invited.

At first, Wilder wasn't sure what he had. The director had suffered through disastrous audience previews of two of his biggest successes, *The Lost Weekend* and *Sunset Boulevard,* and *Some Like It Hot* proved vulnerable to the same curse. The first public screening of the film was held at the Bay Theatre in Pacific Palisades, California, following the regular showing of Tennessee Williams's *Cat on a Hot Tin Roof.* Perhaps quieted by the marital discord of Paul Newman and Elizabeth Taylor, the audience did not respond—with the exception of one gentleman laughing uncontrollably in the front row, who just happened to be comedian Steve Allen. After the screening, fellow director Joseph L. Mankiewicz came up to Wilder, put his arm around his shoulder, and said consolingly, "Well, it happens to all of us."

Recalls Lemmon, "Of all the films that I've done, including the rotten ones, *Some Like It Hot* had the worst preview that I was at. Why? Who knows? But the interesting thing was standing in the lobby afterward and just watching Billy surrounded by all of the [Mirisch] brothers—offering suggestions, saying it's much too long, it can't hold, you've got to cut ten, fifteen minutes out of this film because they're leaving in droves, et cetera. Billy just listened very politely, didn't have much to say—which is unusual for Billy—and went back and took exactly one short scene out, a scene that came after the last scene you see there of the party with the girls in my upper bunk. With a little of the joy juice in me, I'm now so enamored of Marilyn that I go back and jump up in her bunk—only she's switched with Tony. I spill my guts and say, 'I'm a man, I can't stand it, I'm nuts about you,' and I take my wig off and she turns over and it's Tony. I grab the wig, put it on my head, and say, 'You wouldn't hit a girl, would you?' It was one long monologue, a beauty. It was a very good scene but it was just one scene too many, Billy felt, in that sequence. Other than that, he didn't touch the film. He was smart enough to go on his own instincts rather than the reaction of that particular audience. It previewed again in Westwood the next week, over the Mirisches' collective dead bodies, and you couldn't hear the lines, the people were screaming so much. It was a smash."

The first appearance of Lemmon and Curtis tottering in their high heels at the railway station was such a hit, in fact, that Wilder went back and added every take he had shot of them. Anyone who watches carefully today will see that they pass the same three railroad cars several times.

The film opened in March 1959 to nearly universal raves. John Mc-Carten in *The New Yorker* called it "a jolly, carefree enterprise in which some of the old phrenetic nonsense of Mack Sennett is restored to the screen." Arthur Knight in *Saturday Review* thought the laughs harked back "to those glorious days of screwball comedy and the Marx Brothers." A. H. Weiler in *The New York Times* found the film overlong but "often outrageously funny . . . a rare, rib-tickling lampoon." *Time* initially gave the movie a mild review, but, as Diamond delighted to point out, by December hailed it as "the best comedy of the year."

The first week's box office was somewhat disappointing, but grosses continued to build with the critics' praise and strong audience word of mouth. Not everyone was a champion of the film, however. In Kansas, the movie's release was delayed by two months when the state's three-woman Board of Review refused to approve the picture until cuts totaling 105 feet were made in the shipboard love scene between Monroe and Curtis. The Memphis Board of Censors also rejected the film, but agreed to pass it uncut if showings were restricted to adults only; UA eventually got them to agree to a "Not Recommended for Children" advisory. Fired up by the movie's flirtations with transvestism and homosexuality, Bishop McNulty, chairman of the Episcopal Committee for Motion Pictures, Radio and TV, wrote an angry letter to Motion Picture Producers and Distributors Association of America president Eric Johnston, calling *Some Like It Hot* a "flagrant violation of the spirit and letter of the Production Code" and predicting "a film of this type can only help to provoke greater support for those in favor of legal censorship."

Ultimately, the movie took in $15 million, becoming one of the top hits of 1959. It was such a popular success that Arthur Krim and NBC discussed a TV series based on the film and overseen by Wilder; that never materialized, but twenty years later the Tom Hanks sitcom *Bosom Buddies* used the same basic idea. In the 1959 Oscar race, *Some Like It Hot* earned six nominations, including Lemmon for Best Actor, Wilder for Best Director and Wilder and Diamond for Best Adapted Screenplay, but, faced with the *Ben-Hur* juggernaut, won only one: Orry-Kelly's costumes.

With *Some Like It Hot* now a box-office smash, Wilder felt free to air some of his production headaches in an interview with *New York Herald Tribune* columnist Joe Hyams, suggesting he deserved a Purple Heart for making two films with Monroe. "I am eating better," he reported. "My back doesn't ache anymore. I am able to sleep for the first time in months." Asked if he'd ever consider doing another project with Monroe, Wilder joked, "I have discussed this project with my doctor and my psychiatrist, and they tell me I am too old and too rich to go through this again."

The director's blunt jibes prompted Arthur Miller to send an angry telegram scolding Wilder for forcing his wife to work full days during the early stage of her pregnancy, and in effect blaming him for the miscarriage she suffered twelve hours after the final shooting day. "Now that the hit for which she is so largely responsible is in your hands and its income to you is assured, this attack upon her is contemptible," Miller's telegram raged, branding Wilder unjust and cruel.

Wilder fired back with his own telegram, arguing, "This is a small world with very sharp ears. Ever since the early days of shooting, when rumors of Marilyn's unprofessional conduct first leaked out, I have been besieged by newspapermen from as far as London, Paris and Berlin for a statement. I have staved them off, I have avoided them, I have lied to them. As for the story in the *New York Herald Tribune*, the conclusions reached by the columnist from his own research would have been twice as vicious had I not submitted to the interview." The director expressed sorrow for his star's recent loss, but denied any responsibility: "The fact is that the company pampered her, coddled her and acceded to all her whims. The only one who showed any lack of consideration was Marilyn, in her treatment of her co-stars and her co-workers." Wilder's parting shot was a nasty one: "Had you, dear Arthur, been not her husband but her writer and director, and been subjected to all the indignities I was, you would have thrown her out on her can, thermos bottle and all, to avoid a nervous breakdown. I did the braver thing. I had a nervous breakdown."

Miller then wired another telegram, demanding an apology. "The simple truth is that whatever the circumstances she did her job and did it superbly," Miller contended, "while your published remarks create the contrary impression without any mitigation. . . . She is not the first actress who must follow her own path to a performance."

Wilder finally relented, but in typically impish fashion: "Dear Arthur. In order to hasten the burial of the hatchet I hereby acknowledge that good wife Marilyn is a unique personality and I am the Beast of Belsen but in the immortal words of Joe E. Brown quote Nobody is perfect end quote."

Monroe herself was urged by composer Matty Malneck to patch things up with Wilder following a recording session in New York for a *Some Like It Hot* title song that was never used. She placed a long-distance call to Los Angeles, which Audrey Wilder picked up. Told Billy wasn't in, Monroe hesitated, then said: "Well, when you see him, will you give him a message from me? Please tell him to go fuck himself." After a pause, she added: "And my warmest personal regards to you, Audrey."

Wilder and Monroe's professional love/hate relationship continued over the next two years. Star and director reunited at a gala luncheon held on the 20th Century–Fox lot in honor of visiting Soviet leader Nikita Khrushchev. A robust-looking Monroe embraced and kissed her *Some Like It Hot* director, and Wilder even began to entertain thoughts of casting her in the title role of *Irma la Douce*, the French stage hit he had recently acquired for the movies. Meeting up the next year at a party following a sneak preview of *The Apartment*, Wilder came right out and asked Monroe to consider playing Irma.

But Wilder's acid tongue got him in Dutch with Monroe once again. In an interview with Art Buchwald for the *Herald Tribune*, he joked about reading *War and Peace* and *Les Miserables* during the hours his star kept him waiting. He added, "It takes a real artist to come on the set and not know her lines and give the performance she did." The rift between Wilder and Monroe never really healed, and the part of Irma went to the star of *The Apartment*, Shirley MacLaine.

After Monroe's death, Wilder refused to subscribe to the popular notion that she was a victim of Hollywood exploitation. He felt "appalled" by the cult surrounding "Saint Marilyn," calling her "the meanest woman I have ever met around this town."

Now, from a distance of three decades, Wilder takes a more compassionate, almost contradictory view of his impossible star. "If she was alive today, would I still make pictures with her? Yes, I would, because of the joy of her performance, which was something that was inborn. She was a wonderful, wonderful character to write for comedy—she knew the points to make without Strasberg and without advisers always on the set."

"In spite of everything, I loved her very much," Wilder recently told director Helmut Dietl in Germany's *Stern* magazine. "Her lifelong problem was that she fell in love so quickly. She was not the kind of woman a sex bomb is supposed to be, and it wore her out. . . . She never found anyone who understood her, she was completely incapable of normal communication. She was a mixture of pity, love, loneliness and confusion."

APPEARING AT NEW YORK'S NINETY-SECOND STREET YMHA in 1994 to promote his autobiography, Tony Curtis, then sixty-eight and still capable of making his fans' hearts flutter, said of Billy Wilder: "He's an extraordinary filmmaker, a very kind and sweet man, yet with a strain of . . . not bitterness, but brittleness." Asked later to elaborate on that comment, Curtis says, "I think the brittleness comes from, perhaps, his Austrian background, and leaving Austria [*sic*] before the Nazis. I have a feeling that maybe that overshadows part of his being safe and alive in America. I'm not sure, but it seems to me that he must be relieved that he left the country when he did, and maybe there's some guilt in that. I'm only juxtaposing my ideas about it. But he is a very sensitive and a very delicate man in so many ways. . . . He wants everybody to love him, and he's kind of surprised when somebody is offended or hurt by what he says or does. That's the interesting thing about him.

"He used to scare the shit out of me," Curtis goes on to confess. "But with that fear came a love and affection for him. He was like my daddy. And you know, during the making of the film, I didn't think he liked me as much as everybody else in the movie. I don't know what it makes me, but because of that, I always worked harder to get him to like me and be nice to me.* Maybe that's the way you get a good performance out of people.

"I'm just thrilled that I ended up in *one* of his films, and maybe the best he ever made," the veteran star concludes. "I'm really proud that I contributed to that movie. In my own personal sense of who I am and what I represent, it means a lot to me."

IT APPEARS WILDER *DID* LIKE LEMMON BEST. "WE HAD THE first screening of *Some Like It Hot* at Bill Paley's house in Long Island," the actor recalls. "In the car on the way out, Billy started talking to me about *The Apartment*. So here I am, I've just finished one film that has not been seen, and Billy is already saying he wants me to play the lead in the next film. Sensational!"

The idea for *The Apartment* had been formulating in Wilder's mind ever since he had seen David Lean's *Brief Encounter* in 1946. Based on a one-act play by Noël Coward, the British romantic classic concerned an affair between two married people. Wilder, always looking for that fresh perspective on the human condition, started wondering about one of the film's minor characters.

Years ago, in an interview with French critic Michel Ciment, Wilder described the impulse that led him from *Brief Encounter* to *The Apartment*. "Surely, one can make superficial films on the theme of success, like *42nd Street*, where the star breaks a leg and the understudy pulls off a triumph. But the understudy is in fact a tedious character. The interesting character, and one who is not treated, is the star who breaks her leg and sees the unknown take her place. That is, in a sense, the subject of *All About Eve*. To show the reverse of the coin, that is what counts. In *Brief Encounter*, for example, the subject treated is the liaison between a man and a married woman. The lovers meet in the apartment of a friend of the hero. Me, I

---

* Toward the end of production, Curtis decided to cheer up his beleaguered director by hiring a stripper to replace the machine-gun-wielding gangster who pops out of a birthday cake during the mob convention. In the middle of shooting the scene, the buxom party girl rose from the cake, headed straight for Wilder and gave him a big kiss, leaving the director uncharacteristically speechless.

think that the interesting character is the friend who returns to his home and finds the bed still warm, he who has no mistress."

Wilder never developed this notion very far, realizing he'd be up against the censorship restrictions of the forties and fifties. Then, the memory of a 1951 Hollywood scandal helped crystallize the idea. Film producer Walter Wanger had shot agent Jennings Lang, who was sleeping with Wanger's wife, actress Joan Bennett, and reports had filtered in that Lang's love nest was the apartment of an unmarried subordinate at the agency. Wilder and Diamond brainstormed. What if the lending of the apartment wasn't an act of friendship, but a career move? Now the concept had a little edge—something to do with what it takes to get ahead in corporate America.*

A visual inspiration was director King Vidor's 1928 silent classic *The Crowd*, which Wilder had named as his fifth favorite film of all time in an early-fifties poll. Centered on a young clerk who toils in a giant insurance-company office, the picture wowed twenties audiences with its opening scenes depicting an ordinary worker amid hordes of anonymous extras.

The beginning of *The Apartment* is Wilder's modern-day homage to *The Crowd*. Lemmon narrates over aerial shots of New York City, followed by a pan up the fictional Consolidated Life building. We're told that Consolidated is one of the top five companies in the country, with 31,259 employees in its home office—"more than the entire population of Natchez, Mississippi, or Gallup, New Mexico." Our first glimpse of the nineteenth-floor office where Lemmon's character, insurance accountant C. C. "Bud" Baxter, works is a stunner: a sea of identical desks and busy employees that seems to retreat back into infinity. Built on the same Goldwyn Studio soundstage that housed the catfish-row set in *Porgy and Bess*, the mammoth office set heightened its effect by using tiny desks at the back, manned by dwarves (according to Wilder) and even tinier toy desks with cutout figures. After directing 350 extras rushing for the elevators, Wilder declared, in a nod to *Ben-Hur*, "This is my chariot race."

---

* In his autobiography, Tony Curtis claims *The Apartment* was inspired by his use of his friend Nicky Blair's pad to conduct his extramarital flings; columnist Sidney Skolsky heard about the arrangement, wrote it up as a movie treatment and sold it to Wilder, Curtis says.

In a piece he wrote for *The New York Times*, Diamond revealed that his partner originally conceived *The Apartment* as a play, then decided his vision of that huge office space could be realized only on the big screen. The film medium could also better emphasize the contrast between Baxter's cavernous workplace and the drab bachelor apartment he comes home to at night—sometimes very late at night. "It's not that I'm overly ambitious," Baxter says about his long office hours. "It's just a way of killing time, until it's all right for me to go home. You see, I have this little problem with my apartment. . . ."

It all began innocently enough when Baxter was going to night classes and lent his apartment key to a colleague from New Jersey who needed a place to change into a tuxedo before a hotel banquet. But then, "all sorts of guys were suddenly going to banquets." Now, Baxter has four weekly regulars, all randy married men, all higher-ups promising to "put in a good word" for the accountant with the personnel boss, Sheldrake (Fred Mac-Murray).* But when Sheldrake hears about the apartment, he wants it for himself. In exchange for the key, Baxter gets what he's been hungering for: a promotion to second administrative assistant and a private office with a window.

Everything's swell in Baxter's world until the night of the office Christmas party. There, he discovers that Fran Kubelik (Shirley MacLaine), the pert elevator operator he has a crush on, is Sheldrake's mystery mistress. It's a bad night for Fran, too, as Sheldrake's bitter secretary Miss Olsen (Edie Adams) informs her that she's just the latest in a long line of office conquests—including Miss Olsen. Baxter goes off on a bender and picks up a daffy barfly; meanwhile, back at the apartment, Fran takes an overdose of sleeping pills after Sheldrake confirms what a louse he is by offering her a hundred-dollar bill as a Christmas present.

The following scene may be the riskiest of Wilder's career, as Baxter brings home his addled date and discovers Fran lying unconscious in his bed. "There was a delicate balance there between drama and comedy," Diamond noted, "and we were afraid that if we got a laugh in the wrong place, the whole picture would go out the window." Diamond had reason

---

* Sheldrake was also the name of the studio executive Joe Gillis was so desperate to win over in *Sunset Boulevard*.

to be concerned, since this tricky plot element came from him—years earlier, a woman had committed suicide in the apartment of an acquaintance of Diamond's, as a gesture of revenge.

With Fran's suspenseful recovery, *The Apartment* becomes that much richer. The elevator operator and the accountant develop an intimate bond over the course of two days, and Baxter is ready to take her off Sheldrake's hands (as he rather indelicately puts it) until Sheldrake tells him his wife has kicked him out and he is planning to resume the affair (while still playing the field). The personnel boss then rewards Baxter for keeping Fran's suicide attempt a secret by making Baxter his personal assistant. But when Sheldrake asks Baxter for the apartment key for a New Year's Eve date with Fran, his new assistant gives him his key to the executive washroom and announces "I'm all washed up around here." When Fran hears what Baxter's done, she deserts Sheldrake and hurries to the apartment and the now unemployed accountant.

THE CASTING OF JACK LEMMON IS CRUCIAL TO THE SUCCESS of *The Apartment*. As scripted, C. C. Baxter has few redeeming qualities, and he seems to have no interior life apart from his desire to advance his standing at the company. As his opening narration reveals, he's essentially a numbers cruncher, rattling off statistics about New York City and Consolidated Life as if figures are all that's needed to describe his place in this world. Baxter never reflects on the larger scheme of things, which is why it's so easy for him to lend his apartment key to his superiors for their extramarital dalliances. Even these assignations become part of Baxter's systematized order, mere dates and times in his weekly calendar, divorced from their seedy, flesh-and-juice realities. This "time-share" arrangement has robbed Baxter of a private life: Even on those rare nights when he has the apartment to himself, he sits alone with a frozen dinner, searching in vain for something on his TV other than westerns and endless commercial interruptions.

Unlike Wilder's earlier antiheroes, the roles created for Lemmon aren't schemers, but pathetic victims of other people's machinations. Like Jerry in *Some Like It Hot*, Baxter lacks the nerve to fight back once people see how easily he can be taken advantage of. And, like Jerry, Baxter sniffs out a potential reward for his timid acquiescence: For Jerry, it's the "security" of settling down with a millionaire, even if he is a man; for Baxter, it's the promise of a sudden ascent to a private windowed office on the twenty-seventh floor. Baxter is the perfect corporate soldier: cooperative, unreflective, and blindered not only by his empty worship of career advancement but by his glib acceptance of his bosses' childish sexual games. "He's actually innocent, he is a Forrest Gump," says Wilder, always ready with a contemporary reference point.

Baxter is also a shlemiel and, by his complicity, a heel. Yet, in Lemmon's artful hands, the character is instantly likable and empathetic. It's a performance that would set the pattern for so many of Lemmon's roles in the 1960s and '70s: the well-meaning white-collar drone who falls prey to his own eagerness to master the corporate game. Aided by Wilder's oppressive mise-en-scène, the deeply flawed Baxter becomes an urban Everyman, someone whose struggle a 1960s audience of Organization Men (and forgiving women) could connect with.

Lemmon's performance is expertly modulated, his first chance to show the range that would enable him to alternate between comedy and drama so successfully later in his career. His comic moments in *The Apartment* are among his best: the lengthy scene at his desk as he rearranges his apartment bookings so he can get a night's sleep, all while fighting a fresh cold; his drunken haze on Christmas Eve; the celebrated spaghetti-cooking scene in which he uses a tennis racket as a strainer.* But Lemmon also delivers powerful emotions, whether frantically working to revive the unconscious Miss Kubelik, or gazing tenderly into the elevator girl's eyes, or realizing there's a limit to how far he'll sink to get to the top.

Putting an adorably young Shirley MacLaine opposite Lemmon also helped make Baxter that much more sympathetic. "There are any number of actresses in Hollywood who can be sexy or funny or sad," Diamond stated at the time, "but we knew of only one who could be all three simultaneously—Shirley MacLaine." The vivacious actress-singer-dancer, then twenty-five, had recently earned her first Oscar nomination for her quirky role as a good-time girl in *Some Came Running* and was making news as the

---

* Barbara Diamond says Wilder always credited that gag to her husband, because he never liked it himself.

only female member of the Rat Pack, the exclusive clique of Vegas swingers headed up by her *Running* costars, Frank Sinatra and Dean Martin.

MacLaine—still a movie box-office name and concert draw, and a best-selling author in her spare time—says she saw only twenty-nine screenplay pages when she started *The Apartment*, but "I admired the social statement Billy was making, and the extraordinary sophistication he brought to making that statement. And I liked the idea that Fran was caught in this maze, like everyone else in the film."

Meeting Billy Wilder was a decisive moment in MacLaine's life. The two films she made with him, MacLaine declares, "confirmed that I was a star and that I could act." The actress says she learned a lot about timing from Wilder, and that "there are details of your performance that you're never aware of. . . . I had a habit of clicking my tongue when I did *The Apartment*—he must have cut out twenty-five of those. Billy never misses a thing—sometimes he's diplomatic about it, sometimes not. Bob Fosse is the only other director I know who was as detail-oriented. Most others are involved with emotional generalities and esoterics. With Billy, the emotion the audience feels is orchestrated by specifics that you're aware of."

As Lemmon recalls it, MacLaine got a tough early lesson in Wilder's methodology. "The first day of shooting on *The Apartment*, Billy got one thing very straight with Shirley, because Shirley was used to getting a little loose with the dialogue at times. Now there's nothing unprofessional about that, because with other writers every actor does that, in film and very often in the theater. Actors used to do it in the theater, and that's why they made the law that you can't make a change without the approval of the author. They don't have that in film, unless the individual writer has it in his contract. And all too often the writers don't even come to the set. She liked the feeling of spontaneity, and not necessarily saying the lines word for word. The first scene that Shirley had was when she was in an elevator, early on in the film going up and down, doors are opening and closing, people are getting on and off, and it's a pretty long, complicated scene for her—which she did beautifully. However, she was not saying the lines at first. And she didn't know about Billy, this was her first time. And Billy kept saying, 'Say the words!' And she says, 'You mean exactly—' 'Exactly!' Sweat's beginning to fly, because she's got a million of them, two full pages of stuff. And finally, when she did get a good take, all the way through, Billy turned to Izzy and Izzy whispered something to Billy, and Billy said, 'Let's do it just once more—you forgot the word "and" on the second page.' And he really made her do it again. And then he gave her a kiss. But, by God, she never came in and started to ad-lib or drop any words from that day on. She came to me afterward and I said, 'Hot dog! You learned! It's just with Billy, you don't do it.' And she said, 'God, I wish somebody told me.' "

Though vehemently protective of his and Diamond's words, Wilder remained open to creative suggestions, as both MacLaine and Lemmon affirm. "He's the only director who, when he found something you said personally that made sense for the character, would go back and reshoot," MacLaine notes. The actress says that when Wilder discovered she had learned gin rummy from her Rat Pack cronies, he incorporated her new talent into the character of Fran. The result is some touching card-playing moments between Lemmon and MacLaine, and the memorable antisentimental closing line, "Shut up and deal."

Recalls Lemmon, "I'd pop into the office any time I got an idea, and Billy would always stop me and say, 'Don't tell me. I might misunderstand. *Show* me.' And he was always wide open. Even though he was the writer and the director and there was no gray area of misinterpretation, he would always let any actor bring whatever they had to offer, and very often would accept it. I have seen him take suggestions for a scene from a prop man— that had nothing to do with the props—and say, 'Hey, that's a good idea,' and use it. Which is really amazing. What it shows, interestingly enough, is a great security."

Lemmon in fact contributed one of *The Apartment*'s best sight gags, when Baxter, struggling with a bad cold, is summoned to Sheldrake's office for the first time. Lemmon took his prop nose spray and had it filled with milk—"because nose spray won't show in black-and-white film. Sheldrake says, 'So we're going to make sure this never happens again. Am I right?' And I say, 'Oh yes, sir!' And I squeeze my hands like that and— Pssheeww!—the stuff went across the screen right onto Fred's nose. Fred did not bat an eyeball."

Reflecting on his onscreen relationship with MacLaine in *The Apartment*, Lemmon says, "I always like to say that what Billy did so successfully was to grow a rose in a garbage pail, because he told a romance, he made you care about these two people, with their flaws—it's interesting that both of them are flawed and he made you care about them. At the same time, he made a hell of a lot of personal comment about our business society and our mores and behavior, and made the best picture of the year."

After *Some Like It Hot*, people may have been expecting another frenetic comedy from the pairing of Wilder and Lemmon. What they got instead was a daring hybrid of comedy, drama and social criticism. At the 1982 Film Society of Lincoln Center tribute to Wilder, Shirley MacLaine analyzed the elements that collide in a picture like *The Apartment:* "In a Wilder film, nobody is spared that Wilder X-ray cynical wit. As a matter of fact, there is no institution so sacrosanct that it can't be punctured by Billy's sense of humor. I'm rather glad he hasn't put his talents to the life story of Mother Teresa yet. . . . Billy Wilder's films are so savagely funny that we're usually too busy laughing to notice that he's really telling an underlying truth about human beings. The Wilder touch goes beyond cynicism. I think what he's been doing all these years is making movies about reality, undermined by the best punch lines in the business."

Wilder himself insists, "I don't regard *The Apartment* as a comedy. It's a slice of life that seemed very naturalistic. We were never opening our mouths wide trying to be funny and doing Ritz Brothers routines. It could happen to anybody."

Nowhere is *The Apartment* more serious than in its depiction of Fran Kubelik's suicide attempt. Once before, in *Sabrina*, Wilder had employed suicide in a comedy, but there the attempt was more the result of an adolescent crush and more obviously halfhearted. Here, Wilder means it, and the process by which Baxter and his good-hearted next-door neighbor, Dr. Dreyfuss, save the girl is deliberately painful to watch. Talking to critic Michel Ciment, Wilder bridled at criticism of the brutality of the scene. "I had three doctors on the stage to whom I asked what one does with a patient who has taken twenty-five sleeping pills. They told me that to keep someone awake it is absolutely necessary that you slap them, feed them coffee and make them walk without stopping. They even told me: It is necessary to hit harder."

Fran's desperate act is like a slap in the face to Baxter, who gradually begins to understand the human consequences of his obsession with hollow success. Does he really want to aspire to be like Sheldrake and his fellow philanderers—especially Sheldrake, who can't be bothered with this messy mistress situation as his suburban family gathers around the Christmas tree? Or, as Dr. Dreyfuss advises, wouldn't he rather learn how to be a mensch, "a human being"?

Interestingly, *The Apartment* is one of the few Wilder films to include explicitly Jewish characters. Dr. Dreyfuss, engagingly played by Jack Kruschen,* and his disapproving wife (Naomi Stevens) are employed as local color and comic relief—never seeing Baxter's superiors, they believe he's entertaining different women every night—but they also provide the movie's moral compass. "Be a mensch" becomes the film's overriding theme, as Wilder juxtaposes the compassion of Baxter's down-to-earth Jewish neighbors with the self-centered decadence of his waspy workaday world.

Being a mensch has its price, however. At the end, both Baxter and Fran are out of work, and there's no guarantee that their love will conquer the hardships that lie ahead. The movie's final moments perfectly encapsulate the movie's mixture of light and darkness. Fran ecstatically runs along the street and up the stairs to the apartment, then stops short when she hears what she thinks is a gunshot—Baxter has told her of his own youthful suicide attempt by pistol. After pounding frantically on his door, she's greeted by her savior—and a wickedly gushing bottle of newly opened champagne.

As usual with Wilder, the script is meticulously layered—each character plays a significant role in the mechanism of the plot, as do meaningful objects like the keys that continually change hands throughout the movie. One of Wilder and Diamond's most effective uses of visual and narrative shorthand features Fran's broken compact mirror: Baxter finds it in the apartment and returns it to Sheldrake, never suspecting who the owner is. Later, as he's trying on a fancy executive bowler, Fran lends him the compact. Peering into the glass, Baxter's image of Fran is instantly shattered, and the audience sees this crucial moment of revelation symbolically reflected in the very same cracked mirror.

Also adding to the movie's texture is Alexandre (now billed as Alexander) Trauner's production design, especially his office set and persuasive

---

* A UA suggestion that the doctor be played by Groucho Marx was quickly rejected by the filmmakers as a potential vaudeville turn.

depiction of a cluttered New York City bachelor apartment. And teeming through the film is a large and extremely well-chosen cast, from Ray Walston, David Lewis, Willard Waterman and David White as Baxter's "clients," to Hope Holiday as his hilarious Christmas Eve desperation date. Third-billed Fred MacMurray is perfectly despicable and insinuating as Sheldrake, perhaps his best screen performance after Walter Neff in *Double Indemnity*. The role was originally intended for Paul Douglas, who suffered a fatal heart attack before production began, and once again Wilder had to use all his powers of persuasion to get MacMurray to come aboard. Wilder says MacMurray told him he couldn't possibly play the part of a man having an illicit affair with an elevator girl, "and at Christmas yet," because he was under contract to Walt Disney. "I'm playing that meshuggene professor with the Volkswagen," Wilder claims the actor protested. "They will never forgive me." But Wilder prevailed. "Everything is possible if you've just got a certain amount of charm," he says.

IN AN UNUSUAL CIRCUMSTANCE, THE TIME FRAME OF *THE Apartment* nearly matches its shooting schedule. The story begins in November 1959, as did the initial filming at such New York locations as Central Park, West Sixty-ninth Street, and the outside of the Majestic Theatre, where Baxter waits in vain for Fran to join him for a performance of *The Music Man*. Shooting then resumed in late November at the Goldwyn Studio, on sets costing a total of $400,000, and concluded in February.

When it came time to preview the picture, both Wilder and Diamond were nervous. Diamond agonized over reaction to the suicide scene, while Wilder felt the second half of the movie was "humpbacked," with too many revelation scenes coming too close together. But, as Barbara Diamond remembers, "there was an enormous party planned at Romanoff's after the first preview. You don't usually do that, so somebody must have thought they had something very good here." The optimists were right—the preview was a smash.

Critical reaction to *The Apartment* was more mixed, ranging from the highest praise to low mutterings of disgust. *Time* pointedly called it "the funniest movie made in Hollywood since *Some Like It Hot*," adding that this time there was "something serious and sad" amid the belly laughs. *News-*

week, too, deemed it "among the finest comedies Hollywood has turned out," while Bosley Crowther concluded that Wilder had taken a morally dubious premise and turned it into "a gleeful, tender and even sentimental film." At the *New York Post*, Archer Winsten proclaimed *The Apartment* "one of the season's funniest, boldest comedies" and "good clean satire," predicting "this comedy will be a success, except among bluenoses."

There were a lot of what Winsten would call bluenoses lurking among the critics. Hollis Alpert in *Saturday Review* branded *The Apartment* "a dirty fairy tale," objecting to "a streak of meanness and cynicism in the story" while also complaining that "all is sickeningly sweet in the end." Wilder couldn't win either way. Over at *The New Yorker*, John McCarten thought Wilder and Diamond had never decided how they really felt about Baxter's "turning his home into a kind of brothel for his bosses." Calling the characters "gray-flannel beatniks," he huffed, "if you want them, take them."

A Chicago critic, Ann Marsters, told Wilder to his face that he had made a dirty picture, warning that the public's acceptance of "unsavory" subjects in films and plays "may mean an alarming indication of our lowering moral standards." The headline to her *Chicago American* piece bluntly stated: "Wilder Picture Pretty Revolting." At the *New York Morning Telegraph*, Leo Mishkin used words like "lecherous," "leering," "slimy" and "noisome" to describe *The Apartment*, claiming, "I've seen better jokes scrawled on back fences by small boys."

One of the harshest attacks came from the eminent film critic for *Esquire*, Dwight Macdonald. "*The Apartment* is without either style or taste, shifting gears between pathos and slapstick without any transition," he argued, going on to declare the movie "immoral, that is, dishonest" and wondering whether "Diamond" was a misprint for "Zircon." In a subsequent collection of his criticism, Macdonald noted that his review provoked more dissent than any he wrote for *Esquire* except his pan of *Tom Jones*; he used the occasion to comment, "Although Mr. Wilder is considered a very cynical fellow in Hollywood, he seems to me not cynical enough; he uses bitter chocolate for his icing, but underneath is the stale old cake."

Though many reviewers loved *The Apartment*, no film of Wilder's had provoked such virulently negative reactions since *Ace in the Hole*. Critics either felt that he had gone too far or that he hadn't gone far enough, that the astringency of his work was purely for surface effect. In their eagerness to label Wilder, they refused to accept that an artist could be both skeptical and optimistic about the human animal within the same film.

Calling Wilder "the biggest softie that ever walked," Jack Lemmon observes, "It wouldn't occur to most writers to make a film about the kind of behavior you see in *The Apartment*, at that time especially. They would accept what is the norm; Billy would not. I think in order to satirize something, you have to be sensitive enough to notice it in the first place, and to care about it. And I think Billy notices those things in what is called ordinary, everyday behavior to a greater extent than the average person."

Still bristling at the criticism of his "dirty fairy tale" in a 1979 interview, Wilder said of *The Apartment*, "Did you really think that I went out of my way to dramatize things which did not exist? A society where things like this could not happen?" In his view, *The Apartment* was "a highly moral picture—I had to show two people who were being emancipated, and in order to do that I had to show what they were emancipated [from]."

The Apartment communicated its message to audiences, setting an opening-day record at New York's Plaza Theatre and ultimately tallying more than double its $3 million production budget in domestic box office. The movie's theme music, an old tune Wilder remembered and unearthed, became a hit record for the piano duo Ferrante and Teicher. At year's end, the film shared the New York Film Critics' best picture prize with *Sons and Lovers*, and Wilder split directing honors with that film's Jack Cardiff.

In the Oscar race, Lemmon lost to Burt Lancaster in *Elmer Gantry* and MacLaine to an ailing Liz Taylor in the forgettable *Butterfield 8*, but Wilder had a winning night. First, Gina Lollabrigida presented him with the Oscar for Best Director. Then, playwright Moss Hart and his wife, Kitty Carlisle, handed the original screenplay award to Wilder and Diamond. Finally, Audrey Hepburn announced the Best Picture: *The Apartment*, produced by Billy Wilder. It was only the second time—after Leo McCarey's *Going My Way* victory—that one individual collected three Oscars in a single night. Wilder was at the peak of his filmmaking career. As Moss Hart whispered to him when he stepped up to the podium to claim his second trophy of the evening, "This is the moment to stop, Billy."

SEVENTEEN

Against the Wall

O N Oscar night 1961, Wilder and Diamond charmed
the audience at the Santa Monica Civic Auditorium with two of the
shortest acceptance speeches on record: "Thank you, I. A. L. Diamond."
"Thank you, Billy Wilder." The simplicity of their words reflects the nature of their partnership.

"We developed this Esperanto language between us," says Wilder. "I
knew what he meant, and he knew what I meant, and there was no ranking
like in the army. Most of the time, I would be standing and writing on my
yellow tablet, and he would be sitting at the typewriter. If I came up with
something, and he said I don't think it's right, or he came up with something and I said it wasn't working, without any anger we would just tear it
up and work again and again until both of us loved it." The highest accolade you could get from Diamond, Wilder says, was a placid "Why not?"

Barbara Diamond recalls the dynamic of the relationship: "Billy has the
excess energy of a hyperactive child. He finds it extremely difficult just to
sit. Iz could sit for hours. Billy would pace and walk out—he would disappear from the office and come back in. Billy generates ideas, like *this*. Iz was
analytical. It was a very sound relationship—they thought alike about most
things, but they approached everything they did from opposite directions,
and it meshed very well."

Mrs. Diamond contradicts slightly Wilder's memories of polite disagreements with his partner. "Billy will tell you, and Iz often said, that they used to have tremendous battles, yelling and screaming. But they would go home and come back the next day, and Iz would say, 'I've been thinking about it and you're right,' and Billy would say, 'I've been thinking about it and *you're* right,' and the yelling and screaming would start again. They were both quite able to look at someone else's point of view and adjust. Because it only happened once in the years they worked together, I remember vividly the one time Iz came home extremely unhappy [over an argument they had]. Billy had said to him, 'You can write it any way you want, but I'll shoot it the way I want to do it.' It was the only time in thirty years this ever happened. And I know it happened only once because Iz was so *devastated* by it. So it was a truly good working relationship."

Wilder and Diamond had hoped to follow *The Apartment* with something completely different—a madcap comedy with nostalgic echoes à la *Some Like It Hot* and a brazenly topical backdrop. Wilder conceived the idea while staying at the Ritz Towers on East Fifty-seventh Street during the New York location shooting for *The Apartment*. The hotel wasn't far from the United Nations, where there always seemed to be some kind of Cold War commotion going on. What a perfect setting for a Marx Brothers movie, Wilder thought.

The anarchic trio hadn't made a movie together since the ill-fated *Love Happy* in 1949* and were now all in their early seventies, but that didn't stop Wilder and Diamond from brainstorming. Quickly, they came up with a framework: Groucho, Harpo and Chico would be thieves who plan to rob Tiffany's while the New York City police are distracted by a major event at the U.N. But during their getaway, they are mistaken for the Latvian delegation and provided an unwanted police escort. The climax, of course, would be Marxian chaos at the General Assembly. Wilder told author W. J. Weatherby at the time, "Imagine, we might have the Marx Brothers mixing up all the flags with, say, Nasser coming in under the Star of David. . . . We'll keep the same Marx Brothers technique of playing against a very serious background. We'll try to keep it all—the dignity of the locale, the procedure, the enormity of the problem—with Groucho, Harpo and Chico in the middle of it." Wilder estimated that he and Dia-

* They appeared separately in 1957's *The Story of Mankind*.

mond would have to fabricate some 3,000 jokes to pull off the project successfully.

Wilder described the storyline to Groucho Marx, who immediately embraced the idea and told the director to contact his agent brother Milton (the onetime Gummo in his performing days). If Groucho liked it, Milton said, Harpo would easily go along—and so would inveterate gambler Chico, who always needed the money.

Neither Wilder, Diamond, nor the Mirisches seemed concerned that the comic brothers might be a bit too old for another slapstick romp. Then came a dose of reality: While rehearsing a TV special, Harpo suffered a heart attack. Suddenly, studio insurers were unwilling to take a risk on a $4 million comedy starring three aging legends. Ironically, Harpo lasted for another three years—outliving Chico, who died in 1961. That was the end of *The Marx Brothers at the U.N.*

Irma la Douce, meantime, was still in the formative stage. A hit in Paris and London, the musical comedy about a Paris prostitute was due to open on Broadway in the fall of 1960. Despite its ready-made appeal, *Irma* was about to be given a serious makeover—including the eventual elimination of all its songs. As far as casting, all Wilder knew at this point was that Jack Lemmon would be his male lead. After the experience of making *The Apartment*, the two became closer than ever; in August 1960, Wilder took Lemmon to Paris and acted as his personal guide to the city's museums, shops and bistros—the same kind of crash course in European culture he had given to William Holden after *Stalag 17*. It was there in Paris that Wilder granted Art Buchwald the irreverent interview about Marilyn Monroe that ended her interest in making *Irma*.

Monroe weighed in with her own frank opinions when she was told of Wilder's plans for the United Nations film. "He's a brilliant moviemaker," she declared, "but he worries too much about the box office. A movie of his about the U.N. would have no real teeth. He'd be scared of politics and unpopularity. It's not the right subject for him."

Monroe's verdict notwithstanding, Wilder's next film *was* political and it was certainly the right subject for him, even if it came out at the wrong time. As with *Love in the Afternoon* and *Some Like It Hot*, the new picture had its roots in the director's Berlin days. In 1928, Wilder had enjoyed a production of Hungarian playwright Ferenc Molnàr's one-act comedy *One, Two, Three*, featuring a whirlwind lead performance by German stage star Max Pallenberg. (The Broadway version, translated by Sidney Howard, debuted in September 1930.) Molnàr's original play centers on a Parisian banker who has been looking after the visiting daughter of a Scandinavian millionaire whose account he's trying to land. The banker is suddenly shocked to discover that the girl has been secretly wed these past four months to a socialist taxi driver—and that she's pregnant. What's more, she has just told her parents of her marriage and they're due to arrive that very afternoon. The banker has but one hour to change the girl's cabbie husband into the kind of titled young industrialist a captain of industry would be proud of.

Wilder and Diamond ingeniously expanded on Molnàr's solid framework, giving the action a more specific and topically satirical backdrop. They transformed the European banker into something more intrinsically comic—an American Coca-Cola executive in charge of operations in Berlin. His guest wasn't just a typical teenage girl, but a dizzy, uninhibited Southern belle, the daughter of the head of the Atlanta home office. And her betrothed was no ordinary socialist, but an angry, slogan-spouting, East German Communist firebrand. The Berlin setting gave Wilder an opportunity to film once again in his beloved, bedraggled old home city, while providing the perfect atmosphere to explore the more risible aspects of Cold War posturing.

Production began in Berlin in the early summer of 1961, and soon after Wilder's arrival he was invited to a party hosted by an East German film club in the Soviet sector. *The Apartment* had just been bought for distribution in East Germany, and the Communist movie buffs were thrilled by its vivid portrait of capitalist corruption. "They were tremendously excited about it," recalls Wilder, "especially when—some Russians were there too—I told them: 'A situation like *The Apartment* could happen any place. It happened in Mr. David Lean's picture, *Brief Encounter*. It could happen in Brussels, in Buenos Aires, in Bucharest, it could happen any place—except it could never happen in Moscow.' Oh, I got big applause. Then I said: 'Let me tell you why it could not happen. Because nobody's got his own apartment. You would have to throw out six families.' "

IN BOTH WRITING AND DIRECTING *ONE, TWO, THREE*, Wilder took his cue from Molnár's original stage directions: ". . . an extremely rapid tempo is necessary and even vital to its successful performance. The author insists that the actor entrusted with the role [of the banker] must create what will amount to a world's record for speed. . . . This tempo will depend only partly on swift movement and delivery. It requires an inner intensity as well. He must accomplish everything he does with the almost superhuman celerity of a magician without, however, any lack of poise, presence of mind or precision."

Wilder and Diamond's screenplay put it more succinctly: "This piece must be played *molto furioso*—at a rapid-fire, breakneck tempo. Suggested speed: 100 miles an hour—on the curves—140 miles an hour on the straightaway."

As far as Wilder was concerned, only one American actor could give *One, Two, Three* the breakneck tempo it needed: James Cagney. The director personally called the sixty-one-year-old star at his home in Martha's Vineyard and sold him on the idea of making a comedy in Germany. "I was lucky I got Cagney when he was still working on eight cylinders," Wilder says. But, as much as he admired Cagney's talent, their relationship wasn't as convivial as he'd hoped.

"People say that we did not like each other," Wilder observes. "I was crazy about him. He was just a very opinionated man, very right-wing, not very talkative. He painted—still lifes, like you think he would have painted, like a conservative would paint. But whether you like each other has nothing to do with how good the performance is. I'd do any goddamn thing. He could kick me in the ass. I just wanted his performance."

"There was a beneficent tension on occasion between Cagney and Wilder," says *One, Two, Three* costar Pamela Tiffin. "I think it kept Cagney from getting bored. And, in a certain sense, that kind of competitiveness—after all, Wilder had just won all those Oscars and Cagney was the great old man of the American cinema—it was like two lions eternally circling each other. But it was never unpleasant. There was never any ugliness. With Billy Wilder, there's never bad form.

"I remember once that Wilder wanted Cagney to speak faster," Tiffin continues. "And Cagney spoke faster. And then Wilder wanted it even faster. Of course, Wilder was playful—sometimes it would be a challenge to you or him to see if it could be done. While Cagney thought that if he didn't speak any faster, he would look foolish. Which was not the case, of course—the German crew couldn't have cared less. Cagney said, 'I've always been told to slow down, never to speed up!' "

To get up to speed for the movie, Cagney had a special ritual. Costar Horst Buchholz remembers, "Sometimes when I came in in the morning, very early in the Bavaria Studios in Munich, the lights were still dim, and I heard 'tacka tacka tick tack, tacka tacka tick tack.' I said, 'What's going on in here?' And behind some wall, I found Jimmy Cagney soft-shoeing. I said, 'What the hell are you doing this for?' And he said, 'Oh, it helps me to get that dialogue out as fast as I can.'

As he revealed in his autobiography, Cagney had some misgivings about Wilder's *"molto furioso"* approach: ". . . as I was going along at a hell of a clip, Wilder asked me if I had ever played anything this fast before. I said yes, *Boy Meets Girl*, which Warners had bought for Pat O'Brien and me. Even in 1938 when we made it, Pat and I had been around for many a day, and we knew the absolute need for pacing, letting air in at certain spots to prevent it from being unadulterated rush. We fought the Warners brass on this, and at the points where they won, the results for the picture were sad. I explained this to Wilder, and he said, 'My God, don't frighten me.'

" 'No,' I said, 'but let's benefit from experience. Let's take our time for a spiel, then pick it up and go like hell again.' And this is what we did to a degree. I never saw the picture, but they tell me it was funny. I hope so. It was certainly a lot of hard work."

In fact, the manic dialogue Wilder and Diamond wrote for their star was a killer. In one lengthy take, Cagney's character, newly dubbed C. R. MacNamara, selects and rejects various pieces of wardrobe as he prepares the makeover of his boss's new son-in-law, Otto Ludwig Piffl. Evaluating suits, he barks, "Too loud! Too quiet! All right—but take the padding out of the shoulders! That's not bad. Belt in the back? I thought that went out with high-button shoes!" Cagney brought all his dancer's agility to the intricate routine, but one sentence kept tripping him up: "Where's the morning coat and striped trousers?" "Where's the coat and striped trousers?" he'd ask, or "Where's the morning coat and trousers?" Wilder, forever faithful to the words, showed Cagney no mercy. And when Cagney finally got all the words right, a bit player missed his cue. The sequence took fifty-two takes.

Another big source of tension for Cagney was the movie's Piffl, Horst Buchholz. The handsome, twenty-eight-year-old German stage and screen actor had become an international star with the 1957 drama *The Confessions of Felix Krull,* and crossed over successfully to English-language films with the British thriller *Tiger Bay* and the popular American western *The Magnificent Seven.* Working with veterans like Cagney and Wilder didn't intimidate him; all it did was make him that much more eager to grab his share of attention.

"Horst was naughty," Pamela Tiffin recalls, "but he was so charming and handsome that you forgave him." But there *were* limits. Tiffin says, "Horst was always trying to change the dialogue, and he would try to rotate Cagney so that Cagney's back would be to the camera and Horst would be onscreen. You cannot do that to an old hoofer-actor like Cagney, or to Billy. I didn't understand—all I knew was that when I worked with Horst I was rotating like a merry-go-round. Finally, Wilder said, 'Stop it, Horst!' "

"I never had the slightest difficulty with a fellow actor until the making of *One, Two, Three,*" Cagney said in his memoirs, claiming that if Wilder hadn't taken steps to rein in the young actor, "I was going to knock Buchholz on his ass."

Buchholz, for his part, recalls only one minor infraction, when he added the words "Oh well" or something similar to his dialogue. He remembers Wilder scolding him, "You cannot better a script that Izzy Diamond and I have worked on for eight months by saying, 'Oh well.' If we had thought of 'Oh well,' we would have written it!"

No one, however, had any complaint with the movie's ingenue, eighteen-year-old Pamela Tiffin, whose combination of beauty and comic flair Cagney later compared to that of Carole Lombard, Kay Kendall and Lucille Ball. As the pampered, impetuous, harebrained Coca-Cola heiress Scarlett Hazeltine, the young Oklahoma native brought a robust energy to this unique Wilder heroine.

Retired from movies, Pamela Danon, as she's known today, lives just off Central Park West and is actively involved in New York social and cultural circles. Now in her early fifties, with long, straight white-blonde hair, she radiates charm and has the same girlish, honeysuckle voice of her youth. *One, Two, Three* was her second movie, after a prestigious debut opposite Geraldine Page in the film version of Tennessee Williams's *Summer and Smoke*.

The former Pamela Tiffin vividly remembers her first meeting with Billy Wilder and I. A. L. Diamond. "They had a small, very plain office on the Sam Goldwyn lot—all the best people have plain offices. I think it was on the second floor in those little two-story bungalow buildings. Both men were there and they asked me to read. But they made me feel so comfortable. They were quiet. Of course, they were looking at me and studying me, but in a nice way. It was a workmanlike atmosphere: Are you right for the girl's role? I was very inexperienced as an actress, but I was certainly a young lady, and I felt very comfortable with those two men, each very different. Wilder would be at a desk, but not *behind* the desk, in that sense. And Diamond would always be sitting in a chair off to the side, kind of hunched over, smoking cigarettes madly. You were with highly intelligent people. They dominated that small office, very spartan in its decoration, and there was this electric air, this air of work and focus. And so I read and they liked it. And the reason they liked it, and the reason I read well was quite simple: It was well written. The part was a spoiled and crazy heiress who was a little wild, and it was just so well written that any fool could have done well. They were delighted, and I was delighted."

Listening to Mrs. Danon, it's clear Wilder made a powerful impression on the young starlet. "I have many mental images of him," she says, "but first and foremost it's always elegance. He often wore a certain kind of golfing sweater—I don't know if he played golf or not, but it's a California thing, and most men look ridiculous in them or look like they've been to a sports store on Saturday, but Wilder's casual dress—it's as if he were in white tie. There's something innately elegant physically about Billy Wilder—his posture, his body movements, his carriage. I remember Roddy McDowall used to play a word game of giving colors or textures to people. I think the word 'platinum' would define Billy Wilder, because there's something very cool, very precious, very special, extremely refined about him. He is the consummate European intellectual—who happens to make films. He's extremely sophisticated, and innately debonair. I suppose the definition of debonair would be elegantly witty, and that's what he is."

The actress also recalls how Wilder enjoyed teasing his impressionable new ingenue. "He would say, 'Good moooorning . . . said the sailor to the lady.' Or I would say, 'Mr. Wilder, I have to go to the bathroom,' and he'd add, '. . . said the lady to the sailor.' Which shocked me a little bit. I think he liked to shock me, but it was gentle. He was extremely courtly."

NOT EVERYONE APPRECIATED WILDER'S SENSE OF HUMOR—most especially the East Germans. That became evident when the director filmed a key scene in which Buchholz drives a motorcycle through the Brandenburg Gate into East Berlin. Wilder secured the cooperation of the East Berlin authorities, conveniently forgetting to mention that attached to the exhaust pipe of the motor bike would be an expanding balloon (planted by the Cagney character) with large black letters reading, "Russki Go Home." Unfortunately, weather conditions on the day of filming were poor and Wilder was unable to complete the shot. When he returned to the location the next day, uniformed guards were swarming around the gate and the production was forbidden to enter the Soviet sector. Wilder was only able to film Buchholz driving up to the boundary line, roughly thirty yards from the gate. After doing a test run, he sent a message to the Soviets that they could still be seen in the picture, and expressed his concern that Western audiences viewing the shot might get the impression East Berlin was a police state. The guards promptly made themselves invisible.

Wilder later tried renegotiating with the East Berlin authorities, but they insisted on seeing a script first. The director responded just as he had with Jack Warner and with his bosses at Paramount. "I wouldn't even show my script to President Kennedy," he told the East Berliners.

To complete the Brandenburg Gate scenes, Wilder authorized his production designer, Alexander Trauner, to build a full-scale replica of the structure on the back lot of the Bavaria Studios in Munich, at a cost of $200,000. As with Trauner's re-creation of London's Old Bailey, the bogus gate is altogether convincing.

One month after the border-guard incident, Wilder and company were in the midst of filming new scenes near the gate when news of a Soviet clampdown shocked the world. "I remember I heard it on the radio," Horst Buchholz says. "It was a Sunday and we were off, and Monday we would have continued at the big gate where we had been shooting on Friday.

There were still some scenes left, and on August 13 they started building the Wall. We went out there and only then did it sink in: What's going on? What do we do now?"

"We found thousands of West Berliners milling silently along the border, which had been closed the night before," Diamond recalled. "And suddenly the scenes we had shot there earlier took on a documentary significance, because it might never be possible to duplicate them."

As all the interiors were being shot in Munich, the sudden appearance of the Berlin Wall caused only minor inconveniences to the production. But Wilder, and especially Diamond, began to get the feeling that perhaps their Berlin comedy-in-progress might not play as amusingly as they had originally envisioned. Notes Barbara Diamond, "It's very difficult to write topical jokes when it's six months off in the future before the picture hits the theaters. Who knows how good these jokes are going to be after a while? And then to have a sudden switch like this in the middle of it all . . ."

"It was like making a picture in Pompeii with all the lava coming down," Wilder once said. "Khrushchev was even faster than me and Diamond. We had to make continual revisions to keep up with the headlines."

Toward the end, the production faced another calamity. On a Sunday morning, just a few days before the movie was due to wrap, Horst Buchholz was driving his Porsche when it spun out of control. "I hit I think three trees," the actor says, adding that he owes his life to Billy Wilder. "I was in a coma, and when I woke up in the hospital, I said to the doctors: 'Where are my clothes? I have a meeting at eight with a director and a writer from Los Angeles for the film *Nine Hours to Rama*.' It was already past midnight. The doctor said: 'You have no outward signs that you are hurt, apart from a little bruise on your head, but you may have something internal.' He left the operating room, and only a few days later when I came to myself again, I learned that my wife and Billy were sitting outside. The professor had asked my wife for permission to operate on me—he'd seen from the police photographs of the car that the steering wheel was bent, which meant I may have had internal injuries. And my wife said: 'For God's sake, don't do that, because my husband hates nothing more than somebody cutting him up.' And it was Billy Wilder who turned to my wife and said: 'So what? If there's nothing, he will have a little scar. But if there's something, then it is the last moment—doctors call it the golden hour.' He made my wife consent to this operation. I've never forgotten that. I would have died. In France and in part of Germany, they announced me as already dead."

The production shut down while waiting for news of Buchholz's condition, but ten days later the actor—showing amazing recuperative powers— was in Los Angeles filming his final scenes, in a studio re-creation of Berlin's Tempelhof Airport.

Just before the cast and crew left Munich, Pamela Tiffin saw an unexpectedly tender side to her director. "They were dismantling the office set, and most of the movie took place in the office—how he got away with that, I don't know, because it could have been very boring. And he said, 'Soooo . . .' He'd kind of sidle up to you; he was always watching me out of the corner of his eye. And I said, 'It's going away. I didn't know this was going to happen. We lived here for two months.' I started to cry. I looked at him and he looked upset. And he walked away. And I realized this was all in his mind—anything we see, me, the sets, the desks, the costumes, that was in his mind, and it's gone. I didn't expect him to care about that. I realized, that's a sensitive man."

One member of the company, however, couldn't wait to see the production end. Outside the studio entrance one day, James Cagney opened a letter from a friend to whom he had lent his boat for the summer. Accompanying the letter was a photo of his buddy and some friends out on the water and raising their glasses to the camera. "Thank God you are gainfully employed!" his friend wrote at the bottom of the picture. Cagney stared at the photo with envy. "Then," he recalled, "the assistant director came and said, 'Mr. Cagney, we are ready.' So inside the studio I went, and as they closed the giant doors behind me and I found myself in that great black cavern with just a few spotlights dotted here and there, I said to myself, 'Well, this is it. This is the end. I'm finished.' " Cagney retired to his farm in Dutchess County, New York, and did not make another movie until Milos Forman's *Ragtime*, twenty years later.

WITH THE SINGLE EXCEPTION OF ARLENE FRANCIS AS CAGney's long suffering spouse, everyone in the comic universe of *One, Two, Three* is a zany caricature, whether German, Russian, American Yankee or

Georgia peach. The evenhandedness of the satire is the movie's salvation; by exposing each side's foibles in the pressure cooker of 1960s Berlin, Wilder also reveals their common human arrogance and imperfection. Everyone has a blindered, selfish agenda: MacNamara, with his fierce determination to rise to the top of the Coca-Cola corporate ladder; Piffl, with his humorless faith in Communist dogma; MacNamara's Russian counterparts, who drive a surprisingly hard bargain for Western goods; his German assistant Schlemmer, who lives to be a loyal soldier to his *Führer;* and even Scarlett, spoiled from birth and with nothing on her mind but having a good time.

Of the three nationalities represented in *One, Two Three,* Wilder naturally prefers the Americans—but only because he finds "Coca-Cola imperialism" more amusing than other brands of totalitarianism. As he told Garson Kanin in the mid-1960s, "I happen to think Coca-Cola is funny. . . . And when I drink it, it seems even funnier." With Cagney dominating the screen as he does, the movie could be interpreted as an endorsement of C. R. MacNamara's values, but the character is meant to be a figure of fun—an exaggeration of America's headstrong determination to remake the world in its own product-driven image.

Cagney's counterpart in the Molnár original was equally a fast-talking dynamo with a solution for every crisis—but Molnár's simple joke was that the banker accomplished a miracle makeover in one hour, without missing his train for his vacation in the mountains. At the end, his admiring assistant remarks how wonderful it must be to have all mankind at your disposal. The jaded banker's curtain line: "All mankind ought to be damn well ashamed of itself."

In Wilder and Diamond's version, the joke is different, and more elaborate. MacNamara has much more at stake than trying to catch a train—he's after a long desired promotion to head of European operations in London. (Five years earlier, MacNamara lost his chance when, on his watch, rioters burned down the Middle East bottling plant after the cancellation of a Benny Goodman concert.) The challenge is bigger, too—pugnacious Piffl isn't nearly as compliant as the newlywed in the Molnár one-acter. Wilder and Diamond's wonderfully ironic capper is that MacNamara performs his task too well—the newly westernized Piffl gets the London job MacNamara wanted all along.

Unlike in Molnár, the joke is on MacNamara. Cagney's character joins a parade of Wilder businessmen—Michael in *Bluebeard's Eighth Wife*, Linus in *Sabrina*, Frank in *Love in the Afternoon*, Sheldrake in *The Apartment*—who manipulate the people around them and become ensnared by feelings or circumstances beyond their control. Critics Adrian Turner and Neil Sinyard have pointed out that MacNamara's tornado of energy in *One, Two, Three* also mirrors the forces that drive Kirk Douglas's Tatum in *Ace in the Hole*. "He wants to be going, going . . ." Tatum says to his editor Boot about the cub reporter who idolizes him. "Going where?" is his sober-sided editor's reply. As much as Wilder admires the gung ho spirit of America, he also retains enough of the Old World to see how unreflective his adopted country can be. There *is* something funny about all that Cagney energy being expended in the name of Coca-Cola.

Of course, Wilder doesn't spare the other factions in the Cold War world of *One, Two, Three*. First, there's the Communist delegation MacNamara meets to discuss opening Coca-Cola bottling plants in Russia—three comic types borrowed almost directly from *Ninotchka*. Negotiations nearly break down over who will supply the syrup, until MacNamara reminds the Russians that when they tried their own imitation—Kremlin-Kola: "even the Albanians wouldn't drink it—they used it for sheep-dip." When the Russians try to barter a Bolshoi Ballet tour for Coca-Cola, MacNamara succinctly states the American position: "Please, no culture. Just cash." "The ugly American," mutters Borodenko, emissary from the Soft Drink Secretariat.

Though East-West tensions were an even less likely fount of humor in 1961 than in the 1939 of *Ninotchka*, Wilder stepped in fearlessly. When the East German authorities arrest Piffl in the "Russki Go Home" balloon incident (MacNamara has also planted on him a cuckoo clock that chimes "Yankee Doodle Dandy" and contains a flag-waving miniature Uncle Sam), they torture him by playing over and over again "Itsy Bitsy Teenie Weenie Yellow Polka Dot Bikini," one of the more inane American pop songs of the day. And, when it comes time to rescue Piffl after it's revealed his wife is pregnant, MacNamara gets the Russians involved by pretending to offer up Ingeborg, his buxom German secretary (Lilo Pulver). As Ingeborg dances on a table at the run-down restaurant of East Berlin's Grand Hotel Potemkin, the rapt Russians clap their hands and pound their shoes, and the vibrations cause the room's portrait of Khrushchev to fall, revealing a portrait of Stalin underneath.

Wilder is equally irreverent in his depiction of the German mind-set. Every day, as MacNamara enters the office, his faceless employees rise in unison and stand at attention until he wearily orders, *"Sitzen machen!"* Schlemmer, his bony, toadying assistant, clicks his heels with every reply, even though it drives his boss crazy. "That old Gestapo training?" MacNamara inquires, as Schlemmer swears he was in the underground— the subway, that is, where news of Hitler was supposedly hard to come by. Schlemmer's secret past finally slips out when he recognizes a German newspaperman threatening to expose MacNamara's scheme as his old commanding officer from the SS. As with Rommel in *Five Graves to Cairo*, Erika in *A Foreign Affair* and Colonel Schulz in *Stalag 17*, Wilder refuses to demonize his Nazi characters—a running joke he may be, but Schlemmer remains a rather likable comic figure.

Diamond once described *One, Two, Three* as an attempt to re-create "the kind of fast-paced comedy they were doing in the thirties," something with the momentum of *The Front Page*. It probably contains the highest number of gags per page of any Wilder-Diamond screenplay. If one joke falls flat—as they sometimes do—there's another to take its place in a matter of seconds. The sheer volume leaves an audience panting to keep up.

Mixed among the laughs were countless topical references. "Won't school open soon?" Ingeborg asks, wondering when Scarlett will finally head back to America. "In Georgia?" MacNamara replies. "You never know." The joke, fresh in 1961, is lost on today's younger viewers. So, probably, is MacNamara's admonition to Piffl, half dressed and still threatening to revolt: "Put your pants on, Spartacus!" Wilder and Diamond also couldn't resist having fun with their star's iconic movie past: An angry Cagney holds half a grapefruit up to Buchholz's face, a parody of his famous breakfast scene in *The Public Enemy*, and Red Buttons, in a cameo as a military cop, taunts MacNamara with his best Cagney imitation.

Most of the reviews of *One, Two, Three* expressed astonishment that this Cold War romp worked as well as it does. Dwight Macdonald, who had demolished *The Apartment*, began his *Esquire* notice by asking, "What could be more vulgar, more tasteless than a farce laid in West Berlin whose comic impetus is derived largely from jokes about the Cold War? 'They'll be gagging up lung cancer next,' a friend complained after the preview. I see her point, but I'm ashamed to say that *One, Two, Three* made me laugh more than *Zazie, The Joker* and *The Devil's Eye* [three contemporary comedy imports] put together." The estimable Macdonald concluded that the film skirted vulgarity thanks to its equal-opportunity ridicule and its all-out stylization, so that "one is able to laugh at things which in their headline reality would make one shudder." (Macdonald also took back his crack that Diamond's real name was Zircon.)

In his *New Yorker* rave, Brendan Gill expressed an almost identical sentiment: "We find ourselves incredulously (and perhaps unconscionably) laughing at gags based on events that, when they are reported in the daily papers, suffice to freeze our hearts."

The historian Arthur Schlesinger Jr., then reviewing films for the short-lived magazine *Show*, noted that "Billy Wilder's specialty is skating over thin ice and extracting comedy from materials which, soberly contemplated, are uncomfortably noncomic. I thought that the ice broke under him when he did *The Apartment*. But *One, Two, Three* is audacious, adroit and wholly successful." Schlesinger, in an extravagant mood, went on to add, "One cannot but feel that Mark Twain would have rejoiced in *One, Two, Three*."

Time, The New York Times, The New Republic—all joined in the praise for one of Wilder's most potentially dicey comedies. After the Oscar-winning success of *The Apartment*, there was also a great deal of general press interest in the new Billy Wilder film, which the director masterfully orchestrated. Pamela Tiffin remembers, "When we were there in Germany, he had Hedda Hopper come—all the great freeloading press at the time. Earl Wilson, Leonard Lyons, Sheilah Graham, all the really powerful ones came. Wilder paid great attention to publicity, he understood its function. So, as long as it had to be done, he chose the best and most powerful of the publicity people. He wasn't aloof or standoffish. He worked to publicize his pictures. The attitude was one of very sound business sense, with no illusions, no vanity. And he made sure that people knew it was a Billy Wilder film. I think he understood that he needed to maintain his identity as a working and successful person to survive in the Hollywood corporate world."

Despite all the publicity and good reviews, *One, Two, Three* was a box-office disappointment, taking in roughly $5 million. Wilder and Diamond's worst fears about their comedy were confirmed: The public just wasn't in the mood for a farce set at the scene of an ongoing tragedy.

The final blow came several months after the film's December 1961 debut, in the form of scathing attacks on *One, Two, Three* and the Wilder aesthetic by two soon-to-be-influential film critics, Pauline Kael and John Simon.

Even today, Wilder broods about Kael, and no wonder. The nation's most highly regarded film authority pulled no punches in her spring 1962 *Film Quarterly* essay. "As a member of the audience, I felt degraded and disgusted," she griped. "*One, Two, Three* is overwrought, tasteless, and offensive—a comedy that pulls out laughs the way a catheter draws urine." Kael then went on to cite some examples of the movie's "rancid humor." Admittedly, the list covers some clinkers—including the most adolescent joke in the Wilder canon, when Red Buttons comes upon the dress containing colored "Yankee Go Home" balloons that Schlemmer has used to disguise himself as the bosomy Ingeborg. "Fellas, you won't believe this," he gulps, "but one of them is yellow, one of them is green!" Still, for every painfully dated gag like that one, there are three witty and trenchant punch lines Kael seemed all too eager to overlook.

"In Hollywood it is now common to hear Billy Wilder called the world's greatest movie director," Kael scolded. "This judgment tells us a lot about Hollywood: Wilder hits his effects hard and sure; he's a clever, lively director whose work lacks feeling or passion or grace or beauty or elegance. His eye is on the dollar, or rather on success, on the entertainment values that bring in dollars. But he has never before, except perhaps in a different way in *Ace in the Hole*, exhibited such a brazen contempt for people."

Within months of Kael's salvo, John Simon weighed in with his own dismissal of Wilder in a *Theatre Arts* piece entitled "Belt and Suspenders," comparing the director's "excessive caution" with that of the belt-and-suspender-wearing small-town editor in *Ace in the Hole*. Even in Wilder's best films, Simon scoffed, one finds "characters depending on the whims of the plot, dictated, in turn, by what the public demands, or by what Wilder thinks it demands." Simon refused to believe in the crises of conscience of the protagonists in films like *Sunset Boulevard, Double Indemnity* and *Ace in the Hole*, and what's more, he was convinced Wilder didn't believe in them either.

In a way, Wilder set himself up for these attacks when he told writer Colin Young in a 1959 *Film Quarterly* interview: "It is an absolute cinch to make a film so that it will win first prize at some festival in Zagreb. It is much more difficult to make a film which will have worldwide popularity. I have no interest in making arty films to appeal to a group of critics, full of false aesthetics. There is an international association of them, capable of falling into raptures over Cocteau's dead donkey draped over a piano.* There are filmmakers for these critics too, who have no concern about who is going to pay the bills, no worry about the man who runs the business, who pays the usher's salary. The critics have no idea what precisely Bergman is saying, but they rave about him nevertheless."

Statements like that, in which Wilder so blatantly addressed the commercial concerns of a Hollywood moviemaker, made his artistic credentials more suspect in the eyes of the feisty new breed of film critic. The cinema world was changing, too. The critics of France's *Cahiers du Cinema*, with their *politique des auteurs*, had generated a new awareness of and regard for the work of American B-movie directors functioning at a status level below Wilder's high-profile, big-studio projects. Then, a number of *Cahiers* critics, most notably Jean-Luc Godard, the late François Truffaut,† Claude Chabrol and Jacques Rivette, became filmmakers themselves, creating the low-budget, free-form works of the Nouvelle Vague, which would suddenly turn the "well-made" French studio film into an archaic joke. Along with the Nouvelle Vague, the late 1950s and early 1960s brought a flood of exciting new imports from Europe and Asia into American art houses: the psychological and spiritual explorations of Ingmar Bergman; the phantasmagorical spectacles of Federico Fellini; the studies in ennui of Michelangelo Antonioni; the wide-ranging period and contemporary tales of Akira Kurosawa, to name just the most celebrated.

Wilder had been working in a completely different tradition for some

* Wilder's mention of Jean Cocteau is incorrect. The image appears in Salvador Dalí and Luis Buñuel's *Un Chien andalou.*
† Ironically, as a *Cahiers* critic, Truffaut heaped praise on such lesser Wilder films as *Stalag 17* and *The Seven Year Itch.*

twenty-five years—the Hollywood studio system, in which one's continued existence was tied into one's recognition of the public mood. With perhaps a bit of false modesty, Wilder told *Playboy* in 1963, "I have at no time regarded myself as one of the artistic immortals. I am just making movies to entertain people and I try to do it as honestly as I can." For Wilder, craftsmanship was much more desirable than the conscious pursuit of art. "To be poetic is not enough," he once told French critic Michel Ciment. "It's necessary also to be an engineer, to go to engineering school, to sweat over the planning."

In interviews at the time, Wilder took frequent swipes at the era's foreign-film gods. "Ingmar Bergman to me is very interesting," he commented in 1960, "but only for a limited young audience. For me, his things are déjà vu, for we used every shot he does back in Berlin." Critical praise for filmmakers like Antonioni, he said, was prompting American directors to make longer and slower pictures, on the assumption "that slowness and solemnity are the same thing as profundity." As for Godard, Wilder declared in 1970, "He has *epaté les bourgeois* for so long that they are no longer at all shocked. The only ones who are shocked are the people who put their money into these films. They are shocked and ruined, for sure."

Wilder's love of a strong narrative (and a certain "been there/done that" generational bias) closed him off from some of the more provocative and stylistically revolutionary films of the period, films that have long withstood the test of time. But no one should infer from his aesthetic judgments that he hasn't maintained a keen intellectual curiosity about the film medium. For all his shots at Godard and Antonioni, he was just as inclined to throw bouquets at a Truffaut or a Fellini. He even (apparently) came to have a high regard for Bergman: When the great Swedish director was feted at a Hollywood luncheon in the mid-1970s, Wilder toasted him by saying, "We feel like the personnel in a backwoods hospital when Dr. Christiaan Barnard is making a call." And, when the American movie industry underwent its own revolution in the late sixties, Wilder would lavish praise on many of the films at the forefront, pictures like *Easy Rider* and *Midnight Cowboy* and *Carnal Knowledge*.

Wilder's unashamed embrace of commercial success—and his recent record of box-office hits—made him a prime target of the new generation of critics who felt intellectually superior to the conventions of mainstream

Hollywood movies. But in their eagerness to knock him down a few pegs, they failed to see what he had accomplished within those conventions: consistently groundbreaking work with a strong personal imprint. Who else but Billy Wilder could have made *A Foreign Affair? Sunset Boulevard? Some Like It Hot?* Even *One, Two, Three?*

Wilder's films may not possess the traditional qualities of grace, beauty and elegance as Pauline Kael defined them, but they are certainly not lacking in feeling and passion—the grand delusions of a Norma Desmond, the survivor's grit of an Erika von Schlutow, the sorrow of a Fran Kubelik, the torment of a Don Birnam. And isn't there a kind of grace and beauty and elegance in the noble acts of the wartime heroes in *Arise, My Love* and *Five Graves to Cairo*, the incandescence of the young Audrey Hepburn in *Sabrina* and *Love in the Afternoon*, the polished wit of Wilder's dialogue, the finely honed structure of his screenplays? If, as John Simon said, "Wilder has made some extremely skillful, effective, and, in part, even penetrating films, [but] he has never done anything first-rate," then what, exactly, in American cinema *is* first-rate? Beauty, as the millions of people who continue to discover these films will attest, is truly in the eye of the beholder.

IN 1986, *ONE, TWO, THREE* RECEIVED VINDICATION IN THE unlikeliest of places. Following a successful art-house revival in Paris, the film was re-released in Germany and became something of a phenomenon with young audiences there. As Horst Buchholz describes it, "The director of one of the biggest theaters in Berlin called me and said: 'Please come and see what's happening here. The house is packed, and they all stand up and click their heels and say, *"Sitzen machen!"*' They wave small Russian and American flags, and start talking along with the screen.' The young people turned it into a happening, like *The Rocky Horror Picture Show!*"

Today, in the united Germany, the tensions that suddenly made *One, Two, Three* seem like an ill-timed sick joke are largely nonexistent. Near the Brandenburg Gate, only one hint of the bitter rivalry of the movie's era remains: huge, competing neon signs advertising Coke and Pepsi.

E I G H T E E N

From Irma to Infamy

BILLY WILDER'S TIMING COULDN'T HAVE BEEN WORSE with *One, Two, Three*, but it couldn't have been better with his new project, *Irma la Douce*. Movie-industry columnists questioned his wisdom in mounting a big-budget studio comedy about a Parisian prostitute, but Wilder had always had a pretty clear sense of how much he could get away with. "There's no reason this film should not get a seal [from the Production Code office]," he told the press. "It has no orgies, homosexuals or cannibalism."

Louella Parsons told Jack Lemmon she had seen the show on Broadway and couldn't imagine how it could be cleaned up for the screen. "Audiences are much more mature today and they demand maturer subject matter," he countered. "I think any subject can be handled on the screen today provided it's done in good taste."

But neither Wilder nor Lemmon could be absolutely certain *Irma la Douce* wasn't headed for trouble with the censors. Production Code head Geoffrey Shurlock, on reading the play script in 1959, found it potentially unacceptable on several counts: "Its leading lady is a practicing prostitute who, additionally, falls in love with and lives with the leading man, bearing his child out of wedlock. She is also carrying on a second affair with the leading man who has disguised himself as somebody else. This relationship is not treated with any semblance of the compensating moral values and

voice for morality required by the Code. In addition, there are other elements of low and sordid tone (such as the portrayal of pimps) which would
render this property unacceptable."

Amazingly, *Irma* the film has all those elements and still managed, as
Wilder predicted, to obtain a Production Code seal. How did he do it? In
the words of one of the movie's characters, that's another story.

What did *not* remain of the stage version of *Irma la Douce* was virtually
its entire second act, and every single one of its songs. As Wilder explained
at the time, "I have nothing against music, but the more I went into that
story, the better I thought it was. And for me, the numbers got in the way.
So, first, one of them went, then another one went, then we started talking
that idiocy you hear yourself go on about—you know, an intimate musical,
or play with music—but, more and more, I could see that if I really wanted
to explore all the avenues of this story, there wasn't going to be room for
any numbers. And, one day, I made the decision, and we threw the whole
score out and made it a straight picture. We used some of the music for
underscoring, but that was all. I think it worked out very well."

Diamond was more blunt about the matter, in an interview with Hollywood journalist Joe Hyams. "When we first read the script and heard the
music," he noted, "we didn't like it. We saw the show in Paris and liked the
twist—the double identity of the pimp who becomes a patron only to
become jealous of himself—but we didn't like the show. Here was a musical
with only one girl in it who dances only one dance. The songs stopped the
action and seemed to have nothing to do with the story. Besides, musicals
as such are not our forte."

And so Wilder and Diamond kept the twist they liked and fashioned a
screenplay with only a handful of lines borrowed from the original, like the
darkly comic introductory narration that boasts, "This is a story about
passion, bloodshed, desire and death—everything, in fact, that makes life
worth living," and Irma's risqué comment that "I never remember a face."
The setting was changed from bohemian Montmartre to the bustling pro-
duce-market area of Les Halles. Nestor, an innocent law student in the
play, was transformed into a naïve and laughably high-minded rookie cop.
And, for the film, Irma was given a wild array of streetwalking companions,
among them Kiki the Cossack, Amazon Annie, the Zebra Twins and, in a

Wilder nod to two recent movie hits, Suzette Wong and Lolita (wearing the same heart-shaped sunglasses as Sue Lyon in the Stanley Kubrick film).

In the Wilder-Diamond adaptation, Nestor initiates a raid on the hotel where Irma and the other *poules* (prostitutes) conduct their business, bringing upon himself the wrath of the chief police inspector who is also a regular customer there. Nestor is canned from the force, and returns to the neighborhood as a forlorn, unemployable civilian. At the Chez Moustache bistro, where the *mecs* (pimps) loiter while their girls work the streets, Nestor rises to Irma's defense after her burly *mec* roughs her up. Through sheer tenacity (and a couple of lucky shots), Nestor wins the battle and becomes Irma's de facto *mec*. Irma takes him under her roof and promises to work even harder, but Nestor isn't at all comfortable with the arrangement. Since no self-respecting *mec* is supposed to go out and look for a job, Nestor has to conceive an elaborate scheme to keep his lover off the streets: He disguises himself with a beard, an eyepatch and a fancy dress suit as Lord X, a wealthy, older, pip-pip English aristocrat who becomes Irma's sole client. Even though Lord X's extravagant tips ultimately come back to Nestor, expenses add up for the hapless *mec*, and he is forced to sneak out early each morning to jobs at the meat and fish markets in order to make ends meet. Nestor and Irma's sex life suffers as a consequence, but she puts extra effort into keeping Lord X interested, and before long Nestor becomes wildly, irrationally jealous of his own alter ego. Nestor eventually puts a stop to the madness by throwing his Lord X costume into the Seine, a gesture that backfires badly when he is arrested and convicted of the imaginary aristocrat's murder. Nine months later, Nestor learns that Irma is pregnant, and escapes to reunite with his love. He clears his name by staging a miraculous reappearance of Lord X, then rushes off to the church wedding where he and Irma say "I do" just seconds before she gives birth.

ALONG WITH MARILYN MONROE, WILDER HAD CONSIDERED both Brigitte Bardot and Elizabeth Taylor for the role of Irma la Douce (or Irma the Sweet). But in the end the part went to Jack Lemmon's *Apartment* costar, Shirley MacLaine, whose salary rose appreciably from a flat $175,000 for the first film to $350,000 against a maximum 7.5 percent of gross. "They couldn't have a girl who looks like a hooker who enjoys her work," the star told *Look* magazine. "That's why the standard Hollywood sex symbol in the role would be disastrous. This girl has to be a naïve, wide-eyed, innocent-looking young thing. Like I am."

Of course, as a doted upon member of Frank Sinatra's Rat Pack, MacLaine wasn't quite as innocent as she appeared onscreen, and she makes that special mix of sophistication and girlishness work for the character and for the film. It's there right from the opening credits, as Wilder and Diamond deflect any sense of condescending pity for Irma in three brief vignettes that show various clients asking how a nice girl like her ended up walking the streets. Irma tells each a different elaborate sob story and, as her guilt-ridden johns leave handsome tips, offers a self-assured, mechanical thank-you without even looking at the extra cash. Later, when Nestor asks the same question, Irma complains, "Just the other night, I ran across a man who thought I was too good for this kind of work, and you know what he does for a living? He's a mortician! Now I ask you . . ."

MacLaine and Lemmon prepared for their roles by spending two days observing the routine of a Paris brothel. As Lemmon recalled it, "They were saying *pardonnez moi* every three minutes and booming upstairs. Our eyes were as big as saucers. They were very proud of the fast turnover—it's also an economic matter!"

For its time, *Irma la Douce* is remarkably nonjudgmental about the oldest profession. The script continually ponders *petit bourgeois* attitudes toward prostitution, often through the mouthpiece of Moustache, the worldly bistro owner who argues, "Love is illegal, but not hate—that you can do anywhere, anytime, to anybody." In the end, however, the movie bows to certain *petit bourgeois* conventions as it hastens to get Irma (and her baby) to the altar on time.

Wilder makes Irma's world more palatable to a 1963 audience by emphasizing the artificiality of the piece; it may no longer be a musical, but it still feels like one. It is also Wilder's first color film since *The Spirit of St. Louis.* The film has an exceptionally jaunty score by André Previn (adapting some themes by the original stage composer, Marguerite Monnot), and most of the action takes place on a massive $350,000 re-creation of the Les Halles neighborhood on two soundstages, a tour de force for designer Alexander Trauner. The main set, including the Chez Moustache and the

Hotel Casanova where Irma conducts her business, consisted of forty-eight buildings and three large streets, all marked by Trauner's typical exacting detail. But paradoxically, the set is so spectacular in its authenticity, it only enhances the unreal flavor of the story.

So, too, does Wilder's curious decision not to have any of his actors simulate a French accent. Lemmon, MacLaine, and the entire cast of *mecs* and *poules* are plainly Americans—only Lou Jacobi, the likable but undynamic substitute for Wilder's first choice, the late Charles Laughton, adopts a cultured accent of indeterminate origin in his role as Moustache. Remembers MacLaine, "We had a long talk and decided that everyone should have the same accent. It was a subliminal acknowledgment that it was all artificial anyway."

Production began in August 1962 with ten days of exterior shooting in Paris, during which Jack Lemmon wed the actress Felicia Farr; Billy Wilder and another director close to Lemmon, Richard Quine, shared the duties of best man. The honeymoon ran into a major snag, however, when Lemmon caught an intestinal virus after filming the scene where Lord X emerges from the Seine. Production resumed in Hollywood on October 8 and continued for four months.

ALTHOUGH IT SEEMS TAILOR-MADE TO HIS PENCHANT FOR COMedies of disguise and identity, *Irma la Douce* is not first-rate Wilder. The novelty of the Nestor/Lord X gambit fades long before the story does, and the cast of characters is too broadly drawn to sustain interest over a nearly 2½-hour running time. The main charm of the film lies in the continuing chemistry between Lemmon and MacLaine, especially in the gentle scene in which Nestor first enters Irma's apartment and hangs newspaper pages over the windows to keep the neighbors from spying on their first night together. There's also no shortage of jokey Wilder/Diamond mischief: Moustache's constant references to past adventures as a colonel in Marrakesh, an obstetrician with Albert Schweitzer, a croupier in Monte Carlo, etc., always capped by the phrase, "But that's another story"; or Lord X's description of his war injuries from "those beastly guns" at Navarone and that "ruddy bridge" on the River Kwai that fell down on him. Needless to say, material like this is also license for Wilder to indulge his love of naughty double entendres, as when Lord X mentions how he saw his wife in the garden showing her lover "her begonias."

Irma la Douce opened in June 1963 to a mixture of pans and qualified positive notices. Bosley Crowther expressed astonishment that Wilder had managed to make an "acceptable film" out of the racy stage show, calling it "brisk and bubbly" and "charmingly antic." His only complaint was that the picture was "somewhat one-tracked and overlong." *Life* deemed the film "wildly comic and honestly romantic," while *Newsweek* heaped all of its praise on Lemmon, declaring, "He saves the Wilder reputation—and the picture with it."

The pans simmered with vitriol. Stating upfront that he found prostitution "about as hilarious as muscular dystrophy," Brendan Gill in *The New Yorker* called the Wilder-Diamond script "a model of vulgarity," and conceded only that Lemmon and MacLaine "almost succeed in purging [the movie] of squalor." *Saturday Review* branded the script laborious, vulgar and "too often unfunny." Then there was Leo Mishkin of the *Morning Telegraph*, who had been lobbing tomatoes at Wilder ever since *A Foreign Affair*. The veteran New York critic pronounced the movie "as vulgar, tasteless and revolting a business as has been shown this year, a leering, sniggering exercise in lewdness more properly designed for a stag smoker than for mass commercial exhibition."

One of the most unexpected condemnations of the film came from a fellow filmmaker, Hal Wallis, the producer of *The Story of Louis Pasteur*, *Casablanca*, and *Gunfight at the OK Corral*, who wrote a scathing letter to Production Code chief Shurlock, calling *Irma la Douce* a "salacious, pornographic, distasteful, obscene, offensive piece of celluloid. . . . I have great admiration for Wilder's talents in some of his work, but the only thing I admired in this one was his ability to pull the wool so far over your eyes as to enable him to get a seal on the picture. This is without a doubt the filthiest thing I have ever seen on the screen."

Shurlock responded to Wallis's rant by explaining that the seal was issued only after United Artists had agreed to advertise *Irma* as a film for adults only, with the Code office concluding "that the film would probably be considered more funny than offensive by this restrictive audience." Shurlock went on to note that "we have only received two letters of complaint, yours being the second. As I have said, we were at first somewhat apprehensive about the project. However, the event seems to have justified our action. The picture is evidently going to be one of the top grossers for 1963. And from all we can find out, it is mostly men who complain about it. Women generally seem to find it hilarious."

Surprisingly, considering the tenor of many of the reviews, *Irma la Douce* won a "B" rating ("morally objectionable in part for all") from the Catholic Legion of Decency, after United Artists agreed to make minor cuts. These included an apparent close shot of Irma naked from the waist up (in the final version, her nudity is barely visible as Nestor peers through the wrong end of a pair of binoculars); "pelvic contortions" during the Irma/Lord X seduction scene; and a shot in which an American soldier leaves the Hotel Casanova with the twins on his arms.

As Geoffrey Shurlock noted, *Irma* was a smash with the public. By mid-January 1964, it had taken in $9.5 million in domestic rentals (roughly $19 million in box office) from fewer than 4,400 engagements, with many long runs around the country. *Daily Variety* reported that the film had broken all records in St. Paul, Minnesota, a largely Catholic market where pictures condemned by the Catholic church were invariably banned; the previous record holder was the religious epic *The Robe*. Ultimately, *Irma* counted up some $12 million in domestic rentals, prompting UA executive Arnold Picker to tout it as the highest-grossing comedy in history after *Around the World in 80 Days* (though the all-star road-show attraction *It's a Mad, Mad, Mad, Mad World* would soon surpass it). It was by far the biggest hit Wilder ever enjoyed.

Though it gave another great boost to her career, Shirley MacLaine frankly admits, "I didn't like the movie. I hated things like the cut to a big slab of meat being sliced down the center [as Nestor toils in the market-place]. That was vulgar. And it should have been a musical." In her most recent autobiography, the longtime star also notes, "I didn't understand why I got nominated for an Oscar, and would have been really nonplussed had I won. I knew I wouldn't, but had that happened, I was ready to make a speech for the legalization of the oldest profession in the world."

MacLaine's view of Billy Wilder is constantly teetering between admiration and frank criticism, as if she's still trying to comprehend this key figure in her life. "He abhors sentimentality," she observes. "He was one of the first to warn us against sentimentality." But at the same time, MacLaine feels Wilder's best films are those that show evidence of heart, a quality she largely attributes to the director's mostly unsung collaborator, editor Doane Harrison. "When Doane died, something went out of Billy," the actress attests. "I began to realize what editors were in the lives of great directors. He'd say to Billy, 'You didn't break my heart today—go back and do it again.' "

Back in the 1970s, it didn't take much prodding for MacLaine to brand Wilder a male chauvinist. Today, she's less eager to level the charge. "That's just his Germanic background," she says. "I don't think any of us thought about what it meant at the time."

Speculating on Wilder's rocky relationship with Marilyn Monroe, MacLaine believes the director "was nonsensitive to the insecurities of women who lack self-esteem." MacLaine herself often felt somewhat neglected by Wilder, but she says that was more a function of his professional infatuation with Jack Lemmon. Wilder, it seems, would film take after take of a scene, just to see what his favorite new star would come up with. "I would stay around and watch Jack," MacLaine says, "and I'd think, 'Well, Jack was better in the first take.' Billy *could* be wrong at times."

As MacLaine herself grew more self-confident and strongly opinionated, the gap between her and her former mentor seemed to become only wider; after their two big box-office hits, they never worked together again. Still, it's clear Shirley MacLaine loves Billy Wilder like an imposing father figure. She praises his panache, his wit, his resilience, his dignity. And, with a good-natured touch of self-parody, she adds, "Once in thirteen lifetimes do you come across someone like this."

APART FROM THE VARIOUS HOSTILE REVIEWS HE HAD BEEN RE-ceiving of late, Wilder was drowning in good fortune. Four of his last five pictures had been big box-office hits, with *Irma la Douce* breaking records. He had just signed a new three-picture deal with the Mirisch Company giving him $400,000 against 10 percent of the gross per film, plus an amazing 75 percent of the profits after breakeven. He had six Oscars to his name. No screenwriter in Hollywood was more highly regarded; few directors commanded more respect. His parties were strictly A-list affairs, and when he decided to invest in a restaurant, it became the hottest spot in town, the Bistro. (In fact, the Bistro probably wouldn't have existed without Wilder. When Romanoff's closed in 1962, he coordinated most of the backing for maître d' Kurt Niklaus's new venture, though Wilder's original idea of a simple French restaurant was transformed into something much more grand and luxurious.)

As a filmmaker, Wilder had managed to hold on to his standing while remaining true to his interests and testing the limits of what was acceptable in popular entertainment. Emboldened by the success of *Irma la Douce*, and no doubt stimulated by some of the frank new films that were coming out of places like Britain, Italy, France and Sweden, he decided, with his next film, to see just how bawdy an American movie could be in 1964.

Wilder's source material for the film that came to be known as *Kiss Me, Stupid* was *L'Ora della Fantasia*, a farce by Italian playwright Anna Bonacci that had enjoyed a successful Paris production in 1953, starring Jeanne Moreau and Suzanne Flon. The French version was set in Victorian England; oddly enough, the action was transplanted to 1860s France for the American adaptation, *The Dazzling Hour*, which starred Olivia de Havilland and closed before making it to Broadway.

Bonacci's play concerns a provincial church organist who is desperate to have his new oratorio performed in London. When the lecherous sheriff of London passes through town, the musician tries to win his favor by inviting him to spend the night in close proximity to his wife. Fearing she isn't pretty enough to interest the sheriff, the organist's wife volunteers to trade places with the town prostitute. The composer and the courtesan share an unexpected attraction and throw out the sheriff, who winds up in the arms of the organist's wife. Everyone keeps the night's events to themselves, and the organist is left mystified when his masterwork is given its London premiere.

"It's the same plot we used," said Diamond, "but we were not interested in doing a picture about greed and sex in eighteenth-century [*sic*] England. We wanted to translate it into modern terms."

At the outset, *Kiss Me, Stupid* looked as promising as any Wilder-Diamond project, with three stars at or near the height of their careers. Dean Martin was cast as a caricature of himself known only as Dino, a big TV, movie, concert and recording star who suffers terrible headaches if he doesn't have sex every single night. Kim Novak, for a decade one of the movies' top sex symbols, was set to play Polly the Pistol, a waitress at the forlorn Belly Button café ("Drop In and Get Lost," a neon sign outside advises) who isn't above selling her favors for some extra spending money. And, for the key role of piano teacher and aspiring composer Orville J. Spooner, Wilder landed Peter Sellers, the chameleonlike British comic genius who had just created a sensation playing three characters in Stanley Kubrick's Nuclear Age satire *Dr. Strangelove*. Also on board were Jack Lemmon's wife, Felicia Farr, as Orville's good-hearted wife, Zelda, and the virtually unknown Cliff Osmond as Orville's obsessive songwriting partner, Barney Millsap.

From the first day of shooting on March 6, *Kiss Me, Stupid* was jinxed. United Artists had arranged for some of the nation's leading columnists to be in the audience as Wilder filmed the sequence of Dino's final-night concert performance in Las Vegas (actually, the Earl Carroll Theatre in Hollywood). Unfortunately, no one from the studio told Wilder that the scribes were expecting individual closeups. Joseph LaShelle's Panavision camera raced past the gaggle of gossips, who went home offended—and determined not to give *Kiss Me, Stupid* any play in their columns.

In a March 20 interview with Steve Allen, Peter Sellers positively gushed about his director. "I might say that it's long been my ambition to work with Billy Wilder," he declared. "The two directors I've always wanted to work with are Vittorio De Sica and Billy Wilder. I think Wilder is one of the greatest, if not *the* greatest, comedy directors in the world."

But within days, the working methods of star and director began to clash. Sellers had just come off *Dr. Strangelove* with Stanley Kubrick and *A Shot in the Dark* with Blake Edwards; both directors encouraged their star to toss aside the script and let his comic imagination go wild. Wilder, of course, would have none of that; as always, the screenplay was sacrosanct. Sellers, who by now had become accustomed to directors catering to his whims and mercurial moods, felt unfairly constricted. "I realized that there was no way for me to work within Wilder's system," the actor observed, years later. "Placing oneself entirely in someone's hands, even Wilder's, brilliant as he was, just wasn't right. He and Izzy Diamond's words were golden, but they were very set in their ways."

Though Wilder demanded absolute respect for the script, his sets were anything but monastic—he liked a lively social atmosphere, and visitors were always welcome. This, too, irked Sellers to the point of distraction. "I used to go down on the set," he complained, "and find a Cook's tour of hangers-on and sightseers standing just off the set, right in my line of vision. Friends and relatives of people in the front office came to kibitz on Peter Sellers, actor."

Costar Cliff Osmond says he saw no signs that Sellers was distraught during the month they filmed together. "We were working for someone who was at the top of his craft and his fame, so there was no emotionalism—it was just a bunch of people working together happily. Kim Novak would make cookies at three in the morning and bring them to the set. Peter seemed to be enjoying it—he had a new wife and she'd come visit, dressed up in ruby, jade and diamonds on various days. My guess is that Peter's unhappiness arose after the fact—he probably was unhappy he was replaced."

Four weeks into shooting, on Sunday night, April 5, Sellers suffered a mild heart attack after making love to his wife of less than two months, the actress Britt Ekland (and using amyl nitrate to prolong his performance). The following day, Sellers checked into Cedars of Lebanon Hospital for observation. In the early-morning hours of April 7, his heart suddenly stopped beating; a blood clot from the initial attack had caused a massive coronary. Sellers was attended by two heart specialists—Dr. Rex Kennamer, Elizabeth Taylor's physician, and Dr. Eliot Corday, considered America's top heart surgeon—and the prognosis was not good. The actor suffered seven more heart attacks that day, and at one point was technically dead; he later remembered his soul leaving his body and seeing the white light common to people who have near-death experiences. Somehow, Sellers's heart survived the onslaught, and the actor announced plans for a minimum six-month convalescence in England.

Losing Sellers was a blow to the production, but he wouldn't be altogether missed. "What do you mean, heart attack?" Wilder reportedly said when he first heard the news of Sellers's seizure. "You've got to have a heart before you can have an attack."

On his return to London, Sellers complained to Alexander Walker of the *Evening Standard*, "I have had Hollywood, love. At the studios they give you every creature comfort, except the satisfaction of being able to get the best work out of yourself. America I would go back to gladly tomorrow, but as far as filmland is concerned, I've taken the round trip for good."

Wilder and the rest of the *Kiss Me, Stupid* company took Sellers's words as an unjust personal affront. A few days later, he received a telegram reading, "Talk About Unprofessional Rat Finks," signed by Wilder, Dean Martin, Kim Novak and other members of the cast and crew—a reference to Polly the Pistol's phrase for the men who have dumped on her. The telegram found its way into the gossip columns, and Sellers responded with a full-page ad in *Variety*, arguing, "I did not go to Hollywood to be ill. I went there to work and found, regrettably, that the creative side in me couldn't accept the conditions under which work had to be carried out."

Wilder seems to have blotted out memories of his troubles with Sellers; in his own mind, they worked together only a few days before the actor had his heart attack. Trying to put the best face on their relationship, Wilder says, "I liked him and I worked very well with him. I just don't know whether with that English accent I could have made him work as a small-town piano teacher. But it would have been exciting—I admired him greatly."

Whatever Wilder really thought of Sellers, the production never seriously considered the financially onerous option of shutting down to wait for the actor's return. As the gravity of Sellers's condition made headlines, Wilder began looking for a replacement. One trade paper reported that Tony Randall was a serious candidate; other names bandied about included Bob Hope, Danny Kaye and Tom Ewell. Ray Walston, then finishing up the season on his hit TV fantasy sitcom *My Favorite Martian*, heard the reports and had his agent contact Wilder, with whom he had worked previously on *The Apartment*. By that Thursday, Walston had the part, and filming resumed the following Monday.

For Walston, starring in a Billy Wilder movie was a tremendous break, yet at the same time something bothered him. As he told writer Nick Tosches, "Both my wife and I sat down and read this script, and I said when I finished it, 'It's not good, it's not good.' But one doesn't say that about a Billy Wilder–I. A. L. Diamond script. The feeling was that they would repair it."

Walston claimed he had never seen a Peter Sellers film, and had no intention of looking at the footage that had already been shot. "I wanted my own interpretation," he said, "as directed by Billy Wilder. I couldn't let Sellers's reputation bug me." Twenty-four shooting days out of a total of eighty-five were devoted to redoing scenes Sellers had already filmed.

A less momentous—but painful—mishap befell Kim Novak during the shoot, when she tripped and fell and aggravated a childhood back injury. Initially, she felt fine, but ten days later she was in crippling pain. Her doctor told her to stay in traction for two weeks, but she insisted on returning to work, with the help of pain pills and Novocaine shots. Between scenes, she would stand on a slantboard instead of sitting down.

"My doctor told me not to do anything physical," Novak recalled. "But it had to be. The director, Billy Wilder, is the most considerate man I've ever known, but when he'd ask if it would bother my back, I'd just say, 'Oh no, it's fine.' I didn't want to complain. If you're doing a movie, you can't pamper yourself that way."

Dean Martin, meantime, was predictably irreverent. Ray Walston recalls that on his first day of filming, after Wilder had given Walston some detailed direction, Martin said, in a voice everyone could hear, "Tell the cocksucker to go fuck himself. Do it your own way."

"Dean is a very funny man, and witty," says Felicia Farr. "He was sort of there to make Billy happy. He'd have Billy in stitches, with tears running down his eyes. We'd be shooting, and Dean would say, 'Blackbirds at twelve o'clock,' which meant there were guests on the set. We'd all be looking around. He was adorable. I used to tease him—I used to say, 'I'm gonna give away your myth, that you're heavy into drink and not a serious guy,' because the only thing I saw him do was play golf, when he had a minute. That's about all—I never saw him drunk, or busy with drinking—that was just for his nightclub act."

Kiss Me, Stupid was a choice opportunity for Farr, a charming actress until then best known for her roles in the Delmer Daves westerns *The Last Wagon, Jubal* and *3:10 to Yuma*. Wilder had originally offered Farr the part of the barfly who goes home with C. C. Baxter on Christmas Eve in *The Apartment*, but her agent advised her to turn it down. "He felt it came at such a poor time in the script, when the leading lady is committing suicide.

He thought it would be detrimental for me to do something like that. It was years later that Billy finally talked to me with any civility at all. . . . No, he was always sweet, but his feelings were hurt about it." All was now forgiven—Wilder wrote the part of sweet, sexy Zelda Spooner specifically for his friend, Mrs. Jack Lemmon.

Wilder also gave a huge break to Cliff Osmond, a very tall, very rotund young actor who had played a small part as a cop in *Irma la Douce*. "When I finished *Irma la Douce*," the actor recalls, "Wilder said to me, 'We're going to work again.' I only had three or four lines. I figured he was just being nice. But about seven months later, he called my agent. I came in to see him and he said, 'You thought I was bullshitting you?' I was twenty-six and I thought, My gosh, only a few years ago I was working for a hundred a month in repertory down in Texas."

Unlike some collaborators who experienced Wilder's biting wit, Osmond says the veteran director was quite protective of him. "I think he sensed how fragile I was as a young man, how terribly insecure. Three years removed from college, seven years removed from the inner-city ghetto, having made a tremendous leap in social class and artistic work. I was so insecure about my singing. André Previn [the film's composer and orchestrator]—imagine all that talent having to pull me through a song. I remember a gaffer laughed, and Billy turned to him and said, 'Do you know how to high-jump?' 'What, Billy?' 'Do you high-jump?' He went, 'No.' And Billy said, 'It must be funny to watch you high-jump,' more or less saying, 'Hey, so the kid can't sing.' " Osmond does, however, remember Wilder later telling a colleague, "Cliff Osmond has the musical ear of van Gogh."

KISS ME, STUPID MIGHT BEST BE TERMED A DYSFUNCTIONAL love story. Married to the prettiest girl in town, struggling musician Orville J. Spooner simply can't believe his good fortune—in fact, his disbelief has made him irrationally possessive. Is the milkman leaving mash notes with the buttermilk? Has that pimply-faced fourteen-year-old piano student been taking liberties? Orville's jealousy is like some primitive beast that *must be fed*, but then, so is the ambition of his songwriting partner, the ever hopeful and patently untalented gas-station owner next door, Barney Millsap. Whatever musical gifts Orville may harbor, they're doomed by his sad alliance with a man who writes verses like "I'm a poached egg without a piece of toast/I'm a haunted house that doesn't have a ghost/I'm Vienna without the Viennese/I'm da Vinci without the Mona Lize. . . ."* As crass as his lyrics, Barney all but flashes dollar signs in his eyes when superstar Dino rides into his service station in the arid Nevada town of Climax. If only Dino could hear some of his and Orville's sixty-two tunes, Barney thinks to himself as he dismantles the singer's fuel line and arranges a prolonged pit stop. He quickly devises a plan to keep Dino within listening distance, using Orville's wife as bait. Not Orville's real wife, God forbid, but the local roadhouse's one and only hot number, Polly the Pistol. While Barney makes arrangements to have Polly pose as Zelda Spooner, Orville's job is to pick a fight with his wife and get her off the premises.

The farce mechanism is in high gear even before the masquerade begins. Zelda, never realizing her idol Dino is in her house, gives him a loving pat on the fanny while he's in the shower, thinking it's Orville. Thus, Dino is already primed for Barney's scheme. Getting Zelda angry enough to leave is another story, though. Her angelic devotion propels one of Wilder and Diamond's funniest comic exchanges, as Orville labors desperately to irk Zelda (all the while keeping a Cagney-inspired half grapefruit at the ready) and his wife keeps acquiescing. (She's inclined to agree when Orville complains that her mother looks like Godzilla—later we see why.)

At last, Orville's crazy tirade has the desired effect. Zelda speeds off to her parents just seconds before Polly, suffering from a terrible head cold, arrives to take her place. Even Dino, who surely has seen just about everything, couldn't be prepared for the bizarre dinner party for three that awaits him. It's a combustible trio: Polly, fairly bursting out of her too tight paisley housedress; Dino, a cartoon portrait of lecherousness; and Orville, the seemingly oblivious, all-too-genial husband. Wielding a very phallic bottle of chianti, Orville virtually summons Dino—who doesn't need to be told twice—to go ahead and take liberties. For her part, Polly is indifferent to Dino's Vegasy allure ("I like Andy Williams better," she sniffs) and put off by his constant groping. It's Orville, his love songs, and the momentary fantasy of domestic bliss that she finds charming.

* Amazingly, the songs in *Kiss Me, Stupid* are really previously unpublished (for good reason) ditties by George and Ira Gershwin.

Just as Nestor in *Irma la Douce* becomes illogically jealous of his own alter ego, Orville begins to behave as if Polly really *were* his wife and reverts to his old paranoid self—only this time, there's a real interloper making a play for his (pretend) spouse. "Does he really think he can buy my wife for a song?" Orville rants. "Him and his rat pack. They think they own the earth, riding around in their white chariots, raping and looting and wearing cuffs on their sleeves. To them, we're just a bunch of squares, straight men, civilians. Any time they want to move in, we're supposed to run up a white flag, hand over our homes and our wives and our liquor!" With one of America's most celebrated hedonists as his hapless target, Orville can finally vent his crazy rage. Literally thrown out of the Spooner house, the humiliated Dino heads for the only other action in town, at the seedy Belly Button.

Polly starts to berate Orville for blowing the chance of a lifetime, but he urges her not to break the spell. "Tonight," he tells her, "we're Mr. and Mrs. Orville J. Spooner!" Together, like an old married couple, they do some perfunctory postparty cleanup—Polly makes sure to wipe away the chianti Dino's poured in her shoe—and head for the bedroom.

Kiss Me, Stupid soon turns into *Double Infidelity*. Unbeknownst to Orville, Zelda has returned home at the height of the soiree. Through the front door, she has spied her husband and Polly dancing and carousing— but failed to see Dino, slumped out of sight. So, for probably the first time in her wholesome life, Zelda drowns her troubles at the Belly Button. The virtuous wife gets stinking drunk, and is deposited by the management in Polly's trailer in the lot next door. When she comes to, she finds Dino hovering at the door, looking for action. The good wife figures out from Dino's tale of woe what's really been going on at the Spooner house, and she determines in her own pragmatic way to set things right, making sure to plug her spouse's songwriting talent while (apparently) indulging her own private fantasy. The next morning, Zelda greets Polly and gives her the $500 Dino has left on the night table—the kind of windfall that will finally enable her to buy a car and leave the unarousing town of Climax. When, a few days later, Orville hears his song "Sofia" sung by Dino on national television, he is dumbfounded. In another of Wilder's trademark closing punch lines, Zelda turns to her hapless husband and purrs, "Kiss me, stupid."

BY ANY YARDSTICK, *KISS ME, STUPID* IS AN AUDACIOUS movie. American comedies had become increasingly suggestive in the early 1960s, but Wilder and Diamond's script "dropped over the edge," in Barbara Diamond's words. "They were trying to make a 'taste-free' picture, I always say, as opposed to tasteless."

Wilder's gags were never more blunt; even today, some of the movie's double entendres have the potential to shock. "It's not very big but it's clean," Orville volunteers when Polly first enters his home. "While you're plugging the song . . ." is how Barney starts to describe his plan to entice Dino—no need to complete *that* sentence. Within *Kiss Me, Stupid*'s sex-obsessed environment, inspired in part by Orville's dementia, most everything acquires an extra patina of tawdriness—from the phallic cacti outside the Spooner house to Polly's TV-western-addicted parrot, whose favorite utterance is "Bang! Bang!"

Even more startling is the film's intimation that adultery can be redemptive. Orville's willingness to suspect the worst of his wife only reveals how little he knows her. No doubt his ardor is genuine, but it's the emotion of a collector of fine objects, not that of a genuinely loving husband. The Spooners' marriage is itself something of a farce.

When Polly the Pistol enters his domain, Orville discovers, perhaps for the first time, how to *talk* to a woman. She may be a hooker, but that's as much a designated role as the part of enticing wife she's been hired to play. Orville is able to relax and open up with the B girl in a way we haven't seen in his moments with Zelda. Freed from the proprieties and the proprietariness of his marriage, the songwriter becomes a sensual and compassionate man—at least for one night. Even if he's been changed just slightly, Orville's marriage can only be improved by this moment of "weakness."

The next morning, Orville's suffering begins anew. "I'm contemplating suicide," he tells Polly as they part. "Look at me. Yesterday, a solid citizen, a blood donor, a signer of petitions. Today, the way of all flesh." There's a certain hypocrisy in Orville's eagerness to bed down with Polly after all his protestations of love for Zelda, but his wife is willing to see the night's developments as a fair and equitable exchange. "Whatever he did, he did it for you," Polly tells Zelda in their morning-after trailer encounter. "Whatever I did, I did it for him," Zelda retorts.

THOUGH WILDER CAN'T RESIST AIMING HIS CAMERA AT KIM Novak's tightly wrapped posterior (at one point, he has her demonstrate the hula-hoop hip swivel in loving closeup), *Kiss Me, Stupid* is much more sympathetic to the plight of its women than that of its men. Novak's working-class-accented, cold-in-the-nose performance may be a bit broad, but she achieves real moments of poignance. A former manicurist at New York's Plaza Hotel, Polly fell in love with a hula-hoop salesman, who disappeared after proposing and bringing her to Nevada. Hardened by life in Climax, Polly unthaws when she hears Orville's love song—the same song that made Zelda fall for her husband. Still bruised by her close brush with marriage, Polly is profoundly touched when Orville suggests she be Mrs. Spooner for one night—rather than something seamy, it's one of the tenderest moments of Wilder's career. For once, Polly the Pistol is treated like a person with feelings, and her fortunes are about to become even brighter.

Zelda is too good to be true, but there's something brewing beneath her surface wholesomeness. She alone can see the Orville who's worthy of her complete devotion—the Orville who, to court her, gave blood three times a week at the blood bank where she worked, the Orville who wrote the love song that won her over, the Orville who took her away from her harpy of a mother. One suspects from her unflappable demeanor that Zelda may even be somewhat charmed and complimented by her husband's jealous tirades. He may not feel he's worthy of such a woman, but Zelda clearly enjoys the prospect of sex with this man—watch how her fingers beckon seductively as she lies down and coos, "Come to bed."

Unlike the ineffectual Orville and the ham-handed Barney, it's Zelda who ultimately thinks on her feet (so to speak) and clinches the opportunity of her husband's lifetime—she's the real Wilder hustler in *Kiss Me, Stupid*. "You can't sing that song ["Sofia"]," she baits Dino while posing as Polly the Pistol. "I told Orville to send it to somebody younger, like the Beatles." "The Beatles!" Dino grimaces. "I sing better than all of them put together, and I'm younger . . . than all of them put together." After seducing the man she has worshiped since her days as president of her high school's Dino fan club, Zelda then sets to work on reforming her errant husband. With Barney as her co-conspirator, she fools Orville into believing their marriage is over and sets up a phony appointment with a divorce lawyer one flight up from Pringle's hardware store, at the very same time Dino will introduce "Sofia" on his TV variety show. As a crowd of entertainment-starved Climaxites ogles the TVs in Pringle's front window, Dino gives an innocuous account of how he met sudden hometown heroes "Miller and Spoonsap," concluding with the ultimate show-biz credo, "If you've got what it takes, sooner or later somebody will take what you've got." Zelda rolls her eyes at that one, knowing a little something about give-and-take herself. Having taken the measure of her former idol, she'll cheerfully settle for her innocent, confused, "stupid" spouse.

The true butts of the jokes in *Kiss Me, Stupid* are its men, slaves to their sex organs or to their imagined role as dominant partner in marriage. Zelda's final words to Orville just reaffirm his situation throughout the film—out of touch, out of control, totally befuddled. Whatever good comes out of his encounter with Dino is a matter of lucky chance and has nothing to do with Orville's own hapless charade. The only quality that keeps the songwriter from being a complete loser is his central core of kindness—a saving grace best perceived by both Zelda and Polly.

Then there's Dino. Just as Wilder cast Gloria Swanson and Marilyn Monroe as archetypal versions of themselves in *Sunset Boulevard* and *The Seven Year Itch*, he uses Dean Martin in a broad exaggeration of his Rat Pack image. (Though Dino's surname is never mentioned, there are explicit references to the leader of the pack: "That Sinatra kid missing again?" Dino jokes when confronted by the roadblock that leads him to Climax. "You should do it more like Sinatra would," Zelda urges in their trailer encounter. "I'm trying all the time," Dino moans.) With Martin's good-natured consent, Wilder creates a devastating portrait of a celebrity's psyche—the star as self-centered, uncontrollable satyr.

OTHER HOLLYWOOD COMEDIES OF THE DAY COULD SMIRK about wayward husbands, blonde sexpots next-door, and the precious virginity of a certain middle-aged box-office queen named Doris Day. Yet, however ribald their content, the mise-en-scène of those films is virtually straight out of Disney—bright candy colors, innocuously peppy music, performances aimed at the kids in the balcony.

Kiss Me, Stupid would have none of that. Filmed in stark black-and-white Panavision by Joseph LaShelle, the movie has a desperate, melancholy edge that is anything but soothing to a viewer accustomed to the frothy sex tease of a *Lover, Come Back* or an *Under the Yum Yum Tree*. As designed by Alexander Trauner, Climax is a desolate place, from the dusty neighborhood where Orville and Barney eke out their modest living, to the morose ambiance of the Belly Button bar, to the downtown "nightlife" of Pringle's TV display. One immediately flashes on other Wilder hellholes that drive their inhabitants to extreme measures: the noir-ish Los Angeles of *Double Indemnity*, the sun-baked New Mexico of *Ace in the Hole*, the drab, impersonal New York of *The Apartment*. Orville, Zelda, Polly and Dino may be acting out roles in a farce, but the backdrop holds out the promise of true madness and sorrow.

KISS ME, STUPID PROVED TO BE A BENCHMARK FILM FOR both of the movie industry's big watchdogs, the Production Code Administration and the Catholic Legion of Decency. Wilder had stopped submitting scripts to the PCA in the mid-1950s, after it approved Mervyn LeRoy's film of *The Bad Seed*, in the wake of turning down Wilder's earlier proposed treatment of the hit Broadway play about a murderous little girl. Vowing never to be frustrated by the organization again, Wilder refused to let the PCA evaluate potentially troublesome films like *Some Like It Hot*, *The Apartment* and *Irma la Douce* until they were finished.

The Production Code Administration, meantime, had never been so vulnerable. As audiences began to support more risqué films, the industry—especially the feisty independent producers and distributors—was taking more gambles with movie content and blithely letting the PCA handle the fallout from local censors and religious groups. PCA chief Geoffrey Shurlock had recently learned a lesson in modern audience tastes when he rejected the script for *Tom Jones*, based on its many violations of the Code, then found himself quietly approving the film after it passed muster with the Legion of Decency. When *Tom Jones* became a critical and popular hit *and* won the Oscar, it only made it clearer to Shurlock that the Code needed some fine-tuning. But that wasn't going to happen anytime soon; the PCA's parent organization, the Motion Picture Association of America, was essentially functioning without a leader, since the 1962 death of its president, Eric Johnston. Left without recourse for change, Shurlock decided to take a more daredevil approach to Code precepts.

After screening *Kiss Me, Stupid*, Shurlock shocked his colleagues by announcing he was giving the picture the Code seal. "If dogs want to return to their vomit," he allegedly declared, "I'm not going to stop them." His public statements, however, were of a more gentlemanly nature: "Wilder has had a series of extremely successful pictures," he noted, "all of which dealt with provocative subjects, and his treatment has been accepted. In giving the seal, we were betting on his track record that this one would be, too. The jury is still out on this picture. We must wait to see how the audiences react, but it will be a lesson to all of us if the audience rejects this picture."

In fact, audience reactions at the first sneak previews in New York and Los Angeles in mid-October 1964, and preliminary objections from the Legion of Decency, were ominous enough to prompt Wilder to go back and reshoot the trailer scene between Dean Martin and Felicia Farr. "In the original scene," Farr remembers, "I'm trying to sell my husband's song and I start singing, and he's kissing me and I push him away, still singing, and we just go out of the bottom of the frame. She's absolutely aloof from him, which is very, very funny, because he's coming on like gangbusters and she's just singing. How they could have taken it seriously, I have no idea. But they quarreled with the notion of an American housewife giving herself—or the intimation is, *selling* herself—for her husband." The revamped scene ends with Dino falling asleep while Zelda gives him a back massage. But those who want to read something more into the sequence can easily do so: Zelda wakes up the next morning bare-shouldered under the bedcovers—and there's still that $500 on the night table.

United Artists and Monsignor Thomas F. Little of the Legion of Decency, meanwhile, continued to haggle over individual lines of dialogue and visual outrages like Kim Novak's cleavage (which the monsignor felt could be "shadowed in" by technical means). Among the gags the Legion objected to was Dino's suggestion that he step out into the garden with Mrs. Spooner, where "she can show me her parsley." Advised UA's Robert Benjamin to Wilder, "The use of any other vegetable other [sic] than parsley would satisfy them because several female members of the committee felt there was something particularly suggestive in the use of parsley." "What do they want—broccoli?" was Wilder's reaction.

Producer Harold Mirisch said the filmmakers tried their best to placate the Church. "We made a lot of changes, but they insisted on more of them. It would have meant bringing Kim Novak back to reshoot and we couldn't do that." (Novak was then in England making *The Amorous Adventures of Moll Flanders*.)

All together, Monsignor Little listed ten "sine qua non" violations that had to be removed before the Legion would approve the film. Ultimately, the two parties reached an impasse, and the Legion went ahead and branded *Kiss Me, Stupid* with a "C," or "condemned," rating. Not since Elia Kazan's *Baby Doll* in 1956 had the Church given an American studio film this mark of disgrace. Contrasting Wilder's latest film with *The Apartment*, which it called "effective comic satire," the Legion, in its official statement, deemed *Kiss Me, Stupid* "a thoroughly sordid piece of realism which is esthetically as well as morally repulsive. Crude and suggestive dialogue, a leering treatment of marital and extramarital sex, a prurient preoccupation with lechery compound the film's bald condonation of immorality."

The Legion also noted that the film's planned holiday release was "a commercial decision bereft of respect for the Judaeo-Christian sensibilities of the majority of the American people," and expressed astonishment that the picture had received a Code seal. In a pointed attack on the PCA, the Legion stated, "It is difficult to understand how such approval is not the final betrayal of the trust which has been placed by so many in the organized industry's self-regulation."

Publicly, Shurlock defended his decision, arguing that the outcome of the Dino-Zelda trailer scene is left to the imagination, and that "on the basis of Walston's remorse, the picture doesn't condone extramarital relations."

But behind the scenes, Shurlock admitted to PCA assistant director Jack Vizzard, "I passed this picture with my eyes wide open. I did it to precipitate a crisis. Now maybe we've got it. Somebody had to rupture the Code in so conspicuous a manner that they'd [the motion picture industry] have to do something about it. Because if this is the kind of movies they want to make, if the companies are going to put up the money for this kind of stuff and then expect me to try to stop them, they're crazy."

Even before the Legion of Decency issued its condemnation, a nervous United Artists took its name off the picture and opted to release it through its Lopert Pictures subsidiary, normally the province of foreign art films. That decision resulted in a different and more limited release pattern; in Los Angeles, for instance, the premiere run of *Kiss Me, Stupid* was shifted from the famed Grauman's Chinese Theatre to the more specialized Vogue and Fine Arts venues. Whether or not the film was appropriate holiday fare, the pre-Christmas opening date produced one disastrous consequence: Every year at mid-December, America's Catholics were asked to stand up in church and pledge to boycott movies targeted by the Legion of Decency. This year, all the focus would be on that home-grown offender, *Kiss Me, Stupid.*

Ironically, just before the film opened, Wilder was basking in one of the most prestigious honors of his career to date: a sixteen-film retrospective of his work at New York's Museum of Modern Art. Richard Griffith, curator of MOMA's film department, called the filmmaker "the most precise, indeed relentless, chronicler of the postwar American scene, in shade as well as light, that the movies have produced." He praised Wilder's movies for having "a sharp-edged light of truth that seems the product of long observation of and involvement with the American ethos on all its levels." These were the last kind words Wilder would hear for quite some time.

"Wilder Dirty-Joke Film Stirs a Furor," blared *Life* magazine a month later, offering a blow-by-blow account of *Kiss Me, Stupid*'s rocky reception. "For years Billy Wilder has walked the shaky tightrope between sophistication and salaciousness," wrote Thomas Thompson, later the author of true-crime books like *Blood and Money.* "But with *Kiss Me, Stupid,* he has fallen off with a resounding crash." Thompson deemed the film "a titanic dirty joke, an embarrassment to audiences, the performers and the industry which produced it." In the past, *Life* had run a number of good-natured photo spreads of Wilder at work and moments from his films; now, it took the opportunity to publish a portfolio entitled "Racy Scenes Pass the Code," focusing on the movie's various seductions and making special mention that two scenes take place in the bathroom.

The majority of the nation's film critics shared *Life*'s indignant tone, relying heavily on derogatory "s" words like sleazy, squalid and smutty. *Time* called the movie "one of the longest traveling-salesman stories ever committed to film." "A repellent, oversized trifle," scoffed Brendan Gill in *The New Yorker*. *Films in Review* went so far as to wonder, "Is senility setting in or has [Wilder] always been not quite bright?" *New York Herald Tribune* critic Judith Crist declared *Kiss Me, Stupid* "the slimiest movie of the year" and, with consummate taste, speculated that Peter Sellers must have suffered his heart attack after seeing the entire script. Crist also used the occasion to do some retroactive sniping, questioning the moral tone of earlier Wilder triumphs. About *Some Like It Hot*, she said, "For every raucous and/or ribald masquerade joke, there is another that involves a transvestite leer, a homosexual in-joke or a perverse gag." On *The Apartment*: "The heroine is a tramp whom we are supposed to bleed for simply because her most recent and most permanent client refused to pay (payment involved divorce and marrying her)."

At the *New York Times*, A. H. Weiler joined the chorus of pans, labeling the film coarse, vulgar, obvious and "pitifully unfunny." A few weeks later, head critic Bosley Crowther, in an article on the Production Code controversy, came at the movie from a slightly different angle, calling its portrait of greed and its consequences "as moral as a preacher's Sunday sermon," but hampered by "the seamy way in which the film is made and played." *Cue*'s William Wolf, meantime, complained about having to write his review twice, insisting that the original Dino-Zelda trailer scene was "the one aspect that gave the film what nugget of value it had."

The most significant minority report on *Kiss Me, Stupid* was filed by Joan Didion, then film critic for *Vogue*. "It is a profoundly affecting film," she declared, "as witnessed by the number of people who walk out on it. What makes the picture so affecting, what makes people walk out when they will sit through and even applaud the real tastelessness, the true venality of pictures like *The Pink Panther* or *Bedtime Story*? They walk out, I suspect, because they sense that Wilder means it. . . . The Wilder world is one seen at dawn through a hangover, a world of cheap double entendre and stale smoke and drinks in which the ice has melted: the true country of despair."

(In gratitude, Wilder sent Didion a note reading: "I read your piece in the beauty parlor while sitting under the hair dryer, and it sure did the old pornographer's heart good.")

The response to *Kiss Me, Stupid* overseas, by contrast, was downright cordial. In London, *The Times* noted in its headline, "Wilder Returns in His Best Farcical Form," and hailed the movie's "cheery bad taste." J. H. Fenwick, in the august British film magazine *Sight and Sound*, said, "If the result isn't as hilarious as it should ideally be, it does nevertheless have moments of being very funny indeed, and it is always fascinatingly watchable." The critic for *The Listener* seemed awed that "some deeply engrained ideas take a terrible beating. Wilder is master of his own universe. He creates the standards by which he wishes to be judged." In Paris, *Variety* reported, critics regarded *Kiss Me, Stupid* as "a good old boulevard farce comedy" in the spirit of Georges Feydeau.

Indeed, *Kiss Me, Stupid* had antecedents going back much farther than Feydeau. "What we were really trying to do was a Restoration comedy in modern dress, but nobody caught on to that," explained Diamond. "A lot of the things that we were criticized for, the names of the characters, the costuming, some of the double entendres, that was a pure attempt to update a Restoration comedy. And like all such comedies, it was a moral and cautionary tale. A jealous husband goes to such extremes to protect his wife's virtue that she winds up losing it. . . . We got great reviews in London and Paris. The critics there realized that we were trying to make a statement about contemporary America. But in this country, the critics were so obsessed with looking for smut that they couldn't see anything beyond that. One television writer came to me and said, 'It reminded me of Congreve's *The Way of the World*,' and I wanted to throw my arms around him, because he understood what we were aiming for.

"I think what it is," Diamond concluded, "people don't like to be told they're corrupt. If they're going to pay money for it, they want to hear that they're honest and loyal and warm and friendly and loveable." Like that other arid heartland tale *Ace in the Hole*, *Kiss Me, Stupid* was sending a message the American public didn't want to ponder.

It's also important to remember that *Kiss Me, Stupid* was derived from an Italian play, and arrived on screens in the wake of earthy Italian sex farces like *Divorce—Italian Style* and *Seduced and Abandoned*, whose director, Pietro Germi, Wilder has praised. If *Kiss Me, Stupid* had been yet another

Italian film import, no doubt it wouldn't have raised such a ruckus—though it still might have been condemned by the Catholic church. From a purely artistic vantage point, *Kiss Me, Stupid*'s "C" rating is something of a badge of honor: As *Newsweek* noted at the time, by late 1964 the "Condemned" list also included such European offenders as *Jules and Jim*, *Breathless*, *Knife in the Water*, *L'Avventura*, *La Notte* and *Saturday Night and Sunday Morning*.

ONE SURPRISING CRITIC OF *KISS ME, STUPID* IS ITS CO-author's widow, Barbara Diamond. "It's a terrible movie," she flat-out declares. "I dislike it because they did not make the movie they started to make. When Iz first told me about the movie, he said they were going to concentrate on the Novak character, and the fact that she came in and blossomed, that she loved every little detail of keeping house and making dinner, and made this enormous change in her life. But the emphasis got shifted, they did not make that movie, whether it would have worked or not. The other mistake is that they should have waited for Peter Sellers to recover, because Ray Walston was too unattractive a person."

It's just possible that the loss of Sellers might have made all the difference to the fate of *Kiss Me, Stupid*. "I love Ray Walston," says Felicia Farr. "He's a dear man and a very talented man, and it was wonderful working with him—I didn't miss Peter at that point. I only missed Peter when I finally saw the picture. I thought: Well, maybe it would have been better with Peter. Maybe he could have gotten over the Legion of Decency problems, made everything so outrageous that they wouldn't have been taken seriously."

"Peter was a classic innocent," observes Cliff Osmond, "and the film demanded a certain innocence. When it shifted to Ray, certain things shifted—certain attitudes, certain sensibilities, and I think it threw it off. After all, Wilder wrote it with certain people in mind. I know I felt I worked a little extra hard, trying to compensate for what was not there without Peter. The whole thing was a little out of whack—it lost a bit of its grace. And a piece like that demanded elegance and grace."

Because Orville's delirium propels the film, an actor of inspired madness was required to keep the momentum going. Walston, a good actor (and better than ever in his current role on TV's *Picket Fences)*, works hard to capture that madness, but it doesn't come as instinctively as it would have to his predecessor. "If Peter Sellers hadn't dropped out," Wilder once said, "it would have been a far better movie, a different movie altogether." Even those stalwarts who love *Kiss Me, Stupid* have to concede the point.

THANKS TO ALL THE CONTROVERSY SURROUNDING IT, *KISS Me, Stupid* had a few good weeks of business in New York, Los Angeles and Chicago, but faded fast. As it made its way around the country, it met strong resistance in communities with a large Catholic presence. In Columbus, Ohio, a campaign of protest letters and phone calls by local church-women resulted in the cancellation of the film's bookings at two downtown theaters. In Warwick, Rhode Island, the board of public safety threatened to suspend the license of a local theater operator if he did not remove the film from his schedule. Wilder himself was targeted on NBC's *Frontiers of Faith* TV series by one Dr. Lycurgus M. Starkey Jr., pastor of the College Avenue Methodist Church in Muncie, Indiana, who stated, "Billy Wilder's movies have overturned all the sexual mores, glorified promiscuity, glamorized prostitution and elevated adultery to a virtue." With so much going against it, *Kiss Me, Stupid* never came close to recouping its $2 million production cost.

Devastated by the scathing response to his film, Wilder immediately left for a long vacation in Europe. "The uproar stunned me," Wilder told journalist Peter Bart in a *New York Times* interview ten months later. "Okay, I had made a bad picture, but why the indignation, why the charges that I had undermined the nation's morals? Suddenly, I was a celluloid Rasputin."

One of the director's first orders of business on returning to Los Angeles was to write to Geoffrey Shurlock and apologize for the trouble he had caused him. "It is obvious that the Legionnaires have been lying in the bushes, biding their time until they could waylay some picture-maker of import and use him as a whipping boy for the entire industry," Wilder stated. Somewhat disingenuously, Shurlock responded, "In your case, please believe me, I was motivated primarily by my esteem and affection for you, over and above the normal call of duty."

Wilder's late friend Walter Reisch once called *Kiss Me, Stupid* "the one thing about which he has no sense of humor." Ernest Lehman remembers walking into Wilder's office on the Goldwyn lot in 1965, "and there were Billy and Iz sitting there together in utter silence. Billy said, 'We're like two parents who've given birth to a mongoloid idiot, and we're afraid to screw again.' "

In subsequent interviews, Wilder has been alternately dismissive and defensive of the film. "It stinks, it always stunk, it was just a complete failure," he bluntly told reporter Joseph Gelmis in October 1966. Two months later, he complained to *Saturday Evening Post* writer Richard Lemon, "I've seen many a picture, believe me, that was far more suggestive and dirty. I don't mind reading a slew of reviews that say it was bad. It probably was bad. But what hurt me was that old pals said I set out deliberately to make a dirty picture. I go out into new territory and dig for oil, and sometimes all that comes up is vinegar. And sometimes the digging operation is so expensive, we try to recoup the losses by selling the vinegar."

Asked today about *Kiss Me, Stupid*, Wilder would rather avoid the subject. "I don't spend too much time analyzing and rethinking after a failure," he insists. "I'm already preparing another failure. Hopefully not. All that chest-beating is a waste of time, it's self-torture."

Argues Wilder, "Once you engage in the making of a movie, and you know after the third day this is not going to work, you still have to finish it. They're not going to put it on the shelf to collect dust—they're going to show that thing. We don't bury our dead. We try to squeeze out the last penny, even if it is way below the standard of the picturemaker, by some miscalculation. It is just wonderful with a play—the plays that never reach New York, by Kaufman and Hart and very successful playwrights. But not with a movie—maybe once every twenty years, something is so bad that somebody very clever takes the negative in the night and buries it. It's very, very difficult when a film looks like it's going to live, like it's going to breathe, and suddenly it just doesn't have . . . not everything has to have magic, but some allure, something. Show me a director who never has a failure, and I'll show you a man who always has done cowardly pictures. A cowardly man just makes pictures that have been made before, and he gets away with it. He's not going to get great reviews, it's barely going to make its money, but, by God, he never had a total failure. Only the man who dares to try a picture which may turn out to be a total disaster, or a total success, that's the man that I like."

One factor that clearly worked against the vastly underrated *Kiss Me, Stupid* was its timing—just slightly ahead of the curve of sexual permissiveness that would overtake America in the mid-1960s. "I remember after the first preview," says Jack Lemmon. "It hadn't gone well and Billy knew it. We were in the back of the theater and he shrugged his shoulders and said, 'Trust me. Within several years, they will be making films that we would now call pornographic.' He was right."

Just five and a half years later, *Kiss Me, Stupid* would be reissued in theaters and submitted for a rating from the Motion Picture Association of America's new Code and Rating system. It earned a PG—all ages admitted, parental guidance suggested. United Artists put its name back on the film. For its 1994 video release, however, *Kiss Me, Stupid* was given a more restrictive PG-13 rating for "sex-related plot material."

NINETEEN

Wilder but Mellower

S LOWLY, WILDER AND DIAMOND RECOVERED THEIR WILL to write, and set to work on a new script entitled *The Fortune Cookie*. "It's about greed, love, compassion, human understanding, but *not* sex," Wilder told *Variety* columnist Army Archerd, in a pointed reference to the *Kiss Me, Stupid* fallout.

Wilder took his inspiration for *The Fortune Cookie* while watching a football game on TV; when a husky fullback ran past the end zone and smashed into an unfortunate spectator, Wilder said to himself, "That's a movie, and the guy underneath is Lemmon." In the film, Lemmon is Harry Hinkle, a CBS-TV cameraman who is in the wrong spot when Cleveland Browns halfback Luther "Boom Boom" Jackson (Ron Rich) barrels off the field during a crucial play. Boom Boom collides with Harry and sends him sailing over some rolled-up tarpaulin; the cameraman seems to be okay but then passes out and has to be taken off the field on a stretcher. The accident is viewed as a golden opportunity by Harry's brother-in-law, Willie Gingrich (Walter Matthau), a lawyer so devious the word "shyster" doesn't begin to do him justice.

Baiting Harry with the possibility of a reconciliation with his greedy ex-wife, Sandy (Judi West), Willie persuades his brother-in-law to fake a spinal injury and paralysis of his left leg and several fingers in order to collect an insurance windfall. Harry grudgingly goes along with the charade, but is riddled with guilt when Boom Boom makes it his personal crusade to oversee the cameraman's physical therapy. Harry's progress is also monitored by dogged private eye Chester Purkey (Cliff Osmond), using hidden microphones and a surveillance camera positioned across the street from the patient's apartment.

When Sandy reenters Harry's life, Boom Boom finds his services are no longer needed and he begins drinking and wrecking his career. Willie ultimately squeezes a $200,000 settlement from the insurance company, but the victory is short-lived after Purkey comes to the apartment on the pretext of collecting his bugging devices and tricks Harry out of his wheelchair by using a racial slur against Boom Boom. By this time, Harry has realized that his ex-wife's return was motivated solely by money, and he gladly restages the event for Purkey's camera. In the closing sequence, Harry confesses his fraud to Boom Boom on the empty nighttime field of Cleveland Municipal Stadium, and the pair make up with a friendly game of two-man football.

IN 1965, WALTER MATTHAU HAD SCORED A MAJOR HIT ON Broadway as the slovenly Oscar Madison in Neil Simon's *The Odd Couple*— Jack Lemmon calls Matthau's stage characterization "the single best comedy performance I'd ever seen in my life." Up till then, Matthau's film work had been mostly dramatic supporting roles, often as a heavy, in films like *Slaughter on Tenth Avenue*, *King Creole*, *Lonely Are the Brave*, *Charade*, *Fail Safe*, and *Mirage*. Wilder, who had wanted Matthau for *The Seven Year Itch* just as the actor was starting his film career, came to *The Odd Couple* already sensing he had the perfect role for Broadway's hottest comedy star.

Remembers Matthau, "I had been given about half a dozen scripts after the notices came out on *The Odd Couple*, and I didn't like any of them. I was judging them the way I judged play scripts, by their literary value—and that's not how you judge a movie. As a matter of fact, you really can't judge a movie—there are too many factors that go into it. But when Billy came to see me in *The Odd Couple* and told me the story of *The Fortune Cookie*, I said, 'Fine, I'm ready.'"

"How we never worked together before, I'll never know," says Lemmon, because we were in the same melting pot of actors who came back after the war. We're approximately the same age—Walt's a couple of years older—but at any rate we were in the same boat. We were both in the early days of live TV and Broadway, but we never did a show together. I did at least five hundred television shows over a period of five or six years, from about 'forty-seven through 'fifty-three, and Walter was doing the same thing and appearing on Broadway. I only did one Broadway show, but I played a lead right off the bat, in a revival of *Room Service*. And Walter was supposed to do it with me, and unfortunately he had a conflict. He worked with Felicia before he worked with me, and we knew each other: "Hi, Jack!" "Hi, Walt!" But we never worked together until *Fortune Cookie*. And, Jesus, it worked from the very first morning—first time, crack out of the barrel, it flowed like we were sitting down at breakfast and just talking with each other. It's that same sort of feeling. It's been a wonderful relationship, and I think it's strengthened by the fact that we not only have an onscreen relationship that works so easily and so well, but personally. And the more that you know someone personally, the easier it is to work with them. The same with our wives, who are like sisters. So as a result, we are extremely close, see each other all the time. And when Walter and I work together, we can change scenes right in the middle, do anything, and the other guy goes along with it.

By the time of *The Fortune Cookie*, Jack Lemmon was a hugely popular movie star, and Matthau was struck by the fact that *he* had the showier role. "I said to Lemmon, 'How come you're doing this part? My part's better than yours.' And he said, 'It's about time.' It's hard to be funny when you're being wheeled around in a wheelchair—it's a reminder to the audience that they're mortal, and that puts a damper on the laughing."

At the 1986 American Film Institute Life Achievement Award ceremony, Lemmon recalled how, on the first day of filming *The Fortune Cookie*, Wilder indulged his penchant for directing by example, acting out an entire long scene while Matthau stood silently by, a blank expression on his face. At the end of Wilder's performance, Matthau dryly observed, "You speak kind of funny. You from out of town?"

"I always found Wilder to be intelligent and reasonable," Matthau asserts. "But the façade may have been German arrogance: 'Here's the way you do it, you take out the cigar, you pull off the wrapper, snap it, you do this, you go left, you go right, you go here, you go there.' *Jawohl!* But if you can't work with that kind of regimentation, then you say, 'Look, Billy, let me take out the cigar, and if you don't like it, I'll do it another way, okay?' And he'll say, 'Fine.' That's what happens.

"To the best of my recollection," says Matthau, "I was a proper student. I listened to the master and did it his way. Oh, I had an argument with him once in a while about a piece of business. I think Billy was used to the actors doing what he said—actually, he was a director because he wanted to protect his writing. There are different directors: Sometimes you get a director who understands the actor's problems. But Billy wasn't one of those directors—he was a director who said: 'Here's a situation, and do it as dramatically as you can.' "

The rapport he had with his two lead actors was a tonic for Wilder, but then, eight weeks into shooting, the production was hit with a crisis that was eerily similar to the Peter Sellers disaster. As with Sellers's collapse and Horst Buchholz's car accident, it happened on a Sunday—Walter Matthau was stricken by a severe heart attack. With so much of the film already completed, Wilder and the Mirisch Company were left with no choice but to wait for their star to recover.

Matthau's wife, Carol, did all she could to keep the film from falling apart by assuring everyone her husband was making good progress. "Oh, he's coming along fine, he's just dandy," Lemmon remembers Carol Matthau reporting. "But, boy, he had a ripper, and you couldn't see him for a long time. My favorite story is, he sent word to me to come immediately and he gave me an envelope, saying, 'I want you to meet Hymie at ten o'clock tomorrow morning across from the entrance to the Goldwyn Studios [where we were shooting]. He'll be in a beat-up old Dodge. He'll come across the street. He'll just look at you and he won't say one word. Hand him the envelope.' The envelope was filled with money that he owed to his bookie and, being in the hospital and not being able to tell them, 'I can't pay you off,' I guess he thought, 'Christ, maybe they're going to come kill me. They'll grab Carol.' Jesus, he was funny. So I did, and I wanna tell you, this funny little fireplug of a guy, about five foot zip, came out of an old Dodge, crossed the street, just looked up at me and raised his eyebrows, *did not say a word.* I pulled the envelope out and said, 'Hymie,?' and he nodded. I gave it to him, and he said thank you as he was walking away. He didn't count it, the envelope was sealed."

After about two months, Matthau returned to finish the film, picking up from a scene in which he runs up the stairs to Harry's apartment, holding the insurance-settlement check. "You see me going upstairs weighing 198 pounds," Matthau noted. "I walk in and I'm 160 pounds."

WHATEVER HIS SIZE, *THE FORTUNE COOKIE* WAS A STAR-making showcase for Matthau. With his slumping posture and squinty eyes always on the lookout for a crooked new angle, the actor turns "Whiplash Willie" into one of Wilder's most unrepentant yet engaging scoundrels. From his very first scene, Matthau defines the character with telling physical gestures—the way he flicks his cigarette ash into a hospital water fountain, or the way his hat rises up on his forehead when he hears that Harry has had a childhood back injury. When his niece and nephew ask for a dime to put into a collection box for unwed mothers, he answers, "Unwed mothers? I'm for that"—a typically irreverent Wilder gag line. Critic Richard Schickel called Matthau "the W. C. Fields of the 1960s," and his Willie Gingrich shares the same kind of indelibly comic orneriness.

Lemmon's part wasn't merely inferior to Matthau's, but impossible to pull off. Not only does he spend the majority of the film on his back or in a wheelchair, but Harry is too patently a loser, easily manipulated by the vultures circling around him. Willie's entire scheme rests upon Harry's continuing obsession with his ex-wife, but Sandy is shown from the very beginning to be such a selfish, unloving vixen that Harry comes across as nothing more than a complete dupe. Newcomer Judi West (whom Wilder cast after seeing her in the Marilyn Monroe role in the national company of Arthur Miller's *After the Fall*) has a fine, brittle, seductive screen presence, but the character Wilder and Diamond wrote should have been given a touch more charm and ambiguity.

The writers also falter in their presentation of black halfback Boom Boom Jackson, a character so good-hearted and earnest he's clearly the product of two older white men anxious not to offend. The fact of his race seems to exist only for the climactic payoff in which Purkey provokes Harry to rise up in anger; otherwise, Boom Boom is embarrassingly colorless.

Wilder and Diamond's script does, however, have an integrity to its social criticism that places it in a continuous line from the superior *The Apartment*. All the characters, with the exception of Boom Boom and, to a degree, Harry, willingly contribute to and take advantage of a certain built-in corruption in the American system; even the nuns in the hospital where Harry is laid up place bets on the Sunday football games and look to Boom Boom for some inside dope. No sooner is Harry hospitalized than his mother is taking a vacation in Florida, his sister is wearing a new fur coat and Willie is tooling around in a new Ford Mustang. When Harry suggests they wait until the insurance claim is paid, Willie retorts, "Who waits nowadays? Take the government—when they shoot a billion dollars' worth of hardware into space—you think they pay cash? It's all on the Diners' Club." Harry, who is motivated only by the battered torch he carries for Sandy, eventually rejects his role in Willie's scam, but it's a sign of how deeply engrained our own corruption is when the moral, uplifting finale of *The Fortune Cookie* seems so much duller than watching Willie Gingrich work his slimy magic.

Like *The Apartment* and *Kiss Me, Stupid*, *The Fortune Cookie* is photographed in wide-screen black-and-white by the gifted Joseph LaShelle, each film depicting its characters' humble living environments with an unsparing crispness. This time, however, production designer Alexander Trauner is nowhere in sight, and the drabness of Harry's apartment—combined with the claustrophobia of his situation—becomes a bit oppressive after a while. In its favor, the story is broken up with intriguing onscreen titles for each new "chapter," while composer André Previn—after exceptionally lively creative contributions to *One, Two, Three*, *Irma la Douce* and *Kiss Me, Stupid*—sets the perfect mood with his bluesy score.

Thanks in large part to Matthau's universally admired performance, *The Fortune Cookie* received the best notices Wilder had collected since *One, Two, Three*. Vincent Canby, in his new post as film critic of the *New York Times*, called the film "a fine, dark, gag-filled hallucination" and "an explosively funny live-action cartoon about petty chiselers." In *Life*, Richard Schickel found it "a jackhammer of a film savagely applied to those concrete areas of the human spirit where cupidity and stupidity have been entrenched for so long. It has all the defects of a power tool—it is crude and noisy and nerve-racking. But it has a virtue that cancels out these faults: it is a bitterly, often excruciatingly funny movie." Schickel went on to proclaim Wilder "just about the only American director of comedy who finds his material not in manufactured 'situations' but in the artful exaggerations of all-too-recognizable human and social traits. His is a cold rather than a warm comic spirit, and therefore not to everyone's taste. But if you can stand the chill, I think you'll find plenty of truth in what he has to say."

Some traditionally tough-to-please pundits were on Wilder's side this time. *The New Yorker* deemed the film "very funny and very cruel," and speculated, "Mr. Wilder has a low opinion of mankind; when he scourges us, I suspect that it is not so much because he hopes to improve us as because he wishes to keep his own despair at bay." Judith Crist proclaimed, "The old Billy Wilder is back with *The Fortune Cookie*." Even the *Morning Telegraph*'s Leo Mishkin, who had been revolted by Wilder's last several films, did an about-face, calling *The Fortune Cookie* a "gleaming, wonderful show."

Filing a minority report was *Saturday Review*'s Hollis Alpert, who was thoroughly delighted by Matthau but severely disappointed by Lemmon and by a Wilder "gone soft."

The Fortune Cookie was at best a modest box-office performer, but it rescued Wilder from the ignominy of *Kiss Me, Stupid* and did wonders for Matthau's movie career. Even though he is essentially the film's costar (and, in England, where the picture was released as *Meet Whiplash Willie*, the title player), Matthau was nominated for the Oscar in the Best Supporting Actor category, and bested such competition as Robert Shaw in *A Man for All Seasons*, James Mason in *Georgy Girl* and George Segal in *Who's Afraid of Virginia Woolf?*. (Wilder and Diamond earned the last Oscar nomination of their career, in the original screenplay category.) At the Academy Awards, Matthau arrived with a cast on his right arm, having fallen off his bicycle the previous Sunday.

WITH THE PAINSTAKING ATTENTION TO DETAIL THAT MARKS his screenplays, it ought to come as no surprise that Billy Wilder would be attracted to detective fiction's most celebrated master of deduction, Sherlock Holmes. Wilder had loved the character since his boyhood in Austria, and planned his first Holmes project back in 1957, when he signed a deal with author Arthur Conan Doyle's estate to produce a Broadway musical based on the sleuth and timed with the centennial of Conan Doyle's birth, in 1959. Wilder hoped to star Rex Harrison, and did some preliminary work with Moss Hart and composers Alan Jay Lerner and Frederick Loewe, but nothing came of the collaboration. In the fall of 1963, flush with the success of *Irma la Douce*, Wilder floated the idea of a *film* musical, again with Lerner and Loewe, starring Peter O'Toole as Holmes and Peter Sellers as his doting colleague, Dr. Watson. But Wilder was unable to pull O'Toole away from his exclusive contract with producer Sam Spiegel, and the *Kiss Me, Stupid* debacle took Sellers off the director's casting list.

"What I plan is a serious study of Holmes," Wilder said in early 1968. "Something in depth. After all, here he was, a most riveting character, a dope addict and a misogynist, yet in all the movies made about him nobody has ever explained why."

Wilder and Diamond read every Holmes mystery and every critical analysis of the great detective they could get their hands on, and discovered that this was one case that wouldn't be easily cracked. Drained of ideas, Diamond split up with Wilder for the first time in ten years, and went to work on the screen adaptation of the hit Broadway comedy *Cactus Flower*. Wilder reunited with his *Witness for the Prosecution* co-writer, Harry Kurnitz, a huge Sherlock Holmes fan, but the pair called it quits after half a year of work. Another collaboration with British playwright John Mortimer was also short-lived.

Then, one day, Wilder came up with a conceit that recharged his imagination: Sherlock Holmes meets the Loch Ness monster! Of course, it wouldn't really be the fabled sea creature, but a camouflaged experimental submarine. Wilder proposed the idea to Diamond, and the game was once more afoot.

One of the reasons the Holmes script took so long to take shape was that Wilder and Diamond weren't basing it on any of the existing Conan Doyle stories. *The Private Life of Sherlock Holmes* was exactly what its title described: an unveiling of the man behind the myth, as revealed in a series of confidential cases from the journals of the ever loyal Watson: "The Curious Case of the Upside Down Room," "The Singular Affair of the

Russian Ballerina," "The Dreadful Business of the Naked Honeymooners" and "The Adventure of the Dumbfounded Detective."*

Wilder regarded these individual adventures as similar to movements in a symphony and, indeed, part of his inspiration was a musical one. At one of Walter Reisch's annual Christmas parties a few years earlier, Wilder told Miklos Rozsa how much he admired the violin concerto Rozsa wrote in 1953 for the virtuoso Jascha Heifetz, and that he hoped to use it in a film someday. As the Sherlock Holmes project began to take shape, Wilder called in his *Lost Weekend* composer and made a formal request. He said that he often listened to music while working on a script; for example, while writing the closing scene in *Sunset Boulevard* where Norma Desmond descends the stairs as Salome, he played Richard Strauss's "Dance of the Seven Veils" from *Salome*. Wilder asked the film's composer, Franz Waxman, to write something similar but, Wilder said, "no matter how good the music was that Franz composed, it wasn't the music I had in my ears." The director told Rozsa, "This time it will be different. I have been listening to your music while [writing] the script and that is the music I want." Rozsa agreed to come aboard Wilder's project about the violin-playing sleuth, and enjoyed adapting his work to the movie's various moods: The first movement came to represent Holmes's cocaine addiction; the poignant second movement became the love theme; and the swirl of the final movement accompanied the Loch Ness monster intrigue.

Wilder and Diamond's screenplay came in at 260 pages, and was planned as a 165-minute road-show extravaganza, "with an intermission to give your kidneys a break," Wilder charitably added. The director had never before attempted a road-show picture, the kind of special-event movie that played for only two shows a day, with reserved seats and higher ticket prices. Some of the most successful movies of the 1960s had been road shows, including *Lawrence of Arabia*, *My Fair Lady*, *The Sound of Music*, and *Dr. Zhivago*; with Sherlock Holmes, Wilder felt he finally had a subject worthy of the same lavish, big-ticket treatment.

The film's budget was $10 million—the highest of Wilder's career—and the gamble was made even greater by his decision to cast two relatively

---

* For a time, Wilder and Diamond toiled on an episode involving Holmes's famed nemesis Moriarty, but ultimately abandoned the idea.

unknown British actors in the lead roles. Robert Stephens, the new Holmes, was a respected member of Laurence Olivier's National Theatre company, perhaps most familiar to American movie audiences for his role as an artist in *The Prime of Miss Jean Brodie*, playing opposite his Oscar-winning wife, Maggie Smith. "I'd never seen Stephens except for twenty minutes in the bar of the Connaught Hotel," Wilder told a reporter at the time, "but I thought, What's good enough for Larry Olivier is good enough for me." For a time, Wilder's Watson was going to be veteran British actor Richard Attenborough, but the role ended up going to the little-known Colin Blakely, whom some American film buffs might have recognized from the 1960s British imports *Saturday Night and Sunday Morning* and *This Sporting Life*.

Justifying his casting choices, the director told *Parade* magazine, "In today's market, familiar star faces keep audiences away. They know what's coming from these people. They know what to expect. They're tired of the same old characterizations." Surprising words from a man who had worked with some of the great icons in Hollywood history. Did Wilder really believe what he was saying about the drawing power of stars? Or was it that stars weren't what they used to be? Or that Wilder's clout wasn't what it used to be?

The Private Life of Sherlock Holmes began production at London's Pinewood Studios in May 1969, with additional location work in Inverness, Scotland. Production designer Alexander Trauner was back on the payroll, and again dazzling onlookers with his authentically detailed re-creations of Baker Street in the 1880s and the Victorian clutter of Holmes's living room. The beautifully muted color wide-screen cinematography was the work of Christopher Challis, who had been camera operator on Michael Powell's classic dance fantasy *The Red Shoes*, and went on to become Powell's cinematographer on such films as *The Elusive Pimpernel* and *The Tales of Hoffmann*.

Challis, whose recent credits were *Two for the Road*, *Those Magnificent Men in Their Flying Machines* and the Mirisch Company's *A Shot in the Dark*, says the British *Holmes* crew "were all a bit in awe" of Billy Wilder. "It was sort of formal for the first couple of days. It was all 'Mr. Wilder' and he called me 'Mr. Challis,' and we'd set a shot up, and Freddie [Cooper] the camera operator always said, 'Would you like to look through the finder,

Mr. Wilder?' After about three days, we were lighting quite a complicated tracking shot, and Freddie said, 'Mr. Wilder, would you like to have a look through while I operate and see if it's what you want?' Billy looked at him and said, 'Freddie, let's cut out all this technical crap. I don't know what you're talking about.' He said, 'I'm not technical. I don't know how the radio works when you shut the window.' It was a marvelous remark. And from that moment on, everything changed—it was on a more intimate and different level.

"Billy came in every morning with Izzy Diamond. He always arrived on time, but as soon as he arrived on the set, he said, 'Just a minute, fellows, I've got to go to the can.' And he used to disappear for ten minutes—that was his ritual—then he'd come back. Then he always had coffee, he loved Viennese coffee and he'd offer it to anybody, and he used to chat and tell marvelous stories. He's terribly funny. He did that for half an hour before we ever started work.

"Because he was a writer and knew exactly the importance of every line of dialogue, he played material on people's backs and in long shot. A lot of modern directors would shoot it fifteen different ways, in the hope that they could sort something out at the end. He didn't do that—he didn't cover it at all. He shot very, very economically in terms of footage. So although he took quite a long time, in fact we did a lot of work every day."

Challis feels Wilder's talent is more oriented to the verbal than the visual. "He knew whether it was right or wrong when he saw it, but he couldn't really tell you exactly how he wanted it to look beforehand," Challis notes. As an example, the cameraman cites a night sequence at Loch Ness, when Queen Victoria comes to visit. The cast and crew spent three nights filming the scene on location, even though Challis had warned his director it was too dark to make out the backgrounds. "We went to see the rushes in Inverness," Challis recalls, "and Billy said, 'It's not what I want—I've got to see the hills and the mountains behind.'" And so, Wilder put Alexander Trauner to work, building a Loch Ness set under more controlled conditions at Pinewood.

The Private Life of Sherlock Holmes had a luxuriously lengthy shoot of six months, but during that time an awful chill came over the big Hollywood studios. A number of costly road-show attractions were not merely failing to live up to expectations, they were outright disasters. The first shock wave came in 1968, as Julie Andrews broke her string of hit movie musicals with *Star!*, a lavish biography of entertainer Gertrude Lawrence that left audiences completely indifferent. Then, 1969 brought the failure of Joshua Logan's *Paint Your Wagon*, starring Clint Eastwood and Lee Marvin, and, most startling of all, Gene Kelly's gaudy film of the Broadway smash *Hello, Dolly!*, which not even Barbra Streisand could save.

After a disappointing preview of *Sherlock Holmes*, United Artists panicked—suddenly, the Great Wilder Road Show seemed like a very unsound idea. UA told Wilder and the Mirisches they would have to pare down the film to a running time suitable for normal theatrical engagements. Wilder, who had final cut, at first refused, but UA insisted it would never release the road-show version, and the director gave in.

Wilder today is surprisingly willing to accept a portion of the blame. "We discussed how we were going to cut it," he says, "but I had to go to Europe and start preparing a new picture and I could not control it anymore. I was very unhappy about it, because it got to be too long. I didn't quite catch the atmosphere, I did not quite *get* Sherlock Holmes. Robert Stephens was a very good actor, and Dr. Watson—they were very good. I just . . . it did not have enough character and enough mystique and enough audience involvement in one case. It's not one of my best remembrances. The sets were going up and I was still fighting with the script. It was an abortion.

"The next time I saw it, it was cut already. They just cut like they cut for television. It lost everything. I just didn't have the energy. I felt guilty— I didn't do a good job, so maybe they had some right to operate on the thing. But they didn't operate—they just killed it altogether." Coughing up a small crumb of praise, Wilder finally admits, "I think it was one of my better-shot pictures. It was elegant."

According to Diamond, the first rough cut of *Sherlock Holmes* ran 3 hours and 20 minutes, more than a half hour longer than Wilder originally expected. Because the film consisted of discrete episodes, the studio had a relatively easy time taking the ax to Wilder's handiwork. Two complete chapters were eliminated: the 15-minute "Naked Honeymooners" episode and the half-hour "Upside Down Room" sequence (which includes an unrelated comic interlude on a train). Also cut were a modern-day prologue in which Watson's grandson (also played by Blakely) is given the box containing the "unpublished" Holmes stories and an intriguing flashback to Holmes's student days at Oxford. According to the film's editor, Ernest Waller, "Upside Down Room" was the first to go, followed—with some regret by the producers—by the more expensive "Naked Honeymooners." The final release version clocked in at 2 hours and 5 minutes, with the remaining episodes no longer given individual names.

A recent attempt to track down the deleted portions of *The Private Life of Sherlock Holmes* for its laser-disc edition proved only marginally successful. The 1994 Image Entertainment disc of the film includes the soundtrack (but no picture) for the "Upside Down Room" episode, and the picture (but no sound) for the "Naked Honeymooners" segment.

Based on this partial evidence, "The Dreadful Business of the Naked Honeymooners" sequence was by far the most dispensable. Even taking into account the absence of sound (the laser-disc presentation is subtitled), it is one predictable, protracted joke, a tepid bit of naughtiness featuring the first glimpse of nudity in a Wilder movie.

By contrast, "The Upside Down Room"—the original script's first episode—is a real loss. Even without the visuals, it is the film's most pointed exploration of the main characters' relationship, as Watson fabricates a comically nonsensical crime scene to divert Holmes from his cocaine habit.

Also revealing is the deleted Oxford sequence, filmed at the university itself. As an undergraduate, Holmes and his teammates win a rowing race against Cambridge and celebrate by chipping in to buy a prostitute for one lucky lottery winner. The victor is Holmes, who goes to the rendezvous reluctantly, since he already has a huge crush on a beautiful girl he's seen near the campus. Of course, the girl is the very same prostitute, a shock that sends the young Holmes fleeing in the other direction. "It seems so idiotic in retrospect," Holmes reflects. "Everybody at Oxford knew she was one of the girls working for the local madam—except yours truly, who prided himself on his powers of observation and deduction."

Holmes's college anecdote is virtually identical to the story from Wilder's Vienna youth as told by biographer/analyst/amateur detective Maurice Zolotow in 1977. Again, Wilder readily admits to frequenting prostitutes as a young man, but categorically rejects any direct connection between Holmes's fictional trauma and his own experience. In the wake of Zolotow's Freudian deductions, no doubt Wilder is relieved that the Oxford episode is presumed lost.

CONTRARY TO ITS DIRECTOR'S CLAIMS, *THE PRIVATE LIFE OF Sherlock Holmes* remains quite coherent and engaging in its truncated form. The main difference is one of tone: The two missing cases were largely comedic in nature, making the existing version seem that much more somber and elegiac. Now, only one comic episode remains: "The Singular Affair of the Russian Ballerina." The contents of the prologue are folded into the opening credits, as various items familiar to Holmes fans are removed from a safety-deposit box. (Holmes's syringe points to the credit "Written by Billy Wilder and I. A. L. Diamond.") The detective's arrival at 221b Baker Street from the "Upside Down Room" opens the movie, and the scene fades as he prepares to administer a shot of cocaine. In the film's new chronology, the next scene finds the partners invited to attend a performance of *Swan Lake* by the Imperial Russian Ballet (conducted onscreen by none other than Miklos Rozsa). There, Holmes is cornered by prima ballerina Petrova (played by real-life dancer Tamara Toumanova), who is searching for a genius to become the father of her first child. Prior candidates included Tolstoy ("too old"), Nietzsche ("too German") and, most disastrous of all, Tchaikovsky ("Women not his glass of tea," in the words of the ballet-company director, Rogozhin). Holmes extricates himself from this awkward situation by telling Petrova that, as "a bachelor living with another bachelor for the last five years," he shares something in common with Tchaikovsky. Word spreads around the ballet company, ruining the wonderful evening Watson has been having with the female members of the troupe. (In a funny sight gag, the male dancers gradually replace the line of women Watson has been cavorting with.) Back home, the doctor explodes at Holmes for tarnishing his good reputation, then pauses a moment to inquire, "I hope I'm not being presumptuous, but there *have* been women in your life?" Holmes replies, "The answer is yes. You're being presumptuous."

With this motif established, the central preoccupation of the pared-down *Private Life of Sherlock Holmes* becomes the great detective's relation-ship with the opposite sex. In one of Wilder's most audacious gambits—this was 1970, after all—the filmmaker keeps Holmes's sexuality ambiguous well into the movie's main episode. This story begins with the arrival on Holmes's doorstep of a dazed, shivering woman suffering from temporary amnesia after being knocked out and dumped into the Thames. In time, Holmes discovers that her name is Gabrielle Valladon, and she has come from Brussels to London in search of her missing engineer husband, Emile. While helping Gabrielle, Holmes is warned by his brother, Mycroft, who is involved in espionage for the British government, to stay away from this particular case. Sherlock, of course, disobeys, and the investigation takes him to Inverness, Scotland, with Gabrielle posing as his wife and Watson as his valet. There, after sorting through such baffling clues as dead canaries, angry midgets and a mechanical Loch Ness monster (and confirming the death of Gabrielle's husband), Holmes is once again summoned by his brother. By this time, Sherlock has pretty much figured out that the mon-ster is actually camouflage for a small fighting sub being developed by the British Navy. But it comes as a complete, devastating shock when Mycroft informs him that his traveling companion is not the widow of Emile Val-ladon, but Ilse von Hoffmanstahl, one of Germany's top secret agents, who has been using Holmes and his deductive genius to track down the experi-mental sub. But Mycroft, too, is at the mercy of a woman: When Queen Victoria comes to inspect the sub and realizes the "unsporting" nature of this new weapon of war, she orders it destroyed. (Mycroft manages to sink it with Ilse's German contacts aboard.) Thanks to Holmes's intervention, Ilse is exchanged for a British spy rather than sent to prison, but months later the detective is saddened to learn that she has been caught spying in Japan and executed by a firing squad. The movie ends with a despondent Holmes retreating to his room, syringe in hand.

In an era of revisionist westerns like *The Wild Bunch* and *Little Big Man* and revisionist gangster films like *Bonnie and Clyde*, *The Private Life* is Wil-der's revisionist Sherlock Holmes film. Though he's still as adept at inter-preting the most trivial of details, this particular Holmes is largely ineffectual, unaware that his brother is tracking his every move and com-pletely duped by Ilse's elaborate charade. As critics Neil Sinyard and Adrian Turner have pointed out, Ilse is most likely modeled after Irene Adler, the devious female at the center of "A Scandal in Bohemia," one of the two cases the detective was unable to solve.

As zany and convoluted as the clues to the Loch Ness mystery are, Wilder's interest clearly lies elsewhere: in exploring Holmes's misogyny and exposing his vulnerability to the machinations of a brilliant opponent when that opponent happens to be of a different sex. "Women are never to be entirely trusted, not the best of them," Ilse/Gabrielle quotes Holmes from one of Watson's *Strand* magazine accounts as they travel together by train to Inverness. This is where the Oxford flashback would have appeared; in its place, Wilder has Holmes recount two anecdotes partially explaining his attitude toward women. The most affectionate woman he knew, he tells Gabrielle, was merely leading him on in order to steal cyanide from his lab and put it in her husband's steak-and-kidney pie. Holmes then reveals that his fiancée—the daughter of his violin teacher—caught influenza and died, twenty-four hours before their wedding. "It just proves my contention that women are unreliable—and are not to be trusted," he adds, masking whatever pain the trauma caused him.

Significantly, the train scene comes just after Wilder has tipped his hand regarding Ilse, showing her signaling with her parasol to her fellow German agents. Thus, *we* now know that Holmes's beautiful client indeed can't be trusted and spend the remainder of the film waiting for the detective to see through her. He never does.

Unlike Phyllis in *Double Indemnity*, Lorraine in *Ace in the Hole* or, most recently, Sandy in *The Fortune Cookie*, Ilse is a sympathetic double-crosser. Her motives are largely professional, mingled with the thrill of going up against the world's most celebrated sleuth. She leaves Holmes convinced he's been on to her the whole time. "I'm sorry I didn't give you a closer game," she apologizes. "Close enough," Holmes replies, too embarrassed to reveal the truth. The irony of the moment is that while Holmes has fallen in love with Ilse's innocent, victimized alter ego, he's even more smitten by the marvelous conspirator she really is—even if she has soundly humiliated him. That Ilse, too, feels deeply for Holmes is revealed by the fact that when she died, it was under the pseudonym Mrs. Ashdown, the same name she adopted while traveling as Holmes's wife.

The Private Life of Sherlock Holmes is thus Wilder's most subtle and sophisticated variation on the romantic masquerades played between men and women. It's also one of his most heartfelt and poignant pieces of work: Rather than end the film on a jaunty comic note, Wilder remains true to Ilse and the impact of her death on Holmes, as the detective once again seeks release through his addiction.

Visually, *The Private Life of Sherlock Holmes* may be the most handsome film of Wilder's career, with an unstressed feel for the period and splendid use of its Scottish locations. And even if there's no real star magic onscreen, the cast is solid. Tall, lean Robert Stephens is physically right for the role of Holmes, and if he seems more effete than predecessors like Basil Rathbone and Raymond Massey, that's all part of Wilder's conception. (This Holmes even appears to have a liking for mascara.) Stephens ably captures the ennui and melancholy of the "private" Holmes, but his delivery of Wilder and Diamond's gag lines tends to have a certain lilting sameness.* Colin Blakely, meanwhile, is the perfect Watson, giving strong competition to the memory of Nigel Bruce in the successful film series that ran from 1939 through 1946. Blakely's Watson is less of a fool than Bruce's, but he's equally excitable and impetuous. Wilder gives Blakely the biggest share of the movie's comic duties, and the actor never lets him down—he's especially hilarious wallowing in the attention of the Russian ballerinas. Along with being a terrific foil, Blakely possesses an innate decency that keeps Watson always believable and human. It's sad that this consistently fine actor died so young in 1987, at the age of fifty-seven.

The French actress Geneviève Page, perhaps best known for her role as the madam in Luis Buñuel's *Belle de Jour* a few years earlier, never really generates the kind of sexual tension the film needs, but she still makes an elegant and lovely figure of mystery as Gabrielle/Ilse. Hammer horror-movie veteran Christopher Lee, who had previously played the detective in 1962's *Sherlock Holmes and the Deadly Necklace*, shows what a good and subtle actor he can be as Holmes's haughty sibling, Mycroft, and New Zealand–born character actor Clive Revill is very amusing as the officious Russian ballet impresario.

---

* Stephens revealed in his autobiography (*Knight Errant*, published just before his death in 1995) that he was so unhappy with his own performance and so unnerved by Wilder that he suffered a breakdown and attempted suicide.

THE PRIVATE LIFE OF SHERLOCK HOLMES OPENED AT Radio City Music Hall on October 29, 1970, to extremely mixed reviews. Focusing in on the picture's playful questions about the Holmes-Watson relationship, Vincent Canby of *The New York Times* called the movie "comparatively mild Billy Wilder and rather daring Sherlock Holmes, not a perfect mix, perhaps, but a fond and entertaining one." Kathleen Carroll of New York's *Daily News* gave *Holmes* 3 ½ stars, declaring it "an elegant, delightfully amusing film." A mildly diverted *Newsweek* deemed the film "pleasant in a rather elementary way," but *Time*, in a mock excerpt from Dr. Watson's journals, called it listless and disappointing. Andrew Sarris, while judging the movie's wit, performances and mystery elements all to be inferior, still found the picture rather moving. Pauline Kael complained that "Wilder has made a detective picture that fails to whet our curiosity," rather missing the point that the goofy assortment of clues in the film isn't meant to be taken all that seriously; they're just a means of prolonging the movie's main concern, the Holmes/Ilse relationship. Arthur Knight in *Saturday Review* also carped about the handling of the mystery, and seemed genuinely offended by both the ballerina sequence and the movie's characterization of Holmes as something of a bumbler.

Typically, Wilder was better treated abroad. *Punch* critic Richard Mallett said, "The whole thing is very good value," while Tom Milne of London's *The Observer* immediately placed the film on his ten-best list. "Paradoxical as always," Milne noted perceptively, "in upsetting the Sherlock applecart Wilder has made a film which comes full circle through a generous helping of his acid wit to become an affectionate *hommage*."

Whatever the reason—lack of stars, tepid reviews, out-of-fashion filmmaking—*The Private Life of Sherlock Holmes* did dismal business; in fact, it was the first Thanksgiving attraction at Radio City Music Hall to be withdrawn before the actual holiday. By the end of its abbreviated national run, this $10 million production had taken in a paltry $1.5 million. Coming so soon after the debacle of *Kiss Me, Stupid*, the failure of *The Private Life of Sherlock Holmes* was a blow from which Wilder's career never recovered.

WILDER STILL HAD ENOUGH CACHET WITH THE MIRISCH COM-
pany to move right into preparations for *Avanti!*, the screen version of a
1968 Broadway play by Samuel Taylor, the author of *Sabrina Fair*. It was a
curious choice for someone in need of a box-office comeback: Taylor's play
had received indifferent reviews and played a scant twenty-one performances.

"Taylor was a very talented playwright," says Jack Lemmon, "but Billy
did not consider this to be a terrific play—and I don't think it was received
as a terrific play. But he did feel, as is so often the case, that it could make a
better film than it did a play."

Iz Diamond was off on a separate movie project—adapting the hit
Broadway comedy *40 Carats*—so Wilder teamed with Julius J. Epstein, co-
author of the legendary *Casablanca*. The two veterans got nowhere. Then,
for a few weeks, Wilder reunited with Norman Krasna, with whom he had
had a short-lived partnership between *Ace in the Hole* and *Stalag 17*. Again,
the chemistry wasn't there. Wilder then turned to Luciano Vincenzoni, one
of the writers of the Italian comedy *Seduced and Abandoned*, who contributed some of the Italian dialogue. Vincenzoni stayed on as a general adviser
on local customs, but as soon as Iz Diamond was available, Wilder was
relieved to have him back.

The screenplay of *Avanti!* isn't as radical an overhaul of the play as
Wilder's treatment of Taylor's *Sabrina Fair*, but it makes some substantial
changes. The bare bones of the plot remain: An American businessman
comes to Italy to retrieve the body of his father, who has died suddenly in a
car accident. There, he meets the daughter of a woman who also perished
in the crash, and discovers that his father had an ongoing extramarital affair
with his unfortunate passenger. The legacy is then passed on to the next
generation, as the son and the daughter become caught up in their own
illicit romance.

Wilder and Diamond completely reconceived the main protagonist,
here named Wendell Armbruster III, turning him from a fairly sympathetic
romantic lead into an irascible xenophobe, as driven as James Cagney's
C. R. MacNamara in *One, Two, Three*. Where in the play the character is
immediately enchanted by his father's mistress's pretty daughter, the film's

Wendell is antagonistic to the odd, zaftig British woman who seems to be following him all over Italy. What had been a simple, straightforward romance becomes a more interesting clash of cultures and sensibilities.

Wilder has suggested that Wendell is the man Jack Lemmon's C. C. Baxter might have become if he hadn't seen the light in *The Apartment*. "There are many of these men in America," he told French critic Michel Ciment, "these young guys who drink pretty good, drive a Cadillac, go to the club, play golf. . . . They have a luxurious life, two telephones in their car, and suddenly they discover that their existence is empty, that they have no one to talk to and nothing to say on the telephone, and that it doesn't make much difference if the stocks go up three points or go down. It's the reestimation of our values that this film addresses."

The unlikely catalyst for Wendell's reawakening is Pamela Piggott, a slightly overweight boutique clerk from London. Pamela has no luck introducing herself to this rude man as they travel on the same train and boat to the island of Ischia to identify the bodies of their parents; when Wendell discovers their common purpose, he's deeply apologetic. But as Pamela describes how the departed pair took a room together at the Excelsior hotel and spa every summer for the past ten years, Wendell's embarrassment turns to rage. "You mean all the time we thought he was over here getting cured, he was getting laid?" he shouts, more disturbed by his father's secret life than by the fact of his death.

The industrialist proceeds with his mission of cutting through the country's voluminous red tape and getting his father's body back to America on time for a massive funeral to be attended by Henry Kissinger and other dignitaries. Pamela, meanwhile, wonders why they can't simply bury the lovers together in Ischia. When the bodies suddenly disappear, Wendell is convinced Pamela is the culprit, and tries to get to the bottom of things by inviting her to dinner as a "last salute" to their parents. Midway through the meal, the businessman is called away to negotiate a settlement with the real robbers—the Trotta family, owners of the vineyard where Wendell's father crashed his car. On returning to the restaurant at dawn, Wendell is met by a drunken Pamela, who suggests ending the evening the way their parents would have—by swimming out to their favorite rock and sunbathing in the nude. Diving in after Pamela, Wendell is forced to shed not only his clothes, but his preconceptions about this daffy, endearing Englishwoman.

Circumstances conspire to bring Wendell and Pamela even closer together. Bruno, a hotel valet who was deported from America and longs to go back, is trying to blackmail the businessman with photos of his nude antics, but Bruno's pregnant Sicilian girlfriend hears of his plans to abandon her and shoots him dead inside Pamela's room. When Pamela's luggage is temporarily moved into Wendell's room, she misinterprets the situation, causing Wendell to realize he really does love her in return. In the end, he agrees to Pamela's plan to have their parents buried in Italy, while Bruno gets his wish to return to America—in the Armbruster coffin. Wendell and Pamela say good-bye, but it's likely they'll continue their parents' tradition and reunite in Ischia the following summer.

AVANTI! RETURNS TO A THEME THAT APPEARS IN WILDER films ranging from *A Foreign Affair* to *One, Two, Three,* from *The Emperor Waltz* to *Sabrina* and *Love in the Afternoon*—the often comically mismatched relationship between Europe and America, particularly America as represented by its capitalist true believers. *Avanti!*'s link to *Sabrina* is particularly strong, and not merely because of the Samuel Taylor connection. Wendell is much like Linus Larrabee (whose personality is more Wilder's creation than Taylor's), an aloof industrialist whose outlook is changed by a working-class woman with a liberated, "European" approach to living.

With all his affection for America and the creature comforts of Beverly Hills, Wilder is still very much a European—witness his impulse to "educate" people like William Holden and Jack Lemmon in the riches of his native continent's culture, indeed to lecture anyone within earshot on international cuisine, art, fashion, furnishings, what have you. It can be daunting. Barbara Diamond remembers, "We once did a tour through Europe publicizing a movie—the Wilders, Iz and I, Jack Lemmon and the Mirisches. And Billy was very much our fearless leader. Now we *were* on a schedule—you meet the press, you go to a screening, you meet the press again, you have dinner with local UA people. It does have to move like an army, and Billy is a natural leader. But he also does tend to tell you what you're supposed to do. And when he is in Europe, he doesn't want you to be too visibly American. Jack and I were sitting on the terrace of a hotel in Zurich one afternoon, having a Coca-Cola—which is not a thing that you should do. And Billy walked out the door of the hotel, and Jack and I didn't even look at each other—we just took the Coca-Colas and put them under the table. And Jack went, 'What am I doing? If I want to have a Coke, I can have a Coke. This is the man who made me drink raspberry juice and beer in Berlin!' It isn't that he ever would have said to us, 'Shame on you, you're drinking a Coca-Cola.' It's just that he intimidates as a natural consequence of what he is. He's a force."

In Wilder films, every rich American, no matter how far back the money goes, is still a nouveau riche American—and most every European, no matter what their background, still possesses an innate savoir faire. Pamela Piggott may be a plump, unworldly clerk, but Wilder is very much on her side: While Wendell bulldozes his way through Ischia, always focused on the task at hand, Pamela finds consolation for her grief in the beauty of the island where her mother died. Making small talk before entering the morgue, Wendell points to a bouquet in Pamela's hand and says, "Pretty flowers—what are they?" "In Italian, they're called *trombochine*," she replies. "What are they called in English?" asks Wendell. "Daffodils," Pamela answers in astonishment. The exchange speaks volumes.

In casting Wendell, Wilder once again turned to his pal Jack Lemmon, who manages to suppress his natural likability for the first half of the film. "Most of my characters are flawed," Lemmon insists, "which is great—it gives them a chance to grow and to learn." But Lemmon concedes that Wendell was something else: "a rich, snotty prig. He might have been a decent-looking guy, and civil and so forth, but he definitely had delusions of grandeur and, socially at least, was very class-conscious for an American. He felt that he was above people, that money counted, et cetera, and one behaved a certain way or that was *it*. . . . She was just nothing but a future charwoman, the young English girl, as far as he was concerned."

Casting that English girl was a challenge. Wilder and Diamond, inspired by a Dorothy Parker short story about an overweight woman in love, thought that giving Miss Piggott a weight problem would add an extra dimension to the character. But, as Wilder discovered, "it's difficult to find someone twenty pounds overweight, someone you make fun of who is nonetheless adorable, and finally erotic."

At one point, an agent suggested his client, the former child star Hayley Mills. "I asked him her weight," Wilder remembers. "He said she was slim like a wire. I explained that the role required someone twenty pounds overweight, upon which—you know agents—he told me she had problems with her weight." Eventually, Wilder lit upon Hayley's older sister, Juliet Mills, familiar to American TV audiences from the recent sitcom *Nanny and the Professor*. Juliet Mills was also slim but less petite; eager to land the role, she agreed to put on twenty-five pounds by adopting a diet consisting largely of pasta, desserts and heavy cream. Although the script makes a big deal of Pamela's struggle with her extra poundage— Wendell cruelly refers to her as "fat ass" at one point—the attractive Mills remains, at worst, very pleasingly plump.

A third key role, that of the unflappably efficient hotel manager Carlucci, was filled by Clive Revill, the comical Russian ballet official from *Sherlock Holmes*. Wilder had considered casting an accomplished Italian comedian such as Nino Manfredi, Alberto Sordi or Romolo Valli, but decided their lack of mastery of the English language would slow down the rhythms of his script. "They would not have been returning the serve quickly enough to Lemmon, on the other side of the net," he noted. Revill not only has the Wilder-Diamond rhythms down pat, but makes a wonderfully persuasive Italian. Wilder gave Revill the key to the character—an uninhibited bisexual in the Taylor original—by describing him as "the Toscanini" of the Grand Hotel Excelsior, a crisis-master who only sleeps during the off-season.

Wilder filmed *Avanti!* entirely in Italy, with interiors at Rome's Safa Palatino studios and exteriors along the Amalfi coast and on the islands of Capri and Ischia, with cast and crew housed at the Hotel Excelsior Vittoria in Sorrento. Stating that "all Italians seem to be born actors anyway," Wilder cast a number of local citizens in small roles, including his sixty-two-year-old driver as an elderly baron with a keen appetite for women. The location shoot paid handsome dividends; for a Viennese-American, Wilder shows a vivid appreciation for the Italian people and their way of life. Speaking with French critic Michel Ciment during the making of the film, the director declared, "I am not just photographing views of Ischia, or things of that kind, but blending them into a dramatic story, a context. I would not have been able to do this anywhere but Italy. There are also some financial reasons—it would have been more expensive in America. The same goes for when I film the interiors in Rome: The look is Italian. If I transported the bed, the sofa, the vase of flowers to a Hollywood studio, it would not have the same aspect."

Of course, this wouldn't be a Wilder film without some benign jabs at his Italian hosts: the convolutions of the government bureaucracy; the sacred three-hour lunch breaks; the cheerful corruption of the Trotta brothers; the moustachioed Sicilian maid out for revenge; the heliport official who longs for the days of Mussolini (the Italian equivalent to Schlemmer in *One, Two, Three*). Most of these gags, however, are at the expense of Wendell, underlining his "ugly American" arrogance, impatience and generally poor attitude.* For all their flaws, the Italians of *Avanti!* are genuine and open to life in a way Wendell can't hope to be until he sets aside his mission and learns to see things through the eyes of his philandering but enlightened father.

"It's actually a love story between a son and his father," Wilder told Michel Ciment. "[Wendell] begins to understand a father whom he has never thought about, of whom he was only an employee in a large company. He is closer to his father dead than when he was living." The father-son theme may be relatively rare for Wilder (though it's there in places like the Neff-Keyes relationship in *Double Indemnity)*, but Wendell's odyssey has strong ties to other familiar Wilder motifs. When Wendell pretends to court Pamela to cajole information from her, he's just another gigolo, feigning love out of his own selfish motives. And when the couple don their deceased parents' clothes, it's the beginning of a masquerade that eventually leads them to "become" their parents and, in effect, bring their love back to life.

If, by 1972, *Avanti!* seemed like an old-fashioned romantic comedy to some, it's worth remembering that the film is no less unjudgmental about

---

* Wilder indulges his liberal Democratic sympathies by making it clear Wendell's a Republican with powerful connections to the Nixon administration, including the boorish State Department official (Edward Andrews) who intervenes in the movie's final half-hour.

adultery than the heretical *Kiss Me, Stupid* of just eight years earlier. And, to this day, how many romantic comedies revolve around the retrieval of two parental corpses and include murder among their subplots?

Indeed, *Avanti!*'s high point is Wilder's most risky mixture of darkness and light, pathos and comedy, since the suicide scene in *The Apartment*. Directed with great wit and delicacy, it's the sequence in which Wendell and Pamela come to identify their parents' bodies at the Ischia morgue. Wilder counterpoints the gravity of their task with the lanky coroner's hilariously elaborate ritual of removing rubber stamps, stamp pads, even a sponge and water spray bottle, from his coat pocket; stamping two sets of triplicate forms; gluing on tiny white strips of paper, etc.: Wilder and Italian actor Pippo Franco choreograph the comedy brilliantly. At the same time, the lighting and composition of visual elements inside the morgue give the scene a haunting, sad, wistful beauty. The careful, successful balancing of contradictory emotions finds Wilder in complete, unshowy but impressive control of his craft.

Equally memorable, for completely different reasons, is the first nude scene of Wilder's—and Jack Lemmon's—career (not counting the deleted "Naked Honeymooners" sequence from *Sherlock Holmes*). It's all played for comedy, as Wendell jumps into the Bay of Naples after Pamela and loses his shorts in the process. Lying on the rock where their parents used to sunbathe, the two have their first real intimate moment of conversation— Wendell admitting that he's often too tired to make love to his wife, Pamela confessing that she tried to eat herself to death after her boyfriend left her for "a thin girl from Kensington." When a fishing boat passes by, Pamela sits up and waves; Wendell, in a foolishly protective gesture, takes off his socks and holds them in front of her nipples. Mills thought Lemmon was more nervous about the nude scene than she was; her biggest concern, she said, was the tiny marine animals nipping at her bare bottom.

AVANTI! OPENED ON DECEMBER 17, 1972, TO LARGELY NEGative reviews. Vincent Canby, usually a Wilder fan, called it "in almost every respect, terrible." *Saturday Review* critic Arthur Knight branded it "a disaster." *Cue*'s Donald J. Mayerson declared, "It is hard to believe that this sour chianti has come from the rich vineyards of Billy Wilder and I. A. L. Diamond." Less virulent notices came in from *Time* magazine critic Jay Cocks, who pronounced *Avanti!* "passingly pleasant," and the *New York Times*'s daily reviewer A. H. Weiler, who found it "intermittently funny, charming, cute and, unfortunately, overlong." Current *Times* film critic Janet Maslin, then writing for the *Boston Phoenix*, was also kinder than most to the film, proclaiming that Lemmon "gives one of his all-time best performances." Also filing minority reports were *Variety*, calling *Avanti!* a "top-notch comedy," and, significantly, former Wilder dissenter Andrew Sarris, who was charmed by the Lemmon–Mills romance.

No doubt much of the negative reaction stemmed from the high expectations surrounding a new Billy Wilder film; few critics were prepared for something so deceptively slight and sentimental. *Avanti!*'s biggest offense, however, was its length. Clocking in at 2 hours and 24 minutes, the film betrays some residual hubris from Wilder's glory days—conventional wisdom says that light romantic comedies aren't meant to be this long. But then, *Avanti!* isn't merely a light romantic comedy—Wilder also wants to portray the emotional awakening of an American archetype, and he's not about to be rushed. The film's leisurely (though never plodding) pace also complements its frantic American vs. easygoing Italian sentiments. Once you've taken its running time into account, *Avanti!* holds many pleasures: a supremely entertaining and resourceful performance by Jack Lemmon; charming work by Juliet Mills; exquisite photography by Luigi Kuveiller; and buoyant direction by Billy Wilder. It's a woefully underrated film.

Avanti! took in a modest $4.5 million and, as is often the case with his box-office flops, Billy Wilder became one of its toughest critics. It was "too mild, too soft, too gentle," he said. "The picture was fifteen years too late, if it should have been done at all." Maybe if Wendell's father had been found in the car with a bellhop—*then* it might have broken some ground, he declared.

AFTER FOUR BOX-OFFICE DISAPPOINTMENTS IN A ROW, OF varying sizes, for the Mirsch Company and United Artists, Wilder was

inclined to say yes when Universal Pictures executive Jennings Lang* asked
if he'd be interested in directing Jack Lemmon and Walter Matthau in a
remake of the classic Ben Hecht–Charles MacArthur newspaper comedy,
The Front Page. By coincidence, Wilder and Diamond had already been
exploring the idea of doing something in the spirit of classic American film
farces like *Nothing Sacred, Roxie Hart* and *Libeled Lady.* "It just so happened
that these were all newspaper stories. Nobody has made this kind of picture
recently," Diamond noted.

The project first took root when Paul Monash, producer of *Butch Cassidy and the Sundance Kid,* saw a spirited production of the play at London's
Old Vic and decided it would make a terrific movie—notwithstanding the
fact that two terrific movies of *The Front Page* already existed. Back in 1931,
director Lewis Milestone followed his landmark *All Quiet on the Western
Front* with a visually inventive *Front Page* starring Pat O'Brien and Adolphe
Menjou. Nine years later, Howard Hawks turned ace reporter Hildy Johnson into a feisty female, and cast Rosalind Russell opposite Cary Grant in
the screwball-comedy classic retitled *His Girl Friday.* But that was decades
ago; now, with the 1930s Chicago caper *The Sting* making a fortune for
Universal, and Watergate turning reporters into modern-day folk heroes,
The Front Page looked like a newly hot property.

When Monash's first directing choice, Joseph L. Mankiewicz, turned
him down, executive producer Lang suggested the man who first brought
Lemmon and Matthau together in *The Fortune Cookie.* It was a long over-
due reunion: Wilder had almost been part of the film with which the team
of Lemmon and Matthau is most closely identified, 1968's *The Odd Couple.*
As Lemmon told *Film Comment,* "Billy and Walter and I were going to be
partners in this thing, and split it three ways. But: Nobody had asked Mr.
Paramount—[Charles] Bluhdorn. And they had not asked Neil Simon.
First of all, Neil would hardly want anybody to start fucking around with
his script. (Billy, obviously, would want some changes.) Number two: Mr.
Bluhdorn personally hauls me into the studio and says, 'Why do I want
Billy Wilder? Why should I *pay* Billy Wilder? I've got you and Walter and
this great script—I don't *need* Billy Wilder.' That was it. And Billy just said

---

* Lang was the former agent whose shooting by producer Walter Wanger in 1951 helped
inspire *The Apartment.*

to Walter and me, while they were futzin' around: 'Look, you guys go to the dance without me.' " Gene Saks became the director.

Wilder had also been searching for a solo starring vehicle for Matthau since his breakthrough in *The Fortune Cookie*; one such project, Franz Lehár's *The Count of Luxembourg* (once meant for Danny Kaye), fell through when the Mirisch Company refused to give Wilder the right to take it elsewhere if United Artists didn't like the screenplay.

The Front Page was one of the most successful stage comedies of its era, a raucous, bawdy, irreverent look at Chicago newspapermen who will do just about anything for a scoop. Hecht and MacArthur based the two main characters, Hildy Johnson and conniving editor Walter Burns, on people they had known from their own reporting days—Hilding Johnson of the defunct *Chicago Herald-Examiner*, and the paper's managing editor, Walter Howey. Soon after the play begins, Hildy announces that he's quitting the news game and taking a job in advertising, working for the uncle of his fiancée, Peggy. Hildy's plans to leave for New York (Philadelphia in Wilder's version) are temporarily put on hold when convicted killer and anarchist Earl Williams, slated to be hanged the next morning, escapes from police custody and Hildy gets an exclusive on how he did it. The story becomes even hotter when Earl crashes through the courthouse pressroom window while everyone but Hildy is gone. Hildy and Walter conspire to keep the convict hidden in a fellow reporter's rolltop desk until they can spread the news of his capture in the morning edition. Walter, meantime, labors to keep his prize reporter distracted from his obligations to his fiancée, at one point stooping to kidnap Hildy's future mother-in-law. Earl Williams's hiding place is discovered and Walter and Hildy are arrested for harboring a fugitive, but just in time the journalists discover that the corrupt mayor and sheriff have been illegally harboring a messenger from the governor who holds a last-minute reprieve for Williams. Hildy is free to catch the train east, and Walter gives him his watch as a going-away present; in the play's famous closing line, Walter contacts the police at the first stop out of Chicago, crying, "The son of a bitch stole my watch!"

"This is not only the funniest comedy written during the decade of the 1920s, but one of the best-constructed comedies ever written," Wilder told film critic Roger Ebert during production. "It is as tight as a drum. We are making no changes lightly. Every morning when we come out on the set we say, Hecht and MacArthur would have been proud of us."

To *Daily Variety* columnist Army Archerd, Wilder confessed some anxieties. "I love the twenties," he said. "And I hate *Hamlet* in turtleneck. But it will be an enormous ordeal to make a proper picture out of the play. If I do it the way it was, I choke it to death, and if I open it up—I bleed it to death."

Wilder and Diamond opted to risk bleeding over asphyxiation: At least half the film's dialogue is new, as are many of its situations. It's an open question how proud or happy Hecht and MacArthur would have been.

The Front Page's new adapters completely eliminated the character of Peggy's harridan of a mother, and added an extremely green substitute reporter hired by Walter just to irk Hildy. They also gave Peggy a job singing and playing the organ at the Balaban & Katz movie theater; in a new scene, Walter visits Peggy backstage in the guise of Hildy's probation officer and tries to scare her off with the news that her betrothed is a flasher.

Like the 1931 Milestone film, Wilder's *Front Page* shows a key encounter that is only referred to in the play, as a Professor Eggelhofer from Vienna examines Earl Williams and borrows the sheriff's gun in order to reenact Williams's accidental shooting of a black police officer. Wilder and Diamond expand on the incident, heightening the comedy with gleeful digs at Freudian psychology. "You wanted to kill your father and sleep with your mother," Eggelhofer tells Williams, who complains to the sheriff, "If he's going to talk dirty . . ." Reenacting the crime, Eggelhofer is shot in the groin, and demands to be taken to a clinic in Vienna because he doesn't trust American doctors. On the way to Chicago's Passavant Hospital, the patient's stretcher rolls out of the ambulance as it swerves to avoid a line of speeding police cars. The last we see of Eggelhofer, he's careening down a steep Chicago street screaming, "Fruitcakes! Fruitcakes!" Fifty years after being shown the door, Wilder again gets his revenge on Freud.

Hecht and MacArthur's play may have been "tight as a drum," but Wilder and Diamond still couldn't resist tinkering with its construction. The most satisfying change occurs near the end, as the bumbling sheriff brings about his own downfall by ordering a raid on the same Chinese brothel where the mayor has squirreled away the governor's emissary, the one with the reprieve for Williams. In the play, the messenger simply stumbles back into the action.

Wilder and Diamond were a good match for the corrosive sensibility of Hecht and MacArthur; it's often hard to tell where one team leaves off and the other begins. Hildy's speech about the indignities of being a reporter—"waking people up in the middle of the night to ask them what they think of Aimee Semple McPherson, stealing pictures off old ladies of their daughters that get raped in Oak Park"—could have come from Wilder's own reminiscences of his reporting days in Vienna, but it's taken almost intact from the play.

On other occasions, Wilder and Diamond's dialogue contributions are fairly obvious. The film includes several off-color comments about the Chinese brothel, and when Hildy tells Walter, "The only time you get it up is when you put the paper to bed," again that's the Wilder bluntness at work. There's also a passing salute to *Some Like It Hot* (which is also set in 1929 Chicago), as Hildy confesses to sending his rival reporters to the wrong garage after the St. Valentine's Day massacre. Wilder and Diamond even indulge in a Watergate reference, as Walter pictures Earl Williams "twisting slowly, slowly in the wind"—a phrase stolen from Nixon White House aide John Ehrlichman.

Although he didn't originate the project, *The Front Page* had deep resonances for Wilder, since it takes place in the same era when he himself was a working journalist. Wilder told writer Nora Sayre that, in those days, a reporter was "a mixture of a private eye and a poet. If you were any good, you could improve the story. You felt that you were an inventor, a discoverer, an explorer, a dramatist. You let yourself go: The story started as something rather simple, and you blew it up into *The Three Musketeers*. Then there was the around-the-clock dedication—no family life for the lone wolf—and the camaraderie and the rivalry in the newsroom. And the reporters were either in conflict or in cooperation with the police. As we've shown in *The Front Page*, the police are prone to protect the guilty."

Like *Ace in the Hole*, *The Front Page* presents a world where just about everyone in a position of power is corrupt. Some reporters play along with the status quo, but for others part of the joy of being a newspaperman is exposing corruption, not so much out of moral conviction but because mendacity makes such good copy. Hildy Johnson is one of the best at this game, and all Walter Burns's scheming is motivated by the knowledge that reporting is what Hildy is *meant* to do, not settling into domesticity and writing dumb ad slogans.

The Front Page's central relationship is the bond between Hildy and Walter, a love-hate situation so potent that Howard Hawks made Hildy Walter's ex-wife in *His Girl Friday*. Wilder accentuates the "love story" aspect of *The Front Page* in a more veiled manner, through his portrayal of one of the comedy's buffoons, *Tribune* reporter Bensinger. In the play, Bensinger is a high-strung hypochondriac; Wilder and veteran actor David Wayne conspire to make the reporter a more blatant gay stereotype who practically skips out of the pressroom. Even for the year 1974, this mincing character is offensive, but he *does* serve a thematic purpose. Early in the film, as the reporters sing a farewell song to Hildy, Bensinger sidles up to *Examiner* cub reporter Rudy Keppler and puts his arm around his shoulder insinuatingly. This seemingly gratuitous gag is echoed later when Peggy storms into the pressroom and tries to coax Hildy away from his typewriter, where he is feverishly composing his front-page Earl Williams story. "Cigarette me," Hildy says to Walter, who lights a smoke, puts it in his star reporter's mouth, and caresses his shoulder. Like a lover.

At moments like these, Wilder is in full command, but *The Front Page* is one of his more uneven films. Lemmon is smoothly professional, but a little too old for a role that calls for a whirlwind of energy. (Rosalind Russell and Pat O'Brien each had a lot more zip in the earlier versions.) Matthau, however, competes well against the memory of suave but shifty Adolphe Menjou in the 1931 version—the unscrupulous Walter Burns, after all, is like a better-heeled Willie Gingrich. Of all the screen Burnses, the grizzled Matthau is probably closest to the original conception of a hard-boiled newsman—there's no sense even comparing him with Cary Grant in *His Girl Friday*, where the character was reconceived as a romantic lead.

In the spirit of the old Preston Sturges and Frank Capra comedies, Wilder assembled some of the best character types available for the secondary roles. Charles Durning, Allen Garfield, Dick O'Neill, Herbert Edelman, Noam Pitlik and Lou Frizzell make a persuasive kennel of newshounds; Harold Gould is a dashing crook as the mayor; a young Susan Sarandon shows great charm in the rather thankless role of Peggy; and

Martin Gabel is very amusing as Dr. Eggelhofer. The film is nearly stolen, however, by Austin Pendleton, who plays Earl Williams as America's most gentle anarchist, a shy, stammering eccentric who giggles at the thought of sending a package of explosives to J. P. Morgan. At the 1982 Lincoln Center tribute to Billy Wilder, Pendleton recalled the director's reaction to his first take on the film: "He sweetly said, 'I can't let that be shown—it isn't truthful.' Anyone who's ever acted in a film will understand how much one appreciates a director for pointing that out." Whether or not it's the result of Wilder's quiet scolding, Pendleton gives the film's most original and witty performance.

At the other extreme is Carol Burnett, obviously cast on the basis of her TV stardom, and all at sea in the role of Williams's sometime lover, the streetwalker Molly Malone. Fulfilling a longtime wish to work with Billy Wilder and Jack Lemmon, the gifted sketch comedienne discovered she didn't have a clue how to play this noncomedic role. In the right hands, Molly should provide a poignant counterpoint to the cynical banter of the pressroom, with her outrage at the exploitation of Williams and her shocking leap from the pressroom window in an attempt to save his life. But Burnett brings no sense of reality to this admittedly problematic character; her shrill performance is no more subtle than her TV sketch work. Burnett knew it wasn't working, but was too embarrassed to ask Wilder for help. "I enjoyed the movie," Burnett said. "I just didn't enjoy that woman I played who kept running in and out of it—the one who never stopped yelling." About a year later, the actress was forced to relive the trauma when she flew cross-country and discovered that *The Front Page* was the in-flight movie. After the film ended, she got on the stewardess's intercom and apologized to her fellow passengers for her lackluster work.

Also landing in the debit column is the late Vincent Gardenia, an often engaging actor who gives a one-note, all-shouting performance as the inept sheriff. Pauline Kael commented that Gardenia reminded her of Chicago mayor Richard Daley—which may have been a conscious choice on Wilder's part, since the movie features an overzealous police raid on the headquarters of the Friends of American Liberty.

With sets by veteran production designer Henry Bumstead, fresh from *The Sting*, and cinematography by Jordan Cronenweth, who would later photograph the remarkable *Blade Runner*, *The Front Page* captures the period with artful ease—it's like a Technicolor answer to *Some Like It Hot.* But, oddly, the film projects less energy than its two predecessors. Jack Lemmon thinks he knows why: "I wish that Billy had been a little looser as the writer and let us overlap and charge it more—and screw the lines! But Billy the writer, I know, does not like to have any of his words not heard. I would have liked to have seen all of the guys overlapping to the point where you lost some of the dialogue. We would bite the cues, but we wouldn't overlap them, and we should have."

THE FRONT PAGE OPENED ON DECEMBER 17, 1974, TO A broad spectrum of critical opinion. "Absolutely surefire entertainment," raved *Saturday Review*'s Hollis Alpert. "A refreshing refurbishment for our time," cheered Judith Crist. "Lively, refreshingly caustic and easily one of the funniest films of the year," said the New York *Daily News*'s Kathleen Carroll, bestowing 3½ stars on the film. At *The New York Times*, Vincent Canby quibbled about the tempo, but declared, "This *Front Page* displays a giddy bitterness that is rare in any films except those by Mr. Wilder. It is also, much of the time, extremely funny." Andrew Sarris, in a long piece that picked apart the racism and misogyny of the original play, had strong reservations concerning Lemmon and Matthau, but he announced, "Those of us who have been busy reappraising Wilder's career in the 1960s and '70s must acknowledge *The Front Page* with gratitude. For one thing, it is refreshing to find a director who is still making talkies instead of gawkies, and who thus still believes in the spoken word as a vehicle of expression. For another, Wilder's unique blend of cynicism and passion seems much more profound than it once did. More profound and more contemporary."

Pauline Kael, in contrast to Sarris, still considered the play a masterpiece, "a sustained high" when performed right. "That's what the new movie version isn't," she argued. "The overlapping, hollering lines, which were funny in the past because they were so precise, are bellowed chaotically now and turned into sheer noise." Jay Cocks at *Time* was also unimpressed. "The sap and the snap are gone," he concluded. "This is a movie conceived with indifference and made with disinterest, like a piece of occupational therapy." Finally, *Variety* took exception to Wilder and Diamond's loosening up of the pressroom language, labeling *The Front Page* "one of the more cheaply vulgar, gratuitously coarse, and embarrassingly strident pictures of the 'liberated' screen."

Perhaps stung by all the comparisons with the Hecht–MacArthur original and its earlier movie incarnations, Wilder later expressed regret about the enterprise. "One should never make a remake of a play that was great," he told *Film Comment* in 1979. Still, this $4 million production did rather well, taking in some $15 million at the box office and ranking twenty-sixth (just ahead of Robert Altman's *Nashville)* in *Variety's* 1975 film-rental listings. It was Wilder's first popular success in eleven years—and destined to be his last.

TWENTY

Parting Shots

I N THE MIDST OF FILMING *THE FRONT PAGE* ON THE UNI-
versal lot, Wilder suffered a terrible loss when a fire broke out at the
Goldwyn Studios, where he maintained his office. Many of his most valuable mementos were "not just burned up, cremated," he told critic Charles
Champlin. "Pictures, letters, scripts, research materials, addresses. I never
kept much of that stuff at home, and it's all gone. People said, 'Were your
Oscars lost?' They're nothing—you send the Academy a check and get
another. But all that irreplaceable, priceless stuff. If you haven't been
through it, you can't really know what it feels like.

"It's probably as well I was working here at Universal when the fire
broke out. I would have rushed back trying to save things, and there wasn't
time. People who tried to drive their cars off the lot didn't even have time
to get around the corner."

Wilder put the loss behind him as quickly as possible. "What I have
learned to do when such things happen to me," he told Maurice Zolotow,
"is to think of a bigger tragedy. For instance—Hitler might have won
World War II."

More than the fire, Wilder's main concern at the time was picking up
the pieces of his career. In a prickly interview with *New York* magazine
writer Jon Bradshaw in late 1975, Wilder came out swinging. "What did
you expect to find when you came here?" he queried the visitor to his new

office at Universal, once Lucille Ball's dressing room. "A broken-down director? A wizened, myopic boob in his dotage? . . . I'm not just functioning in the motion-picture relief home, y'know. I feel just as confident and virile as I did thirty years ago. I can still hit home runs."

Despite the moderate success of *The Front Page*, Wilder was clearly anxious to prove something. Extending the baseball metaphor, he summed up his recent stats. "*Irma la Douce* was a home run, but that was during the 1963 season. *Kiss Me, Stupid* was a strike-out on three straight strikes. . . . *The Fortune Cookie* was a scratch bunt. I just got on. *Sherlock Holmes* was a strike-out, an expensive error. *Avanti!* was a strike-out too, though it was a double in Europe. My last film, *The Front Page*, was a single. It was a nice hit and drove in a run or two, but that was all. It was solid, but hell, I used to hit the solid stuff over the fences." Wilder swore he was just going through a slump. "I did not suddenly become an idiot," he argued. "I did not suddenly unlearn my craft. It's a dry spell. Occasionally, the vineyards produce a bad vintage."

Just as *The Front Page* evoked his most acclaimed comedy, *Some Like It Hot*, Wilder's next project would echo his most celebrated drama, *Sunset Boulevard*. The director had been tinkering with an idea for a movie about the Mayer Hollywood dynasty, which he jokingly named *The Foreskin Saga*, when he heard that actor-turned-novelist Tom Tryon was coming out with a new book about Hollywood called *Crowned Heads*. Out of this collection of interlocking tales, Wilder was especially intrigued by a story called "Fedora." Universal bought the film rights to Tryon's book, and Wilder and Diamond set to work on the screenplay. It was the first all-out drama the team had ever attempted, and the first of Diamond's entire career.

Tryon's tale centers on a legendary Hollywood goddess, born in the Soviet Republic of Georgia, who emerged from a seventeen-year hiatus as ravishing as ever, and finally ended her life in seclusion on the island of Crete. The story begins just after Fedora's death, as celebrity journalist Barry Detweiller describes his last encounter with the mysterious beauty at her island villa. There, he uncovered the bizarre truth behind Fedora's comeback: The woman who made that spectacular return to the screen was not Fedora but her daughter, secretly born out of wedlock and groomed to take the star's place after her quack doctor's experimental beauty injections permanently destroyed her magnificent face. Taking on the identity of her lover's dead mother, Fedora watched as her daughter matched her stardom but proved unable to cope with her impossible real-life role and became increasingly dependent on drugs to ease her anguish.

As was their habit, Wilder and Diamond made some decisive changes to Tryon's story. The reporter became a down-on-his-luck movie producer who had a long-ago one-night stand with Fedora and hopes to persuade her to star in his new film of *Anna Karenina*, haplessly retitled *The Snows of Yesteryear*. In Tryon's version, Detweiller is summoned to the villa and asked to read his new novel to the half-blind "countess"; sharply observant, he figures out who is the real Fedora and gets the scoop of the century when the movie legend unburdens herself to him. Wilder and Diamond instead opted for intrigue and suspense, with Detweiler (now minus an "l") sneaking around the villa and even getting knocked unconscious for a critical portion of the movie's complex time scheme. In all, Tryon's straightforward storytelling, basically one long monologue, is transformed into something much more intricate and dramatic.

In September 1976, Wilder and Diamond turned in their first draft. But, just as the sudden failure of big road-show attractions had prompted United Artists to take the ax to *Sherlock Holmes*, Universal's experience with two 1976 flops about old Hollywood, *Gable and Lombard* and *W. C. Fields and Me*, impelled the studio to rethink its commitment to *Fedora*.

" 'Turnaround,' one of the ugly new words that sprang up in Hollywood," is how Wilder described the outcome. "After I finished the script, I got a short little telephone call from Universal to tell me they were not going to continue the project. I folded my tent and started offering the script around town and got a unanimous *no*. Nowadays, you have to go out and get the money to make your picture. By the time you're ready to direct, you're totally exhausted. In the olden, marvelous days, when those illiterate moguls were running the studios, we were spared all that."

After suffering the humiliating rejection of Hollywood, Wilder gave the okay for his agent, Paul Kohner, to look for European backing. Thus, the majority of *Fedora*'s $6.7 million production budget came from a Munich-based tax-shelter company, Geria Film. Wilder recalled his meeting with his German investors in an amusing story he told to *Film Comment*: "Now I come to Germany and they give me a party and, my God, old UFA is going to rise again. And one of the guys at Geria gets up and says, 'Herr

Wilder, we read the script, it's very interesting. I just would like to ask you a question. The picture plays in Greece, it plays in France, and there's a small scene in Hollywood. Why do you want to shoot it in Munich?' And I said, 'Do you know a man in America by the name of Willie Sutton? He started robbing banks when he was sixteen years old and now, at the age of seventy-eight, he has been in jail for forty-eight years. Now he's caught again and the judge asks him, 'Mr. Sutton, why do you keep robbing banks?' And Willie Sutton says, 'Because that's where the money is.' And so I told them, 'I'm making it in Munich because that's where the money is.' The guy very seriously looked at me and said, 'You're not going to *rob* us, are you, Herr Wilder?' "

Universal, meantime, wanted to protect its initial investment by retaining the right of first refusal to distribute the picture. Wilder repaid Universal out of his own pocket to avoid any further possible embarrassment.

The film was now scheduled to begin shooting in June 1977, and the first step was finding the right location for Fedora's mystery-shrouded villa. Wilder, Diamond and Alexander Trauner scoured Crete, but eventually found the house they needed on Madouri Island, off the coast of Levkàs near the village of Nydri. Just a short distance away was Scorpios, the retreat of the late Aristotle Onassis. The villa was used only one month a year, and had just the dilapidated grandeur Wilder was looking for.

Casting was another matter. "We need Garbo, age thirty-five, and Spencer Tracy, age fifty. Any ideas?" Wilder asked the *New York Times.* Initially, Wilder dreamed of hiring Marlene Dietrich as the aged, wheelchair-bound "Countess Sobryanski," with Faye Dunaway—whom he considered something of a Dietrich lookalike—as her daughter, the bogus Fedora. He sent a copy of the script to Dietrich, who returned it registered and special delivery, "as if she couldn't get rid of it fast enough," says Wilder. Attached was a note simply saying: "How could you possibly think . . . !" Perhaps it was the idea of playing a scarred old woman, or the fact that the film hinged on a mother-daughter relationship too uncomfortably close to Dietrich's with her daughter, Maria Riva, but Dietrich's decision was obviously final.

Dunaway also proved unavailable, and Wilder continued his search for a young actress who could convincingly play a screen legend. "I have known Garbo, Swanson, Dietrich, Lombard and Monroe," he said, "and today there is nobody like them left in Hollywood." New to Hollywood was a beautiful Swiss actress named Marthe Keller, who first garnered international attention in French director Claude Lelouch's *And Now My Love* and had recently been featured in the thrillers *Marathon Man* and *Black Sunday*. Next up was her biggest American role to date, opposite her offscreen lover Al Pacino in the race-car drama, *Bobby Deerfield*. After director Sydney Pollack screened a rough cut of the film for him, Wilder decided to take a chance on this actress seemingly on the brink of stardom.

Wilder's initial intention was to have Keller play both the old and young Fedora and her daughter, Antonia. The director recalls, "We were about two days before shooting [actually, it was closer to several weeks] and we did a test—we put a mask on her to make her old and she started crying. It turned out that she had been in an automobile accident and all the nerves were exposed. She was screaming with pain, so we could not use it. So we needed two actresses."

At Keller's suggestion, Wilder then cast Hildegard Knef as the aged "countess." Back in 1971, the German-born Knef had enjoyed a major U.S. success with her autobiography, *The Gift Horse*, which recounted her amazing odyssey. A teenage actress in propaganda films, she fell in love with a UFA official groomed by Goebbels, and followed him to the Russian front disguised as a man. There, she and her lover were captured and she never saw him again. Knef made such an impression in the postwar German film *Murderers Among Us* that David O. Selznick beckoned her to Hollywood. After a brief American film career, she returned to Europe and solidified her international stardom.

In *The Gift Horse*, Knef recalled being invited to Wilder's house for dinner shortly after her arrival in Hollywood. Her description of the man she called "a conqueror in the New World" was remarkably vivid: "The round close-cropped head, the taut blank face and eyes that missed little and proscribed much, the cynical, ready-for-sarcasm mouth, the nasal voice and staccato dialogue presented a picture of an alert sovereign, a victor mistrustful of the vanquished. . . . His house was beautiful in an unfussy way, with bookshelves to the ceiling, African wood carvings, Toulouse-Lautrecs, and a built-in, well-stocked bar. Standing behind it was a dark-haired apparition named Audrey who looked like the immaculate beauties in the film magazines." Knef remembered how Wilder, as a joke, barked

"Speak German!" to his companion, and Audrey puts her hands on her hips and "made gargling guttural noises which sounded like the hoarse barking of the oddly dressed officers in the anti-German films."

Wilder apparently bore no grudge against Knef for her frank portrait, but he was merciless during her makeup tests. "Let's go for the extreme in deterioration," he told makeup artist Tom Smith, "and then find a happy medium." Mischievously consoling Knef, he advised, "Be brave, Hilde. Remember what Charles Laughton had to go through in *The Hunchback of Notre Dame.*"

Absent the star power of a Dietrich or a Dunaway, Wilder recruited his friend William Holden for the part of Barry "Dutch" Detweiler; it was their first film together since *Sabrina*, some twenty-three years earlier. The onetime matinee idol's features had grown increasingly craggy through years of hard drinking, but Holden was still a formidable name, having just earned his third Oscar nomination for the Paddy Chayefsky TV-news satire, *Network*. Holden's presence also invited comparisons to *Sunset Boulevard*, a film *Fedora* was already mirroring in provocative ways.

Wilder finally got to work with José Ferrer, his original choice for the part of Don Birnam in *The Lost Weekend* more than thirty years earlier, casting him as the egotistical and rather mad Dr. Vando. And, for *Fedora's* stern, devoted assistant, Miss Balfour, he chose Frances Sternhagen, a respected New York stage actress who had impressed him in the Broadway production of *Equus*. Sternhagen, who won her second Tony Award in 1995 in a revival of *The Heiress*, recalls her first meeting with Wilder after flying into Munich for makeup tests. "I said to Mr. Wilder, 'I would like to talk to you sometime about my character.' And he said [imitating his Austrian accent], 'Oh, you do just what you did in *Equus*, that was fine.' And that was all he said. I just thought, 'Oh, uh, okay.' "

Sternhagen was later joined in Europe by her husband and four young children, and she remembers, "Billy was darling with my children. He called one of my little boys his mascot—John would occasionally be the a.d. [assistant director], at age nine. What amazed me was how dear and childlike and funny and unpretentious Billy was. I just found him delightful."

There was only one disappointment. "At one point," the actress remembers, "I asked Bill Holden what it was like working on *Network*, which he had just come off. He said, 'Oh, it was great—every scene was a little play. We'd rehearse the whole thing before we shot it.' And I said, 'God, it's so sad that Billy doesn't do that.' And Holden said, 'He used to.' But Billy felt such pressure getting the thing under budget that the only rehearsal we got was placement, right before we shot, so that we'd know where the camera was. And I know Marthe Keller was quite distressed about it, because she had so much to do."

For the first time since the forgotten *Mauvaise Graine*, Wilder was directing a film without an American studio's support system, a demeaning circumstance for someone of his reputation. He'd always been an economical filmmaker, but the finite resources of his German backers created new tensions, and certainly didn't allow the luxury of exploring a character the way an actress like Keller demanded. "I didn't feel at all connected to the part of Fedora," Keller said afterward, "because Billy Wilder never discussed anything. You had to do what he said and I felt a bit like a marionette. He's a wonderful director, but of another school."

"It was terribly hard for her," Sternhagen declares. "She had just come off *Bobby Deerfield*, and Syd Pollack is somebody who loves to work with actors, and she had had such a wonderfully secure and stimulating experience that she felt really abandoned at times. Also, just when you were preparing as an actor to shoot a very tense scene, Billy would be making jokes with the crew—because he's a very funny man. I remember one in particular: " 'Miriam found Moses in the bullrushes and brought him home to the Pharaoh, and the Pharaoh said, "What an ugly kid!" And she said, "He looked really good in the rushes!" ' That was the kind of thing Billy would say as we were trying to prepare."

Clearly, there was no great love lost between Wilder and Keller. "She's not a very good actress—she's Swiss," Wilder says, as if the latter comment explains everything. Keller, according to writer Rex McGee's detailed eyewitness account of the production, had trouble enunciating certain words in the script, and when Wilder spoke some of the lines out loud to hear how they sounded, Keller thought he was trying to dictate her line readings. One scene, in which Antonia parodies her mother's acting style, turned out so poorly it was cut from the film.

Some of Wilder's frustration with Keller stemmed from his inability to stick to the plan to have one actress play the old, the young and the fake

Fedora—a snag that ultimately hurt the film. During post-production, Wilder concluded that Keller and Knef's voices didn't sound alike enough to pull off the illusion that both were Fedora, and that *someone*'s vocal performance would have to be replaced. Not wanting to appear to favor either Keller or Knef, Wilder made the extraordinary decision to hire a third actress to loop their lines: Inga Bunsch, who had worked with Keller on the Berlin stage and sounded a bit like her better-known colleague. Knef was furious: "First he destroys my face," she fumed, "now he takes away my voice. What else is left?" Keller's agent also protested, but when Wilder showed his star the undoctored film and samples of Bunsch's dubbing work, Keller admitted that something had to be done about the dissimilarity between her voice and Knef's. She did, however, insist that Wilder retain her voice for the scenes where Antonia is not trying to be Fedora.

Eventually, Wilder mollified his two stars by letting Keller loop both characters in the French version, and having Knef, who was a huge star in Germany, do the same for the German version. But not everyone was happy. During the final mixing of the English-language tracks, both editor Fredric Steinkamp and composer Miklos Rozsa argued in favor of restoring Knef's feisty vocal performance; Inga Bunsch's looping of the old woman, they argued, was too mononotous. Wilder, however, refused to jeopardize the delicate compromise he'd worked out.

LIKE *SUNSET BOULEVARD*, *FEDORA* HAS A FADED MOVIE LEGend living in seclusion, and William Holden as a desperate interloper who unintentionally sparks a tragedy. But Wilder also sees a key difference: The film is "not just about the madness of a star. Fedora is a very rational and cunning woman who has written a scenario of her life and wants to bring it to the end she planned." Unlike Norma Desmond, the deformed Fedora has given up hope of a return to the screen, but she is able to live it vicariously by robbing her own daughter of her identity.

As *Sunset Boulevard* begins with Joe Gillis dead in a swimming pool, *Fedora* opens with the suicide of its heroine, as she takes her cue from Anna Karenina and leaps in front of an oncoming train. Under the credits, a long procession of admirers comes to mourn the great beauty, her face repaired, as she lies surrounded by floral tributes in the entrance hall to her Paris mansion. Among them is Barry Detweiler, who relates his recent experiences with the movie goddess and her weird entourage. Wilder and Diamond's unusually twisty narrative includes a flashback within a flashback, as Detweiler writes a letter to Fedora reminding her of their first, comical meeting while he was an assistant director on her 1947 MGM costume epic, *Leda and the Swan*. Detweiler is ordered to rearrange the lily pads during a nude bathing scene; as Fedora's glorious body stretches out before him, he wades into the water and lets out a conspicuous yawn. "Tell me, Mr. Detweiler—are you a faggot?" she demands to know later in her dressing room, convinced no *normal* man would yawn before her naked presence. Detweiler explains that he's had a rough evening, and the encounter leads to a one-night stand on the beach at Santa Monica.

The film returns to the more recent past, as Detweiler smuggles a copy of his script into Fedora's villa, and is summoned by the Countess Sobryanski for the express purpose of informing him that a Fedora comeback is out of the question. (Later on, we learn the countess has her own reasons for getting a look at Detweiler.) Fedora, still amazingly beautiful, overhears the conversation, and insists she'd love to play Anna Karenina. Watching the jittery actress chafe against her handlers, and later seeing her violently dragged away after she is found sneaking off to his hotel room, Detweiler becomes convinced that Fedora is being held prisoner in her own villa. Returning to the island unannounced, he is caught snooping by the star's brutish chauffeur and bonked on the head with a poker. (In an early draft, the weapon of choice was Fedora's honorary Oscar.) When he awakens nearly a week later, Fedora is already dead.

Fedora the film is now about two thirds over, and in a daring move reminiscent of Alfred Hitchcock's decision to tell all about the Kim Novak character midway through *Vertigo*, Wilder elects to unmask the secret of his age-defying heroine. "Look at the hands," the countess tells Detweiler during a break in the mourners' procession, pointing as Miss Balfour changes the corpse's ever present white gloves. "Hands are a problem—so are knees," miracle worker Dr. Vando had said when Fedora first offered her gloved hand to Detweiler. But the dead Fedora's hands are those of a young woman; the gloves are there to hide the fact that she's *not* old, and indeed not the real Fedora.

The real Fedora, of course, is the countess, who takes over most of the narration, recounting the horror of Dr. Vando's botched treatment (after twenty years of success) and how she came to see her younger self in her neglected daughter Antonia. The tragedy of Antonia begins with an Oscar, as Henry Fonda* (playing himself, but in the role of President of the Academy) writes to say he is coming over from Cannes to personally present a special Academy Award to the great Fedora. Antonia agrees to double for her mother, with Fedora watching enviously from an upstairs window, and the official photos are printed all over the world. Offers pour in, and Fedora leaps at the chance to be reborn. Antonia studies her mother's pictures religiously and even consents to have her features altered to make her look slightly *older*, before accepting a cameo role in an Italian film, *The Miracle of Santa Cristi*. "Fedora Is Back!" the headlines blare, and all goes well through several more pictures until her double costars opposite Michael York (also playing himself) in *The Last Waltz*. Antonia, still just a girl, falls in love with her leading man, and plans to reveal her charade after the picture is over. But Balfour won't hear of it—that would mean uncovering the truth of Fedora's disfigurement. "You mean it's going to go on like this until the day she dies?" Antonia cries. "No," corrects Balfour. "Until *Fedora* dies. And you are now Fedora." That night, Antonia tries to kill herself with sleeping pills, and Fedora abruptly retires from the screen. Left without an identity, Antonia becomes addicted to drugs, and Detweiler's visit only increases her agitation. Sent to Dr. Vando's clinic in Paris, the girl escapes and ends her life trying to destroy her mother's cursed face.

Having unburdened herself to Dutch (the fact that she knows his nickname means she remembers him after all), Fedora prepares the mansion's grand entrance hall for the waiting mourners—the two o'clock show. "You sure know how to throw yourself a funeral," Detweiler wisecracks. "Endings are very important," Fedora counters. "That's what people remember—the last exit, the final closeup." Before the end credits roll, Detweiler reveals that the real Fedora died eight months later, still in the guise of Countess Sobryanski. "The news rated one short paragraph in the local paper," he notes.

* In an early draft, Wilder planned on casting his friend, former Academy President Gregory Peck.

TOM TRYON'S PREMISE IS, OF COURSE, PREPOSTEROUS, AND many reviews of *Fedora* seemed unable to look beyond that plain fact. What Wilder saw in *Fedora*, however, was a chance to make another Hollywood Gothic, to apply his old German expressionist palette once again to the excesses of the illusion factory. Holden's narration is the tip-off: Just as almost thirty years earlier, he sized up the demented grandeur of Norma Desmond, here he's just as caustic about "that spooky entourage" of Fedora's. Desmond's musty mansion and Fedora's shrouded island villa share a forbidding aura out of horror films, and *Fedora* is peppered with movie-chiller imagery: Fedora's panicked eyes darting back and forth beneath her bandages after Vando's experiment goes awry; the menacing way in which Antonia's protectors surround and suffocate her, like a coven of vampires or soul snatchers.

Fedora also shares with *Sunset Boulevard* a healthy skepticism about the intoxication of stardom. Having worked with many of the most fabled Hollywood icons, Wilder has seen stardom from the inside, and understands its cost. "I'll tell you what becomes a legend most," Fedora declares in response to an inquiry from the famed fur ad campaign. "Not to linger on beyond your time. Monroe and Harlow—they were the lucky ones." Like Norma Desmond, Fedora tries to defy time, to hold on to the beauty that has become her identity—the battle appears to be lost until her daughter naïvely takes on the role of permanent understudy. Fiercely devoted Balfour, disreputable Dr. Vando—they also draw their identity from the maintenance of the Fedora myth; behind every great star, there's a flock of handlers who would be nothing without them.

Detweiler, too, is both painfully aware of the passage of time and hoping to reclaim some legitimacy from Fedora. "The kids with beards have taken over," he complains in a last-ditch attempt to win the countess's approval of his film project. It's tempting to equate Barry Detweiler with Billy Wilder (even the names sound alike): Both are older filmmakers looking for a comeback, both favor sporty straw hats, both like to quote Sam Goldwyn ("In life, you have to take the bitter with the sour"), and both are dependent on tax-shelter money. But Detweiler's biggest claim to fame is a picture called *Chinaman's Chance*, and Wilder would never be caught hawking a project named *The Snows of*

Yesteryear. Like Joe Gillis, Dutch Detweiler is a Hollywood hustler of debatable talent—but an aging one.

FEDORA WAS AN ACT OF CHUTZPAH, AND WILDER KNEW IT. "This would make a much better picture than the script I brought you," Detweiler tells Fedora after promising to keep her story a secret. "Yes," she replies, "but who would you get to play it?" That moment is Wilder's acknowledgment of the difficulty of trying to film a story of Hollywood legends in the year 1977—especially when you're making it in Europe under a tax-shelter arrangement.

Despite Wilder's harsh judgment, Marthe Keller isn't a terrible actress—just a very uneven one, under the circumstances. Regrettably, her least successful scene is among her most important—Detweiler's initial visit to the villa to pitch his *Anna Karenina* project. Even after taking into account that Antonia/Fedora is hopped up on amphetamines, Keller's arm-flailing, shouting interpretation of her character's turmoil is too broad, too busy. "Always the actress," the countess smirks, but the audience remains unconvinced.

Keller is most effective in the movie's more human moments: She projects just the right imperious attitude of a sheltered star during the witty *Leda and the Swan* flashback, and her joy is infectious when Antonia accepts Fedora's Oscar and rushes upstairs to deliver it to her mother. Both Keller's and Knef's performances, however, are continually marred by Inga Bunsch's dubbing, which gives a tinny, artificial quality to much of the film.

Holden's presence, meanwhile, enriches and deepens the film beyond measure, even if it's a bit of a shock to see how weathered the handsome Joe Gillis has become. José Ferrer is especially diverting as the egomaniacal Dr. Vando, and nearly all the other supporting players are strong: Sternhagen as the rigid Balfour; Mario Adorf as a Greek hotel manager who boasts he once appeared in *Zorba the Greek;* Stephen Collins as the young and rakish Dutch; Hans Jaray as Fedora's old lover, the guilt-ridden Count Sobryanski. Casting Michael York as Antonia's great crush was a bane on the film, however. It's believable enough that this vulnerable girl would fall for a quasi star like York, but this time Wilder's colliding of fiction and reality proved too way-out for most audiences. If Antonia's photo shrine to York wasn't enough to set them giggling, the sight of York placing a rose on Fedora's corpse got them every time. Wilder later said he regretted the shot and wished he had removed it from the film.

As filmmaking, *Fedora* is often stunning. Wilder's budget limitations certainly don't affect his lavish staging of Fedora's funeral (filmed at the same Studios de Boulogne near Paris where he shot *Love in the Afternoon*), and he and cinematographer Gerry Fisher make magnificent use of their Greek island locations. The early scenes in which Detweiler spies on the inhabitants of the villa signal a new, looser filmmaking style for the seventy-one-year-old director, as Wilder shoots Dutch's point-of-view with a long lens, with the action partially obscured. The flashback to Fedora's botched operation is another stylistic high point; the staging, tempo and performances bring out the full horror of the moment.

Finally, even though this is Wilder and Diamond's first "serious" film, there remain plenty of examples of their caustic wit. Buttering up Vando, Detweiler says, "When I think of the job you did on Generalissimo Franco and Coco Chanel and Paul Getty—" "No names, please," the loony doctor replies. Fedora laments about never winning an Oscar in competition—she lost one year to "the one who played that nun with tuberculosis." And, in the movie's best encapsulation of how far Hollywood and the culture have come, Fedora observes, "Remember those days—moral turpitude? You could have six husbands, but you couldn't have an illegitimate child. Now you can have six children and no husband—and who cares?"

FEDORA COMPLETED ITS SIXTY-DAY SHOOTING SCHEDULE ON August 31, 1977. Two months later, Lorimar Productions struck an unusual agreement with the producers: In exchange for handling the sale and promotion of *Fedora* in North America and certain other territories, Lorimar would be given an "above-the-title" presentation credit on the film. In March, Wilder screened a cut of just over two hours for Lorimar chairman Merv Adelson and president Lee Rich. The reaction was muted, at best. Wilder and editor Fredric Steinkamp trimmed the picture by twelve minutes, and the first public preview was held on May 12, 1978, accompanying the Walter Matthau comedy *House Calls*, at the State Theatre in Santa

Barbara. The audience was with the movie for the first half, but as the byzantine details of Fedora's ruse were explained, some in the crowd began to titter, with Michael York and the rose getting the biggest laugh.

Later that month, *Fedora* had its official premiere at the Cannes Film Festival—the climax of a Wilder retrospective—and the disparity between the American and the European view of its director was never more apparent. French and Italian critics loved the movie, but the Yank press was underwhelmed.

That fall, Lorimar made an oral agreement with Allied Artists (the independent company that handled *Love in the Afternoon*) to distribute the new Billy Wilder film. But, early in 1979, Allied backed away from the deal. "They gave us a print and we thought we had a deal," an Allied executive told *Variety*. "But when it came down to hammering out a final contract, we found we were so far apart it was pointless to continue." Shortly afterward, United Artists, Wilder's old longtime distributor, came to the rescue and picked up the film—motivated partly by a new exclusive distribution pact between UA and Lorimar.

Almost a year after its Cannes debut, *Fedora* opened at the 300-seat Cinema Studio I on New York's Upper West Side, trailed by talk of its distribution troubles and of inappropriate laughter at screenings. The reviews were among the most sharply divided of Wilder's career. Two *New York Times* critics trumpeted the movie. Janet Maslin, in a review that seemed to relish the film's excesses, called *Fedora* "a fabulous relic . . . , a proud, passionate remembrance of the way movies used to be, and a bitter smile at what they have become." Vincent Canby found it "hugely entertaining," and optimistically predicted that "it should restore Wilder to something like permanent favor or, at least, the favor that doesn't dissolve simply because a new picture doesn't duplicate the success of the last." Stephen Farber in *New West* magazine contended, "It's too leisurely for many audiences, and too florid for some of the shortsighted, smart-ass critics who pride themselves on being hip. Yet I think it will stand as one of the most haunting films ever made about Hollywood."

At *The New Yorker*, Penelope Gilliatt found the movie "inadequate" but decided that Wilder was being more subtly satirical than most people realized. Andrew Sarris called the movie "too gimmicky," but also lectured his readers that *Fedora* "can be understood and appreciated only in the context of an entire career as a testament of twilight." *Time*'s Richard Schickel, after declaring that "we are asked to accept a melodramatic manner of storytelling and characterization that is outmoded by at least a quarter of a century," admitted, "in some perverse way, *Fedora* is an entertaining film. . . . The energy of the determinedly unfashionable informs [Wilder and Diamond's] work, and almost redeems it."

Both the *New York Post* and *Daily News* put the phrase "old hat" in their headlines, with the *Daily News*'s Kathleen Carroll offering perhaps the movie's most scathing assessment: "It is a positively antiquated, arthritic-looking movie that is extremely painful to watch because it shows that Wilder is not only completely out of touch with his times, but that his talents have sadly deteriorated."

On the strength of the *New York Times* raves, *Fedora* broke the house record at the Cinema Studio I, with $22,749 in its opening week. But the movie quickly tapered off and barely got distributed around the country. Wilder accused United Artists of releasing the film "in a perfunctory and insulting way and spending about $625 on an advertising campaign." Because the film performed well in France and Germany, he believed *Fedora* would turn a small profit. But unfortunately, he told the *New York Times*, "a picture that shows a small profit is regarded as a washout."

Even before *Fedora* opened, Wilder admitted, "If I had it to do over again, I would rewrite 60 percent of it, and I would test and test and test [for the lead role]." Today, the director says, "I feel like if that picture were a person in a crowd, I would not put my arms around it. I would just say, 'Hey, how are you? We had a good time, didn't we?' "

In a sad postscript, two years after the release of *Fedora*, William Holden—one of Billy Wilder's closest actor friends—died after stumbling drunk in his apartment and hitting his head on the sharp corner of a table. "I really loved Bill," Wilder told writer Stephen Farber, "but it turned out I just didn't know him. If somebody had said to me, 'Holden's dead,' I would have assumed that he had been gored by a water buffalo in Kenya, that he had died in a plane crash approaching Hong Kong, that a crazed jealous woman had shot him and he drowned in a swimming pool. But to be killed by a bottle of vodka and a night table—what a lousy fade-out for a great guy."

AFTER THE FADE-OUT OF *FEDORA*, WILDER WAS FEELING more and more alienated from his own industry. Commenting on one recent blockbuster, he joked, *"Grease* is what I call an $11,000 picture. If you gave me $11,000, I would go to see it." The youth culture was now dominating movies, and Wilder felt, "I fit in absolutely nowhere. Some directors might say, 'If they want youth-oriented pictures, I can do that too.' Well, I can't. If you compose waltzes, you cannot suddenly start writing disco. It's going to sound phony."

Six years had now passed since the release of *The Front Page*, with one little-seen film to show for it. No wonder Wilder responded favorably when producer Jay Weston invited him to reteam with Jack Lemmon and Walter Matthau on *Buddy Buddy*, a remake of the 1973 French farce *L'Emmerdeur* (released to fair business in America as *A Pain in the A . . .*).

For the first time since *Ninotchka*, Wilder would be reporting to work at Metro-Goldwyn-Mayer—a radically changed MGM from the grand and glossy film factory he remembered. In the early 1970s, under new owner Kirk Kerkorian and his hand-picked president, James Aubrey, the financially strapped studio had taken extreme measures to reduce its debt, selling off large portions of its back lot and, to the amazement of movie lovers, auctioning off much of its store of costumes and props—many of them antiques sold for a fraction of their true value. All through the decade, MGM released just a handful of films per year, a sad whimper replacing its trademark lion's roar. After the blockbuster success of films like *Jaws* and *Star Wars*, however, Kerkorian sought to increase the studio's output and hired David Begelman, a former Columbia production chief recently at the center of a bizarre forgery-and-embezzlement scandal, to oversee MGM's stepped-up production. Among the first projects Begelman green-lighted was *Buddy Buddy*.

The French original was written by Francis Veber and directed by Edouard Molinaro, both Oscar-nominated for their 1979 international comedy smash, *La Cage aux Folles*. Lino Ventura, a veteran Italian actor specializing in tough guys, plays Milan, a professional hit man assigned to dispose of an informer who is about to testify in a major government scandal. Jacques Brel, the popular French entertainer and composer, is Pignon, a klutzy shirt salesman hoping to reconcile with his wife, who has dumped him for her psychiatrist. When his spouse refuses to meet him, Pignon decides to hang himself from an overhead water pipe in the bathroom of his hotel. By chance, Milan is in the next room, preparing to fire on the courthouse across the street. Pignon's suicide attempt fails when the water pipe breaks, and Milan takes it upon himself to keep the hapless husband from creating any more disturbances. Pignon believes he has found a true friend, but the more he "bonds" with the disgruntled hit man, the more hellish Milan's day becomes. After a series of comic disasters, Pignon discovers the rifle in Milan's room and refuses to give it back. In the resulting struggle, he accidentally discharges the weapon, setting off a massive police assault on the hotel room. The movie ends with the pair as prison cellmates—at Pignon's request.

Wilder and Diamond wrote their version in a faster-than-usual three months. Pignon was now Victor Clooney, a CBS censor whose journalist wife left him after researching a *60 Minutes* investigation of the Institute for Sexual Fulfillment (their motto: "Ecstasy Is Our Business") and falling in love with its eccentric founder, Dr. Zuckerbrot. Milan was rechristened Trabucco. Many of the gags were taken directly from the French original: the water-pipe fiasco; a woman in labor interrupting the assassin's plans; the accidental injection of the hit man with a powerful sedative meant for the husband. But Wilder and Diamond made a crucial change in the final reel: Instead of preventing the hit, Victor (Lemmon) volunteers to complete the job for the groggy Trabucco (Matthau). A poor shot, Victor winds up killing a police officer, never realizing that it's actually the informer in disguise. (Wilder and Diamond also aimed to make Victor's act more acceptable by turning the stoolie into a sleazy Mafia henchman.) Instead of prison, Trabucco winds up on a tropical island, enjoying perfect bliss until pesky Victor washes ashore—a fugitive from justice, having blown up the sex institute.

Exteriors for the hotel and courthouse square where much of the action revolves were filmed in the town of Riverside, about an hour out of Los Angeles. The courthouse was real; the hotel, a Spanish-style structure was not—this extremely convincing façade was built on the site of a parking lot. One sequence called for Lemmon to climb onto a ledge four stories above the square; an unseen safety belt would protect him from falling. Before Lemmon volunteered to do the stunt himself, the seventy-four-year-old Wilder, determined to prove there was no danger, walked onto the ledge himself—without the belt.

Another stunt, however, almost ended in catastrophe. Late in the film, Victor and Trabucco escape the police swarming the hotel by diving down a laundry chute. The bottom of the chute was built roughly two stories above the stage floor, and Lemmon and Matthau were to slide through and land on a platform containing a huge mattress. The stars returned from lunch before most of the crew, and saw the laundry-chute setup. Matthau told Lemmon, "Let's try this out—I'll go first." Unfortunately, the platform had not yet been placed in the proper position. Matthau went down the chute, landed on the edge of the mattress, rolled backward and fell headfirst onto the stage. In a flash, Lemmon was by his side. Matthau was lying on his back, with his neck tilted to the side and his hand over his heart. "He was saying, over and over, 'Oh God, I'm dying, I'm dying,' and he meant it," Lemmon recalls. "I took my jacket off and very carefully I lifted his head, just to get it off the stage floor. You know, you're not aware of the silly things you may say. I put my coat under him and I said, 'Walter, are you comfortable?' And he said, 'I make a living.' I couldn't believe it."

"Did I break anything? Let me see," ponders Matthau when asked about the incident. "I fell down about eight feet and landed on my back and my head, on a concrete floor. I was hobbling around with crutches for about three weeks. I was in the hospital for three days. Nothing very serious, but very inconvenient." According to one published report, Matthau suffered a fractured collarbone and an impacted rib; a double performs the stunt in the finished film.

Matthau declares, "Even today, I say: Every time I work with Lemmon or Wilder, I get either a heart attack or double pneumonia or I break my elbow or I get an ulcer or I fall down and break my back. But it's just superstition, kidding around—like saying: I was using a Waterpik when I had my heart attack; therefore, I will never use a Waterpik again."

Accidents aside, Matthau could still be a handful on the set, picking apart his own work and that of his director. "I saw the original French picture," he says. "An actor named Lino Venturi [*sic*] played my role, and there's no way I could do it as well as he. He was very good. I maybe was thinking as I was doing it, I would like to do it like Lino Venturi. Maybe I was trying to imitate him. But I enjoyed the picture. I remember an argument I had with Billy. In the picture, I spoke with a faint New York Italian accent—like, 'Hello, Mr. Green. Dis is Mr. Brown. Lemme talk to Mr. White.' And then, there was a scene where I had to turn my collar around and pretend I was a priest, talking with an Irish accent. So I said to Billy: 'Billy, if this guy has got such a great Irish accent, how come he's not an actor? Why is he a hit man?' He said: 'Just say it!' He couldn't answer, see?"

For his part, Lemmon sensed that the working atmosphere had changed since the glory days of *Some Like It Hot* and *The Apartment.* "I did get the feeling after *Fortune Cookie*, starting around *Avanti!* and in *Buddy Buddy*, that Billy was pushing a little more. I may be wrong. But I felt that Billy was getting a little more didactic in his staging, trying to be a little more exact in what he wanted out of each scene, that there was a little less freedom for the actors. Whether that was conscious or unconscious, because he was trying to make it exactly right, I don't know—it may be this is only in my mind. But I felt it a little bit, and I think that Walter felt it."

THE MAIN PROBLEM WITH *BUDDY BUDDY* IS THAT IT JUST isn't very funny. Wilder may have seen some potential in the hardened-killer/innocent-shlemiel dynamic of the original, but the gimmick never blossoms into anything more resonant. Victor and Trabucco don't evolve over the course of the film, and Wilder and Diamond's attempts at social satire—a lamebrained hippie, the leering portrait of the sex institute—feel dated and strained. Edouard Molinaro's film at least had a core of realism—especially in the performance of Lino Ventura—that provided a satisfying counterpoint to the comedy. *Buddy Buddy* is artificial from the get-go, as it labors to take an *Odd Couple* situation to its furthest extreme.

To his credit, Matthau does his best to inhabit the part of Trabucco. Never cracking a smile or betraying any sentiment, he remains absolutely true to the demands of the character. The one element he's unable to control is the familiarity factor: No matter how hard he tries, he can't escape being Walter Matthau.

Lemmon, meantime, combines the neurosis of *The Odd Couple*'s Felix Ungar with the priggishness of *Avanti!*'s Wendell Armbruster, and the result feels less than fresh. The bright talent of comic actress Paula Prentiss is barely tapped in the role of Lemmon's ex-wife, while the intense German actor Klaus Kinski is woefully unfunny as the sex guru. Watching *Buddy Buddy* is a disheartening experience; now that Wilder characters can say the "f" word at will, the thrill of the battle is gone—and so is a great film-maker's inspiration.

Buddy Buddy opened on December 11, 1981, to mostly negative reviews, though some critics were kinder to the film than it really deserved. Vincent Canby found it "slight but irresistible" and "the lightest, breeziest comedy any one of them [Wilder, Lemmon or Matthau] has been associated with in years." In another puzzling pronouncement, the *New York Post*'s Archer Winsten called *Buddy Buddy* "an ingratiating throwback to the kind of pictures [Wilder, Diamond, Lemmon and Matthau] used to make." In *Time*, Richard Corliss said, "If Wilder's antique vehicle is no more than serviceable, it is ever at the service of two meticulous *farceurs*, and Lemmon and Matthau are never less than funny." In a review titled "Some Like It Not," *Newsweek*'s David Ansen found Wilder and Diamond's stabs at social commentary extremely dated but had high praise for Matthau's performance. *New York*'s David Denby also blanched at many of the gags, but noted, "Wilder and Diamond are so far out of touch that they sustain their own sour-stomached purity." Rex Reed, with his taste for overwrought metaphor, said the film "just lies there, like a dry goldfish gasping for oxygen on a nylon carpet," and that Lemmon and Matthau "both end up looking like squealing, sweating hysterics climbing the walls of a padded cell." Perhaps the most painful evaluation came from *Variety*, which declared, *"Buddy Buddy* is undoubtedly the weakest of Billy Wilder's twenty-five Hollywood pictures, a comedy of sustained mirthlessness." The opening blurb consisted of two words: "Duddy Duddy." *Variety*'s verdict was borne out by the box-office gross, an unimpressive $6 million.

During production, Lemmon had told *Variety*'s Army Archerd that *Buddy Buddy* was "the best comedy script I've read since *Some Like It Hot*." Later, in retrospect, he admitted the film "didn't work at all," likening it to a Broadway show done with top talent that closes in one night. "One wonders how so many talented and experienced people can all be so wrong at the same time about the same thing."

Wilder, meanwhile, speculated that the Lemmon–Matthau combination may not have been right for this particular project. "It was probably wrong to use two comedians," he noted. "After two weeks of shooting, I realized that the killer should have been cast with a hit man instead of a comic. With Clint Eastwood instead of Walter Matthau."

At the charity premiere of *Buddy Buddy* in Westwood, California, Wilder frankly discussed with a reporter from *Women's Wear Daily* the insecurities of a septuagenarian filmmaker in the new Hollywood: "Little did I know when I started in films that I was walking a tightrope over an abyss. Now I know how deep it is. I'm more apprehensive now than I was when I started." Undaunted, Wilder said he had several new projects in the works. "If I make another next summer," he declared, "I'll be happy. I like to make pictures after the Super Bowl and before the World Series." It's been fourteen summers since then, and Billy Wilder still talks of making another picture.

TWENTY-ONE

A Final Closeup

I HAVE ABSOLUTELY NO INTENTION OF RETIRING. AS FAR as I'm concerned, this here ball game is going into extra innings," Billy Wilder assured the black-tie audience at the Film Society of Lincoln Center tribute in his honor on May 3, 1982.

But Wilder also acknowledged that the ground rules were different from the ones he used to know. "Hollywood has changed a lot," he noted. "Today, half the people you run into are on their way to China to set up a coproduction deal, the other half are on their way to Cedars-Sinai for a quadruple bypass. As a matter of fact, the entire industry is in intensive care. So who do they call in to save the patient? Lawyers, agents, supermarket operators, soft-drink distributors—those are the people who decide what picture gets made and what doesn't. They approach it very scientifically—computer projections, marketing research, audience profiles—and they always come up with the same answer: 'Get Richard Pryor—he's hot this week.' The truth, of course, is that pictures are launched out of a gut feeling—and the prerequisite is that you have guts."

In Wilder's heyday, those gut decisions were usually made by one unpredictable, sometimes undereducated, but resolute mogul. Now, they're made by an amorphous mass of executives, and there's always the danger that, as Wilder says, "after a year and a half you have been kissing the wrong ass all along."

Wilder likens today's studio to a Ramada Inn: "You hire the sound-stage, the editing rooms and dubbing theaters, then you get out." Often manning the inn is a green-looking clerk; Wilder hates the idea of having to go in and sell his project to a young executive he may recognize as the former mailboy at the William Morris Agency.

Back in the studio era, Wilder insists, "We had more fun. We had, disposed over this here area, fiefdoms. There was the castle of Louis B. Mayer, there was Warner Brothers, Paramount was there on Melrose. We did not meet. We had families. I remember one day, I was having dinner with the wife of Bill Goetz, the daughter of Louis B. Mayer. And I told her, come Monday I've got to go to Berlin to do a picture called *One, Two, Three.* 'Who is in it?' she asked. I said, 'Jimmy Cagney.' And she said, 'Who? I don't know him.' And I said, 'What do you mean you don't know him?' [I explained who he was] and she told me, 'My father absolutely forbade us to look at any Warner Brothers pictures, because they were all about gangsters and about the ugly side of human behavior.' She truly did not know him."

Just as the studios have become one big blur of package deals, the larger world that Billy Wilder once knew has also been homogenized. "You go to London or Paris or Berlin," he says, "they have changed, and not for the better. I dream of it the way it was in 1930, but, especially now with the fax and the rapid method of traveling, the mystique of America—or of Europe for the Americans—has evaporated. There's almost nobody that I know who has not been in Europe—they know the hotels, they know the restaurants, they copy the Americans, the Americans copy the Japanese, blah, blah, blah. It's become one, flattened-out globe where people are all living almost the same way. It's not that big a contrast. When I met some-body from America when I was a newspaperman, it was a tremendous event for me, even if he was pretty stupid: 'This man, this man is an American!' "

The movies, too, have lost much of their mystique for Wilder. "Those ugly things that are very necessary and make people extremely rich—I'm talking about special effects—I can't do that, I can't direct car crashes," Wilder complains. "But slowly now, I have a feeling people are coming back to the content of a picture, to the exploration of a character a little bit more in depth. By this time, as far as plots are concerned, I think we're done. Now we're doing remakes. There's a picture of mine called *Double*

Indemnity—they remade it five times, but none of those is any better.* Why don't they show the original? Let them do the *Jurassic Park*s, that's fine. But with all those millions that they make, they should put a small sum aside and let talented people make pictures for a million or two million."

That sort of industry largesse isn't about to happen anytime soon. Neither is the kind of deal that will allow Billy Wilder the one condition he absolutely demands: final cut. After the failure of *Fedora* and *Buddy Buddy*, and the grumblings that Wilder was out of step with the times, the right of final cut is likely the biggest sticking point that has kept the director in forced retirement since 1981.

Wilder and Diamond continued to write after *Buddy Buddy*, working on feature ideas that Wilder has always refused to divulge. Of all the lost opportunities, one stands out. "I was very much interested in doing *Schindler's List*," Wilder reveals, "for the reason that most of my family died in Auschwitz. But I could not get to the property because Universal had already bought it for Mr. Spielberg, and that was good enough for me. He did a great, wonderful picture. That was the one I was going to end my career with, but it did not come to be."

Probably the closest Wilder came to getting a new film off the ground was in early 1986, when Jerry Weintraub, the flamboyant new chairman of United Artists, invited him to be a special consultant and gave him a large office at the company. Wilder's assignment was to advise young filmmakers signed by UA, and to develop his own material for possible production. But UA's Oscar-winning alumnus was shocked by the quality of the material Weintraub was bringing in and the films he had inherited from the previous administration. In his book, *Fade Out: The Calamitous Final Days of MGM*, Peter Bart reports on a rough-cut screening Wilder and Weintraub attended of one such film, Brian De Palma's mobster comedy *Wise Guys*. When the lights came up, the UA chair turned to his adviser for suggestions. Blunt as ever, Wilder announced, "This picture is a big pile of shit. Perhaps I could tell you how to make it into a smaller pile of shit, but it would still be shit!" Wilder's tenure at the new UA was short-lived.

Wilder summoned as much optimism as he could for the future of the

---

* Though *Double Indemnity* has been much imitated, it was literally remade only once, as a 1973 TV movie.

Hollywood movie when he was awarded the fourteenth annual American Film Institute Life Achievement Award that March (following the Directors Guild's D. W. Griffith Award for lifetime achievement the previous year). Noting the rise of sophisticated new technologies, he declared, "Someday, somebody is going to press a button and send a signal to a satellite which in turn will light up five million screens, all the way from Albania to Zanzibar. All the hardware is there, beautifully programmed. Bravo! Except for one little detail. What about the software? What are we going to *do* on all those screens? Who is going to write it? Who is going to direct it? Who is going to act it? For all I know, these wise guys are trying right now to supplant the human factor, [with] microchips that will replace the human brain and the human heart. Mechanical gadgets that can simulate emotions, dreams, laughter, tears. Well, so far they have not succeeded—not yet, anyway. So relax, fellow picturemakers. We are not expendable. The fact is, the bigger they get, the more irreplaceable *we* become. For theirs may be the kingdom, but ours is the power and the glory."

Wilder also took the opportunity to pay tribute to departed colleagues—Ernst Lubitsch, Arthur Hornblow, Charles Brackett, Doane Harrison and Harold Mirisch—and faces that were gone but not forgotten. "Gary Cooper. William Holden. Ty Power. Gloria Swanson. Humphrey Bogart. Erich von Stroheim. Marilyn Monroe. Eddie Robinson. Maurice Chevalier. Charles Laughton. Man, what a picture He could cast up there—with a score by Beethoven, naturally, and sets by Michelangelo, and additional dialogue by W. Shakespeare.

"And, of course," he added, "ultimately it will all wind up in a turnaround."

Jack Lemmon, the evening's lively host, risked his friendship by imitating the honoree's accent (always a sore point with Wilder) and cataloguing the unusual number of heart attacks and accidents connected with the director's films. "I cannot tell you how pleased I am to *be* here tonight!" Lemmon joked, as Wilder gave an embarrassed shrug.

Audrey Hepburn, Walter Matthau, Ginger Rogers, Jimmy Stewart, Fred MacMurray, Tony Curtis and Carol Burnett all saluted their director, and I. A. L. Diamond brought down the house with the line, "This business has come a long way . . . but why should I depress you?" Representatives of the new Hollywood like Steven Spielberg and Sylvester Stallone were present that night, and Whoopi Goldberg and Jessica Lange both swore that they'd love to star in the next Billy Wilder picture.

No one stepped forward that night with the backing for such a movie, but the honors and awards kept coming. In the spring of 1988, before a worldwide television audience, Jack Lemmon presented to Wilder the Academy of Motion Picture Arts and Sciences's prestigious Irving G. Thalberg Memorial Award for "consistent high quality of production." Wilder's salute to the Mexicali customs official who permitted his return to Hollywood was a highlight of the evening, and he ended his speech with a personal message: "I hope you're watching, I. A. L., because part of this is yours. So get well, will you?"

I. A. L. Diamond had been diagnosed with multiple myeloma—a cancer of the bone marrow—four years earlier, but hadn't told Wilder about his illness until about a month before the Oscar telecast, when he became too sick to work. On April 21, 1988, just ten days after the Academy Awards ceremony, Wilder lost his partner of three decades. "It was a tremendous sledgehammer blow," Wilder says. A few days after the memorial service, the director told writer Howard Rodman, "He used to sit in that chair there, the Eames chair. Raymond Chandler said in one of his books, 'Nothing is as empty as an empty swimming pool.' Well, nothing is as empty as this Eames chair right now.

"The way we had plotted this script, the script about our lives, was that being twelve or fourteen years older, I was supposed to go first. And, as you see, that didn't happen."

Diamond also may have supplied more edge to the partnership than many people realized. "The person who was really cynical and really had a jaundiced view of the world was my husband," says his widow. "A lot of things that Billy had to apologize for were things that came rolling out of Iz's mouth. Iz was absolutely, completely honest, and absolutely, completely intolerant of all the little accommodations to truth and integrity that people make."

If getting a new film off the ground had been a struggle before, now it was doubly hard. "Diamond was, in the words of my beloved wife, the world's greatest collaborator, with the possible exception of Quisling," Wilder declares. The director still tells journalists he wants to make another picture, but without Diamond his determination isn't nearly as strong. "He is absolutely irreplaceable," Wilder laments. "I don't know anybody now that I would like to work with."

Working without a collaborator, at this stage in his life, is a challenge. "I started the idea of collaborating when I first arrived in America, because I could not speak the language. I needed somebody who was responsible, who had some idea of how a picture is constructed. Then I found out that it's *nice* to have a collaborator—you're not writing into a vacuum, especially if he's sensitive and ambitious to create a product of some value."

WILDER CONTINUES TO DEVELOP FILM IDEAS ON HIS OWN, and he still maintains a small second-floor office on Brighton Way, in the heart of the Beverly Hills shopping district. Original prints by Ellsworth Kelly and Frank Stella adorn the walls. A bookcase holds his six Oscars and copies of his screenplays, bound in leather. Wilder answers his own phone and works at a large desk strewn with papers, correspondence and all kinds of tantalizing memorabilia. Behind his head is an amusing photo of the director from 1958, chugging along the train platform from *Some Like It Hot*, doing his best imitation of Marilyn Monroe's hurried wiggle.

The artworks in Wilder's office merely scratch the surface of his massive holdings. The filmmaker's collecting mania began in childhood with buttons, stamps and coins, and blossomed during his ghostwriting period in Berlin when he bought a poster by Toulouse-Lautrec for the equivalent of eight dollars. Other posters and lithographs followed, all left behind in his flight from Germany. Once he and Charles Brackett enjoyed their first success, the bug bit him again—he replaced his collection of Toulouse-Lautrec posters, and bought his first drawing by Picasso for $900. Before long, Wilder was part of the elite Hollywood circle of art connoisseurs.

"Josef von Sternberg had a wonderful collection, including some great German painters," Wilder recalls. "I got very friendly with Sternberg—I discussed art with him for hours and hours. Then, of course, there was Eddie Robinson. There were quite a few collectors. I caught on rather early, thank God, and as my salary went up a bit, I started buying better paintings and swapping paintings."

According to Wilder, "There were very few dealers in Los Angeles then. When I was on location in New York or Paris or London, I would always pick up something. Days we weren't working, I would go on a buying spree fourteen hours a day. I bought a George Grosz painting for a carton of cigarettes in 1945."

The Wilder collection mushroomed, with works by Picasso, Matisse, Renoir, Klee, Miró, Léger, Braque, Dufy, Dubuffet, Rouault, Camille Pissarro, Schiele, Klimt and Kirchner; sculptures by Giacometti, Calder and Henry Moore; box constructions by Joseph Cornell; pieces by modern masters like David Hockney, Saul Steinberg, Larry Rivers, Balthus, Wayne Thiebaud and Milton Avery; plus a wide-ranging selection of pre-Columbian and African sculpture, French primitives, Roman busts, bentwood furniture, Tiffany lamps, patent models and assorted *tchotchkes.* "I don't call myself a collector," Wilder once said. "I call myself an accumulator."

Over the years, the "accumulator" had made some remarkably astute purchases. He discovered Joseph Cornell before most of the world did, and picked up some of his oddly evocative boxes for a song. In Paris in the fifties, he was viewing a Miró exhibition at the Galerie Maeght when he accidentally broke a glass case; to mollify the owner, he offered to buy a Giacometti nude for a thousand dollars—several decades later, the sculpture sold for a million.

Since 1959, Billy and Audrey had been living in a roomy twelfth-story apartment on Wilshire Boulevard near Westwood, and after thirty years their home was literally wall-to-wall art. Nearly every available wall space showcased a masterwork, and if you weren't careful, a Calder mobile might poke you in the eye. Paintings and posters were stacked upright in the hallways, the closets were stuffed with art, and the overflow was sent to a storage facility. Audrey had learned to live with her husband's obsession, but there *were* limits: Sometimes, Billy would drive around for weeks with a valuable new acquisition in the trunk of his car before daring to bring it up to the apartment.

Then one night, according to Wilder, "while making my way to the can, I stumbled over a Henry Moore bronze and right smack into a de Staël oil. While they were applying a splint to my big toe, I decided right then and there to get rid of everything I had. Everything absolutely unnecessary."

In another version of the story, Wilder explained, "I wanted to test my willpower. I kept reading about those fantastic sales, those incredible prices. So one day I said to my wife, 'Let me call their bluff.' "

The result was the great Wilder auction of 1989. Samples of the collection were exhibited in Paris, Geneva, Zurich and Tokyo, and a more comprehensive showing was held for two days in September at the Beverly Hills Hotel in Los Angeles, attracting scores of the celebrated and the curious. On November 13, ninety-four works were put up for sale at Christie's in New York, including Wilder's most valued acquisition, Picasso's *Head of a Woman*, a 1921 pastel of the artist's first wife, Olga Koklova. The collection was particularly notable for its many female nudes (including several explicit Egon Schiele watercolors) and for its smart eclecticism, covering a wide range of twentieth-century movements.

In interviews at the time, Wilder gave more reasons why he was selling off so many of his holdings. "A collection needs to grow with the times, or it becomes like an old suit—you love it, but the moths have eaten it. It needed new stuff. Unfortunately, I found things I desperately wanted, but today there is an additional zero at the end of the price. Besides, you know the cliché about being possessed by possessions. We worried that the people in the apartment above ours would let the bathtub overflow. And insurance—I don't have to tell you. I felt I needed a liberation from responsibility."

On another occasion, Wilder was more blunt about the matter. "I'm sick of watching all my friends die and their art auctioned off much to the delight of their heirs. This way, my heirs will get the money, but I'll get the laughs."

Wilder had plenty of reason to laugh that day at Christie's: The collection brought in an astounding $32.6 million. The only disappointment was the Picasso; with an estimated value of $7 million, it sold for a mere $4.8 million. Two Mirós went for more than $2.5 million apiece, and record prices were set for twelve artists, including $2 million for Balthus's *La Toilette*, the near life-sized nude of a pubescent girl that had formerly hung in Wilder's bedroom. In all, the director found the event "less nerve-racking than a film preview."

Wilder's timing was exquisite: Not only did he sell at the height of the market, but he was saved the anguish of seeing his most valuable pieces threatened by a major early-morning fire that erupted in his fourteen-story apartment building just before Christmas. Audrey smelled the smoke first, and Billy jokes that she made sure to pack up her jewelry before waking him to leave. Four hundred firefighters fought the blaze for more than four hours, and 150 people were evacuated from the building and surrounding homes. Billy's remaining artworks—and Audrey's jewelry—were unharmed.

Over the years, Wilder has become close friends with a number of celebrated artists—including the late Charles Eames, David Hockney and Saul Steinberg. According to Hockney, he and Wilder could talk for hours "about pictures, all kinds: stills, moving, painted, drawn, collaged. His sharp eye doesn't miss much; he knows that form and content are one." As for Wilder's critiques of films, Hockney finds them "subtle and . . . very amusing, especially of the ones he hasn't seen."

Wilder himself has something of a second career as an artist, collaborating on whimsical pieces that strike his imagination. With the artist Richard Saar, he executed a series of zany sculptures including *Stallone's Typewriter*, an old Underwood done up in camouflage colors, with an American-flag roller, keys painted with red, white and blue stars, and rifle shells where the shift keys should be. In December 1993, the Louis Stern Gallery, just a few doors down from the filmmaker's office, presented "Billy Wilder's Marché aux Puces," an exhibition featuring more works for sale from Wilder's ever growing collection. Alongside playful works by Steinberg, Hockney and Botero and paintings by Picasso, Rouault and Utrillo, the "Marché" spotlighted new pieces conceived by Wilder and executed by Palm Springs artist Bruce Houston. The centerpiece of the show was Wilder and Houston's *Variations on the Theme of Queen Nefertete II*, small plaster busts of the Egyptian queen encased in Plexiglas: Nefertete as Einstein, Nefertete as Groucho Marx, a fat Botero Nefertete, a wiry Modigliani Nefertete, a Warhol Nefertete with a Campbell's Soup headpiece, Nefertetes done in the styles of Matisse, Picasso, Dubuffet. "The whole idea is to have fun," Wilder said of his debut as a curator/artist.

As Wilder moved deeper into his eighties, his awards and honors seemed to increase exponentially. In December 1990, he joined Katharine Hepburn, Dizzy Gillespie, soprano Risë Stevens and composer

Jule Styne at the White House, as part of the annual Kennedy Center Honors tribute to great Americans in the performing arts. The following year, he was the recipient of the Writers Guild of America West/Directors Guild of America's first annual Preston Sturges Award and the subject of a thirty-five-film retrospective at New York's premier repertory film theater, Film Forum. A less formal honor came from critic Andrew Sarris, who, in a public mea culpa in *Film Comment*, declared that Wilder belonged in his personal pantheon of Hollywood directors, and not the demeaning "Less Than Meets the Eye" category of old.

In 1992, it was the European Film Academy's turn to present their native son with a Lifetime Achievement Award; the next year, Wilder traveled to Germany to accept the Berlin Film Festival's Golden Bear for Lifetime Achievement, an award he was originally supposed to collect at the festival's extensive 1980 Wilder retrospective. That fall, it was back to the White House, as President Bill Clinton presented Wilder with the National Medal of Arts, in a ceremony also honoring cultural figures like Arthur Miller, Ray Charles, William Styron, Robert Rauschenberg and Cab Calloway. The year ended with the first Lifetime Achievement Award in Screenwriting from PEN, the professional writers' association.

The tributes continued to flow. At the 1994 Academy Awards ceremony, Spanish director Fernando Trueba, in accepting the foreign-language Oscar for his film *Belle Epoque*, noted that he "would like to believe in God so that I could thank him, but I just believe in Billy Wilder—so thank you, Billy Wilder." "I wish he hadn't said that," the director reacted. "People start crossing themselves when they see me."

Later that spring, Wilder returned to Vienna to be feted at an official dinner by Austrian Chancellor Franz Vranitzky, who said he hoped his guest would come to know "a new Austria." Wilder charmed the chancellor by telling him he had a movie role for him if he were interested.

By early 1995, the veteran filmmaker was virtually drowning in encomiums: the Los Angeles Film Critics' Career Achievement Award, a fellowship from the British Academy of Film and Television Arts, and the National Board of Review's first annual Billy Wilder Award for lifetime achievement in directing.

Wilder garnered yet more attention from the London, Los Angeles and New York openings of *Sunset Boulevard*, Andrew Lloyd Webber's $13 million musical extravaganza. Two other Wilder classics had been reworked as Broadway musicals: *The Apartment* became Burt Bacharach's *Promises, Promises* in 1968, and *Some Like It Hot* turned into *Sugar* in 1973. But *Sunset Boulevard* was an event, the latest undertaking by the British composer/showman responsible for the boundlessly successful *Cats* and *The Phantom of the Opera*, among other international smashes.

Back in the mid-1950s, Gloria Swanson had developed her own musical of Wilder's film (with a happy ending!), but the project died when Paramount refused to grant permission for the stage show. (A recording of the score survives at the University of Texas's Swanson archives.) Lloyd Webber's version had been in the works since the mid-1970s, and gathered momentum in the early nineties. In the summer of 1992, the composer sent Wilder a courtesy copy of the musical's book, adapted by playwright and Oscar-winning screenwriter Christopher Hampton. Wilder wrote back to Lloyd Webber, "I think you did a marvelous job. Let me congratulate you on a very ingenious idea: You left the original script alone, you did not try to *improve* it."

Amazingly, even though much of Wilder and Brackett's original dialogue remains in the show, Wilder does not make a cent from *Sunset Boulevard* the musical; Paramount owns the property outright. "Do not worry about the financial recompense for the guys who made the original movie," Wilder told Lloyd Webber in the same letter. "I know those power people at Paramount, as well as in the other studios. They have their pockets made of rubber—so they can steal soup."

A few months before the show's July 1993 London premiere, writer Stephen M. Silverman caught Wilder in a prickly mood. "I'm just going to sit back," he said of the hoopla. "If it's terrific, I say, 'Well, of course. It was based on a very good picture.' If it stinks, I say, 'Now, you see how people can fuck it up?'" Of Lloyd Webber's craft, Wilder opined, "I'm not saying he writes great music. He'll have one good song: tra-la-le-de-la-da. One song. He provides a whole special atmosphere, a kind of magic for enveloping you. That's originality. People pay for that."

Billy and Audrey attended the London opening with Nancy Olson and her husband, Alan Livingston, and the creator of Norma Desmond seemed genuinely touched. "We had tears in our eyes," he told Army Archerd. "Remember, we had patterned the young girl after Audrey. It was a very sentimental journey. I was thinking back forty-five years—to be alive to see the play, it was like seeing old friends." In all, Wilder pronounced the show "a very lush, a very well-done production."

The show received mixed reviews in London, as it later did in Los Angeles and New York. But Lloyd Webber appeared to have another block-buster. Prior to the Los Angeles opening, the composer and his team re-vised and streamlined the show, incorporating some suggestions made by Wilder himself. With Glenn Close starring as Norma Desmond, *Sunset Boulevard* was an L.A. sensation, but abruptly ended its run there when Lloyd Webber rejected Close's replacement, Faye Dunaway. The com-poser also bruised the ego of the London star, Patti LuPone, by reversing his original plan to have her play Norma Desmond in New York and opting for Close instead.

Sunset Boulevard made its New York debut on November 17, 1994, to the largest advance sale in Broadway history: $37.5 million. Over the course of Glenn Close's run, this deeply flawed show proved critic-proof. The production is undeniably sumptuous, but Lloyd Webber's score—with the exception of two effective ballads—is clunky. Close, during her tenure, held the stage, but her big, Kabuki-like performance was closer to Carol Burnett than Gloria Swanson. As for Alan Campbell's white-bread Joe Gillis, the less said the better. The not-so-secret ingredient powering *Sun-set Boulevard*'s success is Wilder's original story—the shooting of Joe Gillis can still elicit gasps from a 1990s audience.

Sunset Boulevard is not the only Wilder retread currently on view. Late 1995 brought a new Paramount version of *Sabrina* (again, Wilder says, without any recompense), directed by Sydney Pollack, with Harrison Ford in the Humphrey Bogart role, newcomer Julia Ormond filling in for Au-drey Hepburn, and talk-show host Greg Kinnear (!) in the shadow of Wil-liam Holden. A new version of *Love in the Afternoon* is also in the works. "Right now I'm king of the remakes," Wilder boasts.

Thanks to new venues like cable "classic-movie" networks, videocas-settes and laser discs, the Wilder originals are more visible than ever. Even some of the late films, pictures like *The Private Life of Sherlock Holmes*, *Avanti!* and *Fedora*, are gathering their cults. "Yes, I have a very small cult of admirers," the put-upon director joked around the time of *Fedora*. "One of these days I will take them to Guyana. . . ."

"LONG BEFORE BILLY WILDER WAS BILLY WILDER, HE BE-
haved as though he were Billy Wilder," Audrey once said, by way of
explaining her husband's sometimes abrupt manner. Wilder can still intimidate, and he still has a justifiably strong ego, but there's also a gentle, self-
mocking side to this Hollywood giant that people don't always see.

"This is what happened to me," he swears, "on a rainy evening outside
the Spago restaurant. There are always autograph hounds, with the autograph book and the camera and the fountain pen that does not write. One
rainy night, there were very few people, and one of them came up to me
and said: 'Mr. Wilder, I would like an autograph. As a matter of fact, I'd
like three of your autographs.' 'Why three?' He says, 'Because for three
Wilders I can get one Spielberg!' "

Interviewed near his eighty-ninth birthday, Billy Wilder again shows
how sharp, funny—and gracious—he can be. "I have a little inner-ear
infection," he confides. "Vertigo. And vertigo without Kim Novak is
nothing."

Even with vertigo, Wilder's wit never fails him. But behind the humor,
there's always another, more complex mechanism operating. "Deep down,
Billy is quite serious," declares his friend and contemporary, director Fred
Zinnemann. "It's just that he doesn't like to show it too often. But those
funny films of his, if you stop and think about it, have a great deal of
meaning in contemporary terms. I think he was an enormously important
influence."

"He really is like an older brother and a father—part father, part older
brother," says Jack Lemmon of his relationship with Wilder. "What I've
learned from him goes so far beyond just film or acting or writing and
directing—it's about living, about values, about art. I mean, this man has
interests, he's got antennae out for everything under the sun, not just
his work. He's broadened my horizons a great deal, far beyond just
film."

As anyone who's ever tried to pin down Billy Wilder for an interview
can attest, he continues to be quick, restless, actively engaged with the
world. Making films was a way of channeling all that energy and intellectual
curiosity, and those films just happened to change an industry. "Every
picture's a new adventure," he says, and if time and a fickle movie business

have conspired to rob him of new adventures, it's more our loss than his. Wilder has seen Hollywood from the bottom up, like Joe Gillis, and from the top down, like Norma Desmond—but unlike his two tragic players, he's survived with his wits and his renown intact. Rich and rewarding as his motion-picture legacy is, Billy Wilder will always be his own greatest creation.

ACKNOWLEDGMENTS

BILLY WILDER INITIALLY DECLINED TO PARTICIPATE IN this new book on his life and his films, but from the very first minute of our first meeting, he was extraordinarily kind, gracious and full of lively opinions and memories. Looking at least a decade younger than his age, the still energetic Hollywood legend greeted me at the door of his Beverly Hills office and immediately put me at ease. "It's good that we met," he said, two hours later, "because I may be a little less bellicose—or whatever you want to call it—than people have made me out to be."

Although he has not authorized this critical biography, Mr. Wilder was tremendously cooperative, making time for me during my visits to Los Angeles and offering an open invitation for follow-up phone interviews. Without his courtesy and generosity, this book would not have been possible.

I was also fortunate to secure interviews with a number of Mr. Wilder's greatest surviving stars. Jack Lemmon, one of the director's closest friends and collaborators, proved every bit as warm and engaging as his public image, and another Wilder buddy, Walter Matthau, was playfully gruff and entertaining. Shirley MacLaine, Tony Curtis and Kirk Douglas all offered sharp insights, and I enjoyed delightful interviews with such stellar Wilder players as Horst Buchholz, Pamela (Tiffin) Danon, the late Tom Ewell,

Felicia (Farr) Lemmon, Nancy (Olson) Livingston, Cliff Osmond and Frances Sternhagen.

Barbara Diamond, the widow of Mr. Wilder's longtime writing partner I. A. L. Diamond, welcomed me into her home and provided a rare, intimate view of the dynamics of one of Hollywood's great screenwriting teams. Veteran writer-producer Ernest Lehman, Billy Wilder's writing partner on *Sabrina*, was also helpful and generous beyond measure. I was privileged to speak with two of Mr. Wilder's great filmmaking contemporaries, both extremely giving of their time: Oscar-winning director Fred Zinnemann and horror-genre master Curt Siodmak. It was also a special treat to talk with two superb cinematographers: Hollywood veteran Charles Lang and British lensman Christopher Challis.

Two members of Billy Wilder's "inner circle" deserve my special gratitude. Irene Heymann of the Paul Kohner Agency gently cleared the way toward my first meeting with the formidable director, and Mr. Wilder's assistant, Steve Forleo, provided keen insights and enthusiastic support.

In Berlin, Wolfgang Jacobsen and Gero Gandert at the Stiftung Deutsche Kinemathek offered kind encouragement and valuable leads, and I am indebted to the Kinemathek's Rosemarie van der Zee, Walther Seidler, Eva Orbanz and the entire library and archive staff for providing research materials and allowing me to view several rare films co-written by Billy Wilder in Germany. I saw even more Wilder-scripted films at Berlin's Bundesarchiv Filmarchiv, and my thanks go to Dr. Holgar Theuerkauf and his staff for their many courtesies. I'm also grateful to Volker Schlöndorff, the film director and head of Germany's Babelsberg Studios, for kindly supplying me with a video copy of the marvelous series of interviews he conducted with Mr. Wilder in the late 1980s.

In Los Angeles, Sam Gill, Fay Thompson and the helpful staff of the Academy of Motion Picture Arts and Sciences' Margaret Herrick Library provided extremely valuable script, production and Production Code materials from Mr. Wilder's Hollywood films. Thanks also to Ned Comstock and the staff of the University of Southern California's Cinema/TV Library for guiding me to some very useful Wilder-related holdings.

In New York, the staff of the Billy Rose Theatre Collection at the Library of the Performing Arts unearthed many important materials, including several obscure play scripts that inspired Wilder movies; special thanks go to my friend and colleague David Bartholomew for putting up with all my small but vital requests. Charles Silver at the Museum of Modern Art's Film Study Center was patient and helpful, as were Mary Corliss and Terry Geesken in the Department of Film's Stills Collection. At the Film Society of Lincoln Center, Wendy Keys very kindly took the time to show me a recording of the society's 1982 tribute to Billy Wilder.

Thanks to Ben Brewster of the State Historical Society in Madison, Wisconsin, for providing access to its United Artists Collection, and to the staff of the British Film Institute in London for maintaining such an indispensable film-research library. I am also indebted to Stacy Bias and David Pfeiffer of the National Archives in Washington, D.C., for providing a treasure trove of documents related to Billy Wilder's duties with the U.S. Army's Psychological Warfare Division in Germany.

I am very grateful to Bob and Jimmy Sunshine, publishers of *The Film Journal*, for their warm encouragement and for allowing me both the space and the time to devote to my first book. Loving thanks go to my mother, Helen Lally, for her unwavering support, and to the rest of the Lally family.

A very special thank-you to four of my closest friends, all of whom contributed more to this project than they know. Cole Gagne brought his boundless film knowledge and sharp editing skills to his reading of my manuscript, helping me avoid some foolish gaffes while keeping my morale lifted high. Ed Kelleher enthusiastically supported this venture from day one, and suffered my constant barrage of Wilderiana with patience and humor. John Loughery's friendship, guidance and example were key to the very existence of this book. And Robert Sheff (aka "Blue" Gene Tyranny) not only proved a meticulous translator, but took a deep and lively interest in the subject matter.

The energy and exuberance of my agent, Faith Hamlin, are a wonder to behold, and I am deeply grateful to my editor, Cynthia Vartan, for her acuity and patience, her much needed encouragement and her enthusiasm for the work of Billy Wilder.

For advice, support and favors large and small, my gratitude also goes to Alessandra Bocco, Charlotte Brown at UCLA, film historian and lecturer Richard Brown, Frank de Falco and Vicki Feldman, Donna Dickman, Marjorie Ewell, Bruce Feld, Film Forum programmer extraordinaire Bruce

Goldstein, David Graham, Chris Grunden, Harry Haun, Jeff Hill at Clein + White, Leonard Hirshan at the William Morris Agency, Don Kelleher, Bill Kenly, Rebecca Lieb, John Littell, Connie McCauley at Jalem Productions, Maitland McDonagh, Jim McHugh, Howard Mandelbaum and the staff of Photofest, Jonathan Marder, Phyllis Mayes, Myron Meisel, Sheryl Miller, the staff of the Newtown Theatre, Arthur Neuhauser, David Noh, Dale C. Olson, Etain O'Malley, Tom Orefice, Teresa Park, Beth Porter, Allen Reuben of Culver Pictures, Cynthia Rose, Michael Riordan, Juliet Rozsa, Thelma Schoonmaker-Powell, Ingrid Schieb-Rothbart of Goethe House, Fred Specktor at Creative Artists Agency, John Springer, the staff of the Louis Stern Gallery, Paige Taylor, Doris Toumarkine, Jennifer Walsh, Wendy Weinstein and Peter Wood.

Wilder Times also owes thanks to the groundbreaking work of previous Wilder biographers and interviewers, particularly the late Maurice Zolotow, Hellmuth Karasek, Volker Schlöndorff and Andreas Hutter.

A final additional thank-you must go to Billy Wilder for the sheer pleasure his films have provided over countless viewings. From celebrated classics like *Some Like It Hot, Sunset Boulevard* and *Double Indemnity*, to overlooked gems like *A Foreign Affair, Kiss Me, Stupid* and *The Private Life of Sherlock Holmes*, his body of work is the truest inspiration behind *Wilder Times*.

FILMOGRAPHY

AS WRITER

Der Teufelsreporter (*The Daredevil Reporter*) (Deutsch Universalfilm Verleih, 1929): Directed by Ernst Laemmle. Written by BW. Cast: Eddie Polo, Gritta Ley, Robert Garrison.

Menschen am Sonntag (*People on Sunday*) (Steinfilm GmbH, 1930): Directed by Robert Siodmak. Screenplay by BW, from an idea by Curt Siodmak. Produced by Moritz Seeler. Photography: Eugen Schüfftan. Assistant directors: Fred Zinnemann, Edgar G. Ulmer. Cast: Brigitte Borchert, Christl Ehlers, Erwin Splettstösser, Wolfgang von Waltershausen, Annie Schreyer.

Der Mann, der seinen Mörder sucht (*The Man Who Looked for His Murderer*) (UFA, 1931): Directed by Robert Siodmak. Screenplay by BW, Curt Siodmak, Ludwig Hirschfeld, based on the play by Ernst Neubach. Produced by Erich Pommer. Music by Friedrich Holländer. Cast: Heinz Rühmann, Lien Dreyers, Raymund Janitschek.

Ihre Hoheit befiehlt (*Her Majesty Commands*) (UFA, 1931): Directed by Hanns Schwarz. Screenplay by BW, Paul Frank, Robert Liebmann. Cast: Willy Fritsch, Käthe von Nagy, Reinhold Schünzel. [U.S. remake: *Adorable* (Fox, 1933): Directed by William Dieterle. Screenplay by George Marion Jr., Jane Storm. Cast: Janet Gaynor, Henri Garat.]

Seitensprünge (*Extramarital Escapade*) (UFA, 1931): Directed by Stefan Székely. Screenplay by Ludwig Biro, B. E. Luthge, Karl Noti, from an idea by BW. Produced by Joe Pasternak. Cast: Oskar Sima, Gerda Maurus, Paul Vincenti, Jarmila Marton, Otto Wallburg.

Der falsche Ehemann (*The Counterfeit Husband*) (UFA, 1931): Directed by Johannes Guter. Screenplay by BW, Paul Frank. Cast: Johannes Riemann, Maria Paudler, Gustav Waldau, Jessie Vihrog.

Emil und die Detektive (*Emil and the Detectives*) (UFA, 1931): Directed by Gerhard Lamprecht. Screenplay by BW, based on the novel by Erich Kästner. Cast: Fritz Rasp, Rolf Wenkhaus, Käte Haack, Inge Landgut.

Es war einmal ein Walzer (*Once There Was a Waltz*) (AAFA, 1932): Directed by Viktor Janson. Screenplay by BW. Music by Franz Lehár. Cast: Marta Eggerth, Rolf von Goth, Ernst Verebes.

Ein blonder Traum (*A Blonde Dream*) (UFA, 1932): Directed by Paul Martin. Screenplay by BW, Walter Reisch. Produced by Erich Pommer. Cast: Lilian Harvey, Willy Fritsch, Willi Forst, Paul Hörbiger.

Scampolo, ein Kind der Strasse (*Scampolo, a Girl of the Street*) (Bayerische Filmgesellschaft, 1932): Directed by Hans Steinhoff. Screenplay by BW, Max Kolpe, based on the play by Dario Niccodemi. Produced by Lothar Stark. Music by Franz Wachsmann. Cast: Dolly Haas, Karl Ludwig Diehl, Oskar Sima, Paul Hörbiger.

Das Blaue vom Himmel (*The Blue from the Sky*) (AAFA, 1932): Directed by Viktor Janson. Screenplay by BW, Max Kolpe. Cast: Marta Eggerth, Hermann Thimig, Ernst Verebes.

Madame wünscht keine Kinder (*Madame Wants No Children*) (Europa Filmverleih, 1933): Directed by Hans Steinhoff. Screenplay by BW, Max Kolpe, based on the novel by Clement Vautel. Produced by Lothar Stark. Cast: Georg Alexander, Liane Haid, Erika Glässner.

Was Frauen träumen (*What Women Dream*) (Bayerische Filmgesellschaft, 1933): Directed by Geza von Bolvary. Screenplay by BW, Franz Schulz. Cast: Nora Gregor, Gustav Fröhlich, Kurt Horwitz, Peter Lorre. [U.S. remake: *One Exciting Adventure* (Universal, 1934): Directed by Ernst L. Frank. Screenplay by William Hurlbut, William B. Jutte. Cast: Binnie Barnes, Neil Hamilton, Eugene Pallette.]

Music in the Air (Fox, 1934): Directed by Joe May. Screenplay by BW, Howard I. Young, based on the operetta by Oscar Hammerstein II, Jerome Kern. Produced by Erich Pommer. Cast: Gloria Swanson, John Boles, Douglass Montgomery, June Lang, Al Shean, Reginald Owen.

Lottery Lover (Fox, 1935): Directed by William Thiele. Screenplay by BW, Franz Schulz, from a story by Siegfried M. Herzig, Maurice Hanline. Produced by Al Rockett. Cast: Lew Ayres, Pat Paterson, Peggy Fears, Sterling Holloway.

Champagne Waltz (Paramount, 1937): Directed by A. Edward Sutherland. Screenplay by Frank Butler, Don Hartman, based on a story by BW, H. S. Kraft. Produced by Harlan Thompson. Cast: Fred MacMurray, Gladys Swarthout, Jack Oakie.

Bluebeard's Eighth Wife (Paramount, 1938): Produced and directed by Ernst Lubitsch. Screenplay by BW, Charles Brackett, from the play by Alfred Savoir. Cinematography: Leo Tover. Music by Frederick Hollander. Cast: Claudette Colbert, Gary Cooper, Edward Everett Horton, David Niven, Elizabeth Patterson, Herman Bing.

Midnight (Paramount, 1939): Directed by Mitchell Leisen. Screenplay by BW, Brackett, from a story by Edwin Justus Mayer, Franz Schulz. Produced by Arthur Hornblow Jr. Cinematography: Charles B. Lang Jr. Edited by Doane Harrison. Music by Frederick Hollander. Cast: Claudette Colbert, Don Ameche, John Barrymore, Mary Astor, Francis Lederer, Hedda Hopper, Rex O'Malley, Elaine Barrie, Monty Woolley. [Remade by Leisen as *Masquerade in Mexico*, 1945.]

What a Life (Paramount, 1939): Directed by Jay Theodore Reed. Screenplay by BW, Brackett, based on the play by Clifford Goldsmith. Cinematography: Victor Milner. Cast: Jackie Cooper, Betty Field, John Howard, Janice Logan, Lionel Stander, Hedda Hopper.

Ninotchka (MGM, 1939): Directed by Ernst Lubitsch. Screenplay by BW, Brackett, Walter Reisch, from a story by Melchior Lengyel. Cinematography: William Daniels. Cast: Greta Garbo, Melvyn Douglas, Ina Claire, Bela Lugosi, Sig Ruman, Felix Bressart, Alexander Granach. [Remade as the musical *Silk Stockings*, 1957.]

Rhythm on the River (Paramount, 1940): Directed by Victor Schertzinger. Screenplay by Dwight Taylor, from a story by BW, Jacques Théry. Produced by William LeBaron. Cinematography: Ted Tetzlaff. Cast: Bing Crosby, Mary Martin, Basil Rathbone, Oscar Levant, William Frawley.

Arise, My Love (Paramount, 1940): Directed by Mitchell Leisen. Screenplay by BW, Brackett, from a story by Benjamin Glazer, John S. Toldy. Adaptation by Jacques Théry. Produced by Arthur Hornblow Jr. Cinematography: Charles B. Lang Jr. Edited by Doane Harrison. Cast: Claudette Colbert, Ray Milland, Walter Abel, Dennis O'Keefe.

Hold Back the Dawn (Paramount, 1941): Directed by Mitchell Leisen. Screenplay by BW, Brackett, from a story by Ketti Frings. Produced by Arthur Hornblow Jr. Cinematography: Leo Tover. Edited by Doane Harrison. Cast: Charles Boyer, Olivia de Havilland, Paulette Goddard, Victor Francen, Walter Abel, Rosemary DeCamp.

Ball of Fire (Goldwyn, 1941): Directed by Howard Hawks. Screenplay by BW, Brackett, from the story *From A to Z* by BW, Thomas Monroe. Produced by Samuel Goldwyn. Cinematography: Gregg Toland. Edited by Daniel Mandell. Music by Alfred Newman. Cast: Gary Cooper, Barbara Stanwyck, Oscar Homolka, Dana Andrews, Henry Travers, S. Z. Sakall, Richard Haydn, Tully Marshall, Leonid Kinskey, Dan Duryea. [Remade by Hawks as the Danny Kaye musical *A Song Is Born*, 1948.]

UNCREDITED HOLLYWOOD SCREENPLAY CONTRIBUTIONS

Under Pressure (1935): Directed by Raoul Walsh.

Tales of Manhattan (1942) (uncredited story concept): Directed by Julien Duvivier.

The Bishop's Wife (1947): Directed by Henry Koster.

AS WRITER/DIRECTOR

Mauvaise Graine (*Bad Seed*) (Compagnie Nouvelle Commerciale, 1933): Directed by BW, Alexander Esway. Screenplay by Esway, H. G. Lustig, Max Kolpe, from a story by BW. Produced by Eduoard Corniglion-Molinier. Music by Franz Wachsmann. Cast: Danielle Darrieux, Pierre Mingand, Raymonde Galle.

The Major and the Minor (Paramount, 1942): Screenplay by BW, Brackett, suggested by the play *Connie Goes Home* by Edward Childs Carpenter and the story "Sunny Goes Home" by Fannie Kilbourne. Produced by Arthur Hornblow Jr. Cinematography: Leo Tover. Edited by Doane Harrison. Art directors: Hans Dreier, Roland Anderson. Cast: Ginger Rogers, Ray Milland, Rita Johnson, Robert Benchley, Diana Lynn, Lela Rogers. [Remade as *You're Never Too Young*, 1955.]

Five Graves to Cairo (Paramount, 1943): Screenplay by BW, Brackett, based on the play *Hotel Imperial* by Lajos Biro. Produced by Brackett. Cinematography: John F. Seitz. Edited by Doane Harrison. Art directors: Hans Dreier, Ernst Fegte. Music by Miklos Rozsa. Cast: Franchot Tone, Anne Baxter, Erich von Stroheim, Akim Tamiroff, Fortunio Bonanova, Peter Van Eyck.

Double Indemnity (Paramount, 1944): Screenplay by BW, Raymond Chandler, based on the novella by James M. Cain. Produced by Joseph Sistrom. Cinematography: John F. Seitz. Edited by Doane Harrison. Art directors: Hans Dreier, Hal Pereira. Music by Miklos Rozsa. Cast: Barbara Stanwyck, Fred MacMurray, Edward G. Robinson, Porter Hall, Jean Heather, Tom Powers, Byron Barr, Fortunio Bonanova.

The Lost Weekend (Paramount, 1945): Screenplay by BW, Brackett, based on the novel by Charles R. Jackson. Produced by Brackett. Cinematography: John F. Seitz. Edited by Doane Harrison. Art directors: Hans Dreier, Earl Hedrick. Music by Miklos Rozsa. Cast: Ray Milland, Jane Wyman, Howard Da Silva, Philip Terry, Doris Dowling, Frank Faylen.

The Emperor Waltz (Paramount, 1948): Screenplay by BW, Brackett. Produced by Brackett. Cinematography: George Barnes. Edited by Doane Harrison. Art directors: Hans Dreier, Franz Bachelin. Music by Victor Young. Cast: Bing Crosby, Joan Fontaine, Roland Culver, Lucile Watson, Richard Haydn, Sig Ruman.

A Foreign Affair (Paramount, 1948): Screenplay by BW, Brackett, Richard L. Breen, from a story by David Shaw. Produced by Brackett. Cinematography: Charles B. Lang Jr. Edited by Doane Harrison. Art directors: Hans Dreier, Walter Tyler. Music by Frederick Hollander. Cast: Jean Arthur, Marlene Dietrich, John Lund, Millard Mitchell, Peter von Zerneck.

Sunset Boulevard (Paramount, 1950): Screenplay by BW, Brackett, D. M. Marshman Jr. Produced by Brackett. Cinematography: John F. Seitz. Editorial supervisor: Doane Harrison. Edited by Arthur Schmidt. Art directors: Hans Dreier, John Meehan. Music by Franz Waxman. Cast: William Holden, Gloria Swanson, Erich von Stroheim, Nancy Olson, Jack Webb,

Fred Clark, Cecil B. De Mille, Hedda Hopper, Buster Keaton, Anna Q. Nilsson, H. B. Warner.

Ace in the Hole (aka *The Big Carnival*) (Paramount, 1951): Screenplay by BW, Lesser Samuels, Walter Newman. Produced by BW. Cinematography: Charles B. Lang Jr. Edited by Doane Harrison, Arthur Schmidt. Art directors: Hal Pereira, Earl Hedrick. Music by Hugo Friedhofer. Cast: Kirk Douglas, Jan Sterling, Bob Arthur, Porter Hall, Richard Benedict, Ray Teal, Frank Cady.

Stalag 17 (Paramount, 1953): Screenplay by BW, Edwin Blum, based on the play by Donald Bevan, Edmund Trzcinski. Produced by BW. Cinematography: Ernest Laszlo. Editorial adviser: Doane Harrison. Art directors: Hal Pereira, Franz Bachelin. Music by Franz Waxman. Cast: William Holden, Don Taylor, Otto Preminger, Robert Strauss, Harvey Lembeck, Neville Brand, Peter Graves, Sig Ruman, Richard Erdman, Gil Stratton Jr.

Sabrina (Paramount, 1954): Screenplay by BW, Samuel Taylor, Ernest Lehman, based on the play *Sabrina Fair* by Taylor. Produced by BW. Cinematography: Charles B. Lang Jr. Editorial adviser: Doane Harrison. Edited by Arthur Schmidt. Art directors: Hal Pereira, Walter Tyler. Music by Frederick Hollander. Cast: Humphrey Bogart, Audrey Hepburn, William Holden, John Williams, Walter Hampden, Martha Hyer, Marcel Dalio. [Remade by Sydney Pollack, 1995.]

The Seven Year Itch (20th Century–Fox, 1955): Screenplay by BW, George Axelrod, based on Axelrod's play. Produced by BW, Charles K. Feldman. Associate producer: Doane Harrison. Cinematography: Milton Krasner. Art directors: Lyle Wheeler, George W. Davis. Music by Alfred Newman. Cast: Marilyn Monroe, Tom Ewell, Evelyn Keyes, Sonny Tufts, Robert Strauss, Oscar Homolka, Carolyn Jones, Doro Merande.

The Spirit of St. Louis (Warner Bros., 1957): Screenplay by BW, Wendell Mayes, based on the book by Charles A. Lindbergh. Produced by Leland Hayward. Associate producer: Doane Harrison. Cinematography: Robert Burks, J. Peverell Marley. Edited by Arthur Schmidt. Art director: Art Loel. Production consultant/montage: Charles Eames. Music by Franz

Waxman. Cast: James Stewart, Murray Hamilton, Patricia Smith, Marc Connelly.

Love in the Afternoon (Allied Artists, 1957): Screenplay by BW, I. A. L. Diamond, based on the novel *Ariane* by Claude Anet. Produced by BW. Associate producers: William Schorr, Doane Harrison. Cinematography: William Mellor. Art director: Alexander Trauner. Musical adaptation: Franz Waxman. Cast: Gary Cooper, Audrey Hepburn, Maurice Chevalier, Van Doude, John McGiver.

Witness for the Prosecution (United Artists, 1957): Screenplay by BW, Harry Kurnitz, based on the play and novel by Agatha Christie. Adaptation: Larry Marcus. Produced by Arthur Hornblow Jr. Cinematography: Russell Harlan. Art director: Alexander Trauner. Edited by Daniel Mandell. Music by Matty Malneck. Cast: Tyrone Power, Marlene Dietrich, Charles Laughton, Elsa Lanchester, John Williams, Henry Daniell, Ian Wolfe, Una O'Connor, Norma Varden.

Some Like It Hot (United Artists/The Mirisch Company, 1959): Screenplay by BW, Diamond. Produced by BW. Associate producers: Doane Harrison, Diamond. Cinematography: Charles B. Lang Jr. Edited by Arthur Schmidt. Art director: Ted Haworth. Music by Adolph Deutsch. Cast: Marilyn Monroe, Tony Curtis, Jack Lemmon, Joe E. Brown, George Raft, Pat O'Brien, Nehemiah Persoff, Joan Shawlee, Billy Gray.

The Apartment (United Artists/Mirisch, 1960): Screenplay by BW, Diamond. Produced by BW. Associate producers: Harrison, Diamond. Cinematography: Joseph LaShelle. Art director: Alexander Trauner. Edited by Daniel Mandell. Music by Adolph Deutsch. Cast: Jack Lemmon, Shirley MacLaine, Fred MacMurray, Ray Walston, David Lewis, Jack Kruschen, Edie Adams, Joan Shawlee, Hope Holiday, Naomi Stevens, Willard Waterman, David White, Johnny Seven.

One, Two, Three (United Artists/Mirisch, 1961): Screenplay by BW, Diamond, from the one-act play by Ferenc Molnar. Produced by BW. Associate producers: Diamond, Harrison. Cinematography: Daniel Fapp. Art director: Alexander Trauner. Edited by Daniel Mandell. Music by André Previn. Cast: James Cagney, Horst Buchholz, Pamela Tiffin, Arlene

Francis, Lilo Pulver, Howard St. John, Hanns Lothar, Leon Askin, Red Buttons.

Irma la Douce (United Artists/Mirisch, 1963): Screenplay by BW, Diamond, based on the play by Alexander Breffort. Produced by BW. Associate producers: Diamond, Harrison. Cinematography: Joseph LaShelle. Art director: Alexander Trauner. Edited by Daniel Mandell. Music by André Previn, Marguerite Monnot. Cast: Jack Lemmon, Shirley MacLaine, Lou Jacobi, Bruce Yarnell, Herschel Bernardi, Hope Holiday, Joan Shawlee, Grace Lee Whitney, Tura Santana, Harriet Young, Cliff Osmond, Bill Bixby, James Caan.

Kiss Me, Stupid (United Artists/Mirisch, 1964): Screenplay by BW, Diamond. Produced by BW. Associate producers: Harrison, Diamond. Cinematography: Joseph LaShelle. Production designer: Alexander Trauner. Edited by Daniel Mandell. Music by André Previn. Songs by George and Ira Gershwin. Cast: Dean Martin, Kim Novak, Ray Walston, Felicia Farr, Cliff Osmond, Barbara Pepper, Doro Merande, Howard McNear, Henry Gibson, Tommy Nolan, Alice Pearce, Mel Blanc.

The Fortune Cookie (United Artists/Mirisch, 1966): Screenplay by BW, Diamond. Produced by BW. Associate producers: Diamond, Harrison. Cinematography: Joseph LaShelle. Art director: Robert Luthardt. Edited by Daniel Mandell. Music by André Previn. Cast: Jack Lemmon, Walter Matthau, Ron Rich, Cliff Osmond, Judi West, Lurene Tuttle, Harry Holcombe, Les Tremayne, Marge Redmond.

The Private Life of Sherlock Holmes (United Artists/Mirisch, 1970): Screenplay by BW, Diamond, based on characters created by Arthur Conan Doyle. Produced by BW. Associate producer: Diamond. Cinematography: Christopher Challis. Production designer: Alexander Trauner. Edited by Ernest Walter. Music by Miklos Rozsa. Cast: Robert Stephens, Colin Blakely, Genevieve Page, Christopher Lee, Irene Handl, Tamara Toumanova, Clive Revill, Stanley Holloway, Mollie Maureen.

Avanti! (United Artists/Mirisch, 1972): Screenplay by BW, Diamond, based on the play by Samuel Taylor. Produced by BW. Cinematography: Luigi Kuveiller. Art director: Ferdinando Scarfiotti. Edited by Ralph E.

Winters. Music by Carlo Rustichelli. Cast: Jack Lemmon, Juliet Mills, Clive Revill, Edward Andrews, Gianfranco Barra, Franco Angrisano, Pippo Franco, Giselda Castrini.

The Front Page (Universal, 1974): Screenplay by BW, Diamond, based on the play by Ben Hecht, Charles MacArthur. Produced by Paul Monash. Cinematography: Jordan S. Cronenweth. Art directors: Henry Bumstead, Henry Larrecy. Edited by Ralph E. Winters. Music by Billy May. Cast: Jack Lemmon, Walter Matthau, Carol Burnett, Susan Sarandon, Vincent Gardenia, Austin Pendleton, David Wayne, Allen Garfield, Charles Durning, Harold Gould, Herbert Edelman, Martin Gabel, Jon Korkes, Cliff Osmond, Dick O'Neill, Lou Frizzell, Noam Pitlik, Paul Benedict, Doro Merande.

Fedora (United Artists, 1979): Screenplay by BW, Diamond, based on the story in Thomas Tryon's *Crowned Heads*. Produced by BW. Associate producer: Diamond. Cinematography: Gerry Fisher. Production designer: Alexandre Trauner. Edited by Fredric Steinkamp. Music by Miklos Rozsa. Cast: William Holden, Marthe Keller, Hildegard Knef, José Ferrer, Frances Sternhagen, Mario Adorf, Stephen Collins, Michael York, Henry Fonda, Hans Jaray, Gottfried John, Arlene Francis.

Buddy Buddy (MGM, 1981): Screenplay by BW, Diamond, based on the screenplay *L'Emmerdeur* by Edouard Molinaro, Francis Veber. Produced by Jay Weston. Executive producer: Alain Bernheim. Cinematography: Harry Stradling Jr. Production designer: Daniel A. Lomino. Music by Lalo Schifrin. Cast: Jack Lemmon, Walter Matthau, Paula Prentiss, Klaus Kinski, Dana Elcar, Miles Chapin, Joan Shawlee.

SOURCE NOTES

Abbreviations are used for the following reference sources:

AMPAS   Academy of Motion Picture Arts and Sciences
BW   Billy Wilder
ICD   Information Control Division, Motion Picture Branch, National Archives, Washington, D.C.
KL   Kevin Lally
UA   United Artists Collection, State Historical Society, Madison, Wisc.
USC   University of Southern California Cinema/TV Library

PROLOGUE: A WILDER OUTLOOK

". . . the aim of a film . . .": Rasner and Wulf, p. 49.
"When people walk out . . .": BW to KL, Sept. 17, 1993.
"Every picture I make . . .": John McDonough, "For 44 Years, Billy Wilder's Given Movies New Direction," *Chicago Tribune*, April 20, 1986, sect. 13, p. 8.
"Billy is called . . .": Jack Lemmon to KL, Dec. 2, 1993.

1: A BOY NAMED BILLIE

"I grew up . . .": BW to KL, March 4, 1994.
"My father . . .": Ibid.

BW's memories of World War I: BW to KL, Oct. 25, 1994.

"My father was a dreamer . . .": Karasek, p. 34.

"But he was not as old . . .": Ibid., p. 36.

"I remember hearing . . .": Zolotow, p. 25.

Billie's date with Greta: Karasek, p. 37.

"There are many aspects to Austria . . .": BW to KL, Sept. 17, 1993.

2: THE VIENNA BEAT

"Hey, I would like you to meet . . .": Joseph McBride and Todd McCarthy, "Going for Extra Innings," *Film Comment* 15, no. 1 (Jan./Feb. 1979), p. 43.

"[Zolotow] came up . . .": BW to KL, Sept. 17, 1993.

". . . I was pretty good . . .": BW to KL, April 12, 1995.

Hans Liebstockl story: Karasek, p. 44.

Reisch reminiscence: Richard Lemon, "Well, Nobody's Perfect . . . ," *Saturday Evening Post*, Dec. 17, 1966, p. 36.

BW's encounter with Freud: BW to KL, April 12, 1995.

"Whiteman gave four concerts . . .": BW to KL, Sept. 17, 1993.

"I said, 'Gee . . .' ": Ibid.

"Berlin was the dream . . .": Karasek, p. 47.

3: BERLIN STORIES

Prince Youssopoff story: Zolotow, p. 33.

"You can scarcely breathe . . .": Karasek, p. 52.

BW's gigolo account: BW, "Waiter, Bring Me a Dancer—The Life of a Gigolo," *Berliner Zeitung am Mittag*, January 1927 (translated by Robert Sheff).

". . . I had the best dialogue . . .": Karasek, p. 61.

"A ghostwriter . . .": BW to KL, Sept. 17, 1993.

Franz Schulz stories: Ibid.

Succoth story: Karasek, p. 53.

"Since I was young and romantic . . .": Interview with BW, *Playboy* 10, no. 6 (June 1963), p. 66.

"Who cares about the war!": BW television interview with Charles Champlin, "Champlin on Film," Z Channel Partnership, 1988.

BW's account of the creation of Film Studio 1929: BW, "Wie wir unseren Studio-film drehten" ("How We Shot Our Studio Film"), *Montag Morgen*, Feb. 10, 1930 (translated by Robert Sheff).

Curt Siodmak's account: Curt Siodmak, *Unfinished Ruminations* (autobiography in progress, courtesy of the author).

"We bluffed him . . .": "Wie wir unseren Studio-film drehten."

"I was trying to find a story . . .": Curt Siodmak, *Unfinished Ruminations*.

The greatest rivalry: Robert Siodmak and Blumenberg, p. 42.

Curt Siodmak's response: Curt Siodmak, *Unfinished Ruminations*.

Edgar G. Ulmer's comments: Interview in *Cahiers du Cinema*, c. 1961 (translated by Robert Sheff).

Brigitte Borchert's memories: *SDK* [Stiftung Deutsche Kinemathek] *Newsletter*, no. 4 (June 1993) (translated by Robert Sheff).

"We work at a fevered tempo . . .": BW, "Wir vom Filmstudio 1929" ("We of Film Studio 1929"), *Tempo*, no. 169 (June 23, 1929) (translated by Robert Sheff).

"It was a shallow time . . .": BW to KL, Oct. 25, 1994.

"At first we thought about young . . .": "Wie wir unseren Studio-film drehten."

"Gliese shot so much film . . .": Robert Siodmak and Blumenberg, p. 42.

". . . the one who owns the football . . .": Higham and Greenberg, p. 245.

"It's very simple . . .": Fred Zinnemann to KL, Jan. 10, 1994.

Lost negative story: Zinnemann, p. 16.

Zinnemann's duties: Fred Zinnemann to KL, Jan. 10, 1994.

"All of us were pretty much amateurs": Ibid.

"They did the same story in Italy . . .": Curt Siodmak to KL, June 29, 1993.

"We project it . . .": "Wie wir unseren Studio-film drehten."

"people applauded like crazy . . . The news . . .": Robert Siodmak and Blumenberg, p. 44.

"For somebody who . . .": BW to KL, Oct. 25, 1994.

4: DREAMS AND NIGHTMARES

"We were just getting going . . .": BW to KL, Oct. 25, 1994.

"I locked myself . . .": Robert Siodmak and Blumenberg, p. 45.

BW's encounter with Liebmann: BW to KL, Oct. 25, 1994.

Siodmak on the "grotesque film": Robert Siodmak, "Grotesque und Tonfilm" ("The Grotesque and Sound Film"), *UFA-Feuilleton*, no. 6 (Feb. 11, 1931) (translated by Robert Sheff).

"We amused ourselves . . .": Rühmann, p. 124.

"We worked at Pommer's villa . . .": Curt Siodmak to KL, June 29, 1993.

BW on Pommer: BW to KL, Oct. 25, 1994.

Kästner's criticisms: Kevin Macdonald, p. 75.

Hans Feld on BW: Hans Feld in "Salut für Billy Wilder" ("Salute to Billy Wilder"), *Der Tagesspiegel*, Berlin, May 24, 1987.

"Do I have to talk . . .": BW to KL, Oct. 25, 1994.

"The other day, I saw . . .": Rasner and Wulf, p. 18.

BW on musical conventions: Ibid, p. 22.

". . . the best popular German scriptwriter . . .": BW to KL, Oct. 25, 1994.

"Back then . . .": Rasner and Wulf, p. 25.

BW on Hans Steinhoff: Ibid., p. 21.

"nobody took Hitler . . .": BW to KL, Sept. 17, 1993.

5: ESCAPE TO PARIS

"We were saying . . .": BW to KL, Sept. 17, 1993.

"A lot of my friends . . .": Aljean Harmetz, "Seven Years Without Directing, and Billy Wilder Is Feeling Itchy," *The New York Times*, Oct. 3, 1988, p. C21.

Max Kolpe's recollections: "Salüt fur Billy Wilder" ("Salute to Billy Wilder"), *Der Tagesspiegel*, Berlin, May 24, 1987.

"We had to improvise . . .": BW to KL, April 12, 1995.

"live on the streets . . .": Higham and Greenberg, p. 245.

". . . a forerunner of Nouvelle Vague . . .": Karasek, p. 95.

"It got very good reviews . . .": BW to KL, April 12, 1995.

"I cannot say that it made me happy": Karasek, p. 94.
". . . deals were made at the Café Fouquet . . .": BW to KL, April 12, 1995.
"My dream all along . . .": Ibid.

6: HOLLYWOOD HUSTLE

". . . We came to save our lives": Gene D. Phillips, interview with BW, *Film/Literature Quarterly*, Winter 1975, p. 4.
"Like a fool . . .": BW to KL, April 12, 1995.
BW on *Pam-Pam:* BW to KL, March 4, 1994.
BW on Peter Lorre: Ibid.
Ann Little's and the Chateau Marmont's desk clerk's recollections: Sarlot and Basten, p. 50.
"I was here . . .": Karasek, p. 130.
"I forgot to notify Miss Little . . .": BW to KL, Sept. 17, 1993.
BW on Paramount: Ibid.

7: TEAMWORK

BW on the pajama scene: Lincoln Barnett, "The Happiest Couple in Hollywood," *Life*, Dec. 11, 1944, p. 106.
BW on Lubitsch touch re sign in shop: Karasek, p. 171.
BW on Lubitsch and censorship: BW to KL, Sept. 17, 1993.
". . . two plus two . . .": "Billy, How Did You Do It? Billy Wilder in Conversation with Volker Schlöndorff," *Arena* series, BBC-TV, 1988 (courtesy of Volker Schlöndorff).
BW on Charles Brackett: BW to KL, March 4, 1994.
Mitchell Leisen on BW: Chierichetti, p. 129.
BW on Mitchell Leisen: Zolotow, p. 69.
"*Midnight* is perfect . . .": Ibid.

8: GARBO LAUGHS

Garbo and Lubitsch exchange: d'Acosta, p. 240.
Lubitsch on Garbo's inhibitions: Bainbridge, p. 204.

"She played it beautifully . . .": Ibid., p. 205.

"I've always wanted to see Odessa . . .": Lincoln Barnett, "The Happiest Couple in Hollywood," *Life*, Dec. 11, 1944, p. 109.

Garbo's high spirits: d'Acosta, p. 306.

BW's chance meeting with Garbo: BW to KL, July 6, 1994.

Luigi Luraschi letter: AMPAS Production Code Administration File.

Joseph Breen letter: AMPAS Production Code Administration File.

Leisen on the Production Code: Chierichetti, p. 149.

Ray Milland on Brackett and Wilder: Ibid., p. 153.

"We got many letters . . .": BW to KL, Sept. 17, 1993.

9: THE DIRECTING ITCH

Details of Ketti Frings screenplay proposal: AMPAS script file and Production Code Administration file.

Casting Olivia de Havilland: Chierichetti, p. 171.

"I was a pest . . .": BW to KL, March 4, 1994.

". . . the value of people . . .": BW to KL, Sept. 17, 1993.

BW on Howard Hawks: Ibid.

Gary Cooper's complaints: Swindell, p. 237.

BW and Sam Goldwyn: Berg, pp. 363, 426.

"I was the number-two writer . . .": BW to KL, March 4, 1994.

". . . 'We'll give Wilder a picture . . .' ": BW to KL, July 6, 1994.

"You tell Ginger Rogers . . .": Lincoln Barnett, "The Happiest Couple in Hollywood," *Life*, Dec. 11, 1944, p. 111.

"wonderful sense of the ridiculous": Rogers, p. 292.

BW on the *Lolita* connection: BW to KL, July 6, 1994.

"I've directed fifty pictures . . .": Zolotow, p. 106.

"I've learned how to shoot elegantly . . .": BW to KL, Sept. 17, 1993.
  BW on Doane Harrison: Ibid.

"My God, those were the great naïve days . . .": Higham and Greenberg, p. 247.

10: LOVE, WAR AND MURDER

BW on Erich von Stroheim: BW to KL, Oct. 25, 1994.

"You know, he was not an actor . . .": Ibid.

"There was something very odd . . .": Higham and Greenberg, p. 247.

"An audience always senses . . .": Zolotow, p. 109.

"We would have nothing . . .": AMPAS production file.

"a top-notch melodrama . . .": Madsen, *Billy Wilder*, p. 66.

". . . entertaining hunk of celluloid . . .": Gene D. Phillips, interview with BW, *Film/Literature Quarterly*, Winter 1975, p. 6.

Joseph Breen's letter: AMPAS Production Code Administration file.

"Too grisly": BW to KL, Sept. 17, 1993.

Wilder's secretary: Brunette and Peary, p. 128.

Cain on the Hayes Office letter: David Hanna, "Hays Censors Rile Jim Cain," *Los Angeles Daily News*, Feb. 14, 1944.

"It's not only the principle . . .": Ibid.

Chandler on Cain: MacShane, *Life of Raymond Chandler*, p. 101.

BW's first impression of Chandler: Karasek, p. 259.

"He had that idiotic idea . . .": "Billy, How Did You Do It? Billy Wilder in Conversation with Volker Schlöndorff," *Arena* series, BBC-TV, 1988.

"He did not like me very much . . .": BW to KL, April 12, 1995.

"It was a letter of complaint . . .": Moffat, p. 46.

"Magnanimously . . .": Karasek, p. 262.

Chandler's letter to Hamish Hamilton: MacShane, ed., *Selected Letters of Raymond Chandler*, p. 237.

"Chandler had no idea . . .": BW to KL, April 12, 1995.

"my story was done very slapdash . . .": Brunette and Peary, p. 125.

Cain on seeing the film: Ibid.

The Cain-Chandler story conference: Ibid., p. 127.

"I'm a very good dialogue writer . . .": BW to KL, July 6, 1994.

"I heard some of the best wit . . .": MacShane, *Life of Raymond Chandler*, p. 110.

"the status of an assistant . . .": Raymond Chandler, "Writers in Hollywood," *Atlantic Monthly* 176, November 1945, p. 50.

"Of course he was invited . . .": Karasek, p. 264.

"Without question . . .": Peter Forster, "Gentle Tough Guy," *John O'London's Weekly* 62, March 6, 1953, p. 189.

George Raft's lapel: Moffat, p. 48.

Convincing Fred MacMurray: BW to KL, Sept. 17, 1993.

Barbara Stanwyck's reservations: Smith, p. 169.

"She was a terrific performer . . .": BW to KL, Feb. 7, 1995.

"to complement her anklet . . .": Smith, p. 170.

"We hired Barbara Stanwyck . . .": Ibid.

"at my age . . .": Robinson, p. 236.

"dirtying up" the sets: Phillips interview with BW, p. 6.

"you couldn't have a more meaningful scene . . .": BW to KL, July 6, 1994.

"I was very proud of the scene . . .": Ibid.

"I went to get my car . . .": "Billy, How Did You Do It?"

"Mr. McCarey . . . stumbled perceptibly": Schickel, p. 68.

"a dull son of a bitch": "Dialogue on Film: Billy Wilder and I. A. L. Diamond," *American Film* 1, no. 9 (July/Aug. 1976), p. 45.

11: LOST AND REDEEMED

BW discussing *The Lost Weekend*'s attraction: BW to KL, March 4, 1994.

"Y. Frank Freeman . . .": BW to KL, Sept. 17, 1993.

Joe Breen's complaints: AMPAS Production Code Administration file.

Stanley Barr letter: AMPAS Production Code Administration file.

Brackett's defense: Alton Cook, "Film Probes the Mind of an Alcoholic," *New York World Telegram*, Oct. 28, 1944, p. 7.

"How many of us . . .": Eileen Creelman, "Charles Brackett and Billy Wilder Discuss the Filming of 'The Lost Weekend,'" *New York Sun*, Oct. 14, 1944.

BW on Don Birnam's sexuality: BW to KL, March 4, 1994.

Ray Milland's recollections: Milland, pp. 211–16.

Brackett on Jane Wyman: "Brackett and Wilder Discuss Filming."

Doris Dowling's comments: Eileen Creelman, "Doris Dowling Discusses Her First Movie, 'The Lost Weekend,' Due Soon at the Rivoli," *New York Sun*, Nov. 24, 1945.

BW on New York location filming: Billy Wilder, "The Case for the American Film," *America* (State Dept. publication), c. 1946.

Milland explodes: Milland, p. 218.

"The bat-and-mouse sequence . . .": Higham and Greenberg, p. 249.

"The people laughed . . .": Karasek, p. 286.

"I've sworn off . . .": BW interview with Richard Brown, "Reflections on the Silver Screen," American Movie Classics network, 1993.

Henry Ginsberg's comments: Ibid.

Miklos Rozsa's comments: Rozsa, p. 148.

"If they would have given *me* . . .": BW interview with Brown.

BW's army interview: Karasek, p. 303.

"Everything was terribly clandestine.": Ibid., p. 304.

"It looked like the end of the world . . .": Ibid., p. 310.

Searching for his father's grave: "Billy, How Did You Do It? Billy Wilder in Conversation with Volker Schlöndorff," *Arena* series, BBC-TV, 1988.

BW on anti-Semitism: BW to KL, Sept. 17, 1993.

BW on Bergen-Belsen: "Billy, How Did You Do It?"

The preview of *Death Mills*: Ibid.

Audience reaction to *Death Mills*: ICD files.

"I never met a single Nazi . . .": Karasek, p. 313.

"Monet, Manet . . .": Zolotow, p. 232.

BW's "Propaganda Through Entertainment" report: ICD files.

Eric T. Clarke's memo: Ibid.

". . . with an opponent like Paley . . .": Karasek, p. 321.

BW on German reconstruction: Thomas M. Pryor, "End of a Journey: William Wilder, Writer-Director, Reports on Movie Activities in Germany," *The New York Times*, Sept. 23, 1945, sect. 2, p. 3.

"The Kidney": Ibid.

"Charlie and I . . .": Ibid.

Russell Holman's comments: AMPAS Production Code Administration file.

British trailer: Ibid.

"London is on a praise binge . . .": Wiley and Bona, p. 150.

". . . the cheapest stuff he could buy": "The Case for the American Film." Charles Jackson's praise: " 'Lost Weekend's' Author Loves the Movie," *P.M. New York*, Nov. 25, 1945, p. 3.

Public reaction to Ray Milland: Oliver Jensen, " 'Lost Weekend' Hangover: Milland Is Haunted by Alcoholic He Portrayed," *Life*, March 11, 1946, p. 17.
"It's Four Roses . . .": Wiley and Bona, p. 155.
House of Seagrams ad: Ibid., p. 153.

12: FOREIGN AFFAIRS

"Believe me . . .": Zolotow, p. 209.
"I'd worship the ground . . .": Ibid., p. 210.
"My daddy . . .": Zolotow, p. 142.
Details of Wilder and Brackett's office: Lincoln Barnett, "The Happiest Couple in Hollywood," *Life*, Dec. 11, 1944, p. 103.
"No good deed goes unpunished": Karasek, p. 337.
BW on Technicolor: Ibid., p. 340.
"There is one great difference . . .": Aljean Harmetz, "Seven Years Without Directing, and Billy Wilder Is Feeling Itchy," *The New York Times*, Oct. 3, 1988, p. C21.
"Painting trees red . . .": Robert Mundy and Michael Wallington, "Interview With Billy Wilder," *Cinema*, no. 4 (October 1969), p. 21.
Ernst Lubitsch sees *The Emperor Waltz*: Eyman, p. 350.
"No more Lubitsch . . .": BW in *Action!* (magazine of the Screen Directors Guild of America), November 1967.
Details on *Love in the Air* screen treatments: AMPAS script file.
". . . you can't refuse Billy Wilder": Dietrich, p. 228.
"She hated the character . . .": Riva, p. 595.
Luraschi memo: AMPAS production file.
Dietrich on Lund and Arthur: Riva, p. 595.
Jean Arthur's mythical closeup: "Dialogue on Film: Billy Wilder and I. A. L. Diamond," *American Film* 1, no. 9 (July/Aug. 1976), p. 37.
Filming Arthur's drunk scene: Karasek, p. 343.
"in rotten taste": Agee, p. 311.
"The rise and fall . . .": Corliss, p. 145.
"The affair with the German girl? . . .": BW to KL, Sept. 17, 1993.
"If you are wondering how . . .": Ibid.

Production Code objections: AMPAS Production Code Administration file.

"This is the kind of film . . .": Corliss, p. 145.

"thoughtlessly brutalizes": Sarris, p. 166.

Phone call from Jean Arthur: Karasek, p. 344.

Schulberg attack: Stuart Schulberg, "A Communication: A Letter About Billy Wilder," *Quarterly of Film, Radio and Television* 7, no. 4 (Summer 1952), p. 434.

"I was in the army . . .": BW to KL, Sept. 17, 1993.

"They loved it . . .": BW to KL, March 4, 1994.

13: PARTNERS AT SUNSET

"Wilder, Marshman and I . . .": Charles Brackett, "Putting the Picture on Paper" (undated lecture, AMPAS *Sunset Boulevard* file).

"Suppose the old dame shoots the boy?": Phil Koury, "How Script for 'Sunset Boulevard' Was Born," *The New York Times*, July 2, 1950.

"I was never mistaken for an undertaker . . .": BW to KL, Sept. 17, 1993.

"Only part of Betty Schaefer's story . . .": Nancy Olson to KL, Dec. 18, 1994.

BW and Mary Pickford: Rosenfeld, p. 159.

Gloria Swanson's objections: Zolotow, p. 161.

"If they ask you to do ten . . .": Swanson, p. 479.

William Holden's eagerness: Thomas, p. 60.

Holden's hesitation: Zolotow, p. 163.

BW on Holden's performance: BW to KL, Sept. 17, 1993.

"He had seen my screen test . . .": Nancy Olson to KL.

"extremely friendly . . .": Ibid.

Erich von Stroheim's driving: Swanson, p. 483.

BW on Cecil B. De Mille: Gene D. Phillips, interview with BW, *Film/ Literature Quarterly*, Winter 1975, p. 9.

De Mille's extra closeup: David Freeman, "Sunset Boulevard Revisited," *The New Yorker*, June 21, 1993, p. 77.

"Waxworks is right": Swanson, p. 483.

"The Paramount-Don't-Want-Me Blues": AMPAS Production Code Administration file.

Swanson on art imitating life: Swanson, p. 481.

". . . Do you know Bill Holden? . . .": Thomas, p. 61.

". . . a bit ghoulish": Swanson, p. 483.

"What made it work . . .": David Gritten, "A New Turn for 'Sunset Boulevard,' " *Los Angeles Times*, June 27, 1993, "Calendar" sect., p. 8.

"was one of those pictures . . .": BW to KL, Sept. 17, 1993.

"This was very risky storytelling . . .": Nancy Olson to KL.

"I had a party planned . . .": Swanson, p. 484.

Olson on Swanson and von Stroheim: Graham Wells, "40 Years Ago: 'Sunset Boulevard' Dazzles Expectant Crowds," *Memories*, Aug./Sept. 1990.

"We had the ending . . .": BW to KL, Sept. 17, 1993.

Audience reactions to the morgue scene: Karasek, p. 354.

"I've never seen so many prominent people . . .": Higham and Greenberg, p. 250.

"These affairs are known . . .": Swanson, p. 484.

"You bastard! . . .": Zolotow, p. 168.

"It was not anti-Hollywood . . .": BW interview with Richard Brown, "Reflections on the Silver Screen," American Movie Classics network, 1993.

"Swanson didn't get it . . .": BW to KL, Sept. 17, 1993.

"It slowly dawned on me . . .": Swanson, p. 259.

"I had played the part too well . . .": Ibid.

Olson on Holden: "William Holden: The Golden Boy," Wombat Prod. documentary, *Crazy About the Movies* series, Cinemax network, 1989.

"Billy was a little in awe of Charles . . .": Barbara Diamond to KL, Sept. 14, 1993.

"Collaboration is like a box of matches . . .": BW to KL, Sept. 17, 1993.

Charles Brackett on the breakup: Kanin, p. 178.

Herbert G. Luft's criticisms: Herbert G. Luft, "A Matter of Decadence," *Quarterly of Film, Radio and Television* 7, no. 1 (Fall 1952), p. 65.

Brackett defends Wilder: Charles Brackett, "A Matter of Humor," *Quarterly of Film, Radio and Television* 7, no. 1 (Fall 1952), pp. 66–69.

"I cannot imagine . . .": Kanin, p. 180.

"The sooner the bulldozers . . .": Wood, p. 78.

Details of Audrey and Billy's wedding: Zolotow, pp. 214–15.

"Working with Billy . . .": Kirk Douglas to KL, April 18, 1994.

"Behind my back . . .": BW to KL, Sept. 17, 1993.

"It was a very good picture . . .": BW to KL, March 4, 1994.

"Having been at it . . .": "Billy, How Did You Do It? Billy Wilder in Conversation with Volker Schlöndorff," *Arena* series, BBC-TV, 1988.

"I've often thought . . .": Kirk Douglas to KL.

Walter Newman's reflections: Froug, p. 78.

14: DIRECT FROM BROADWAY

Dietrich and astrology: Karasek, p. 325.

Swifty Lazar on Audrey Wilder: Zolotow, p. 222.

"I always make things very tough . . .": Philip K. Scheuer, "Wilder Seeks Films 'with Bite' to Satisfy 'Nation of Hecklers,' " *Los Angeles Times*, Aug. 20, 1950, p. 26.

"He is the black marketeer . . .": BW to KL, Feb. 7, 1995.

"I was not a blind, idiotic patriot . . .": BW to KL, Sept. 17, 1993.

"I looked on in amazement . . .": Huston, p. 135.

"I was young and stupid . . .": Kirk Douglas to KL, April 18, 1994.

"Second choice again?": Thomas, p. 79.

"Sometimes opening up a play . . .": Gene D. Phillips, interview with BW, *Film/Literature Quarterly*, Winter 1975, p. 10.

". . . one of the easiest films of my life . . .": "Billy, How Did You Do It? Billy Wilder in Conversation with Volker Schlöndorff," *Arena* series, BBC-TV, 1988.

BW on Otto Preminger: Ibid.

William Holden on the Oscar race: Thomas, p. 82.

BW's dispute with Paramount: BW to KL, March 4, 1994.

Germany's *Stalag 17* disclaimer: "German Censors at Last Okay 'Stalag 17' Pic," *Variety*, Feb. 10, 1960.

"little more than his butler": Zolotow, p. 181.

"We made four important stops . . .": Thomas, p. 95.

Ernest Lehman reminisces: Ernest Lehman to KL, Sept. 11, 1993.

Cary Grant story: Tony Curtis to KL, Nov. 11, 1993.

"Virtue is not photogenic": BW to KL, Sept. 17, 1993.

"I kind of liked the idea . . .": Ibid.

"Wilder is the kind of Prussian German . . .": Goodman, p. 265.

"I learned from the master . . .": Ibid., p. 266.

"I saw the test . . .": BW to KL, Feb. 7, 1995.

"After so many drive-in waitresses . . .": Goodman, p. 271.

"He bore his agony . . .": Karasek, p. 385.

Production Code objections to George Axelrod's play: AMPAS Production Code Administration file.

The hairpin gambit: BW interview with Richard Brown, "Reflections on the Silver Screen," American Movie classics network, 1993.

"the look of death": Spoto, *Marilyn Monroe*, p. 284.

"She was shaking like hell . . .": Ibid., p. 283.

"it was worth going through hell . . .": BW to KL, March 4, 1994.

"I have an Aunt Ida . . .": Zolotow, p. 258.

Tom Ewell on Marilyn Monroe: Norton Mockridge, "I Love My Wife, But . . . ," *New York World Telegram and Sun Saturday Magazine*, Jan. 22, 1955, p. 10.

Testing Walter Matthau: BW interview with Brown.

"Yeah, I did a screen test . . .": Walter Matthau to KL, Dec. 3, 1993.

"is a very good actor": BW interview with Brown.

BW's romance with Evelyn Keyes: Viertel, p. 52.

"Billy is, was . . .": Patrick McGilligan, "Irony," interview with George Axelrod, *Film Comment* 31, no. 6, November/December 1995, p. 14.

"Billy gave me . . .": Ibid.

"He's a wonderful director . . .": Aline Mosby interview with Marilyn Monroe, *Hollywood Citizen-News*, Nov. 8, 1954.

15: FINDING A DIAMOND

BW meets Charles Lindbergh: Aline Mosby, "Lindbergh and the Bus," *Beverly Hills Citizen*, Feb. 26, 1957.

"I was interested . . .": BW to KL, Feb. 7, 1995.

"Wouldn't it be embarrassing . . .": Zolotow, p. 194.

James Stewart's campaign for the role of Lindbergh: Eleanor Harris, "How Jimmy Stewart Learned to Be Lindbergh," *The American Weekly*, Jan. 1, 1956, p. 7.

"My first instinct . . .": Joe Hyams, "This Is Hollywood," *New York Herald Tribune*, Jan. 9, 1956.

Leland Hayward's letter to Warner Bros.: USC *Spirit of St. Louis* file.

Stewart's unhappiness: Ibid.

"There is no escaping . . .": Ibid.

"The technical problems . . .": Higham and Greenberg, p. 252.

"the most disastrous failure . . .": Zolotow, p. 314.

"The editor said . . .": Jack Lemmon to KL, Dec. 2, 1993.

The Wilder-Diamond combination: Barbara Diamond to KL, Sept. 14, 1993.

BW on Cary Grant: BW to KL, Sept. 17, 1993.

Doris Vidor on Aly Khan: Zolotow, p. 199.

". . . why not be in Paris? . . .": "Why Not Be in Paris?," *Newsweek*, Nov. 26, 1956, p. 108.

"How proud I would be . . .": Walker, *Audrey*, p. 140.

Audrey Wilder in cast: BW to KL, Feb. 7, 1995.

"I never knew . . .": Woodward, p. 162.

"When you watched me . . .": BW to KL, March 4, 1994.

Cooper's "astounding" looks: Maychick, p. 140.

Legion of Decency objection: AMPAS Production Code Administration file.

Dispute over the title: "Billy, How Did You Do It? Billy Wilder in Conversation with Volker Schlöndorff," *Arena* series, BBC-TV, 1988.

Mirisch Company objectives: Balio, p. 161.

"If we had to invent someone . . .": Letter from Arthur Hornblow to Edward Small, Edward Small Collection, USC.

". . . he said the promise of the show . . .": Ibid.

Harry Kurnitz on BW: Harry Kurnitz, "Billy the Wild," *Holiday*, June 1964, pp. 93–95.

"something much deeper": Helmut Dietl, "Billy, Wie Has Du Das Gemacht? ("Billy, How Did You Do It?"), interview with BW in *Stern*, July 3, 1992, p. 36 (translated by Robert Sheff).

"she was a great cook . . .": BW to KL, Oct. 25, 1994.

"She was Mother Teresa . . .": "Billy, Wie Has Du Das Gemacht?," p. 36.

"the cleverest man I ever met": Karasek, p. 351.

". . . a master builder . . .": Dietrich, p. 127.

"They were good friends . . .": Riva, p. 648.

Dietrich on *Witness*, Power and Laughton: Riva, p. 680.

"She was a great lighting technician . . .": "Billy, How Did You Do It?"

"It is not easy to teach Cockney . . .": Bach, p. 385.

". . . donkey work . . .": Callow, p. 242.

Laughton rehearsing: BW interview with Richard Brown, "Reflections on the Silver Screen," American Movie Classics network, 1993.

"you can tell how good an actor is . . .": Higham, p. 205.

BW on Tyrone Power: Arce, *Secret Life of Tyrone Power*, pp. 252–53.

"The reality . . .": Thomas M. Pryor, "Hollywood Canvas," *The New York Times*, Aug. 7, 1957.

"Christie plotted . . .": BW to KL, March 4, 1994.

"I get bored . . .": Ibid.

"We killed them in Berlin . . .": Edward Small Collection, USC.

"I hate the noise . . .": "Billy, How Did You Do It?"

"We laughed all the way . . .": Arce, *Secret Life of Tyrone Power*, p. 254.

Laughton by swimming pool: Callow, p. 272.

"When I'm in Paris . . .": "Billy, How Did You Do It?"

16: HOTTER THAN EVER

"All the Mirisch Company . . .": Interview with BW, *Playboy*, 10, no. 6 (June 1963), p. 61.

"We got a print . . .": Stanley Kauffmann, "Landmarks of Film History: *Some Like It Hot*," Horizon, Winter 1972, p. 66.

"Fresh from the experience . . .": Barbara Diamond to KL, Sept. 14, 1993.

"an absolute question of life and death": Gene D. Phillips, interview with BW, *Film/Literature Quarterly*, Winter 1975, p. 10.

"Suddenly, we were in business . . .": Froug, p. 163.

"Boy, we were really . . .": Jack Lemmon to KL, Dec. 2, 1993.

"You can't make it work . . .": Zolotow, p. 203.

"The only way to play it . . .": Widener, p. 167.

"It never dawned on me . . .": Tony Curtis to KL, Nov. 11, 1993.

"Mr. Curtis . . .": "Billy, How Did You Do It? Billy Wilder in Conversation with Volker Schlöndorff," *Arena* series, BBC-TV, 1988.

"You didn't want . . .": Curtis and Paris, p. 163.

"I enjoyed seeing . . .": Tony Curtis to KL.

"If I do it in color . . .": Ibid.

"You had to go through Paula . . .": Curtis and Paris, p. 167.

Rights of Man story: I. A. L. Diamond, "Marilyn Monroe and the 30-Proof Coffee Break," *Chicago Tribune Magazine*, Jan. 12, 1986, p. 23; and Zolotow, p. 263.

BW on Monroe's erratic performance: "Billy, How Did You Do It?"

"I did not dare . . .": BW to KL, April 12, 1995.

"We were in midflight . . .": Guiles, p. 239.

Curtis on Monroe: Tony Curtis to KL.

Lemmon on Monroe: Jack Lemmon to KL.

"the actor's actor . . .": Widener, p. 167.

"Hell, the man can do anything . . .": C. Robert Jennings, "Twist of Jack Lemmon," *Coronet*, Aug. 1966.

"never stopped to think . . .": Widener, p. 167.

"In general . . .": Jack Lemmon to KL.

Curtis on his performance: Tony Curtis to KL.

"a huge, wonderful plus . . .": Curtis and Paris, p. 160.

"It's not even Cary Grant . . .": Tony Curtis to KL.

Monroe's disdain for Sugar: Spoto, *Marilyn Monroe*, p. 402.

"Nothing was ever quite as frantic . . .": Barbara Diamond to KL.

"No matter how much . . .": BW interview with Richard Brown, "Reflections on the Silver Screen," American Movie Classics network, 1993.

"She never shows up . . .": Spoto, *Marilyn Monroe*, p. 405.

The preview: "Monroe and the 30-Proof Coffee Break," p. 26.

"Of all the films . . .": Jack Lemmon to KL.

Religious and censor-board objections: AMPAS Production Code Administration file.

"I am eating better . . .": Zolotow, p. 264.

Monroe's message to Wilder: "Monroe and the 30-Proof Coffee Break," p. 26.

"It takes a real artist . . .": Art Buchwald, "Billy Wilder Eats Some Crow," *Los Angeles Times*, Aug. 7, 1960.

"the meanest woman . . .": Marika Aba, "Billy Wilder: He Chose Hollywood," *Los Angeles Times*, March 3, 1968.

"If she was alive today . . .": BW to KL, April 12, 1995.

"In spite of everything . . .": Helmut Dietl, "Sie Dampfte Nur So Vor

Sex" ("She Only Smoked Before Sex"), Interview with BW in *Stern*, Aug. 6, 1992, p. 34 (translated by Robert Sheff).

Curtis on Wilder: Tony Curtis to KL.

"We had the first screening . . .": Jack Lemmon to KL.

"Surely, one can make superficial films . . .": Michel Ciment, "Entretien avec Billy Wilder" ("Conversation with Billy Wilder"), *Positif*, no. 120 (Oct. 1970), p. 15 (translated by Ed Kelleher).

Walter Wanger inspiration: Froug, p. 164.

"This is my chariot race": I. A. L. Diamond, " 'Apartment' with View," *The New York Times*, June 12, 1960.

". . . a delicate balance . . .": Froug, p. 160.

Suicide inspiration: Barbara Diamond to KL.

". . . a Forrest Gump": BW to KL, Feb. 7, 1995.

"There are any number of actresses . . .": " 'Apartment' with View."

MacLaine on *The Apartment* and BW: Shirley MacLaine to KL, Sept. 14, 1993.

MacLaine's first day of shooting: Jack Lemmon to KL.

"He's the only director . . .": Shirley MacLaine to KL.

"I'd pop into the office . . .": Jack Lemmon to KL.

Lemmon on the nose-spray gag: Michael Wilmington, "Saint Jack," *Film Comment*, (March/April 1993), p. 15.

". . . rose in a garbage pail . . .": Jack Lemmon to KL.

"I don't regard . . .": BW to KL, Feb. 7, 1995.

"I had three doctors . . .": "Entretien avec Billy Wilder," p. 11.

BW on Fred MacMurray's reservations: Harold Lloyd Master Seminar with BW, American Film Institute, March 3, 1986.

"Although Mr. Wilder . . .": Dwight Macdonald, p. 312.

". . . the biggest softie . . .": Jack Lemmon to KL.

"Did you really think . . .": Joseph McBride and Todd McCarthy, "Going for Extra Innings," *Film Comment* 15, no. 1 (Jan./Feb. 1979), p. 46.

17: AGAINST THE WALL

"We developed this Esperanto language . . .": BW to KL, Sept. 17, 1993.

Barbara Diamond on the Wilder-Diamond relationship: Barbara Diamond to KL, Sept. 14, 1993.

BW on the Marx Brothers film: Weatherby, p. 85.

"He's a brilliant moviemaker . . .": Ibid.

BW on *The Apartment* in Moscow: BW to KL, March 4, 1994.

BW on James Cagney: Ibid.

Pamela Tiffin's comments: Pamela Tiffin Danon to KL, Feb. 3, 1995.

Horst Buchholz's comments: Horst Buchholz to KL, April 6, 1994.

"as I was going along . . .": Cagney, p. 154.

"I never had the slightest . . .": Ibid., p. 155.

"We found thousands . . .": I. A. L. Diamond, " 'One, Two, Three': Timetable Test," *The New York Times*, Dec. 17, 1961.

"It's very difficult . . .": Barbara Diamond to KL.

". . . like making a picture in Pompeii . . .": Interview with BW, *Playboy* 10, no. 6 (June 1963), p. 64.

Cagney retires: Cagney, p. 156.

"I happen to think . . .": Kanin, p. 185.

". . . fast-paced comedy . . .": Froug, p. 164.

BW on "art" films: Colin Young, "The Old Dependables," *Film Quarterly* 13, no. 1 (Fall 1959), p. 4.

"I have at no time . . .": Interview with BW, *Playboy*, 10, no. 6 (June 1963), p. 64.

"To be poetic . . .": Michel Ciment, "Entretien avec Billy Wilder" ("Conversation with Billy Wilder"), *Positif*, no. 120 (Oct. 1970), p. 6 (translated by Ed Kelleher).

BW on Ingmar Bergman: Richard Gehman, "Charming Billy," *Playboy* 7, no. 12 (Dec. 1960), p. 167.

BW on Antonioni: Stephen Watts, "Fast Talker," *The New York Times*, March 4, 1962, sect. 2, p. 7.

BW on Godard: "Entretien avec Billy Wilder," p. 6.

BW's toast to Bergman: Kohner, p. 176.

18: FROM IRMA TO INFAMY

"There's no reason . . .": Joe Hyams, "Poor 'Irma' Left Without a Song," *New York Herald Tribune*, Oct. 21, 1962.

"Audiences are . . .": Louella O. Parsons, "Jack Lemmon—A Multi-Talented Trouper," *New York Journal-American*, Sept. 2, 1962.

Geoffrey Shurlock's objections: AMPAS Production Code Administration file.

"I have nothing against music . . .": Kanin, p. 185.

"When we first read . . .": "Poor 'Irma' Left Without a Song."

"They couldn't . . .": Joseph Roddy, "Shirley MacLaine: New-style Star Tries a Rough Role," *Look*, Jan. 29, 1963, p. 61.

"They were saying . . .": C. Robert Jennings, "Twist of Jack Lemmon," *Coronet*, Aug. 1966.

"We had a long talk . . .": Shirley MacLaine to KL, Sept. 14, 1993.

Hal Wallis–Geoffrey Shurlock exchange: AMPAS Production Code Administration file.

"I didn't like the movie . . .": Shirley MacLaine to KL.

"I didn't understand . . .": MacLaine, p. 350.

MacLaine on BW: Shirley MacLaine to KL.

"It's the same plot . . .": Froug, p. 165.

"I might say that it's long been . . .": Lewis, p. 672.

"I realized . . .": Ibid., p. 674.

"I used to go . . .": Alexander Walker London *Evening Standard* interview with Sellers, quoted in ibid., p. 673.

Cliff Osmond's comments: Cliff Osmond to KL, Sept. 16, 1993.

"What do you mean . . .": Lewis, p. 673.

"I have had Hollywood . . .": Walker interview, quoted in ibid., p. 674.

"I liked him . . .": BW to KL, April 12, 1995.

Ray Walston on the script: Tosches, p. 374.

"I wanted . . .": Murray Schumach, "Sellers' Fill-in Finds Pace Hectic," *The New York Times*, April 25, 1964.

Kim Novak's accident: Kleno, pp. 203–6.

Dean Martin's ribbing: Tosches, p. 374.

Felicia Farr's comments: Felicia Farr to KL, Jan. 4, 1994.

". . . a 'taste-free' picture . . .": Barbara Diamond to KL, Sept. 14, 1993.

"If dogs . . .": Vizzard, p. 304.

"Wilder has had . . .": Thomas Thompson, "Wilder's Dirty-Joke Film Stirs a Furor," *Life*, Jan. 15, 1965, p. 55.

Legion of Decency objections and Shurlock's response: AMPAS Production Code Administration file.

"I passed this picture . . .": Vizzard, p. 305.

"I read your piece . . .": Richard Lemon, "Well, Nobody's Perfect . . . ," *Saturday Evening Post*, Dec. 17, 1966, p. 30.

"What we were really trying . . .": Froug, p. 165.

"It's a terrible movie . . .": Barbara Diamond to KL.

"If Peter Sellers . . .": Interview with Joseph Gelmis, *Newsday*, Oct. 15, 1966.

"The uproar stunned me . . .": Interview with Peter Bart, *The New York Times*, Nov. 7, 1965.

Wilder-Shurlock correspondence: AMPAS Production Code Administration file.

"the one thing . . .": "Well, Nobody's Perfect . . . ," p. 30.

". . . 'We're like two parents . . .' ": Ernest Lehman to KL, Sept. 11, 1993.

"It stinks . . .": Gelmis interview.

"I've seen . . .": "Well, Nobody's Perfect . . . ," p. 30.

"I don't spend . . .": BW to KL, Sept. 17, 1993.

"Once you engage . . .": Ibid.

". . . after the first preview . . .": Jack Lemmon to KL, Dec. 2, 1993.

19: WILDER BUT MELLOWER

"It's about greed . . .": Army Archerd, "Just for *Variety*," *Daily Variety*, Nov. 26, 1965.

"That's a movie . . .": Jack Lemmon, quoted in Baltake, p. 167.

Walter Matthau's comments: Walter Matthau to KL, Dec. 3, 1993.

Jack Lemmon's comments: Jack Lemmon to KL, Dec. 2, 1993.

"You see me going upstairs . . .": Zolotow, p. 243.

"What I plan . . .": Roderick Mann, "Movie-Maker Billy Wilder Is Ready for Sherlock Holmes," *Los Angeles Herald-Examiner*, March 10, 1968, p. C-3.

"no matter how good . . .": Miklos Rozsa, quoted in *Films in Review*, Dec. 1970, p. 633.

"with an intermission . . .": Wood, p. 232.

". . . What's good enough for Larry Olivier . . .": Mark Shivas, "Wilder—'Yes, We Have No Naked Girls,' " *The New York Times*, Oct. 12, 1969, sect. 2, p. 4.

"In today's market . . .": Lloyd Shearer, "The Decline and Fall of Hollywood," *Parade*, May 10, 1970, p. 5.

Christopher Challis comments: Christopher Challis to KL, May 25, 1995.

"We discussed how . . .": BW to KL, March 4, 1994.

"Taylor was . . .": Jack Lemmon to KL.

"There are many . . .": Michel Ciment, "Entretien avec Billy Wilder (à propos d'*Avanti!*)" ("Conversation with Billy Wilder) *Positif*, no. 155 (January 1974), p. 7 (translated by Ed Kelleher).

"We once did a tour . . .": Barbara Diamond to KL, Sept. 14, 1993.

"Most of my characters . . .": Jack Lemmon to KL.

Casting Juliet Mills: "Entretien . . . *Avanti!*," p. 5.

"They would not . . .": Ibid.

"all Italians . . .": United Artists production notes.

marine animals: Widener, p. 228.

"too mild . . .": "Dialogue on Film: Billy Wilder and I. A. L. Diamond," *American Film* 1, no. 9 (July/Aug. 1976), p. 44.

"It just so happened . . .": Joseph McBride, "In the Picture: *The Front Page*," *Sight and Sound* 43, no. 4 (Autumn 1974), p. 212.

Lemmon on *The Odd Couple*: Michael Wilmington, "Saint Jack," *Film Comment*, 29, no. 2 (March-April 1993) p. 18.

"This is not only . . .": Roger Ebert, "Wilder Turning Out Another 'Front Page'," *New York Post*, May 31, 1974, p. 20.

"I love the twenties . . .": Army Archerd, "Just for *Variety*," *Daily Variety*, Aug. 15, 1973.

". . . a private eye and a poet . . .": Nora Sayre, "Falling Prey to Parodies of the Press," *The New York Times*, Jan. 1, 1974, p. 8.

Carol Burnett's reflections: Tamborelli, p. 301.

"I wish that Billy . . .": Jack Lemmon to KL.

"One should never . . .": Joseph McBride and Todd McCarthy, "Going for Extra Innings," *Film Comment* 15, no. 1 (Jan./Feb. 1979), p. 48.

20: PARTING SHOTS

"not just burned up . . .": Charles Champlin, "Wilder Still Working Without a Net," *Los Angeles Times*, July 14, 1974, p. 78.

"What I have learned . . .": Zolotow, p. 237.

"What did you expect . . .": Jon Bradshaw, " 'You Used to Be Very Big.' 'I Am Big. It's the Pictures That Got Small.'," *New York*, Nov. 24, 1975, pp. 39, 43.

" 'Turnaround' . . .": Aljean Harmetz, "At 73, Billy Wilder's Bark Still Has Plenty of Bite," *The New York Times*, June 29, 1979, p. C12.

"Now I come to Germany . . .": Joseph McBride and Todd McCarthy, "Going for Extra Innings," *Film Comment* 15, no. 1 (Jan./Feb. 1979), p. 42.

"We need Garbo . . .": Guy Flatley, "At the Movies," *The New York Times*, Sept. 3, 1976.

"as if she couldn't . . .": Karasek, p. 482.

"I have known Garbo . . .": Rex McGee, "The Life and Hard Times of *Fedora*," *American Film* 4, no. 4 (Feb. 1979), p. 19.

"We were about two days . . .": BW to KL, March 4, 1994.

Hildegard Knef on BW: Knef, pp. 189–90.

"Let's go for the extreme . . .": "The Life and Hard Times of *Fedora*," p. 19.

Frances Sternhagen's comments: Frances Sternhagen to KL, June 7, 1995.

"I didn't feel . . .": Dan Yakir, "Fedora: Another 'Uneasy' Role for Marthe Keller," *New York Post*, April 13, 1979, p. 27.

"She's not . . .": BW to KL, March 4, 1994.

"First he destroys . . .": "The Life and Times of *Fedora*," p. 31.

"not just about . . .": "At 73, Billy Wilder's Bark Still Has Plenty of Bite," p. C12.

Details of early *Fedora* screenings: "The Life and Times of *Fedora*," p. 32.

"They gave us a print . . .": "Allied Artists Out of 'Fedora'; Wilder Pic Back with Lorimar," *Variety*, n.d. (c. February 1979).

". . . perfunctory and insulting . . .": "At 73, Billy Wilder's Bark Still Has Plenty of Bite," p. C12.

"If I had it . . .": "The Life and Times of *Fedora*," p. 32.

"I feel like . . .": BW to KL, March 4, 1994.

"I really loved Bill . . .": Stephen Farber, "Wilder: A Cynic Ahead of His Time," *The New York Times*, Dec. 6, 1981, p. D21.

"*Grease* is . . .": Stephen Farber, "Magnificent Obsession," *New West*, May 7, 1979.

Lemmon recalls Matthau's accident: *Late Show with David Letterman*, CBS, Jan. 1994.

Matthau's comments: Walter Matthau to KL, Dec. 3, 1993.

"I did get the feeling . . .": Jack Lemmon to KL, Dec. 2, 1993.

"the best comedy script . . .": Army Archerd, "Just for *Variety*," *Daily Variety*, Feb. 9, 1981.

"didn't work at all . . .": Baltake, p. 255.

"It was probably wrong . . .": Karasek, p. 467.

"Little did I know . . .": *Women's Wear Daily*, Dec. 11, 1981, p. 20.

21: A FINAL CLOSEUP

"after a year . . .": Joseph McBride and Todd McCarthy, "Going for Extra Innings," *Film Comment* 15, no. 1 (Jan./Feb. 1979), p. 44.

"You hire the soundstage . . .": Nigel Andrews, "Still Sparkling on Sunset," *Financial Times* (London), Nov. 14, 1992.

"We had more fun . . .": BW to KL, Sept. 17, 1993.

"You go to London . . .": Ibid.

"Those ugly things . . .": Ibid.

BW on *Schindler's List:* BW to KL, Feb. 7, 1995.

BW as UA consultant: Bart, p. 243.

". . . sledgehammer blow": BW to KL, Sept. 17, 1993.

"He used to sit . . .": Howard Rodman, "I. A. L.," *Village Voice*, June 14, 1988, p. 71.

"The person who was . . .": Barbara Diamond to KL, Sept. 14, 1993.

"Diamond was . . .": BW to KL, Sept. 17, 1993.

"I started the idea . . .": Ibid.

"Josef von Sternberg . . .": BW to KL, Oct. 25, 1994.

"There were very few . . .": Susan Reed and Doris Bacon, "Director Billy Wilder Puts His Legendary $22 Million-or-So Art Collection on the Auction Block," *People*, Nov. 13, 1989.

"I don't call . . .": Malcolm N. Carter, "Great Private Collections: The Obsessions of Billy Wilder," *Saturday Review*, Dec. 1980, p. 60.

"while making my way . . .": BW, catalogue introduction to "Billy Wilder's Marché aux Puces," Louis Stern Gallery, Dec. 15, 1993–Jan. 31, 1994.

"I wanted to test . . .": "Director Billy Wilder . . . Auction Block."

"A collection needs . . .": Ibid.

"I'm sick of watching . . .": Michael Blowen, "The Art of Billy Wilder," *Boston Globe*, Oct. 22, 1989, p. 82.

David Hockney on BW: Army Archerd, "Just for *Variety*," *Daily Variety*, Sept. 27, 1989, p. 2.

"I wish he hadn't . . .": Kevin Thomas, " 'I Just Believe in Billy Wilder,' " *New York Post*, March 26, 1994, p. 17.

"I think you did . . .": *Variety*, July 19, 1993, p. 44.

"I'm just going . . .": Stephen M. Silverman, interview with BW, *Mirabella*, June 1993, p. 18.

"We had tears . . .": Army Archerd, "Just for *Variety*," *Daily Variety*, July 14, 1993, p. 2.

". . . king of the remakes": Pat Kirkham, "Saul Bass and Billy Wilder in Conversation," *Sight and Sound*, June 1995, p. 21.

". . . cult of admirers . . .": Stephen Farber, "Magnificent Obsession," *New West*, May 7, 1979.

Autograph story: BW to KL, Sept. 17, 1993.

". . . Vertigo . . .": BW to KL, April 12, 1995.

"Deep down . . .": Fred Zinnemann to KL, Jan. 10, 1994.

". . . an older brother . . .": Jack Lemmon to KL, Dec. 2, 1994.

"Every picture's . . .": BW to KL, March 4, 1994.

BIBLIOGRAPHY

Agee, James. *Agee on Film*. New York: Grosset & Dunlap, 1969.

Arce, Hector. *Gary Cooper: An Intimate Biography*. New York: William Morrow, 1979.

————. *The Secret Life of Tyrone Power*. New York: William Morrow, 1979.

Axelrod, George. *The Seven Year Itch* (play). New York: Dramatists Play Service, 1953.

Bach, Steven. *Marlene Dietrich: Life and Legend*. New York: William Morrow, 1992.

Bainbridge, John. *Garbo*. Garden City, N.Y.: Doubleday, 1955.

Balio, Tino. *United Artists: The Studio That Changed Hollywood*. Madison: University of Wisconsin Press, 1987.

Baltake, Joe. *Jack Lemmon: His Films and Career*. New York: Citadel, 1986.

Bart, Peter. *Fade Out: The Calamitous Final Days of MGM*. New York: Anchor, 1991.

Berg, A. Scott. *Goldwyn: A Biography*. New York: Ballantine, 1990.

Bevan, Donald, and Edmund Trzcinski. *Stalag 17* (play). New York: Dramatists Play Service, 1951.

Breffort, Alexandre, and Marguerite Monnot. *Irma la Douce* (stage musical). English version by Julian More, David Heneker, Monty Norman. 1960. Courtesy of Billy Rose Theatre Collection, New York Public Library for the Performing Arts–Lincoln Center.

Brunette, Peter, and Gerald Peary. Interview with James M. Cain in *Backstory: Interviews with Screenwriters of Hollywood's Golden Age*. Berkeley: University of California Press, 1986.

Cagney, James. *Cagney by Cagney*. New York: Doubleday, 1976.

Cain, James M. *Double Indemnity*. 1943. Reprint, New York: Vintage, 1989.

Callow, Simon. *Charles Laughton: A Difficult Actor*. New York: Grove, 1988.

Challis, Christopher. *Are They Really So Awful? A Cameraman's Chronicle*. London: Janus, 1995.

Chierichetti, David. *Hollywood Director: The Career of Mitchell Leisen*. New York, Curtis Books, 1973.

Christie, Agatha. *Witness for the Prosecution* (play). New York: Samuel French, 1954.

Christie's New York. *The Billy Wilder Collection* (catalogue). 1989.

Corliss, Richard. *Talking Pictures: Screenwriters in the American Cinema*. 1975. Reprint, Woodstock, N.Y.: Overlook, 1985.

Coursodon, Jean-Pierre, with Pierre Sauvage. *American Directors*. Vol. I. New York: McGraw-Hill, 1983.

Current Biography, 1984.

Curtis, Tony, and Barry Paris. *Tony Curtis: The Autobiography*. New York: William Morrow, 1993.

Curtiss, Thomas Quinn. *Von Stroheim*. New York: Farrar, Straus & Giroux, 1971.

d'Acosta, Mercedes. *Here Lies the Heart*. London: Andre Deutsch, 1960.

Dick, Bernard F. *Billy Wilder*. Boston: Twayne, 1980.

Dickens, Homer. *The Complete Films of Marlene Dietrich*. New York: Citadel, 1992.

———. *The Films of Gary Cooper*. New York: Citadel, 1970.

Dietrich, Marlene. *Marlene*. New York: Avon, 1990.

Douglas, Kirk. *The Ragman's Son: An Autobiography*. New York: Simon & Schuster, 1988.

Durgnat, Raymond. *The Crazy Mirror: Hollywood Comedy and the American Image*. New York: Horizon Press, 1970.

Eisner, Lotte. *The Haunted Screen*. Translated by Roger Greaves. Berkeley: University of California Press, 1969.

Eyles, Allen. *James Stewart*. New York: Stein & Day, 1984.

Eyman, Scott. *Ernst Lubitsch: Laughter in Paradise*. New York: Simon & Schuster, 1993.

Ferrer, José, Ketti Frings, and Nancy Mitford. *The Dazzling Hour* (adaptation of Anna Bonacci's play, *L'Ora della Fantasia*). 1954. Courtesy of Billy Rose Theatre Collection, New York Public Library for the Performing Arts–Lincoln Center.

Fischer, Dennis. "Curt Siodmak." In *Backstory 2: Interviews with Screenwriters of the 1940s and 1950s*, edited by Pat McGilligan. Berkeley: University of California Press, 1991.

Friedrich, Otto. *City of Nets: A Portrait of Hollywood in the 1940s*. New York: Harper & Row, 1986.

Froug, William. *The Screenwriter Looks at the Screenwriter*. New York: Dell, 1972.

Gardner, Gerald. *The Censorship Papers: Movie Censorship Letters from the Hays Office 1934 to 1968.* New York: Dodd, Mead, 1987.

Giannetti, Louis. *Masters of the American Cinema.* Englewood Cliffs, N.J.: Prentice-Hall, 1981.

Goodman, Ezra. *The Fifty-Year Decline and Fall of Hollywood.* New York: Simon & Schuster, 1961.

Greenberg, Joel. "Walter Reisch." In *Backstory 2: Interviews with Screenwriters of the 1940s and 1950s,* edited by Pat McGilligan. Berkeley: University of California Press, 1991.

Guiles, Fred Lawrence. *Norma Jean: The Life of Marilyn Monroe.* New York: Paragon House, 1993.

Hecht, Ben, and Charles MacArthur. *The Front Page* (play). New York: Samuel French, 1928.

Higham, Charles. *Charles Laughton: An Intimate Biography.* Garden City, N.Y.: Doubleday, 1976.

Higham, Charles, and Joel Greenberg. *The Celluloid Muse: Hollywood Directors Speak.* Chicago: H. Regnery, 1969.

Hunter, Allan. *Walter Matthau.* New York: St. Martin's, 1984.

Huston, John. *An Open Book.* New York: Knopf, 1980.

Jackson, Charles. *The Lost Weekend.* New York: Farrar & Rinehart, 1944.

Kanin, Garson. *Hollywood.* New York: Limelight Editions, 1984.

Karasek, Hellmuth. *Billy Wilder: Eine Nahaufnahme (Billy Wilder: A Closeup).* Hamburg: Hoffmann und Campe, 1992 (Excerpts used in this book translated by Robert Sheff).

Kästner, Erich. *Emil and the Detectives.* New York: Doubleday, Doran, 1937 (translated by May Massee).

Katz, Ephraim. *The Film Encyclopedia.* 2d ed. New York: HarperCollins, 1994.

Kazan, Elia. *Elia Kazan: A Life.* New York: Anchor, 1989.

Kleno, Larry. *Kim Novak on Camera.* San Diego: A. S. Barnes, 1980.

Knef, Hildegard. *The Gift Horse: Report on a Life.* New York: McGraw-Hill, 1971.

Kobal, John. *People Will Talk.* New York: Knopf, 1985.

Kohner, Frederick. *The Magician of Sunset Boulevard: The Improbable Life of Paul Kohner, Hollywood Agent.* Palos Verdes, Calif.: Morgan Press, 1977.

Kracauer, Siegfried. *From Caligari to Hitler: A Psychological History of the German Film.* Princeton, N.J.: Princeton University Press, 1947.

Lanchester, Elsa. *Elsa Lanchester Herself.* New York: St. Martin's, 1983.

Lazar, Irving. *Swifty: My Life and Good Times.* New York: Simon & Schuster, 1995.

Lehman, Ernest. *Screening Sickness and Other Tales of Tinseltown.* New York: Perigee, 1982.

Lewis, Roger. *The Life and Death of Peter Sellers.* London: Century, 1994.

Lindbergh, Charles A. *The Spirit of St. Louis.* New York: Charles Scribner's Sons, 1953.

Lloyd, Ann, ed. *Movies of the Fifties.* London: Orbis, 1982.

Luhr, William. *Raymond Chandler and Film.* Tallahassee, Fla.: Florida State University Press, 1991.

Macdonald, Dwight. *On Movies.* New York: Berkley, 1971.

Macdonald, Kevin. *Emeric Pressburger: The Life and Death of a Screenwriter.* London: Faber & Faber, 1994.

McGilligan, Patrick. *Cagney: The Actor as Auteur.* New York: Da Capo, 1979.

MacLaine, Shirley. *My Lucky Stars: A Hollywood Memoir.* New York: Bantam, 1995.

MacShane, Frank. *The Life of Raymond Chandler.* New York: Penguin, 1976.

MacShane, Frank, ed. *Selected Letters of Raymond Chandler.* New York: Columbia University Press, 1981.

Madsen, Axel. *Billy Wilder.* Bloomington: Indiana University Press, 1969.

———. *Stanwyck.* New York: HarperCollins, 1994.

Mailer, Norman. *Marilyn.* New York: Warner, 1975.

Marling, William H. *Raymond Chandler.* Boston: Twayne, 1986.

Mast, Gerald. *The Comic Mind: Comedy and the Movies.* Indianapolis: Bobbs-Merrill, 1973.

Matthau, Carol. *Among the Porcupines: A Memoir.* New York: Ballantine, 1993.

Maychick, Diana. *Audrey Hepburn: An Intimate Portrait.* New York: Birch Lane, 1993.

Milland, Ray. *Wide-Eyed in Babylon.* New York: William Morrow, 1974.

Miller, Frank. *Censored Hollywood: Sex, Sin and Violence on Screen.* Atlanta: Turner, 1994.

Moffat, Ivan. "Billy Wilder" In *The World of Raymond Chandler,* edited by Miriam Gross. New York: A&W Publishing, 1977.

Molnár, Ferenc. *One, Two, Three* (one-act play). English version by Sidney Howard. 1930. Courtesy Billy Rose Theatre Collection, New York Public Library for the Performing Arts–Lincoln Center.

Mosley, Leonard. *Lindbergh: A Biography.* Garden City, N.Y.: Doubleday, 1976.

Perry, George. *Sunset Boulevard: From Movie to Musical.* New York: Henry Holt, 1993.

Pickard, Roy. *Jimmy Stewart: A Life in Film.* New York: St. Martin's, 1992.

Pogue, Leland. *The Hollywood Professionals.* Vol. 7, *Wilder and McCarey.* San Diego: A. S. Barnes, 1980.

Previn, André. *No Minor Chords: My Days in Hollywood.* New York: Doubleday, 1991.

Quirk, Lawrence J. *The Complete Films of William Holden*. New York: Citadel, 1986.

Randall, Richard S. *Censorship of the Movies: The Social and Political Control of a Mass Medium*. Madison: University of Wisconsin Press, 1968.

Rasner, Heinz-Gerd, and Reinhard Wulf. " 'Ich nehm das alles nicht so ernst . . .'—Gespräch mit Billy Wilder" (" 'I Don't Take It All So Seriously . . .'—A Conversation With Billy Wilder"). In *Billy Wilder's Filme*. Berlin: Verlag Volker Speiss, 1980. (Excerpts used in this book translated by Robert Sheff.)

Riva, Maria. *Marlene Dietrich*. New York: Ballantine, 1992.

Robinson, Edward G., with Leonard Spigelgass. *All My Yesterdays*. New York: Hawthorn, 1973.

Rogers, Ginger. *Ginger: My Story*. New York: HarperCollins, 1991.

Rosenfeld, Paul. *The Club Rules: Power, Money, Sex, and Fear—How It Works in Hollywood*. New York: Warner, 1993.

Rozsa, Miklos. *Double Life*. New York: Wynwood Press, 1989.

Rühmann, Heinz. *Heinz Rühmann: Das Was's*. Berlin, Frankfurt, Vienna: Ullstein, 1982. (Excerpts used in this book translated by Robert Sheff.)

Sarlot, Raymond, and Fred E. Basten. *Life at the Marmont*. Santa Monica, Calif.: Roundtable Publishing, 1987.

Sarris, Andrew. *The American Cinema: Directors and Directions 1929–1968*. New York: Dutton, 1968.

Schickel, Richard. *Double Indemnity*. London: British Film Institute, 1992.

Seidman, Steve. *The Film Career of Billy Wilder*. Boston: G. K. Hall, 1977.

Sinyard, Neil, and Adrian Turner. *Journey Down Sunset Boulevard: The Films of Billy Wilder*. Ryde, Isle of Wight: BCW Publishing, 1979.

Siodmak, Robert, and Hans C. Blumenberg. *Zwischen Berlin und Hollywood* (*Between Berlin and Hollywood*). Munich: Herbig, 1980. (Excerpts used in this book translated by Robert Sheff.)

Skenazy, Paul. *James M. Cain*. New York: Continuum, 1989.

Smith, Ella. *Starring Miss Barbara Stanwyck*. New York: Crown, 1985.

Spoto, Donald. *Blue Angel: The Life of Marlene Dietrich*. New York: Doubleday, 1992.

———. *Marilyn Monroe: The Biography*. New York: HarperCollins, 1993.

Swanson, Gloria. *Swanson on Swanson*. New York: Random House, 1980.

Swindell, Larry. *The Last Hero: A Biography of Gary Cooper*. Garden City, N.Y.: Doubleday, 1980.

Tamborelli, J. Randy. *Laughing Till It Hurts: The Complete Life and Career of Carol Burnett*. New York: William Morrow, 1988.

Taylor, John Russell. *Strangers in Paradise: The Hollywood Emigrés, 1933–1950*. New York: Holt, Rinehart and Winston, 1983.

Taylor, Samuel. *Avanti!* (play). 1968. Courtesy Billy Rose Theatre Collection, New York Public Library for the Performing Arts–Lincoln Center.

———. *Sabrina Fair* (play). New York: Dramatists Play Service, 1954.

Thomas, Bob. *Golden Boy: The Untold Story of William Holden*. New York: St. Martin's, 1983.

Toland, John. *Adolf Hitler*. New York: Doubleday, 1976.

Tosches, Nick. *Dino: Living High in the Dirty Business of Dreams*. New York: Doubleday, 1992.

Truffaut, François. *The Films in My Life*. Translated by Leonard Mayhew. New York: Simon & Schuster, 1978.

Tryon, Thomas. *Crowned Heads*. New York: Knopf, 1976.

Tyler, Parker. *Magic and Myth of the Movies*. New York: Simon & Schuster, 1948.

Viertel, Peter. *Dangerous Friends: Hemingway, Huston and Others*. New York: Doubleday, 1992.

Vizzard, Jack. *See No Evil: Life Inside a Hollywood Censor*. New York: Simon & Schuster, 1970.

Walker, Alexander. *Audrey: Her Real Story*. New York: St. Martin's, 1994.

———. *Peter Sellers: The Authorized Biography*. London: Weidenfeld & Nicolson, 1981.

Weatherby, W. J. *Conversations with Marilyn*. New York: Paragon House, 1992.

Weinberg, Herman G. *The Lubitsch Touch: A Critical Study*. New York: Dover, 1977.

Widener, Don. *Lemmon*. New York: Macmillan, 1975.

Wilder, Billy, and I. A. L. Diamond. *The Apartment and The Fortune Cookie: Two Screenplays*. New York: Praeger, 1971.

———. *Some Like It Hot* (screenplay). New York: Signet, 1959.

Wiley, Mason, and Damien Bona. *Inside Oscar: The Unofficial History of the Academy Awards*. 2d ed. New York: Ballantine, 1987.

Wood, Tom. *The Bright Side of Billy Wilder, Primarily*. Garden City, N.Y.: Doubleday, 1970.

Woodward, Ian. *Audrey Hepburn*. New York: St, Martin's, 1986.

Zinnemann, Fred. *Fred Zinnemann: An Autobiography—A Life in the Movies*. New York: Charles Scribner's Sons, 1992.

Zolotow, Maurice. *Billy Wilder in Hollywood*. New York: Limelight, 1987.

Major Wilder-Related Articles Not Cited in Source Notes

Allen, Tom. "Bracketting Wilder." *Film Comment*, May/June 1982.

Brown, Vanessa. "Broadcast to Kuala Lumpur" (interview). *Action*, Nov./Dec. 1970.

Columbus, Chris, "Wilder Times" (interview). *American Film*, March 1986.

Domarchi, Jean, and Jean Douchet. "Entretien avec Billy Wilder" (interview). *Cahiers du Cinema*, Aug. 1962.

Farber, Stephen. "The Films of Billy Wilder." *Film Comment*, Winter 1971.

Higham, Charles. "Cast a Cold Eye: The Films of Billy Wilder." *Sight and Sound*, Spring 1963.

McBride, Joseph, and Michael Wilmington. "The Private Life of Billy Wilder." *Film Quarterly*, Summer 1970.

Morris, George. "The Private Films of Billy Wilder." *Film Comment*, Jan./Feb. 1979.

Mundy, Robert. "Wilder Reappraised." *Cinema*, Oct. 1969.

Sarris, Andrew. "Billy Wilder: Closet Romanticist." *Film Comment*, July/Aug. 1976.

———. "Why Billy Wilder Belongs in the Pantheon." *Film Comment*, July/Aug. 1991.

Spiller, David. "A World of Wilder." *London Magazine*, June 1968.

Wilder, Billy. "One Head Is Better Than Two," *Films and Filming*, Feb. 1957.

INDEX

Abbott, Bud, 164, 286
Abel, Walter, 99
Abend, Der, 33
Abenteuer der Thea Roland, Das, 44n
Academy of Motion Picture Arts and
    Sciences, 415
Ace in the Hole, 9, 209–15, 216, 218,
    221, 247, 255, 266, 306, 320,
    323, 324, 346, 351, 371, 374,
    385
Adams, Edie, 298
Adam's Rib, 244
Adelson, Merv, 402
Adler, Alfred, 11
Adorable, 41
Adorf, Mario, 401
Adventure of Thea Roland, The, 44n
Adventures of a Ten-Mark Note, The, 29
Adventures of Robin Hood, The, 102
Advise and Consent, 224, 250
Affairs of Anatol, The, 192
African Queen, The, 108, 265
After the Fall, 360

Agee, James, 161, 172, 176, 182, 203
Airport 1975, 204
All About Eve, 203, 296
Allan, Rupert, 287
Allen, Steve, 291, 336
Allied Artists, 256–57, 264, 403
All Quiet on the Western Front, 23, 31,
    51, 161, 382
Alpert, Hollis, 255, 306, 362, 388
Altman, Robert, 389
Ameche, Don, 75
American Cinema, The (Sarris), 183
American Film Institute, 414
Amorous Adventures of Moll Flanders,
    The, 348
Anatomy of a Murder, 224, 250
Anchors Aweigh, 20
And Now My Love, 394
Andrews, Dana, 106
Andrews, Edward, 379n
Andrews, Julie, 367
Anet, Claude, 257
Anna Christie, 66, 86

Anna Karenina, 82

Ansen, David, 409

Answered Prayers (Capote), 217

Anti-Semitism, 7, 51, 53–54, 153

Antonioni, Michelangelo, 324, 325

Apartment, The, 151, 231, 294, 296–
    307, 309, 310, 311, 320, 322,
    329, 339, 346, 348, 350, 361,
    375, 380, 381n, 408, 421

Arce, Hector, 270

Archerd, Army, 356, 384, 409, 421

Arch of Triumph, 56

Ariane, 257, 259

Arise, My Love, 18, 90–97, 111, 120,
    326

Arnheim, Rudolf, 34

Around the World in 80 Days, 167, 253,
    333

Arsenic and Old Lace, 121

Arthur, Bob, 209

Arthur, Jean, 147, 173, 175, 177, 180,
    181, 183

Asphalt, 59

Astaire, Fred, 110, 260

Astor, Mary, 76, 79

Atlantic Monthly, 133

Attenborough, Richard, 365

Aubrey, James, 405

Aus dem Tagebuch einer schönen Frau,
    44n

Austin, Gene, 15

Avanti!, 231, 374–81, 391, 408, 422

Avery, Milton, 417

Avventura, L', 352

Axelrod, George, 240, 241, 245, 246,
    247, 274, 277

Ayres, Lew, 66

Baal, 25

Baby Doll, 348

Bacall, Lauren, 159

Bacharach, Burt, 421

Bad Seed, 56–58, 66, 346, 396

Balaban, Barney, 144, 233

Balázs, Béla, 29

Baldinger, David, 2

Baldinger, Eugenia. *See* Wilder,
    Eugenia

Ball, Lucille, 314, 391

Ball of Fire, 105–7, 108, 111, 185

Balthus, 417, 418

Bank Holiday, 32

Bardot, Brigitte, 329

Barnes, Binnie, 51

Barnes, Howard, 88, 139, 161

Barnett, Lincoln, 86

Barr, Stanley, 144

Barrie, Elaine, 79

Barris, Harry, 164

Barrymore, John, 75, 76, 79

Bart, Peter, 353, 413

Batman (TV), 224

Battleship Potemkin, The, 125

Battle with the Dragon, The, 37–38

Baxter, Anne, 119, 124

Beast with Five Fingers, The, 34

Beckmann, Max, 14

Bedtime Story, 350

Begelman, David, 405

Behrman, S. N., 82, 86

Bekessy, Imre, 10

Bella Epoque, 420

Belle de Jour, 372

Bell for Adano, A, 248

Bells of St. Mary's, The, 162

Benchley, Robert, 113, 116, 148

Benedict, Richard, 209

Ben-Hur, 293, 297

Benjamin, Robert, 265, 347

Bennett, Joan, 297

Bergman, Ingmar, 324, 325
Bergman, Ingrid, 56, 156
Bergner, Elisabeth, 257
Berlin, the Symphony of a Great City, 29
Berliner Zeitung am Mittag (B.Z.), 15, 16–17, 39
Berlin Wall, 317
Best Years of Our Lives, The, 156
Bevan, Donald, 219
Big Carnival, The, 214
Big Sleep, The (Chandler), 127, 128
Billy Wilder Award, 420
Biro, Lajos, 118–19
Biro, Ludwig, 42
Bishop's Wife, The, 108
Bitter Rice, 165
Bizarre Bizarre, 34
Black Cat, The, 34
Black Narcissus, 42
Black Sunday, 394
Blade Runner, 387
Blair, Nicky, 297n
Blakely, Colin, 365, 372
Blaue vom Himmel, Das, 49
Blind Husbands, 121, 192
Blockade, 93
Blond Dream, A, 45–47
Blood and Money (Thompson), 349
Blood and Sand, 270
Bloodbrothers, 215
Blue Angel, The, 37, 39, 55, 272
Bluebeard, 34
Bluebeard's Eighth Wife, 70, 72, 74–75, 76, 79, 143, 231, 259, 320
Bluebeard's Ten Honeymoons, 141
Blue Dahlia, The, 165
Blue from the Sky, The, 49
Bluhdorn, Charles, 382
Blum, Edwin, 218–19, 226
Blumenberg, Hans C., 27

Bobbitt, Lorena, 213
Bobby Deerfield, 394, 396
Bogart, Humphrey, 221, 229, 232–33, 236–37, 238, 239, 245, 257, 260, 414, 422
Bolvary, Geza von, 50
Bomba, the Jungle Boy, 256
Bonacci, Anna, 335
Bonanova, Fortunio, 124
Bonnie and Clyde, 370
Borchert, Brigitte, 27, 30
Borger, Hanus, 154
Born Yesterday, 203
Börsen Courier, 15, 21
Bosom Buddies (TV), 292
Boston Phoenix, The, 381
Boyer, Charles, 17, 55, 56, 57, 98, 101–2, 109, 251
Boy Meets Girl, 313
Brackett, Charles
  background and personality of, 71–72
  on Raymond Chandler, 133
  defense of Wilder films by, 206, 213–14
  as producer of *The King and I*, 239, 259
  professional breakup with Wilder, 204–7, 216
  working relationship with Wilder, 71–74, 125, 126, 142
  writing collaborations with Wilder
    Arise, My Love, 90–97
    Ball of Fire, 106–7
    The Bishop's Wife, 108
    Bluebeard's Eighth Wife, 74–75
    The Emperor Waltz, 166–67, 172
    Five Graves to Cairo, 118–19, 125
    A Foreign Affair, 172–73, 175, 181, 182

Brackett, Charles (*cont'd*)
    Hold Back the Dawn, 100–104
    The Lost Weekend, 142, 144–46,
      147, 161, 162
    The Major and the Minor, 110–11,
      115, 116
    Midnight, 75–79
    Ninotchka, 82–88
    Sunset Boulevard, 186–90, 200
    What a Life, 79–80
Bradshaw, Jon, 390
Brandauer, Klaus Maria, 275
Brandenberg Gate, 316, 326
Brando, Marlon, 225, 255
Braun, Curt, 19
Breakfast at Tiffany's, 246
Breathless, 48, 352
Brecht, Bertolt, 23, 25, 66
Breen, Joseph, 94, 95, 125–27, 144
Breen, Richard, 173n, 206
Brel, Jacques, 405
Bridge on the River Kwai, The, 108, 275
Bridges of Toko-Ri, The, 233
Brief Encounter, 296, 311
Bringing Up Baby, 105, 232
Briskin, Sam, 62
British Board of Censors, 160
Broidy, Steve, 256, 264
Bronnen, Arnolt, 25
Brown, Joe E., 284, 285, 290
Brown, Vanessa, 244
Bruce, Nigel, 372
Brynner, Yul, 219n, 259
Buchholz, Horst, 313, 314, 316–18,
    326, 359
Buchman, Sidney, 62
Buchwald, Art, 294, 310
Buddy Buddy, 405–10, 413
Bühne, Die, 10
Bumstead, Henry, 387

Bunsch, Inga, 397, 401
Buñuel, Luis, 324n, 372
Burnett, Carol, 387, 414, 422
Burschenlied aus Heidelberg, Ein, 37
Burton, Richard, 225, 266
Busoni, Ferruccio, 22
Bus Stop, 246, 265
Butch Cassidy and the Sundance Kid,
    382
Butler, Frank, 69
Butterfield 8, 307
Butterworth, Charles, 116n
Buttons, Red, 321

Cabinet of Dr. Caligari, The, 23
Cactus Flower, 363
Cage aux Folles, La, 405
Cagney, James, 134, 312–14, 318,
    319, 320, 321, 374, 412
Cahiers du Cinema, 27, 324
Cain, James M., 62, 125–26, 128,
    130–32, 138, 162, 219
Caine, Michael, 257n
Calloway, Cab, 420
Camille, 218–19
Campbell, Alan, 422
Canadian Pacific, 191
Canby, Vincent, 361, 373, 380, 388,
    403, 409
Cannes Film Festival, 166, 403
Can of Beans, A, 188
Capote, Truman, 217, 274
Capra, Frank, 62, 273, 386
Cardiff, Jack, 307
Cardinal, The, 224
Carlisle, Kitty, 307
Carmen Jones, 224
Carnal Knowledge, 325
Carné, Marcel, 34
Carney, Art, 175

Carpenter, Edward Childs, 110

Carroll, Kathleen, 373, 388, 404

Caruso, Enrico, 67

Casablanca, 118, 332, 374

Cat Ballou, 215

Catbird Seat, The, 277

Catholic Legion of Decency, 245, 264, 333, 346, 347–49

Cat on a Hot Tin Roof, 291

Cats, 421

Censorship

  Catholic Legion of Decency and, 245, 264, 333, 346, 347–49

  Episocopal Committee for Motion Pictures and, 292

  in Germany, 158, 226

  in Great Britain, 160–61

  Lubitsch films and, 73

  Motion Picture Association of America and, 292, 346–47, 355

  See also Production Code Administration

Cerf, Bennett, 274

Chabrol, Claude, 324

Challis, Christopher, 365, 366

Champagne Waltz, 68–69, 134, 167

Champion, 211

Champlin, Charles, 390

Chandler, Raymond, 127–34, 145, 165, 415

Chanel, Coco, 67

Chaplin, Charles, 6, 15, 39, 94, 198, 265

Charade, 357

Charles, Ray, 420

Charley's Aunt, 278

Chayefsky, Paddy, 395

Chevalier, Maurice, 166, 260, 261, 262, 414

Chicago American, 306

Chicago Herald-Examiner, 383

Chierichetti, David, 78

Children of Paradise, 252

Christie, Agatha, 265, 267, 269, 271

Ciment, Michel, 296, 303, 325, 375, 378, 379

Cinderella, 76

CinemaScope, 241, 253

Citizen Kane, 124

Claire, Ina, 83

Clark, Kenneth, 100

Clarke, Eric T., 158–59

Clift, Montgomery, 190, 199, 225

Clinton, Bill, 239, 420

Close, Glenn, 422

Cocks, Jay, 381, 388

Cocteau, Jean, 324n

Cohn, Harry, 62, 173, 255–56, 266, 280

Colbert, Claudette, 72, 74–75, 79, 82, 91, 94, 96, 245

College Scandal, 72

Collins, Floyd, 208–9

Collins, Stephen, 401

Colpet, Max. *See* Kolpe, Max

Columbia Pictures, 62, 90, 255–56, 266, 279

Comedian, The, 228

Communist witch-hunts, 220–21

Concentration camps, 153–54

Confessions of a Nazi Spy, 93–94

Confessions of Felix Krull, The, 314

Connery, Sean, 257n

Connie Goes Home, 110

Coogan, Jackie, 15

Cooper, Freddie, 365–66

Cooper, Gary, 72–73, 74–75, 104–7, 156, 245, 254, 259–60, 261, 262, 263, 264, 414

Cooper, Jackie, 79

Cooper, Merian C., 68
Coppicus, George, 67
Corday, Eliot, 337
Corliss, Richard, 176, 183, 409
Cornell, Joseph, 417
Corner, James, 79
Corniglion-Molinier, Edouard, 56
Coronet, 285
Cosmopolitan, 227
Costello, Lou, 164, 286
Cotten, Joseph, 229
Counterfeit Husband, The, 40, 41–42
Count of Luxembourg, The, 166, 383
Country Girl, The, 238
Cover Girl, 156
Cowan, Lester, 68
Coward, Noël, 269, 296
Creature from the Black Lagoon, The, 241
Criss Cross, 34
Crist, Judith, 350, 362, 388
Cronenweth, Jordan, 387
Crosby, Bing, 69, 140, 162, 167, 168, 169
Cross-section films, 29
Crowd, The, 297
Crowned Heads (Tryon), 391–92
Crowther, Bosley, 96, 107, 115, 123, 124, 139, 161, 171, 182, 213, 225, 238, 245, 254, 263, 274, 306, 332, 350
Cue magazine, 161, 170, 183, 263, 274, 350, 380
Cukor, George, 65, 82, 189, 244
Culver, Roland, 168
Curtis, Tony, 66, 224, 228, 279, 280–84, 285, 286–88, 290, 292, 295–96, 297n, 414
Curtiz, Michael, 99, 113

d'Acosta, Mercedes, 81, 87
Daily Variety, 333, 384
Daisy Kenyon, 223
Daley, Richard, 387
Dalí, Salvador, 324n
Dancing Pirate, The, 68
Danon, Pamela. *See* Tiffin, Pamela
Daredevil Reporter, The, 24
Dark Mirror, The, 34
Darrieux, Danielle, 56–57
Da Silva, Howard, 148
Daves, Delmer, 339
Davis, Bette, 203
Davis, Elmer, 150–51
Day, Doris, 345
Day-Lewis, Daniel, 143
Dazzling Hour, The, 335
Dean, James, 194
Death Mills, 154–55
Death Takes a Holiday, 77
de Havilland, Olivia, 98, 102–4, 218, 335
De Mille, Cecil B., 67, 77, 192, 193, 198, 200, 202, 223
Denby, David, 409
De Palma, Brian, 413
De Sica, Vittorio, 336
Destry Rides Again, 20
De Sylva, Buddy, 135, 142, 143, 146
Detour, 34
Deval, Jacques, 81
Devil's Eye, The, 322
Deyers, Lien, 38
Diamond, Barbara, 204, 258, 278, 288–89, 300n, 305, 308–9, 317, 343, 352, 376–77
Diamond, I. A. L. "Izzy"
  background and personality of, 257–59
  quip on modern film industry, 414

as screenwriter for *40 Carats*, 374
working relationship with Wilder, 258–59, 278, 308–9, 315, 415–16
writing collaborations with Wilder
  The Apartment, 298, 301, 304, 305, 306, 307
  Buddy Buddy, 406, 409
  Fedora, 391, 392
  The Fortune Cookie, 356, 361, 362
  The Front Page, 381–82, 383–85
  Irma la Douce, 328–29
  Kiss Me, Stupid, 335, 336, 351
  Love in the Afternoon, 264
  One, Two, Three, 314, 315, 317, 319, 321, 322
  The Private Life of Sherlock Holmes, 363, 364, 366, 367
  Some Like It Hot, 278–79, 282, 286, 288, 293
Diary of Anne Frank, The, 222
Didion, Joan, 350–51
Diehl, Karl Ludwig, 48
Dieterle, William, 88, 113
Dietl, Helmut, 268, 295
Dietrich, Marlene
  as film star in Germany, 31, 39, 49
  friction with Audrey Wilder, 217
  friendship with Billy Wilder, 23, 217, 267–68, 276
  Wilder films and
    A Foreign Affair, 9, 173–75, 177, 180, 183, 184
    professional criticisms of, 268–69
    proposed as one-legged prostitute in, 218
    proposed for *Fedora*, 393
    Witness for the Prosecution, 265, 266, 268–71, 272, 274–75
di Frasso, Dorothy, 263

DiMaggio, Joe, 243
Divorce—Italian Style, 351
Dix, Otto, 14
Dodsworth, 156
Domenica d'Agusto, 32
Dommnici, Itek. *See* Diamond, I. A. L.
Donovan's Brain (Siodmak), 34
Double Indemnity, 9, 47, 124, 125–40, 141, 171, 190, 193, 194, 205, 209, 212, 219, 305, 324, 346, 371, 379, 412–13
Douglas, Kirk, 209, 211–12, 213, 214, 221–22, 266, 320
Douglas, Melvyn, 83, 87, 92
Douglas, Paul, 305
Dowling, Constance, 147, 165
Dowling, Doris, 147, 163, 164, 165
Doyle, Arthur Conan, 363
Doyle, Jack, 99
Dozier, William, 104, 127, 205
Dracula, 195
Drei von der Tankstelle, Die, 19
Dr. Mabuse, the Gambler, 14
Dr. Strangelove, 336
Dr. Zhivago, 364
Dunaway, Faye, 393, 422
Dupont, E. A., 113
Duran, D. A., 235
Durbin, Deanna, 20
Durning, Charles, 386
Duryea, Dan, 141
Dwan, Allan, 20–21, 24

Eames, Charles, 207, 208, 252, 419
Eames, Ray, 207
Earrings of Madame De, 57
Eastwood, Clint, 367, 410
Easy Living, 77
Easy Rider, 325

Ebert, Roger, 383
Eddy, Nelson, 147
Edelman, Herbert, 386
Edwards, Blake, 66, 336
Ehlers, Christl, 30
Ehrlichman, John, 385
Eisenhower, Dwight D., 157, 173
Ekland, Britt, 337
El Cid, 141
Ellington, Duke, 219
Elmer Gantry, 307
Elusive Pimpernel, The, 365
Emil and the Detectives, 40, 42–44, 45
Emmerdeur, L', 405
Emperor Waltz, The, 167–72, 184, 223, 376
Encore, 67
Englund, Ken, 77
Enter Madame, 72
Episcopal Committee for Motion Pictures, 292
Epstein, Julius J., 374
Equus, 395
Esquire, 306, 321
Es war einmal ein Walzer, 47–48
Esway, Alexander, 56
European Film Academy, 420
European Film Fund, 88
Evans, Ray, 193
Evening Standard (London), 337
Every Day's a Holiday, 116n
Ewell, Tom, 240, 241, 243, 244, 245, 338
Executive Suite, 227, 228, 229, 234
Exodus, 224
Extramarital Escapade, 40, 42
Eyman, Scott, 171

Fade Out: The Calamitous Final Days of MGM (Bart), 413

Fail Safe, 357
Fairbanks, Douglas, 6, 20, 265
Fairbanks, Douglas, Jr., 274
Faktor, Emil, 21
Falcon Takes Over, The, 127
Fallen Angel, 223
Fall of the Roman Empire, The, 141
Falsche Ehemann, Der, 40, 41–42
Family Plot, 239
Fanfares of Love, 277
Faraway So Close, 39
Farber, Stephen, 403, 404
Farewell My Lovely (Chandler), 127
Farr, Felicia, 331, 336, 339–40, 347, 352
Faylen, Frank, 145
Fedora, 392–404, 405, 413, 422
Feld, Hans, 44
Feldman, Charles, 240, 241, 245
Fellini, Federico, 324, 325
Fenwick, J. H., 351
Ferrer, José, 146, 219, 395, 401
Ferrer, Mel, 238
Feydeau, Georges, 351
Field, Betty, 79
Film Comment, 382, 389, 392, 420
Filmography of Billy Wilder, 429–37
Film Quarterly, 323, 324
Films in Review, 350
Film Society of Lincoln Center, 411
Film Studio 1929, 25, 28–29, 33
Fisher, Gerry, 402
Fitzgerald, Barry, 140
Fitzgerald, Geraldine, 103
Fitzgerald, Scott, 145
Five Fingers, 57
Five Graves to Cairo, 118–25, 136, 171, 191, 321, 326
Flon, Suzanne, 335
Florey, Robert, 118

Fonda, Henry, 109, 399
Fontaine, Joan, 168
Foolish Wives, 121, 192
Forbidden Paradise, 189
Ford, Glenn, 266
Ford, Harrison, 422
Foreign Affair, A, 9, 174–85, 187, 193, 205, 206, 212, 221, 272, 274, 321, 376
Foreign Correspondent, 94
Forever Amber, 223
Forman, Milos, 318
Forst, Willi, 37, 45–46
Fortune Cookie, The, 9, 114, 165, 356–62, 371, 383, 391, 408
40 Carats, 364
42nd Street, 296
For Whom the Bell Tolls, 104
Fosse, Bob, 301
Fox Pictures. *See* 20th Century-Fox
Francis, Arlene, 274, 318
Franco, Pippo, 380
Frank, Bruno, 66
Frank, Paul, 40, 41
Frankenstein, 195
Franklin, Sidney, 81
Franz Josef, Emperor, 3, 167, 168, 170
Freeman, Y. Frank, 143, 214
Freud, Sigmund, 11
Freund, Karl, 29
Frey, Sam, 125
Friendly Persuasion, 256, 264
Frings, Ketti, 91, 99–100
Frings, Kurt, 99, 100
Fritsch, Willy, 40, 45
Frizzell, Lou, 386
Fröhlich, Gustav, 50
From A to Z, 105
From Caligari to Hitler, 34

From Here to Eternity, 35, 225, 241
From the Diary of a Beautiful Woman, 44n
Frontiers of Faith (TV), 353
Front Page, The, 47, 250, 321, 382–89, 390, 391, 405
Funny Face, 260

Gabel, Martin, 387
Gable, Clark, 245, 254, 257
Gable and Lombard, 392
Galitzenstein, Herr, 22–23
Galle, Raymond, 57
Garbo, Greta, 66, 81–83, 86–87, 89, 111, 166, 259, 267, 393
Gardenia, Vincent, 387
Gardner, Ava, 266
Garfield, Allen, 386
Garland, Judy, 221
Garrett, Oliver H. P., 67
Garrison, Robert, 24
Gaynor, Janet, 41
Gaynor, Mitzi, 279
Geller, James, 125
Gellhorn, Martha, 91
Gelmis, Joseph, 354
George White's Scandals, 163
Georgy Girl, 362
Gere, Richard, 215
Geria Film, 392
German Self-Censorship Board, 226
Germany
    film industry in, 14, 19–20, 23, 40, 54–55, 158, 159, 226, 392–93
    Nazi takeover in, 51–55
    post–World War II, 152–59
Germi, Pietro, 351
Gershwin, George and Ira, 341n
Getty, J. Paul, 194

Ghostwriting, 19–20, 23–24, 37, 55, 66

Gibbons, Cedric, 136

Gibraltar, 67

Gibson, Hoot, 6

Gift Horse, The (Knef), 394–95

Gigolo exposé, 16–18

Gilbert, John, 199

Gilded Lily, The, 96

Gill, Brendan, 322, 332, 350

Gillespie, Dizzy, 419

Gilliatt, Penelope, 403

Ginsberg, Henry, 150, 190, 205

Girl Can't Help It, The, 244

Girl from Jones Beach, The, 257

Givenchy, Hubert de, 238

Glazer, Benjamin, 90–91

Gliese, Rochus, 30, 31

Godard, Jean-Luc, 324, 325

Goddard, Paulette, 98

Goebbels, Joseph, 51, 55, 152, 394

Goetz, William, 108, 412

Going My Way, 140, 162

Goldberg, Whoopi, 415

Golden Boy, 190

Gold Rush, The, 162

Goldsmith, Clifford, 79

Goldwyn, Samuel, 22, 104–5, 107–8, 111, 245, 400

Golem, The, 30

Gone with the Wind, 88, 102, 109, 161, 244

Goodbye, Mr. Chips, 88

Goodman, Ezra, 236

Gordine, Fiorenzo, 165

Gould, Harold, 386

Goulding, Edmund, 82

Graham, Sheila, 322

Grande Illusion, La, 122

Grand Hotel, 82, 99

Grant, Cary, 87, 142, 228–29, 232, 259, 263, 287, 382, 386

Grapes of Wrath, The, 161

Graves, Peter, 224

Gray, Judd, 130

Grease, 405

Great Caruso, The, 20

Great Dictator, The, 94

Great Flamarion, The, 141

Great McGinty, The, 104

Greed, 121, 213

Gregor, Nora, 50

Griffith, D. W., 139, 265

Griffith, Richard, 349

Grosz, George, 14, 23, 417

Gunfight at the OK Corral, 332

Gunga Din, 92

Gurney, Bud, 254

Guys and Dolls, 258

Haas, Dolly, 48

Habsburg, Otto von, 3

Hall, Porter, 209

Hamburger, Philip, 203

Hamilton, Hamish, 130

Hammell, John, 126

Hammerstein II, Oscar, 65, 274

Hammett, Dashiell, 128, 145

Hampton, Christopher, 421

Hanks, Tom, 292

Happy Time, The, 227

Harari, Robert, 173

Harding, Tonya, 213

Hardy, Oliver, 218

Harrison, Doane, 113–14, 124, 233, 334, 414

Harrison, Rex, 274, 363

Hart, Moss, 274, 307, 363

Hart, William S., 6

Hartman, Don, 69, 228

Hartwig, Hella, 53–55, 68, 151
Harvey, Lilian, 45, 47, 154
Havoc, June, 174
Hawks, Howard, 105, 190, 257, 382, 386
Hays, Will, 95
Hays Office, 125–27, 134, 138, 144, 160
  See also Production Code Administration
Hayward, Leland, 111, 248–50, 252–54, 274
Hayworth, Rita, 109, 156, 255, 266
Head, Edith, 238
Head of a Woman (Picasso), 418
Heaven Can Wait, 171
Hecht, Ben, 381, 384, 389
Heifetz, Jascha, 364
Heiress, The, 395
Hello, Dolly!, 239, 367
Hemingway, Ernest, 60, 91, 104, 111
Henry Aldrich for President, 80
Hepburn, Audrey, 48, 166, 227, 228, 229, 230, 232, 236–39, 259–60, 262, 263, 277, 307, 326, 414, 422
Hepburn, Katharine, 147, 237, 419
Her Majesty Commands, 40–41
Hernandez, Helen, 166, 205
Heston, Charlton, 221, 254
Heymann, Werner Richard, 41
High Noon, 19, 35, 263, 265
High Window, The (Chandler), 127
Hindenburg, Paul von, 52
Hirschfeld, Al, 48
Hirschfeld, Ludwig, 37
His Girl Friday, 105, 250, 382, 386
Hitchcock, Alfred, 94, 138, 139, 162, 171, 227, 252, 273, 398
Hitler, Adolf, 51–55

Hitlerjunge Quex, 51
Hockney, David, 417, 419
Hoffman, Dustin, 143
Hold Back the Dawn, 17, 63, 98–104, 106, 128, 179, 212, 251
Holden, Ardis. *See* Marshall, Brenda
Holden, William
  affair with Audrey Hepburn, 237–38
  death of, 404
  on filming *Network*, 395–96
  friendship with Wilder, 204, 226, 227, 229, 236, 310, 376
  Oscar given to, 225
  in Wilder films
    Fedora, 397, 401
    Sabrina, 229, 230, 232, 233, 236, 237–38
    Stalag 17, 222, 225
    Sunset Boulevard, 17, 190, 194, 201, 204, 422
Holiday, Hope, 305
Holiday magazine, 267
Hollander, Frederick, 39, 55, 174, 177, 182
Holliday, Judy, 203, 246
Hollis, Alpert, 263
Hollywood Reporter, The, 161, 254
Holman, Libby, 190
Holman, Russell, 160, 174
Homolka, Oscar, 245
Honeymooners, 176
Hoover, Herbert, 4
Hope, Bob, 104, 162, 279, 338
Hopper, Hedda, 193, 322
Hornblow, Arthur, Jr., 77, 78, 90, 100, 101, 109, 110, 116, 265–66, 270, 274, 414
Horne, Lena, 218
Horton, Edward Everett, 74

Horwitz, Kurt, 50
Hotel Ansonia, 55–56
Hotel Imperial, 118
House Calls, 402
Houseman, John, 228
House Party (TV), 254
Houston, Bruce, 419
Howard, Sidney, 311
Howey, Walter, 383
Hughes, Howard, 259
Hunchback of Notre Dame, The, 269, 395
Hustler, The, 34
Huston, John, 109n, 134, 221, 244, 256–57
Hutchinson, Josephine, 163
Hyams, Joe, 293, 328

Idiot's Delight, 94
I Have Loved You, 36
Ihre Hoheit befiehlt, 40–41
I Kiss Your Hand, Madame, 31, 36
Informer, The, 161, 213
Inge, William, 246
In Harm's Way, 250
Inspector General, The, 266
Intolerance, 125
Iribe, Judith, 67, 75, 89–90, 116–17, 164–65
Iribe, Paul, 67, 77n
Irma la Douce, 9, 111, 275, 294, 310, 327–33, 334, 335, 340, 346, 361, 363, 391
It Happened One Night, 238
It's a Mad, Mad, Mad, Mad World, 333
I Walked With a Zombie, 34
I Wanted Wings, 100

Jackson, Charles, 142, 145–46, 147, 148, 161–62

Jacobi, Lou, 331
Jaray, Hans, 401
Jaws, 405
Jazz Singer, The, 36
Jenkins, William, 194
Jezebel, 156
Joe Palooka series, 62
Johnson, Hilding, 383
Johnson, Nunnally, 126
Johnson, Rita, 111
Johnston, Eric, 292, 347
Joker, The, 322
Jolson, Al, 36
Jolson Story, The, 244
Journey to the Center of the Earth, 206
Joyless Street, The, 14
Jubal, 339
Jud Suss, 152
Jules and Jim, 352
Julia, 35
Julius Caesar, 225
Jungle, The, 214
Jurassic Park, 69, 413

Kael, Pauline, 181, 182n, 323, 326, 373, 387, 388
Kampf mit dem Drachen, Der, 37–38
Kanin, Garson, 205, 319
Karasek, Hellmuth, 276
Kästner, Erich, 42–43
Kauffmann, Stanley, 278
Kaye, Danny, 147, 166, 278, 338, 383
Kazan, Elia, 165, 238, 348
Keaton, Buster, 6, 39, 193, 200
Keller, Marthe, 394, 396–97, 401
Kelly, Ellsworth, 416
Kelly, Gene, 190, 221, 266, 367
Kelly, Grace, 238
Kendall, Kay, 274, 314
Kennamer, Rex, 337

Kennedy, Joseph, 191
Kerkorian, Kirk, 405
Kern, Jerome, 65
Kerr, John, 249
Keyes, Evelyn, 244
Khan, Aly, 259
Khrushchev, Nikita, 294, 317
Kid, The, 15
Kilbourne, Fanny, 110
Killer Bees, The, 204
Killers, The, 34
King and I, The, 206, 239, 259
King Creole, 357
King Kong, 68
King of Kings, The, 67, 77n, 193
Kingsley, Sidney, 62
Kinnear, Greg, 422
Kinski, Klaus, 409
Kipling, Rudyard, 257
Kissinger, Henry, 375
Kiss Me, Stupid, 9, 335–55, 356, 361,
    362, 363, 373, 379, 391
Kiss of Death, 250
Kitty Foyle, 110, 111
Knef, Hildegard, 394–95, 397, 401
Knickerbocker Holiday, 147
Knife in the Water, 352
Knight, Arthur, 292, 373, 380
Kohner, Paul, 20, 24, 88, 392
Koklova, Olga, 418
Kolpe, Max, 44, 48, 49, 55, 56
Korda, Alexander, 49
Koster, Henry, 44n, 113
Kracauer, Siegfried, 29, 34
Kraft, Hy, 68
Krasna, Norman, 62, 218, 374
Krauss, Werner, 152
Krim, Arthur, 264–65, 292
Krock, Arthur, 130
Krupp, Alfried, 54

Kruschen, Jack, 304
Kubrick, Stanley, 329, 336
Kurnitz, Harry, 266–67, 271, 272,
    363
Kurosawa, Akira, 324
Kuveiller, Luigi, 381

Ladd, Alan, 134, 165
Ladykillers, The, 40
Laemmle, Carl, 24, 65
Lake, Veronica, 100
Lamarr, Hedy, 193
Lamprecht, Gerhard, 43
Lancaster, Burt, 221, 225, 254, 307
Lanchester, Elsa, 266, 274
Land of the Pharaohs, 266–67
Lang, Anton, 152
Lang, Charles, 78, 96, 184
Lang, Fritz, 14, 23, 25, 55, 61n
Lang, Jennings, 297, 382
Langdon, Harry, 285
Lange, Jessica, 415
LaShelle, Joseph, 336, 346, 361
Last Command, The, 118
Last Laugh, The, 14, 23, 45
Last Mile, The, 99
Last Tango in Paris, 181, 182n
Last Train from Madrid, 93
Last Wagon, The, 339
Laughton, Charles, 56, 61, 109, 208,
    266, 268, 269–70, 274–76,
    331, 395, 414
Laura, 223
Laurel, Stan, 218
Lawrence, Gertrude, 367
Lawrence of Arabia, 108, 364
Lazar, Irving "Swifty," 217, 233, 236,
    239–40, 258
Lean, David, 275, 296, 311
LeBorg, Reginald, 62

Lederer, Charles, 250
Lederer, Francis, 75
Lee, Christopher, 372
Léhar, Franz, 47, 383
Lehman, Ernest, 228–29, 233–35, 236, 237, 238, 239, 258, 262, 354
Leigh, Janet, 66
Leigh, Vivien, 88
Leisen, Mitchell, 77–79, 90, 92, 95–96, 100, 101, 102
Lelouch, Claude, 394
Lembeck, Harvey, 223, 225
Lemmon, Felicia. See Farr, Felicia
Lemmon, Jack
   on Izzy Diamond, 257–58
   friendship with Wilder, 310, 355, 376–77, 414, 423
   on Marilyn Monroe, 284
   marriage to Felicia Farr, 331
   Oscar nomination for, 293
   professional relationship with Wilder, 334, 387–88, 415
   in Wilder films
      The Apartment, 297, 299–302, 307
      Avanti!, 377, 380, 381
      Buddy Buddy, 405, 406–9
      The Fortune Cookie, 357–60
      The Front Page, 382, 386, 387–88
      Irma la Douce, 327, 330, 331
      Some Like It Hot, 279–82, 284–86, 290, 291–92, 293, 296
Lemon, Richard, 354
Lengyel, Melchior, 81
Lerner, Alan Jay, 204, 274, 363
LeRoy, Mervyn, 346
Lewis, David, 305
Lewis, Jerry, 235, 286
Lewis, Sinclair, 60

Lewton, Val, 198
Libeled Lady, 382
Liberty, 130
Liebmann, Robert, 37, 40, 43, 44
Liebstockl, Hans, 10
Liedtke, Harry, 36
Life magazine, 151, 162, 166, 183, 186, 225, 332, 349–50, 361
Lights of New York, 36
Liliom, 55
Lindbergh, Charles, 246, 248–49, 255
Lindsay-Hogg, Edward, 103
Listener, The, 351
Little, Ann, 64, 68
Little, Thomas F., 347–48
Little Big Man, 370
Little Caesar, 135
Little Foxes, The, 156
Little Women, 65
Litvak, Anatole, 185
Livingston, Alan, 421
Livingston, Jay, 193
Livingston, Nancy. *See* Olson, Nancy
Lloyd, Harold, 39
Loch Ness monster, 363, 364, 370
Loewe, Frederick, 363
Logan, Joshua, 265, 367
Lolita, 112
Lollabrigida, Gina, 307
Lombard, Carole, 314
Lonely Are the Brave, 357
Look magazine, 330
Loos, Mary, 171
Lopert Pictures, 349
Lord Love a Duck, 246
Lorimar Productions, 402, 403
Lorre, Peter, 50, 55, 64
Los Angeles Herald & Express, 270
Los Angeles Times, 219, 250
Lost Weekend, The, 124, 142–50, 159–

62, 163, 165, 166, 193, 201, 212, 260, 291, 364, 395

Lottery Lover, 66

Louis Stern Gallery, 419

Louisville Courier-Journal, 209

Loved One, The, 219n

Love Happy, 309

Love in the Afternoon, 18, 48, 59, 102, 226, 231, 252, 257, 259–64, 278, 310, 320, 326, 376, 402, 403, 422

Love in the Air, 172–73

Love Me or Leave Me, 20

Lover, Come Back, 346

Lowe, Edmund, 66

Lubitsch, Ernst
death of, 172
as director of *Bluebeard's Eighth Wife*, 70, 72, 74–75
as director of *Ninotchka*, 80, 81–88
on Greta Garbo, 82–83
as Hollywood immigrant, 61
influence on Wilder's work, 57, 73, 84–85, 101, 113, 167, 171–72, 259, 262
unfinished films by, 223
Wilder's screenplays for, 72–75, 84–88

Luft, Herbert G., 206

Lund, John, 173, 175, 180

LuPone, Patti, 422

Luraschi, Luigi, 94, 126, 174

Lustig, Hanns G., 56

Luthge, B. E., 42

Lux Video Theatre (TV), 254

Lydon, Jimmy, 80

Lynn, Diana, 111

Lyon, Sue, 329

Lyons, Leonard, 322

Lytess, Natasha, 243

M, 45, 50

MacArthur, Charles, 381, 384, 389

Macdonald, Dwight, 306, 321–22

MacKenna, Kenneth, 239–40

MacLaine, Shirley, 9, 294, 298, 301–303, 307, 329–30, 331, 333–34

MacMurray, Fred, 69, 103, 134–36, 140, 190, 209, 298, 305, 414

Madame Dubarry, 189

Madame Wants No Children, 49–50, 51

Magnificent Seven, The, 314

Main, Marjorie, 164

Major and the Minor, The, 102n, 110–16, 118, 120, 126

Male and Female, 189, 192

Mallett, Richard, 373

Malneck, Matty, 294

Maltese Falcon, The, 109, 134

Man Between, The, 266

Manchurian Candidate, The, 246

Mandel, Joseph. *See* May, Joe

Man for All Seasons, A, 35, 362

Manfredi, Nino, 378

Mankiewicz, Joseph L., 203, 274, 291, 382

Mann, Anthony, 141

Mann, der seinen Mörder sucht, Der, 37, 38–39

Mann, Thomas, 23, 66

Mannhof, Emil, 99

Mansfield, Jayne, 244, 254

Mantz, Paul, 253

Man Who Knew Too Much, The, 252

Man Who Looked for His Murderer, The, 37, 38–39

Man Who Would Be King, The, 257

Man with the Golden Arm, The, 215, 224

Marathon Man, 394

March, Fredric, 134

Marcus, Larry, 266
Marcuse, Ludwig, 66
Marshall, Brenda, 226, 238
Marshman, D. M., Jr., 186–87, 207
Marsters, Ann, 306
Martin, Dean, 235, 286, 301, 335, 338, 339, 345, 347
Martin, Mary, 69
Martin, Paul, 46
Marty, 265, 277
Marvin, Lee, 367
Marx, Groucho, 304n, 310
Marx Brothers, 309–10
Marx Brothers at the U.N., The, 310
Maslin, Janet, 381, 403
Mason, James, 362
Masquerade device, 75, 120, 289, 379
Massey, Raymond, 372
Matthau, Carol, 359
Matthau, Walter
  Oscar given to, 362
  professional relationship with Wilder, 358–59, 407
  as star in *The Odd Couple*, 357, 382
  in Wilder films
    Buddy Buddy, 405, 406, 407–8, 409
    The Fortune Cookie, 356, 357–60, 361, 362
    The Front Page, 381, 382, 386
    screen test for *The Seven Year Itch*, 244
Mauvaise Graine, 56–58, 66, 346, 396
May, Joe, 58–59, 61, 64
Mayer, Carl, 23, 29, 37, 45
Mayer, Edwin Justus, 75
Mayer, Louis B., 125, 202, 412
Mayerling, 57
Mayerson, Donald J., 380
Mayes, Wendell, 250

McCarey, Leo, 140, 162, 221
McCarten, John, 213, 254, 292, 306
McCarthy era witch-hunts, 220–21
McClure, Robert A., 152
McCrea, Joel, 96n
McDowall, Roddy, 315
McGee, Rex, 396
McGiver, John, 261
McLaglen, Victor, 66
McNulty, Bishop, 292
McTeague, 121
Meet Whiplash Willie, 362
Melody of the Heart, 36
Memo to a Movie Producer, 99
Menjou, Adolphe, 15, 382, 386
Menschen am Sonntag, 27–34, 36–37, 43, 84, 225
Merande, Doro, 241
Merry Andrew, 278
Metro-Goldwyn-Mayer, 80, 81, 228, 239, 278, 390, 405
Metropolis, 14, 25, 43
MGM. *See* Metro-Goldwyn-Mayer
Midnight, 75–79, 91, 120
Midnight Cowboy, 325
Milestone, Lewis, 382
Milland, Ray, 91, 95, 96, 111, 116, 118, 142, 146–49, 159, 162
Miller, Arthur, 281, 290, 291, 293–94, 360, 420
Mills, Hayley, 378
Mills, Juliet, 378, 380, 381
Milne, Tom, 373
Mingand, Pierre, 57
Mirage, 357
Miranda, Isa, 118
Mirisch, Harold, 256, 264, 281, 348, 414
Mirisch, Marvin, 256
Mirisch, Walter, 256

Mirisch Company, 264–65, 277, 334, 359, 365, 374, 381, 383

Miró, Joan, 417, 418

Mishkin, Leo, 182–83, 306, 332, 362

Mister Roberts, 248, 279

Mitchell, Millard, 176

Mix, Tom, 6

Mock, John, 235

Molinaro, Edouard, 405, 408

Molnár, Ferenc, 11, 55, 166, 311, 312, 319, 320

Monash, Paul, 382

Monkey Business, 257

Monnot, Marguerite, 330

Monogram Pictures, 256

Monroe, Marilyn
divorce from Joe DiMaggio, 243
marriage to Arthur Miller, 290–91, 293–94
photogenic quality of, 263, 290
professional relationship with Wilder, 243–44, 281–84, 290, 293–94, 310, 334
in Wilder films
The Seven Year Itch, 240, 241–44, 245–46, 345
Some Like It Hot, 279, 281–84, 287, 288

Monroe, Thomas, 105, 107

Montag Morgen, 24–25, 26, 27, 30

Montgomery, Douglass, 65

Montgomery, Robert, 72

Moore, Henry, 417

Moore, Roger, 266

Moreau, Jeanne, 335

More the Merrier, The, 173

Morning Telegraph, 182, 332, 362

Mortimer, John, 363

Motion Picture Association of America, 292, 346–47, 355

See also Production Code Administration

Mrs. Miniver, 156

Mr. Smith Goes to Washington, 88, 173

Mummy's Ghost, The, 62

Murderers Among Us, 394

Murders in the Rue Morgue, 118

Murnau, F. W., 14, 45, 61

Music Corporation of America (MCA), 279

Music in the Air, 65, 167, 189

Music Man, The, 305

Mutiny on the Bounty, 269

My Fair Lady, 364

My Favorite Martian (TV), 338

My Favorite Spy, 147

My Left Foot, 143

My Living Doll, 165

My Sister and I, 277

Nabokov, Vladimir, 112

Nachtausgabe, 14–15

Nagy, Käthe von, 40

Nanny and the Professor (TV), 378

Nashville, 389

Nation, 161

National Medal of Arts, 420

Nazis, 51–55, 151, 152, 154, 155

Nebenzahl, Heinrich, 25

Negri, Pola, 118, 189

Network, 395

Neubach, Ernst, 37

Newman, Paul, 34, 291

Newman, Walter Brown, 208–9, 210, 214–15

New Republic, The, 322

Newsweek, 203, 274, 305, 332, 352, 373, 409

New West magazine, 403

New York Daily News, 373, 388, 404

New Yorker, The, 71, 182, 203, 213, 225, 254, 263, 274, 292, 306, 322, 332, 350, 362, 403
New York Evening Sun, 145, 147
New York Herald Tribune, 88, 139, 161, 293, 294, 350
New York magazine, 390, 409
New York Morning Telegraph, 306
New York Post, 115, 182, 305, 404, 409
New York Times, The, 88, 96, 115, 123, 139, 159, 171, 202, 213, 275, 292, 298, 322, 350, 353, 361, 373, 381, 388, 393, 403, 404
New York World Telegram, 144
Niagara, 206
Niccodemi, Dario, 48
Nichols, Mike, 239
Nielsen, Asta, 6
Nijinksy, Vaslav, 108
Niklaus, Kurt, 335
Nilsson, Anna Q., 193
Nine Hours to Rama, 317
Ninotchka, 11, 18, 81–88, 92, 156, 206, 259, 320, 405
Norris, Frank, 121
North by Northwest, 239
No Strings, 227
Nothing Sacred, 382
Noti, Karl, 42
Notte, La, 352
Nouvelle Vague, 324
Novak, Kim, 9, 254, 335–36, 337, 338, 339, 344, 347, 348, 398
Nugent, Frank S., 88
Nun's Story, The, 35

Oberon, Merle, 274
O'Brien, Pat, 289, 313, 382, 386
Observer (London), 373
Octopus, The, 214

Odd Couple, The, 357, 382, 408
O'Hara, John, 255
Old Dark House, The, 195
Oliver, Lawrence, 365
Olson, Nancy, 188, 191, 199, 200, 204, 421
Olympia, 166
Onassis, Aristotle, 393
Once There Was a Waltz, 47–48
One, Two, Three, 11, 42, 165, 231, 311, 312–23, 326, 327, 361, 376, 412
One Exciting Adventure, 51
O'Neill, Dick, 386
One Touch of Venus, 266
Only Angels Have Wings, 105, 173
On the Waterfront, 108, 238
Operation Candybar, 174
Ora della Fantasia, L', 335
Ormond, Julia, 422
Osmond, Cliff, 336, 337, 340, 352, 357
Othello, 146, 165
O'Toole, Peter, 363
Ouspenskaya, Maria, 90
Ox-Bow Incident, The, 161

Pabst, G. W., 14, 61n
Pacino, Al, 394
Page, Geneviève, 9, 372
Page, Geraldine, 315
Paige, Satchel, 201
Paine, Thomas, 282
Paint Your Wagon, 367
Paley, William S., 156, 158, 159, 296
Pal Joey, 255
Pallenberg, Max, 311
Pam-Pam, 59, 62–63
Parade magazine, 365
Paramount Pictures, 68–70, 90–91,

94, 97, 100, 109–10, 129, 139, 140, 143–44, 150, 160, 167, 169, 186, 193, 205, 214, 227, 247, 421, 422

Parker, Dorothy, 62, 145, 377

Parks, Larry, 244

Parsons, Louella, 193, 327

Pasternak, Joe, 20, 24, 65

Patricide, 25

PCA. *See* Production Code Administration

Peck, Gregory, 134, 399n

Pendleton, Austin, 387

People on Sunday, 27–34, 36–37, 43, 84, 225

Père Goriot (Balzac), 187

Perfect Furlough, The, 66

Perils of Pauline, The, 173

Persoff, Nehemiah, 289

Petersen, Verita, 236

Phantom from Space, 141

Phantom Lady, 34

Phantom of the Opera, The, 421

Picasso, Pablo, 416, 417, 418

Piccadilly Jim, 72

Picker, Arnold, 333

Picket Fences (TV), 352

Pickford, Mary, 188–89, 202, 264–65

Picnic, 265

Pink Panther, The, 350

Pioneer Films, 67–68

Pit, The, 214

Pitlik, Noam, 386

Plaisir, Le, 57

Playboy magazine, 215, 325

Polaire, Hal, 282

Pollack, Sydney, 394, 396, 422

Polo, Eddie, 24

Polonaise, La, 90, 97

Pommer, Erich, 19, 38, 40, 46, 47, 55, 65, 67, 109, 118, 174, 184

Porgy and Bess, 224, 297

Postman Always Rings Twice, The, 62, 125

Potemkin, 45

Powell, Dilys, 274

Powell, Michael, 42, 365

Power, Tyrone, 219, 266, 268, 270–71, 274, 275, 414

Preminger, Otto, 215, 223–24, 250

Prentiss, Paula, 408

Pressburger, Emeric, 42–43

Previn, André, 330, 340, 361

Prime of Miss Jean Brodie, The, 365

Princess O'Rourke, 147, 218

Private Life of Henry VIII, The, 118, 269

Private Life of Sherlock Holmes, The, 9, 363–73, 391, 422

Production Code Administration (PCA)

  Ace in the Hole and, 211

  Arise My Love and, 94–95

  Double Indemnity and, 125–27, 134, 138

  A Foreign Affair and, 182

  Hold Back the Dawn and, 101

  institution of film rating system by, 355

  Irma la Douce and, 327–28, 332–33

  Kiss Me, Stupid and, 346–49

  The Lost Weekend and, 144, 160

  Love in the Afternoon and, 264

  Lubitsch films and, 73

  The Seven Year Itch and, 240–41

  Some Like It Hot and, 292

  Stalag 17 and, 224

  Sunset Boulevard and, 198

  See also Censorship

Promises, Promises, 421
Pryor, Richard, 411
Pryor, Thomas M., 202
Psycho, 138
Public Enemy, The, 321
Pulver, Lilo, 320
Punch, 373

Quai des Brumes, 34, 252
Quarterly of Film, Radio and Television, 206
Queen Christina, 82
Queen Kelly, 121, 191–92
Querschnitt, 15
Quine, Richard, 331

Raft, George, 134, 288, 289
Rage of Paris, The, 57
Ragtime, 318
Raiders of the Lost Ark, 92
Raikes, Glenn, 163
Rain Man, 143
Randall, Tony, 338
Rasp, Fritz, 43
Rathbone, Basil, 69, 372
Rat Pack, 301, 302, 330, 345
Rauschenberg, Robert, 420
Razor's Edge, The, 270
Rebel Without a Cause, 194
Redbook, 255
Redl, Colonel Alfred, 275, 277
Red River, 190
Red Shoes, The, 42, 365
Reed, Jay Theodore, 80
Reed, Rex, 409
Reed, Sir Carol, 32
Regeneration, 193
Reinhardt, Gottfried, 81, 88
Reinhardt, Max, 26, 81, 82, 223

Reisch, Walter, 11, 46, 53, 56, 82, 85, 86, 88, 109, 206, 353, 364
Remarque, Erich Maria, 20, 23, 56
Renoir, Jean, 122, 176, 417
Revill, Clive, 372, 378
Revue of the Month, 15
Rhythm on the River, 69
Rich, Lee, 402
Rich, Ron, 356
Riefenstahl, Leni, 51
Riemann, Johannes, 41
Rights of Man, The (Paine), 282
Ring des Nibelungen, Der, 2
Riskin, Robert, 62
Riva, Maria, 174, 268, 393
Rivers, Larry, 417
Rivette, Jacques, 324
Roach, Hal, 113
Road-show pictures, 364, 366–67
Robe, The, 225, 333
Roberts, Ralph Arthur, 272
Robeson, Paul, 109, 146, 219
Robin Hood, 20
Robinson, Edward G., 109, 135, 140, 414, 416
Robinson, Edward G., Jr., 289
Robles, Gabriel, 99
Rocky Horror Picture Show, The, 326
Rodgers, Richard, 227
Rodman, Howard, 415
Rogers, Buddy, 188–89
Rogers, Ginger, 109, 110–11, 115–16, 414
Rohe, Miles van der, 23
Roman Holiday, 227, 229, 237
Rommel, Erwin, 119, 121, 123
Ronde, La, 57
Room Service, 358
Roosevelt, Franklin, 100, 220
Rose of the Rancho, 72

Ross, Frank, 175
Ross, Harold, 71
Rowlands, Gena, 244
Roxie Hart, 111, 382
Royal Scandal, A, 223
Rozsa, Miklos, 150, 162, 364, 369, 397
Rühmann, Heinz, 38, 39
Ruman, Sig, 168, 223
Russell, Jane, 254
Russell, Rosalind, 382, 386
Ruttmann, Walter, 29

Saar, Richard, 419
Sabrina, 18, 48, 102, 179, 227–39, 260, 262, 283, 303, 320, 326, 376, 395, 422
Sabrina Fair, 227, 374
Sadie Thompson, 189
Saks, Gene, 383
Salome, 192, 196, 198, 364
Samson and Delilah, 192, 193, 194
Samuels, Lesser, 209, 210
Sanders, George, 141
Sarandon, Susan, 386
Sarris, Andrew, 58, 183, 212, 373, 381, 388, 403, 420
Saturday Evening Post, 71, 112, 354
Saturday Night and Sunday Morning, 352, 365
Saturday Review, 213, 214, 255, 263, 274, 292, 306, 332, 362, 373, 380, 388
Savoir, Alfred, 70
Sayre, Nora, 385
Scampolo, a Girl of the Street, 48–49, 51, 55
Scarface, 105
Scarlet Pimpernel, The, 118
Schary, Dore, 62, 228

Schickel, Richard, 360, 361–62, 404
Schiele, Egon, 6, 417, 418
Schindler's List, 413
Schlesinger, Arthur, Jr., 322
Schnitzler, Arthur, 11
Schoedsack, Ernest B., 68
Schorr, William, 205
Schreyer, Annie, 30
Schüfftan, Eugen. *See* Shuftan, Eugene
Schulberg, Stuart, 184
Schulz, Franz, 19–20, 50, 55, 66, 75
Scott, Randolph, 191
Screen Directors Guild, 221
Seberg, Jean, 48
Seduced and Abandoned, 351, 374
See Here Private Hargrove, 266
Seeler, Moritz, 24, 25, 30, 33, 35
Segal, George, 362
Seidlin, Oskar, 154
Seitensprünge, 40, 42
Seitz, John F., 124, 136, 149, 195
Sellers, Peter, 336–38, 339, 350, 352–53, 359, 363
Selznick, David O., 61n, 82, 126, 139–40, 280, 394
Selznick, Irene, 274
Selznick International Pictures, 147
Sennett, Mack, 189, 198, 292
Sergeant York, 105
Settember, Tony, 165
Seven Year Itch, The, 114, 165, 240–46, 247, 279n, 281, 345, 357
Shadow of the Thin Man, 266
Shaw, David, 172
Shaw, Irwin, 172
Shaw, Robert, 362
Shaw, Sam, 242
Sherlock Holmes and the Deadly Necklace, 372

Sherlock Holmes. See *Private Life of Sherlock Holmes, The*
Sherwood, Robert E., 94
Short, Martin, 65
Shot in the Dark, A, 336, 365
Show magazine, 322
Shuftan, Eugene, 24, 25, 30, 31, 32, 34
Shurlock, Geoffrey, 240, 327, 332–33, 346–47, 348, 353
Sight and Sound, 351
Silverman, Stephen M., 421
Simon, John, 323, 326
Simon, Neil, 357, 382
Simpson, O. J., 213
Sinatra, Frank, 279, 301, 330
Since You Went Away, 139
Sinyard, Neil, 320, 370
Siodmak, Curt, 26–27, 32, 34, 37, 40, 61, 194
Siodmak, Robert, 25, 26, 27, 30, 31, 32, 33, 34, 37, 38, 39, 61
Sistrom, Joe, 110, 126–27, 128, 130
Skolsky, Sidney, 297n
Slaughter on Tenth Avenue, 357
Slezak, Walter, 44
Small, Edward, 265–66
Smith, Jack, 15
Smith, Maggie, 365
Smith, Tom, 395
Snow Creature, The, 141
Snow White and the Seven Dwarfs, 105
Snyder, Ruth, 130
Solomon and Sheba, 265, 266, 275
Somebody Up There Likes Me, 239
Some Came Running, 300
Some Like It Hot, 39, 42, 47, 111, 279–94, 296, 299, 303, 305, 309, 310, 346, 350, 385, 388, 391, 408, 409, 416, 421

Sons and Lovers, 307
Sordi, Alberto, 378
Sound of Music, The, 239, 364
South Pacific, 248, 279
Spellbound, 162
Spiegel, Sam, 108–9, 274, 363
Spielberg, Steven, 273, 413, 415
Spiral Staircase, The, 34
Spirit of St. Louis, The, 247–55, 257, 259, 330
Stagecoach, 88
Stalag 17, 219–26, 229, 245, 310, 321, 374
Stallone, Sylvester, 415
Stallone's Typewriter, 419
Stanwyck, Barbara, 9, 106, 107, 135, 202
Stapenhorst, Günther von, 43
Star!, 367
Starkey, Lycurgus M., Jr., 353
Star Wars, 405
State Fair, 206
State of the Union, 248
Steinberg, Saul, 72, 417, 419
Steinhoff, Hans, 51
Steinkamp, Fredric, 397, 402
Stella, Frank, 416
Stephens, Robert, 365, 367, 372
Sterling, Jan, 9, 209, 211–12
Sternberg, Josef von, 416
Sternhagen, Frances, 395–96, 401
Stern magazine, 295
Stevens, Naomi, 304
Stevens, Risë, 419
Stewart, James, 141, 249, 251, 252–54, 255, 414
Sting, The, 382, 387
Storms of Passion, 6
Story of Louis Pasteur, The, 332
Strasberg, Lee, 281

Strasberg, Paula, 281–82
Strauss, Johann, 3
Strauss, Richard, 11, 364
Strauss, Robert, 223, 225, 245
Streisand, Barbra, 367
Stroheim, Erich von, 119, 121–24, 141, 191–92, 198, 200, 223, 236, 414
Student Song from Heidelberg, A, 37
Stunde, Die, 10–13
Sturges, Preston, 77, 104, 109, 113, 115, 386
Styne, Jule, 419
Styron, William, 420
Sugar, 421
Sullavan, Margaret, 227, 230
Sullivan, Francis L., 266
Summer and Smoke, 315
Sun Also Rises, The, 270
Sunday in August, 32
Sundowners, The, 35
Sunrise, 23, 30
Sunset Boulevard, 1, 17, 58, 109, 114, 124, 181, 182n, 186–204, 205, 206, 207, 212, 215, 216, 223, 247, 255, 291, 298n, 324, 345, 364, 391, 395, 397, 400, 420–22
Sutton, Willie, 393
Svabó, István, 275
Swan Lake, 369
Swanson, Gloria, 65, 70, 189, 190, 191–92, 195–96, 198, 199–200, 202, 203–4, 215, 345, 414, 421, 422
Swanson, H. N., 126, 128–29
Sweet Smell of Success, 227, 228, 265, 277
Swerling, Jo, 62
Szekely, Stefan, 42

Tales of Hoffman, The, 365
Tales of Manhattan, 109
Talking Pictures (Corliss), 183
Taming of the Shrew, The, 74, 227n
Tamiroff, Akim, 119, 124
Taylor, Davidson, 156, 158
Taylor, Dwight, 69
Taylor, Elizabeth, 291, 307, 329, 337
Taylor, Sam, 227n
Taylor, Samuel, 227, 238, 240, 374, 376
Tea and Sympathy, 249
Teal, Ray, 210
Technicolor, 169, 387
Tempo, 15, 28–29, 39
Ten North Frederick, 206
Teufelsreporter, Der, 24
That Lady in Ermine, 223
Theatre Arts, 323
Théry, Jacques, 67, 69, 91
Thiebaud, Wayne, 417
Thiele, William, 66
Thing, The, 250
This Sporting Life, 365
Thoeren, Robert, 277
Thomas, Bob, 190, 225
Thompson, Thomas, 349
Those Magnificent Men in Their Flying Machines, 365
3:10 to Yuma, 339
Three from the Filling Station, 19
Three Musketeers, The, 385
Three of a Kind (Cain), 126
Threepenny Opera, The, 61n
Tiffin, Pamela, 312, 314–16, 318, 322
Tiger Bay, 314
Time magazine, 236, 238, 245, 292, 305, 322, 350, 373, 381, 388, 404, 409
Times, The (London), 274, 351

Time to Kill, 127
Titanic, 206
To Be or Not to Be, 223
Today (TV), 254
Today's Cinema, 215
Todd, Mike, 167, 253
Todesmuhlen, 154–55
To Each His Own, 173
To Have and Have Not, 159
Toilette, La (Balthus), 418
Toldy, John S., 90–91
Tom Jones, 306, 346
Tone, Franchot, 119, 124
Toscanini, Arturo, 67
Tosches, Nick, 338
Toulouse-Lautrec, Henri de, 416
Toumanova, Tamara, 369
Tovarich, 81–82
Tracy, Spencer, 134, 393
Trauner, Alexander, 252, 271, 304, 316, 330–31, 346, 361, 365, 366, 393
Treasure of the Sierra Madre, The, 213
Triumph of the Will, 51
Trouble with Harry, The, 171
Trueba, Fernando, 420
Truffaut, François, 324, 325
Truth or Consequences (TV), 254
Tryon, Tom, 391–92, 400
Trzcinski, Edmund, 219
Turner, Adrian, 320, 370
Turpin, Ben, 155
Twain, Mark, 322
20th Century-Fox, 64, 191, 206, 207, 240, 245, 281
Twentieth Century, 105
Two for the Road, 365
Two Guys from Milwaukee, 257
Two Guys from Texas, 257

Ulmer, Edgar, 25, 26, 27, 30, 31, 34, 194
Under Pressure, 66
Under the Yum Yum Tree, 346
Under Your Spell, 223
Uninvited, The, 126
United Artists, 264–65, 279, 333, 336, 347, 349, 355, 367, 383, 403, 404, 413
Universal Pictures, 65–66, 381, 392, 393
Up in Arms, 147

Valentino, Rudolph, 124
Valli, Romolo, 378
Vanderbilt, Cornelius, Jr., 15
Van Eyck, Peter, 119, 121
Varden, Norma, 271
Variations on the Theme of Queen Nefertete II, 419
Variety, 115, 139, 172, 238, 246, 264, 338, 351, 356, 381, 388, 389, 403, 409
Variety Girl, 173
Vautel, Clement, 49
Veber, Francis, 405
Veidt, Conrad, 88, 153
Ventura, Lino, 405, 407, 408
Verne, Jules, 167
Verneuil, Louis, 277
Vertigo, 227, 398
Victoria, Olive, 15
Vidor, Doris, 259
Vidor, King, 297
Viertel, Berthold, 66
Viertel, Peter, 245
Viertel, Salka, 66, 88
Vincenzoni, Luciano, 374
Vizzard, Jack, 348
Vogue, 350

von Stroheim, Erich. *See* Stroheim, Erich von
Vranitzky, Franz, 420

Wachsmann, Franz. *See* Waxman, Franz
Wald, Jerry, 255, 256
Walker, Alexander, 227, 337
Walking Down Broadway, 121
Waller, Ernest, 368
Wallis, Hal, 332
Walsh, Raoul, 66, 193
Walston, Ray, 304, 338–39, 352–53
Walt Disney Company, 305
Walter, Ernest, 372n
Waltershausen, Wolfgang von, 30
Wanger, Walter, 297, 381n
Warner, H. B., 193
Warner, Jack, 103, 126, 245, 250, 253, 254, 255, 316
Warner Brothers, 254, 255
Was Frauen träumen, 50–51, 55
Waterman, Willard, 305
Waters, Ethel, 109
Watson, Lucile, 168
Waugh, Evelyn, 219n
Waxman, Franz, 44, 55, 58, 203, 364
Wayne, David, 386
Way of the World, The, 351
W. C. Fields and Me, 392
Weatherby, W. J., 309
Webb, Clifton, 274
Webb, Jack, 197
Webber, Andrew Lloyd, 420, 421–22
Weiler, A. H., 292, 350, 381
Weintraub, Jerry, 413
Welles, Orson, 165
Wenders, Wim, 39
West, Judi, 9, 356, 360
West, Mae, 116n, 186, 188, 255

Weston, Jay, 405
West Side Story, 239
What a Life, 79–80
What Women Dream, 50–51, 55
Where the Sidewalk Ends, 223
Whirlpool, 223
White, David, 305
Whiteman, Paul, 12–13, 15
Whitney, Cornelius Vanderbilt, 68
Whitney, John Hay, 68
Whitten, Gladys, 243
Who's Afraid of Virginia Woolf?, 239, 362
Wichita, 264
Wiener Tagblatt, 10
Wild Bunch, The, 370
Wilder, Audrey, 163–64, 184–85, 187–88, 207–8, 216–18, 226, 260, 291, 294, 394–95, 417, 419, 423
Wilder, Billy
    as army colonel in Europe, 151–59
    arrives in Hollywood, 61–70
    art collection of, 416–19
    birth and childhood of, 1–6
    children of, 90, 165, 217–18
    filmography of, 429–37
    in Film Studio 1929, 24–34
    as freelance writer, 15–18
    as French film director, 56–58
    as German screenwriter, 23–24, 37–51
    as ghostwriter, 19–20, 23–24, 37, 55, 66
    as gigolo, 16–18
    Holocaust film by, 154–55
    in law school, 8–9
    learns film directing, 105, 113–14
    marriage to Audrey, 207–8, 216–18, 260, 417

Wilder, Billy (*cont'd*)
  marriage to Judith, 75, 89–90, 116–17, 164–65
  in Mexicali, 63–64
  Nazi takeover and, 51–55
  as newspaper reporter, 9–13, 14–15
  Oscar nominations for, 88, 104, 107, 139, 162, 203, 215, 225, 238, 274, 293, 362
  Oscars given to, 162, 307
  salaries earned as director, 116, 136, 151, 174–75, 266, 277
  as teenager, 6–7
  travels to America, 59–60
Wilder, Eugenia, 1, 2, 8, 153
Wilder, Judith. *See* Iribe, Judith
Wilder, Max, 1–5, 21
Wilder, Victoria, 90, 165, 166, 218
Wilder, Vincent, 90
Wilder, Willie, 1, 60, 140–41
Williams, John, 166, 230, 235
Williams, Tennessee, 291, 315
Wilson, Earl, 322
Winchell, Walter, 243
Winsten, Archer, 115, 182, 306, 409
Wise Guys, 413
Wistful Widow of Wagon Gap, The, 164
Witness for the Prosecution, 179, 265–75, 279n, 363
Wizard of Oz, The, 88
Woche, Die, 26

Wodehouse, P. G., 72
Wolf, Manny, 70
Wolf, William, 350
Wolfe, Thomas, 60
Wolf Man, The, 34
Women's Wear Daily, 410
Wonderful Lies of Nina Petrowna, The, 28n
Wood, Natalie, 254
"Writers in Hollywood" (Chandler), 133
Wuthering Heights, 88, 156
Wyler, William, 113, 156, 162, 172, 221, 227, 237, 256
Wyman, Jane, 147

York, Michael, 399, 401–2, 403
Young, Audrey. *See* Wilder, Audrey
Young, Colin, 324
Young Lions, The, 172
Youssopoff, Prince, 15–16

Zaharoff, Sir Basil, 11
Zanuck, Darryl F., 207, 241, 245
Zaza, 193
Zazie, 322
Zinnemann, Fred, 19, 27, 30–31, 34–35, 225, 241, 423
Zolotow, Maurice, 8–9, 12, 20, 78, 115, 116n, 135, 164, 166, 188, 189, 190, 205, 368–69, 390